Human Emotions: A Reader

Human Emotions: A Reader

Edited by
Jennifer M. Jenkins, Keith Oatley, and Nancy L. Stein

BLACKWELL
Publishers

Copyright © Jennifer M. Jenkins and Keith Oatley, 1998

First published 1998

2 4 6 8 10 9 7 5 3 1

Blackwell Publishers Inc.
350 Main Street
Malden, Massachusetts 02148
USA

Blackwell Publishers Ltd
108 Cowley Road
Oxford OX4 1JF
UK

Library of Congress Cataloging-in-Publication Data

Human emotions : a reader/edited by Keith Oatley, Jennifer M. Jenkins, and Nancy L. Stein
    p.   cm.
    Includes bibliographical references and index.
    ISBN 0–631–20747–3 (hardcover : alk. paper). — ISBN 0–631–20748–1 (pbk. : alk. paper)
    1. Emotions. I. Oatley, Keith. II. Jenkins, Jennifer M. III. Stein, Nancy L.
  BF531.H785 1998
  152.4—dc21

                                        97–38756
                                           CIP

British Library Cataloguing in Publication Data

A CIP catalogue record for this book is available from the British Library.

Typeset in Garamond on 10.5/12.5pt by PureTech India Ltd, Pondicherry.
Printed in Great Britain by T. J. International, Padstow, Cornwall

This book is printed on acid-free paper

Contents

Figures

Tables

Preface

This book is an introduction to the understanding of human emotions from the perspective of empirical and theoretical research. With our introductions to each part and to each article, it offers an approach in which the main story is carried by original writings – including some classical articles and some that represent the latest thinking in the field.

The book can be used as a textbook. It also provides a set of research readings to accompany *Understanding Emotions*, by Oatley and Jenkins, when that book is used as a text in university and college courses. In table 1 at the end of this preface, we indicate the chapters of *Understanding Emotions* for which each selection here is an appropriate accompaniment. For the most part we concentrate on empirical articles: for a set of review articles that covers the field, we recommend Lewis and Haviland (1993).

A word about our approach and biases

Compiling a reader involves selection, and selection depends on theoretical positions and biases. It would, for instance, be possible to put together a good volume from the social constructivist position – the idea that human emotions are for the most part constructed quite differently in different societies from social practices and language. Harré and Parrott (1996) have indeed recently published an excellent collection of this kind, and we recommend their reader to any who wish to explore, or teach within, the social constructivist approach.

Although we respect this approach, and although there is material relevant to it in this reader, we have taken the view that emotions have an evolutionarily developed biological basis, which acts as a set of start-up processes on which culture and individual development then build. Culture and individual development take the rather plastic potential of what is given genetically to produce the emotions that we recognize in ourselves and our acquaintances, in our own culture, and in the cultures of others.

In our approach, we regard the theory of evolution as fundamental to understanding emotions, and this brings into focus the question of universals in human emotions, alongside evidence of differences among individuals and among cultures.

A note on the format and content of the readings

In general we have included selections that will be accessible to readers at the university undergraduate level; the majority of them are also accessible to the non-specialist reader although technical material, such as statistical tests of significance, is included in some of the readings. We have excluded abstracts from journal articles: these are seldom comprehensible until after one has read the paper. To conserve space we have also excluded most footnotes, authors' acknowledgements, and the like; those needing to see such material should consult the original articles.

References

Harré, R., & Parrott, W. G. (1996). *The emotions: Social, cultural and biological dimensions.* London: Sage.

Lewis, M., & Haviland, J. M. (Eds.) (1993). *Handbook of emotions.* New York: Guilford.

Oatley, K., & Jenkins, J. M. (1996). *Understanding emotions.* Oxford, UK, and Cambridge, MA: Blackwell.

Table 0.1. Chapters of *Understanding Emotions* by Oatley & Jenkins, keyed to readings in this book.

Chapter numbers and chapter headings in *Understanding Emotions*	Selections in this book
1 Approaches to understanding	1 Darwin; 2 James; 3 Freud.
2 Cultural understandings of emotions	5 Briggs; 6 Jankowiak & Fischer.
3 Evolution of emotions	7 Ekman & Friesen; 8 Russell & Fernandez-Dols.
4 What is an emotion?	4 Lazarus; 9 Oatley & Johnson-Laird; 22 Frijda.
5 Brain mechanisms of emotion	10 LeDoux; 11 Davidson; 12 Damasio et al.
6 Development of emotions	13 Hiatt et al.; 14 Lewis.
7 Individual differences in the development of emotionality	15 Dunn et al.; 16 Kagan et al.; 17 Caspi et al.; 18 Tomkins.
8 Emotions and psychopathology in childhood	19 Jenkins & Smith; 26 Patterson et al.
9 Functions and effects of emotions in cognition and persuasion	23 Isen et al.; 24 Mathews; 25 Salovey & Mayer.
10 Emotions in social relationships	20 Sherif; 21 Gottman;
11 The role of emotions in adult psychopathology	27 Brown et al.; 28 Stein et al.
12 Psychotherapy, consciousness, and narrative	29 Pennebaker et al.; 30 Kavanagh.

Introduction

Emotions are central to human life. Love – in sexual relationships, in parent–child relationships, and in friendships – is as important to most of us as anything else. Fear – for instance, of offending people in our social group – continues to be a fundamental part of our heritage as humans. One can go through other emotions in the same way: anger, sadness, disgust, hope, pride, shame, contempt, and so forth.

Emotions must have been salient to almost every human being who has ever lived. They have been of central concern to the world's religions, to many of the great philosophers, and to the tellers of stories in many different societies, as people have reflected upon the human condition. But, despite this, emotions have only recently become a subject of intense research. During the growth of modern psychology, for instance, emotions were at first a Cinderella subject. We heard of their existence, but perception, learning, thinking, personality, and suchlike subjects occupied the stage.

All that has changed. Emotions have entered the research drama, in psychology, psychiatry, education, sociology, anthropology, linguistics, modern philosophy, and related disciplines. New insights and understandings have been substantial. We offer some of them in our introductions and in the readings contained in this book.

Distinguishing different kinds of emotional states

It is worth distinguishing among emotions, moods, and dispositions. Emotions are usually sudden. We become angry at someone who behaves badly towards us, or terrified when we are crossing the road and are almost hit by a truck. In such incidents the emotion interrupts our previous activity and organizes our minds to deal with the event.

What we call moods are not usually so sudden. They are emotional states, but they may last for hours or even months. In the mood of happiness we feel engaged in what we are doing – perhaps in conversation with a friend or in doing something creative. When we feel sad we dwell on the loss that has caused it. Intrusions that would disrupt the mood are resisted, and we put off other matters. If we are depressed we avoid being taken out of ourselves.

Emotional dispositions – loving someone over the years, being cheerful and optimistic, being a generally aggressive person, or feeling embittered – are usually thought of as traits of personality, and as bases for individual differences. Such dispositions too have emotional bases, and are rather like prolonged moods.

With a sudden emotion we usually know what caused it, and this event or person then becomes the focus of our thoughts. This focus of thought is called the object of the emotion. But with a mood we may not know what started it, so we may be anxious without knowing why, a state called free-floating anxiety, or we may be irritable without any specific object. The roots of personality traits are usually even more obscure, often having begun in childhood with temperament (a genetic bias) in conjunction with a particular early upbringing.

Technically speaking then, the world of emotions includes short-term emotions, longer-term moods, and very long-term emotional dispositions of personality. The likelihood is that all are produced by the same kinds of brain processes.

The older term for emotions, moods, traits, and emotion-based preferences (likes and dislikes) is "affect." Also, speaking technically, when an intense mood lasts for more than two weeks, when it is disabling so that a person can no longer cope with the ordinary tasks of life and when it resists change by most kinds of outside events, it is termed an emotional disorder, sometimes called an affective disorder or a mood disorder. If the person is inappropriately high and happy we say he or she is manic. If the person is low, sad, or despairing, we say he or she is depressed. If the person is fearful, panicky, or lacking all confidence, we say he or she has an anxiety disorder (see e.g. DSM-IV, American Psychiatric Association, 1994, for more exact definitions). And if someone has a lifelong emotional trait that is disabling to the self or destructive to others we talk (again in terms of DSM-IV) of a personality disorder; so, for instance, people with anti-social personality disorder are habitually angry, aggressive, and uncaring towards others.

Notice too that the drugs given for many psychiatric disorders are designed to alter moods. Antidepressants such as Prozac are designed to make one less despairing. Tranquillizers such as Valium are designed to make one less anxious. Many so-called recreational drugs also affect moods: alcohol is an anxiety reducer, probably the one in the widest use. Mood-altering drugs work on brain states without affecting the outside world, so although they influence how we experience people and events, the alterations of mood are themselves object-less.

Emotions often have both mental and bodily aspects. When happy we typically experience a certain mental state, happy thoughts, and a desire to continue what we are doing. We exhibit bodily exuberance, perhaps including expressions of smiling and laughter. When we are sad become preoccupied, with thoughts that are difficult to dispel; our body may droop, we may cry, we may withdraw from social activities. Although some researchers have questioned whether any one aspect (the experience, the compulsive thoughts, the urge to act in some particular way, or the expressions of face and body) is scientifically essential to decide that an emotion exists, our best understanding is that an emotion or mood may include all of such mental and bodily aspects, but often only some of them.

One of the issues that makes emotions challenging to researchers is that the mental aspects of emotions and moods are first-person experiences, while bodily and behavioral aspects are visible mainly to others. If you think about your own emotions it is usually the mental aspects and the object of the emotion which are salient – thoughts of the person with whom you have fallen in love, angry feelings of wanting to get even, anxious forebodings about a future event. But when you think about another person's emotions, behavioral aspects provide the information, along with the context in which they occur: "He was fidgeting and unable to look people in the eye at the meeting"; or, "Her eyes were full of tears when she talked about her daughter." How far first-person accounts and observer accounts can be reconciled is still a matter of research.

Ambivalence towards the emotions

Here is the most persistently puzzling aspect of our Western attitude to emotions. We have profound ambivalence toward them.

On the one hand emotions are what make us most distinctively human. What is more important to human life than love – of parents, of lovers, of children, of friends? What is more important to the integrity of self and society than the ability to act well despite fear? What is more important to understanding ourselves than knowing how we really feel – the sources and objects of our emotions? In such values we seek to know our emotions and to understand them.

On the other hand, with almost equal force, we distrust emotions. We wonder about anger, contempt, and fear as destructive forces. Such elements devastate families, just as they foment war between communities and between nations. There are greed and disdain, which make for endless misery among powerless minorities. There are shame and humiliation, which drive people to rage and desperate acts.

What thinkers, writers, and researchers on emotions have believed down the ages is that there is something both profound and non-obvious about emotions, about how they arise, about how to understand them, and about how to deal with them. It is in this spirit that we offer these thoughts and readings.

Reference

American Psychiatric Association (1994). *Diagnostic and statistical manual of mental disorders, Fourth edition: DSM- IV.* Washington, DC: American Psychiatric Association.

PART I

History and Culture

History and Culture

The Western tradition of thought about emotions

For most of the the last 2300 years in the West it has been self-evident that to understand emotions, one must understand them as kinds of thought that affect us strongly. The idea was explained by Aristotle: "The emotions," he wrote in his book *Rhetoric* (1378a, 20–22), "are all those feelings that so change [people] as to affect their judgements, and that are also attended by pain or pleasure." How do such feelings arise? Aristotle continues to explain: typically they arise from events and from the way we evaluate events: "Anger may be defined as an impulse, accompanied by pain, to a conspicuous revenge for a conspicuous slight directed without justification towards what concerns oneself or towards what concerns one's friends" (1378a, 32–35).

So the evaluations which are emotions are usually about events in relation to our concerns. They are usually caused by the unexpected, and they usually urge us towards some plan of action. They are unlike non-emotional plans, such as, "I'll pick up some milk on my way home from work." There is nothing compulsive about this. I could equally well think: "We can manage without more milk until tomorrow." Emotional urges have a compulsive aspect – the aspect that Aristotle calls an impulse.

It is the compulsive aspects of emotions – the single-mindedness of being in love, the inescapable bitterness of feeling rejected, the consuming pursuit of vengeance – that give rise to both our positive and negative attitudes toward emotions in Western societies. Starting in the later part of the nineteenth century, researchers began to focus on the bodily aspect of emotions, which promised to help understand more about how emotions affect us involuntarily. These bodily aspects, including expressions of the face and voice, moreover, promised also to be invaluable to researchers because they could be observed reliably. They could become the stuff of natural science.

Three founding fathers

The founding fathers of modern research on emotions – Darwin, James, Freud (selections 1, 2, and 3) – started our repertoire of methods for studying emotions. Darwin founded ethology with his observation of emotional expressions in natural settings. James emphasized physiological changes in the body which, with the invention of electronics, were later to be measured and traced in such devices as polygraphs. Freud offered the method of listening to what people said about their emotional lives. Again later technology emerged, audio and video recording, which allowed this method to be used for research purposes.

Each of these founders offered an important insight on emotions: Darwin showed they connect us to our own prehistory, James that they are involved in monitoring our bodies, Freud that they may need to be discussed with others in order to be understood.

Appraisal: a central issue in emotion

We come now to the important issue of appraisal, introduced into research on emotions by Magda Arnold (e.g. Arnold and Gasson, 1954). She took up Aristotle's idea that emotions were based on evaluations of events in relation to what was personally and interpersonally important in life, and combined it with some of St Thomas Aquinas's insights. Here are two quotations from Arnold and Gasson's paper:

> We suggest that an emotion or an affect can be considered *as the felt tendency towards an object judged suitable, or away from an object judged unsuitable, reinforced by specific bodily changes according to the type of emotion* . . .
>
> *Judged.* – The individual must perceive and judge the object in relation to himself (as suitable or unsuitable, good or bad for himself) before an emotion can arise. The emotion will follow this judgement, whether or not it is correct. (p. 294)

Arnold and Gasson's idea was, therefore, that emotions are judgements of the *relation* of objects and events to goals, to what Frijda (1986) has called "concerns."

Think about it like this: whereas visual perception is about how we see the outside world, whereas a feeling of thirst is about the inner world, emotions are different. They mediate between outer and inner worlds. As an example imagine an event, the arrival of a loved one with whom we are much concerned, a source of happiness. If she departs and we are concerned about her absence, we feel sad. So emotions are those psychological states or processes that relate events to concerns. In modern research on emotions there is probably no more important concept than this.

A principal function of emotions, then, is to direct attention to any event that is relevant to any concern that is important to us. So in this sense emotions are like burglar alarms. If an alarm goes off, it alerts us to an event related to our concern for security. It may not tell us exactly what has happened. The alarm may have

Table 0.2. Emotions as a function of appraisal features suitable–unsuitable, and object present–absent (slightly modified from Arnold & Gasson, 1954)

	Emotions toward object (whether absent or present)	Object absent	Object present
For impulse emotions			
Object judged suitable (good)	love	desire	joy
Object judged unsuitable (bad)	hate	dislike	sadness
For contending emotions			
(when there is some difficulty)			
Object judged suitable (good)		hope	
Object judged unsuitable (bad)		fear	anger

been triggered falsely by a malfunction or by the cat. But having been alerted, our previous activity is interrupted, and our priority is to attend to the signal. This priority takes over our consciousness and some of our actions.

Putting this the other way round, if you are aware of an emotion in yourself, you should know that something is happening that is important to you. We do not always know our goals and aspirations, or admit them to ourselves or others, but where there is an emotion there is a concern.

Since Arnold's work, many studies have been conducted in which subjects have assessed emotional incidents in terms of a set of features of appraisal (e.g. whether the event was conducive to a goal or concern, whether it was pleasant, and so forth) in order to show how judgements that range over a set of features determine what emotion would occur. Arnold and Gasson have pointed the way towards this, for instance, with features of suitable–unsuitable, and of the object of the emotion being absent or present, in table 2. The "object" in such emotions is more frequently human than non-human.

It is possible to argue with these characterizations. You might regard sadness not as the emotion of some bad object being present, but of a good object being absent. You might then make alterations to this table. You might also consider a paper by Smith and Ellsworth (1987) who used a larger set of appraisal features to study the emotions of students taking an exam and later receiving their marks. Alternatively you might consider the large international study of Scherer (1997) in which 2921 people in 37 countries were asked to recall recent experiences of the emotions of joy, sadness, fear, anger, disgust, shame, and guilt, and then rate each experience on a set of appraisal dimensions.

There are many papers we could have chosen to represent this line of thinking. One would have been the famous paper by Schachter and Singer (1962) that became for many years the foundation of research on emotions, in which the authors offered the theory that the bodily accompaniment of an emotion is not specific, but is a general arousal. They proposed that an emotion IS this general arousal plus a labelling of the events (a kind of appraisal) in which the arousal took place. Empirically speaking Schachter and Singer's theory did not fare well (see e.g. Reisenzein, 1983). But modifications of it are very much alive, for instance in Mandler's (1984) prominent theory of emotion as violation of an expectation, and in current interests of social psychologists in misattribution effects, in which an emotion derived from one setting is experienced and applied to another; see Clore (1992).

To represent appraisal theory we offer a piece by Lazarus (selection 4) whose approach became influential. Other aspects of appraisal are represented in selections elsewhere in this reader (Oatley & Johnson-Laird, and Stein et al.; selections 9 and 28).

The influence of culture

A culture is a set of ideas, concepts, and practices, shared by people who live in a particular society. As Howard (1991) has proposed: "a culture can be thought of as a community of individuals who ... share particular interpretations as central to their lives and action ... the young learn to tell the dominant stories of their cultural group" (p. 190). Aspects of the self, including the self's emotions, are formed in any society from culturally recognizable narratives people tell themselves and others.

When you come to Freud's narrative of the story told him by Katharina (selection 3) notice that his concern as therapist was first to understand a story, then to make suggestions to fill in gaps caused by emotional disturbances, and to produce an improved story without such gaps but with a meaning that was recognizable to the person whom it concerned, and also to others.

In general, then, narratives provide us with many of our ideas of the objects and meanings of emotions. Narrative, as Bruner (1986) has proposed, is one of the fundamental modes of human thinking, in which we understand human action as it encounters vicissitudes from which emotions result.

Differences of emotions in different cultures

Much thinking and research on emotions is based on the assumption that emotions are the same everywhere, that cross-cultural differences are small. But is this so?

What if we visited a society of the past? As L. P. Hartley said in the first line of *The Go-between*: "The past is foreign country: they do things differently there." For such historical excursions we leave the possibilities to you – possibilities include poems, plays, and novels. On the subject of love and courtship, one possibility would be to make an imaginary visit to medieval times in Europe via C. S. Lewis's (1936) book *The Allegory of Love*. Or, from 200 years ago, experience the social rituals of courtship and family life in English middle-class society in Jane Austen's (1813) *Pride and Prejudice*.

Or what if we were to travel to a contemporary society not much touched by Western culture? What if we were to visit a group of Inuit people living a traditional way of life in the Arctic? Would emotions and the stories people tell about them be the same there? We start our consideration of cross-cultural differences in emotions with just such a visit, by Jean Briggs (selection 5), who wrote the first anthropological book devoted solely to emotions.

Briggs's story is of how Utku selves and North American selves are shaped. Her book's title, *Never in Anger*, refers to her finding that the adult Utku people she visited never expressed anger interpersonally, whereas in North America injustice as well as frustration give rise rather easily to anger which is expressed quite often. How can people be so different?

One thinks of an anthropologist going to a remote society, and bringing back stories of what it is like to be a member of that society. But, by the time one is an adult, even when one learns the language of a society, it is very difficult to become a full member of that society's culture. One remains, as it were, a Martian. The goal of becoming a member of another society within a few months or years cannot be reached.

Inadvertently almost, Briggs hit on a different idea, and invented an important anthropological method. Her idea was to attend to disconcerting incidents of culture shock, when the assumptions of her culture collided with those of the culture she visited. This method illuminates both the emotional assumptions of another society and of our own, pointing up the contrast between the two.

Universals of emotion

The method of culture shock focuses on differences, but there are also similarities among societies. Darwin introduced the idea that emotions were much the same the world over. As part of the evidence for this, he used responses to a set of printed questionnaires that he had sent to missionaries and administrators, asking them to make specific observations for him of the emotional expressions of people around the world (selection 1). Shared human characteristics are known as universals, and there is good evidence that there are universals of mind and behavior, not just of anatomy and physiology (Brown, 1991).

The other cross-cultural selections of part I pursue mainly the question of universals of human emotions, but how much emphasis should we place on similarities of emotions among cultures, and how much on differences?

To answer such questions it is sensible to adopt the suggestion of Mesquita and Frijda (1992), from their review of cross-cultural differences and similarities, to consider different phases of the process of an emotion separately. Mesquita and Frijda's phases are: (i) antecedent events; (ii) coding and representation of these events (cf. Briggs, selection 5); (iii) appraisal (cf. Lazarus, selection 4); (iv) physiological response patterns (cf. Gottman, selection 21); (v) action readiness (cf. Frijda, selection 22); (vi) overt emotional behavior (cf. Jankowiak & Fischer, selection 6) together with expressions (cf. Ekman & Friesen, selection 7, and Russell & Fernandez-Dols, selection 8); and (vii) the ways in which emotions are regulated (cf. Freud, selection 3). See Stein et al. (selection 28) for a somewhat different account of the phases of emotion.

This section of the reader started with Darwin's work on expression (selection 1); the last two selections close the section with modern research on this theme. Research on facial expressions did more than draw attention to a specific aspect of emotions; it showed how emotions could be studied within experimental paradigms. It is a mark of the success of this method that there has recently been a new wave of research on expression, and that interpretation of studies of the kind that Ekman and Friesen pioneered (selection 7) has become controversial. Selection 8 gives an indication of this controversy.

At the same time as newer studies of expression have begun to emerge, however, with the advent of cognitive psychology, behavioral issues have ceased to be of such overwhelming importance. Research on other issues in the domain of emotions has taken its place alongside research on expression. Despite this, it is not an exaggeration to say that studying the face and its expressions has been instrumental in putting research on emotions onto the accepted research agenda of scientific psychology.

References

Aristotle (circa 330 BCE). *Rhetoric and Poetics*, trans. W. R. Roberts. New York: Random House.

Arnold, M. B., & Gasson, J. A. (1954). Feelings and emotions as dynamic factors in personality integration. In M. B. Arnold & J. A. Gasson (Eds.), *The human person* (pp. 294–313). New York: Ronald.

Austen, J. (1813). *Pride and prejudice*. London: Dent (current edition, 1906).

Briggs, J. L. (1970). *Never in anger: Portrait of an Eskimo family*. Cambridge, MA: Harvard University Press.

Brown, D. E. (1991). *Human universals*. Philadelphia: Temple University Press.

Bruner, J. (1986). *Actual minds, possible worlds*. Cambridge, MA: Harvard University Press.

Clore, G. L. (1992). Cognitive phenomenology: Feelings and the construction of judgement. In L. L. Martin & A. Tesser (Eds.), *The construction of social judgement* (pp. 133–163). Hillsdale, NJ: Erlbaum.

Darwin, C. (1872). *The expression of the emotions in man and animals*. Modern paperback edition, Chicago: University of Chicago Press (1965).

Ellsworth, P. C., & Smith, C. A. (1988). From appraisal to emotion: Differences among unpleasant feelings. *Motivation and Emotion, 12*, 271–302.

Freud, S., & Breuer, J. (1895). *Studies on hysteria. The Pelican Freud Library, Vol. 3*. (Eds. J. Strachey, A. Strachey, & A. Richards). London: Penguin (current edition, 1974).

Frijda, N. H. (1986). *The emotions*. Cambridge: Cambridge University Press.

Hartley, L. P. (1953). *The go-between*. London: Hamish Hamilton.

Howard, G. (1991). Culture tales: A narrative approach to thinking, cross-cultural psychology, and psychotherapy. *American Psychologist, 46*, 187–197.

James, W. (1884). What is an emotion? *Mind, 9*, 188–205.

Lewis, C. S. (1936). *The allegory of love: A study in medieval tradition*. Oxford: Oxford University Press.

Lutz, C. A. (1988). *Unnatural emotions: Everyday sentiments on a Micronesian atoll and their challenge to Western theory*. Chicago: University of Chicago Press.

Mandler, G. (1984). *Mind and body: Psychology of emotions and stress*. New York: Norton.

Mesquita, B., & Frijda, N. (1992). Cultural variations in emotions: A review. *Psychological Bulletin, 112*, 179–204.

Reisenzein, R. (1983). The Schachter theory of emotion: two decades later. *Psychological Bulletin, 94*, 239–264.

Schachter, S., & Singer, J. (1962). Cognitive, social and physiological determinants of emotional state. *Psychological Review, 69*, 379–399.

Scherer, K. (1997). Profiles of emotion-antecedent appraisal: testing theoretical predictions across cultures. *Cognition and Emotion, 11*, 113–150.

Smith, C. A., & Ellsworth, P. C. (1987). Patterns of appraisal and emotion in relation to taking an exam. *Journal of Personality and Social Psychology, 52*, 475–488.

CHAPTER *1*

The Expression of the Emotions in Man and Animals

Charles Darwin

Charles Darwin wrote The Expression of the Emotions in Man and Animals *in a few months, although his note-taking and research for it extended over more than 30 years. Darwin's life project was to show that every species of plant and animal was derived from another species by small modifications. The human mind was central to his project, because if human beings had been created specifically in God's image, with the human mind and its emotions quite separate from anything else in nature, then most people would not really care about evolution. But if mind and emotions had been derived by gradation from those of other animals, then evolution would provide a foundation of our understanding of what it is to be human, of our relations with the natural world, and of our relations with each other.*

Darwin wanted to show that the human mind differed only in degree from the minds of other animals. He chose to fight his first battles on gradual evolution on a field that excluded humans, so in The Origin of Species *he scarcely mentioned them. He waited until this battle was almost won, by his friends who included Thomas Henry Huxley, before he brought forward his two books on human psychology. In* The Descent of Man, *he showed that many psychological features that we humans might like to think are unique to us, like love, memory, and intelligence, are present in lower animals. In* The Expression of Emotions *he showed that some aspects of lower animal life, and of infancy, are still present in adult humans. The key idea in his book on emotions is that emotional expressions are derived from some earlier time, in evolution or infancy, but in adults they occur whether or not they are of any use.*

We have taken our selection from the second edition of The Expression of Emotions, *which had some minor corrections made by Darwin's son Francis. The selection concludes with one of the sentences expressing the central idea of the book, that the actions which are now seen as expressions of emotion are performed in adults "even when not of the least use."*

Charles Darwin, *The expression of the emotions in man and animals*. Second edition, ed. Francis Darwin. London: John Murray, 1890, pp. 9–12, 14–20, 28–30, 39–41.

References

Darwin, C. (1859). *On the origin of species by means of natural selection.* London: Murray.
—— (1871). *The descent of man and selection in relation to sex.* London: Murray.
—— (1872). *The expression of the emotions in man and animals* (first edition). London: Murray; reprinted 1965, Chicago: University of Chicago Press.

Mr Herbert Spencer, in treating of the Feelings in his *Principles of Psychology* (1855), makes the following remarks: "Fear, when strong, expresses itself in cries, in efforts to hide or escape, in palpitations and tremblings; and these are just the manifestations that would accompany an actual experience of the evil feared. The destructive passions are shown in a general tension of the muscular system, in gnashing of the teeth and protrusion of the claws, in dilated eyes and nostrils, in growls; and these are weaker forms of the actions that accompany the killing of prey." Here we have, as I believe, the true theory of a large number of expressions; but the chief interest and difficulty of the subject lies in following out the wonderfully complex results. I infer that some one (but who he is I have not been able to ascertain) formerly advanced a nearly similar view, for Sir C. Bell says, "It has been maintained that what are called the external signs of passion, are only the concomitants of those voluntary movements which the structure renders necessary." Mr Spencer has also published a valuable essay on the Physiology of Laughter, in which he insists on "the general law that feeling passing a certain pitch, habitually vents itself in bodily action"; and that "an overflow of nerve-force undirected by any motive, will manifestly take first the most habitual routes; and if these do not suffice, will next overflow into the less habitual ones." This law I believe to be of the highest importance in throwing light on our subject.

All the authors who have written on Expression, with the exception of Mr Spencer – the great expounder of the principle of Evolution – appear to have been firmly convinced that species, man of course included, came into existence in their present condition. Sir C. Bell, being thus convinced, maintains that many of our facial muscles are "purely instrumental in expression"; or are "a special provision" for this sole object. But the simple fact that the anthropoid apes possess the same facial muscles as we do, renders it very improbable that these muscles in our case serve exclusively for expression; for no one, I presume, would be inclined to admit that monkeys have been endowed with special muscles solely for exhibiting their grimaces. Distinct uses, independently of expression, can indeed be assigned with much probability for almost all the facial muscles.

Sir C. Bell evidently wished to draw as broad a distinction as possible between man and the lower animals; and he consequently asserts that with "the lower creatures there is no expression but what may be referred, more or less plainly, to their acts of volition or necessary instincts." He further maintains that their faces "seem chiefly capable of expressing rage and fear." But man himself cannot express love and humility by external signs, so plainly as does a dog, when with drooping ears, hanging lips, flexuous body, and wagging tail, he meets his beloved master. Nor can these movements in the dog be explained by acts of volition or necessary instincts, any more than the beaming eyes and smiling cheeks of a man when he meets an old friend. If Sir C. Bell had been questioned about the expression of affection in the dog, he would no doubt have answered that this animal had been created with special instincts, adapting him for association with man, and that all further enquiry on the subject was superfluous [...]

In order to acquire as good a foundation as possible, and to ascertain, independently of common opinion, how far particular movements of the features and gestures are really expressive of certain states of the mind, I have found the following means the most serviceable. In the first place, to observe infants; for they exhibit many emotions, as Sir C. Bell remarks, "with extraordinary force"; whereas, in after life, some of our expressions "cease to have the pure and simple source from which they spring in infancy."

In the second place, it occurred to me that the insane ought to be studied, as they are liable to the strongest passions, and give uncontrolled vent to them. I had, myself, no opportunity of doing this, so I applied to Dr Maudsley, and received from him an introduction to Dr J. Crichton Browne, who has charge of an immense asylum near Wakefield, and who, as I found, had already attended to the subject. This excellent observer has with unwearied kindness sent me copious notes and descriptions, with valuable suggestions on many points; and I can hardly over-estimate the value of his assistance. I owe also, to the kindness of Mr Patrick Nicol, of the Sussex Lunatic Asylum, interesting statements on two or three points.

Thirdly, Dr Duchenne galvanized, as we have already seen, certain muscles in the face of an old man, whose skin was little sensitive, and thus produced various expressions which were photographed on a large scale. It fortunately occurred to me to show several of the best plates, without a word of explanation, to above twenty educated persons of various ages and both sexes, asking them, in each case, by what emotion or feeling the old man was supposed to be agitated; and I recorded their answers in the words which they used. Several of the expressions were instantly recognized by almost every one, though described in not exactly the same terms; and these may, I think, be relied on as truthful, and will hereafter be specified. On the other hand, the most widely different judgments were pronounced in regard to some of them. This exhibition was of use in another way, by convincing me how easily we may be misguided by our imagination; for when I first looked through Dr Duchenne's photographs, reading at the same time the text, and thus learning what was intended, I was struck with admiration at the truthfulness of all, with only a few exceptions. Nevertheless, if I had examined them without any explanation, no doubt I should have been as much perplexed, in some cases, as other persons have been.

Fourthly, I had hoped to derive much aid from the great masters in painting and sculpture, who are such close observers. Accordingly, I have looked at photographs and engravings of many well-known works; but, with a few exceptions, have not thus profited. The reason no doubt is, that in works of art, beauty is the chief object; and strongly contracted facial muscles destroy beauty. The story of the composition is generally told with wonderful force and truth by skilfully given accessories.

Fifthly, it seemed to me highly important to ascertain whether the same expressions and gestures prevail, as has often been asserted without much evidence, with all the races of mankind, especially with those who have associated but little with Europeans. Whenever the same movements of the features or body express the same emotions in several distinct races of man, we may infer with much probability, that such expressions are true ones, – that is, are innate or instinctive. Conventional expressions or gestures, acquired by the individual during early life, would probably have differed in the different races, in the same manner as do their languages. Accordingly I circulated, early in the year 1867, the following printed queries with a request, which has been fully responded to, that actual observations, and not memory, might be trusted. These queries were written after a considerable interval of time, during which my attention had been otherwise directed, and I can now see that they might have been greatly improved. To some of the later copies, I appended, in manuscript, a few additional remarks:

(1) Is astonishment expressed by the eyes and mouth being opened wide, and by the eyebrows being raised?

(2) Does shame excite a blush when the colour of the skin allows it to be visible? and especially how low down the body does the blush extend?

(3) When a man is indignant or defiant does he frown, hold his body and head erect, square his shoulders and clench his fists?

(4) When considering deeply on any subject, or trying to understand any puzzle, does he frown, or wrinkle the skin beneath the lower eyelids?

(5) When in low spirits, are the corners of the mouth depressed, and the inner corner of the eyebrows raised by that muscle which the French call the "Grief muscle"? The eyebrow in this state becomes slightly oblique, with a little swelling at the inner end; and the forehead is transversely wrinkled in the middle part, but not across the whole breadth, as when the eyebrows are raised in surprise.

(6) When in good spirits do the eyes sparkle, with the skin a little wrinkled round and under them, and with the mouth a little drawn back at the corners?

(7) When a man sneers or snarls at another, is the corner of the upper lip over the canine or eye tooth raised on the side facing the man whom he addresses?

(8) Can a dogged or obstinate expression be recognized, which is chiefly shown by the mouth being firmly closed, a lowering brow and a slight frown?

(9) Is contempt expressed by a slight protrusion of the lips and by turning up the nose, with a slight expiration?

(10) Is disgust shown by the lower lip being turned down, the upper lip slightly raised, with a sudden expiration, something like incipient vomiting, or like something spit out of the mouth?

(11) Is extreme fear expressed in the same general manner as with Europeans?

(12) Is laughter ever carried to such an extreme as to bring tears into the eyes?

(13) When a man wishes to show that he cannot prevent something being done, or cannot himself do something, does he shrug his shoulders, turn inwards his elbows, extend outwards his hands and open the palms; with the eyebrows raised?

(14) Do the children when sulky, pout or greatly protrude the lips?

(15) Can guilty, or sly, or jealous expressions be recognized? though I know not how these can be defined.

(16) Is the head nodded vertically in affirmation, and shaken laterally in negation?

Observations on natives who have had little communication with Europeans would be of course the most valuable, though those made on any natives would be of much interest to me. General remarks on Expression are of comparatively little value; and memory is so deceptive that I earnestly beg it may not be trusted. A definite description of the countenance under any emotion or frame of mind, with a statement of the circumstances under which it occurred, would possess much value.

To these queries I have received thirty-six answers from different observers, several of them missionaries or protectors of the aborigines, to all of whom I am deeply indebted for the great trouble which they have taken, and for the valuable aid thus received. I will specify their names, &c., towards the close of this chapter, so as not to interrupt my present remarks. The answers relate to several of the most distinct and savage races of man. In many instances, the circumstances have been recorded under which each expression was observed, and the expression itself described. In such cases, much confidence may be placed in the answers. When the answers have been simply yes or no, I have always received them with caution. It follows, from the information thus acquired, that the same state of mind is expressed throughout the world with remarkable uniformity; and this fact is in itself interesting, as evidence of the close similarity in bodily structure and mental disposition of all the races of mankind.

Sixthly, and lastly, I have attended, as closely as I could, to the expression of the several passions in some of the commoner animals; and this I believe to be of paramount importance, not of course for deciding how far in man certain expressions are characteristic of certain states of mind, but as affording the safest basis for generalization on the causes, or origin, of the various movements of Expression. In observing animals, we are not so likely to be biased by our imagination; and we may feel safe that their expressions are not conventional.

From the reasons above assigned, namely, the fleeting nature of some expressions (the changes in the features being often extremely slight); our sympathy being easily aroused when we behold any strong emotion, and our attention thus distracted; our imagination deceiving us, from knowing in a vague manner what to expect, though certainly few of us know what the exact changes in the countenance are; and lastly, even our long familiarity with the subject, – from all these causes combined, the observation of Expression is by no means easy, as many persons, whom I have asked to observe certain points, have soon discovered. Hence it is difficult to determine, with certainty, what are the movements of the features and of the body, which commonly characterize certain states of the mind. Nevertheless, some of the doubts and difficulties have, as I hope, been cleared away by the observation of infants – of the insane, – of the different races of man, – of works of art, – and lastly, of the facial muscles under the action of galvanism, as effected by Dr Duchenne.

But there remains the much greater difficulty of understanding the cause or origin of the several expressions, and of judging whether any theoretical explanation is trustworthy. Besides, judging as well as we can by our reason, without the aid of any rules, which of two or more explanations is the most satisfactory, or are quite unsatisfactory, I see only one way of testing our conclusions. This is to observe whether the same principle by which one expression can, as it appears, be explained, is applicable in other allied cases; and especially, whether the same general principles can be applied with satisfactory results, both to man and the lower animals. This latter method, I am inclined to think, is the most serviceable of all. The difficulty of judging of the truth of any theoretical explanation, and of testing it by some distinct line of investigation, is the great drawback to that interest which the study seems well fitted to excite.

Finally, with respect to my own observations, I may state that they were commenced in the year 1838; and, from that time to the present day, I have occasionally attended to the subject. At the above date, I was already inclined to believe in the principle of evolution, or of the derivation of species from other and lower forms. Consequently, when I read Sir C. Bell's great work, his view, that man had been created with certain muscles specially adapted for the expression of his feelings, struck me as unsatisfactory. It seemed probable that the habit of expressing our feelings by certain movements, though now rendered innate, had been in some manner gradually acquired. But to discover how such habits had been acquired was perplexing in no small degree. The whole subject had to be viewed under a new aspect, and each expression demanded a rational explanation. This belief led me to attempt the present work, however imperfectly it may have been executed [...]

General principles of expression

I will begin by giving the three Principles, which appear to me to account for most of the expressions and gestures involuntarily used by man and the lower animals, under the influence of various emotions and sensations. I arrived, however, at these three Principles only at the close of my observations. They will be discussed in the present and two following chapters in a general manner. Facts observed both with man and the lower animals will here be made use of; but the latter facts are preferable, as less likely to deceive us. In the fourth and fifth chapters, I will describe the special expressions of some of the lower animals; and in the succeeding chapters those of man. Everyone will thus be able to judge for himself, how far my three principles throw light on the theory of the subject. It appears to me that so many expressions are thus explained in a fairly satisfactory manner, that probably all will hereafter be found to come under the same or closely analogous

heads. I need hardly premise that movements or changes in any part of the body,
– as the wagging of a dog's tail, the drawing back of a horse's ears, the shrugging
of a man's shoulders, or the dilatation of the capillary vessels of the skin, – may all
equally well serve for expression. The three Principles are as follows.

I. *The principle of serviceable associated Habits.* – Certain complex actions are of
direct or indirect service under certain states of the mind, in order to relieve
or gratify certain sensations, desires, &c.; and whenever the same state of
mind is induced, however feebly, there is a tendency through the force of
habit and association for the same movements to be performed, though
they may not then be of the least use. Some actions ordinarily associated
through habit with certain states of the mind may be partially repressed
through the will, and in such cases the muscles which are least under the
separate control of the will are the most liable still to act, causing movements which we recognize as expressive. In certain other cases the checking of one habitual movement requires other slight movements; and these
are likewise expressive.
II. *The principle of Antithesis.* – Certain states of the mind lead to certain habitual
actions, which are of service, as under our first principle. Now when a
directly opposite state of mind is induced, there is a strong and involuntary
tendency to the performance of movements of a directly opposite nature,
though these are of no use; and such movements are in some cases highly
expressive.
III. *The principle of actions due to the constitution of the Nervous System, independently from
the first of the Will, and independently to a certain extent of Habit.* – When the
sensorium is strongly excited, nerve-force is generated in excess, and is
transmitted in certain definite directions, depending on the connection of
the nerve-cells, and partly on habit: or the supply of nerve-force may, as it
appears, be interrupted. Effects are thus produced which we recognize as
expressive. This third principle may, for the sake of brevity, be called that
of the direct action of the nervous system [...]

Another familiar instance of a reflex action is the involuntary closing of the eyelids
when the surface of the eyes is touched. A similar winking movement is caused
when a blow is directed towards the face; but this is an habitual and not a strictly
reflex action, as the stimulus is conveyed through the mind and not by
the excitement of a peripheral nerve. The whole body and head are generally
at the same time drawn suddenly backwards. These latter movements, however,
can be prevented, if the danger does not appear to the imagination imminent;
but our reason telling us that there is no danger does not suffice. I may mention
a trifling fact, illustrating this point, and which at the time amused me. I put my
face close to the thick glass-plate in front of a puff-adder in the Zoological
Gardens, with the firm determination of not starting back if the snake struck at
me; but, as soon as the blow was struck, my resolution went for nothing, and I
jumped a yard or two backwards with astonishing rapidity. My will and reason
were powerless against the imagination of a danger which had never been
experienced.

The violence of a start seems to depend partly on the vividness of the imagination, and partly on the condition, either habitual or temporary, of the nervous system. He who will attend to the starting of his horse, when tired and fresh, will perceive how perfect is the gradation from a mere glance at some unexpected object, with a momentary doubt, whether it is dangerous, to a jump so rapid and violent, that the animal probably could not voluntarily whirl round in so rapid a manner. The nervous system of a fresh and highly-fed horse sends its order to the motory system so quickly, that no time is allowed for him to consider whether or not the danger is real. After one violent start, when he is excited and the blood flows freely through his brain, he is very apt to start again; and so it is, as I have noticed, with young infants.

A start from a sudden noise, when the stimulus is conveyed through the auditory nerves, is always accompanied in grown-up persons by the winking of the eye-lids. I observed, however, that though my infants started at sudden sounds, when under a fortnight old, they certainly did not always wink their eyes, and I believe never did so. The start of an older infant apparently represents a vague catching hold of something to prevent falling. I shook a pasteboard box close before the eyes of one of my infants, when 114 days old, and it did not in the least wink; but when I put a few comfits into the box, holding it in the same position as before, and rattled them, the child blinked its eyes violently every time, and started a little. It was obviously impossible that a carefully-guarded infant could have learnt by experience that a rattling sound near its eyes indicated danger to them. But such experience will have been slowly gained at a later age during a long series of generations; and from what we know of inheritance, there is nothing improbable in the transmission of a habit to the offspring at an earlier age than that at which it was first acquired by the parents.

From the foregoing remarks it seems probable that some actions, which were at first performed consciously, have become through habit and association converted into reflex actions, and are now so firmly fixed and inherited, that they are performed, even when not of the least use, as often as the same causes arise, which originally excited them in us through the volition.

CHAPTER *2*

The Principles of Psychology

William James

In 1884 William James wrote a famous article entitled "What is an emotion?" Darwin's book was quite well known, but James's article was the beginning of a new era in research on emotions. In it, James answered his question with a new theory, that an emotion is not the cause of anything. It is an effect. It is a kind of perception. With vision and hearing we perceive things in the outside world. In an emotion we perceive a specific pattern within the world of our own body. This view has become known as the peripheral theory of emotions, because an emotion depends on nerve signals indicating the state of the body (the periphery) often contrasted with central theories (e.g. Cannon, 1927) which maintain that emotions arise in the brain, i.e. centrally, and cause certain kinds of behavior.

James is still considered America's premier psychologist. The pieces of work by which he is best known are his theory of emotion and his 1890 textbook, The Principles of Psychology *(from which we have taken our selection).*

In his 1890 chapter on emotions, James acknowledged that the Danish psychologist, Carl Lange, had independently published a similar theory in the year following James's own first article on the subject. It is for this reason that the theory is correctly known as the James–Lange theory of emotions.

References

Cannon, W. B. (1927). The James-Lange theory of emotion: a critical examination and an alternative theory. *American Journal of Psychology, 39,* 106–124.
James, W. (1884). What is an emotion? *Mind, 9,* 188–205.

William James, *The Principles of Psychology*. New York: Henry Holt, 1890 (reprinted by Dover Publications, New York, 1950), vol. 2, pp. 442–454. Reprinted with permission.

The emotions

In speaking of the instincts it has been impossible to keep them separate from the emotional excitements which go with them. Objects of rage, love, fear, etc., not only prompt a man to outward deeds, but provoke characteristic alterations in his attitude and visage, and affect his breathing, circulation, and other organic functions in specific ways. When the outward deeds are inhibited, these latter emotional expressions still remain, and we read the anger in the face, though the blow may not be struck, and the fear betrays itself in voice and color, though one may suppress all other sign. *Instinctive reactions and emotional expressions thus shade imperceptibly into each other. Every object that excites an instinct excites an emotion as well.* Emotions, however, fall short of instincts, in that the emotional reaction usually terminates in the subject's own body, whilst the instinctive reaction is apt to go farther and enter into practical relations with the exciting object.

Emotional reactions are often excited by objects with which we have no practical dealings. A ludicrous object, for example, or a beautiful object are not necessarily objects to which we *do* anything; we simply laugh, or stand in admiration, as the case may be. The class of emotional, is thus rather larger than that of instinctive, impulses, commonly so called. Its stimuli are more numerous, and its expressions are more internal and delicate, and often less practical. The physiological plan and essence of the two classes of impulse, however, is the same.

As with instincts, so with emotions, the mere memory or imagination of the object may suffice to liberate the excitement. One may get angrier in thinking over one's insult than at the moment of receiving it; and we melt more over a mother who is dead than we ever did when she was living. In the rest of the chapter I shall use the word *object* of emotion indifferently to mean one which is physically present or one which is merely thought of.

It would be tedious to go through a complete list of the reactions which characterize the various emotions. For that the special treatises must be referred to. A few examples of their variety, however, ought to find a place here. Let me begin with the manifestations of Grief as a Danish physiologist, C. Lange, describes them:

> The chief feature in the physiognomy of grief is perhaps its paralyzing effect on the voluntary movements. This effect is by no means as extreme as that which fright produces, being seldom more than that degree of weakening which makes it cost an effort to perform actions usually done with ease. It is, in other words, a feeling of weariness; and (as in all weariness) movements are made slowly, heavily, without strength, unwillingly, and with exertion, and are limited to the fewest possible. By this the grieving person gets his outward stamp: he walks slowly, unsteadily, dragging his feet and hanging his arms. His voice is weak and without resonance, in consequence of the feeble activity of the muscles of expiration and of the larynx. He prefers to sit still, sunk in himself and silent. The tonicity or "latent innervation" of the muscles is strikingly diminished. The neck is bent, the head hangs ("bowed down" with grief), the relaxation of the cheek- and jaw-muscles makes the face look long and narrow, the jaw may even hang open. The eyes appear large, as is always the case where the *orbicularis* muscle is paralyzed, but they may often be partly

covered by the upper lid which droops in consequence of the laming of its own *levator*. With this condition of weakness of the voluntary nerve- and muscle-apparatus of the whole body, there coexists, as aforesaid, just as in all states of similar motor weakness, a subjective feeling of weariness and heaviness, of something which weighs upon one; one feels "downcast," "oppressed," "laden," one speaks of his "weight of sorrow," one must "bear up" under it, just as one must "keep down" his anger. Many there are who "succumb" to sorrow to such a degree that they literally cannot stand upright, but sink or lean against surrounding objects, fall on their knees, or, like Romeo in the monk's cell, throw themselves upon the earth in their despair.

But this weakness of the entire voluntary motor apparatus (the so-called apparatus of "animal" life) is only one side of the physiology of grief. Another side, hardly less important, and in its consequences perhaps even more so, belongs to another subdivision of the motor apparatus, namely, the involuntary or "organic" muscles, especially those which are found in the walls of the blood-vessels, and the use of which is, by contracting, to diminish the latter's calibre. These muscles and their nerves, forming together the "vaso-motor apparatus," act in grief contrarily to the voluntary motor apparatus. Instead of being paralyzed, like the latter, the vascular muscles are more strongly contracted than usual, so that the tissues and organs of the body become anaemic. The immediate consequence of this bloodlessness is pallor and shrunkenness, and the pale color and collapsed features are the peculiarities which, in connection with the relaxation of the visage, give to the victim of grief his characteristic physiognomy, and often give an impression of emaciation which ensues too rapidly to be possibly due to real disturbance of nutrition, or waste uncompensated by repair. Another regular consequence of the bloodlessness of the skin is a feeling of cold, and shivering. A constant symptom of grief is sensitiveness to cold, and difficulty in keeping warm. In grief, the inner organs are unquestionably anaemic as well as the skin. This is of course not obvious to the eye, but many phenomena prove it. Such is the diminution of the various secretions, at least of such as are accessible to observation. The mouth grows dry, the tongue sticky, and a bitter taste ensues which, it would appear, is only a consequence of the tongue's dryness. [The expression "bitter sorrow" may possibly arise from this.] In nursing women the milk diminishes or altogether dries up. There is one of the most regular manifestations of grief, which apparently contradicts these other physiological phenomena, and that is the weeping, with its profuse secretion of tears, its swollen reddened face, red eyes, and augmented secretion from the nasal mucous membrane.

Lange goes on to suggest that this may be a reaction from a previously contracted vaso-motor state. The explanation seems a forced one. The fact is that there are changeable expressions of grief. The weeping is as apt as not to be immediate, especially in women and children. Some men can never weep. The tearful and the dry phases alternate in all who can weep, sobbing storms being followed by periods of calm; and the shrunken, cold, and pale condition which Lange describes so well is more characteristic of a severe settled sorrow than of an acute mental pain. Properly we have two distinct emotions here, both prompted by the same object, it is true, but affecting different persons, or the same person at different times, and *feeling* quite differently whilst they last, as anyone's consciousness will testify. There is an excitement during the crying fit which is not without a certain pungent pleasure of its own; but it would take a genius for felicity to discover any dash of redeeming quality in the feeling of dry and shrunken sorrow. – Our author continues:

> If the smaller vessels of the lungs contract so that these organs become anæmie, we have (as is usual under such conditions) the feeling of insufficient breath, and of oppression of the chest, and these tormenting sensations increase the sufferings of the griever, who seeks relief by long drawn sighs, instinctively, like every one who lacks breath from whatever cause.
>
> The anaemia of the brain in grief is shown by intellectual inertia, dullness, a feeling of mental weariness, effort, and indisposition to work, often by sleeplessness. Indeed it is the anaemia of the motor centres of the brain which lies at the bottom of all that weakening of the voluntary powers of motion which we described in the first instance.

My impression is that Dr Lange simplifies and universalizes the phenomena a little too much in this description, and in particular that he very likely overdoes the anaemia business. But such as it is, his account may stand as a favorable specimen of the sort of descriptive work to which the emotions have given rise.

Take next another emotion, Fear, and read what Mr Darwin says of its effects:

> Fear is often preceded by astonishment, and is so far akin to it that both lead to the senses of sight and hearing being instantly aroused. In both cases the eyes and mouth are widely opened and the eyebrows raised. The frightened man at first stands like a statue, motionless and breathless, or crouches down as if instinctively to escape observation. The heart beats quickly and violently, so that it palpitates or knocks against the ribs; but it is very doubtful if it then works more efficiently than usual, so as to send a greater supply of blood to all parts of the body; for the skin instantly becomes pale as during incipient faintness. This paleness of the surface, however, is probably in large part, or is exclusively, due to the vaso-motor centre being affected in such a manner as to cause the contraction of the small arteries of the skin. That the skin is much affected under the sense of great fear, we see in the marvellous manner in which perspiration immediately exudes from it. This exudation is all the more remarkable, as the surface is then cold, and hence the term, a cold sweat; whereas the sudorific glands are properly excited into action when the surface is heated. The hairs also on the skin stand erect, and the superficial muscles shiver. In connection with the disturbed action of the heart the breathing is hurried. The salivary glands act imperfectly; the mouth becomes dry and is often opened and shut. I have also noticed that under slight fear there is strong tendency to yawn. One of the best marked symptoms is the trembling of all the muscles of the body; and this is often first seen in the lips. From this cause, and from the dryness of the mouth, the voice becomes husky or indistinct or may altogether fail. "Obstupui steteruntque comae, et vox faucibus haesit." ... As fear increases into an agony of terror, we behold, as under all violent emotions, diversified results. The heart beats wildly or must fail to act and faintness ensue; there is a death-like pallor; the breathing is labored; the wings of the nostrils are widely dilated; there is a gasping and convulsive motion of the lips, a tremor on the hollow cheek, a gulping and catching of the throat; the uncovered and protruding eyeballs are fixed on the object of terror; or they may roll restlessly from side to side, *huc illuc volens oculos totumque pererrat*. The pupils are said to be enormously dilated. All the muscles of the body may become rigid or may be thrown into convulsive movements. The hands are

alternately clenched and opened, often with a twitching movement. The arms may be protruded as if to avert some dreadful danger, or may be thrown wildly over the head. The Rev. Mr. Hagenauer has seen this latter action in a terrified Australian. In other cases there is a sudden and uncontrollable tendency to headlong flight; and so strong is this that the boldest soldiers may be seized with a sudden panic.

Finally take Hatred, and read the synopsis of its possible effects as given by Sig. Mantegazza:

Withdrawal of the head backwards, withdrawal of the trunk; projection forwards of the hands, as if to defend one's self against the hated object; contraction or closure of the eyes; elevation of the upper lip and closure of the nose, – these are all elementary movements of turning away. Next threatening movements, as: intense frowning; eyes wide open; display of teeth; grinding teeth and contracting jaws; opened mouth with tongue advanced; clenched fists; threatening action of arms; stamping with the feet; deep inspirations – panting; growling and various cries; automatic repetition of one word or syllable; sudden weakness and trembling of voice; spitting. Finally, various miscellaneous reactions and vaso-motor symptoms: general trembling; convulsions of lips and facial muscles, of limbs and of trunk; acts of violence to one's self, as biting first or nails; sardonic laughter; bright redness of face; sudden pallor of face; extreme dilatation of nostrils; standing up of hair on head.

Were we to go through the whole list of emotions which have been named by men, and study their organic manifestations, we should but ring the changes on the elements which these three typical cases involve. Rigidity of this muscle, relaxation of that, constriction of arteries here, dilatation there, breathing of this sort or that, pulse slowing or quickening, this gland secreting and that one dry, etc., etc. We should, moreover, find that our descriptions had no absolute truth; that they only applied to the average man; that every one of us, almost, has some personal idiosyncrasy of expression, laughing or sobbing differently from his neighbor, or reddening or growing pale where others do not. We should find a like variation in the objects which excite emotion in different persons. Jokes at which one explodes with laughter nauseate another, and seem blasphemous to a third; and occasions which overwhelm me with fear or bashfulness are just what give you the full sense of ease and power. The internal shadings of emotional feeling, moreover, merge endlessly into each other. Language has discriminated some of them, as hatred, antipathy, animosity, dislike, aversion, malice, spite, vengefulness, abhorrence, etc., etc.; but in the dictionaries of synonyms we find these feelings distinguished more by their severally appropriate objective stimuli than by their conscious or subjective tone.

The result of all this flux is that the merely descriptive literature of the emotions is one of the most tedious parts of psychology. And not only is it tedious, but you feel that its subdivisions are to a great extent either fictitious or unimportant, and that its pretences to accuracy are a sham. But unfortunately there is little psychological writing about the emotions which is not merely descriptive. As emotions are described in novels, they interest us, for we are made to share them. We have grown acquainted with the concrete objects and emergencies which call them forth, and any knowing touch of introspection which may grace the page meets with a quick and feeling response. Confessedly literary works of aphoristic philosophy also flash lights into our emotional life, and give us a fitful delight. But as far as "scientific psychology" of the emotions goes, I may have been surfeited by too much reading of classic works on the subject, but I should as lief read verbal descriptions of the shapes of the rocks on a New Hampshire farm as toil through them again. They give one nowhere a central point of view, or a deductive or generative principle. They distinguish and refine and specify *in infinitum* without ever getting on to another logical level. Whereas the beauty of all truly scientific work is to get to ever deeper levels. Is there no way out from this level of individual description in the case of the emotions? I believe there is a way out, but I fear that few will take it.

The trouble with the emotions in psychology is that they are regarded too much as absolutely individual things. So long as they are set down as so many eternal and sacred psychic entities, like the old immutable species in natural history, so long all that *can* be done with them is reverently to catalogue their separate characters, points, and effects. But if we regard them as products of more general causes (as "species" are now regarded as products of heredity and variation), the mere distinguishing and cataloguing becomes of subsidiary importance. Having the goose which lays the golden eggs, the description of each egg already laid is a minor matter. Now the general causes of the emotions are indubitably physio-logical. Prof. C. Lange, of Copenhagen, in the pamphlet from which I have already quoted, published in 1885 a physiological theory of their constitution and con-ditioning, which I had already broached the previous year in an article in *Mind*. None of the criticisms which I have heard of it have made me doubt its essential truth. I will therefore devote the next few pages to explaining what it is. I shall limit myself in the first instance to what may be called the *coarser* emotions, grief, fear, rage, love, in which every one recognizes a strong organic reverberation, and afterwards speak of the *subtler* emotions, or of those whose organic reverberation is less obvious and strong.

Emotion follows upon the bodily expression in the coarser emotions at least

Our natural way of thinking about these coarser emotions is that the mental perception of some fact excites the mental affection called the emotion, and that this latter state of mind gives rise to the bodily expression. My theory, on the contrary, is that *the bodily changes follow directly the perception of the exciting fact, and that our feeling of the same changes as they occur* IS *the emotion*. Common-sense says, we lose our fortune, are sorry and weep; we meet a bear, are frightened and run; we are insulted by a rival, are angry and strike. The hypothesis here to be defended says that this order of sequence is incorrect, that the one mental state is not immedi-ately induced by the other, that the bodily manifestations must first be interposed between, and that the more rational statement is that we feel sorry because we cry, angry because we strike, afraid because we tremble, and not that we cry, strike, or tremble, because we are sorry, angry, or fearful, as the case may be. Without the bodily states following on the perception, the latter would be purely cognitive in form, pale, colorless, destitute of emotional warmth. We might then see the bear, and judge it best to run, receive the insult and deem it right to strike, but we should not actually *feel* afraid or angry.

Stated in this crude way, the hypothesis is pretty sure to meet with immediate disbelief. And yet neither many nor far-fetched considerations are required to mitigate its paradoxical character, and possibly to produce conviction of its truth.

To begin with, no reader of the last two chapters will be inclined to doubt the fact that *objects do excite bodily changes* by a preorganized mechanism, or the farther fact that *the changes are so indefinitely numerous and subtle that the entire organism may be called a sounding-board*, which every change of consciousness, however slight, may make reverberate. The various permutations and combinations of which these organic activities are susceptible make it abstractly possible that no shade of emotion, however slight, should be without a bodily reverberation as unique, when taken in its totality, as is the mental mood itself. The immense number of parts modified in each emotion is what makes it so difficult for us to reproduce in cold blood the total and integral expression of any one of them. We may catch the trick with the voluntary muscles, but fail with the skin, glands, heart, and other viscera. Just as an artificially imitated sneeze lacks something of the reality, so the attempt to imitate an emotion in the absence of its normal instigating cause is apt to be rather "hollow."

The next thing to be noticed is this, that *every one of the bodily changes, whatsoever it be*, is FELT, *acutely or obscurely, the moment it occurs*. If the reader has never paid attention to this matter, he will be both interested and astonished to learn how many different local bodily feelings he can detect in himself as characteristic of his various emotional moods. It would be perhaps too much to expect him to arrest the tide of any strong gust of passion for the sake of any such curious analysis as this; but he can observe more tranquil states, and that may be assumed here to be true of the greater which is shown to be true of the less. Our whole cubic capacity is sensibly alive; and each morsel of it contributes its pulsations of feeling, dim or sharp, pleasant, painful, or dubious, to that sense of personality that every one of us unfailingly carries with him. It is surprising what little items give accent to these complexes of sensibility. When worried by any slight trouble, one may find that the focus of one's bodily consciousness is the contraction, often quite inconsiderable, of the eyes and brows. When momentarily embarrassed, it is something in the pharynx that compels either a swallow, a clearing of the throat, or a slight cough; and so on for as many more instances as might be named. Our concern here being with the general view rather than with the details, I will not linger to discuss these, but, assuming the point admitted that every change that occurs must be felt, I will pass on.

I now proceed to urge the vital point of my whole theory, which is this: *If we fancy some strong emotion, and then try to abstract from our consciousness of it all the feelings of its bodily symptoms, we find we have nothing left behind*, no "mind-stuff" out of which the emotion can be constituted, and that a cold and neutral state of intellectual perception is all that remains. It is true that, although most people when asked say that their introspection verifies this statement, some persist in saying theirs does not. Many cannot be made to understand the question. When you beg them to imagine away every feeling of laughter and of tendency to laugh from their consciousness of the ludicrousness of an object, and then to tell you what the feeling of its ludicrousness would be like, whether it be anything more than the perception that the object belongs to the class "funny," they persist in replying that the thing proposed is a physical impossibility, and that they always *must* laugh if they see a funny object. Of course the task proposed is not the practical one of seeing a ludicrous object and annihilating one's tendency to laugh. It is the purely speculative one of subtracting certain elements of feeling from an emotional state supposed to exist in its fulness, and saying what the residual elements are. I cannot help thinking that all who rightly apprehend this problem will agree with the proposition above laid down. What kind of an emotion of fear would be left if the feeling neither of quickened heart-beats nor of shallow breathing, neither of trembling lips nor of weakened limbs, neither of goose-flesh nor of visceral stirrings, were present, it is quite impossible for me to think. Can one fancy the state of rage and picture no ebullition in the chest, no flushing of the face, no dilatation of the nostrils, no clenching of the teeth, no impulse to vigorous action, but in their stead limp muscles, calm breathing, and a placid face? The present writer, for one, certainly cannot. The rage is as completely evaporated as the sensation of its so-called manifestations, and the only thing that can possibly be supposed to take its place is some cold-blooded and dispassionate judicial sentence, confined entirely to the intellectual realm, to the effect that a certain person or persons merit chastisement for their sins. In like manner of grief: what would it be without its tears, its sobs, its suffocation of the heart, its pang in the breast-bone? A feelingless cognition that certain circumstances are deplorable, and nothing more. Every passion in turn tells the same story. A purely disembodied human emotion is a nonentity. I do not say that it is a contradiction in the nature of things, or that pure spirits are necessarily condemned to cold intellectual lives; but I say that for *us*, emotion dissociated from all bodily feeling is inconceivable. The more closely I scrutinize my states, the more persuaded I become that whatever moods, affections, and passions I have are in very truth constituted by, and made up of, those bodily changes which we ordinarily call their expression or consequence; and the more it seems to me that if I were to become corporeally anæsthetic, I should be excluded from the life of the affections, harsh and tender alike, and drag out an existence of merely cognitive or intellectual form. Such an existence, although it seems to have been the ideal of ancient sages, is too apathetic to be keenly sought after by those born after the revival of the worship of sensibility, a few generations ago.

Let not this view be called materialistic. It is neither more nor less materialistic than any other view which says that our emotions are conditioned by nervous processes. No reader of this book is likely to rebel against such a saying so long as it is expressed in general terms; and if any one still finds materialism in the thesis now defended, that must be because of the special processes invoked. They are *sensational* processes, processes due to inward currents set up by physical happenings. Such processes have, it is true, always been regarded by the platonizers in psychology as having something peculiarly base about them. But our emotions must always be *inwardly* what they are, whatever be the physiological ground of their apparition. If they are deep, pure, worthy, spiritual facts on any conceivable theory of their physiological source, they remain no less deep, pure, spiritual, and worthy of regard on this present sensational theory. They carry their own inner measure of worth with them; and it is just as logical to use the present theory of the emotions for proving that sensational processes need not be vile and material, as to use their vileness and materiality as a proof that such a theory cannot be true.

If such a theory is true, then each emotion is the resultant of a sum of elements, and each element is caused by a physiological process of a sort already well known. The elements are all organic changes, and each of them is the reflex effect of the exciting object. Definite questions now immediately arise – questions very different from those which were the only possible ones without this view. Those were questions of classification: "Which are the proper genera of emotion, and which the species under each?" or of description: "By what expression is each emotion characterized?" The questions now are *causal:* Just what changes does this object and what changes does that object excite? and "How come they to excite these particular changes and not others?" We step from a superficial to a deep order of inquiry. Classification and description are the lowest stage of science. They sink into the background the moment questions of genesis are formulated, and remain important only so far as they facilitate our answering these. Now the moment the genesis of an emotion is accounted for, as the arousal by an object of a lot of reflex acts which are forthwith felt, *we immediately see why there is no limit to the number of possible different emotions which may exist, and why the emotions of different individuals may vary indefinitely*, both as to their constitution and as to objects which call them forth. For there is nothing sacramental or eternally fixed in reflex action. Any sort of reflex effect is possible, and reflexes actually vary indefinitely, as we know. [As Lange has said:]

> We have all seen men dumb, instead of talkative, with joy; we have seen fright drive the blood into the head of its victim, instead of making him pale; we have seen grief run restlessly about lamenting, instead of sitting bowed down and mute; etc., etc., and this naturally enough, for one and the same cause can work differently on different men's blood-vessels (since these do not always react alike), whilst moreover the impulse on its way through the brain to the vaso-motor centre is differently influenced by different earlier impressions in the form of recollections or associations of ideas.

In short, *any classification of the emotions is seen to be as true and as "natural" as any other*, if it only serves some purpose; and such a question as "What is the 'real' or, 'typical' expression of anger, or fear?" is seen to have no objective meaning at all. Instead of it we now have the question as to how any given "expression" of anger or fear may have come to exist; and that is a real question of physiological mechanics on the one hand, and of history on the other, which (like all real questions) is in essence answerable, although the answer may be hard to find. On a later page I shall mention the attempts to answer it which have been made.

CHAPTER *3*

Studies on Hysteria

S. Freud and J. Breuer

Even people with little interest in psychology have heard of Freud. Many people may now have heard, also, of current controversies on repressed memories of emotional traumas of child-abuse, or of false memory syndrome. Whichever side you may favor in this debate, the thinker who hovers behind it is Freud.

Sigmund Freud devoted himself to understanding how people felt and behaved despite themselves. He founded psychoanalysis, a prototype of all therapies based on the idea that we can change emotional personality traits by understanding ourselves better.

Despite the importance of evolutionary and physiological ideas at the turn of the century, the mental study of emotions with a view to understanding them, and via this understanding to change our personality, has been of long standing in the Western history of ideas. It remains important. Whatever you may think of Freud, one of his lasting accomplishments was to show how the thoughts and feelings of people in states of emotional crisis can be taken seriously (e.g. Gay, 1988).

Freud's method was not to observe people as in the medical practice of his day − think of medical lecture-rooms shaped like theaters in which demonstrations on patients were performed. His innovation was to listen. So what do people say in their psychiatric breakdowns and crises? They talk about their emotions. Among the classics, then, of the study of mental aspects of emotions, are Freud's case histories, the first set of which he published with Breuer in 1895. The selection here, the case of Katharina, is like a short story.

Reference

Gay, P. (1988). *Freud: A life for our time.* London: Dent.

S. Freud and J. Breuer, *Studies on Hysteria* (1895), trans. J. and A. Strachey. *Pelican Freud Library* (Eds. J. Strachey, A. Strachey, and A. Richards), vol. 3. London, Penguin, 1974, pp. 190–201. Reprinted with permission.

Katharina – (Freud)

In the summer vacation of the year 189– I made an excursion into the Hohe Tauern so that for a while I might forget medicine and more particularly the neuroses. I had almost succeeded in this when one day I turned aside from the main road to climb a mountain which lay somewhat apart and which was renowned for its views and for its well-run refuge hut. I reached the top after a strenuous climb and, feeling refreshed and rested, was sitting deep in contemplation of the charm of the distant prospect. I was so lost in thought that at first I did not connect it with myself when these words reached my ears: "Are you a doctor, sir?" But the question was addressed to me, and by the rather sulky-looking girl of perhaps eighteen who had served my meal and had been spoken to by the landlady as "Katharina." To judge by her dress and bearing, she could not be a servant, but must no doubt be a daughter or relative of the landlady's.

Coming to myself I replied: "Yes, I'm a doctor: but how did you know that?"

"You wrote your name in the Visitors' Book, sir. And I thought if you had a few moments to spare…The truth is, sir, my nerves are bad. I went to see a doctor in L—about them and he gave me something for them; but I'm not well yet."

So there I was with the neuroses once again – for nothing else could very well be the matter with this strong, well-built girl with her unhappy look. I was interested to find that neuroses could flourish in this way at a height of over 6000 feet; I questioned her further therefore. I report the conversation that followed between us just as it is impressed on my memory and I have not altered the patient's dialect.

"Well, what is it you suffer from?"

"I get so out of breath. Not always. But sometimes it catches me so that I think I shall suffocate."

This did not, at first sight, sound like a nervous symptom. But soon it occurred to me that probably it was only a description that stood for an anxiety attack: she was choosing shortness of breath out of the complex of sensations arising from anxiety and laying undue stress on that single factor.

"Sit down here. What is it like when you get 'out of breath'?"

"It comes over me all at once. First of all it's like something pressing on my eyes. My head gets so heavy, there's a dreadful buzzing, and I feel so giddy that I almost fall over. Then there's something crushing my chest so that I can't get my breath."

"And you don't notice anything in your throat?"

"My throat's squeezed together as though I were going to choke."

"Does anything else happen in your head?"

"Yes, there's a hammering, enough to burst it."

"And don't you feel at all frightened while this is going on?"

"I always think I'm going to die. I'm brave as a rule and go about everywhere by myself – into the cellar and all over the mountain. But on a day when that happens I don't dare to go anywhere; I think all the time someone's standing behind me and going to catch hold of me all at once."

So it was in fact an anxiety attack, and introduced by the signs of a hysterical "aura" – or, more correctly, it was a hysterical attack the content of which was anxiety. Might there not probably be some other content as well?

"When you have an attack do you think of something? and always the same thing? or do you see something in front of you?"

"Yes. I always see an awful face that looks at me in a dreadful way, so that I'm frightened."

Perhaps this might offer a quick means of getting to the heart of the matter.

"Do you recognize the face? I mean, is it a face that you've really seen some time?"

"No."

"Do you know what your attacks come from?"

"No."

"When did you first have them?"

"Two years ago, while I was still living on the other mountain with my aunt. (She used to run a refuge hut there, and we moved here eighteen months ago.) But they keep on happening."

Was I to make an attempt at an analysis? I could not venture to transplant hypnosis to these altitudes, but perhaps I might succeed with a simple talk. I should have to try a lucky guess. I had found often enough that in girls anxiety was a consequence of the horror by which a virginal mind is overcome when it is faced for the first time with the world of sexuality.

So I said: "If you don't know, I'll tell you how *I* think you got your attacks. At that time, two years ago, you must have seen or heard something that very much embarrassed you, and that you'd much rather not have seen."

"Heavens, yes!" she replied, "that was when I caught my uncle with the girl, with Franziska, my cousin."

"What's this story about a girl? Won't you tell me all about it?"

"You can say *anything* to a doctor, I suppose. Well, at that time, you know, my uncle – the husband of the aunt you've seen here – kept the inn on the —kogel. Now they're divorced, and it's my fault they were divorced, because it was through me that it came out that he was carrying on with Franziska."

"And how did you discover it?"

"This way. One day two years ago some gentlemen had climbed the mountain and asked for something to eat. My aunt wasn't at home, and Franziska, who always did the cooking, was nowhere to be found. And my uncle was not to be found either. We looked everywhere, and at last Alois, the little boy, my cousin, said: 'Why, Franziska must be in Father's room!' And we both laughed; but we weren't thinking anything bad. Then we went to my uncle's room but found it locked. That seemed strange to me. Then Alois said: 'There's a window in the passage where you can look into the room.' We went into the passage; but Alois wouldn't go to the window and said he was afraid. So I said: 'You silly boy! I'll go. I'm not a bit afraid.' And I had nothing bad in my mind. I looked in. The room was rather dark, but I saw my uncle and Franziska; he was lying on her."

"Well?"

"I came away from the window at once, and leant up against the wall and couldn't get my breath – just what happens to me since. Everything went blank, my eyelids were forced together and there was a hammering and buzzing in my head."

"Did you tell your aunt that very same day?"

"Oh no, I said nothing."

"Then why were you so frightened when you found them together? Did you understand it? Did you know what was going on?"

"Oh no. I didn't understand anything at that time. I was only sixteen. I don't know what I was frightened about."

"Fräulein Katharina, if you could remember now what was happening in you at that time, when you had your first attack, what you thought about it – it would help you."

"Yes, if I could. But I was so frightened that I've forgotten everything."

(Translated into the terminology of our "Preliminary Communication" this means: "The affect itself created a hypnoid state, whose products were then cut off from associative connection with the ego-consciousness.")

"Tell me, Fräulein. Can it be that the head that you always see when you lose your breath is Franziska's head, as you saw it then?"

"Oh no, she didn't look so awful. Besides, it's a man's head."

"Or perhaps your uncle's?"

"I didn't see his face as clearly as that. It was too dark in the room. And why should he have been making such a dreadful face just then?"

"You're quite right."

(The road suddenly seemed blocked. Perhaps something might turn up in the rest of her story.)

"And what happened then?"

"Well, those two must have heard a noise, because they came out soon afterwards. I felt very bad the whole time. I always kept thinking about it. Then two days later it was a Sunday and there was a great deal to do and I worked all day long. And on the Monday morning I felt giddy again and was sick, and I stopped in bed and was sick without stopping for three days."

We [Breuer and I] had often compared the symptomatology of hysteria with a pictographic script which has become intelligible after the discovery of a few bilingual inscriptions. In that alphabet being sick means disgust. So I said: "If you were sick three days later, I believe that means that when you looked into the room you felt disgusted."

"Yes, I'm sure I felt disgusted," she said reflectively, "but disgusted at what?"

"Perhaps you saw something naked? What sort of state were they in?"

"It was too dark to see anything; besides they both of them had their clothes on. Oh, if only I knew what it was I felt disgusted at!"

I had no idea either. But I told her to go on and tell me whatever occurred to her, in the confident expectation that she would think of precisely what I needed to explain the case.

Well, she went on to describe how at last she reported her discovery to her aunt, who found that she was changed and suspected her of concealing some secret. There followed some very disagreeable scenes between her uncle and aunt, in the course of which the children came to hear a number of things which opened their eyes in many ways and which it would have been better for them not to have heard. At last her aunt decided to move with her children and niece and take over the present inn, leaving her uncle alone with Franziska, who had meanwhile become pregnant. After this, however, to my astonishment she dropped these threads and began to tell me two sets of older stories, which went back two or three years earlier than the traumatic moment. The first set related to occasions on which the same uncle had made sexual advances to her herself, when she was only fourteen years old. She described how she had once gone with him on an expedition down into the valley in the winter and had spent the night in the inn there. He sat in the bar drinking and playing cards, but she felt sleepy and went up to bed early in the room they were to share on the upper floor. She was not quite asleep when he came up; then she fell asleep again and woke up suddenly "feeling his body" in the bed. She jumped up and remonstrated with him: "What are you up to, Uncle? Why don't you stay in your own bed?" He tried to pacify her: "Go on, you silly girl, keep still. You don't know how nice it is." – "I don't like your 'nice' things; you don't even let one sleep in peace." She remained standing by the door, ready to take refuge outside in the passage, till at last he gave up and went to sleep himself. Then she went back to her own bed and slept till morning. From the way in which she reported having defended herself it seems to follow that she did not clearly recognize the attack as a sexual one. When I asked her if she knew what he was trying to do to her, she replied: "Not at the time." It had become clear to her much later on, she said; she had resisted because it was unpleasant to be disturbed in one's sleep and "because it wasn't nice."

I have been obliged to relate this in detail, because of its great importance for understanding everything that followed. – She went on to tell me of yet other experiences of somewhat later date: how she had once again had to defend herself against him in an inn when he was completely drunk, and similar stories. In answer to a question as to whether on these occasions she had felt anything resembling her later loss of breath, she answered with decision that she had every time felt the pressure on her eyes and chest, but with nothing like the strength that had characterized the scene of discovery.

Immediately she had finished this set of memories she began to tell me a second set, which dealt with occasions on which she had noticed something between her uncle and Franziska. Once the whole family had spent the night in their clothes in a hay loft and she was woken up suddenly by a noise; she thought she noticed that her uncle, who had been lying between her and Franziska, was turning away, and that Franziska was just lying down. Another time they were stopping the night at an inn at the village of N—; she and her uncle were in one room and Franziska in an adjoining one. She woke up suddenly in the night and saw a tall white figure by the door, on the point of turning the handle: "Goodness, is that you, Uncle? What are you doing at the door?" – "Keep quiet. I was only looking for something." – "But the way out's by the *other* door." – "I'd just made a mistake"... and so on.

I asked her if she had been suspicious at that time. "No, I didn't think anything about it; I only just noticed it and thought no more about it." When I inquired whether she had been frightened on these occasions too, she replied that she thought so, but she was not so sure of it this time.

At the end of these two sets of memories she came to a stop. She was like someone transformed. The sulky, unhappy face had grown lively, her eyes were bright, she was lightened and exalted. Meanwhile the understanding of her case had become clear to me. The later part of what she had told me, in an apparently aimless fashion, provided an admirable explanation of her behaviour at the scene of the discovery. At that time she had carried about with her two sets of experiences which she remembered but did not understand, and from which she drew no inferences. When she caught sight of the couple in intercourse, she at once established a connection between the new impression and these two sets of recollections, she began to understand them and at the same time to fend them off. There then followed a short period of working-out, of "incubation," after which the symptoms of conversion set in, the vomiting as a substitute for moral and physical disgust. This solved the riddle. She had not been disgusted by the sight of the two people but by the memory which that sight had stirred up in her. And, taking everything into account, this could only be the memory of the attempt on her at night when she had "felt her uncle's body."

So when she had finished her confession I said to her: "I know now what it was you thought when you looked into the room. You thought: 'Now he's doing with her what he wanted to do with me that night and those other times.' That was what you were disgusted at, because you remembered the feeling when you woke up in the night and felt his body."

"It may well be," she replied, "that that was what I was disgusted at and that was what I thought."

"Tell me just one thing more. You're a grown-up girl now and know all sorts of things . . ."

"Yes, now I am."

"Tell me just one thing. What part of his body was it that you felt that night?"

But she gave me no more definite answer. She smiled in an embarrassed way, as though she had been found out, like someone who is obliged to admit that a fundamental position has been reached where there is not much more to be said. I could imagine what the tactile sensation was which she had later learnt to interpret. Her facial expression seemed to me to be saying that she supposed that I was right in my conjecture. But I could not penetrate further, and in any case I owed her a debt of gratitude for having made it so much easier for me to talk to her than to the prudish ladies of my city practice, who regard whatever is natural as shameful.

Thus the case was cleared up. – But stop a moment! What about the recurrent hallucination of the head, which appeared during her attacks and struck terror into her? Where did it come from? I proceeded to ask her about it, and, as though *her* knowledge, too, had been extended by our conversation, she promptly replied: "Yes, I know now. The head is my uncle's head – I recognize it now – but not from *that* time. Later, when all the disputes had broken out, my uncle gave way to a senseless rage against me. He kept saying that it was all my fault: if I hadn't chattered, it would never have come to a divorce. He kept threatening he would do something to me; and if he caught sight of me at a distance his face would get distorted with rage and he would make for me with his hand raised. I always ran away from him, and always felt terrified that he would catch me some time unawares. The face I always see now is his face when he was in a rage."

This information reminded me that her first hysterical symptom, the vomiting, had passed away; the anxiety attack remained and acquired a fresh content. Accordingly, what we were dealing with was a hysteria which had to a considerable extent been abreacted. And in fact she had reported her discovery to her aunt soon after it happened.

"Did you tell you aunt the other stories – about his making advances to you?"

"Yes. Not at once, but later on, when there was already talk of a divorce. My aunt said: 'We'll keep that in reserve. If he causes trouble in the Court, we'll say that too.'"

I can well understand that it should have been precisely this last period – when there were more and more agitating scenes in the house and when her own state ceased to interest her aunt, who was entirely occupied with the dispute – that it should have been this period of accumulation and retention that left her the legacy of the mnemic symbol [of the hallucinated face].

I hope this girl, whose sexual sensibility had been injured at such an early age, derived some benefit from our conversation. I have not seen her since.

Discussion

If someone were to assert that the present case history is not so much an analysed case of hysteria as a case solved by guessing, I should have nothing to say against him. It is true that the patient agreed that what I interpolated into her story was probably true; but she was not in a position to recognize it as something she had experienced. I believe it would have required hypnosis to bring that about. Assuming that my guesses were correct, I will now attempt to fit the case into the schematic picture of an "acquired" hysteria on the lines suggested by Case 3. It seems plausible, then, to compare the two sets of erotic experiences with "traumatic" moments and the scene of discovering the couple with an "auxiliary" moment. The similarity lies in the fact that in the former experiences an element of consciousness was created which was excluded from the thought-activity of the ego and remained, as it were, in storage, while in the latter scene a new impression forcibly brought about an associative connection between this separated group and the ego. On the other hand there are dissimilarities which cannot be overlooked. The cause of the isolation was not, as in Case 3, an act of will on the part of the ego but *ignorance* on the part of the ego, which was not yet capable of coping with sexual experiences. In this respect the case of Katharina is typical. In every analysis of a case of hysteria based on sexual traumas we find that impressions from the presexual period which produced no effect on the child attain traumatic power at a later date as memories, when the girl or married woman has acquired an understanding of sexual life. The splitting-off of psychical groups may be said to be a normal process in adolescent development; and it is easy to see that their later reception into the ego affords frequent opportunities for psychical disturbances. Moreover, I should like at this point to express a doubt as to whether a splitting of consciousness due to ignorance is really different from one due to conscious rejection, and whether even adolescents do not possess sexual knowledge far oftener than is supposed or than they themselves believe.

A further distinction in the psychical mechanism of this case lies in the fact that the scene of discovery, which we have described as "auxiliary," deserves equally to be called "traumatic." It was operative on account of its own content and not merely as something that revived previous traumatic experiences. It combined the characteristics of an "auxiliary" and a "traumatic" moment. There seems no reason, however, why this coincidence should lead us to abandon a conceptual separation which in other cases corresponds also to a separation in time. Another peculiarity of Katharina's case, which, incidentally, has long been familiar to us, is seen in the circumstance that the conversion, the production of the hysterical phenomena, did not occur immediately after the trauma but after an interval of incubation. Charcot liked to describe this interval as the "period of psychical working-out" [*élaboration*].

The anxiety from which Katharina suffered in her attacks was a hysterical one; that is, it was a reproduction of the anxiety which had appeared in connection with each of the sexual traumas. I shall not here comment on the fact which I have found regularly present in a very large number of cases – namely that a mere suspicion of sexual relations calls up the affect of anxiety in virginal individuals.[1]

Note

1 (*Footnote added* 1924:) I venture after the lapse of so many years to lift the veil of discretion and reveal the fact that Katharina was not the niece but the daughter of the landlady. The girl fell ill, therefore, as a result of sexual attempts on the part of her own father. Distortions like the one which I introduced in the present instance should be altogether avoided in reporting a case history. From the point of view of understanding the case, a distortion of this kind is not, of course, a matter of such indifference as would be shifting the scene from one mountain to another.

CHAPTER *4*

Emotion and Adaptation

R. S. Lazarus

The theorists whom we have introduced so far lacked much sense of purpose for emotions. Darwin said that emotional expressions were manifestations of behavioral mechanisms that once had a purpose, in evolution or infancy, but which in adulthood they did not necessarily retain. James proposed that emotions arose when the business of constructing a piece of behavior was over. Freud concentrated on dysfunctional effects of emotions that affected a person because of something in the past rather than the present. Appraisal theorists were in the new wave of asking what psychological functions emotions might have.

Richard Lazarus was early in studying appraisal. His book of 1966 became a classic, and was influential in studies of stress and coping. He himself was influenced by ideas of the cognitive revolution. In 1992 he published a famous paper, taking the cognitive side in a debate with Zajonc whose research (e.g. Zajonc, Murphy, & Inglehart, 1989) produced striking results upholding the peripheralist ideas of James.

References

Lazarus, R. S. (1966). *Psychological stress and the coping process.* New York: McGraw-Hill.
Lazarus, R. S. (1992). Thoughts on the relation between emotion and cognition. *American Psychologist, 37,* 1019–1024.
Zajonc, R. B., Murphy, S. T., & Inglehart, M. (1989). Feeling and facial efference: Implications of the vascular theory of emotion. *Psychological Review, 96,* 395–416.

R. S. Lazarus, *Emotion and Adaptation.* New York: Oxford University Press, 1991, pp. 121, 131–134, 149–152. Reprinted with permission.

Core relational themes

Person–environment relationships come together with personal meaning and the appraisal process (to be discussed in Chapter 4) in the concept of *core relational themes*. Appraisal involves an appreciation of a particular harm or benefit in the relationship with the environment, with its manifold implications for well-being, action, and coping. Within the cognitive-motivational-relational framework, each negative emotion should suggest research questions about the necessary and sufficient core relational themes at the *molar level*, as well as the necessary and sufficient appraisal components specifying the harms or benefits, and what could be done about them, at the *molecular level*. The latter combine into patterns to produce the core relational themes as a kind of convenient summary, much like the themas of Murray (1935). Considering knowledge and appraisal in terms of *both* molecular components and molar themes provides a clearer understanding of the relationship between appraisal and emotion than a study of either would yield in isolation.

Although person-environment relationships must be sensed and evaluated personally (appraised) by an individual to generate emotions, we can nevertheless speak of them without reference to cognitive activity for the time being if we simply assume for future reference that it is the relationship as appraised subjectively that counts rather than the objective or actual relationship as it is presumably viewed through the eyes of observers.

A core relational theme is simply the central (hence core) relational harm or benefit in adaptational encounters that underlies each specific kind of emotion. There are diverse kinds of harmful relationships, each of which constitutes a core relational theme leading to a distinctive negative emotion. There are also diverse kinds of beneficial relationships, each of which constitutes a core relational theme leading to a distinctive positive emotion. Each individual emotion or emotion family is defined by a specific core relational theme. When its implications for well-being are appraised by the person, each thematic relationship produces an action impulse consistent with the core relational theme and the emotion that flows from it [...] Table 4.1 contains a list of the core relational themes for each emotion in [...]

Appraisal

Primary appraisal concerns whether something of relevance to the person's well-being has occurred. Only if a person has a personal stake in an encounter – say, a short- or long-term goal such as social or self-esteem or the well-being of a loved one – will there be a stressful response to what is happening. To anticipate recent changes in this concept, primary appraisal has now been expanded to include three components: *goal relevance, goal congruence or incongruence,* and *type of ego-involvement.* I have more to say about these components later.

Secondary appraisal concerns coping options – that is, whether any given action might prevent harm, ameliorate it, or produce additional harm or benefit. The

Table 4.1. Core relational themes for each emotion

Anger	A demeaning offense against me and mine.
Anxiety	Facing uncertain, existential threat.
Fright	Facing an immediate, concrete, and overwhelming physical danger.
Guilt	Having transgressed a moral imperative.
Shame	Having failed to live up to an ego-ideal.
Sadness	Having experienced an irrevocable loss.
Envy	Wanting what someone else has.
Jealousy	Resenting a third party for loss or threat to another's affection.
Disgust	Taking in or being too close to an indigestible object or idea (metaphorically speaking).
Happiness	Making reasonable progress toward the realization of a goal.
Pride	Enhancement of one's ego-identity by taking credit for a valued object or achievement, either our own or that of someone or group with whom we identify.
Relief	A distressing goal-incongruent condition that has changed for the better or gone away.
Hope	Fearing the worst but yearning for better.
Love	Desiring or participating in affection, usually but not necessarily reciprocated.
Compassion	Being moved by another's suffering and wanting to help.

fundamental issue being evaluated is: "What, if anything, can I do in this encounter, and how will what I do and what is going to happen affect my well-being?" (see Janis & Mann, 1977, for a parallel analysis). To distinguish among the individual emotions, three secondary appraisal components are needed – namely, *blame or credit, coping potential,* and *future expectations*. I return to these later.

Because all encounters with the environment are continually changing and generating feedback about the psychological situation, primary and secondary appraisal are also continually changing, which is why emotions are always in flux. Feedback about the environment, or from one's own actions and reactions, constitutes new information to be evaluated. I refer to the process of further evaluation as *reappraisal* (Lazarus, 1966). It is distinguished from appraisal only by coming later, and so it is basically no different from other kinds of appraisal except for its history and the self-generated feature of cognitive- or emotion-focused coping, which, like defenses, are appraisals that are constructed by the mind to regulate emotional distress or protect one's ego-identity (see Chapter 3). The term *reappraisal* also implies the continuous nature of a person's evaluations of transactions with the environment and emphasizes their responsiveness to feedback [...]

Primary and secondary appraisal components

I am now ready to examine the six appraisal components, which I will use in chapters 6 and 7 to explore the appraisal pattern for each individual emotion. These have been chosen with two purposes in mind. First, I aim to integrate my earlier work on psychological stress theory with the present cognitive-motivational-relational theory of emotions (for example, one of the secondary appraisal components refers to conditions relevant to coping). Second, I have also drawn on concepts that either borrow or parallel the burgeoning work of others on appraisal and emotion.

There are three forms of primary appraisal and three of secondary appraisal, which overlap with some of the cognitive dimensions proposed by Frijda (1986), Roseman (1984), Scherer (1984a, 1984b), and Smith and Ellsworth (1985, 1987). These can be considered components of appraisal (Lazarus & Smith, 1988) rather than of knowledge. The three *primary appraisal* components are goal relevance, goal congruence or incongruence, and type of ego-involvement.

Goal relevance refers to the extent to which an encounter touches on personal goals – that is, whether or not there are issues in the encounter about which the person cares or in which there is a personal stake. If there is no goal relevance, there cannot be an emotion; if there is, one or another emotion will occur, depending on the outcome of the transaction.

Goal congruence or incongruence refers to the extent to which a transaction is consistent or inconsistent with what the person wants – that is, it either thwarts or facilitates personal goals. If it thwarts, I speak of goal incongruence; if it facilitates, I speak of goal congruence. Goal congruence leads to positive emotions; goal incongruence to negative ones. The specific emotion depends, however, on additional secondary appraisal components.

Type of ego-involvement refers to diverse aspects of ego-identity or personal commitments. I listed six in chapter 3 including self- and social-esteem, moral values, ego-ideals, meanings and ideas, other persons and their well-being, and life goals, all collected within the rubric of ego-identity. As we will see in chapters 6 and 7, ego-identity is probably involved in all or most emotions, but in different ways depending on the type of ego-involvement that is engaged by a transaction. To illustrate with several examples: In anger, one's self- or social-esteem is being assaulted; in anxiety, the threat is existential (to meaning structures in which one is invested); in guilt, it is violation of a moral value one is sworn to uphold; in shame, it is a failure to live up to one's ego-ideals; in sadness, it is loss of any or all of the six types of ego-identity; in happiness, it is an overall sense of security and well-being; and in pride – a kind of opposite of anger – it is an enhancement of the self- and social-esteem aspect of ego-identity; and so on.

The three components of *secondary appraisal* are *blame or credit* (which can be external – that is, directed at someone else – or internal – that is, directed at oneself), *coping potential*, and *future expectancy*.

Blame and *credit* derive from knowing who is accountable or responsible for frustration; if this knowledge is accompanied by the knowledge that the frustrating act was under the accountable person's control, credit or blame is assigned.

Coping potential refers to whether and how the person can manage the demands of the encounter or actualize personal commitments (cf. Folkman & Lazarus, 1980, 1985; Folkman, Lazarus, Dunkel-Schetter, DeLongis, & Gruen, 1986; Folkman, Lazarus, Gruen, & DeLongis, 1986; Folkman & Lazarus, 1990; Lazarus & Folkman, 1987). I emphasize that coping potential is not actual coping but only an evaluation by a person of the prospects for doing or thinking something that will, in turn, change or protect the person-environment relationship.

Future expectancy has to do with whether for any reason things are likely to change psychologically for the better or worse (i.e. becoming more or less goal congruent).

This is a good place to emphasize one more time that the concepts of blame and credit, and those of accountability and imputed control, illustrate the interplay of knowledge and appraisal in the generation of an emotion. Accountability and imputed control are components of knowledge; blame and credit are components of appraisal. Knowledge is often indeterminate with respect to personal implications and does not generate emotion without a further process of evaluation of its personal implications for one's well-being. (See also a complex and subtle attributional analysis of the effects of praise and blame by Meyer [1992] which shows that how it is taken by the recipient and observer depends on the context and cognitive maturity.) Knowing that we are accountable for something socially valued does not create pride unless we have also accepted credit for it. For example, we cannot readily take credit if what has happened was accidental. Similarly, others frustrating us does not result in blame unless we also believe that they were in control of their actions; if they couldn't have done otherwise under the circumstances, we resist blaming them and feeling anger toward them, though we may cast around for others to blame. We will see how this works specifically in anger, pride, and other emotions in chapters 6 and 7.

Notice that the appraisal components are ordered in such a way that they proceed from very broad decisions – for example, whether or not there will be an emotion (goal relevance), whether the emotion will be positive or negative (goal congruence or incongruence) – gradually narrowing down to a precise discrimination between one emotion and another. As the options are narrowed, it becomes possible to say that only one emotion is possible in this context. This decision-tree pattern will be used in chapters 6 and 7 in identifying the appraisal patterns for each individual emotion.

Since I argue that appraisals are not sequential (unlike Scherer's 1984a, 1984b, analysis), why do I use a decision-tree format, which invites the image of a person going stepwise down the list of appraisal components until the specific desiderata of a single emotion have been reached? The answer is that a decision-tree format helps the reader to understand the theoretical or explanatory logic of appraisal but does not describe how a person goes about appraising in the real world. It is a didactic device rather than a portrayal of how things work. There is, of course, no established answer about how appraisal decisions are actually made. However, I would like to make two points about this:

First, we do not have to go through the entire appraisal process every time a new adaptational encounter is faced. When we have previously learned the contingencies between certain conditions and their consequences for well-being, instantaneous appraisals will then be made in response to minimal cues, based on our knowledge of these contingencies. Much in life is a restatement of past struggles, which as a feature of our personal history is an integral part of the emotion process (see chapter 8). In effect, many appraisal decisions have already been all but made, and need only the appropriate environmental cue to trigger them. Deliberation is not needed to appraise these instances, because the appraisal patterns have, as it were, already been set in advance.

Second, goal hierarchies and belief patterns prime the person to be sensitive to some circumstances and not others. This priming is a prior process that speeds up the appraisal and makes it selective. This is better addressed in the next section, however, under the rubric of meaning.

In any event, even though I have presented it and used it in chapters 6 and 7 as a decision tree, we must not see the appraisal process as a sequential or stepwise process of scanning the components in any fixed order. Very rapidly, perhaps even simultaneously, we draw on a variety of stored information about the environment, person variables, and their relational meaning. How this is done remains something of a mystery, but we must indeed automatically do something similar to what I have described, or else the emotion process would not be adaptive and our emotional lives would be much more chaotic than they are [...]

References

Folkman, S., & Lazarus, R. S. (1980). An analysis of coping in a middle-aged community sample. *Journal of Health and Social Behavior, 21*, 219–239.

—— (1990). Coping and emotion. In N. Stein, B. Leventhal, & T. Trabasso (Eds.), *Psychological and biological approaches to emotion* (pp. 313–332). Hillsdale, NJ: Erlbaum.

Folkman, S., Lazarus, R. S., Dunkel-Schetter, C., DeLongis, A., & Gruen, R. (1986). The dynamics of a stressful encounter: Cognitive appraisal, coping, and encounter outcomes. *Journal of Personality and Social Psychology, 50*, 992–1003.

Folkman, S., Lazarus, R. S., Gruen, R., & DeLongis, A. (1986). Appraisal, coping, health status, and psychological symptoms. *Journal of Personality and Social Psychology, 50*, 572–579.

Frijda, N. H. (1986). *The emotions.* Cambridge: Cambridge University Press.

Lazarus, R. S. (1966). *Psychological stress and the coping process.* New York: McGraw-Hill.

—— (1981a). The stress and coping paradigm. In C. Eisdorfer, D. Cohen, A. Kleinman, & P. Maxim (Eds.), *Models for clinical psychopathology* (pp. 177–214). New York: Spectrum.

Lazarus, R. S., & Folkman, S. (1984). *Stress, appraisal and coping.* New York: Springer.

—— (1987). Transactional theory and research on emotions and coping. In L. Laux & G. Vossel (Special Eds.), Personality in biographical stress and coping research. *European Journal of Personality, 1*, 141–169.

Lazarus, R. S., & Launier, R. (1978). Stress-related transactions between person and environment. In L. A. Pervin & M. Lewis (Eds.), *Perspectives in interactional psychology* (pp. 287–327). New York: Plenum.

Lazarus, R. S., & Smith, C. A. (1988). Knowledge and appraisal in the cognition-emotion relationship. *Cognition and Emotion, 2*, 281–300.

Meyer, W.-U. (1992). Paradoxical effects of praise and blame on perceived ability and affect. In W. Stoege & M. J. Hewstone (Eds.), *European Review of Social Psychology, 3*, 259–283.

Murray, H. A. (1938). *Explorations in personality.* New York: Oxford University Press.

Roseman, I. (1984). Cognitive determinants of emotion: A structural theory. In P. Shaver (Ed.), *Review of personality and social psychology*: Vol. 5. *Emotions, relationships, and health* (pp. 11–36). Beverly Hills, CA: Sage.

Scherer, K. R. (1984a). On the nature and function of emotion: A component process approach. In K. R. Scherer & P. Ekman (Eds.), *Approaches to emotion* (pp. 293–317). Hillsdale, NJ: Erlbaum.

———(1984b). Emotion as a multicomponent process: A model with some cross-cultural data. In P. Shaver (Ed.), *Review of personality and social psychology: Vol. 5. Emotions, relationships, and health* (pp. 37–63). Beverly Hills, CA: Sage.

Smith, C. A., & Ellsworth, P. C. (1985). Patterns of cognitive appraisal in emotion. *Journal of Personality and Social Psychology, 48,* 813–838.

———(1987). Patterns of appraisal and emotion related to taking an exam. *Journal of Personality and Social Psychology, 52,* 475–488.

CHAPTER *5*

Never in Anger: Portrait of an Eskimo Family

Jean L. Briggs

Jean Briggs spent seventeen months, between June 1963 and March 1965, in an Inuit (Eskimo) family, who lived on the banks of Back River as it enters Chantry Inlet, near the Arctic circle, some 1300 miles north of Winnipeg, Canada. Her research project had at first been to learn about shamanism – indigenous religious and healing practices – only to find when she arrived that her hosts had become Christians thirty years previously. They assured her that any shamans must now be either in hell or in hiding. Only by accident, therefore, did she decide to find out about emotions in the family in which she stayed.

Brigg's book has become the classic study of the emotional life of a group living in a traditional way of life, little touched by Western industrialization or consumerism. Other anthropological studies of emotions, e.g. Lutz (1988), owe much to Briggs's pioneering work.

In this selection Yiini is the Inuit pronunciation of Brigg's first name, Jean; Inuttiaq is the head of the family who adopted her, with whom she stayed; Allaq is his wife; Saarak is their third daughter, aged about three when she arrived (a fourth child was born during Briggs's stay). Kaplunas are white people. An iglu is a house made of snow in which the entire family lives during the winter months when the temperature goes down to between 30 and 70 degrees Fahrenheit below zero. Compared with outside, the interior of an iglu is cosy, but still has to be kept below freezing so that its roof and walls do not melt. A qaqmaq is a circular dwelling built in the autumn, with walls of ice or snow but roofed with a tent.

Reference

Lutz, C. A. (1988). *Unnatural emotions: Everyday sentiments on a Micronesian atoll and their challenge to Western theory*. Chicago: University of Chicago Press.

Jean L. Briggs, *Never in Anger: Portrait of an Eskimo Family*. Cambridge, MA: Harvard University Press, 1970, pp. 226–232, 274–279, 283–285. Reprinted with permission.

I Stranger and guest: graciousness

In retrospect, my relationship with the Utku seems to divide approximately into three phases, in which from the Utku point of view I was first a stranger and curiosity, then a recalcitrant child, and finally a confirmed irritant. This does not mean that I was never liked. I was, at times. Days and weeks passed very harmoniously, but I want to describe here the less harmonious aspects of the relationship, which illuminate the ways in which the Utku handled the problems created by my presence.

The initial phase of the relationship I have already described in part. In this period I was treated with all the solicitude that is accorded an honored guest. When I visited in the Eskimo tents, I was given the softest seat, often a seat on the family ikliq, and, like the always privileged children, I was offered milk and sugar in my tea. My interests were tended equally in my own tent. When I offered food to my visitors, they never took advantage of my ignorance of an owner's pre-rogatives; I was always urged to serve myself first, the largest pieces of the bannock that I hospitably fried were always urged upon me, and if I offered to share a meal with a visitor, the latter never failed to ask whether I had finished eating, before he took the pot I held out to him. My fish supply was always replenished before I felt the need, and often even the usual division of labor between men and women stood in abeyance as men offered to fetch me water from the river or to refuel my primus.

To be sure, such solicitous acts were not wholly altruistic. Neither did they necessarily signify that I was liked. They were, not surprisingly, motivated in part by fear (*ilira*), which was admitted only months later, and by a desire for profit, if a word of such exploitative connotations can be used of the very moderate requests that Utku make of their wealthy kapluna visitors. My hosts expected to be rewarded for their solicitude, both by my goodwill in a broad sense and by the tangible expression of that goodwill: a share in my kapluna supplies. As Inuttiaq put it once when I thanked a young man for repairing a tear in my tent wall: "If you are grateful, make tea." In the early days, before I was integrated into Utku life to the point where I might reasonably be expected to share my goods as a participating member of the community, people did not often ask for gifts; however, in addition to the services they performed for me, they besieged me daily with small bone and wood objects, nearly all the crude result of an hour or two of work: miniature models of fishhooks, fishing jigs, fish spears, seals, airplanes, and sleds, which their makers wished to trade for "a little bit" of tobacco, tea, sugar, milk, flour, or oats. Generous at first, I quickly became alarmed when I saw how quickly and in what quantity these trade goods were manufactured; but each request was so modest, and the Utku set such a precedent for generosity in their treatment of me that it was difficult – as I am sure they hoped it would be – to refuse them.

So in this early period of my stay, I was both guest and provider; and I played another role, as well, that of comedian. My curious appearance and manner were closely, though covertly, observed and gave the community endless amusement. The unpronounceable plant names that I was required to repeat for entertainment on my first meeting with the married couple were brought out on other occasions, too, together with other known tongue-twisters, like the intensifying form "-hlkha," which I could never pronounce except as "-lzga." "Yiini," someone would observe, with a twinkle, "Niptaihlkha (it's terribly foggy)." And when I, knowing full well the nature of the game, obligingly agreed: "Eee, yes, indeed, it's terribly foggy: niptailzga," then my audience would be overcome with laughter, in which I was expected to join. Amaaqtuq once remarked to me: "You're nice (*quvia*) because you're comical (*tiphi*)."

So convivial was the laughter of the Utku and so gracious their attempts to smooth the unknown ground for me that I am chagrined to remember how thorny this first period was. Of course it could not have been otherwise. In such a new and strange situation it was impossible even to stimulate the composure that the Eskimos would have approved of and that would have made the relationship between us comfortable and harmonious. I was afraid in those first weeks: afraid of freezing to death, of going hungry, of being seriously ill and unable to reach help. All of these fears, natural enough in anyone who undertakes to isolate himself in a completely foreign environment, were aggravated in my case by the exaggerated warnings with which I had been bombarded before setting out on my venture. I had been at pains to conceal from my well-wishers that their anxieties had borne fruit, but they had. By the time I arrived at Back River I was not at all convinced that my undertaking was rational and feasible. Long before the temperature reached zero, I had acquired three frost-reddened toes and twelve chilblains on my hands, which convinced me that I would never be able to survive the winter temperatures of 30 to 70 degrees below zero. The fear itself, of course, added to my chill, lowering my body temperature perceptibly and causing me to curse futilely at my anxiety.

My fear of food shortage was not quite as realistic, in a material sense, as the fear of cold. Though I had been alarmed in Ottawa by reports of "recurrent famines" at Back River, that myth had been exploded by a sensible priest in Gjoa Haven, who had experience of the region. The value that my kapluna food supplies had for me, therefore, was primarily symbolic. It was hard to accustom myself to a diet of raw fish, eaten skin, scales, and all. I never did succeed in mastering the skin, but at first I tried, valiantly, though the scales stuck in my throat and the slime made me retch. Fish were usually plentiful, and I was rarely really hungry; nevertheless I craved the solace of oatmeal, dates, boiled rice, and bannock, and much of the time my secret thoughts crept guiltily around one problem: how best to create opportunities for gorging myself on these familiar foods without having to share them with the visitors who were so generous with their own food. It is hard for anyone who has not experienced isolation from his familiar world to conceive the vital importance of maintaining symbolic ties with that world and the sense of deprivation that results from their absence. One can be driven to lengths that seem ludicrous once one is safely back on home ground. Unpacking on my return, I was amazed to find eight sesame seeds that I had hoarded, carefully wrapped in tinfoil, for an emergency: a time of emotional starvation. Food provided many comforts beyond the fundamental satisfaction of a full stomach. Whenever anything went awry; whenever I failed to make myself understood; when Saarak wailed at the sight of me; or when the cries of the seagulls reminded me of home, my solace was food. Though I did not know it at the time, my dependence on food as a solace was very Eskimo; the problems were that I preferred my kapluna foods to the plentiful fish, and that the demand of the Eskimos for my limited supplies was great.

Frightened as I was of cold and hunger, mishaps seemed to occur constantly, and the smallest one assumed momentous proportions in my imagination. When I discovered that I had left my gun on the plane that brought me in; when I found that I had bought all the accoutrements of a fishnet but had neglected to buy the net itself; when I learned that I had been misinformed about the date at which the Utku normally move to their winter campsite and that as a consequence I had brought too little kerosene to the autumn site; when I understood Allaq to tell me that the caribou hides I had brought were not suitable for my winter clothing, ridiculous as it seems to me now, I was filled with panic. I had no realistic image of what the winter would be like, no idea whether the Utku would deal with it in ways that I could tolerate, and, worse, no way of allaying my apprehension, since I could not speak Eskimo.

Equally appalling, however, was the thought of giving up and going home, after having stubbornly resisted all those well-meant warnings. "I told you so"s rang in my imagination and hardened my resolve. Nevertheless, the conflicting wishes and fears hammered for expression and, on occasion, made it difficult to smile in proper Eskimo fashion.

My spontaneous reaction to any sort of strain is tearfulness. I tried to suppress that reaction, knowing from previous experience with Eskimos that equanimity in the face of difficulty is a high virtue and that tearfulness is not to be countenanced; nevertheless I am certain that all too frequently I was unsuccessful in concealing my distress. The first such incident that I remember occurred on a Sunday morning, shortly after the return of the caribou hunters to the camp at the Rapids. A number of Pala's kin, including Inuttiaq, were drinking tea in my tent at eight in the morning when Nilak and his family appeared in the entrance. Nilak was oddly dressed: from underneath his short parka a plaid wool bathrobe flowed over his trousers. It was a costume that he affected every Sunday at that time, but I had not seen it before. He and his wife and daughter each carried a small calico bag containing, as I later found, a Bible and a prayerbook. I was puzzled, both by the bathrobe and by the mysterious calico bags, but no one volunteered an explanation. People sat and drank tea, and every hour or half-hour one of the men asked me: "What time is it?" I suspected that a church service was in the offing; it was, after all, the first Sunday since Inuttiaq's return from the caribou hunt. It was a dismal day in my private world, I can no longer remember why, and my anticipation of the forthcoming service did little to cheer me. On the contrary, the reticence of my visitors intensified my depression and made me feel altogether isolated. Though I very much wanted the opportunity to observe the religious behavior of the camp, I was sure they would not invite me to join them. So when I pronounced the time to be 10:30, and Inuttiaq confirmed my suspicion – "we are going to pray at 11" – I asked if I might come. Inuttiaq's face and Pala's went blank. The words of their reply were incomprehensible to me, but their reluctance, their hesitation, were evident enough. I felt a spasm cross my face. Nothing was said on either side, but when the company rose to leave at eleven, Inuttiaq turned to me: "We are going to pray. You, too." And so, restored to cheer, I accompanied the others.

Tactful compliance was the characteristic response of the Utku in those early days, whenever resentment, fatigue, or anxiety brought the tears close to the surface or made my voice sharp. Such breaches of emotional decorum occurred fairly frequently, too, all precipitated by the fear of cold and hunger, and by the difficulty of communicating with my Eskimo hosts. Concerned about the effects of my untoward behavior, I recorded a number of these incidents even though at the time I had no idea how right I was to worry about Utku reactions. Now that I know how strongly they disapproved of volatility, I am astonished that they continued to respond with graciousness and, instead of withdrawing from me, continued to court me in a friendly manner when I was in a mood to permit it.

My moodiness in the early days, and the reactions of the Utku to it, are exemplified by my relationship with Pala, who subsequently became my grandfather. For various reasons, Pala attracted more of my impatience than did the rest of his kin in those first days. Nevertheless, Pala, like his kin, gave no sign that he was offended by my snappishness. Perhaps it would be more accurate to say that neither he nor the others showed offense in any way that was recognizable to me at that time.

In part, the friction between Pala and me arose from my unpleasant suspicion that he cast a covetous eye on my possessions. Though it never occurred to me that he might actually take something of mine (and neither he nor anyone else ever did), nevertheless I did not find his attitude attractive. There was a game he used to play with me, in which he pretended to steal from me, always ostentatiously showing me his action: "Yiini, watch!" or in which he pretended to reach for an object I was holding: a boot, a spoon, a piece of bannock. "Mine? Mine?" he would inquire, extending his hands with fingers curled in mock aggressiveness, his eyes and mouth wide in simulation of greed. And when I, entering into the comedy, made a great show of pulling the "stolen" object back, or hiding the object reached for, with exaggerated exclamations of alarm or umbrage, Pala and the others present laughed with the greatest merriment. Others, taking their cue from Pala, used occasionally to play the same game with me, but Pala was its creator and chief actor, and it seemed clear to me that his real wishes were being expressed under cover of a joke.

Of all my possessions, tobacco was what Pala most craved, and it was tobacco that created the greatest tension between us. It was not necessarily that he craved it more than other people, but his wish to have it was certainly more clearly expressed. His visits were more conspicuously correlated than were other people's with the state of my tobacco supply; he was the only person who ever made the performance of a service *contingent* on receiving tobacco, and he was the only one who ever demanded, "More!" when, on request, I filled the men's tobacco pouches of a morning. His "greediness," for such I felt it to be, contrasted with Inuttiaq's attitude; Inuttiaq more than once stopped me when his pouch was half full: "That's enough; more later today or tomorrow." [...]

IV The fishermen: crisis

At the time I went to live with the Utku, Chantrey Inlet was becoming increasingly known among sports fishermen in the provinces of Canada and in the United States. Every year in July and August small charter airlines in Ontario and Manitoba, which cater to sportsmen, flew men in, for a price incredible to me, to spend two or three or five days fishing for arctic char and salmon trout at the Rapids. Until a year or so before my arrival only a few had come each summer, perhaps five or six, but then they had begun to come in numbers. Fifteen or twenty, the Utku calculated, had come in 1963, and in 1964, when I was there, forty came, not all at once but in groups ranging in size from two or three to approximately fifteen. One or more of these groups was with us constantly from July 26 until August 23. They camped across the river from us, out of sight behind a point of land, and their outboard motors sputtered up and down the river from dawn to dark.

Some of these fishermen and their guide, a Canadian named Ray, kept to themselves on their side of the river. They traded generously with the Eskimos when the latter went to offer bone toys in exchange for tea, tobacco, and fishhooks, but otherwise they largely ignored the native inhabitants of the Inlet. The Utku – it was Nilak, Pala, Inuttiaq, and, later, Ipuituq, who were camped by the rapids that summer – liked Ray. He was a mild-mannered man, who had been bringing fishing parties to the Inlet for several years and who treated the Eskimos with dignity.

Individuals in other groups were less innocuous. Hard drinking, cigar smoking, and gruff-voiced, lacking in gentleness and sensitivity, they were the antithesis of everything Eskimo. They stared at the Eskimos; visited the Eskimo camp and photographed people without asking permission; peered into the tents; and when the Eskimos tried to trade for the coveted tea, tobacco, and fishhooks, one or two of these kaplunas offered instead strings of pink beads and other useless items, which the Eskimos were too timorous and too polite to refuse. The Eskimo women were particularly afraid (*kappia, iqhi*) of one of the plane pilots who, they said, had "wanted a woman" the previous year and had made his wishes known distinctly.

The Utku did not fail to notice differences among the fishermen and to judge some of them kinder (*quya*) than others, but whatever dislike they felt showed neither in avoidance nor, of course, in aggressive acts. The Eskimos looked forward with excitement to the coming of the kaplunas in July. As soon as the ice left the river, they began to listen for planes and, as they sat together on the gravel in front of the tents, they filed away at bits of caribou antler, shaping them into miniature replicas of fishhooks, pipes, knives, and other objects to trade to the kaplunas. Their talk was of tea and tobacco and of other things – food and clothing – which they had received from the fishermen in the past in very generous amounts, and which they hoped to receive again. When a plane was heard they hurried with one accord to the other side of the river in order to be present when the kaplunas landed, to help with the unloading of the plane, and to watch the strangers. Regardless of the quality of the men who had arrived, regardless of how the Utku felt about them, they treated all alike with the same obliging acquiescence with which they had treated me on my arrival. Their courtesy did not fail even when the kaplunas took advantage of their mildness to treat them in ways that I considered most humiliating. One champion wrestler picked up Mannik and held him horizontally, by shoulder and thigh, over his head: for a television ad, he explained to me. Mannik, who knew nothing of what was happening until he found himself in the air, giggled. On another occasion a loud-voiced man staggered off the plane, steeped in champagne, and wove his way over to Pala, whom he had singled out as the Eskimo "chief." Hugging Pala warmly, he inquired what his name was and invited him in incoherent English to be his friend. Pala, to my astonishment, understood the man to ask his name and replied "Peeterosi" (Peter, his Christian name). "Ha ha, Peeterosi!" roared the drunken kapluna. "Ha ha, Peeterosi! Le's be frens, I like Eskimos, nice Eskimos," and he stroked Pala's head, while Pala laughed mildly and resisted not at all. The other Utku watched, expressionless, in the background.

When we returned to our camp, later, I discovered that the Utku did have a way of retaliating against the kaplunas' condescending behavior; they made fun of it. They taught Saarak to imitate the drunken fisherman, and for months she ran from person to person, on request, stroking their heads and laughing with kapluna boisterousness in her piping voice: "Ha ha ha, Peeterosi, ha ha ha!" But even when I saw this mockery, my feelings were not relieved. I was ashamed of being a kapluna among such kaplunas, and I was humiliated on behalf of the Eskimos who watched, smiled, nodded, and submitted.

Yet I did not identify entirely with the Eskimos, and this fact made the situation even more painful. In spite of myself, I was drawn to the men camped across the river. Except for an exasperatingly brief conversation with a passing police officer in May, I had seen no member of my own culture and heard no English since the previous November. Neither had I tasted any kapluna food other than the few items: bannock, tea, rice, raisins, and chocolate, that I stocked in meagre quantities. Most trying of all, perhaps, I had had no mail since March, except for a few pitiful items, mostly bills and advertisements for camping equipment, which the police officer had brought in May. I deplored the insensitive ways of the men, and yet I was starved for the sights and sounds of my own world that they represented and for the familiar food that symbolized that world and that they had brought in enormous quantities.

But more detrimental to my peace of mind than the sudden sharp awareness of my deprivations was the fact that, since I was the only bilingual present, the members of each camp expected me to mediate with the other on their behalf. I often tangled the two languages hopelessly in my distress, unable to muster a coherent sentence in either one. It was not too hard to help the Utku in their attempts to trade with the kaplunas, since I almost always felt the Eskimos' requests reasonable. Difficulty arose only if a fisherman countered with beads a request for tea. Then I was tempted to demur on behalf of the unresisting Eskimo. Far more awkward were the requests that the kaplunas made of me. I was supposed to explain to Mannik why he had been so summarily hoisted skyward; to ask Nilak for his braided boot laces, though I knew no wool was to be had for replacements; and to negotiate with Allaq and with Niqi for the manufacture of fur mittens, though I knew that hides suitable for mittens were scarce and that our own winter mitten material would be used. The Eskimos would never refuse.

Most painful of all the transactions that I was expected to mediate were negotiations for the loan of the two Eskimo canoes. Once, each Utku family had owned a kapluna-style canoe of wood and painted canvas. The Canadian government had provided them after the famine of 1958, in order to encourage the Utku to depend more heavily on their rich fish resources than they had formerly done. One by one the canoes had been damaged and now either lay beached for lack of repair material or had been burned for firewood. Inuttiaq's and Pala's were the only two usable canoes remaining to our camp. During the spring, the canoes were used to transport the household goods up and down the river in the long series of moves, and during the summer and early autumn the men anchored them in midriver at the foot of the rapids and fished from them more efficiently than they could have fished from the shore. The canoes were used also to set and check the nets in the open river before freeze-up, and to ferry people back and forth across the river on various errands: to fetch birch twigs, which grew more plentifully on the far side of the river, to bring in needed possessions from caches, and to visit other families camped nearer the mouth of the river. The canoes had innumerable uses; without them Utku life would have been greatly constricted. Just how constricted I discovered when the kaplunas asked to borrow the boats.

All the groups, both the pleasanter ones and the less pleasant ones, wanted the use of these canoes. The kaplunas had two aluminum boats of their own, but these were not large enough to enable all of the men to go fishing at once. The ins and outs of the negotiations that I was forced to conduct are too complicated to record here, but the result was that from July 26, when the first plane arrived, until August 15, when the last large party of fishermen left, we seldom had the use of both of our canoes and sometimes we had the use of neither. The kaplunas suggested that to compensate us for the loan of the canoes, which prevented us from fishing as we would have done, they would bring us the fish that *they* caught during the day; Ray also offered to feed us a meal of kapluna food every evening. Of course, it was impossible to know what Inuttiaq and Pala thought of this plan when it was proposed, but they agreed to it with alacrity. I myself thought it sounded like a reasonable solution to the conflict of interests, one that would involve minimal discomfort for the Utku. In fact, however, the effects of the arrangement were more inconvenient than I had foreseen [...]

The strength of Inuttiaq's desire to retain his canoe, for whatever reason, appeared a few days after the first group had returned it. We were expecting another group of fishermen to arrive as soon as the clouds lifted. Knowing this, and knowing that Inuttiaq had been restless without his canoe, I tried to assure him that the kaplunas would not take it amiss if he refused to lend it again. If he wished, I said, I would tell them; and I warned him that if they used the boat when they were drunk, they might break it. Inuttiaq responded strongly. "I don't want to lend my canoe," he said. "I want to fish in it. If those kaplunas ask to borrow my canoe tell them they can't. The kapluna leader gave us those canoes because he cares for (*naklik*) us. It's Eskimos he cares for, not kaplunas, because we live under more difficult conditions (*ayuq*), and he said that if any harm came to those canoes, the people who damaged them would be stabbed with something metal – I forget exactly what – something metal, yes? It will hurt." He made a stabbing gesture in the air and turned to Allaq for confirmation, which she silently gave. Little did I suspect how much trouble my literal interpretation of Inuttiaq's instruction that day was to cause me.

The fishermen arrived in due course, and shortly thereafter they came for a canoe. Trouble began almost at once, but I was not aware of it. The Utku did not lend their best canoe, Inuttiaq's; they lent Pala's, which was slightly leaky; but even so, I was annoyed at their compliance. I wished they had refused to lend either and, in my irritation, when the kapluna guide asked me for assurance that the Eskimos would really use the fish he offered as rental payment for the canoe, I replied that the Eskimos had not used the kapluna fish before when they were given, and probably would not do so now. Pala's fourteen-year-old son, Ukpik, freshly arrived in camp after a winter at school in Inuvik, listened, expressionless, to my remarks.

The rest of the day passed uneventfully. As usual when they had the use of a canoe, the men spent a large part of their time at the kapluna camp, but they returned with less booty than sometimes; this trip leader did not believe in "spoiling the natives." Next morning early, I woke to hear the sound of an outboard approaching, and kapluna voices down at the shore. Anxious not to lose an opportunity to use my native tongue, I dressed and joined the men, Eskimo and white, who clustered at the edge of the beach. Inuttiaq and Pala approached me as I went toward the group. "The kaplunas are going to borrow the other canoe," they told me. "They say they will return it when they are through with it."

The kapluna trip leader corroborated what Pala had said. "That first canoe is no good," he said; "it has a hole in it, so we have to borrow this other one." There was, indeed, a sizeable rent in the canvas, which had certainly not been there when we loaned it and which made the canoe unusable. The two men who had come with the guide were already attaching the outboard to Inuttiaq's canoe, as Inuttiaq and the other Utku men watched.

I exploded. Unsmilingly and in a cold voice I told the kapluna leader a variety of things that I thought he should know: that if he borrowed the second canoe we would be without a fishing boat, that if this boat also was damaged we would be in a very difficult position, since a previous guide had forgotten to bring on his return trip the repair materials that Inuttiaq had traded for, and that we would be unable to buy materials ourselves until the strait froze in November. I also pointed out the island where our supplies of tea, sugar, and kerosene were cached and mentioned our inability to reach it except by canoe. Then, armed with my memory of Inuttiaq's earlier instructions, I told the guide that the owner of that second canoe did not wish to lend it.

The guide was not unreasonable; he agreed at once that if the owner did not wish to lend his canoe, that was his option: "It's his canoe, after all." Slightly soothed, I turned to Inuttiaq, who stood nearby, expressionless like the other Utku. "Do you want me to tell him you don't want to lend your canoe?" I asked in Eskimo. "He will not borrow it if you say no."

Inuttiaq's expression dismayed me, but I did not know how to read it; I knew only that it registered strong feeling, as did his voice, which was unusually loud: "Let him have his will!"

I hoped my voice was calm when I replied to Inuttiaq: "As you like," but I was filled with fury at kapluna and Inuttiaq alike, as well as at myself for having undertaken the futile role of mediator, and my tone was icy when I said to the guide: "He says you can have it." Turning abruptly, I strode back to my tent, went to bed, and wept in silence.

CHAPTER *6*

A Cross-cultural Perspective on Romantic Love

W. R. Jankowiak and E. F. Fischer

Romantic love has been proposed as a good example of a culturally constructed emotion. Averill (1985) made a persuasive case to that effect, arguing that this emotion, with its feeling of supreme valuation of the other, of commitment, and of altruistic feelings, was invented by Dante in thirteenth-century Florence. So compelling has this idea become that, instead of parents choosing marital partners for their children, now in the West the individual's own experience of falling in love has become the basis of choosing whom to live with "till death us do part."

What if romantic love were universal in human societies? Then, as with Darwin's cross-cultural evidence, we might be swayed towards the hypothesis that it was not a culturally constructed invention, but was founded upon some biological base. And if this were the case, how would we understand the different bases for marriage in different societies?

The reading we offer here will not solve this debate, but what Jankowiak and Fischer have done is to take a useful step. If you want to pursue further the question of whether there are universals in sexual matters you might like to contrast two articles about jealousy. One is by Hupka (1991) who maintains that, although there might well be something universal about jealous feelings concerning what people value, the Western sexual scenario of such feelings is not universal. The other article is by Daly, Wilson, and Weghorst (1992) who claim that not only is male sexual jealousy universal, but that it is based on strong evolutionary grounds.

References

Averill, J. R. (1985). The social construction of emotion: with special reference to love. In K. J. Gergen & K. E. Davis (Eds.), *The social construction of the person* (pp. 89–109). New York: Springer Verlag.

W. R. Jankowiak and E. F. Fischer, A cross-cultural perspective on romantic love. *Ethnology, 31* (1992), pp. 149–155. Reprinted with permission.

Daly, M., Wilson, M., & Weghorst, S. J. (1982). Male sexual jealousy. *Ethology and Socio-biology, 3*, 11–27.

Hupka, R. B. (1991). The motive for the arousal of romantic jealousy: its cultural origin. In P. Salovey (Ed.), *The psychology of jealousy and envy* (pp. 252–270). New York: Guilford.

The anthropological study of romantic (or passionate) love is virtually nonexistent due to the widespread belief that romantic love is unique to Euro-American culture. This belief is by no means confined to anthropology. The historian Philippe Ariès (1962), for example, argues that affection was of secondary importance to more utilitarian ambitions throughout much of European history. Lawrence Stone (1988: 16) goes further, insisting that "if romantic love ever existed outside of Europe, it only arose among the nonwestern nation-states' elite who had the time to cultivate an aesthetic appreciation for subjective experiences." Underlying these Eurocentric views is the assumption that modernization and the rise of individualism are directly linked to the appearance of romantic notions of love.

The validity of an affectionless past is challenged by some historians who draw upon the insights of an earlier generation of anthropologists (e.g. Lowie, 1950; Westermark, 1922) to argue that European preindustrial courtship was neither cold, aloof, nor devoid of affection (Gillis, 1988; MacDonald, 1981; MacFarlane, 1987; Pollock, 1983). However, much of this revisionist work continues to explain instances of romantic love as a basis for marriage, ignoring the role romantic love plays in affairs (see Stearns & Stearns, 1985). Consequently, little has been done to alter the prevalent opinion that romantic love is a European contribution to world culture.

Paul Rosenblatt (1966, 1967), a psychologist, in a pioneering series of holocultural investigations, correlated modes of cultural transmission and social organization to the emergence of romantic love as a basis for marriage. Writing within the 1960s functionalist milieu, he assumed like almost everyone else that the social construction of reality had a corresponding impact on the construction and expression of private sentiment. In effect, one assumed the other (see also Coppinger & Rosenblatt, 1968).

The premise of much of this research is apparent: cultural traditions bind the individual emotionally into a web of dependency with others, thereby rechannelling or defusing the intensity of an individual's emotional experience. This web of dependency, in turn, undermines the individual's proclivity to fantasize about a lover or the erotic (Averill 1980; de Rougement 1974; Dion & Dion 1988; Endleman 1989; Hsu 1981).

Recently, some evolutionary-oriented anthropologists and psychologists have explored the possibility that romantic love constitutes a human universal (Buss, 1988; Fisher, 1987; Tennov, 1984). These researchers argue that humans have evolved the propensity to experience romantic love which can be recognized by a sudden, unrestrained passion often resulting in the individual entering into an immediate, if short-term, commitment. In this view romantic love centers on a biological core that is expressed as love and enacted in courtship (Perper, 1985). Concurring, Liebowitz (1983) draws upon biochemical research that suggests that the giddiness, euphoria, optimism, and energy lovers experience in early stages of infatuation is caused by increased levels of phenylethylamine (PEA), an amphet-amine-related compound that produces mood-lifting and energizing effects (see also Fisher, 1987). This evolutionary perspective suggests that romantic love arises from forces within the hominid brain that are independent of the socially con-structed mind. From this perspective, romantic love must be present, in some form or another, within every culture.

This paper draws upon Murdock and White's (1969) Standard Cross-Cultural Sample (SCCS) of 186 societies in order to identify those cultures in which romantic love, at least within the domain of private experience, is present or absent. Unlike the previous holocultural studies, whereby only the normative sphere was examined, we focused on both the idiosyncratic and the normative for evidence of romantic love presence.

By romantic love we mean any intense attraction that involves the idealization of the other, within an erotic context, with the expectation of enduring for some time into the future (see Lindholm, 1988). Romantic love stands in sharp contrast to the companionship phase of love (sometimes referred to as attachment) which is characterized by the growth of a more peaceful, comfortable, and fulfilling relationship; it is a strong and enduring affection built upon long-term association (Hatfield, 1988; Liebowitz, 1983).

Methodology

The data for this project come primarily from the works recommended in the Standard Cross-Cultural Sample (SCCS). By first consulting these authorities, we sought to control for Galton's problem.

Our research procedure was to first examine the collective works of the ethnographic authorities recommended by Murdock and White. If that material proved vague and therefore inconclusive, we then analyzed, whenever possible, the culture's folklore. When no folklore was available, other supplemental ethno-graphies were examined, provided that the culture's subsistence system, social structure, and cosmological system had not undergone any significant transforma-tion. For example, because Lizot (1985) and Chagnon (1983) both worked among unacculturated Yanomamo, Lizot's account of Yanomamo love experience is cited as confirmation that romantic love was not an unknown experience. On the other hand, the present-day Siriono social organization and subsistence base bears only a faint resemblance to the previous generation. The fact that Stearman (1987) found evidence of romantic love among contemporary town-dwelling Siriono does not mean that some of the forest-dwelling Siriono also experienced romantic love. Consequently, her study could not be used to supplement Holmberg's (1969) account.

A culture was dropped from our sample if: (1) there was no reliable or relevant source material available; (2) the SCCS's primary or supplemental authorities did not discuss courtship, marriage, or family relations; and (3) the inability of the coders to agree whether a specific passage conclusively indicated romantic love's presence (N = 1). Using these criteria, twenty cultures were dropped, leaving us with a sample universe of 166 societies.

Besides the usual difficulties in finding reliable source material, our primary methodological problem arose from the absence of any clear and consistent usage of the terms love, lovemaking, and lovers. Because ethnographers often fail to distinguish between love and sexual intercourse, it is unclear if they are referring to passionate love or only using a common metaphor for sexual intercourse. In order to distinguish between behaviors motivated solely out of lust or physical satisfaction from those motivated by romantic love, additional indices were required. Thus the presence of romantic love in a culture was coded only when the ethnographer made a clear distinction between lust and love, and then noted the presence of love. There was, however, one exception. If the ethnographer claimed that romantic love was not present, yet provided a folktale or an incident that demonstrated passionate involvement, his or her interpretation was rejected. Only two such discrepancies appeared in our sample population (i.e. Manus, Pakistan).

In over 250 ethnographic and folkloric studies examined not a single researcher explicitly defined romantic love. Those ethnographers who insisted that the phenomenon did not exist rarely noted which psychological attitudes or behavioral traits were absent. This lacuna arose from overlooking the exceptional or non-normative act, as well as from failing to distinguish between lust and the two fundamental types of love experience romantic and companionship love.

The most problematic cross-cultural studies are those that use high inferences indices. We were at pains therefore to find richly texture illustrations of romantic love's presences. Because many ethnographies did not supply such cases, we relied upon other indicative clues or indices.

The criteria (listed below) are similar to those used in previous cross-cultural studies that sought to document the ecological and social factors responsible for the emergence of romantic love as a basis for marriage. These studies examined specific acts (e.g. elopement, love magic, and love songs) that suggest choice for attachment and thus the presence of passionate affection.

With the exception of love magic, we used similar indices. It is important to stress, however, that we recorded as positive only those cases where the ethnographer recorded an expressive motive (i.e. mutual affection) and not an instrumental motive (i.e. meat for sex). If the ethnographer simply reported the presence of elopement, but did not supply additional information concerning the individual's motivation, then that culture was coded as romantic love absent. In this way, our criteria are more precise than previous cross-cultural studies of romantic love. Moreover, unlike previous cross-cultural studies, we read whenever possible a culture's folklore. This proved to be the most fruitful means to document the presences of the romantic love. Finally, to determine the presence or absence of romantic love, only the initial phase of involvement (i.e. less than two years) was examined. The phase of the love relationships was determined through examining the ethnographic context. Unless one of the indicators discussed below was present, we never inferred romantic love's presence.

The following indicators were used to assess the presence of romantic love within a culture during the first two years of involvement (marriage or other):

1 accounts depicting personal anguish and longing;
2 the use of love songs or folklore that highlight the motivations behind romantic involvement;
3 elopement due to mutual affection;
4 native accounts affirming the existence of passionate love; and
5 the ethnographer's affirmation that romantic love is present.

On the basis of the above indicators, each of the 166 societies were coded and labelled as either (a) love present or (b) love absent. The presence of any one of these indicators was taken as evidence of the presence of romantic love. Each researcher photocopied the page(s) on which he found indicators of romantic love. At a later date, the researchers independently recoded each other's original coding to insure reliability. Unresolved disagreements (n = 1) were dropped from the sample.

Results

Table 6.1. Culture area and romantic love

	Romantic love	
	+	−
Circum-Mediterranean	22 (95.7%)	1 (4.3%)
Sub-Saharan Africa	20 (76.9%)	6 (23.1%)
East Eurasia	32 (94.1%)	1 (5.9%)
Insular Pacific	27 (93.1%)	2 (6.9%)
North America	24 (82.8%)	5 (17.2%)
South & Central America	22 (84.6%)	4 (15.4%)

Discussion

To provide a more revealing illustration of our findings, three ethnographic examples that are highly representative of the entire sample set are presented below to highlight the intensity, commitment, pathos, and romantic idealization of the other. The examples illustrate through indigenous representations of romantic love (see #1 and #2), and provide a case in which an ethnographer clearly distinguished between passionate love and lust (see #3).

(1) Nisa, a Kung woman, who lived in a hunting and gathering society in the Kalahari desert, clearly differentiated between passionate and companionship love by drawing a distinction between a husband and a lover. Nisa notes that the former relationship is "rich, warm and secure. The [latter] is passionate and exciting, although often fleeting and undependable" (Shostak, 1981: 267). Nisa adds that "when two people come together their hearts are on fire and their passion is very great. After a while, the fire cools and that's how it stays" (Shostak, 1981: 269).

(2) John Turi (1931), in his autobiography, commented on some of the behavioral manifestations of infatuation that befell many Lapp herders during courtship. He writes that "the mind is often a little wild, especially in those who have that sort of blood. The explanation of why some folk have such weak blood that it is rather easy to upset them is that some people are of such an amorous nature that at the time they can think of nothing else...And some folk are still in love afterwards, but it is not everyone who is in love afterwards."

(3) During the Sung dynasty (928–1233) the most popular tale among both the literary and nonliterate population was that of the *Jade Goddess*. It is a tale about Chang Po who falls in love with a woman who is already engaged. When he felt that "the greatest desire of his was beyond him" (Lin, 1961: 75), he loses interest in work and lapses into a prolonged despair, a love-despair that closely resembles that which was being discussed in the Romance poems of Europe at the same time. Finally, he confronts the girl about his love and discovers she has similar feelings. They elope. After awhile, however, suffering from poverty and isolation, they decide to return home. On the night they are to leave, Chang Po draws the girl into his arms and says "since heaven and earth were created you were made for me and I will not let you go. It cannot be wrong to love you" (Lin, 1961: 74). In several ways, this tale runs parallel to the Tristan and Isolde folk-legend and variations in its clear-eyed delineation of romantic love (see Jankowiak, 1992).

Although at least one incident of passionate love was documented in 147 out of 166 cultures or more than 88.5 percent; no evidence was found for its existence in 19 (11.5 percent) of the cultures. Of the nineteen cases in which romantic love was not found, for example, only one ethnographer (Holmberg, 1969) makes the distinction between romantic love and lust and then proceeds to deny the presence of romantic love. The other eighteen ethnographies note that sexual affairs do occur, but do not explore the motive for entering into these, and thus we are unable to determine if romantic love is one of the motives. These cultures are coded "romantic love not present." Nonetheless, we believe that these negative cases arise from ethnographic oversight rather than any set of cultural norms that prevent an individual from experiencing romantic affection. There are two explanations that may account for the African cultural area as having the higher percentage of inconclusiveness. First, the absence of folklore. For example, we were able to find folklore material for only 4 out of the 26 African cultures. More importantly, we were not able to find any folklore for the 7 cultures classified as inconclusive. Second, in many African cultures passionate affection is expressed in a variety of nonverbal idioms seldom studied by an earlier generation of ethnographers (James Bell, personal communication).

It is important to note that not everyone within a culture falls in love. This seldom occurs even in the so-called romantic cultures (i.e. Euro-American cultures) that celebrate passionate entanglements in its literature, films, and mythology. By the same token, this should not undermine our finding that in almost every culture there are some individuals who, often in the face of severe negative sanctions, do fall in love.

Romantic love may in fact be muted, though never entirely repressed, by other cultural variables. Because researchers have rarely studied the relative frequency in which a person falls in and out of love, it is unclear if romantic love is experienced with less frequency in those cultures that deny or disapprove of the emotional experience. The relative frequency in which members of a community experience romantic love may very well depend upon that culture's social organization and ideological orientation. Thus a greater proportion of Americans, compared to Yanomamo or Tiv, may actually experience romantic love. We suspect that this is the case. However, until this is substantiated through further field research, it remains only a hypothesis.

Conclusion

The fact that we are able to document the occurrence of romantic love in 88.5 percent of the sampled cultures stands in direct contradiction to the popular idea that romantic love is essentially limited to or the product of Western culture. Moreover, it suggests that romantic love constitutes a human universal, or at the least a near-universal.

The proposal that romantic love is a near-universal rests in part on subjective appraisal since there is no definitive boundary that marks near-universals. Brown (1991) suggests that a 95 percent distribution might, by analogy with statistical tests of significance be a convenient marker of a near universal. Though our sample has less than a 95 percent distribution of instances of romantic love, we have argued that the distribution is actually larger. We furthermore concur with a position stated by Brown (1991: 44) that the distinction between universals and near-universals is often unimportant: "a near universal is universal enough."

If romantic love is a human universal, then it is important to explore its emic manifestations, within a variety of cultural settings. To date, this has seldom been done (Abu-Lughod, 1986; Cancian, 1987), thus our understanding of the cross-cultural variation in the styles of romantic expression is lacking.

At present there is no consensus concerning the relationship between cognition, emotion, and behavior. Romantic involvement is one sphere of human interaction that is in need of analysis. It is a project that will require the assistance of ethnographers who, in drawing a distinction between private experience and cultural expression of that experience, are able to enhance our understanding of the interplay between, on the one hand, the biopsychological factors that affect the perception of stimuli and, on the other, the culturally patterned attitudes that structure the framework for social action; thereby contributions will be made to anthropology's historical mission to study both the particular and the universal aspects of human experience.

References

Abu-Lughod, L. (1986). *Veiled sentiments*. Berkeley: University of California Press.
Ariès, P. (1962). *Centuries of childhood: A social history of family life* (Trans. R. Baldick) New York: Knopf.
Averill, J. (1980). A constructivist view of emotion. In R. Plutchik & H. Kellerman (Eds.), *Emotion: theory, research and experience* (Eds.), (pp. 305–337). New York: Academic Press.
Brown, D. (1991). *Human universals*. Philadelphia Temple University Press.

Buss, D. (1988). Love acts: The evolutionary biology of love. In R. Sternberg & M. Barnes (Eds.), *The psychology of love* (pp. 100–118) New Haven: Yale University Press.

Cancian, F. (1987). *Love in America.* Cambridge: Cambridge University Press.

Chagnon, N. (1983). *Yanomamo: The fierce people.* New York: Holt.

Coppinger, R., & Rosenblatt, P. (1968). Romantic love and subsistence dependence of spouses. *Southwestern Journal of Anthropology, 24*: 310–318.

Dion, K. L., & Dion, K. K. (1988). Romantic love: individual and cultural perspectives. In R. Sternberg & M. Barbnes (Eds.), *The psychology of love* (pp. 264–289). New Haven: Yale University Press.

Endleman, R. (1989). *Love and sex in twelve cultures.* New York: Psyche Press.

Fisher, H. (1987). The four-year itch. *Natural History, 10*, 12–16.

Gillis, J. R. (1988). From ritual to romance: toward an alternative history of love. In C. Stearns & P. Stearns (Eds.), *Emotion and social change,* (pp. 87–122) New York: Holmes & Meier.

Hatfield, E. (1988). Passionate love and companionate love. In R. Sternberg & M. Barners (Eds.), *The psychology of love* (pp. 191–217). New Haven: Yale University Press.

Holmberg, A. (1969). *People of the Long Bow.* Garden City: Natural History Press.

Hsu, F. (1981). *Americans and Chinese: passage to difference.* Honolulu: University Press of Hawaii.

Jankowiak, W. (1992). *Sex, death and hierarchy in a Chinese city: an anthropological account.* New York: Columbia University Press.

Liebowitz, M. R. (1983). *The chemistry of love.* Boston: Little, Brown.

Lin, Y. (1961). *The Lolo of Llang Shan.* New Haven: Yale University Press.

Lindholm, C. (1988). Lovers and leaders: A comparison of social and psychological models of romance and charisma. *Social Science Information,* 1–27.

Lizot, J. (1985). *Tales of the Yanomami.* Cambridge: Cambridge University Press.

Lowie, R. (1950). *Social organization.* New York: Rinehart

MacDonald, M. (1981). *Mystical Bedlam: madness, anxiety and healing in seventeenth-century England.* Cambridge: Cambridge University Press.

MacFarlane, A. (1987). *The culture of capitalism.* Oxford: Blackwell.

Mead, M. (1930). *Growing up in New Guinea.* New York: New American Library.

Murdock, G. P., and White, D. (1969). Standard cross-cultural sample. *Ethnology, 8,* 329–369.

Perper, T. (1985). *Sex signals: the biology of love.* Philadelphia: ISI Press.

Pollock, L. (1983). *Forgotten children: parent-child relations from 1500 to 1800.* Cambridge: Cambridge University Press.

Rosenblatt, P. (1966). A cross-cultural study of child rearing and romantic love. *Journal of Personality and Social Psychology, 4,* 336–338.

—— (1967). Marital residence and the functions of romantic love. *Ethnology, 6,* 471–480.

Rougemont, D. de (1974). *Love in the Western world* (Trans. M. Belgion). New York: Pantheon.

Shostak, M. (1981). *Nisa.* Cambridge, MA: Harvard University Press.

Stearman, A. (1987). *No longer nomads: the Siriono revisited.* Latham, MD: Hamilton Press.

Stearns, P., and Stearns, C. (1985). Emotionology: clarifying the history of emotions and emotions standards. *American Historical Review,* 90, 813–836.

Stone, L. (1988). Passionate attachments in the West in historical perspective. In W. Gaylin & E. Person (Eds.), *Passionate attachments,* (pp. 15–26). New York: Free Press.

Tennov, D. (1984). *Love and limerance.* New York: Stein & Day.

Turi, J. (1931). *Turi's book of Lappland.* Oosterhout: Anthropological Publications.

Westermarck, E. (1922). *The history of human marriage,* vols I–III. New York: Allerton Book Co.

CHAPTER *7*

Constants across Culture in the Face and Emotion

P. Ekman and W. V. Friesen

Starting in the 1950s Sylvan Tomkins (see his selected works, 1995) began proposing that faces were central not just to the expression of human emotions but, via feedback, to their experience. (We republish a piece of Tomkins's writing as selection 18.) You can think of his idea of bodily feedback as based on James's theory: if we smile, part of the reason for feeling happy is because we perceive the changes in our face, and this perception gives rise to, and then amplifies, the feeling of happiness. Paul Ekman and Carroll Izard were strongly influenced by Tomkins, and both began studies of facial expressions – of happiness, sadness, anger, and so forth, at about the same time.

Ekman and Friesen have been pioneers in modern empirical work on emotions. Subsequent to the paper selected here, they have devoted much effort to describing each individual muscle movement in facial expressions, so that facial emotions could be reliably recognized by means of a coding system (FACS, Ekman & Friesen, 1978). Alternative coding systems (e.g. MAX) for facial expressions have been developed by Izard (1979). These coding systems have become measurement standards, and they enable facial expressions to be recognized from video film. Although Izard too has conducted cross-cultural research, he has focused more on the development of facial expressions in infancy (see Izard, 1991).

References

Ekman, P., & Friesen, W. V. (1978);. *Facial action coding system: a technique for the measurement of facial movement.* Palo Alto: Consulting Psychologists Press.

Izard, C. E. (1991). *The psychology of emotions.* New York: Plenum.

P. Ekman and W. V. Friesen, Constants across cultures in the face and emotion. *Journal of Personality and Social Psychology, 17* (1971), 124–129. Copyright © 1971 by the American Psychological Association. Reprinted with permission.

—— (1979). *The maximally discriminative facial movement coding system (MAX)*. Newark: University of Delaware, Office of Instructional Technology.

Tomkins, S. S. (1995). *Exploring affect: the selected writings of Sylvan S. Tomkins* (Ed. E. V. Demos). New York: Cambridge University Press.

Prolonged and at times heated controversy has failed to demonstrate whether facial behaviors associated with emotion are universal for man or specific to each culture. Darwin (1872) postulated universals in facial behavior on the basis of his evolutionary theory. Allport (1924), Asch (1952), and Tomkins (1962, 1963) have also postulated universals in emotional facial behavior, although each writer offered a different theoretical basis for his expectation. The culture-specific view, that facial behaviors become associated with emotion through culturally variable learning, received support from Klineberg's (1938) descriptions of how the facial behaviors described in Chinese literature differed from the facial behaviors associated with emotions in the Western world. More recently, Birdwhistell (1963) and LaBarre (1947) have argued against the possibility of any universals in emotional facial behavior, supplying numerous anecdotal examples of variations between cultures.

Ekman (1968) and Ekman and Friesen (1969) considered these contradictory viewpoints within a framework which distinguished between those elements of facial behavior that are universal and those that are culture-specific. They hypothesized that the universals are to be found in the relationship between distinctive patterns of the facial muscles and particular emotions (happiness, sadness, anger, fear, surprise, disgust, interest). They suggested that cultural differences would be seen in some of the stimuli, which through learning become established as elicitors of particular emotions, in the rules for controlling facial behavior in particular social settings, and in many of the consequences of emotional arousal.

To demonstrate the hypothesized universal element, Ekman and Friesen (1969) conducted experiments in which they showed still photographs of faces to people from different cultures in order to determine whether the same facial behavior would be judged as the same emotion, regardless of the observers' culture. The faces were selected on the basis of their conformity to Ekman, Friesen, and Tomkins's a priori descriptions of facial muscles involved in each emotion. College-educated subjects in Brazil, the United States, Argentina, Chile, and Japan were found to identify the same faces with the same emotion words, as were members of two preliterate cultures who had extensive contact with Western cultures (the Sadong of Borneo and the Fore of New Guinea), although the latter results were not as strong (Ekman, Sorenson, & Friesen, 1969). Izard (1968, 1969), working independently with his own set of faces, obtained comparable results across seven other culture-language groups.

While these investigators interpreted their results as evidence of universals in facial behavior, their interpretation was open to argument; because all the cultures they compared had exposure to some of the same mass media portrayals of facial behavior, members of these cultures might have learned to recognize the same set of conventions, or become familiar with each other's different facial behavior.

To overcome this difficulty in the interpretation of previous results, it is necessary to demonstrate that cultures which have had minimal visual contact with literate cultures show similarity to these cultures in their interpretation of facial behavior. The purpose of this paper was to test the hypothesis that members of a preliterate culture who had been selected to insure maximum visual isolation from literate cultures will identify the same emotion concepts with the same faces as do members of literate Western and Eastern cultures.

Method

Subjects

Members of the Fore linguistic-cultural group of the southeast Highlands of New Guinea were studied. Until 12 years ago, this was an isolated, Neolithic, material culture (Gajdusek, 1963; Sorenson & Gajdusek, 1966). While many of these people now have had extensive contact with missionaries, government workers, traders, and United States scientists, some have had little such contact. Only subjects who met criteria established to screen out all but those who had minimal opportunity to learn to imitate or recognize uniquely Western facial behaviors were recruited for this experiment. These criteria made it quite unlikely that subjects could have so completely learned some foreign set of facial expressions of emotion that their judgments would be no different from those of members of literate cultures. Those selected had seen no movies, neither spoke nor understood English or Pidgin, had not lived in any of the Western settlement or government towns, and had never worked for a Caucasian (according to their own report); 189 adults and 130 children, male and female, met these criteria. This sample comprises about 3 percent of the members of this culture.

In addition to data gathered from these more visually isolated members of the South Fore, data were also collected on members of this culture who had had the most contact with Westerners. These subjects all spoke English, had seen movies, lived in a Western settlement or government town, and had attended a missionary or government school for more than a year; 23 male adults, but no females, met these criteria.

Judgment task

In a pilot study conducted one year earlier with members of this same culture, a number of different judgment tasks were tried. The least Westernized subjects could not be asked to select from a printed list of emotion terms the one that was appropriate for a photograph, since they could not read. When the list was repeated to them with each photograph, they seemed to have difficulty remembering the list. Further, doubts remained about whether the meaning of a particular emotion concept was adequately conveyed by translating a single English word into a single South Fore word. Asking the subject to make up his own story about the emotions shown in a picture was not much more successful, although the problems were different. Subjects regarded this as a very difficult task, repeated probes were necessary, and as the procedure became lengthy, subjects became reluctant.

To solve these problems, it was decided to employ a task similar to that developed by Dashiell (1927) for use with young children. Dashiell showed the child a group of three pictures simultaneously, read a story, and told the child to point to the picture in which the person's face showed the emotion described in the story. The advantages of this judgment task in a preliterate culture are that (*a*) the translator recounts well-rehearsed stories which can be recorded and checked for accurate translation; (*b*) the task involves no reading; (*c*) the subject does not have to remember a list of emotion terms; (*d*) the subject need not speak, but can point to give his answer; and (*e*) perfect translation of emotion words is not required since the story can help provide connotations.

Emotion stories

With the exception of the stories for fear and surprise, those used in the present study were selected from those which had been most frequently given in the pilot study. Considerable care was taken to insure that each story selected was relevant to only one emotion within the Fore culture, and that members of the culture were agreed on what that emotion was. Since the stories told by the pilot subjects for fear and surprise did not meet these criteria, the authors composed stories for these emotions based on their experience within the culture. The stories used are given below:

Happiness: His (her) friends have come, and he (she) is happy.
Sadness: His (her) child (mother) has died, and he (she) feels very sad.
Anger: He (she) is angry; or he (she) is angry, about to fight.
Surprise: He (she) is just now looking at something new and unexpected.
Disgust: He (she) is looking at something he (she) dislikes; or He (she) is looking at something which smells bad.
Fear: He (she) is sitting in his (her) house all alone, and there is no one else in the village. There is no knife, axe, or bow and arrow in the house. A wild pig is standing in the door of the house, and the man (woman) is looking at the pig and is very afraid of it. The pig has been standing in the doorway for a few minutes, and the person is looking at it very afraid, and the pig won't move away from the door, and he (she) is afraid the pig will bite him (her).

Pictures and emotions

The six emotions studied were those which had been found by more than one investigator to be discriminable within any one literate culture (cf. Ekman, Friesen, & Ellsworth, in press, for a review of findings). The photographs used to show the facial behavior for each of the six emotions had been judged by more than 70 percent of the observers in studies of more than one literate culture as showing that emotion. The sample included pictures of both posed and spontaneous behavior used by Ekman and Friesen (1968), Frijda (1968), Frois-Wittmann (1930), Izard (1968), Engen, Levy, and Schlosberg (1957), and Tomkins and McCarter (1964). A total of 40 pictures were used of 24 different stimulus persons, male and female, adult and child. The photographs were prepared as 3 × 5 inch prints, cropped to show only the face and neck.

Story–photographs trial

A single item consisted of an emotion story, a correct photograph, in which the facial behavior shown in the photograph was the same as that described in the story, and either one or two incorrect photograph(s). Adult subjects were given two incorrect pictures with each correct picture; children were given only one because of a shortage of copies of the stimuli.

Because of a limitation on the number of available photographs, and upon the subjects' time, not all of the possible pairings of correct and incorrect photographs were tested. Instead, the subjects were presented with some of the presumably more difficult discriminations among emotions. The emotion shown in at least one of the incorrect photographs was an emotion which past studies in literate cultures had found to be most often mistaken for the correct emotion. For example, when *anger* was the emotion described in the story, the incorrect choices included *disgust, fear,* or *sadness,* emotions which have been found to be often mistaken for anger. The age and sex of the stimulus persons shown in the correct and incorrect photographs were held constant within any trial.

No one subject was given all the emotion discriminations, because again the stimuli would have been too few and the task too long. Instead, subjects from different villages were required to make some of the same and some different discriminations. Subjects were shown from 6 to 12 sets of photographs, but no picture appeared in more than one of the sets shown to any one particular subject. A subject's task included making at least three different emotion discriminations; the same story was told more than once, with differing correct and incorrect photographs, and often requiring discrimination among differing sets of emotions. For example, the anger story might have been read once with Anger Picture A, Sadness Picture B, and Fear Picture C; the same anger story might have been read again to the same subject, but now with Anger Picture D, Disgust Picture E, and Surprise Picture F.

Procedure

Two-person teams conducted the experiment. A member of the South Fore tribe recruited subjects, explained the task, and read the translated stories; a Caucasian recorded the subjects' responses. Three such teams operated at once within a village; one team with a male Caucasian worked with male adult subjects; the two others with female Caucasians worked with the female adult subjects and the children. In most instances, almost all members of a village participated in the experiment within less than 3 hours.

Considerable practice and explanation was given to the translators. They were told that there was no correct response and were discouraged from prompting. Repeated practice was given to insure that the translators always repeated the stories in the same way and resisted the temptation to embellish. Spot checks with tape recordings and back translations verified that this was successful. The Caucasians, who did know the correct responses, averted their faces from the view of the subject, looking down at their recording booklet, to reduce the probability of an unwitting experimenter bias effect. Data analysis did not reveal any systematic differences in the responses obtained with different translators.

Results

No differences between male and female subjects were expected, and no such differences had been found in the literate culture data. In this New Guinea group, however, the women were more reluctant to participate in the experiment, and were considered by most outsiders to have had less contact with Caucasians than the men. The number of correct responses for each subject was calculated separately for males and females and for adults and children. The *t* tests were not significant; the trend was in the direction of better performance by women and girls. The data revealed no systematic differences between male and female subjects in the discrimination of particular emotions, or in relation to the sex of the stimulus person shown on the photographs. In the subsequent analyses, data from males and females were combined.

Table 7.1 shows the results for the least Westernized adults for each emotion discrimination. Within each row, the percentage of subjects who gave the correct response for a particular discrimination between three emotions was calculated across all subjects shown that particular discrimination, regardless of whether the photographs used to represent the three emotions differed for individual subjects. Within each row, each subject contributed only one response, and thus the sum of responses was derived from independent subjects. However, the rows are not independent of each other. Data from a given subject appear in different rows, depending upon the particular discriminations he was asked to make. If a group of subjects was requested to discriminate the same emotion from the same two other emotions more than once, only one randomly chosen response was included in the table.

A binomial test of significance assuming chance performance to be one in three showed that the correct face was chosen at a significant level for all of the discriminations (rows) except that of fear from surprise. Twice, fear was not discriminated from surprise, and once surprise was chosen more often than fear, even though the story had been intended to describe fear. A binomial test assuming chance to be one in two (a more conservative test, justified if it was thought that within a set of three pictures, there may have been one which was obviously wrong) still yielded significant correct choices for all but the fear-from-surprise discriminations.

The results for the most Westernized male adults were almost exactly the same as those reported in table 7.1 for the least Westernized male and female adults. The number of correct responses for each subject was calculated; the *t* test showed no significant difference between the most and least Westernized subjects. Again, the only failure to select the correct picture occurred when fear was to be distinguished from surprise.

Table 7.2 shows the results for the children, tabulated and tested in similar fashion. The children selected the correct face for all of their discriminations. Through an oversight, the one discrimination which the adults could not make,

Table 7.1. Adult results

Emotion described in the story	Emotions shown in the two incorrect photographs	No. Ss	% choosing correct face
Happiness	Surprise, disgust	62	90**
	Surprise, sadness	57	93**
	Fear, anger	65	86**
	Disgust, anger	36	100**
Anger	Sadness, surprise	66	82**
	Disgust, surprise	31	87**
	Fear, sadness	31	87**
Sadness	Anger, fear	64	81**
	Anger, surprise	26	81**
	Anger, happiness	31	87**
	Anger, disgust	35	69*
	Disgust, surprise	35	77**
Disgust (smell story)	Sadness, surprise	65	77**
Disgust (dislike story)	Sadness, surprise	36	89**
Surprise	Fear, disgust	31	71*
	Happiness, anger	31	65*
Fear	Anger, disgust	92	64**
	Sadness, disgust	31	87**
	Anger, happiness	35	86**
	Disgust, happiness	26	85**
	Surprise, happiness	65	48
	Surprise, disgust	31	52
	Surprise, sadness	57	28[a]

* $p < .05$.
** $p < .01$.
[a]Subjects selected the surprise face (67%) at a significant level ($p < .01$, two-tailed test).

Table 7.2. Results for children

Emotion described in the story	Emotion shown in the one incorrect photograph	No. Ss	% choosing the correct face
Happiness	Surprise	116	87*
	Sadness	25	96*
	Anger	25	100*
	Disgust	25	88*
Anger	Sadness	69	90*
Sadness	Anger	60	85*
	Surprise	33	76*
	Disgust	27	89*
	Fear	25	76*
Disgust (smell story)	Sadness	19	95*
Disgust (dislike story)	Sadness	27	78*
Surprise	Happiness	14	100*
	Disgust	14	100*
	Fear	19	95*
Fear	Sadness	25	92*
	Anger	25	88*
	Disgust	14	100*

* $p \leq .01$.

fear from surprise, was not tried with the children. The percentages reported in table 7.2 are generally higher than those in table 7.1, but this is probably due to the fact that the children were given two photographs rather than three, and chance performance would be 50 percent rather than about 33 percent. Six and 7-year-old children were compared with 14- and 15-year-olds, by the same procedures as described for comparing males and females. No significant differences or trends were noted.

Discussion

The results for both adults and children clearly support our hypothesis that particular facial behaviors are universally associated with particular emotions. With but one exception, the faces judged in literate cultures as showing particular emotions were comparably judged by people from a preliterate culture who had minimal opportunity to have learned to recognize uniquely Western facial expressions. Further evidence was obtained in another experiment, in which the facial behavior of these New Guineans was accurately recognized by members of a literate culture. In that study, visually isolated members of the South Fore posed emotions, and college students in the United States accurately judged the emotion intended from their videotaped facial behavior. The evidence from both studies contradicts the view that all facial behavior associated with emotion is culture-specific, and that posed facial behavior is a unique set of culture-bound conventions not understandable to members of another culture.

The only way to dismiss the evidence from both the judgment and posing studies would be to claim that even these New Guineans who had not seen movies, who did not speak or understand English or Pidgin, who had never worked for a Caucasian, still had *some* contact with Westerners, sufficient contact for them to learn to recognize and simulate culture-specific, uniquely Western facial behaviors associated with each emotion. While these subjects had some contact with Westerners, this argument seems implausible for three reasons. First, the criteria for selecting these subjects makes it highly improbable that they had learned a "foreign" set of facial behaviors to such a degree that they could not only recognize them, but also display them as well as those to whom the behaviors were native. Second, contact with Caucasians did not seem to have much influence on the judgment of emotion, since the most Westernized subjects did no better than the least Westernized and, like the latter, failed to distinguish fear from surprise. Third, the women, who commonly have even less contact with Westerners than the men, did as well in recognizing emotions.

The hypothesis that there are constants across cultures in emotional facial behavior is further supported by Eibl-Eibesfeldt's (1970) films of facial behavior occurring within its natural context in a number of preliterate cultures. Evidence of constants in facial behavior and emotion across cultures is also consistent with early studies which showed many similarities between the facial behavior of blind and sighted children (Fulcher, 1942; Goodenough, 1932; Thompson, 1941). Universals in facial behavior associated with emotion can be explained from a number of nonexclusive view points as being due to evolution, innate neural programs, or learning experiences common to human development regardless of culture (e.g. those of Allport, 1924; Asch, 1952; Darwin, 1872; Huber, 1931; Izard, 1969; Peiper, 1963; Tomkins, 1962, 1963). To evaluate the different viewpoints will require further research, particularly on early development.

The failure of the New Guinean adults to discriminate fear from surprise, while succeeding in discriminating surprise from fear, and fear from other emotions, suggests that cultures may not make *all* of the same distinctions among emotions, but does not detract from the main finding that most of the distinctions were made across cultures. Experience within a culture, the kinds of events which typically elicit particular emotions, may act to influence the ability to discriminate particular pairs of emotions. Fear faces may not have been distinguished from surprise faces, because in this culture fearful events are almost always also surprising; that is, the sudden appearance of a hostile member of another village, the unexpected meeting of a ghost or sorcerer, etc.

The growing body of evidence of a pan-cultural element in emotional facial behavior does not imply the absence of cultural differences in the face and emotion. Ekman (1968) and Ekman and Friesen (1969) have suggested that cultural differences will be manifest in the circumstances which elicit an emotion, in the action consequences of an emotion, and in the display rules which govern the management of facial behavior in particular social settings. Izard (1969) agrees with the view that there are cultural differences in the antecedent and consequent events, and has also found evidence suggesting differences in attitudes about particular emotions.

References

Allport, F. H. (1924) *Social psychology.* Boston: Houghton Mifflin.

Asch, S. E. (1952) *Social psychology.* Englewood Cliffs, NJ: Prentice-Hall.

Birdwhistell, R. L. (1963). The kinesic level in the investigation of the emotions. In P. H. Knapp (Ed.), *Expression of the emotions in man.* New York: International Universities Press.

Darwin, C. (1872). *The expression of the emotions in man and animals.* London: Murray.

Dashiell, J. F. (1927). A new method of measuring reactions to facial expression of emotion. *Psychological Bulletin, 24,* 174–175.

Eibl-Eibesfeldt, I. (1970). *Ethology, the biology of behavior.* New York: Holt, Rinehart & Winston.

Ekman, P. (1968). Research findings on recognition and display of facial behavior in literate and nonliterate cultures. *Proceedings of the 76th Annual Convention of the American Psychological Association, 3,* 727 (summary).

Ekman, P., & Friesen, W. V. (1968). Nonverbal behavior in psychotherapy research. In J. Shlien (Ed.), *Research in psychotherapy.* Vol. 3. Washington, DC.: American Psychological Association.

—— (1969). The repertoire of non-verbal behavior – Categories, origins, usage and coding. *Semiotica, 1,* 49–98.

Ekman, P., Friesen, W. V., & Ellsworth, P. (1972). *Emotion in the human face: Guidelines for research and integration of findings.* New York: Pergamon Press.

Ekman, P., Friesen, W. V., & Tomkins, S. S. (1971), Facial affect scoring technique: a first validity study. *Semiotica, 3,* 37–58.

Ekman, P., Sorenson, E. R., & Friesen, W. V. (1969). Pan-cultural elements in facial displays of emotions. *Science, 164,* 86–88.

Engen, T., Levy, N., & Schlosberg, H. (1957). A new series of facial expressions. *American Psychologist, 12,* 264–266.

Frijda, N. H. (1968). Recognition of emotion. In L. Berkowitz (Ed.), *Advances in experimental social psychology.* New York: Academic Press.

Frois-Wittmann, J. (1930). The judgment of facial expression. *Journal of Experimental Psychology, 13,* 113–151.

Fulcher, J. S. (1942). "Voluntary" facial expression in blind and seeing children. *Archives of Psychology, 38,* 272.

Gajdusek, D. C. (1963). Kuru. *Transactions of the Royal Society of Tropical Medicine and Hygiene, 57,* 151–169.

Goodenough, F. L. (1932). Expression of the emotions in a blind-deaf child. *Journal of Abnormal and Social Psychology, 27,* 328–333.

Huber, E. (1931). *Evolution of facial musculature and facial expression.* Baltimore: Johns Hopkins Press.

Izard, C. E. (1968). Cross-cultural research findings on development in recognition of facial behavior. *Proceedings of the 76th Annual Convention of the American Psychological Association,* 3, 727 (summary).

—— (1969). The emotions and emotion constructs in personality and culture research. In R. B. Cattell (Ed.), *Handbook of modern personality theory.* Chicago: Aldine Press.

Klineberg, O. (1938). Emotional expression in Chinese literature. *Journal of Abnormal and Social Psychology, 33,* 517–520.

LaBarre, W. (1947). The cultural basis of emotions and gestures. *Journal of Personality, 16,* 49–68.

Peiper, A. (1963). *Cerebral function in infancy and childhood.* New York: Consultants Bureau.

Rosenberg, S., & Gordon, A. (1968). Identification of facial expressions from affective descriptions: a probabilistic choice analysis of referential ambiguity. *Journal of Personality and Social Psychology, 10,* 157–166.

Sorenson, E. R., & Gajdusek, D. C. (1966). The study of child behavior and development in primitive cultures. A research archive for ethnopediatric film investigations of styles in the patterning of the nervous system. *Pediatrics,* 37(1, pt. 2).

Thompson, J. (1941). Development of facial expression of emotion in blind and seeing children. *Archives of Psychology, 37,* 264.

Tomkins, S. S. (1962). *Affect, imagery, consciousness.* Vol. 1. *The positive affects.* New York: Springer.

—— (1963). *Affect, imagery, consciousness.* Vol. 2. *The negative affects.* New York: Springer.

Tomkins, S. S., & McCarter, R. (1964). What and where are the primary affects? Some evidence for a theory. *Perceptual and Motor Skills, 18,* 119–158.

CHAPTER *8*

What does a Facial Expression Mean?

J. A. Russell and J. M. Fernández-Dols

Although for a long time it had been widely accepted that Ekman's and Izard's interpretation of evidence on facial expressions was essentially correct, in the last few years other voices have been heard advocating other interpretations. Most radically, Fridlund brought out a series of articles and a book (1994) based on ethological principles, in which he argued that facial expressions do not necessarily signal emotions, but something like intentions. In the same year Russell (1984) published a controversial paper in which he argued that the evidence for facial expressions being universals based on a small set of specific emotions was not as strong as had been supposed. Ekman (1994) and Izard (1994) both replied to the critique.

We present here a selection by Russell and Fernández-Dols from a recent book edited by them (1997), in which they write about what they call the Facial Expression Program of research (the program inaugurated by Ekman and Izard) and then (in the selection here) summarize Russell's argument. They conclude that there is evidence of universals in human facial expressions, but of a more limited kind than had been claimed. There are, moreover, not one but several kinds of theory that might explain this evidence.

References

Ekman, P. (1994). Strong evidence for universals in facial expressions: a reply to Russell's mistaken critique. *Psychological Bulletin, 115*, 268–287.

Izard, C. E. (1994). Innate and universal facial expressions: evidence from developmental and cross-cultural research. *Psychological Bulletin, 115*, 288–299.

Fridlund, A. J. (1994). *Human facial expression: an evolutionary view.* San Diego: Academic Press.

J. A. Russell and J. M. Fernández-Dols, What does a facial expression mean? In J. A. Russell and J. M. Fernández-Dols (Eds.), *The Psychology of Facial Expression*. New York: Cambridge University Press, 1997, pp. 14–17. Reprinted with permission.

Russell, J. A. (1980). A circumplex model of affect. *Journal of Personality and Social Psychology, 39*, 1161–1178.

Russell, J. A. (1994). Is there universal recognition of emotion from facial expression? A review of methods and studies. *Psychological Bulletin, 115*, 102–141.

Universality

For many, the most convincing and exciting accomplishment of the Facial Expression Program was dramatic evidence for the universality of the facial expression of emotion. To establish this conclusion would require the establishment of three related propositions:

1   The same patterns of facial movement occur in all human groups.
2   Observers in different societies attribute the same specific emotions to those universal facial patterns.
3   Those same facial patterns are, indeed, manifestations of those very emotions in all human societies.

Writers have not always distinguished among these three. For instance, Ekman (1980) published photographs of aboriginal people in New Guinea smiling, frowning, weeping, and so on. Ekman then concluded in favor of universality – "Ultimately, however, the best argument for universality is made by the faces of the New Guineans" (p. 12) – without specifying which aspect of universality was actually established. Of course, the existence of facial patterns per se addresses only Proposition 1.

Proposition 1 has been largely assumed to be true, although its empirical examination might be highly revealing. Proposition 2 has received great attention. Proposition 3 has been curiously ignored; independent evidence on 3 is much needed, since 3 would not necessarily be true even if 1 and 2 were established. (This last point might be dismissed by incredulous readers, and so let us be clear: There is now no evidence showing that, in a number of different societies, happy people smile, angry people frown, disgusted people wrinkle their noses, and so on. See Fernández-Dols & Ruiz-Belda and Frijda & Tcherkassof, chapters 11 and 4 respectively in *The Psychology of Facial Expression* for discussions of this topic.)

Now consider the evidence on Proposition 2. Figure 8.1 provides a summary of relevant results from cross-cultural judgment studies using a standard method. The figures given are "recognition scores" (the percentage of observers who pick the predicted label). The first set of bars comes from Western literate societies (largely college students). The numbers are impressive (far above chance, represented in figure 8.1 by white horizontal lines). The second set of bars comes from non-Western societies (although still largely college students). This second set of scores is reliably lower than the first but still high. Now turn to the third set, which comes from more isolated samples of non-Western observers (uneducated, indeed illiterate). These observers agreed on attributing happiness to the smiles but yielded noticeably lower recognition scores with all other photographs.

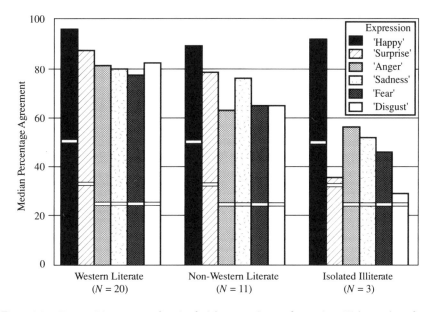

Figure 8.1. Recognition scores for six facial expressions of emotion. Values taken from Russell (1994). White horizontal bars represent level expected by chance alone. N is number of groups

Clearly, both Western and non-Western observers conform to prediction to a greater degree than would be expected by chance. At the same time, the recognition scores are proportional to the amount of Western influence and may have been inflated by a series of method factors: exaggerated posed expressions, within-subject design, and a forced-choice response format (not to mention experimenter influence, Sorenson, 1975, 1976). (For example, in Russell's 1994 data, the within-subject design resulted in an 11-percentage-point increase in average recognition score over that achieved in a between-subjects design.)

So, return to the third set of bars, and picture each bar falling even a small amount each time an inflationary method factor is removed. It remains to be seen which if any of the bars would remain above chance. Whatever the answer to that question, there also remains the matter of their interpretation.

Suppose that all recognition scores remain above chance even when technical problems are overcome. There would still be various alternative explanations for the nonrandom associations, including that of the Facial Expression Program (Izard, chapter 3, *The Psychology of Facial Expression*) but also including alternatives to it (e.g. Fernández-Dols & Carroll, Frijda & Tcherkassof, Russell, Smith, & Scott, chapters 12, 4, 13, and 10 respectively).

The most parsimonious account of all evidence we now have on how facial expressions are produced and interpreted is something called *Minimal Universality*. It is outlined in table 8.1. The phrase may sound like an oxymoron, but the paradox may stem from the presupposition that we face an either–or choice: either randomness (the null hypothesis used in the statistical tests carried out in the cross-cultural studies) or full universality. Like the nature–nurture dichotomy, this choice is simplistic. Minimal Universality predicts a certain amount of cross-cultural

Table 8.1   Minimal universality

Assumptions
1. Certain patterns of facial muscle movement occur in all human beings.
2. Facial movements are coordinated with psychological states (actions, preparation for actions, physical states, emotional states, cognitive states, and other psychological conditions).
3. Most people everywhere can infer something of another's psychological state from facial movement, just as they can from anything else that other person does.
4. People in Western cultures have a set of beliefs in which specific types of facial actions are expressions of specific types of emotion.

Some caveats
1. Facial actions are not necessarily signals.
2. Facial action is not necessary or sufficient for emotion. Facial action is not necessarily more associated with emotions than with other psychological states.
3. What inferences are made in one culture, or by one individual, need not coincide exactly with inferences made in another culture or by another individual.
4. People in all cultures need not share Western beliefs about the specific associations of emotions and facial actions.
5. Western beliefs about the association between facial expressions and emotions are not necessarily valid.

Predictions
1. Photographs of facial movements will be associated with psychological state with agreement that is greater than chance.
2. People are sometimes accurate in the inferences that they make on the basis of facial movements.
3. There will be similarities across cultures in what is inferred from facial movements.

similarity in interpreting facial expressions without postulating an innate emotion signaling system. Calling this position *minimal* is meant to emphasize that at least this much universality appears to exist. The question for the future, then, is: What can be established beyond Minimal Universality?

Needless to say, the topic of universality remains controversial. See Russell (1994, 1995) for an elaboration of the analysis just presented. See Izard (1994) and Ekman (1994) for an alternative analysis. See van Brakel (1994), Cornelius (1996), Oatley and Jenkins (1996), and Parkinson (1995) for independent reviews [...]

References

Brakel, J. van (1994). Emotions: A cross-cultural perspective on forms of life. In W. M. Wentworth & J. Ryan (Eds.), *Social perspectives on emotion*. Vol. 2. Greenwich: JAI Press.
Cornelius, R. R. (1996). *The science of emotion*. Upper Saddle River, NJ: Prentice-Hall.
Ekman, P. (1980). *The face of man: expressions of universal emotions in a New Guinea village*. New York: Garland STPM Press.

——(1994). Strong evidence for universals in facial expression: a reply to Russell's mistaken critique. *Psychological Bulletin, 115*, 268–287.

Oatley, K., & Jenkins, J. M. (1996). *Understanding emotion.* Cambridge, MA: Blackwell.

Parkinson, B. (1995). *Ideas and realities of emotion.* London: Routledge.

Russell, J. A. (1994). Is there universal recognition of emotion from facial expression? *Psychological Bulletin, 115*, 102–141.

——(1995). Facial expressions of emotion: What lies beyond minimal universality? *Psychological Bulletin, 118*, 379–391.

Schachter, S., & Singer, J. E. (1962). Cognitive, social, and physiological determinants of emotional state. *Psychological Review, 69*, 379–399.

Sorenson, E. R. (1975). Culture and the expression of emotion. In T. R. Williams (Ed.), *Psychological anthropology* (pp. 361–372). Chicago: Aldine.

Wierzbicka, A. (1992). *Semantics, culture, and cognition.* New York: Oxford.

PART II

Evolution and Processes

Evolution and Processes

It was Darwin, of course, who established the theory of evolution by natural selection. Many people, with or without reading Darwin's (1872) book *The Expression of the Emotions*, therefore assume that he proposed that emotions confer some selective advantage. But as you will see from selection 1, he did not. His book had the polemical purpose of arguing against those who held that God had created the human and every other species specially and perfectly. Darwin argued against this by demonstrating that at least some emotional expressions were imperfect, and that therefore we humans were based not on a distinct creation, but have descended from some earlier and lower form.

Because of his purpose Darwin could not stress functions of emotions. But now that his theory is widely accepted, we can consider these. Here is the general argument, which has been made by a number of recent writers on emotions. Emotions, being based on the relation between events and concerns (goals) help adapt an animal to its environment. A clear case is fear. When afraid an animal, including a human animal, is in a state of what Frijda (1986) calls "action readiness" of a particular kind – a kind to meet danger. It stops what it is doing, freezes (becomes immobile), scans the environment for signs of danger or safety, and prepares to escape, or possibly to fight.

Why do we have this pattern? The evolutionary answer is that stopping the current action and freezing has been important where predators have been part of the environment, because predators, like other animals, are sensitive to movement. An animal that remains immobile therefore increases its chance of remaining undetected. The fearful attention to signs of danger or safety in the environment functions to monitor the situation, to see whether if danger recedes one can get on with what one was doing, or if it comes closer to decide on the moment to make a run for it, or to fight (for more of this argument see Le Doux, selection 10).

It is not that fearful behavior is always successful in avoiding danger, but that on average during evolution it has been better than not freezing, not attending to signs of danger in the environment, and not preparing to escape or fight. Animals who possess fear, and its repertoire of response readiness, will be more likely to survive and reproduce. Hence the state and its response repertoire is passed on genetically.

Although there are some questions about the individual adaptiveness of some emotional states in psychopathology, comparable arguments can be made about other emotions, including the emotions of sexual attraction on which courtship is based; see, for instance, Fisher (1992), and the emotions of attachment of infants to parents, together with the emotions of maternal care which enable mammals and birds to bring immature youngsters to the point of being able to look after themselves; see, for instance, Bowlby (1971).

Although human emotions have properties that are as fundamental to human life as our ability to walk, Darwin was partly correct in his argument. Human evolution branched from that of our nearest relatives, the chimpanzees, perhaps 5 million years ago. It was following this branching that upright walking developed among human ancestors, and also that brains became much larger than those of animals in the line that led to chimpanzees. For most of that time humans and pre-humans are likely to have lived nomadically, perhaps in groups of extended family members. Therefore, many parts of the repertoire of human emotional responses may be adapted to ancient nomadic ways of life in small face-to-face-groups.

Settlements and cities began to be built only 10,000 or 12,000 years ago, a mere 400 or 500 generations, a quarter of a percent of the 200,000 generations during which our ancestors were evolving since branching from the chimpanzee line. So for 99.75 of the period of evolution of our specifically human line, our ancestors lived without fixed houses, without cultivation of food, without money, without industrial goods. They also lived without needing to take much notice of any beyond the 10 to 30 individuals in their immediate group and perhaps up to about 200 other individuals who might be known and encountered from time to time in travels across a territory or range. So the human environment of evolutionary adaptedness (as it is called) is not the environment in which most of us now live. The theory that emotions have a strong evolutionary basis has a number of implications, some of which depend on this idea that our ancestors lived in ways different from those in which most of us now live.

First there are theories about how the emotional repertoire of human beings has come about. Prominent among these is the theory of MacLean (e.g. 1993) who based his idea on what ethologists call species-specific behavior repertoires. He postulates three main phases: (i) the repertoire of reptiles that includes basic patterns of sleeping, waking, foraging, defending territory, and reproducing; (ii) a new repertoire of early mammals whose infants were live-born, and were suckled and reared by parents (this is added to the repertoire of reptiles); (iii) the repertoire of higher mammals, including humans, which includes expanded memory and thought, as well as both the previous repertoires. At each stage MacLean identifies a part of the brain that evolved to accomplish the new repertoires, with a large development in the second stage of the limbic system that is thought to subserve the emotions.

Second are ideas of what emotions do, based upon evolutionary theory. One such is represented in this reader by a paper of Oatley and Johnson-Laird (selection 9). In this theory it is proposed that the repertoire of emotions, thought to be human universals, each evolved to serve a particular function in the life of a wide range of mammals, not just humans, rather as explained for fear at the beginning of the introduction to part II.

The third implication of evolutionary theory is that evidence on how human emotions work is available not just from humans but from other primates. An example of research on social life and mechanisms of the limbic system is the work of Raleigh and others (1991) who show how increasing monkeys' brain serotonin makes them more likely to become dominant in their social group; the experiment helps to explain some of the effects of Prozac (Kramer, 1993), a drug which makes more serotonin available in the human brain. It acts as an anti-depressant, and also enhances confidence. Also based on the idea of specific emotional processes in the limbic system is the work of LeDoux (selection 10) who proposes that in a mechanism possessed by most mammals, the amygdala, acts as an emotional computer that performs appraisals of the kind discussed in part I.

The fourth kind of implication of evolutionary theory is that there will be universal physiological substrates of emotions. The argument is that whereas asking people about their emotions provides only soft data, hard data arise from brain science, more closely tied to biology, which is closer to the genetically provided programs of human emotions. This argument is not entirely correct because, for instance, different kinds of emotional experience in the lifetime of the individual can profoundly change brain structure. Nevertheless, interest in physiological and neurological accounts of emotions rests on the premise of universals. As representatives of this area, we have papers by Davidson (selection 11) and by Damasio and others (selection 12).

References

Bowlby, J. (1971). *Attachment and loss.* Vol. 1. *Attachment.* London: Hogarth Press (reprinted by Penguin, 1978).

Darwin, C. (1872). *The expression of the emotions in man and animals.* Chicago: University of Chicago Press (1965).

Fisher, H. E. (1992). *Anatomy of love.* New York: Norton.

Frijda, N. H. (1986). *The emotions.* Cambridge: Cambridge University Press.

Kramer, P. D. (1993). *Listening to Prozac.* New York: Viking.

Lutz, C. A. (1988). *Unnatural emotions: everyday sentiments on a Micronesian atoll and their challenge to Western theory.* Chicago: University of Chicago Press.

MacLean, P. D. (1993). Cerebral evolution of emotion. In M. Lewis & J. M. Haviland (Eds.), *Handbook of Emotions* (pp. 67–83). New York: Guilford.

Raleigh, M. J., McGuire, M. T., Brammer, G. L., Pollack, D. B., & Yuwiler, A. (1991). Serotonergic mechanisms promote dominance acquisition in adult male vervet monkeys. *Brain Research, 559,* 181–190.

CHAPTER *9*

The Communicative Theory of Emotions

K. Oatley and P. N. Johnson-Laird

Around 1985 Keith Oatley and Philip Johnson-Laird decided to embark on some theoretical work on emotions, Oatley from the point of view of understanding their role in plans and action, Johnson-Laird to fill a gap in his research with George Miller, Language and Perception. *In that book, although the semantics of most other domains had been treated in detail, the semantics of emotions was left to one side.*

As well as his work on emotions, Johnson-Laird is known for his research on reasoning, including its relation to consciousness and emotions e.g. Mental Models *and* The Computer and the Mind. *Oatley's book on the role of emotions in intended action, drawing on the collaboration with Johnson-Laird, is* Best Laid Schemes.

The result of the collaboration was a series of joint papers on the communicative theory of emotion, exploring the idea that the function of emotions is to communicate both to ourselves and others. The paper we excerpt here has much in common with appraisal theories (selections 4 and 28) and with Ekman and Friesen's postulation of a small number of basic emotions (selection 7). We include it in this section because it is based on an evolutionary way of thinking about emotions that has become increasingly influential.

References

Johnson-Laird, P. N. (1983). *Mental models: towards a cognitive science of language, inference, and consciousness.* Cambridge: Cambridge University Press.
—— (1988). *The computer and the mind.* Cambridge, MA: Harvard University Press.

K. Oatley and P. N. Johnson-Laird, The communicative theory of emotions: empirical tests, mental models, and implications for social interaction. In L. L. Martin and A. Tesser (Eds.), *Striving and Feeling: Interactions among goals, affect, and self-regulation.* Mahwah, NJ: Erlbaum, 1996, pp. 363–366, 372–380. Reprinted with permission.

Miller, G. A., & Johnson-Laird, P. N. (1976). *Language and perception.* Cambridge, MA: Harvard University Press.

Oatley, K. (1992). *Best laid schemes: the psychology of emotions.* New York: Cambridge University Press.

Emotions are at the center of human mental and social life. They integrate subjective experience, bodily changes, planned action, and social relating. We have proposed a theory (Oatley & Johnson-Laird, 1987) in which we integrated the biological approach to emotions deriving from Darwin (1872) and the cognitive science approach applied to emotions by Simon (1967). We proposed that emotions are communicative: they are based on signals within the brain that set it into distinct modes that reflect priorities of goals and that predispose toward appropriate classes of action. Such action includes expressive behavior that communicates emotions to other people.

Our theory has led to empirical studies and has provoked controversy; certain tenets have been shown to be wrong, so it needs revision. Our aim here is to present a revised version of the theory, to show how it accords with new evidence, and to draw out consequences for aspects of human emotional life that we did not originally consider. First, we briefly restate the original theory and its account of the semantics of emotion words. Next, we consider criticisms and tests of the theory, and then its relations with other theories. A revised version of the theory follows. Finally, we frame some conjectures to deal with attachment, psychopathology, emotions in reaction to entertainment, and the interaction between emotions and intellectual performance.

Emotions as managing goals: the communicative theory

Emotions are typically caused by cognitive evaluations that may be conscious or unconscious. According to the communicative theory, each kind of evaluation gives rise to a distinct signal that propagates through the multiple processors of cognitive architecture to produce a basic emotion. This signal is evolutionarily old and simple. It has no internal structure, and in this sense it is not propositional: It does not carry semantic information. Its function is to control the organization of the brain, to make ready mechanisms of action and bodily resources, to direct attention, to set up biases of cognitive processing, and to make the issue that caused the emotion salient in consciousness. The phenomenological experience of this signal is a distinctive feeling of happiness, sadness, anger, or some other emotional state.

In a typical emotional experience, people are aware of an emotion and of some aspects of the evaluation that gave rise to it. Thus the experience depends on two separate signals: the emotion signal and a propositional signal of the evaluation that caused it. The theory allows for dissociations between these two kinds of signal. On the one hand, people may be unaware of the emotion signal, and hence unaware of their emotional state. On the other hand, a person may experience an emotion but without realizing its cause, or why it is so intense.

There is good evidence that emotions can sometimes be caused by purely bodily changes. For instance, Strack, Martin, and Stepper (1988) showed that subjects asked to hold a pencil between their teeth were made mildly happy – the manipulation unobtrusively provided facial feedback like that of smiling. Moreover, Schiff and Lamon (1989) showed that contracting the left side of the face causes sadness, and contracting the right side causes more positive emotions; these manipulations work without conscious mediation, probably by differentially affecting (respectively) right or left hemispheric activation. We believe that physiological changes can be highly ambiguous to their experiencers. Such changes can occur for many reasons: a nonpropositional signal of emotion can occur although the subject does not know its cause, autonomic effects can occur because the subject has drunk too much coffee, feedback of expressions of emotion can be mimicked, differential activation of right and left hemispheres can occur, physical activity can cause changes that the subject feels but does not understand. Where there is ambiguity about any inner perturbation, experimental manipulation of the outer environment can suggest causes for it. It has been shown in many experiments that interpretations of inner states can be labile, and that people can misattribute their causes – a bodily state can be interpreted as a mood and it is affected by the context (Clore & Parrott, 1991).

Although experimentally demonstrated effects point to important processes, they need to be balanced by other kinds of investigation of how episodes of emotion are caused in everyday life. Later in this chapter we present some evidence on everyday emotions. To anticipate: In ordinary life most episodes of emotion are caused in obvious ways by evaluations of events in relation to goals – e.g. something we are working on goes well and we feel happy, someone slights us and we feel angry. In the usual course of events emotions have objects, and we know what caused them. Usually, according to our theory, the emotion signal and the information about its object and/or what caused it are tied together.

For our original theory (Oatley & Johnson-Laird, 1987) we derived a small number of basic emotions from our analysis of the evolutionary origins of emotions in the ontology of social mammals. We proposed that the social life of mammals revolves around a small number of significant individuals: parents and offspring, mates, predators and prey, cooperators in food acquisition, rivals. Important events arise as actions occur to achieve goals concerning such individuals.

This idea led us to postulate five basic emotions that arise at the junctures of such action sequences, corresponding to significant changes in relation to goals. They corresponded to states referred to in English, approximately, as happiness, sadness, anger, fear, and disgust. Thus achievement of subgoals elicits happiness, which prompts the person to continue the current activity until the goal is reached when he or she can stop; loss of a goal elicits sadness, which prompts disengagement from the goal; frustration elicits anger and aggressive striving to reach the goal or to avenge a wrong; threats, dangers, and conflicts of goals elicit fear (or the corresponding mood of anxiety) and hence freezing, flight, or fight; contaminating or toxic substances elicit disgust leading to repulsion and withdrawal. Our line of thinking converged with that of Ekman (1989), which was based on his discovery of pan-culturally recognized facial expressions for these same five emotions, along with a sixth, surprise, that we did not regard as separate because it can occur with

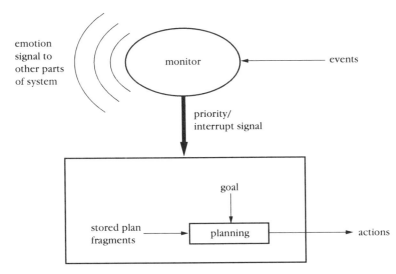

Figure 9.1. Diagram of the emotion system that monitors the status of goal-plan complexes. When an event occurs that indicates that the probability of reaching the goal has changed substantially, the monitoring system sends out a nonpropositional signal that changes the priority of the current plan (indicated by the thicker arrow), and modulates other parts of the brain.

any event in relation to a goal. For us the precise number of basic emotions is less important than the hypothesis that each kind of emotion has specific functions and that mechanisms that evolved to serve these functions map diverse events into a small set of emotional modes.

According to our original theory, when an event occurs that is important in relation to a goal, its cognitive evaluation either maintains (as a mood) the brain's present activities, or switches them (in a discrete emotion) into a new emotional mode appropriate to the event. We agree with Carver and Scheier (1990; Carver, Lawrence, & Scheier, chapter 9 of *Striving and Feeling*) that emotions are based on a system that monitors progress toward goals. Our version is depicted in figure 9.1. We disagree with Carver and Scheier's idea that affect derives continuously from rates of change of such progress. We believe that elicitation of emotions is more discrete; we think an emotion arises when an event indicates that the probability of attaining a goal has become discriminably better or worse than expected. So when some line of action is going well, when events are being dealt with successfully, when problems are being solved with resources that are at hand, when subgoals are being attained, the emotion signal produces a mood of happiness that encourages us to continue what we are doing. When the goal is achieved the person stops that activity. As Chaiken, Liberman, and Eagly (1989) concluded, people stop what they are doing when they reach "a sufficient degree of confidence that they have accomplished their processing goals." The process is not entirely straightforward, however, because, as Martin, Ward, Achee, and Wyer (1993) have shown, under some circumstances the pleasantness of a mood can itself be a goal, the feeling of happiness can itself be interpreted and used to determine whether or not to continue with an activity.

Carver and Scheier propose a positive-negative dimension, as in a servo-regulator, with a positive affective signal stopping activity because a goal state has been achieved and a negative one generating movement to reduce the error. By contrast, we propose that happiness is usually the mood of active engagement in what one is doing (cf. Csikszentmihalyi, 1990; also see later for our own evidence) and encourages one to continue until the goal is reached, or in non-goal-directed activities while the activity lasts. According to our formulation people usually stop not because of a happy emotion but because a goal is reached or an interruption occurs. Moreover, in contrast to Carver and Scheier, we postulate distinct kinds of negative emotion, because during evolution it has been possible to discriminate among negative events and because appropriate responses to different classes of negative event are very different. For instance, disengagement from a goal that is sadly lost is quite different from the striving of anger [...]

Biological theories and evidence

The communicative theory derives from the design of cognitive agents that could operate with multiple goals, which are often achieved in cooperation or competition with other people, in a world of which the agents' knowledge is incomplete and their mental models often incorrect. Yet, remarkably, it has converged with theories drawing on quite independent literatures. One of these is due to Tooby and Cosmides (1990). They proposed a theory similar to ours, though specified in less detail, from considerations of evolutionary biology. Another is LeDoux's (1990, 1993) neurophysiological account. He argued on the basis of conditioning experiments that the amygdala is an emotional computer that evaluates the emotional significance of stimuli. These stimuli may either be very simple percepts (aspects of a sound or sight) or they may depend on conscious recognition of meaning and significance. In either case, the amygdala transmits to other parts of the brain a signal that is not verbal but that functions to alter attention and to initiate physiological responses to the emotionally significant event.

Advances in understanding neurochemical systems have indicated that peptides can have effects that the communicative theory postulated for nonpropositional emotion signals (Panksepp, 1993). The signals for fear are the clearest: Bradwejn (1993) showed that if the peptide cholecystokinin (CCK) is injected into people in small quantities, it can cause free-floating fear. Patients describe resulting feelings as identical to panic attacks. Further evidence shows that CCK modulates some neural systems, and that its emotional effects are based on physiological (not artifactual) mechanisms.

Still other recent discoveries bear out the communicative theory's prediction that emotions can be induced without any conscious, informational content. In a study of the psychopathology of epilepsy, MacLean (1993) concluded that a small number of basic emotions can exist independently of semantic content in the auras of temporal lobe epilepsy. He writes that six kinds of emotions occur in these auras: desire, fear, anger, dejection (sadness), gratulant feelings (feelings of happiness, insight, or achievement), and feelings of affection. Often there is a sense of great conviction, and: "*Significantly, these feelings are free-floating, being completely unattached to any particular thing, situation, or idea*" (p. 79, emphasis in original).

An evaluation of the original communicative theory

The original communicate theory of emotions had some virtues. It is a member of a family of theories expressing views that are plausible to others. It survived, with some knocks, a first round of empirical tests, and it has made successful predictions: about emotions being caused by goal-relevant events, about emotions occurring without conscious cause, and about the effects of emotions on the current plan. The evidence has shown the theory was wrong in two substantial respects: Its treatment of the emotions of disgust and hatred was mistaken and its prediction that mixtures of emotions would be rare was incorrect. It also neglected the secondary evaluation of emotional experiences. We therefore propose a revision.

The revised communicative theory of emotions: foundational issues

What emotions are basic?

In our revised theory we still accept the functional role of emotions as both internal and external communications and believe that the four most common basic emotions (the *big four* as we are tempted to call them) correspond approximately to the English terms: happiness, sadness, anger, and fear. They are basic emotions in the sense that we described earlier. People can experience them without knowing their cause and without their having any apparent object. They also occur as free-floating emotions in epileptic auras. These four emotions are the foundation of moods and even perhaps of certain personality types. Their existence is acknowledged at a conceptual level by most people in most cultures. In ordinary life these four emotions can be, and usually are, experienced with a knowledge of their cause, so one usually knows why one feels happy, sad, angry, or afraid. The majority of emotion terms in European languages and, we believe, in other languages combine reference to a basic emotion and to an indication that the person knows its cause. Thus glad means that one is happy and knows why, disappointment is sadness about a known event, and so forth. We have considered English terms. Our analysis also translates well into Italian (Johnson-Laird & Oatley, 1988), and our interpretation is moderately consistent, we believe, with the results of Reisenzein (1995), using German translations.

In the revised theory, we propose that in addition to these four, there are five further emotions that are basic in the sense of being founded on innate, biological substrates: attachment, parental love, sexual attraction, disgust, and interpersonal rejection. What distinguishes them from the first set of four emotions is that they necessarily have objects. They can only be experienced in relation to someone or something. Attachment occurs between offspring and parent; parental love occurs toward offspring, and erotic attraction occurs between sexual partners (Shaver, Hazan, & Bradshaw, 1988). The emotions of disgust and personal rejection likewise must have objects. We were wrong to postulate that disgust can be free-floating; one can only feel disgust at something or someone. In the emotion of personal rejection, with its cognates of disdain and contempt, one always rejects someone. Frijda (personal communication, 1994) has said that our revised theory would be more elegant if we had added to the emotions that can be acausal (happiness, sadness, anger, and fear) just two types of emotion that are object-related – an emotion of attraction or desire (that would include the various kinds of love) and an emotion of repulsion or withdrawal (that would include both disgust and interpersonal rejection). We are very tempted by this idea. We had suggested it previously (Johnson-Laird & Oatley, 1992), and it would make our set of basic emotions correspond exactly to those suggested by MacLean (1983). We regard the classification of object-related emotions as tentative. Our (slight) preference for thinking that there may be several kinds of object-related emotions of desire is due to the persuasion of Shaver and others' (1988) argument that three quite different systems underlie love of intimates, and our preference for more than one emotion of rejection is due to persuasion by Rozin, Haidt, and McCauley's (1993) account of disgust in comparison with the emotions of inter-individual rejection described by Goodall (1986) in her study of chimpanzees at Gombe, who began systematically killing a subgroup of chimpanzees, formerly companions, who had separated from the main group. The subgroup began to be treated as a different species, somewhat like prey, quite differently from how ingroup members were treated in angry fights for dominance.

It may be that there is no single term in English for the emotion of personal rejection. Cognates include contempt, disdain, and hatred (as in *race-hatred*). But although *hatred* seems in some ways a good name for this mode, in English the term is used more widely – this may have contributed to the results on this term that Reisenzein (1995) found which were so discrepant with our theory. Larocque (personal communication, 1994) collected an example from each of 25 English speakers of an experience of hatred; in her corpus the common attribute of hatred was an intense negative emotion (there were examples of anger, fear, disgust, and interpersonal rejection) with no way of doing anything about the eliciting situation. On the basis of this we should regard the ordinary usage of the English term *hatred* as a superordinate for intense negative emotions where lack of control is salient.

Mental models as mediating emotions

If happiness, sadness, anger, and fear usually have objects, and emotions such as love and rejection necessarily have objects, then what is the psychological nature of these objects, which we become aware of via perception? Perceptual processes occur unconsciously; what they yield are mental models of the world (Marr, 1982; Oatley, Sullivan, & Hogg, 1988). Craik (1943) speculated that thinking is a process of manipulating such models; there is now considerable evidence in favor of this hypothesis and of the hypothesis that verbal comprehension yields analogous models (Johnson-Laird, 1983, 1993).

The essential characteristic of a model, as opposed to other proposed forms of mental representation, is that it has a structure that corresponds to the structure of what it represents. But it always represents only some aspects. It is necessarily incomplete, so it is compatible with more than one possibility. This fact is brought home perceptually by the existence of visual illusions. As far as emotions are concerned this means that as well as the phenomena of the emotions of happiness, sadness, anger, and fear, being able to occur (although rarely) without the subject knowing the cause, the necessarily object-related emotions can be detached from one object and reattached to another that has some attributes of the model. If a Jane falls in love with John then she falls in love with her idea of him, or if Jack rejects people of a different skin color than his own, anyone fitting this minimal description will serve as object.

Self-awareness depends also depends on a model: on a model of the self (Johnson-Laird, 1993) and on the ability to embed one model within another, as when one becomes aware of oneself as perceiving the world. Models of the self are essential to meta-cognition, and indeed for the maintenance of the sense that one has a coherence and integrity over time. Yet, these models of the self are also always incomplete and sometimes erroneous (Oatley, 1992; Singer & Salovey, 1993).

Attachment, parental love, and sexual attraction The role of models is central not only to the experience of object-directed emotions but also to their development. Infant attachment requires a model of the caregiver. Bowlby (1971) wrote of "internal working models" of relationships with attachment figures, and this concept has become central to understanding attachment (Bretherton, 1985; Main, 1991). Bowlby believed that a healthy child should develop a single coherent model of an attachment figure. To account for incoherence in the thought of emotionally disturbed people, Bowlby (1973) argued that they suffer from "multiple models." Psychoanalytic thinkers of the school of object relations (Fairbairn, 1952) hold a similar theory. People with partly unconscious disjunctive models can behave unpredictably to themselves and others, as first one model and its interpretations are invoked and then, in a different emotional situation, another and quite different model. The difficulty of reasoning coherently in disjunctive situations is manifest in laboratory studies of deductive reasoning (Bauer & Johnson-Laird, 1993; Johnson-Laird, Byrne, & Schaeken, 1992) and in judgment and decision-making (Shafir & Tversky, 1992).

Tesser and Cornell (1991) showed how self-esteem may work through a hierarchical system, the components of which all affect a single high-level variable that a person tries to maintain. Adults must maintain hierarchies of models in order to cope with the representation of propositional attitudes, such as one person's beliefs about another's beliefs, meta-cognitive abilities, self-awareness, as well as self-esteem. The development of such representations is being actively explored (Halford, 1993; Stern, 1985).

There are several important aspects of mental models for the revised communicative theory of emotions. Infants' models of caregivers are likely to be formed early in life. To start with they need merely recognize caregivers and detect presence or absence. As a result of interactions, an initial model becomes a model of the relationship between the self and the caregiver. The model of the relationship comes to accommodate emotions other than the feeling of attachment, for instance, temporary losses of the caregiver give rise to sadness, anger of the caregiver gives rise to feelings of fear which can then become represented in the model. The model becomes the means by which the individual predicts the behavior of significant people and influences interactions with them. Comparably, parents must become emotionally attached to, and preoccupied with, their offspring. Every parent knows the problems of children not conforming to a model he or she has of them. Sexual attraction, too, is mediated by models; their role can be seen not only in initial idealizations that occur in romantic love but in the emotions of disappointment that occur when the actual other does not fulfill expectations. In idealization, a person uses a model that is closer to his or her object of desire than to any real person. Recently Hazan and Shaver (1987) and others proposed that adult love is based on infant models of attachment.

Disgust and personal rejection   The other basic emotions that have objects are disgust and personal rejection. In our original theory we had assumed that disgust could be free-floating and also the basis of interpersonal rejection. We now accept that there are no feelings of free-floating disgust: Disgust always has an object (Rozin et al., 1993). We had confused it with the physiological state of nausea, as brought on by, say, seasickness. Disgust is undoubtedly an emotion with a biological base. Rozin and others reported many ingenious studies that demonstrate the importance of an individual's models in eliciting disgust. Thus their subjects felt disgusted by a plastic fly in their drink, even knowing that it was clean and not a real fly. One of the most potent elicitors of disgust is the idea of wearing a sweater that belonged to Hitler, even though subjects are assured that it has been thoroughly cleaned.

A further modification is to distinguish between disgust and the emotion of interpersonal rejection. Disgust is rooted in gustatory aversion (as Rozin and others proposed), whereas interpersonal rejection is a reaction to someone shunned who can be treated as less than human. Although, as Darwin (1872) pointed out, the two emotions are very close, a distinction between them is borne out by the existence of distinct facial expressions for disgust and contempt (Ekman & Friesen, 1986).

Goals of basic object-directed emotions   All five object-related emotions serve clear goals in the life of the species: attachment, parental love, and sexual attraction are the bases of rearing young and reproduction; disgust protects the body from infection and other kinds of contamination. Interpersonal rejection (contempt or hatred) seems perhaps more questionable, but several human paleontologists have seen lethal intergroup conflict as an important part of hominid evolution (Stringer & Gamble, 1993).

Mixtures of emotions

In our original theory we allowed that mixed emotions could occur but thought that one emotion mode would tend to inhibit others. Hence, mixtures should be ephemeral. The evidence shows this was wrong. A plausible revision of the theory is that individuals can react to events by making more than one cognitive evaluation, and such evaluations can create distinct emotions in parallel or in rapid alternation. With loss of a loved one, one may feel both sad at the loss and angry at what was responsible for it. Threats from a hostile person may induce both anger and anxiety – a combination that may be quite stable if it induces conflict between approach and avoidance (Dollard & Miller, 1950). Happiness on achieving subgoals can be accompanied by anxiety about what follows when the goal is achieved.

One consequence of mixtures of emotions is that they make ready for disparate courses of action. Individuals who feel both angry and fearful tend both to advance aggressively and to flee. Such conflicts may be apparent in conflicting facial expressions, a phenomenon that Ekman and O'Sullivan (1991) reported in terms of "impure" emotions, such as smiling while lying but letting small facial signs of anxiety leak out. Mixtures occur often in relation to aggression (Lorenz, 1967). Aggressive actions occur when a predator kills prey. Goodall (1986) observed some prey-killing actions (e.g. biting and tearing flesh) among the chimpanzees that started killing out-group members. Anger relates to within-group aggression, whereas the emotions of personal rejection relate to aggression against outsiders and to treating them as nonmembers of the species. But with aggression sharing parts of the action repertoire, mixtures of anger and interpersonal rejection are not surprising.

The hypothesis that separate evaluations lead to dual emotions has empirical implications. First, in children it indicates increasing cognitive ability to entertain distinct cognitive evaluations of different aspects of the same state of affairs. Harris (1989) reported a study in which children were told a story about a dog that gets lost and later returns with a wounded ear. Older children say they feel happy at the dog's return and sad about its injury; younger children report just one emotion. Second, the complexity of contemporaneous but distinct cognitive evaluations calls for processing at a relatively high level in mental architecture. We can postulate that mixed feelings would not occur without knowing something about their cause. An interesting special case would be mixed feelings with awareness of the cause of only one of the emotions.

Mixtures can also arise from secondary evaluations. A primary evaluation evokes an emotion, then secondary evaluations of what to do about the situation can include new emotions about the original one. Oatley and Duncan (1992) found examples such as guilt about being angry and anger with the self about being fearful. Emotions need not just follow one another like beads on a string; they can overlay one another like strata.

One final thought about mixed feelings: Granted the existence of stable mixtures, it is perhaps surprising how few words in English denote mixed emotions. In the everyday conception of emotions we have a natural grasp of distinct emotions and generally refer to mixtures by indicating the emotions that occur in them.

A summary of the revised theory

We have now outlined a new version of our communicative theory. We will here restate the main functions of emotions in relation to goals.

Evaluation of goal-relevant events   Emotions typically arise from evaluations of events relevant to goals. These evaluations occur within a hierarchy of parallel processors, and they may be conscious or unconscious. They give rise to nonpropositional signals within the brain that induce and maintain emotion modes.

Emotions have signal functions, to ourselves and to others An emotion usually implies the existence of a goal, which may be unconscious, and of an event evaluated as relevant to a goal.

Readiness and the management of goals Emotions function to manage plans and goals: maintaining readiness of ongoing activity in happy moods, interrupting such activity and changing readiness to act in a different plan where a negative emotion occurs. Just as within the individual cognitive system, emotions and moods maintain goal-plan complexes that involve other people. Happiness, attachment emotions, and love induce and maintain cooperation. Sadness is the emotion of disengagement from a relationship. Anger sets up a script for competition, aggression, and perhaps renegotiation of the relationship. Interpersonal fear signals deference. Contempt and disdain signal withdrawal from relationship.

Cognitive organization Each kind of emotion produces a distinctive mode of brain organization that includes distinctive attentional characteristics, biases of memory, and characteristics of problem solving.

Emotions inject the problem that prompted them into consciousness They induce conscious rumination. That such preoccupation can lasts a long time indicates the importance of the cognitive changes that must occur with serious emotions, such as falling in love or coping with death or separation from someone who was close.

The principal changes to our original theory are as follows:

1 Four basic emotions, although their causes are usually known, can be experienced acausally: happiness, sadness, anger, and fear.
2 Five other basic emotions are necessarily object-related, each requires a known object (although they can be experienced toward objects without knowing why): attachment, parental love, sexual attraction, disgust, and personal rejection.
3 The object of an emotion is experienced via a mental model, a schematic, partial, and sometimes erroneous, representation that corresponds in structure to what it represents, a person or object in the world.
4 Secondary evaluations of events occur. These can give rise to sequences of changing emotions as people review what they can do about a situation. Some emotions may depend on secondary evaluation. For some closely held goals, it may take a long time to understand that a goal is lost and must be relinquished.
5 Mixtures of emotions occur. Although one emotion mode may inhibit others, different interpretative evaluations of the same situation, or secondary evaluations of an emotional experience as it unfolds, can lead to stable mixtures of emotions, and these can elicit conflicting kinds of readiness to act [...]

References

Bauer, M. I., & Johnson-Laird, P. N. (1993). How diagrams can improve reasoning. *Psychological Science, 4*, 372–378.

Bendix, E. H. (1966). *Componential analysis of general vocabulary: the semantic structure of a set of verbs in English, Hindi, and Japanese*. The Hague: Mouton.

Biason, A. (1993). *Emotional responses of high-school students to short stories*. Unpublished doctoral dissertation, University of Toronto.

Bowlby, J. (1971). *Attachment and loss*: Vol. 1. *Attachment*. London: Hogarth Press (reprinted by Penguin, 1978).

Bowlby, J. (1973). *Attachment and loss*: Vol. 2. *Separation: Anxiety and anger*. London: Hogarth Press (reprinted by Penguin, 1978).

Bradwejn, J. (1993). Neurobiological investigations into the role of cholecystokinin in panic disorder. *Journal of Psychiatry and Neuroscience, 18*, 178–188.

Bretherton, I. (1985). Attachment theory: Retrospect and prospect. In I. Bretherton & E. Waters (Eds.), *Growing points in attachment: Theory and research. Monographs of the Society for Research in Child Development, 50* (1–2, serial no. 209).

Carver, C. S., & Scheier, M. F. (1990). Origins and functions of positive and negative affect: a control process view. *Psychological Review, 97*, 19–35.

Chaiken, S., Lieberman, A., & Eagly, A. H. (1989). Heuristic and systematic information processing within and beyond the persuasion context. In J. S. Uleman & J. A. Bargh (Eds.), *Unintended thought: limits of awareness, intention and control* (pp. 212–252). New York: Guilford.

Chwelos, G. (1992). *Emotion elicitation models: a comparative study*. Unpublished master's thesis, University of Toronto.

Chwelos, G., & Oatley, K. (1994). Appraisal, computational models, and Scherer's expert system. *Cognition and Emotion, 8*, 245–257.

Clore, G. L., & Parrott, W. G. (1991). Moods and the vicissitudes: Thoughts and feelings as information. In J. P. Forgas (Ed.), *Emotion and social judgements* (pp. 107–123). Oxford: Pergamon Press.

Conway, M. A., & Bekerian, D. A. (1987). Situational knowledge and emotions. *Cognition and Emotion, 1*, 145–191.

Csikszentmihalyi, M. (1990). *Flow: The psychology of optimal experience*. New York: HarperCollins.

Darwin, C. (1872). *The expression of the emotions in man and the animals*. Chicago: University of Chicago Press (reprinted 1965).

Dollard, J., & Miller, N. E. (1950). *Personality and psychotherapy*. New York: McGraw-Hill.

Ekman, P. (1989). The argument and evidence about universals in facial expressions of emotion. In H. Wagner & A. Manstead (Eds.), *Handbook of social psychophysiology* (pp. 143–164). Chichester: Wiley.

Ekman, P., & O'Sullivan, M. (1991). Who can catch a liar? *American Psychologist, 46*, 913–920.

Ellsworth, P. (1991). Some implications of cognitive appraisal theories of emotion. In K. T. Strongman (Ed.), *International Review of Studies on Emotion* (pp. 143–161). Chichester: Wiley.

Fairbairn, W. R. D. (1952). *Psychoanalytic studies of the personality*. London: Routledge & Kegan Paul.

Frijda, N. H. (1986). *The emotions*. Cambridge: Cambridge University Press.

Goodall, J. (1986). *The chimpanzees of Gombe: Patterns of behavior*. Cambridge, MA: Harvard University Press.

Halford, G. S. (1993). *Children's understanding: The development of mental models*. Hillsdale, NJ: Erlbaum.

Harris, P. L. (1989). *Children and emotion: The development of psychological understanding*. Oxford: Blackwell.

Hazan, C., & Shaver, P. (1987). Romantic love conceptualized as an attachment process. *Journal of Personality and Social Psychology, 52*, 511–524.

Johnson-Laird, P. N. (1983). *Mental models: Towards a cognitive science of language, inference, and consciousness.* Cambridge: Cambridge University Press.

—— (1993). *Human and machine thinking.* Hillsdale, NJ: Erlbaum.

Johnson-Laird, P. N., Byrne, R. M. J., & Schaeken, W. (1992). Propositional reasoning by model. *Psychological Review, 99,* 418–439.

Johnson-Laird, P. N., & Oatley, K. (1988). Il significato delle emozioni: una teoria e un' analisi semantica. In V. D'Urso & R. Trentin (Eds.), *Psicologia delle emozioni* (pp. 119–158). Bologna: Il Mulino.

—— (1989). The language of emotions: an analysis of a semantic field. *Cognition and Emotion, 3,* 81–123.

—— (1992). Basic emotions, rationality, and folk theory. *Cognition and Emotion, 6,* 201–223.

Jones, G. V., & Martin, M. (1992). Conjunction in the language of emotions. *Cognition and Emotion, 6,* 369–386.

Lazarus, R. S. (1991). *Emotion and adaptation.* New York: Oxford University Press.

LeDoux, J. E. (1993). Emotional networks in the brain. In M. Lewis & J. M. Haviland (Eds.), *Handbook of emotions* (pp. 109–118). New York: Guilford.

LeDoux, J., Ciccetti, P., Xagoraris, A., & Romanski, L.R. (1990). The lateral amygdaloid nucleus: sensory interface pf the amygdala in fear conditioning. *Journal of Neuroscience, 10,* 1062–1069.

Lorenz, K. Z. (1967). *On aggression.* (M. Latzke, Trans.). London: Methuen.

MacLean, P. D. (1993). Cerebral evolution of emotion. In M. Lewis & J. M. Haviland (Eds.), *Handbook of emotions* (pp. 67–83). New York: Guilford.

Marr, D. (1982). *Vision.* San Francisco: W. H. Freeman.

Martin, L. L., Ward, D. W., Achee, J. W., & Wyer, R. S. (1993). Mood as input: people have to interpret the motivational implications of their moods. *Journal of Personality and Social Psychology, 64,* 317–326.

Nisbett, R., & Ross, L. (1980). *Human inference: Strategies and shortcomings of social judgement.* Englewood Cliffs, NJ: Prentice-Hall.

Oatley, K. (1992). *Best laid schemes: The psychology of emotions.* New York: Cambridge University Press.

Oatley, K., & Duncan, E. (1992). Incidents of emotion in daily life. In K. T. Strongman (Ed.), *International Review of Studies on Emotion* (pp. 250–293). Chichester: Wiley.

—— (1994). The experience of emotions in everyday life. *Cognition and Emotion, 8,* 369–381.

Oatley, K., & Johnson-Laird, P. N. (1987). Towards a cognitive theory of emotions. *Cognition and Emotion, 1,* 29–50.

—— (1992). Terms of emotion: The inferences that can be drawn. *Revista de Psicologia Social, 7,* 97–104.

Oatley, K., Sullivan, G. D., & Hogg, D. (1988). Drawing visual conclusions from analogy: A theory of preprocessing, cues and schemata in the perception of three dimensional objects. *Journal of Intelligent Systems, 1,* 97–133.

Ortony, A., Clore, G. L., & Collins, A. (1988). *The cognitive structure of emotions.* New York: Cambridge University Press.

Ortony, A., & Turner, T. J. (1990). What's basic about basic emotions? *Psychological Review, 97,* 431–461.

Panksepp, J. (1993). Neurochemical control of moods and emotions: Amino acids to neuropeptides. In M. Lewis & J. M. Haviland (Eds.), *Handbook of emotions* (pp. 87–107). New York: Guilford.

Reisenzein, R. (1995). On Oatley and Johnson-Laird's theory of emotions and hierarchical structures. *Cognition and Emotion, 9,* 383–416.

Roseman, I. J. (1991). Appraisal determinants of discrete emotions. *Cognition and Emotion, 5,* 161–200.

Rozin, P., Haidt, J., & McCauley, C. R. (1993). Disgust. In M. Lewis & J. M. Haviland (Eds.), *Handbook of emotions* (pp. 575–594). New York: Guilford.

Russell, J. A. (1991). In defense of a prototype approach to emotion concepts. *Journal of Personality and Social Psychology, 60*, 37–47.

Scherer, K. R. (1988). Criteria for emotion antecedent appraisal: A review. In V. Hamilton, G. H. Bower, & N. H. Frijda (Eds.), *Cognitive perspectives on emotion and motivation* (pp. 89–126). Dordrecht: Kluwer.

——(1993). Studying the emotion-antecedent appraisal process: An expert system approach. *Cognition and Emotion, 7*, 325–355.

Schiff, B. B., & Lamon, M. (1989). Inducing emotion by unilateral contraction of facial muscles: A new look at hemispheric specialization and the experience of emotion. *Neuropsychologia, 27*, 923–935.

Shafir, E., & Tversky, A. (1992). Thinking through uncertainty: Nonconsequential reasoning and choice. *Cognitive Psychology, 24*, 449–474.

Shaver, P., Hazan, C., & Bradshaw, D. (1988). Love as attachment: The integration of three behavioral systems. In R. J. Sternberg & M. L. Barnes (Eds.), *The psychology of love* (pp. 68–99). New Haven, CT: Yale University Press.

Singer, J. A., & Salovey, P. (1993). *The remembered self: Emotion and memory in personality.* New York: Free Press.

Smith, C. A., Haynes, K. N., Lazarus, R. S., & Pope, L. K. (1993). In search of "hot" cognitions: attributions, appraisals and their relation to emotion. *Journal of Personality and Social Psychology, 65*, 916–929.

Stein, N. L., Trabasso, T., & Liwag, M. (1993). The representation and organization of emotional experience: unfolding the emotion episode. In M. Lewis & J. M. Haviland (Eds.), *Handbook of emotions* (pp. 279–300). New York: Guilford.

Stern, D. (1985). *The interpersonal world of the infant.* New York: Basic Books.

Strack, F., Martin, L. L., & Stepper, S. (1988). Inhibiting and facilitating conditions of the human smile: a nonobtrusive test of the facial feedback hypothesis. *Journal of Personality and Social Psychology, 54*, 768–777.

Tesser, A., & Cornell, D. P. (1991). On the confluence of self processes. *Journal of Experimental Social Psychology, 27*, 501–526.

Tooby, J., & Cosmides, L. (1990). The past explains the present: Emotional adaptations and the structure of ancestral environments. *Ethology and Sociobiology, 11*, 375–424.

Wiener, B., & Graham, S. (1989). Understanding the motivational role of affect: Lifespan research from an attributional perspective. *Cognition and Emotion, 3*, 401–419.

Wilson, T. D., Laser, P. S., & Stone, J. I. (1982). Judging the predictors of one's own mood: Accuracy and the use of shared theories. *Journal of Experimental Social Psychology, 18*, 537–556.

CHAPTER *10*

The Emotional Brain

J. Le Doux

Joseph Le Doux has become well known recently for his neuroscientific work on emotions. He has proposed that the amygdala, an area usually regarded as part of this system, is uniquely important in emotions. Although most of the research done on this region is based on the single emotion of fear, Le Doux has written that the amygdala may also be involved with other emotions, including positive ones. He then adds a word of caution, because although "one might be tempted to conclude that the amygdala is the centerpiece of an emotional system of the brain" (Le Doux, 1995: 222), it is too early to draw this conclusion. More research is needed.

What is exciting about Le Doux's work, however, is that for fear at least it seems possible that "Functions mediated by the amygdala are likely to be the neural instantiation of the emotional process known as appraisal," (Le Doux, 1995: 223). If this hypothesis is correct, it would link neuroscientific methods to that important process in which events evaluated in relation to concerns.

Reference

Le Doux, J. E. (1995). Emotion: clues from the brain. *Annual Review of Psychology, 46*, 209–235.

For whom the bell tolls

If your neighbor's dog bites you, you will probably be wary every time you walk by his property. His house and yard, as well as sight and sound of the beast, have become emotional stimuli for you because of their association with the unpleasant event. This is fear conditioning in action. It turns meaningless stimuli into warning

J. Le Doux, *The Emotional Brain: The mysterious underpinnings of emotional life*. New York: Simon & Schuster, 1997, pp. 141–146, 149–150, 157–159, 161–165. Reprinted with permission.

signs, cues that signal potentially dangerous situations on the basis of past experiences with similar situations.

In a typical fear conditioning experiment, the subject, say a rat, is placed in a small cage. A sound then comes on, followed by a brief, mild shock to the feet. After very few such pairings of the sound and the shock, the rat begins to act afraid when it hears the sound: It stops dead in its tracks and adopts the characteristic freezing posture – crouching down and remaining motionless, except for the rhythmic chest movements required for breathing. In addition, the rat's fur stands on end, its blood pressure and heart rate rise, and stress hormones are released into its bloodstream. These and other conditioned responses are expressed in essentially the same way in every rat, and also occur when a rat encounters its perennial arch-enemy, a cat, strongly suggesting that, as a result of fear conditioning, the sound activates the neural system that controls responses involved in dealing with predators and other natural dangers.

Fear conditioning is a variation on the procedure discovered by Ivan Pavlov around the turn of the century.[1] As everyone knows, the great Russian physiologist observed that his dogs salivated when a bell was rung if the sound of the bell had previously occurred while the dog had a juicy morsel of meat in its mouth. Pavlov proposed that the overlap in time of the meat in the mouth with the sound of the bell resulted in the creation of an association (a connection in the brain) between the two stimuli, such that the sound was able to substitute for the meat in the elicitation of salivation.

Pavlov abhorred psychological explanations of behavior and sought to account for the anticipatory salivation physiologically, without having to "resort to fantastic speculations as to the existence of any subjective state in the animal which may be conjectured on analogy with ourselves." He thus explicitly rejected the idea that salivation occurred because the hungry dogs began to think about the food when they heard the bell. In this way Pavlov, like William James, removed subjective emotional states from the chain of events leading to emotional behavior.

Pavlov called the meat an unconditioned stimulus (US), the bell a conditioned stimulus (CS), and the salivation elicited by the CS a conditioned response (CR). This terminology derives from the fact that the capacity of the bell to elicit salivation was conditional upon its relation to the meat, which elicited salivation naturally, which is to say, unconditionally. Applying these terms to the fear conditioning experiment described above, the tone was the CS, the shock was the US, and the behavioral and autonomic expressions were the CRs. And in the language used in the previous chapter to describe the stimuli that initiate emotional behaviors, a US is a *natural trigger* while a CS is a *learned trigger*.

Fear conditioning does not involve response learning. Although rats freeze when they are exposed to a tone after but not before conditioning, conditioning does not teach the rats how to freeze. Freezing is something that rats do naturally when they are exposed to danger. Laboratory-bred rats who have never seen a cat will freeze if they encounter one.[2] Freezing is a built-in response, an innate defense response, that can be activated by either *natural or learned triggers*.

Fear conditioning opens up channels of evolutionarily shaped responsivity to new environmental events, allowing novel stimuli that predict danger (like sounds made

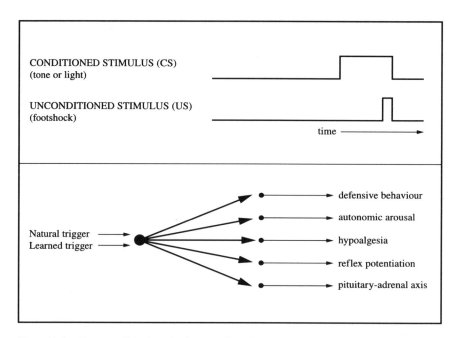

Figure 10.1. Fear conditioning. In fear conditioning an unconditioned stimulus (typically a brief, mild footshock) is delivered at the end of the conditoned stimulus (Usually a tone or light). After a few pairings, the conditioned stimulus acquires the capacity to elicit a wide variety of bodily responses. Similar responses occur in the presence of natural dangers that are innately programmed into the brain. For example, in the presence of either a conditioned fear stimulus or a cat, rats will freeze and exhibit blood pressure and heart rate changes, alterations in pain responsivity, more sensitive reflexes, and elevation of stress hormones from the pituitary gland. Because rats do not require prior exposure to cats to exhibit these responses, the cat is a *natural* trigger of defense responses for rats. And because the tone only elicits these responses after fear conditioning, it is a *learned* trigger. Similar patterns of defense responses occur in humans and other animals when exposed to fear triggers (natural and learned). Studies of nonhuman animals can thus illuminate important aspects of fear reactivity in humans.

by an approaching predator or the place where a predator was seen) to gain control over tried-and-true ways of responding to danger. The danger predicted by these *learned trigger stimuli* can be real or imagined, concrete or abstract, allowing a great range of external (environmental) and internal (mental) conditions to serve as CSs.

Conditioned fear learning occurs quickly, and can occur after a single CS–US pairing. An animal in the wild does not have the opportunity for trial-and-error learning. Evolution has arranged things so that if you survive one encounter with a predator you can use your experience to help you survive in future situations. For example, if the last time a rabbit went to a certain watering hole it encountered a fox and barely escaped, it will probably either avoid that watering hole in the future or the next time it goes there it will approach the scene with trepidation, taking small cautious steps, searching the environment for any clue that might signal that a fox is near.[3] The watering hole and fox have been linked up in the rabbit's brain, and being near the watering hole puts the rabbit on the defensive.

Not only is fear conditioning quick, it is also very long-lasting. In fact, there is little forgetting when it comes to conditioned fear. The passing of time is not enough to get rid of it.[4] Nevertheless, repeated exposure to the CS in the absence of the US can lead to "extinction." That is, the capacity of the CS to elicit the fear reaction is diminished by presentation of the CS over and over without the US. If our thirsty but fearful rabbit has only one watering hole to which it can go, and visits it day after day without again encountering a fox, it will eventually act as though it never met a fox there.

But extinction does not involve an elimination of the relation between the CS and US. Pavlov observed that a conditioned response could be completely extinguished on one day, and on the next day the CS was again effective in eliciting the response. He called this "spontaneous recovery."[5] Recovery of extinguished conditioned responses can also be induced. This has been nicely demonstrated in studies by Mark Bouton.[6] After rats received tone-shock pairings in one chamber, he put them in a new chamber and gave them the tone CS over and over until the conditioned fear responses were no longer elicited – the conditioned fear reaction was completely extinguished. He then showed that simply placing the animals back in the chamber where the CS and US were previously paired was enough to *renew* the conditioned fear response to the CS. Extinguished conditioned fear responses can also be *reinstated* by exposing the animals to the US or some other stressful event.[7] Spontaneous recovery, renewal, and reinstatement suggest that extinction does not eliminate the memory that the CS was once associated with danger but instead reduces the likelihood that the CS will elicit the fear response.

These findings in rats fit well with observations on humans with pathological fears (phobias).[8] As a result of psychotherapy, the fear of the phobic stimulus can be kept under control for many years. Then, after some stress or trauma, the fear reaction can return in full force. Like extinction, therapy does not erase the memory that ties fear reactions to trigger stimuli. Both processes simply prevent the stimuli from unleashing the fear reaction [...]

Measure for measure

Once the meaning of a stimulus has been modified by fear conditioning, the next occurrence of the stimulus unleashes a whole host of bodily responses that prepare the organism to deal with the impending danger about which the stimulus warns. Any of these can be used to measure the effects of conditioning.

For example, when a conditioned fear stimulus occurs, the subject will typically stop all movement – it will freeze.[9] Many predators respond to movement[10] and withholding movement is often the best thing to do when danger is near.[11] Freezing can also be thought of as preparatory to rapid escape when the coast clears, or to defensive fighting if escape is not possible. Since the muscle contractions that underlie freezing require metabolic energy, blood has to be sent to those muscles. Indeed, the autonomic nervous system is strongly activated by a conditioned fear stimulus, producing a variety of cardiovascular and other visceral responses that help support the freezing response. These also help the body prepare for the escape or fighting responses that are likely to follow.[12] Additionally, stress hormones are released into the bloodstream to further help the body cope with the threatening situation.[13] Reactivity to pain is also suppressed, which is useful since the conditioned stimulus often announces a situation in which the probability of bodily harm is high.[14] And reflexes (like eye-blink or startle responses) are potentiated, allowing quicker, more efficient reactions to stimuli that normally elicit protective movements.[15]

These various responses are part of the body's overall adaptive reaction to danger and each has been used to examine the brain systems involved in conditioned fear responses. For example, David Cohen[16] has studied the brain pathways of fear conditioning in pigeons using heart rate responses, and Bruce Kapp,[17] Neil Schneidermann and Phil McCabe[18] and Don Powell[19] have used heart rate responses in rabbits. Michael Fanselow[20] has used freezing and pain suppression in rats as measures, while Michael Davis[21] has exploited the potentiation of reflexes by a fear eliciting conditioned stimulus, also in rats. Orville Smith[22] has studied fear conditioning in baboons, measuring a variety of cardiovascular responses in conjunction with measures of movement inhibition. And in my research on the brain mechanisms of fear conditioning, I've made simultaneous measurements of freezing and blood pressure responses in rats.[23]

The amazing fact is that it has not really mattered very much how conditioned fear has been measured, or what species has been studied, as all of the approaches have converged on a common set of brain structures and pathways that are important. Although there are some minor differences and controversies over some of the details, in broad outline there is remarkable consensus. This contrasts with studies of the neural basis of many other behaviors, where slight changes in the experimental procedure or the species can result in profound differences in the neural systems involved. Fear conditioning is so important that the brain does the job the same way no matter how we ask it to do it [...]

Almond joy

The amygdala is a small region in the forebrain, named by the early anatomists for its almond shape (amygdala is the Latin word for almond). It was one of the areas of the limbic system and had long been thought of as being important for various forms of emotional behavior – earlier studies of the Klüver-Bucy syndrome had pointed to it, as had electrical stimulation studies (see below).

The discovery of a pathway that could transmit information directly to the amygdala from the thalamus suggested how a conditioned fear stimulus could elicit fear responses without the aid of the cortex. The direct thalamic input to the amygdala simply allowed the cortex to be bypassed. The brain is indeed a complex mesh of connections, but anatomical findings were taking us on a delightful journey of discovery through this neuronal maze.

I wasn't really looking for the amygdala in my work. The dissection of the brain's pathways just took me there. But my studies, when they first started coming out, fit nicely with a set of findings that Bruce Kapp had obtained concerning a subregion of the amygdala – the central nucleus. Noting that the central nucleus has connections with the brain stem areas involved in the control of heart rate and other autonomic nervous system responses, he proposed that this region might be a link in the neural system through which the autonomic responses elicited by a conditioned fear stimulus are expressed. And when he lesioned the central nucleus in the rabbit, his hypothesis was confirmed – the lesions dramatically interfered with the conditioning of heart rate responses to a tone paired with shock.[24]

Kapp went on to show that stimulation of the central amygdala produced heart-rate and other autonomic responses, strengthening his idea that the central nucleus was an important forebrain link in the control of autonomic responses by the brain stem. However, he also found that stimulation of the central nucleus elicited freezing responses, suggesting that the central amygdala might not just be involved in the control of autonomic responses, but might be part of a general-purpose defense response control network.

Indeed, subsequent research by several laboratories has shown that lesions of the central nucleus interfere with essentially every measure of conditioned fear,

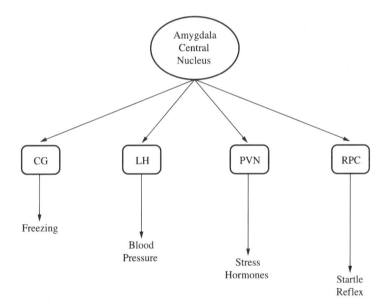

Figure 10.2. Different outputs of the amygdala control different conditioned fear responses. In the presence of danger or stimuli that warn of danger, behavioral, autonomic, and endocrine responses are expressed, and reflexes are modulated. Each of these responses is controlled by a different set of outputs from the central nucleus of the amygdala. Lesions of the central nucleus block the expression of all these responses, whereas lesions of the output pathways block only individual responses. Selected examples of central amygdala outputs are shown. Abbreviations: CG, central gray; LH, lateral hypothalamus; PVN, paraventricular hypothalamus (which receives inputs from the central amygdala directly and by way of the bed nucleus of the stria terminalis); RPC, reticulo-pontis caudalis.

including freezing behavior, autonomic responses, suppression of pain, stress hormone release, and reflex potentiation.[25] It was also found that each of these responses are mediated by different outputs of the central nucleus.[26] For example, I demonstrated that lesions of different projections of the central nucleus separately interfered with freezing and blood pressure conditioned responses – lesions of one of the projections (the periaqueductal gray) interfered with freezing but not blood pressure responses, whereas lesions of another (the lateral hypothalamus) interfered with the blood pressure but not the freezing response.[27] And while lesions of a third projection (the bed nucleus of the stria terminalis) had no effect on either of these responses, other scientists later showed that lesions of this region interfere with the elicitation of stress hormones by the CS[28] [...]

The low and the high road

The fact that emotional learning can be mediated by pathways that bypass the neocortex is intriguing, for it suggests that emotional responses can occur without the involvement of the higher processing systems of the brain, systems believed to be involved in thinking, reasoning, and consciousness. But before we pursue this notion, we need to further consider the role of the auditory cortex in fear conditioning.

In the experiments described so far, a simple sound was paired with a shock. The auditory cortex is clearly not needed for this. But suppose the situation is somewhat more complex. Instead of just one tone paired with a shock, suppose the animal gets two similar tones, one paired with the shock and the other not, and has to learn to distinguish between them. Would the auditory cortex then be required? Neil Schneidermann, Phil McCabe, and their colleagues looked at this question in a study of heart rate conditioning in rabbits.[29] With enough training, the rabbits eventually only expressed heart rate responses to the sound that had been associated with the shock. And when the auditory cortex was lesioned, this capacity was lost. Interestingly, the auditory cortex lesions did not interfere with conditioning by blocking responses to the stimulus paired with the shock. Instead, the cortically lesioned animals responded to both stimuli as if they had each been paired with the shock.

These findings make sense given what we know about the neurons in the thalamus that project to the amygdala as opposed to those that provide the major inputs to the auditory cortex.[30] If you put an electrode in the brain, you can record the electrical activity of individual neurons in response to auditory stimulation. Neurons in the area of the thalamus that projects to the primary auditory cortex are narrowly tuned – they are very particular about what they will respond to. But cells in the thalamic areas that project to the amygdala are less picky – they respond to a much wider range of stimuli and are said to be broadly tuned. The Beatles and Rolling Stones (or, if you like, Oasis and the Cranberries) will sound the same to the amygdala by way of the thalamic projections but quite different by way of the cortical projections. So when two similar stimuli are used in a conditioning study, the thalamus will send the amygdala essentially the same information, regardless of which stimulus it is processing, but when the cortex processes the different stimuli it will send the amygdala different signals. If the

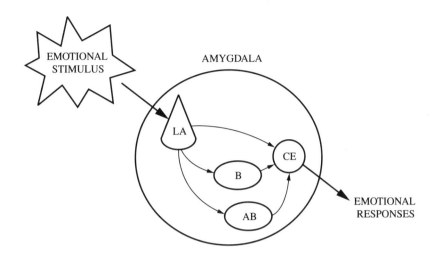

Figure 10.3. Organization of information-processing pathways in the amygdala. The lateral nucleus (LA) is the gateway into the amygdala. Stimuli from the outside world are transmitted to LA, which then processes the stimuli and distributes the results to other regions of the amygdala, including the basal (B), accessory basal (AB), and central nuclei (CE). The central nucleus is then the main connection with areas that control emotional responses. As shown in figure 10.2, different outputs of the central nucleus regulate the expression of different responses.

cortex is damaged, the animal has only the direct thalamic pathway and thus the amygdala treats the two stimuli the same – both elicit conditioned fear.

The quick and the dead

Why should the brain be organized this way? Why should it have the lowly thalamic road when it also has the high cortical road?

Our only source of information about the brains of animals from long ago is the brains of their living descendants. Studies of living fish, amphibians, and reptiles suggest that sensory projections to rudimentary cortical areas were probably relatively weak compared to projections to subcortical regions in primordial animals.[31] In contemporary mammals, the thalamic projections to cortical pathways are far more elaborate and important channels of information processing. As a result, it is possible that in mammals the direct thalamic pathway to the amygdala is simply an evolutionary relic, the brain's version of an appendix. But I don't think this is the case. There's been ample time for the direct thalamo-amygdala pathways to have atrophied if they were not useful. But they have not. The fact that they have existed for millions and millions of years side by side with thalamocortical pathways suggests that they still serve some useful function. But what could that function be?

Although the thalamic system cannot make fine distinctions, it has an important advantage over the cortical input pathway to the amygdala. That advantage is time. In a rat it takes about twelve milliseconds (twelve one-thousandths of a second)

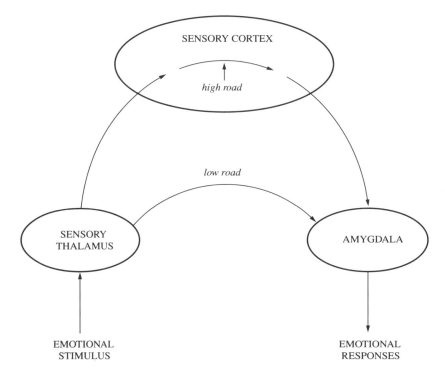

Figure 10.4. The low and the high roads to the amygdala. Information about external stimuli reaches the amygdala by way of direct pathways from the thalamus (the low road) as well as by way of pathways from the thalamus to the cortex of the amygdala. The direct thalamo-amygdala path is a shorter and thus a faster transmission route than the pathway from the thalamus through the cortex to the amygdala. However, because the direct pathway bypasses the cortex, it is unable to benefit from cortical processing. As a result it can only provide the amygdala with a crude representation of the stimulus. It is thus a *quick* and *dirty* processing pathway. The direct pathway allows us to begin to respond to potentially dangerous stimuli before we fully know what the stimulus is. This can be very useful in dangerous situations. However, its utility requires that the cortical pathway be able to override the direct pathway. It is possible that the direct pathway is responsible for the control of emotional responses that we don't understand. This may occur in all of us some of the time, but may be a predominant mode of functioning in individuals with certain emotional disorders.

for an acoustic stimulus to reach the amygdala through the thalamic pathway, and almost twice as long through the cortical pathway. The thalamic pathway is thus faster. It cannot tell the amygdala exactly what is there, but can provide a fast signal that warns that something dangerous may be there. It is a quick and dirty processing system.

Imagine walking in the woods. A crackling sound occurs. It goes straight to the amygdala through the thalamic pathway. The sound also goes from the thalamus to the cortex, which recognizes the sound to be a dry twig that snapped under the weight of your boot, or that of a rattlesnake shaking its tail. But by the time the cortex has figured this out, the amygdala is already starting to defend against the snake. The information received from the thalamus is unfiltered and biased toward evoking responses. The cortex's job is to prevent the inappropriate response rather than to produce the appropriate one. Alternatively, suppose there is a slender curved shape on the path. The curvature and slenderness reach the amygdala from the thalamus, whereas only the cortex distinguishes a coiled up snake from a curved stick. If it is a snake, the amygdala is ahead of the game. From the point of view of survival, it is better to respond to potentially dangerous events as if they were in fact the real thing than to fail to respond. The cost of treating a stick as a snake is less, in the long run, than the cost of treating a snake as a stick.

So we can begin to see the outline of a fear reaction system. It involves parallel transmission to the amygdala from the sensory thalamus and sensory cortex. The subcortical pathways provide a crude image of the external world, whereas more detailed and accurate representations come from the cortex. While the pathway from the thalamus only involves one link, several links are required to activate the amygdala by way of the cortex. Since each link adds time, the thalamic pathway is faster. Interestingly, the thalamo-amygdala and corticoamygdala pathways converge in the lateral nucleus of the amygdala. In all likelihood, normally both pathways transmit signals to the lateral nucleus, which appears to play a pivotal role in coordinating the sensory processes that constitute the conditioned fear stimulus. And once the information has reached the lateral nucleus it can be distributed through the internal amygdala pathways to the central nucleus, which then unleashes the full repertoire of defensive reactions. Although I have mainly discussed my own work, research by others (especially Michael Davis, Michael Fanselow, Norman Weinberger, and Bruce Kapp) has also contributed significantly to our understanding of the neural basis of fear conditioning[32][...]

Notes

1   Pavlov (1927).
2   D. C. Blanchard & R. J. Blanchard (1972).
3   R. J. Blanchard et al. (1993); D. C. Blanchard & R. J. Blanchard (1988).
4   Campeau, Liang, & Davis (1990); Gleitman & Holmes (1967).
5   Pavlov (1927).
6   Bouton (1994); Bouton & D. Swartzentruber (1991).
7   Campbell & Jaynes (1966).
8   Jacobs & Nadel (1985); Marks (1987).
9   Freezing occurs in many species in response to sudden danger [Marks (1987)] but has been studied as a conditioned response mostly in rats.
10 Von Uexkull (1934).
11 Archer (1979).
12 Cannon (1929); Hilton (1979); Mancia & Zanchetti (1981).
13 Mason (1968); van de Kar et al. (1991).
14 Bolles & Fanselow (1980); Watkins & Mayer (1982); Helmstetter (1992).
15 Brown, Kalish, & Farber (1951); Davis (1992b); Weisz, Harden, & Xiang (1992).
16 D. H. Cohen (1980).
17 Kapp et al. (1992).
18 McCabe et al. (1992).
19 Powell & Levine-Bryce (1989).

20 Fanselow (1994).
21 Davis (1992).
22 O.A. Smith et al. (1980).
23 Le Doux (1994), (1995).
24 Kapp's work was seminal in starting this field. In 1979 he published the first study showing the lesions of the central nucleus of the amygdala disrupt fear conditioning. Later studies used stimulation, tracing, and unit recording techniques to show without a doubt that the central amygdala was an important structure in fear conditioning (summarized in Kapp, Pascoe, & Bixler [1984]).
25 The effects of central nucleus of the amygdala lesions are summarized in Kapp et al. (1990); Davis (1992); Le Doux (1993); Le Doux (1995).
26 Kapp et al. (1990); Davis (1992); Le Doux (1993); Le Doux (1995).
27 Le Doux et al. (1988).
28 T. S. Gray et al. (1993).
29 Jarrell et al. (1987).
30 For discussion of processing differences between auditory thalamus and cortex in fear conditioning, see Weinberger (1995); Bordi & Le Doux (1994a); Bordi & Le Doux (1994b).
31 Nauta & Karten (1970); Northcutt & Kaas (1995).
32 Kapp et al. (1992); Davis et al. (1992); Fanselow (1994) Weinberger (1995). For an alternative interpretation of the role of the thalamic pathway, see Campeau & Davis (1995). For a rebuttal of their interpretation see Corodimas and LeDoux (1995).

References

Adolphs, R., Tranel, D., Damasio, H., and Damasio, A. R. (1995). Fear and the human amygdala. *Journal of Neuroscience 15*, 5879–5891

Aggleton, J. P. (1992). *The amygdala: Neurobiological aspects of emotion, memory, and mental dysfunction.* New York: Wiley- Liss.

Archer, J. (1979). Behavioral aspects of fear. In W. Sluckin (Ed.), *Fear in animals and man.* New York: Van Nostrand Reinhold.

Bandler, R., Carrive, P., & Zhang, S. P. (1991). Integration of somatic and autonomic reactions within the midbrain periaqueductal grey: Viscerotopic, somatotopic and functional organization. *Progress in Brain Research, 87*, 269–305.

Bechara, A., Tranel, D., Damasio, H., Adolphs, R., Rockland, C., & Damasio, A. R. (1995). Double dissociation of conditioning and declarative knowledge relative to the amygdala and hippocampus in humans. *Science, 269*, 1115–1118.

Blanchard, D. C., & Blanchard, R. J. (1972). Innate and conditioned reactions to threat in rats with amygdaloid lesions. *Journal of Comparative Physiological Psychology, 81*, 281–290.

——(1988). Ethoexperimental approaches to the biology of emotion. *Annual Review of Psychology, 39*, 43–68.

Blanchard, R. J., Yudko, E. B., Rodgers, R. J., & Blanchard, D. C. (1993). Defense system psychopharmacology: an ethological approach to the pharmacology of fear and anxiety. *Behavioural Brain Research, 58*, 155–166.

Bolles, R. C., and Fanselow, M. S. (1980). A perceptual- defensive-recuperative model of fear and pain. *Behavioral and Brain Sciences 3*, 291–323.

Bordi, F., & Le Doux, J. E. (1994a). Response properties of single units in areas of rat auditory thalamus that project to the amygdala. I: Acoustic discharge patterns and frequency receptive fields. *Experimental Brain Research, 98*, 261–274.

—— (1994b). Response properties of single units in areas of rat auditory thalamus that project to the amygdala. II: Cells receiving convergent auditory and somatosensory inputs and cells antidromically activated by amygdala stimulation. *Experimental Brain Research, 98*, 275–286.

Bouton, M. E. (1994). Conditioning, remembering, and forgetting. *Journal of Experimental Psychology: Animal Behavior Processes, 20*, 219–231.

Bouton, M. E., & Swartzentruber, D. (1991). Sources of relapse after extinction in Pavlovian and instrumental learning. *Clinical Psychology Review, 11*, 123–140.

Brown, J. S., Kalish, H. I., & Farber, I. E. (1951). Conditioned fear as revealed by magnitude of startle response to an auditory stimulus. *Journal of Experimental Psychology, 41*, 317–328.

Campbell, B. A., & Jaynes, J. (1966). Reinstatement. *Psychological Review, 73*, 478–480.

Campeau, S. & Davis, M. (1995). Involvement of subcortical and cortical afferents to the lateral nucleus of the amygdala in fear conditioning measured with fear-potentiated startle in rats trained concurrently with auditory and visual conditioned stimuli. *Journal of Neuroscience, 15*, 2312–2327.

Campeau, S., Liang, K. C., & Davis, M. (1990). Long-term retention of fear-potentiated startle following a short training session. *Animal Learning and Behavior, 18*, 462–468.

Cannon, W. B. (1929). *Bodily changes in pain, hunger, fear, and rage*. Vol. 2. New York: Appleton.

Cohen, D. H. (1980). The functional neuroanatomy of a conditioned response. In R. F. Thompson, L. H. Hicks, & B. Shuyrkov (Eds.), *Neural mechanisms of goal-directed behavior and learning*, pp. 283–302. New York: Academic Press.

Corodimas, K. P., & Le Doux, J. E. (1995). Disruptive effects of posttraining perirhinal cortex lesions on conditioned fear: contributions of contextual cues. *Behavioral Neuroscience, 109*, 613–619.

Damasio, A. (1994). *Descartes's error: Emotion, reason, and the human brain*. New York: Grosset/Putnam.

Darwin, C. (1872). *The expression of the emotions in man and animals* (Chicago: University of Chicago Press, reprinted 1965).

Davis, M. (1992a). The role of amygdala in conditioned fear. In J. P. Aggleton (Ed.), *The amygdala: Neurobiological aspects of emotion, memory, and mental dysfunction* (pp. 255–306). New York: Wiley-Liss.

—— (1992b). The role of the amygdala in fear-potentiated startle: implications for animal models of anxiety. *Trends in Pharmacological Science, 13*, 35–41.

Everitt, B. J., & Robbins, T. W. (1992). Amygdala – ventral striatal interactions and reward related processes. In J. Aggleton (Ed.) *The Amygdala: Neurobiological aspects of emotion, memory and mental dysfunction* (pp. 401–429). New York: Wiley-Liss.

Fanselow, M. S. (1994). Neural organization of the defensive behavior system responsible for fear. *Psychonomic Bulletin and Review, 1*, 429–438.

Fanselow, M. S., & Kim, J. J. (1994). Acquisition of contextual Pavlovian fear conditioning is blocked by application of an NMDA receptor antagonist DL-2-amino-5-phosphono-valeric acid to the basolateral amygdala. *Behavioral Neuroscience, 108*, 210–212.

Fuster, J. M. (1989). *The prefrontal cortex*. New York: Raven.

Gleitman, H., & Holmes, P. A. (1967). Retention of incompletely learned CER in rats. *Psychonomic Science, 7*, 19–20.

Gloor, P., Olivier, A., & Quesney, L. F. (1981). The role of the amygdala in the expression of psychic phenomena in temporal lobe seizures. In Y. Ben-Ari (Ed.), *The amygdaloid complex* (pp. 489–498). New York: Elsevier/North-Holland Biomedical Press.

Goldman-Rakic, P. S. (1993). Working memory and the mind. In *Mind and brain: Readings from Scientific American magazine* (pp. 66–77). New York: Freeman.

Gray, T. S., Piechowski, R. A., Yracheta, J. M., Rittenhouse, P. A., Betha, C. L., & van der Kar, L. D. (1993). Ibotenic acid lesions in the bed nucleus of the stria terminalis attenuate conditioned stress induced increases in prolactin, ACTH, and corticosterone. *Neuroendocrinology, 57*, 517–524.

Greenberg, N., Scott, M., & Crews, D. (1984). Role of the amygdala in the reproductive and aggressive behavior of the lizard. *Physiology and Behavior, 32*, 147–51.

Halgren, E. (1992). Emotional neurophysiology of the amygdala within the context of human cognition. In J. Aggleton (Ed.), *The amygdala: Neurobiological aspects of emotion, memory, and mental dysfunction* (pp. 191–228). New York: Wiley-Liss.

Hamann, S. B., Stefanacci, L., Squire, L., Adolphs, R., Tranel, D., Damasio, H., & Damasio, A. (1996). Recognizing facial emotion. *Nature, 379*, 497.

Helmstetter, F. (1992). The amygdala is essential for the expression of conditioned hypoalgesia. *Behavioral Neuroscience, 106*, 518–528.

Hilton, S. M. (1979). The defense reaction as a paradigm for cardiovascular control. In C. M. Brooks, K. Koizuni, & A. Sato (Eds.), *Integrative functions of the autonomnic nervous system*, (pp. 443–49). Tokyo: University of Tokyo Press.

Jacobs, W. J., & Nadel, L. (1985). Stress-induced recovery of fears and phobias. *Psychological Review, 92*, 512–531.

Jarrell, T. W., Gentile, C. G., Romanski, L. M., McCabe, P. M., & Schneiderman, N. (1987). Involvement of cortical and thalamic auditory regions in retention of differential brady-cardia conditioning to acoustic conditioned stimuli in rabbits. *Brain Research, 412*, 285–294.

Kaada, B. R. (1967). Brain mechanisms related to aggressive behavior. In C. Clemente & D. B. Lindsley (Eds.), *Aggression and defense – Neural mechanisms and social patterns* (pp. 95–133) Berkeley: University of California Press.

Kapp, B. S., Whalen, P. J., Supple, W. F., & Pascoe, J. P. (1992). Amygdaloid contributions to conditioned arousal and sensory information processing. In J. Aggleton (Ed.), *The amygdala: Neurobiological aspects of emotion, memory, and mental dysfunction* New York: Wiley-Liss.

Kapp, B. S., Frysinger, R. C., Gallagher, M., & Haselton, J. (1979). Amygdala central nucleus lesions: effect on heart rate conditioning in the rabbit. *Physiology and Behavior, 23*, 1109–1117.

Kapp, B. S., Pascoe, J. P., & Bixler, M. A. (1984). The amygdala: a neuroanatomical systems approach to its contributions to aversive conditioning. In M. Buttlers & L. R. Squire (Eds.), *Neuropsychology of memory* (pp. 473–88) New York: Guilford.

Kapp, B. S., Wilson, A., Pascoe, J., Supple, W., and Whalen, P. J. (1990). A neuroanatomical systems analysis of conditioned bradycardia in the rabbit. In M. Gabriel & J. Moore (Eds.), *Learning and computational neuroscience: Foundations of adaptive networks*, (pp. 53–90) Cambridge, MA: MIT Press.

LaBar, K. S., Le Doux, J. E., Spencer, D. D., & Phelps, E. A. (1995). Impaired fear conditioning following unilateral temporal lobectomy in humans. *Journal of Neuroscience, 15*, 6846–6855.

Lazarus, R. S. (1966). *Psychological stress and the coping process*. New York: McGraw Hill.

—— (1991). Cognition and motivation in emotion. *American Psychologist, 46*, 352–367.

Le Doux, J. E. (1987). Emotion. In F. Plum (Ed.), *Handbook of Physiology. Section 1: The Nervous System*. Vol. 5. *Higher Functions of the Brain* (pp. 419–460). Bethesda, MD: American Physiological Society.

—— (1993). Emotional memory systems in the brain. *Behavioural Brain Research, 58*, 69–79.

—— (1994). Emotion, memory and the brain. *Scientific American, 270*, 32–39.

—— (1995). Emotion: Clues from the brain. *Annual Review of Psychology, 46*, 209–235.

Le Doux, J. E., Iwata, J., Cicchetti, P., & Reis, D. J. (1988). Different projections of the central amygdaloid nucleus mediate autonomic and behavioral correlates of conditioned fear. *Journal of Neuroscience, 8*, 2517–2529.

Luria, A. (1966). *Higher cortical functions in man*. New York: Basic Books.

Mancia, G., & Zanchetti, A. (1981). Hypothalamic control of autonomic functions. In P. J. Morgane & J. Panksepp (Eds.), *Handbook of the hypothalamus*. Vol. 3. *Behavioral studies of the hypothalamus* (pp. 147–202). New York: Marcel Dekker.

Marks, I. (1987). *Fears, phobias, and rituals: Panic, anxiety and their disorders*. New York: Oxford University Press.

Mason, J. W. (1968). A review of psychoendocrine research on the sympathetic-adrenal medullary system. *Psychosomatic Medicine, 30*, 631–653.

McCabe, P. M., Schneiderman, N., Jarrell, T. W., Gentile, C. G., Teich, A. H., Winters, R. W., & Liskowsky, D. R. (1992). Central pathways involved in differential classical conditioning of heart rate responses. In E. A. Gormenzano (Ed.), *Learning and memory: The behavioral and biological substrates* (pp. 321–346). Hillsdale, NJ: Erlbaum.

Milner, B. (1964). Some effects of frontal lobectomy in man. In J. M. Warren and K. Akert (Eds.), *The Frontal Granular Cortex and Behavior* (pp. 313–334) New York: McGraw-Hill.

Nauta, W. J. H. (1971). The problem of the frontal lobe: a reinterpretation. *Journal of Psychiatric Research, 8*, 167–187.

Nauta, W. J. H., and Karten, H. J. (1970). A general profile of the vertebrate brain, with sidelights on the ancestry of cerebral cortex. In F. O. Schmitt (Ed.), *The neuro-sciences: Second study program* (pp. 7–26) New York: Rockefeller University Press.

Northcutt, R. G., & Kaas, J. H. (1995). The emergence and evolution of mammalian neocortex. *Trends in Neuroscience, 18*, 373–379.

Pavlov, I. P. (1927). *Conditioned reflexes*, (Trans. G. V. Anrep). New York: Dover. [Reprinted 1960.]

Povinelli, D. J., & Preuss, T. M. (1995). Theory of mind: evolutionary history of a cognitive specialization. *Trends in Neuroscience, 18*, 418–424.

Powell, D. A., & Levine-Bryce, D. (1989). A comparison of two model systems of associative learning: heart rate and eyeblink conditioning in the rabbit. *Psychophysiology, 25*, 672–682.

Preuss, T. M. (1995). Do rats have prefrontal cortex? The Rose-Woolsey-Akert program reconsidered. *Journal of Cognitive Neuroscience, 7*, 1–24.

Smith, O. A., Astley, C. A., Devito, J. L., Stein, J. M., & Walsh, R. E. (1980). Functional analysis of hypothalamic control of the cardiovascular responses accompanying emotional behavior. *Federation Proceedings, 39*, 2487–2494.

Stuss, D. T. (1991). Self, awareness, and the frontal lobes: a neuropsychological perspective. In J. Strauss & G. R. Goethals (Eds.), *The self: Interdisciplinary approaches*, New York: Springer.

Tarr, R. S. (1977). Role of the amygdala in the intraspecies aggressive behavior of the iguanid lizard. *Physiology and Behavior, 18*, 1153–1158.

van de Kar, L. D., Piechowski, R. A., Rittenhouse, P. A., & Gray, T. S. (1991). Amygdaloid lesions: differential effect on conditioned stress and immobilization-induced increases in corticosterone and renin secretion. *Neuroendocrinology, 54*, 89–95.

von Uexküll, J. (1934). A stroll through the world of animals and man. In C. H. Schiller (Ed.), *Instinctive behavior: The development of a modern concept*, (pp. 5–80). London: Methuen.

Watkins, L. R., & Mayer, D. J. (1982). Organization of endogenous opiate and nonopiate pain control systems. *Science, 216*, 1185–1192.

Weinberger, N. M. (1995). Retuning the brain by fear conditioning. In M. S. Gazzariga (Ed.), *The cognitive neurosciences* (pp. 1071–1090). Cambridge, MA: MIT Press.

Weisz, D. J., Harden, D. G., & Xiang, Z. (1992). Effects of amygdala lesions on reflex facilitation and conditioned response acquisition during nictitating membrane response conditioning in rabbit. *Behavioral Neuroscience, 106*, 262–273.

CHAPTER *11*

Emotion and Affective Style

R. J. Davidson

The limbic system is often referred to a primitive area of the brain that came into existence with the evolution of the early mammals. But what of the most recently evolved part of the human brain, the cortex? Is it merely, as some writers imply, some computer-like processor working according to laws of logic, and in adult humans keeping the emotions of the lower regions in check? No – the cortex too has emotional functions. We see some of them in this selection from the work of Richie Davidson.

We humans have two sides to our cerebral cortex. Since the nineteenth century, evidence has accumulated that the hemispheres are specialized. If, for instance, a person has a stroke – a hemorrhage – on the left side, that person is often unable to speak, whereas a stroke on the right side usually leaves language intact. But are the hemispheres emotionally different? Davidson has devoted much of his career to answering this question. Activation of the forward parts of the right hemisphere is associated with negative emotions, and of the forward parts of the left with positive and assertive emotions. This holds not only for short-lived emotions but for longer-lasting emotional states, which Davidson calls "affective styles."

In 1995 Davidson co-edited with Paul Ekman a book in which emotion researchers discussed "Fundamental questions" of research on emotions. In this paper of 1992, he summarizes work from his laboratory on issues of emotion and hemispheric asymmetry over the previous fifteen years or so, making connections to work with Ekman (see selection 7) on the relation between expression and hemispheric activation, and also to work on temperament carried out in collaboration with Kagan (see selection 16).

Reference

Ekman, P., & Davidson, R. J. (1995). *The nature of emotion: Fundamental questions.* New York: Oxford University Press.

Emotions have often been conceptualized as reflecting primitive processes that are subserved by correspondingly primitive structures in the brain. This view was endorsed and strengthened by Papez's (1937) pioneering theoretical work in which he described a circuit comprising the hypothalamus, cingulate cortex, hippocampal formation, and their interconnections as forming the anatomical basis of the emotions. McLean (1949) later amplified this view and proposed his concept of the triune brain, with emotions controlled subcortically by the limbic system. This view of the anatomical basis of emotion has had an enormous impact in guiding research on the biology of emotion. Experiments performed within this tradition have usefully underscored the importance of certain subcortical sites in the regulation of emotional behavior. However, this view has also had the ill-fated effect of turning attention away from the potentially important role of various cortical regions in the regulation of emotional behavior. We now know that anterior cortical regions, possibly as a function of their connections with sub-cortical structures, play an important role in the control of emotions (see the review by Kolb & Taylor, 1990). From the very earliest observations on the role of the neocortex in emotion, important functional differences between the two hemispheres of the brain have been noted. This paper will present an overview of theory and research in this emerging area and summarize some of the implications of this work for understanding temperament, personality, and psychopathology.

On the differentiated nature of emotion

Many different behavioral and mental processes contribute to emotion. Sensory and perceptual processes are required to detect emotionally provocative stimuli, cognitive processes are often needed to appraise incoming stimuli, memory functions are sometimes invoked in the generation of emotional responses, and action often accompanies an emotion, functioning to either amplify or attenuate the response. Research on cerebral laterality and emotion has frequently been interpreted to be inconsistent, in part, because of the failure to differentiate among different subcomponents of emotion. It is clear from available research that the hemispheric substrates of the perception of emotional information are different from those associated with the generation of emotional responses (i.e. the experience and expression of emotion) (see Davidson, 1984; Davidson & Tomarken, 1989, for reviews). This paper will focus on the hemispheric substrates of the experience and expression of emotion.

Effects of unilateral cortical lesions on emotional behavior: clinical clues

The earliest suggestions that the left and right cerebral cortex contribute differently to the regulation of emotion came from observations on the effects of unilateral cortical lesions on emotional behavior (e.g. Jackson, 1878). The majority of these reports indicated that damage to the left hemisphere was more likely to lead to what has been termed a catastrophic-depressive reaction compared with comparable damage to the right hemisphere (e.g. Goldstein, 1939). More recent observations have confirmed and extended these early observations (Gainotti, 1972; Sackeim et al., 1982). Of particular importance to the research summarized in this article are studies by Robinson and his colleagues (e.g., Robinson, Kubos, Starr, Rao, & Price, 1984). These investigators have reported that it is damage specifically to the left frontal lobe that results in depressive symptomatology. Among patients with left-hemisphere lesions, they found that the closer the lesion to the frontal pole (assessed on the basis of computed tomographic scan evidence), the more severe the depressive symptomatology. Patients who developed mania subsequent to brain injury were much more likely to have sustained damage to the right hemisphere, sparing the left.

The studies of affective changes in patients with unilateral brain injury suggest that the left frontal region is particularly important for certain forms of positive affect and when this region is damaged, depression is a likely consequence. I have conceptualized the frontal asymmetry as reflecting specialized systems for approach and withdrawal behavior, with the left frontal region specialized for the former and the right frontal region specialized for the latter. Following a brief description of the electrophysiological methods used, data will be presented which demonstrate that systematic changes in activation asymmetry in anterior cortical regions occur in response to experimentally elicited positive and negative emotion.

The use of scalp-recorded measures of brain electrical activity to infer patterns of regional cortical activation

Several important considerations apply in the choice of methods to study regional brain activity underlying emotion. First, the time resolution of the method must match the time scale of the emotional phenomena under study. Spontaneous manifestations of emotion are often brief and frequently unpredictable. For example, many facial expressions of emotion are present for as little as 1 to 2 s, and they can occur at different times for different subjects in response to the same emotionally provocative stimulus. An ideal method of assessing regional brain activity would be one capable of capturing such brief periods marked by specific expressive signs. For other purposes, it is also important to record physiological activity over much longer intervals of time. One of the most exciting new areas in psychophysiological research on emotion is the study of individual differences in emotional reactivity. Such studies often require baseline physiology to be integrated over several minutes in order to obtain a reliable estimate of an individual's characteristic pattern. Thus, with respect to time resolution, the ideal measure would range from subsecond intervals to several minutes.

A second important consideration in the choice of methods to assess regional brain activity is that they be relatively noninvasive. More than most manipulations, the experimental arousal of emotion interacts heavily with contextual factors, and its success depends on the maintanance of an appropriate social context. Invasive procedures, such as certain types of positron emission tomography (PET) imaging, are not very conducive to the arousal and maintenance of positive affect. Also, if common procedures are to be used in research with adults and young children, noninvasive methods are a must.

For these various reasons, most of my work has used scalp-recorded measures of brain electrical activity to make inferences about regional cortical activation. The electroencephalogram (EEG) is noninvasive, has a fast time resolution, and can easily be used with persons of all ages. Moreover, it is suitable for studies of episodic emotional events, as well as stable individual differences. Examples of each of these types of research will be presented later.

The principal measure extracted from the EEG in the research I will highlight in this paper is power in the alpha band, which in adults is defined as activity between 8 and 13 Hz. A wealth of evidence indicates that power in this frequency band is inversely related to activation in adults (Shagass, 1972). In the studies I will describe on infants, power in a lower frequency band was the dependent measure since this represents the functional equivalent of adult alpha activity (Davidson & Fox, 1989; Davidson & Tomarken, 1989). The measures of band power are computed from the output of a Fast Fourier Transform, which decomposes the brain activity into its underlying constituent frequencies.

The effects of specific emotional arousal on brain activity

In collaborative research with Ekman (Davidson, Ekman, Saron, Senulis, & Friesen, 1990; Ekman, Davidson, & Friesen, 1990), normal subjects were exposed to short film clips designed to elicit happiness/amusement and disgust. We chose these emotions for study because of their association with approach and with-drawal behavior respectively. During film viewing, we recorded brain electrical activity and unobtrusively videotaped the subjects' facial behavior. The facial behavior was coded with Ekman and Friesen's (1978) Facial Action Coding System. Using this system, we identified the onset and offset times of different facial expressions of emotion. These times were then entered into our computer system so that brain activity coincident with the expressions could be extracted. Special procedures were used to remove muscle and other artifacts from the EEG (see Davidson, 1988). The EEG data revealed greater right-sided anterior activation (both frontal and anterior temporal) during the disgust than happy facial expression conditions. Notably, 100 percent of the subjects showed the effect in the predicted direction. However, the asymmetry difference between disgust and happy periods was superimposed upon wide-ranging individual differences in the direction and magnitude of asymmetry. As will be described later, these individual differences in asymmetry are relatively stable over time and are associated with different features of dispositional mood and affective reactivity.

With Ekman, I also had the opportunity to compare the brain activity during two types of smiles. One form of smiling includes the contraction of both the zygomatic muscle, which pulls the mouth corners up, and the *orbicularis oculi*, which causes wrinkling in the external canthi (crow's-feet). We have labeled this smile type the Duchenne smile, since it was Duchenne (1862/1990) who first described it in detail and suggested that only this form of smiling was associated with the felt experience of happiness. Other smiles specifically do not include the presence of crow's-feet. Such smiles may be produced in a variety of different situations, and include the masking of negative affect and social signaling in the absence of any felt experience of happiness. Based on our model, we predicted that the Duchenne smiles would be associated with greater left-sided anterior activation compared with other smiles. Measures of frontal and anterior temporal brain activity confirmed this prediction (Ekman et al., 1990). Moreover, only the duration of Duchenne smiles was correlated with self-reports of happiness and amusement; the duration of other smiles was not. A study of 10-month-old infants exposed to episodes of mother and stranger approach also found similar differences in frontal brain asymmetry between Duchenne and other smiles (Fox & Davidson, 1988). In very recent work, Ekman and I (Ekman & Davidson, 1991) had subjects voluntarily produce Duchenne and other smiles and found that they differed significantly in anterior temporal asymmetry in the same direction as was found in the studies examining spontaneous smiling.

We conducted a parallel set of studies with infants to determine at what age differential lateralization for approach- and withdrawal-related emotions emerges (see Davidson & Fox, 1988, for review). In a study with newborn infants (tested within the first 72 hr of life) who were presented with tastes differing in hedonic tone, those tastes associated with facial signs of disgust produced significantly greater right-sided frontal activation compared with a sucrose solution condition, which produced predominantly facial signs of interest (Fox & Davidson, 1986). From these data, it appears that differential anterior lateralization for emotion is present at birth.

Individual differences in asymmetric anterior activation: a biological substrate of affective style

A number of investigators working in the field of lateralization have underscored the distinction between hemispheric specialization and hemispheric activation (e.g. Levy, 1983). Individual differences in hemispheric activation are superimposed upon relatively invariant patterns of hemispheric specialization. Hemispheric specialization refers to the functional efficiency or capability of a hemispheric region. For example, among right-handed individuals, areas in the left temporal lobe are specialized for certain linguistic processes. However, there are differences among people in the degree to which this region might be tonically activated, and these variations in activation patterns have functional consequences. Most germane to this paper are individual differences in activation asymmetry in anterior cortical regions. We have recently found that baseline electrophysiological measures of frontal and anterior temporal activation asymmetry are relatively stable over time, with test-retest correlations varying between .65 and .75 over a 3-week time interval. Moreover, such measures have excellent internal consistency reliabilities, with alpha coefficients in the .90s (Tomarken, Davidson, Wheeler, & Kinney, 1992). In a series of studies in children and adults, we have repeatedly found that baseline frontal asymmetry predicts important qualities of dispositional mood, psychopathology, temperament, reactivity to emotionally provocative events, and other emotion-relevant biological indices. I will briefly summarize key components of this evidence.

In light of the neurological data on the emotional consequences of left anterior lesions, we first studied differences between depressed and nondepressed individuals on EEG measures of frontal asymmetry. We (Schaffer, Davidson, & Saron, 1983) found that subclinically depressed subjects had significantly less left frontal activation compared with their nondepressed counterparts. We have recently observed the same phenomenon in a sample of clinically depressed patients (Henriques & Davidson, 1991). Most important, it appears that the difference between depressed and nondepressed subjects does not depend on the acute symptoms of depression, but rather is a trait difference between the groups, since remitted depressives who are currently normothymic also exhibit hypoactivation in the left frontal region (Henriques & Davidson, 1990).

We have also studied individual differences in anterior asymmetry in normal subjects. As part of a large study, we tested approximately 100 individuals on two occasions, separated by an interval of 3 weeks. With such a large initial sample, we could identify subgroups of subjects with extreme left frontal activation and extreme right frontal activation on both occasions and then compare them on a number of psychological and biological characteristics. We found that the left frontal subjects reported more positive and less negative dispositional affect compared with their right frontally activated counterparts (Tomarken, Davidson, Wheeler, & Doss, 1992).

In three independent studies (Tomarken, Davidson, & Henriques, 1990; Wheeler, Davidson, & Tomarken, 1993), we have also found that subjects with greater baseline right frontal activation report more intense negative affect in response to film clips designed to elicit such emotion compared with subjects showing greater baseline left frontal activation. Subjects with greater baseline left frontal activation tend to report more positive affect in response to positive film clips compared with right frontally activated subjects.

As part of one of the studies referred to above, we collected blood samples from the subjects in the left and right extreme frontal asymmetry groups and assayed the samples for a number of immune measures (Kang et al., 1991). There were three converging lines of evidence which led us to hypothesize possible differences between the groups in immune function. First, a number of reports have indicated that certain subgroups of depressives have compromised immune function (e.g., Schleifer, Keller, Bond, Cohen, & Stein, 1989). Given the findings indicating differences between depressed and nondepressed individuals in frontal activation asymmetry, the finding of decreased immunocompetence among depressives suggested a relation between relative right-sided frontal activation and lowered immune function. Second, several recent studies in which the investigators examined the effects of unilateral cortical lesions on immune function in animals have shown that left-sided lesions result in a much more pronounced impairment in immune function compared with lesions of the right neocortex (e.g. Renoux, Biziere, Renoux, Guillaumin, & Degenne, 1983). Finally, Geschwind's theory (Geschwind & Galaburda, 1985) argued for a strong relation between laterality and immunity based on common influences during embryogenesis. Geschwind proposed that testosterone is the common factor influencing both cerebral asymmetry and immunity. Testosterone delays the development of the left hemisphere and also retards the growth of the thymus.

When we compared extreme right and left frontally activated subjects (Kang et al., 1991), we found that the right-activated group had significantly lower natural killer (NK) cell activity compared with the left-activated subjects. NK activity is one of the measures which best differentiate between depressives and controls and between mice with left versus right neocortical lesions.

In recent work, we have determined that individual differences in frontal activation asymmetry are present within the first year of life (Davidson & Fox, 1989). Earlier, I described a study on the effects of hedonically positive and negative tastes on newborn asymmetry. That study was not designed to examine individual differences. In this more recent work, we assessed whether individual differences in baseline measures of frontal asymmetry predicted an infant's response to a subsequent affective challenge. Among 10-month-old infants, those who cried in response to 1 min of maternal separation had greater right-sided frontal activation during a prior baseline measure (obtained about 30 min before exposure to maternal separation) compared with infants who showed no evidence of crying within the 1-min period. We found no differences in facial signs of positive or negative emotions assessed during the baseline period between babies who subsequently went on to cry and those who did not. Thus, baseline frontal asymmetry predicted reactivity to a subsequent stressful event independent of concurrent mood.

These findings suggested to us that individual differences in frontal asymmetry may be related to early childhood temperament. We are currently in the midst of conducting a longitudinal study of three groups of children. The inhibited group is characterized as shy, wary, and reticent to approach novel objects and people. The uninhibited group is very outgoing and sociable. We have also included a middle group who display intermediate values on the measures used to classify the two extreme groups. The children were first selected on the basis of behavioral measures during a peer play session at 30 months of age (based on the procedures of Kagan, Reznick, & Snidman, 1988). There are approximately 25 children per group. We assessed baseline measures of regional cortical activation at 38 months of age using our quantitative electrophysiological procedures and found that the inhibited children showed significantly less left-sided frontal activation compared with the uninhibited children (Davidson, Finman, Straus, & Kagan, 1991). The middle group fell, predictably, in between. These findings are the first to show that frontal asymmetry is directly related to an important form of childhood temperament. The disposition to approach or not approach novel and unfamiliar objects and people varies greatly among young children. This is among the most stable temperament constructs yet investigated (Reznick et al., 1986) and shows a substantial heritable influence (Matheny, 1989). The pattern of left frontal hypoactivation displayed by the inhibited children is similar to that observed in adult depressives. In this light, it is interesting to note that in a study comparing the offspring of depressed patients and healthy controls, it was found that the incidence of childhood inhibition was significantly higher among offspring of depressives (Kochanska, 1991).

Summary and conclusions

This paper presented a brief overview of recent research on anterior asymmetries associated with emotion, affective style, and temperament. I proposed that the anterior regions of the two cerebral hemispheres are specialized for approach and withdrawal processes, with the left hemisphere specialized for the former and the right for the latter. Data were presented which indicated that the experimental arousal of certain positive and negative emotions is accompanied by phasic shifts in activation in the left and right frontal regions. These state effects are present in the newborn period. I argued that such phasic changes in activation asymmetry are superimposed upon more tonic trait differences among subjects. These individual differences in baseline anterior asymmetry are related to dispositional mood, reactivity to emotionally provocative events, psychopathology, immune function, and temperament. It will be important for future research to characterize both the proximal and the distal causes of this anterior asymmetry. The proximal causes will necessarily require the examination of subcortical and neurochemical contributions. Such studies must be conducted either with animals or in humans using more invasive methods to make inferences about regional brain function (e.g. PET imaging can provide detailed information on metabolic and neurochemical activity throughout the brain). Distal causes will inevitably involve some combination of heritable and early environmental factors. The next decade of research on the hemispheric substrates of emotion should be even more exciting than the previous one has been.

References

Davidson, R. J. (1984). Affect, cognition and hemispheric specialization. In C. E. Izard, J. Kagan, & R. Zajonc (Eds.), *Emotion, cognition and behavior* (pp. 320–365). New York: Cambridge University Press.

—— (1988). EEG measures of cerebral asymmetry: Conceptual and methodological issues. *International Journal of Neuroscience, 39*, 71–89.

—— (1992). Anterior cerebral asymmetry and the nature of emotion. *Brain and Cognition, 20*, 125–151.

Davidson, R. J., Ekman, P., Saron, C. D., Senulis, J. A., & Friesen, W. V. (1990). Approach/withdrawal and cerebral asymmetry: Emotional expression and brain physiology, I. *Journal of Personality and Social Psychology, 58*, 330–341.

Davidson, R. J., Finman, R., Straus, A., & Kagan, J. (1991). *Childhood temperament and frontal lobe activity: Patterns of asymmetry differentiate between wary and outgoing children.* Manuscript submitted for publication.

Davidson, R. J., & Fox, N. A. (1988). Cerebral asymmetry and emotion: developmental and individual differences. In D. L. Molfese & S. J. Segalowitz (Eds.), *Brain lateralization in children: Developmental implications* (pp. 191–206). New York: Guilford Press.

—— (1989). Frontal brain asymmetry predicts infants' response to maternal separation. *Journal of Abnormal Psychology, 98*, 127–131.

Davidson, R. J., & Tomarken, A. J. (1989). Laterality and emotion: an electrophysiological approach. In F. Boller & J. Grafman (Eds.), *Handbook of neuropsychology* (Vol. 3, pp. 419–441). Amsterdam: Elsevier.

Duchenne, G. B. (1990). *The mechanism of human facial expression.* (R. A. Cuthbertson, Ed. and Trans.). New York: Cambridge University Press. (Original work published 1862.)

Ekman, P., & Davidson, R. J. (1991). *The effects of voluntary production of facial expressions on measures of regional brain electrical activity: I. Differentiation among smile types.* Unpublished manuscript.

Ekman, P., Davidson, R. J., & Friesen, W. V. (1990). The Duchenne smile: emotional expression and brain physiology, II. *Journal of Personality and Social Psychology, 58,* 342–353.

Ekman, P., & Friesen, W. V. (1978). *The Facial Action Coding System: A technique for the measurement of facial movement.* Palo Alto, CA: Consulting Psychologists Press.

Fox, N. A., & Davidson, R. J. (1986). Taste-elicited changes in facial signs of emotion and the asymmetry of brain electrical activity in human newborns. *Neuropsychologia, 24,* 417–422.

—— (1988). Patterns of brain electrical activity during facial signs of emotion in ten-month old infants. *Developmental Psychology, 24,* 230–236.

Gainotti, G. (1972). Emotional behavior and hemispheric side of lesion. *Cortex, 8,* 41–55.

Geschwind, N., & Galaburda, A. M. (1985). Cerebral lateralization: Biological mechanisms, associations, and pathology: I. A hypothesis and a program of research. *Archives of Neurology, 42,* 428–459.

Goldstein, K. (1939). *The organism.* New York: American Books.

Henriques, J. B., & Davidson, R. J. (1990). Regional brain electrical asymmetries discriminate between previously depressed and healthy control subjects. *Journal of Abnormal Psychology, 99,* 22–31.

Henriques, J. B., & Davidson, R. J. (1991). Left frontal hypoactivation in depression. *Journal of Abnormal Psychology, 100,* 535–545.

Jackson, J. H. (1878). On the affections of speech from disease of the brain. *Brain, 1,* 304–330.

Kagan, J., Reznick, J. S., & Snidman, N. (1988). Biological bases of childhood shyness. *Science, 240,* 167–171.

Kang, D. H., Davidson, R. J., Coe, C. L., Wheeler, R., Tomarken, A. J., & Ershler, W. B. (1991). Frontal brain asymmetry and immune function. *Behavioral Neuroscience, 105,* 860–869.

Kochanska, G. (1991). Patterns of inhibition to the unfamiliar in children of normal and affectively ill mothers. *Child Development, 62,* 250–263.

Kolb, B., & Taylor, L. (1990). Neocortical substrates of emotional behavior. In N. L. Stein, B. Leventhal, & T. Trabasso (Eds.), *Psychological and biological approaches to emotion* (pp. 115–144). Hillsdale, NJ: Erlbaum.

Levy, J. (1983). Individual differences in cerebral hemisphere asymmetry: Theoretical issues and experimental considerations. In J. B. Hellige (Ed.), *Cerebral hemisphere asymmetry: Method, theory and application* (pp. 465–497). New York: Praeger.

Matheny, A. P., Jr. (1989). Children's behavioral inhibition over age and across situations: genetic similarity for a trait during change. *Journal of Personality, 57,* 215–226.

McLean, P. (1949). Psychosomatic disease and the "visceral brain" and their bearing on the Papez theory of emotion. *Psychosomatic Medicine, 11,* 338–353.

Papez, J. W. (1937). A proposed mechanism of emotion. *Archives of Neurology and Psychiatry, 38,* 725–744.

Renoux, G., Biziere, K., Renoux, M., Guillaumin, J., & Degenne, D. (1983). A balanced brain asymmetry modulates T cell-mediated events. *Journal of Neuroimmunology, 5,* 227–238.

Reznick, J. S., Kagan, J., Snidman, N., Gersten, M., Baak, K., & Rosenberg, A. (1986). Inhibited and uninhibited behavior: a follow-up study. *Child Development, 57,* 660–680.

Robinson, R. G., Kubos, K. L., Starr, L. B., Rao, K., & Price, T. R. (1984). Mood disorders in stroke patients: importance of location of lesion. *Brain, 107,* 81–93.

Sackeim, H. A., Greenberg, M. S., Weiman, A. L., Gur, R., Hungerbuhler, J. P., & Geschwind, N. (1982). Hemispheric asymmetry in the expression of positive and negative emotions. *Archives of Neurology, 39,* 210–218.

Schaffer, C. E., Davidson, R. J., & Saron, C. (1983). Frontal and parietal EEG asymmetries in depressed and non-depressed subjects. *Biological Psychiatry, 18,* 753–762.

Schleifer, S. J., Keller, S. E., Bond, R. N., Cohen, J., & Stein, M. (1989). Major depressive disorder and immunity. *Archives of General Psychiatry, 46*, 81–87.

Shagass, C. (1972). Electrical activity of the brain. In N. S. Greenfield & R. A. Sternbach (Eds.), *Handbook of psychophysiology* (pp. 263–328). New York: Holt, Rinehart and Winston.

Tomarken, A. J., Davidson, R. J., & Henriques, J. B. (1990). Resting frontal brain asymmetry predicts affective responses to films. *Journal of Personality and Social Psychology, 59*, 791–801.

Tomarken, A. J., Davidson, R. J., Wheeler, R. W., & Doss, R. (1992). Relations between individual differences in anterior brain asymmetry and fundamental dimensions of emotion. *Journal of Personality and Social Psychology, 62*, 676–687.

Tomarken, A. J., Davidson, R. J., Wheeler, R. W., & Kinney, L. (1992). Psychometric properties of resting anterior EEG asymmetry: temporal stability and internal consistency. *Psychophysiology, 29*, 576–592.

Wheeler, R. W., Davidson, R. J., & Tomarken, A. J. (1993). Frontal brain asymmetry and emotional relativity: a biological substrate & affective style. *Psychophysiology, 30*, 82–89.

CHAPTER *12*

Somatic Markers and the Guidance of Behavior

A. R. Damasio, D. Tranel, and H. C. Damasio

Antonio Damasio started his book, Descartes' Error, *by describing the famous case of Phineas Gage, an efficient and likable foreman employed in the construction of the Rutland and Burlington railroad. His job included rock blasting to clear a path for the track. On September 13, 1848 a rock had been drilled and the hole filled with gunpowder. Gage tamped it down with an iron rod, an inch and a quarter in diameter. Suddenly there was an explosion. The rod entered Gage's skull beneath the left eyebrow, left via a hole at the top of his head, and landed 50 feet away. Gage bled terribly and his wound became infected, but he was tended by a local doctor, John Harlow. Gage survived, or rather, his body survived. Harlow published the case in 1868. He reported that those who knew the victim said he was "no longer Gage." From being efficient, he was unable to form plans. From being even-tempered and friendly he was impatient, irreverent, and easily angered.*

Damasio and others have found that when their patients suffer damage in the same area of the frontal lobes that were damaged in Phineas Gage, they suffer similar difficulties: problems in planning in the social world and derangement of emotions. Damasio calls them "modern Phineas Gages." His idea is that it is no accident that these difficulties are connected. Knowing whom to trust and how to plan one's life are critically dependent on emotions.

And what was Descartes's error, you may wonder? Damasio says the most famous line in philosophy: "Cogito ergo sum – I think therefore I am," sums up a separation of mind from body in Descartes's writing, and that it is comprehensively wrong. For Damasio, the emotions depend on the body and its reactions in a way that echoes James's hypothesis. Just as Gage after his accident was "no longer Gage," so claims Damasio, we cannot say "I am" merely because we think.

A. R. Damasio, D. Tranel, and H. C. Damasio, Somatic markers and the guidance of behavior: theory and preliminary testing. In H. S. Levin, H. M. Eisenberg, and A. L. Benton (Eds.), *Frontal Lobe Function and Dysfunction.* New York: Oxford University Press, 1991, pp. 217–229. Reprinted with permission.

We can say "I am" only when connected with our body via our emotions. We, the editors, have to say that we think this is a little unfair to Descartes, whose book, Passions of the Soul, *shows that he saw emotions as thoroughly embodied. The paper we present here is a laboratory test of Damasio's idea, with some modern Phineas Gages as subjects.*

References

Damasio, A. R. (1994). *Descartes' error*. New York: Putnam.

Descartes, R. (1649). Passions of the soul. In E. L. Haldane & G. R. Ross (Eds.), *The philosophical works of Descartes*. New York: Dover (current edition 1911).

Harlow, J. M. (1868). Recovery from the passage of an iron bar through the head. Reprinted in *History of Psychiatry, 4* (1993), 274–281.

The theory proposed here evolved as a response to the challenge posed by patient EVR. As has been discussed elsewhere in detail (Eslinger & Damasio, 1985), patient EVR developed profoundly abnormal personality characteristics following a bilateral ablation of ventromedial frontal cortices, which was required for the surgical treatment of a meningioma. Prior to the appearance of the tumor and to surgery (which took place when EVR was age 35), EVR was, from all possible perspectives, a normal individual. He was intelligent, hard-working, successful at securing a steady skilled job and at being promoted for his good performance. He was active in social affairs and was perceived as a leader and example by his siblings, and by others in his community. But the person that emerged after frontal surgery could hardly be more different. EVR has never again been able to maintain a job (he clearly remains skilled enough to hold one, but he cannot be counted on to report to work promptly or to execute all the intermediate steps of the tasks that are expected of him). His ability to plan his activities, both on a daily basis as well as into the future, is severely impaired. The planning may fail to include components that would obviously be advantageous for his future, and include instead peripheral business that is of no possible use. Often, on matters of relatively secondary import, e.g. what to wear, where to shop, what restaurant to go to, EVR is plunged into an endless debate. He is unable to make a rapid choice and, instead, pursues a course of interminable comparisons and successive deliberations among many possible options that become more and more difficult to distinguish. His final response selection, if it ever comes, may end up being random. An especially troubled area for his decision-making has to do with social behaviors and, as a subset of those, with financial planning. It clearly is not easy for EVR to decide which persons are good and which ones are not, in terms of his future life course. A sense of what is socially appropriate, judging from the choices he makes in his "real-life" encounters, is clearly lacking, while it is obvious from his premorbid life and achievement that he once had a keen sense of social appropriateness. His relatives corroborate this, but the ecologic findings make it unequivocal.

In the end, EVR's decision-making and planning are (1) qualitatively different from what they were before, and (2) clearly defective by reference to his own standards as well as those of his direct peers. In the long term, the defect leads to many punishing consequences for EVR. In general, these characteristics of behavior fit the criteria for sociopathy, as defined in the *Diagnostic and Statistical Manual of Mental Disorders* (DSM-III; American Psychiatric Association, 1980) (e.g. "inability to sustain consistent work behavior," "inability to maintain an enduring attachment to a sexual partner," "lack of ability to function as a responsible parent," "defective planning"). The key difference is that EVR's sociopathic personality manifestations appeared in adulthood, after his brain damage, rather than during the development of his personality. Thus, we have tentatively termed his condition "acquired sociopathy." It should be emphasized that there are other important differences between "acquired sociopathy" of the type manifest by EVR and similar patients, and the standard "developmental sociopathy" elaborated in DSM-III, e.g. the latter type of patient has a far greater likelihood of being antisocial in a manner that is harmful to others, while the EVR type is more likely to cause difficulties for the self; hence, parallels between the two conditions are, in part, strictly for heuristic purposes.

Against this background of ravage, we must describe the many aspects of his intellectual profile that remain not only intact but, indeed, outstanding. EVR is not just an intelligent man, but a superiorly intelligent one, a judgment supported by psychometric evidence (on the Wechsler Adult Intelligence Scale-Revised, EVR obtains IQ scores in the top 1–2 percentile [Verbal IQ = 132, Performance IQ = 135]), and by reflection on many hours of structured interviews ranging over varied topics. EVR can distinguish with great subtlety among highly ambiguous concepts, can use deduction and induction fluently, and can comment with charm and irony on myriad daily events. Numerous neuropsychologic tests make these judgments objective (e.g. Shipley-Hartford Vocabulary score = 37/40, Abstractions score = 40/40; Visual-Verbal Test score = 73/84). Naturally, EVR's language processing, at phonemic, lexical, syntactic, and discourse levels, is fully preserved.

Conventional learning and memory are also intact, as can be proven by EVR's perfect acquisition of all manner of events that occur in his daily life, by his perfect recollection of autobiographical details, and by formal neuropsychologic testing (e.g. Wechsler Memory Scale MQ = 145 [99th percentile]; Rey Auditory-Verbal Learning Test Trial 5 score = 14/15 [superior]; Benton Visual Retention Test score = 9/10 correct [superior]; Rey-Osterrieth Complex Figure recall score = 32/36 [99th percentile]). The partial exception to this lies with social knowledge. It might be argued that EVR has a selective memory defect for social knowledge; however, this would not be an accurate statement, because EVR can access social knowledge when he is questioned about it verbally, and even when a social problem is presented to him cast in verbal premises. It is perhaps more accurate to state that learning of social knowledge is impaired, since EVR clearly does not learn from his mistakes, and repeatedly selects response options that lead to negative consequences.

It is not possible to account for EVR's defects on the basis of general impairments of intelligence, memory, language, or perception. Furthermore, EVR and, along with him, other similar patients to whom we will refer as "EVR-like," also lack some subtle but supposedly characteristic signs of frontal lobe dysfunction, which tend to be highly correlated with defective decision-making and planning. For instance, EVR produces perfect scores on the Wisconsin Card Sorting Test, the Category Test, and the World Fluency Test and his performances in paradigms requiring cognitive estimations (Shallice & Evans, 1978) and judgments of recency and frequency (Milner & Petrides, 1984) are flawless. He is not perseverative and he is not impulsive.

How, then, can we explain EVR's peculiar condition?

The theory of somatic markers

Background

We have proposed that although EVR is able to recognize the meaning of social situations, and to imagine possible responses to those situations, he is no longer able to select the most advantageous response, taking into account his autobiography and the contingencies of his environment. In brief, EVR not only possesses but still accesses knowledge about the *manifest* meaning of entities and events (the identity of a person or place), but also knowledge about their *implied* meaning (the positive or negative value of a person or action, possible response options to an event, and the imagined consequences that follow a given response immediately and later).

The distinction between manifest and implied meanings is critical to the understanding of EVR's problem, which we will attempt using as a framework our model for time-locked retroactivation (Damasio, 1989a, b). In this model, any level of meaning is seen as the result of the synchronous evocation of many separate cognitive components, whose ensemble defines entities and events based on their constituent features. The model posits that the co-evocations are the consequence of synchronously activating numerous anatomically separate regions in association cortices. The synchronous activations occur in early cortices that contain the neural inscriptions of component representations and are directed by feedback projections from convergence zones located over multiple cortical regions (interconnected both hierarchically and heterarchically). Because there is no single neuroanatomic region that holds the integrated "image" of a polysensory based set of events, meaning is critically dependent on timing. And because implied meanings require a far larger set of components for their definition than manifest meanings do, the problem of synchronization and subsequent attention looms larger. In short, from this perspective, the response selections required for appropriate decision-making in social cognition and equivalent realms, necessitates the holding on-line, for long periods of time (in the order of several thousand milliseconds), highly heterogeneous sets of cognitive components that must be attended effectively, if a choice is to be made. Where we believe EVR fails is in the *selection of one among many response options*, displayed long after the triggering stimuli were first presented and often even after they are no longer perceivable. It should be noted that the defect in the operations we posit is related to frontal cortical dysfunction, and also, that the frontal cortices have long been presumed to be critical for neural operations in which responses to stimuli must be effected after a delay (Jacobsen, 1935, 1936). The latter notion has played a major role in the theoretic formulations of Fuster (1989) and Goldman-Rakic (1987) regarding frontal lobe function in primates.

The proposed mechanism for the defect

We propose that the response selection impairment is due to a *defect in the activation of somatic markers* that must accompany the internal and automatic processing of possible response options. Deprived of a somatic marker to assist, both consciously and covertly, with response selection, EVR has a reduced chance of responding in the most advantageous manner, and a higher chance of generating responses that will lead to negative consequences. Let us explain with an example.

Imagine yourself confronted by the possibility of accompanying an acquaintance to a particular social event; or the possibility of entering a business partnership with yet another acquaintance. In either case, the premises of the situation (the identities of those involved, their previous relation to you, their social record) will be available to you from previous interactions, drawing on a variety of nonverbal and verbal parcellated knowledge (which, according to the model adduced previously, can be synchronously evoked in separate cortices). The implications of going or not going will also be available to you in all of their complexity, and in an equally distributed neural manner. In short, the premises of the situation, several response options, and several anticipated consequences, must be simultaneously available for your inspection, so that attention can bring them into consciousness.

Going to the social event may mean an immediate advantage, but it may be that the nature of the event implies that you will be criticized for attending it by your friends and relatives, resulting in a future net loss. And yet, you must decide on a course of action. This may be done either with deliberation, or automatically, or somewhere in between. What we are proposing is that normal individuals can be assisted in this complex decision-making process by *the appearance of a somatic signal that marks the ultimate consequences of the response option with a negative or positive somatic state*. In other words, response option "A," regardless of its predictable immediate reward, can evoke a future scenario that is potentially threatening to the individual, and is marked by a negative somatic state. The perceiver would then experience the reenactment of punishment (another way of putting it would be to say that a negative emotion would be felt).

The first effect of the somatic marker would then be to provide the subject with a conscious "gut feeling" on the merits of a given response, and force attention on the positive or negative nature of given response options based on their foreseeable consequences. But in addition, we also posit a second effect, which would be covert and which would modify the state of neural systems that propitiate appetitive or aversive behaviors, e.g. the dopamine and serotonin nonspecific systems that can alter processing in cerebral cortex. This effect would be activated by the somatic marker and would increase or reduce the chances of immediate response, e.g. a negative somatic state would inhibit appetitive behaviors and vice versa, even if the somatic state itself would not be attended to and would thus not be experienced consciously. This, in turn, could increase or reduce the chances of inhibiting a response or facilitating it.

The plausibility of the mechanism

At first glance, it might seem more efficient to have all sorts of decision-making based on a fully rational computation of the merits and disadvantages of each response option. Why should one rely on a seemingly primitive "emotional" signal? The first answer is that, in all likelihood, such mechanisms were successfully developed in other species and have proven to be thoroughly effective in their ecological niches. The second is that the sheer amount of possible response options makes it likely that an assistance device is required to sort out the responses that are more likely to be relevant for the overall goals of the organism in both the short and long term. In other words, an unassisted rational computation of many conflictual response options is probably quite inefficient, e.g. the organism might be paralyzed with indecision, as indeed EVR often is. The third answer has to do with the special value of somatic states in the acquisition of a large range of behaviors than one might call social and personal. This is because the acquisition of such behaviors is closely linked with punishment and reward, brought in by parenting, schooling, peer group influences, and other interactions during development, to ensure that certain key goals of the individual and the species are achieved according to the contingencies set by the social environment. Punishment and reward are perceived modifications of baseline somatic states, which induce perceptions along the range that includes pain and pleasure. It is reasonable to assume that in the same way that punishment and reward mark a given act as valuable or dangerous for the individual during development, and are learned conjunctively, the re-enactment of a state of pain or pleasure triggered by the internal representation of the consequence of a response option would mark that response option as positive or negative. The specific proposal is that the accompanying somatic state would ensure in most circumstances, and in a fairly automatic way, that responses whose consequences would be negative to the individual would be thoughtfully avoided or covertly suppressed.

If the preceding proposal does apply to EVR-type patients, it must be found that they (1) can access implied meanings to the situations in which they act defectively, and (2) fail to activate somatic states to those implied meanings. There is already considerable evidence to support the first requisite, but virtually none to support the second. In a study reported elsewhere (Damasio et al., 1990) and summarized in this chapter, we tested the hypothesis that EVR-type patients are no longer able to mount somatic states to complex stimuli charged with social significance.

Testing the proposal

We studied three subject groups. The first we called *bifrontal*, and comprised five subjects who had bilateral lesions in orbital and lower mesial frontal regions. The second was termed *brain-damaged controls*, and included six subjects who had lesions *outside* the ventromedial frontal cortices. The third consisted of *normal controls*, and included five subjects.

To assess somatic state activation, we utilized the electrodermal skin conductance response (SCR), because the SCR is a biologically and psychologically relevant index of autonomic neural activity (Boucsein, 1988; Edelberg, 1972, 1973; Fowles, 1986), and it reliably indexes the "signal value" of stimuli at both physiologic and psychologic levels (e.g. Bernstein, 1979; Raskin, 1973).

We utilized three categories of stimuli in the experiments: (1) *Elementary unconditioned* ("orienting") stimuli: These were basic "orienting" stimuli that reliably elicit SCRs from normal subjects (Fowles & Schneider, 1978; Raskin, 1973; Stern & Anschel, 1968), such as an unexpected loud hand-clap close to the subject's ears. (2) *Target pictures:* pictures depicting social disaster, mutilation, or nudity. Those pictures have strong "implied" meanings, i.e. they readily evoke emotional responses of pleasure or pain in normal subjects, and elicit high-amplitude, discriminatory SCRs (Greenwald et al., 1989; Lang & Greenwald, 1988). (3) *Nontarget pictures:* pictures depicting neutral material such as bland scenery and abstract patterns. These "nontargets" do not elicit large-amplitude SCRs from normal subjects (Lang & Greenwald, 1988), and they do not have strong "implied" meanings.

The set of 40 pictorial slides (10 targets and 30 nontargets) were randomly ordered and administered twice, consecutively. During the first administration (the PASSIVE response condition), the subject viewed the slides without making any verbal or motor response. During the second (ACTIVE response condition) the subject had to comment on the content of the slide and on the impact it made on the subject.

Following the ACTIVE condition, the subject participated in a short "debriefing" session to verify that the SCR data were not contaminated by inattentiveness or idiosyncratic mores and aesthetics. Questions were asked about the stimulus content and the feelings the subject had experienced while viewing the slides in the PASSIVE versus ACTIVE conditions.

Skin conductance was recorded from both hands, using equipment and techniques described elsewhere (Tranel & A. Damasio, 1988; Tranel & H. Damasio, 1989). The amplitude of the largest SCR that had onset within 1–5 seconds after stimulus onset was measured for both orienting stimuli and for the pictorial stimuli in both conditions.

For each subject we calculated a total of five scores: The average "orienting" SCR, and the average target and nontarget SCR for both response conditions. Averages were based on all available stimulus presentations (including nonresponses counted as zero-amplitude SCRs), and are referred to as "magnitudes" (Venables & Christie, 1980). Nonparametric techniques were utilized for statistical analysis (Siegel & Castellan, 1988), since the data sets did not meet sufficiently the parametric assumptions of homogeneity of variance and normal distribution.

The results of the controls (normals and brain-damaged) and the bifrontals are shown in table 12.1. Statistical analysis of these data indicated the following:

1   There were no differences between the orienting SCRs of the three subject groups (a Kruskal-Wallis one-way analysis of variance by ranks test was nonsignificant [$H = 2.08, p > .30$]).

2   Both the normal and brain-damaged controls showed sharp discrimination between the target and nontarget stimuli with a much larger SCR magnitude

Table 12.1. Skin conductance magnitudes*

	Orienting response	Passive condition		Active condition	
		Target	Nontarget	Target	Nontarget
Normal controls	0.688	0.802	0.077	0.999	0.150
(n=5)	(0.208)	(0.327)	(0.066)	(0.384)	(0.027)
Brain-damaged controls	0.520	0.594	0.137	0.949	0.289
(n = 6)	(0.503)	(0.565)	(0.234)	(0.901)	(0.313)
Bifrontals	0.950	0.125	0.049	0.323	0.074
(n = 5)	(0.347)	(0.145)	(0.088)	(0.294)	(0.153)

* In microSiemens (μS); S.D. in parentheses.

for the targets ($p > .05$, Sign Test), in both the Passive and Active conditions. This effect is in line with previous findings regarding the effects of highly charged visual stimuli on autonomic responses (e.g. Greenwald et al., 1990; Hare et al., 1970; Klorman et al., 1975).

3   The bifrontals failed to generate discriminatory SCRs to the target pictures in the PASSIVE condition ($p = .50$, Sign Test) but in the ACTIVE condition the target versus nontarget SCR magnitudes were significantly different ($p = 0.031$), Sign Test). This indicates that the bifrontals are substantially closer to normals in the ACTIVE condition.

Table 12.2. Skin conductance magnitudes for subject EVR*

Condition	SCR magnitudes (in μS) (S.D.)	
Orienting response	0.650	
	Target	Nontarget
Initial experiment		
Passive	0.003	0.006
	(0.008)	(0.023)
Active	0.598	0.012
	(0.564)	(0.031)
A-B-A reversal experiment		
Passive	0.000	0.004
	(-)	(0.013)
Active	0.718	0.007
	(0.818)	(0.027)
Passive	0.008	0.031
	(0.018)	(0.092)
2-Year follow-up experiment		
Passive	0.002	0.004
	(0.005)	(0.012)
Active	0.576	0.020
	0.356)	(0.042)

* In μ S: S.D. in parentheses.

As an example, the results from subject EVR are presented in detail in table 12.2, together with some ancillary experiments that were used to follow up and firmly document EVR's response patterns.

EVR's orienting SCRs were normal, and his orienting response magnitude was well within the range of the control groups. In the first experiment, however, he demonstrated a marked failure to generate normal SCRs to the target stimuli in the PASSIVE condition. There was no difference between his SCR magnitude for the targets versus the nontargets ($p > .33$, Mann-Whitney U test). In the ACTIVE condition, however, he showed normal discriminatory SCRs to the targets, with a target–nontarget difference that is significant and virtually identical to controls ($z = -3.87, p < .001$, Mann-Whitney U test).

Several months after the initial study, EVR's SCRs were studied in an A-B-A reversal design with a new stimulus set. In this experiment, EVR was first exposed to a PASSIVE condition. An ACTIVE condition immediately followed, and then another PASSIVE condition. The stimulus set was the same across all three sections of this follow-up experiment, i.e. EVR viewed the same stimulus set three times consecutively. Once again, EVR showed normal SCRs to the target pictures only in the ACTIVE condition ($z = -6.28, p < .001$); in both PASSIVE situations, his responses remained severely impaired ($p > .50$ for target–nontarget comparisons in both PASSIVE conditions).

More than 2 years (27 months) after the initial experiment, we conducted a follow-up study of EVR, using still another set of stimuli but the same procedures as for the initial study. The outcome replicated previous findings, as EVR showed excellent SCR discrimination of the target pictures in the ACTIVE condition ($z = -5.76$, $p < .001$), but no discrimination in the PASSIVE condition ($p > .50$).

Comment

When our frontal lobe damaged subjects viewed complex and socially significant stimuli passively, their autonomic responses were abnormal and often were entirely absent. This remarkable and highly reproducible finding suggests that no somatic state was generated in response to the implied meanings that accompany the viewing of those stimuli. The finding cannot be explained by a primary autonomic dysfunction, because stimuli of a simpler and unconditioned nature still elicited normal autonomic responses in the same subjects. Furthermore, when the condition was modified to include an active, verbal commentary on the contents of each stimulus, the subjects did respond to the appropriate stimuli. This clearly reconfirms that the ability to generate autonomic responses has not been compromised, but rather, the mechanism for its triggering has been altered.

It has been shown previously that patients with frontal lobe lesions have defects in autonomic orienting responses (Luria, 1973; Luria & Homskaya, 1970), and a similar outcome has been reported for nonhuman primates with frontal ablations (Kimble et al., 1965). These studies, however, were aimed at measuring overall arousal. Our findings go well beyond this earlier work in demonstrating an autonomic defect that is specific to a certain stimulus type, response condition, and location of lesion.

Neural basis: description of network

The core of damage in EVR-type patients is in the ventromedial sector of the frontal lobe. Both the medial orbital cortices and the lower mesial orbital cortices, along with subjacent white matter, are damaged bilaterally. These cortices, judging from what is known of nonhuman primate neuroanatomy, receive projections that hail from all sensory modalities, directly or indirectly (Chavis & Pandya, 1976; Jones & Powell, 1970; Pandya & Kuypers, 1969; Potter & Nauta, 1979). In turn, they are the only known source of projections from frontal regions toward central autonomic control structures (Nauta, 1971), and such projections have a demonstrated physiologic influence on visceral control (Hall et al., 1977). The ventromedial cortices have extensive bidirectional connections with the hippocampus and amygdala (Amaral & Price, 1984; Goldman-Rakic et al., 1984; Porrino et al., 1981; Van Hoesen et al., 1972; 1975).

This anatomic design is certainly compatible with the role we propose for the ventromedial cortices. We believe these cortices contain convergence zones that hold a record of temporal conjunctions of activity in varied neural units, e.g. sensory cortices, limbic structures. This would be a record of signals from regions that were active simultaneously and that, as a set, defined a given situation. A critical output of the ventromedial convergence zones would be to autonomic effectors such as the amygdala so that, when a given set of inputs to the ventromedial region would obtain, a pertinent output to amygdala would follow. Activation of the amygdala would in turn result in re-enactment of a somatic state whose signal, intensity, and somatic distribution would be pertinent to the sensory set. Finally, the newly enacted somatic state would be perceived by somatosensory cortices in conjunction with the sensory set that had originated the entire cycle and that would have remained on-line.

The systems network necessary for these processes thus includes the following structures: (1) Ventromedial frontal cortices with convergence zones that record combinations of (a) the distributed representations of certain stimuli and the recalled representations they generate, (b) the somatic states that have been prevalently associated with the above; (2) central autonomic effectors, the amygdala in particular, which can activate somatic responses in viscera, vascular bed, endocrine system, and nonspecific neurotransmitter systems; and (3) somatosensory projection systems and cortices, especially those in the nondominant parietal region (see Tranel & H. Damasio, 1989, for preliminary evidence).

It is important to note that the evocation of a somatic marker for stimuli that are unconditioned and far more basic, for instance, a startling noise or a flash of light, requires a different and simpler network. It is possible that autonomic activation could be achieved by direct thalamic projections to amygdala or other autonomic effectors, long before signals about such stimuli would actually reach the cerebral cortex. The complex network outlined previously pertains only to those stimuli whose complexity, in terms of configurations and implications, requires processing in multiple sensory cortices and over longer delays.

131

Extension of the theory to nonsocial decision-making process

Assuming that the brain has available a means to select good responses from bad in social situations, we suspect it is likely that the mechanism has been co-opted for behavioral guidance that is outside the realm of social cognition. The argument here is that nature would have evolved a highly successful mechanism of guidance to cope with problems whose answer might maximize survival or lead to danger. Although a large range of those problems pertains to the social realm directly, it is apparent that many other problems, albeit not social, are indirectly linked to precisely the same framework of survival versus danger, of ultimate advantage versus disadvantage, of ultimate gain and balance versus loss and disequilibrium. It is therefore plausible that a system geared to produce markers and signposts to guide "social" responses would have been adapted to assist with "intellectual" decision-making. Naturally, the somatic markers would not be perceived in the form of "feelings." But they would still act covertly to highlight, in the form of an attentional mechanism, certain components over others, and to direct, in effect, the go, stop, and turn signals necessary for much decision making and planning on even the most abstract of topics.

A final comment is in order regarding the application of the theory and findings previously discussed to a population of psychiatric patients. First, it is possible that "developmental" sociopathy might be due to a developmental defect in the function of the neural system. The defect need not be in the same unit of the system, and need not be as profound. For instance, it might be sufficient to have a higher threshold of activation for somatic states such that most relevant stimuli would produce weak responses. Intriguingly, some evidence is already available in this regard. It has been shown, for example, that sociopaths show poor autonomic conditioning with aversive unconditioned stimuli (e.g. shock), defective autonomic responses in anticipation of aversive stimuli, and even impaired autonomic conditioning to appetitive stimuli (e.g. Hare & Quinn, 1971; Lykken, 1957; for a review, see Hare, 1978). But, in general, the mechanism would be the same. It is important to note that the differences between developmental and acquired sociopaths, namely, the greater benignity of the latter, do not invalidate this proposal. Acquired sociopaths, in spite of their profound defect, have lived a normal premorbid life during which they learned how to deal with social situations normally; developmental sociopaths never did. The previous normality of the system in the acquired sociopath is likely to compensate for the defect in numerous circumstances.

Another psychiatric condition that may be interpreted with the help of these findings is obsessive-compulsive disease. In short, we see it as the very opposite of sociopathy, i.e. a condition in which numerous trivial stimuli are allowed to generate somatic markers that force the attention of the perceiver and call for response implementation. The dysfunction would relate to the same network and, quite particularly, to ventromedial frontal cortices. For instance, it would be reasonable to discover that where ventromedial frontal cortices are damaged in acquired sociopaths, they should be underactive in developmental sociopaths, and probably overactive in obsessive-compulsive patients ("activity" being measured, for instance, by metabolic or cerebral blood flow rates). Along the same perspective, depressed and neurotic patients with a high degree of somatic suffering should reveal overactivity in ventromedial frontal cortices.

References

Amaral, D.G., & Price, J.L. (1984). Amygdalo-cortical projections in the monkey (*Macaca fascicularis*). *Journal of Comparative Neurology, 230*, 465–496.

American Psychiatric Association (1980). *Diagnostic and statistical manual of mental disorders.* 3rd edn. Washington, DC.

Bernstein, A.S. (1979). The orienting response as novelty and significance detector: reply to O'Gorman. *Psychophysiology, 16*, 263–273.

Boucsein, W. (1989). *Elektrodermale Aktivitat: Grundlagen, Methoden und Anwendungen.* New York: Springer-Verlag.

Chavis, D.A., & Pandya, D.N. (1976). Further observations on corticofrontal connections in the rhesus monkey. *Brain Research, 117*, 369–386.

Damasio, A.R. (1989a). The brain binds entities and events by multiregional activation from convergence zones. *Neural Computation, 1*, 123–132.

—— (1989b). Time-locked multiregional retroactivation: a systems-level proposal for the neural substrates of recall and recognition. *Cognition, 33* 25–62.

Damasio, A.R., Tranel, D., & Damasio H. (1990). Individuals with sociopathic behavior caused by frontal damage fail to respond autonomically to social stimuli. *Behavioral Brain Research, 41*, 81–94.

Damasio, H., & Damasio, A.R. (1989). *Lesion analysis in neuropsychology.* New York: Oxford University Press.

Edelberg, R. (1972). The electrodermal system. In N.S. Greenfield, & R.A. Sternbach (Eds.), *Handbook of psychophysiology* (pp. 367–418). New York: Holt, Rinehart & Winston.

—— (1973). Mechanisms of electrodermal adaptations for locomotion, manipulation, or defense. *Progress in physiological psychology*, 5, 155–209.

Eslinger, P.J. & Damasio, A.R. (1985). Severe disturbance of higher cognition after bilateral frontal lobe ablation: Patient EVR. *Neurology*, 35, 1731–1741.

Fowles, D.C. (1986). The eccrine system and electrodermal activity. In M.G.H. Coles, E. Donchin & S.W. Porges (Eds.), *Psychophysiology: Systems, processes, and applications* (pp. 51–96). New York: Guilford Press.

Fowles, D.C. & Schneider, R.E. (1978). Electrolyte effects on measurements of palmar skin potential. *Psychophysiology*, 15, 474–482.

Fuster, J.M. (1989). *The prefrontal cortex.* 2nd edn. New York: Raven Press.

Goldman-Rakic, P.S. (1987). Circuitry of primate prefrontal cortex and regulation of behavior by representational memory. In F. Plum (Ed.), *Handbook of physiology: The nervous system.* Vol. 5 (pp. 373–417). Bethesda, MD: American Physiological Society.

Goldman-Rakic, P.S., Selemon, L.D. & Schwartz, M.L. (1984). Dual pathways connecting the dorsolateral prefrontal cortex with the hippocampal formation and parahippocampal cortex in the rhesus monkey. *Neuroscience*, 12, 719–743.

Greenwald, M.K., Cook, E.W. & Lang, P.J. (1989). Affective judgment and psychophysiological response: Dimensional covariation in the evaluation of pictorial stimuli. *Journal of Psychophysiology*, 3, 51–64.

Hall, R.E., Livingston, R.B. & Bloor, C.M. (1977). Orbital cortical influences on cardiovascular dynamics and myocardial structure in conscious monkeys. *Journal of Neurosurgery*, 46, 638–647.

Hare, R.D. (1978). Electrodermal and cardiovascular correlates of psychopathy. In R.D. Hare, & D. Schalling (Eds.), *Psychopathic behavior: Approaches to research* (pp. 107–143). New York: Wiley.

Hare, R.D. & Quinn, M.J. (1971). Psychopathy and autonomic conditioning. *Journal of Abnormal Psychology, 77,* 223–235.

Hare, R.D., Wood, K., Britain, S. & Shadman, J. (1970). Autonomic responses to affective visual stimuli. *Psychophysiology, 7,* 408–417.

Jacobsen, C.F. (1935). Functions of the frontal association area in primates. *Archives of Neurology and Psychiatry, 33,* 558–569.

—— (1936). Studies of cerebral functions in primates: I. The functions of the frontal association areas in monkeys. *Comparative Psychology Monographs, 13,* 3–60.

Jones, E.G. & Powell, T.P.S. (1970). An anatomical study of converging sensory pathways within the cerebral cortex of the monkey. *Brain, 93,* 793–820.

Kimble, D.P., Bagshaw, M.H. & Pribram, K.H. (1965). The GSR of monkeys during orienting and habituation after selective partial ablations of the cingulate and frontal cortex. *Neuropsychologia, 3,* 121–128.

Klorman, R., Wiesenfeld, A. & Austin, M.L. (1975). Autonomic responses to affective visual stimuli. *Psychophysiology, 12,* 553–560.

Lang, P.J. & Greenwald, M.K. (1988). The international affective picture system standard-ization procedure and initial group results for affective judgments: Technical report 1A. Gainesville, FL: Center for Research in Psychophysiology, University of Florida.

Luria, A.R. (1973). The frontal lobes and the regulation of behavior. In K.H. Pribram & A.R. Luria (Eds.), *Psychophysiology of the frontal lobes* (pp. 3–26). New York: Academic Press.

Luria, A.R. & Homskaya, E.D. (1970). Frontal lobes and the regulation of arousal processes. In D.I. Mostofsky (Ed.), *Attention: Contemporary theory and analysis* (pp. 303–330). New York: Appleton-Century-Crofts.

Lykken, D.T. (1957). A study of anxiety in the sociopathic personality. *Journal of Abnormal and Social Psychology, 55,* 6–10.

Milner, B. & Petrides, M. (1984). Behavioural effects of frontal-lobe lesions in man. *Trends in Neurosciences, 7,* 403–407.

Nauta, W.J.H. (1971). The problem of the frontal lobe: a reinterpretation. *Journal of Psychiatric Research, 8,* 167–187.

Pandya, D.N. & Kuypers, H.G.J.M. (1969). Cortico-cortical connections in the rhesus monkey. *Brain Research, 13,* 13–36.

Porrino, L.J., Crane, A.M. & Goldman-Rakic, P.S. (1981). Direct and indirect pathways from the amygdala to the frontal lobe in rhesus monkeys. *Journal of Comparative Neurology, 198,* 121–136.

Potter, H. & Nauta, W.J.H. (1979). A note on the problem of olfactory associations of the orbitofrontal cortex in the monkey. *Neuroscience, 4,* 316–367.

Raskin, D.C. (1973). Attention and arousal. In W.F. Prokasy, D.C. Raskin (Eds.), *Electro-dermal activity in psychological research* (pp. 125–155). New York: Academic Press.

Shallice, T. & Evans, M.E. (1978). The involvement of the frontal lobes in cognitive estimation. *Cortex, 14,* 294–303.

Siegel, S. & Castellan, N.J. (1988). *Non-parametric statistics for the behavioral sciences,* 2nd edn. New York: McGraw-Hill.

Stern, R.M. & Anschel, C. (1968). Deep inspirations as stimuli for responses of the autonomic nervous system. *Psychophysiology, 6,* 132–141.

Tranel, D. & Damasio, A.R. (1988). Nonconscious face recognition in patients with face agnosia. *Behavioural Brain Research, 30,* 235–249.

Tranel, D. & Damasio, H. (1989). Intact electrodermal skin conductance responses in a patient with bilateral amygdala damage. *Neuropsychologia, 27,* 381–390.

—— (1989). Neuroanatomical correlates of skin conductance responses to "signal" stimuli. *Psychophysiology, 26*, S61.

Van Hoesen, G.W., Pandya, G.N., & (1972). Butters, N. Cortical afferents to the entorhinal cortex of the rhesus monkey. *Science, 175*, 1471–1473.

—— (1975). Some connections of the entorhinal (area 28) and perirhinal (area 35) cortices of the rhesus monkey: II. Frontal lobe afferents. *Brain Research, 95*, 25–38.

Venables, P.H., & Christie, M.J. (1980). Electrodermal activity. In I. Martin, P.H. Venables (Eds.), *Techniques in psychophysiology* (pp. 3–67). New York: Wiley.

PART III

The Development of Emotions in Infancy, the Development of Children's Understanding of Emotions, and Individual Differences in Emotionality

The Development of Emotions in Infancy, the Development of Children's Understanding of Emotions, and Individual Differences in Emotionality

The readings in this section deal with questions such as what develops in children's emotions as they get older, and how these changes come about. Most two-year-olds have temper tantrums. These are rarely seen in ten-year-olds. Five-year-olds feel pride and shame. Such complex emotions are not evident in babies. Preschoolers talk about emotions, but they do not analyze, reflect on experience, confide about emotional events to others in the way that ten-year-olds do. In part III we look at how changes in cognitive development affect how children experience, conceptualize, and talk about emotions, and how individual differences develop.

Cognitive influences on emotion

In the newborn, emotions are at the heart of interactions between babies and their caregivers. Babies' cries of distress bring their parents running to them to solve whatever problem they think has arisen: Is it a cuddle that is needed, a feed, may be a few minutes of play? The first smile six weeks later is a magical moment for a parent. The parent feels drawn in close to the baby, and welcomed as a play partner. The finely tuned interactional dance between parents and their babies is made possible by the presence of negative and positive emotions operating as clear signals about what the babies want in the first months of their lives.

A much debated question is the age at which specific emotions are present in infancy. Some have argued that infants experience the full range of basic emotions – including happiness, surprise, sadness, anger, and fear. Coding schemes for infant facial expressions have been developed (Izard, 1979). Others say that facial expressions may be present but that we can not assume that they are equivalent to emotions. To decide that specific emotions are present we need to link eliciting circumstance and the baby's expression. If something unexpected happens we expect to see surprise. If a person is thwarted in their goal but sees the possibility that the goal will be reinstated, we expect to see anger. The reading by Hiatt and others (selection 13) deals with this issue using an experimental design. The experimenters asked: Do we see the emotion that we expect to see when we expose babies to particular elicitors?

The evidence indicates that all basic emotions, at least in their full form, are unlikely to be present in the first year of life. Over the course of their first couple of years children's capacity to experience and signal a range of basic emotions develops. There is no doubt that facial expressions characteristic of certain emotions are present in the first year. It is also clear that certain emotions are predictably elicited from things that we think should elicit those emotions. For instance, Lewis and others (1990) have shown that happiness is elicited by achievement of a goal at two months old, and Stenberg and Campos (1990) have shown that anger is frequently elicited by arm restraint. It is also clear, however, that children sometimes show expressions that are not appropriate in the context (see selection 13, and for a further discussion of this issue see Camras, 1992). We think it likely that with development, appraisals and patterns of facial and vocal expression become more consistently linked to one another, eventually forming coherent and recognizable emotion packages, as argued by dynamic systems theorists (Fogel et al., 1992).

Between 18 months and 2 years old major changes in children's ability to recognize the self pave the way for more complex emotions. Michael Lewis and his colleagues (selection 14) show that when self-recognition occurs at around 18 months, then embarrassment becomes possible. The self–other distinction, along with the capacity to take the other's perspective, is also essential for the development of empathy. Hoffman (1984) argues that the earliest experience of empathy is a kind of emotion contagion. The newborn baby cries on hearing another baby cry. At the next stage of empathy development children engage in comforting, but they comfort another with the means of comfort they would like themselves. By the age of 3, children show increasing ability to differentiate their own experience from the experience of another and to think about how another person's sources of comfort may be different from their own.

The onset of emotion talk between 18 months and 2 years also has a major impact on children's developing emotionality (Bretherton et al., 1986; Kopp, 1992). Around this age children learn that saying that they are sad, as opposed to just crying, can elicit just as satisfying a cuddle. Small wonder that there is a dramatic drop in the frequency with which children display distressed emotion over the course of the second year of life. The ability to talk about emotions also has a profound impact on children's relationships with parents (Dunn & Brown, 1991). As children become more verbally competent, parents expect children to speak about what they feel rather than exploding into a rage or crying uncontrollably. Emotion talk becomes part of the process of the negotiation of relationships.

At the end of the preschool years another development in cognition alters children's ability to reason about emotions. We know that children reason about internal states (in the form of goals) as early as 3 years old. Stein and Levine (1989) have demonstrated that by age 3 children can predict emotions on the basis of goals. Yet it is still some time before children can represent another's belief state and to know that beliefs about the world affect emotions (Harris, 1993).

Other developments in the metacognition of emotion emerge between 6 and 10 years of age. For instance, between the ages of 6 and 10 children become increasingly adept at masking what they feel. Saarni (1984) studied children who were given a toy that they would not be likely to want, as it was too babyish for them. She observed whether they would mask emotions or simply show their disappointment. The understanding of ambivalence is also something that occurs later in the elementary school years. Harter and Buddin (1987) found that children do not have a well articulated understanding of experiencing two emotions of opposite valence until they are 10 to 11 years old.

Such changes in cognitive ability affect how we experience ourselves emotionally. We become more adept at using emotions instrumentally in the service of our goals. We can think about and weigh up the different emotional components of events. As we learn to analyze emotional experience we come to different understandings of events than those we held at the time that they occurred. With the development of the metacognition of emotion, very different relationships of emotions to the self and to the other also then become possible. We can love someone, though still be frightened of that person, and talk with them about these mixed feelings. And we can tolerate episodes of anger, knowing they can often be resolved. Our ability to recognize and talk about our emotions is an important component of what Salovey and Meyer (selection 25) have called emotional intelligence.

Individual differences

Temperament refers to those individual differences in the constitutional make-up of the child, which are stable over time and across situations. This factor is important in understanding how emotional styles come into being. It has a neurophysiological basis and some degree of heritability (Emde et al., 1992; Goldsmith, 1993). Goldsmith and Campos (1982) have argued that temperament is based on an innate structure that organizes the expression of emotion.

Studies of temperament show that children are born with different propensities to react to events. For instance, some children are more easily angered, others are more fearful, yet others are generally cheerful. These temperaments are by no means immutable but they do constrain possibilities. We see this in the work of Kagan and his colleagues (selection 16). They have looked at children who are unusually shy in early childhood. They have been able to demonstrate considerable continuity of this trait into the school age years. Comparably, Caspi and others (selection 17) show us what happens to angry children over the course of a lifetime. Emotional configurations do change, but there is evidence that the emotional biases with which we are born make one kind of pathway of development more likely for one person and another pathway more likely for another. These emotional biases also influence the ways that others react to us, and hence the opportunities that become available to us over the course of a lifetime.

A further issue of children's developing emotionality is how children are affected by the emotional environments in which they are raised. Children are born into emotional cultures. In some societies it is acceptable for children to cry, in others it is less acceptable (Harkness & Super, 1985). In some families anger works well as a means to achieve a goal (see selection 26), in other families expressions of anger beyond a certain age have no effect, and simply do not occur (selection 5). The ways that families encourage or discourage different expressions of emotion has an important effect on the emotions that children express during interactions.

Children who are exposed, in their families, to more of one emotion than of another, may themselves show more of that emotion over time. Malatesta and Haviland (1982), for instance, found that infants whose mothers showed more anger than other mothers while the infants were three months old, showed more anger than other infants when they were six months old. Jenkins and Smith (selection 19) showed links from anger-based interactions between parents to anger-based interactions in children. When children were exposed to high levels of anger-based parental conflict, their children were more likely to be conflictual and angry in their interactions with peers; comparable results were found for children's interactions with siblings (Jenkins, 1992).

Perhaps parents teach children appraisals that they use themselves. For instance, a parent who is often angry may convey to a child that the world is a hostile place, and that most threats to the person demand retaliation. Such an appraisal pattern would result in the child more frequently experiencing and expressing anger. It may also be that children experience one emotion working for them in the achievement of their goals, where another emotion does not. This mechanism is discussed more fully by Patterson and others (selection 26).

Functional theory in developmental research on emotions

The idea that emotions have functions has been popular in the study of development, and developmentalists have contributed to exploring emotional functions generally (see Campos et al. 1994, also selections 4, 9, 22). The idea is that emotions are integral to person–environment transactions, that they function in the service of our goals. What deserves discussion is why this way of conceptualizing emotion has become important in the study of development.

We think that it is because a functional perspective has encouraged researchers to find new ways to define and investigate emotions. As we have seen in previous sections, operationalizations of emotion have resulted in narrow and discrete aspects of behavior: facial expressions (e.g. selections 7 and 8), or patterns of physiological arousal as predicted by James (selection 2). Although such ways of defining emotion have led to a taming of this complex area, they have also led to some researchers feeling that we have lost something intrinsic. We humans experience emotions as playing a guiding role in every aspect of our lives (see Damasio et al., selection 12). How would we know what was most important to us, what we really valued, without emotions? When we feel happy we have a sense that our lives are going well. When we feel angry, we know something important to us is not happening and we have the sense that there is something that we can do about it.

Such central functions of emotions, although theoretically consistent with many approaches, have not so easily been translated into how people study emotions. What the functional perspective does is to ask us to step back from specific ways in which emotions have been assessed (thinking for instance that facial expression IS the emotion) and to put the person's goals at the center. What is the person trying to do? How are they using facial expression, voice tone, modulation of behavior, in order to manage their relationship to their environment?

This conceptualization leads us to several important challenges. The first issue has to do with developing methods that have as their unit of analysis the meaning of behavior in relation to a person's goals. Instead of simply counting units of behavior, we refocus on what a configuration of behaviors might mean in relation to what a child is trying to accomplish. Attachment researchers have long subscribed to this approach (Sroufe & Water, 1977). The second issue is the focus on the emotion *process* rather than *discrete events*. A momentary facial expression is part of goal-directed behavior, but only a small part. It does not define the whole emotion. The third issue is that we need to move our target of analysis from the individual to the system: the individual in her or his context.

Emotions are intrinsically relational, and yet rarely do our analyses capture the relational component. A baby's expression of anger has an effect on her caregiver. The mother's reaction to the baby's expression changes the baby's goal and perhaps the baby's experience of his or her emotion. On a moment-by-moment basis that baby is interacting with the environment in a goal-directed way; her or his emotions represent flexible strategies that further this environmental transaction.

References

Bretherton, I., Fritz, J., Zahn-Waxler, C., & Ridgeway, D. (1986). Learning to talk about emotions: a functionalist perspective. *Child Development, 57*, 529–548.

Campos, J. J., Mumme, D. L., Kermoian, R., & Campos, R. G. (1994). A functionalist perspective on the nature of emotion. In N. A. Fox (Ed.), *The development of emotion regulation. Monographs of the Society for Research in Child Development* (Vol. 59, 2–3, Serial no. 240, pp. 284–303).

Camras, L. A. (1992). Expressive development and basic emotions. *Cognition and Emotion, 6*, 269–283.

Dunn, J., & Brown, J. (1991). Relationships, talk about feelings, and the development of affect regulation in early childhood. In J. Garber & K. Dodge (Eds.), *The development of emotion regulation and dysregulation* (pp. 89–108). Cambridge: Cambridge University Press.

Emde, R. N., Plomin, R., Robinson, J., Corley, R., DeFries, J., Fulker, D. W., Reznick, J. S., Campos, J., Kagan, J., & Zahn-Waxler, C. (1992). Temperament, emotion and cognition at fourteen months: the MacArthur Longitudinal Twin Study. *Child Development, 63*, 1437–1455.

Fogel, A., Nwokah, E., Dedo, J. Y., Messinger, D., Dickson, K. L., Matusov, E., & Holt, S. A. (1992). Social process theory of emotion: a dynamic systems approach. *Social Development, 2*, 122–142.

Goldsmith, H. H. (1993). Temperament: variability in developing emotion systems. In M. Lewis & J. M. Haviland (Eds.), *Handbook of emotions* (pp. 353–364). New York: Guilford.

Goldsmith, H. H., & Campos, J. (1982). Toward a theory of infant temperament. In R. N. Emde & R. J. Harmon (Eds.), *The development of attachment and affiliative systems*. New York: Plenum Press.

Harris, P. (1993). Understanding Emotion. In M. Lewis & J. M. Haviland (Eds.), *Handbook of Emotions* (pp. 237–246). New York: Guilford.

Harkness, S., & Super, C. M. (1985). Child–environment interactions in the socialization of affect. In M. Lewis & C. Saarni (Eds.), *The socialization of emotions* (pp. 21–36). New York: Plenum Press.

Harter, S., & Buddin, B. (1987). Children's understanding of the simultaneity of two emotions: a five-stage developmental acquistion sequence. *Developmental Psychology, 23*, 388–399.

Hoffman, M. L. (1984). Interaction of affect and cognition in empathy. In C. Izard, J. Kagan, & R. Zajonc (Eds.), *Emotions, Cognition and Behavior* (pp. 103–131). New York: Cambridge University Press.

Izard, C. E. (1979). *The maximally discriminative facial movement coding system (MAX)*. Newark: University of Delaware, Office of Instructional Technology.

Jenkins, J. M. (1992). Sibling relationships in disharmonious homes. In F. Boer & J. Dunn (Eds.), *Children's sibling relationships: Developmental and Clinical Issues* (pp. 125–136). Hillsdale, NJ: Erlbaum.

Kopp, C. B. (1992). Emotional distress and control in young children. In N. Eisenberg & R. A. Fabes (Eds.), *Emotion and its regulation in early development (New Directions in Child Development, no. 55)*, (pp. 41–56). San Francisco: Jossey Bass.

Lewis, M., Alessandri, S. M., & Sullivan, M. W. (1990). Violation of expectancy, loss of control and anger expressions in young infants. *Developmental Psychology, 26*, 745–751.

Lewis, M., Sullivan, M. W., Stanger, C., & Weiss, M. (1989). Self development and self-conscious emotions. *Child Development, 60*, 146–156.

Malatesta, C. Z. & Haviland, J. M. (1982). Learning display rules: the socialization of emotion expression in infancy. *Child Development, 53*, 991–1003.

Rothbart, M. K. (1986). Longitudinal observation of infant temperament. *Developmental Psychology, 22*, 356–365.

Saarni, C. (1984). An observational study of children's attempts to monitor their expressive behavior. *Child Development, 55*, 1504–1513.

Sroufe, L. A., & Water, E. W. (1977). Attachment as an organizational construct. *Child Development, 48*, 1184–1199.

Stein, N. L., & Levine, L. J. (1989). The causal organization of emotional knowledge. *Cognition and Emotion, 3*, 343–378.

Stenberg, C. R., & Campos, J. J. (1990). The development of anger expressions in Infancy. In N. Stein, B. Leventhal, & T. Trabasso (Eds.), *From psychological to biological approaches to emotion* (pp. 247–282). Hillsdale, NJ: Erlbaum.

CHAPTER *13*

Facial Patterning and Infant Emotional Expression

S. W. Hiatt, J. J. Campos, and R. N. Emde

The study that we excerpt here was motivated by an attempt to show a relationship between facial expression and the corresponding basic emotion. At the time that it was carried out, the idea that there was a correspondance between specific facial expressions and the basic emotions was still new. Ekman (see selection 7) had demonstrated such relationships in adults. Hiatt and her collegues were interested in establishing the same correspondance for infants. They conceived an elegant experiment in which babies were exposed to two circumstances designed to elicit happiness, two to elicit surprise, and two to elicit fear, and in this excerpt only the results for happiness and fear are presented, and their facial expressions coded. Two criteria were to be met: The predicted expression should occur more often than any non-predicted expression in response to the specific elicitor, and the predicted expression must be displayed more often in its appropriate eliciting circumstances than in non-predicted circumstances.

The results were mixed, and suggest that there is difficulty arguing that a wide range of discrete emotions is present in young infants. Certainly different expressions are present but it seems that when babies are still young, except for happiness they may not map directly onto internal emotional states. For other evidence that emotions are not well differentiated in infancy see Oster and others (1992). For a quite different perspective on the presence of discrete emotions in infancy see Izard and Malatesta (1987).

References

Izard, C. E., & Malatesta, C. Z. (1987). Perspectives on emotional development. In J. Osofsky (Ed.), *Handbook of Infant Development* (pp. 494–554). New York: Wiley.

S. W. Hiatt, J. J. Campos, and R. N. Emde, Facial patterning and infant emotional expression: happiness, surprise, and fear. *Child Development, 50* (1979), 1021–1027, 1031–1032. Copyright © 1979 by the National Institute of Child Health and Human Development. Reprinted with permission.

Oster, H., Hegley, D., & Nagel, L. (1992). Adult judgements and fine-grained analysis of infant facial expressions: testing the validity of a priori coding formulas. *Developmental Psychology, 28,* 1115–1131.

In the present study, we attempted to extend the prior work on the relationship between facial expressions and discrete emotional states by studying human infants and by eliciting affect expressions in situations which, although induced in the laboratory, are not unlike those encountered in real life. As Ekman and others have acknowledged, much of the previous work on whether facial expressions communicate emotion has presented actor-posed peak facial expressions to judges. Such posed peak expressions solve the problem of whether a judgment of emotion is accurate (accuracy being the agreement between observer's judgment and actor's intent), but posed expressions may bear little relation to facial expression in real-life settings. What studies there are on spontaneous or elicited facial expressions are either methodologically flawed (see Ekman, 1972) or else judge faces on dimensions, rather than on discrete affects. If facial expressions are indeed universal and, by implication, innate (Ekman, 1973; Izard, 1971), infant facial behaviors should be rather similar to those of adults, although immature facial anatomy, the presence of subcutaneous fat, and the greater elasticity of the infant's skin ensure that there will be important differences across ages (Oster & Ekman, 1978).

Furthermore, infant facial expressions are much less likely to be masked. The deliberate disguise of the emotion being expressed by a subject requires the cognitive skill of deferred imitation, a skill that Piaget (1951) describes as developing only in the second year of life. Testing of younger infants thus promises a clearer relationship between expression and eliciting circumstances.

The study of facial expressions in real-life settings and with human infants creates formidable methodological problems. One is how to determine whether an emotion has been elicited and, if so, which one. There are a number of strategies to counter this problem (see Ekman et al., 1972). First of all, although there is rarely a one-to-one correspondence between the presentation of a stimulus and the experience of a discrete emotional state, stimulus circumstances can be chosen according to their previously demonstrated likelihood of eliciting strong emotional reactions at the ages tested. Furthermore, the instigating circumstances can be selected in such a way as to demonstrate convergent and discriminant validity (Campbell & Fiske 1959). That is, instigating events can be selected in pairs, such that, within pairs, emotional reactions (and hence facial behaviors) are predicted to be similar and yet to differ from pairs of events selected to elicit different reactions.

Another problem is how to demonstrate that the instigating event registered on the infant. The failure to observe facial expressions may merely indicate that the stimulus was not effective in eliciting emotion. This problem can be addressed by assessing nonfacial gross motor reactions (instrumental behaviors) which indicate that the stimulus had the desired affective impact.

Additionally, there are two methods of scoring facial expressions which do not necessarily yield the same findings. As Ekman has pointed out (Ekman & Friesen, 1975), facial behavior can be treated as a response, in which case components of facial behavior are scored, or facial behavior can be treated as a stimulus, in which case observer judgment is recorded. We chose to study both and to assess the relationship between the presence of components and the raters' perceptual judgments.

Facial responses were scored using a coding technique based upon facial features described by Ekman and Friesen in *Unmasking the Face* (1975) [...]

In the present study, we tested the differentiation of facial expressions of emotion using two situations designed to elicit happiness, two designed to elicit surprise, and two designed to elicit fear. We hypothesized that we would find evidence for specificity of facial expressions of emotion in infants: the two situations designed to elicit the same emotion were predicted to produce the same facial expressions, and the three sets of situations designed to elicit different emotions were predicted to produce different facial expressions. Fear and surprise were chosen to provide a strong test of the facial patterning hypothesis: prior work has shown these two emotions to be difficult to differentiate in posed expressions (Ekman, 1972). Happiness, on the other hand, has been shown to be easily differentiated [...]

Method

Subjects

There were 27 infants tested (14 male, 13 female), nine each at 10, 11, and 12 months of age. These ages were chosen because the three emotions of interest in this investigation should be readily elicited at this time, as documented in prior research. The data from an additional 10 infants were discarded due to experimenter error ($N = 5$) and fussiness prior to any testing ($N = 5$).

Conditions

Fear: stranger approach (F_{st}) – This condition consisted of a 15-sec period during which a female stranger approached the seated infant from a distance of 1 m to 0.3 m and was based on a paradigm which has produced clear stranger distress in previous work from our lab (see Campos, Emde, Gaensbauer, & Henderson, 1975). As a check on whether the stranger produced the intended behavioral reaction, we included a control condition which consisted of the casual approach of the mother, back turned toward the child, bringing a chair toward the infant. The control condition always preceded the stranger approach.

Fear: visual cliff (F_{vc}) – This condition consisted of 15 sec of direct placement atop the deep side of the visual cliff (model III, Walk & Gibson, 1961). The mother was out of the room, and all trials were initiated with the infant in a quiet state. In order to assess whether the visual cliff elicited behavioral reactions indicative of fear of heights, a locomotor crossing test was administered after the direct placement. Crossing to the mother over the deep side of the cliff was contrasted with crossing to the mother over the shallow side [...]

Happiness: toy game (H_{toy}) – In the H_{toy} condition, the mother activated one of two attractive collapsing figure toys directly in front of the infant. The mother was seated in front of and slightly to the right of the infant and on signal from the experimenter activated the toy. The choice of toys used depended on which appeared to be the more attractive to the child.

Happiness: peek-a-boo (H_{peek}) – This consisted of the mother playing peek-a-boo with her infant. On signal from the experimenter, the mother placed a 500×500-cm white cloth in front of her face, saying "peek-a-boo" as she uncovered her face.

No manipulation checks were deemed appropriate for the two happiness conditions.

Procedure

The infants were brought to the lab on 2 separate days for testing, with one of each of the three emotion situations presented each day. There were three separate orders of testing on each day: FSH, HFS, or SHF, resulting in nine possible orders of testing across the 2 days. Three subjects were assigned to each order of testing.

After the mother was briefed on both day 1 and day 2 as to the specific nature of that day's testing, she was requested to darken her infant's eyebrows with black eyebrow pencil. This allowed for better observation of eyebrow changes.

Facial and gross motor reactions were recorded continuously via two Sony videocameras. One camera was equipped with a zoom lens (f/2.0, 16–24 mm) and focused only on the infant's face and shoulders so as to allow context-free scoring of facial expressions. In the F_{ve} conditions, facial expressions were filmed by a videocamera hidden under the shallow surface but directed upward through the underside of the deep surface at an angle of approximately $60°$. The second camera was equipped with a wide-angle lens and recorded the entire body of the infant, as well as part of the testing situation.

Measurement

There were three different rating tasks, with different sets of raters assigned to each. Two raters assessed nonfacial instrumental behaviors indicative of emotional expression. The behaviors assessed differed for each situation. For the F_{st} condition, the instrumental behaviors coded were the existence of crying, freezing, or bodily withdrawal from the stranger. The instrumental behavior index for F_{ve} consisted of crossing to the mother over either the deep or the shallow surface, with one trial on each side and all trials counterbalanced. An infant was considered wary of the deep side if he refused to cross to the mother within 60 sec or if he took a "detour" route (crossing by any but the most direct route). The instrumental behavior coded for S_{ts} consisted of duration of looking at the novel toy uncovered. This is based on Ramsay and Campos's (1975) finding that a typical surprise reaction due to the presentation of a misexpected event was an increase in looking at the novel toy. Total duration of search behavior was recorded as the instrumental behavior index for the S_{vo} condition. Search was defined as looking under the highchair, to one side of the apparatus, or within the box for the toy which had vanished. Instrumental behaviors for the H_{toy} condition consisted of attempts by the infant to reactivate the toy when given the chance. These included attempting to push the button which made the toy collapse and directly pulling on the toy in order to make it collapse. Instrumental behavior for the H_{peek} condition consisted of attempts by the infant to reactivate the game by uncovering the mother's face after she had repositioned the screen.

Two independent raters judged the occurrence or nonoccurrence of component facial behaviors from three regions of the face: the eyebrow/forehead region, the eyes/lids region, and the nose/mouth region. The components scored are presented in the Appendix and, as mentioned earlier, are similar to those described by Ekman (1972; Ekman & Friesen, 1975). These were scored while viewing, in real time, only the relevant facial region (i.e. two facial regions were blacked out during the rating period). Raters scored any and all changes in facial expressions which occurred during the scoring sequence.

For scoring perceptual judgments, we used two rating tasks. In one, the two raters, scoring independently, were asked to select via a forced-choice method which one of Ekman's six primary emotions (happiness, surprise, anger, fear, disgust, sadness), plus a seventh category of neutral, was being expressed by the infant. In the other rating task, the same raters, again scoring independently, were asked to give a numerical estimate, on a nine-point scale, of their confidence that each of the six categories, plus neutral, was being expressed.

Except for the surprise situations, rating tasks involved 10-sec segments. Each segment, however, began 5 sec before event onset in order for raters to score any change in facial expression. Thus, the total viewed segment was 15 sec in duration. Rating for surprise involved only 5-sec segments but also began 5 sec before event onset. A signal marker visible on the videotape cued the rater about a change from prestimulus to stimulus period.

Results

Reliability data

Reliability between judges proved consistently high for all analyses. For the instrumental behavior assessments, judges were in agreement 96 percent of the time as to whether or not the infant attempted to reactivate either the toy game or the peek-a- boo game. There was perfect agreement on the presence or absence of crossing the deep side of the visual cliff to reach the mother. In the F_{st} condition, the presence or absence of freezing, bodily withdrawal, and crying was agreed upon 93 percent of the time. For the two surprise-eliciting conditions, S_{ts} and S_{vo}, the number of seconds of either looking or search was tabulated and then subjected to product-moment correlations between the two judges. These correlations were .94 and .92 for the S_{ts} and S_{vo} conditions respectively.

The raters were able to make all facial expression judgments reliably. Reliabilities were computed as percentage of perfect agreement of the presence and absence of a specific emotion. A mean reliability of 84 percent (range:

76%–96%) was found for the global judgments task. Correlations of confidence ratings were generally high, the median being .83 (range: .65–.98). Interestingly, for the very exacting task of judging the presence and absence of facial expression components, the percentages of perfect agreement for the raters' initial judgments were 75 percent for the eyebrow/forehead region, 75 percent for the eyes/lids, and 82 percent for the nose/mouth. Disagreements on all judgments were resolved by consensus after reviewing the videotapes.

Instrumental behavior data

The data indicate that the stimulating circumstances did possess affective impact. When the presence or absence of the predicted instrumental behaviors for each of the experimental conditions was compared with the control conditions, significant differences were found. For the F_{st} experimental and control conditions, a Wilcoxon test comparing behavioral ratings yielded significant differences between conditions, $z(1) = 2.02$, $p < .02$. For the F_{ve} condition, Cochran's nonparametric test proved to be significant, $Q(1) = 25.0$, $p < .001$: crossing behavior on both deep and shallow surfaces of the cliff differed, with 23 subjects refusing to cross the deep surface and an additional three showing detour behavior. All 27 subjects crossed to mother on the shallow surface. Differences between experimental and control conditions for the S_{ts} and S_{vo} conditions were likewise significant, t (toy switch) $(26) = -6.38$, $p .001$; t (vanishing object) $(26) = 1.98$, $p < .05$.

Component analyses: facial response patterning

For each of the six eliciting circumstances, the proportion of the 27 subjects who manifested each facial response component was calculated. These data are presented in figures 13.1 and 13.2 for the happiness and fear elicitors, respectively. Within each figure, the components are divided into those from the region of (*a*) the forehead and eyebrow, (*b*) the eyes and lids, and (*c*) the nose and mouth. A broken vertical line separates the set of response components predicted to occur for the emotion we tried to elicit (to the left of the line) from those which were not predicted to occur for that emotion (to the right of the line).

The purpose of this analysis was to demonstrate response specificity for emotion in the human face. Such specificity is demonstrated when two criteria are met, these being (*a*) intratask specificity and (*b*) intertask specificity. For the first criterion to be met, intratask specificity, the "hit" rate (i.e. percent of subjects demonstrating the predicted components) must significantly exceed the "false response" rate (i.e. the percent of subjects demonstrating nonpredicted components) for each eliciting circumstance. For the second criterion to be met, intertask specificity, the hit rate for those components which are predicted to occur in a given situation must significantly exceed the proportion of those same components observed when other emotions were being elicited.

Figure 13.1 presents the results for the happiness conditions. As can be seen, two happiness components – the smile and the presence of wrinkles under the eyelids – were elicited in nearly all the subjects tested in both the H_{peek} (96% and 93% respectively) and H_{toy} (85% and 67% respectively) conditions, while

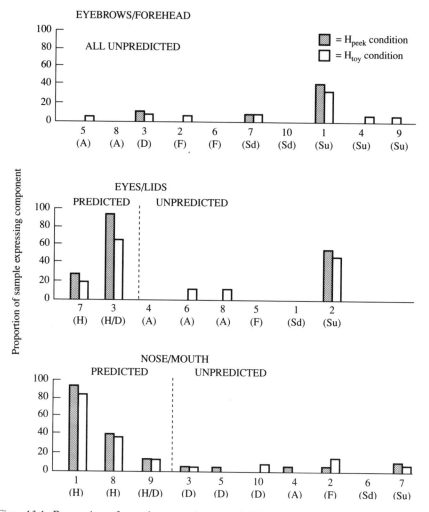

Figure 13.1. Proportion of sample expressing each facial expression component in the two happiness-eliciting conditions. Numbers refer to components described in the Appendix. Letters refer to emotion linked to components.

approximately a third of the subjects showed the predicted nasolabial fold component (41% H_{peek} and 37% H_{toy}). Somewhat fewer showed the crow's-foot pattern around the eyes (30% and 19% respectively), and cheek raising was observed in only 11% of the subjects in each condition. Of the 23 nonpredicted components for all three regions, only two (eyebrow raising and eye opening) were observed in more than three subjects.

Statistical analyses confirmed that both criteria of response specificity were met for the happiness components. Overall, the proportion of the hits for the predicted components was 54% for the H_{peek} condition and 44% for the H_{toy} condition. The false response rates, by contrast, were 6% for the H_{peek} and 7% for the H_{toy} conditions. This produced a highly significant difference between hit and false response rates for each condition: t (26) $= 9.23, p < .001$, for H_{peek};

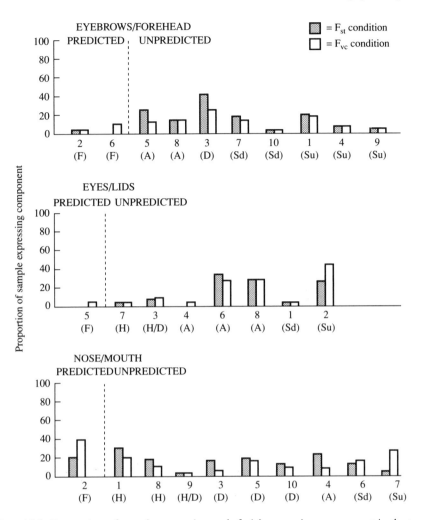

Figure 13.2. Proportion of sample expressing each facial expression component in the two fear-eliciting conditions. Numbers refer to components described in the Appendix. Letters refer to emotion linked to components.

$t(26) = 7.04, p < .001$, for H_{toy}. The proportions of happiness components observed in each of the four other eliciting circumstances were as follows: stranger, 13%; visual cliff, 10%; vanishing object, 1%; and toy switch, 16%. All four proportions proved to be significantly lower in magnitude than the proportion of hits during each of the two happiness conditions by individual t tests $(p < .01)$ [...]

In figure 13.2 are listed the components elicited during the F_{st} and the F_{vc} conditions. These two tasks elicited the smallest proportion of hits of any of the six eliciting circumstances – 6% for the stranger condition and 15% for the visual cliff condition. Only one predicted component – opening of the mouth and stretching back of the lips – was observed in more than three subjects. This component was present in 41% of the subjects in the F_{vc} condition but in only 22% of subjects in the F_{st} condition. In addition, almost all of the remaining, nonpredicted, components were elicited in at least some subjects. Several of the nonpredicted components, especially in the eyes/lids region, were observed in one-third or more of the subjects. Overall, the false response rate for the F_{st} condition was 17% and for the F_{ve} condition was 15%. Contrary to expectation, proportionately more nonpredicted than predicted components were elicited in these conditions. This finding was in fact significant in the F_{st} condition, $t(26) = 4.48$, $p < .001$, although nonsignificant in the F_{ve} condition. Consequently, the criterion of intratask specificity was not met for either the F_{st} or F_{ve} condition.

The F_{ve} condition did, however, meet the criterion of intertask specificity, since this condition elicited significantly more fear components than were elicited in the two surprise and two happiness conditions. Fear responses were rarely observed in the four other eliciting conditions: H_{toy}, 5%; H_{peek}, 1%; S_{ts}, 3%; S_{vo}, 4%. These proportions were all significantly different from the proportion of hits during the F_{ve} task ($p < .05$).

In summary, then, the three sets of conditions differed in the ease with which they elicited facial response patterning. Each of the happiness-eliciting conditions demonstrated both intertask and intratask specificity and, thus, demonstrated the clearest patterning. In addition, both surprise-eliciting conditions demonstrated intratask specificity, but neither succeeded in demonstrating intertask specificity. The poorest response specificity was shown by the two fear-eliciting conditions, neither of which demonstrated intratask specificity. However, by virtue of the fairly low rate of elicitation of fear components in the other two sets of emotion-eliciting conditions, the F_{ve} condition did demonstrate intertask specificity [...]

Discussion

Our study lent strong support to the existence of at least some specific facial patterns of emotion at 10–12 months of age. In addition, it provided further information about the issue of facial response specificity. The raters were able to make all facial expression judgments reliably. Furthermore, there was found to be a relationship between the degree of confidence given for the existence of a particular emotion and the number of predicted components present in the face. Evidence for the existence of more than one emotion (i.e. blends) in the facial patterns was found, as was evidence indicating differential specificity of such response patterns [...]

Furthermore, the data lend support to the challenge of Ekman (1972; Ekman et al., 1972), Izard (1971, 1972, 1977), and Tomkins (1962, 1963) that facial expressions are specific to emotional state. Infant facial expressions were found to be differential in terms of emotion and to possess some generality across emotional situations. Our findings indicated that the component analysis appeared to be the best method for demonstrating facial response patterning. There were, however, task differences in such specificity, as evidenced by the proportions of hit and false response rates. The percent of subjects demonstrating the predicted components was greatest for the two happiness-eliciting conditions (54% for H_{peek} and 44% for H_{toy}) and was lowest for the two fear-eliciting conditions (6% for F_{st} and 15% for F_{ve}) [...]

Appendix

Components scored for three facial regions

Eyebrow/Forehead

1   The brows are raised so that they are curved and high.
2   The brows are raised and drawn together.
3   The brow is lowered, lowering the upper lid.
4   Horizontal wrinkles go across the forehead.
5   The brows are lowered and drawn together.
6   The wrinkles in the forehead are in the center, not across the entire forehead.
7   The inner corners of the eyebrows are drawn up.
8   Vertical lines appear between the brows.
9   The skin below the brow is stretched.
10 The skin below the brow is triangulated, with the inner corner up.

Eyes/Lids

1   The upper eyelid corner is raised.
2   The eyelids are opened; the upper lid is raised and the lower lid is drawn down (the white of the eye-sclera shows above the iris and often below as well).
3   The lower eyelid shows wrinkles below it and may be raised but not tense.
4   The eyes have a hard stare and may have a bulging appearance.
5   The upper lid is raised, exposing sclera, and the lower lid is tensed and drawn up.
6   The lower lid is tensed and may or may not be raised.
7   Crow's-feet wrinkles go outward from the corners of the eyes.
8   The upper lid is tense and may or may not be lowered by the action of the brow.

Nose/Mouth

1   The corners of the lips are drawn back and up; the teeth may or may not be exposed.
2   The mouth is open and the lips are either tensed slightly and drawn back or stretched and drawn back.
3   The upper lip is raised.
4   The lips are in either of two basic positions: pressed firmly together with the corners straight or down, or open, tensed in a squarish shape as if shouting.
5   The lower lip is raised and pushed up to the upper lip or is lowered and slightly protruding.
6   The corners of the lips are down or the lip is trembling.
7   The jaw drops open so that the lips and teeth are parted, but there is no tension or stretching of the mouth.
8   A wrinkle (the nasolabial fold) runs down from the nose to the outer edge beyond the lip corners.
9   The cheeks are raised.
10 The nose is wrinkled.

References

Blurton-Jones, N. (Ed.) (1972). *Ethological studies of child behavior.* Cambridge: Cambridge University Press.

Boucher, J. D., & Ekman, P. (1973). Facial areas and emotional information. *Journal of Communication, 25/2*, 21–29.

Bower, T. G. R. (1967). The development of object permanence: some studies of existence constancy. *Perception and Psychophysics, 2*, 411–418.

Brannigan, C., & Humphries, D. (1969) I see what you mean. *New Scientist*, May 22, pp. 406–408.

Brannigan, C., & Humphries, D. (1972) Human non-verbal behavior, a means of communication. In N. Blurton-Jones (Ed.), *Ethological studies of child behavior.* Cambridge: Cambridge University Press.

Bretherton, I., & Ainsworth, M. D. S. (1974). Responses of one-year-olds to a stranger in a strange situation. In M. Lewis & L. A. Rosenblum (Eds.), *The origins of fear.* New York: Wiley.

Brown, J. S., & Farber, I. E. (1991) Emotions conceptualized as intervening variables with suggestions toward a theory of frustration. *Psychological Bulletin, 48*, 465–495.

Bruner, J. S., & Tagiuri, N. (1954) The perception of people. In G. Lindzey (Ed.), *Handbook of social psychology.* Cambridge, MA: Addison-Wesley.

Campbell, D. T., & Fiske, D. W. (1959). Convergent and discriminant validation by the multitrait-multimethod matrix. *Psychological Bulletin, 56*, 81–105.

Campos, J. J., Emde, R. N., Gaensbauer, T., & Henderson, C. (1975). Cardiac and behavioral interrelationships in the reactions of infants to strangers. *Developmental Psychology, 11*, 589–601.

Camras, L. A. (1977). Facial expressions used by children in a conflict situation. *Child Development, 48*, 1431–1435.

Darwin, C. (1872). *The expression of emotion in man and animals.* London: Murray.

Duffy, E. *Activation and behavior.* (1962). New York: Wiley.

Ekman, P. (1972). Universals and cultural differences in facial expressions of emotion. In J. K. Cole (Ed.), *Nebraska Symposium on Motivation.* Vol. *19* (pp. 207–283). Lincoln: University of Nebraska Press.

—— (1973). Cross-cultural studies of facial expression. In *Darwin and facial expression.* New York: Academic Press.

Ekman, P., & Friesen, W. V. (1975). *Unmasking the face.* Englewood Cliffs, NJ: Prentice-Hall.

—— (1976) Measuring facial movement. *Environmental Psychology and Nonverbal Behavior, 1*, 56–75.

—— (1978). *Facial action coding system.* Palo Alto, CA: Consulting Psychologists Press.

Ekman, P., Friesen, W. V., & Ellsworth, P. (1972). *Emotion in the human face: guidelines for research and an integration of findings.* New York: Pergamon Press.

Ekman, P., Sorenson, E. R., & Friesen, W. V. (1969). Pancultural elements in facial displays of emotions. *Science, 164* (3875), 86–88.

Emde, R. N., & Brown, C. (1978). Adaptation to the birth of a Down's syndrome infant: grieving and maternal attachment. *Journal of the American Academy of Child Psychiatry, 17*, 299–323.

Emde, R. N., Katz, E. L., & Thorpe, J. K. (1978). Emotional expression in infancy, II: Early deviations in Down's syndrome. In M. Lewis & L. Rosenblum (Eds.), *The development of affect.* New York: Plenum.

Emde, R. N., Kligman, D. H., Reich, J. H., & Wade, T. D. (1978). Emotional expression in infancy, I: Initial studies of social signaling and an emergent model. In M. Lewis & L. Rosenblum (Eds.), *The development of affect.* New York: Plenum.

Grant, E. C. (1969). Human facial expression. *Man, 4*, 525–536.

Izard, C. E. (1971). *The face of emotion* New York: Appleton-Century-Crofts.

Izard, C. E. (1972). *Patterns of emotions: a new analysis of anxiety and depression.* New York: Academic Press.

——— (1977). *Human emotions.* New York: Plenum.

Landis, C. (1929). The interpretation of facial expression in emotion. *Journal of General Psychology, 2*, 59–72.

Oster, H., & Ekman, P. (1978). Facial behavior in child development. In A. Collins (Ed.), *Minnesota symposia on child psychology.* Vol. *11.* Hillsdale, NJ: Erlbaum.

Piaget, J. (1951). *Play, dreams and imitation in childhood.* New York: Norton.

Ramsay, D. S., & Campos, J. J. (1975). Memory by the infant in an object notion task. *Developmental Psychology, 11*, 411–412.

Schachter, S. (1970). The assumption of identity and peripheralist-centralist controversies in motivation and emotion. In M. B. Arnold (Ed.), *Feelings and emotion.* New York: Academic Press.

Sherman, M. (1927a). The differentiation of emotional responses in infants, I: Judgments of emotional responses from motion picture views and from actual observation. *Journal of Comparative Psychology, 7*, 265–284.

——— (1927b). The differentiation of emotional responses in infants, II: The ability of observers to judge the emotional characteristics of the crying infants and of the voice of the adult. *Journal of Comparative Psychology, 7*, 335–351.

——— (1928). The differentiation of emotional responses in infants, III: A proposed theory of the development of emotional responses in infants. *Journal of Comparative Psychology, 8*, 385–394.

Tomkins, S. S. (1962). *Affect, imagery, consciousness.* Vol. *1. The positive affects.* New York: Springer.

——— (1963). *Affect, imagery, consciousness.* Vol. *2. The negative affects.* New York: Springer.

Walk, R., & Gibson, E. (1961). A comparative and analytical study of visual depth perception. *Psychological Monographs, 75* (whole no. 519).

Woodworth, R. S., & Schlosberg, H. S. (1954). *Experimental psychology.* New York: Holt.

CHAPTER *14*

Self Development and Self-conscious Emotions

M. Lewis, M. W. Sullivan, C. Stanger, and M. Weiss

An important contribution of Michael Lewis has been to emphasize the role of the self in emotional experience, and to show how particular cognitive capacities are needed before certain kinds of emotional experience are possible. This selection shows how he has demonstrated this kind of effect.

Lewis has found a watershed in emotional development around 18 months of age: the child becomes aware of the self. With this awareness comes the growth of emotions such as embarrassment, which have to do with evaluation of the self.

Shame, on which Lewis (1992) has written a fascinating book, shows a yet more complex cognitive structure. When we feel shame we evaluate our own performance as wanting in comparison to standards that we have internalized. Rather than seeing this as a local failure we evaluate our failure as more global and pervasive. Such evaluations need considerable cognitive capabilities that are in place by the time children are approximately 3 years old.

Reference

Lewis, M. (1992). *Shame: The exposed self.* New York: Free Press.

This article explores the relation between self development as measured by self-recognition and the expression of fear and embarrassment. Fear, but not

M. Lewis, M.W. Sullivan, C. Stanger, and M. Weiss, Self development and self-conscious emotions. *Child Development, 60* (1989), 146–148, 150–152, 153–155. Copyright © by the Society for Research in Child Development. Reprinted by kind permission of Professor Michael Lewis, Institute for the Study of Child Development.

embarrassment, has been considered a primary emotion (Tomkins, 1963). Our general hypothesis is that specific cognition skills are necessary for the emergence of the secondary emotions, although they are not necessary for the primary emotions. In particular, self-referential behavior is not necessary for the emergence of fear but is necessary for the emergence of embarrassment.

The current literature on emotions in the first 2 years focuses on the appearance of what has been called the fundamental or primary emotions (Lewis & Michalson, 1983). These emotions are characterized both by their early appearance and by having prototypic and universal facial expressions. Beyond the appearance of these early emotions, the emergence of other emotions remains relatively uncharted, although some empirical work on pride and guilt, especially within an achievement situation, has recently appeared (Geppert & Kuster, 1983; Heckhausen, 1984).

Theories regarding the origins of the secondary emotions and their dynamics and relation to one another are largely untested, perhaps because measurement methods, operational definitions, and a catalog of possible emotions are not well developed. The appearance of some emotions after the emergence of the primary ones has led to their classification as secondary or derived emotions (Lewis & Michalson, 1983; Plutchik, 1970). The use of the terms primary, secondary, or derived promotes a number of alternative views regarding the course of emotional development. One model presumes that these later emotions are derived from the earlier ones and are composed of combinations of the primary emotions, as all colors are composed from the three primary ones (Plutchik, 1970). Another model considers that these secondary emotions follow the primary ones but are not constructed from these earlier ones (Izard, 1977). Still another model holds that emotions are tied to cognitive processes; those needing the least cognitive support emerge first, and those needing more emerge later (Lewis & Michalson, 1983). To the degree that the earlier, primary emotions contribute to cognitive development, it can be said that they are indirectly related to the secondary or derived emotions (Lewis, Sullivan, & Michalson, 1984).

Although the sequence of emergence of primary emotions has yet to be fully articulated, it seems that by 12 months of age, they all have appeared. Even so, it is not until the middle of the second year that the secondary emotions are observed (Borke, 1971; Lewis & Brooks-Gunn, 1979a; Stipek, 1983). More elaborate cognitive abilities either are necessary for, or occur prior to, the emergence of this new class of emotions – abilities that appear between the end of the first year and the middle of the second year of life.

Figure 14.1 presents a general developmental model. In Stage 1, the primary emotions appear. The timing of the emergence of particular primary emotions is undetermined as yet; interest, joy, physical distress, and disgust expressions appear to be present at or shortly after birth (Izard, 1977). Anger expressions have been observed as early as 4 months (Stenberg, Campos, & Emde, 1983), surprise by 6 months (Charlesworth, 1969), and given the appropriate eliciting circumstances, surprise, anger, fear, and sad expressions can be observed in 10-week-old infants (Sullivan & Lewis, 1989).

In Stage 2, self-referential behavior emerges, although the self system has been undergoing development over the first 2 years of life. Self-other differentiation

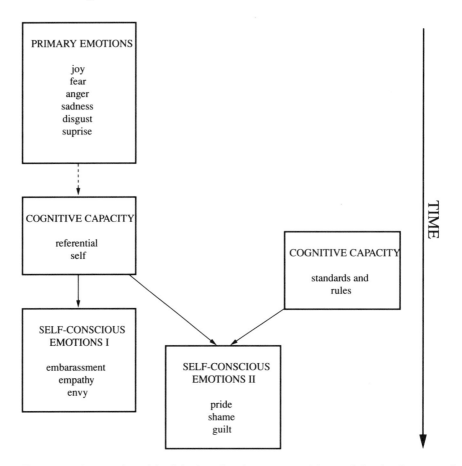

Figure 14.1. A general model of the interface between cognition and the development of self-conscious emotions

appears first followed by object permanence, which appears around 8 months, even though permanence is not consolidated until 18 months or so (Piaget, 1954). Self-referential behavior has a developmental course and appears between 15 and 24 months of age (Bertenthal & Fischer, 1978; Lewis & Brooks-Gunn, 1979b).

The appearance and consolidation of these cognitive skills provide the underpinning for the emergence of Stage 3, the first class of secondary emotions. Self-conscious emotions are characterized by self-referential behavior and include embarrassment, empathy, and perhaps envy. These emotions appear before or around the second birthday. At the same time, children learn about other aspects of their social world, including emotional scripts (Michalson & Lewis, 1985) and rules of conduct that allow them to evaluate their own production and behavior (Kagan, 1981). This leads to the second class of self-conscious emotions – self-evaluative emotions, such as guilt, shame, and pride. Self-evaluative emotions emerge after the self-conscious emotions since they require more cognitive capacity.

In order to observe the relation between self-referential behavior and these secondary emotions, it is necessary (1) to observe the development of two classes of emotion, one associated with primary, the other with self-conscious emotions, and (2) to study their relation to self-referential behavior. The primary emotion of fear (or wariness) will appear early and not require self-referential behavior, while embarrassment should emerge with or following self-referential behavior [...]

[In this excerpt we reprint the second of two studies from the original paper. Because the original description of the second study refers to the first, we have modified the description of the procedures here to include relevant details of the first study. Eds.]

Method

Subjects

The subjects were 44 children, 19 females and 25 males, who were part of a shortterm longitudinal study of emotional development. The mean age of the sample was 22 months (± 2 weeks).

Procedures

Each subject received five emotion-eliciting situations administered in a random order. Each was videotaped, and close-up views of the child's face and upper body were obtained for scoring by two observers. The situations were as follows.

The stranger situation – The child was seated in a small chair in front of a small table, while the mother sat close by in a laboratory room (3 m × 4 m). At a signal an unfamiliar woman, who was not the experimenter, appeared in the door and slowly walked toward the child, taking about 15 sec to reach the infant, where-upon she touched the subject's hand, turned, and left the room.

The mirror situation – The same infants received two different procedures using a mirror. In both situations, the infant was placed in front of a one-way mirror (46 cm × 89 cm) mounted on a large (122 cm × 244 cm) sheet of plywood behind which a video camera was placed.
   In the first procedure, on the experimenter's signal, the infant was placed in front of the mirror by the mother; this provided one of the embarrassment situations. In the second procedure, which provided the measure of self-referential behavior (see below) non-scented rouge was applied to the infants' noses by their mothers, who pretended to wipe their child's face. The children were placed in front of the mirror and their behavior toward the marked nose was observed.

Overcompliment situation – The experimenter initiated interaction with the child, during which she lavishly complimented the child in an effusive manner. A series of four to five compliments were made about the child or his or her appearance. For example, the child was told he was smart, cute, had beautiful hair, and had lovely clothes, etc.

161

Request-to-dance situations (mother and experimenter) – In these two situations, the experimenter handed the mother a small tambourine and asked the mother to coax the child to dance, or did so herself. They each said, "Let's see you dance, dance for me, I'll sing 'Old MacDonald' [or a song familiar to the child]." The dance situation was utilized since conspicuousness is thought to be an elicitor of embarrassment (Buss, 1980). The episode terminated either when the child complied and danced, or upon direct refusal.

Measures

Wariness, fear face, and crying   Wariness was defined as all three of (a) an attentive look characterized by a neutral or sober facial expression, accompanied by (b) a sudden inhibition of all vocal or other behavior, and followed by (c) gaze aversion. A fear face was defined as described int he MAX coding system (Izard & Dougherty, 1982). Crying was also scored. Interobserver reliability, the number of agreements over the number of agreements plus disagreements, was 92% for wariness, 92% for fear face, and 95% for crying.

Embarrassment   The behaviors necessary to score embarrassment were all three of (a) a smiling facial expression followed by (b) gaze aversion, and (c) movement of the hands to touch hair, clothing, face, or other body parts. Interobserver reliability was 87%.

Self-recognition   Touching of the rouge spot on the nose during the mirror–rouge episode was found to be the most reliable indicator od self recognition in numerous studies (Lewis & Brooks-Gunn, 1979a) and served as the index of self-referential behavior. Coding of self recognition was done independently, by different observers from those who coded emotions. Interobserver reliability was 100%.

Results

Table 14.1 presents the numbers and percentage of subjects by sex showing fear face, crying, wariness, and embarrassment for each of the five conditions. Given the frequencies, only wariness and embarrassment were analyzed. Wariness showed an overall condition effect (Cochran Q test, $Q = 30.15$, $p = < .001$) of the five conditions. Given the frequencies, only wariness and embarrassment were analyzed. Wariness showed an overall condition effect (Cochran Q test, $Q = 30.15$, $p = < .001$) such that wariness is more likely in the stranger situation than in any of the others: stranger versus mirror, $\chi^2(1) = 50.22$, $p < .001$; stranger versus compliment, $\chi^2(1) = 17.3$, $p < .001$; stranger versus dance/m, $\chi^2(1) = 60.00$, $p < .001$; stranger versus dance/e, $\chi^2(1) = 22.38$, $p < .01$. Wariness, rather than embarrassment, was seen in the stranger condition ($Z = 4.08$, $p < .01$).

Embarrassment also shows an overall condition effect (Cochran Q test, $Q = 14.04$, $p < .01$) and was less likely to occur in the stranger situation than in any of the others: stranger versus mirror, $\chi^2(1) = 5.78$, $p < .02$; stranger versus

Table 14.1.   Emotional expression by experimental condition

| | | Expression | | | | | | | |
| | | Wary | | Fear | | Cried | | Embarrassed | |
Condition	N	n	%	n	%	n	%	n	%
Stranger:									
Total	44	24	55	0	0	2	5	2	5
Males	25	19	76	0	0	2	8	2	8
Females	19	5	26	0	0	0	0	0	0
Mirror:									
Total	44	2	5	2	5	4	9	11	25
Males	25	1	4	1	5	3	12	6	24
Females	19	1	5	1	4	1	5	5	26
Compliment:									
Total	41	4	10	0	0	1	2	13	32
Males	22	4	18	0	0	0	0	5	23
Females	19	0	0	0	0	1	5	8	42
Dance for mother:									
Total	43	0	0	0	0	4	9	10	23
Males	22	0	0	0	0	3	12	3	13
Females	19	0	0	0	0	1	5	7	37
Dance for experimenter:									
Total	41	2	5	0	0	2	5	13	32
Males	23	2	9	0	0	0	0	4	17
Females	18	0	0	0	0	1	5	9	50

compliment, $\chi^2(1) = 8.99$, $p < .003$; stranger versus dance/m, $\chi^2(1) = 4.92$, $p < .025$; stranger versus dance/e, $\chi^2(1) = 8.99, p < .003$. Embarrassment did not differ by condition.

Self-recognition and emotional behavior

Across conditions, an aggregate count of the number of subjects who showed a range of behavior was obtained (see table 14.2). This range varies from never showing the emotion on any of the four conditions to showing the emotion on each condition. Table 14.2 presents by condition the number and percentage of subjects who showed wary and embarrassment behavior as a function of self-recognition. It was predicted that while there would be no difference between touchers and nontouchers for wary behavior, touchers would show significantly more embarrassed behavior than nontouchers.

The first analysis looked at the numbers of subjects who did and did not show the two emotions across conditions as a function of self-recognition. Of the touchers, seven did not show any embarrassment, while 19 showed embarrassment on at least one condition. Likewise, there were 13 nontouchers who showed no embarrassment, while there were only five nontouchers who showed embarrassment, a significant difference, $\chi^2(1) = 8.08, p < .005$. Of those subjects

Table 14.2. Number of times embarrassment and wariness were observed over the situations used to elicit them

| | Embarrassment (Mirror, Compliment, Dance-M, Dance-E Conditions) | | | | |
	0	1	2	3	4
Total	20	9	7	5	3
Males	14	6	2	2	1
Females	6	3	5	3	2
Touchers	7	7	6	4	2
Nontouchers	13	2	1	1	1

| | Wariness (Stranger Condition) | |
	0	1+
Total	17	27
Males	4	21
Females	13	6
Touchers	10	16
Nontouchers	7	11

Table 14.3. For total sample, those who have attained self-referential behavior (touchers) and those who have not (nontouchers)

| | % of Subjects showing wary or embarrassment | | | | | | | | | |
| | Stranger | | Mirror | | Compliment | | Dance-Exp | | Dance-Mother | |
	W	E	W	E	W	E	W	E	W	E
Total	55	5	5	25	10	32	5	32	0	23
Touchers	54	8	4	31	4	42	8	44	0	27
Nontouchers	56	0	6	17	18	18	0	13	0	18

| | No. of Subjects showing wary or embarrassment | | | | | | | | | |
| | Stranger | | Mirror | | Compliment | | Dance-Exp | | Dance-Mother | |
	W	E	W	E	W	E	W	E	W	E
Total	24	2	2	11	4	13	2	13	0	10
Touchers	14	2	1	8	1	10	2	11	0	7
Nontouchers	10	0	1	3	3	3	0	2	0	3

who showed at least one occasion of embarrassment, approximately 80% touched their noses. Moreover, 32 out of 44 subjects showed the predicted relation between embarrassment and self-recognition. Observation of the number who showed wary behavior as a function of self-recognition revealed no significant differences; only self-recognition is related to embarrassment.

A condition analysis (see table 14.3) revealed that for the stranger condition, there was no significant difference in wariness as a function of self-recognition, while there were several significant (or near significant) effects for embarrassment. Subjects who showed self-recognition also exhibited more embarrassment in the compliment (Fischer's exact, $p < .055$), dance/m (Fischer's exact, $p < .11$), and dance/e (Fischer's exact, $p < .02$) conditions. Thus, the overall effect was replicated by observing each of the conditions individually [...]

Discussion

The general discussion will consider three issues: (1) situations eliciting emotions and measures, (2) the interface of cognition and emotion, and (3) individual and sex differences in the development of embarrassment.

Situations and measures

The data from both studies agree, even though Study 1 varied age. Embarrassment but not wariness, was related to self-recognition when observed either by looking at age changes in the ability to recognize oneself in the mirror or by looking at individual differences in this ability during the period of time when it is being acquired.

The approach of a stranger has long been used as a situation to elicit fear, although wariness rather than fear is usually observed (see Lewis & Rosenblum, 1974). Embarrassment is elicited by situations that produce exposure of the self, although Buss (1980) describes embarrassment also as being elicited by impropriety or lack of social competence, as well as conspicuousness. There are many situations that might be used to elicit this emotion, and we found that four were successful: viewing oneself in the mirror (in both studies), being complimented, and being asked to perform (to dance). Self-conspicuousness is the central feature of these situations. While these situations are different in terms of the amount of embarrassment elicited, they did not produce much wariness/fear. Likewise, few subjects showed embarrassment during stranger approach. These situations, therefore, are adequate to observe embarrassment.

Although the measurement of wariness/fear has been well established, the measurement of embarrassment has received less attention, although since Darwin (1872/1965) it has been described and seen in young children (Amsterdam, 1972; Dixon, 1957; Lewis & Brooks-Gunn, 1979a; Schulman & Kaplowitz, 1977). In this study, the measurement approach used provides an easy criteria for observing its presence.

One problem with using nervous touching as part of the criteria is that this is a behavior also used in the self-recognition measure. In order to eliminate any confusion, we limited our definition of embarrassment to smiling and gaze averting, a procedure used by some (Buss, 1980). Using this new measure to compare embarrassment with self-recognition resulted in findings quite similar to those when nervous touching is included. Under this measurement procedure, many more subjects would be said to show embarrassment. For example, in Study 1, 21 rather than 10 subjects showed embarrassment. Although the numbers of subjects increase, the percentage of subjects who show embarrassment, without using nervous touching as a criteria, and who show self-recognition is 78%, while 22% show embarrassment and no self-recognition. These figures are similar to the findings using nervous touching; thus, there is no reason to believe that our definition of embarrassment affects the results reported.

The role of cognition and affect

We have suggested that in order for all secondary emotions, both self-conscious and self-evaluative, to emerge, a referential self is necessary. It is important to note that a self system and its development consists of several features (Lewis & Brooks-Gunn, 1979b). While details of this system are still being worked out (see, e.g., Pipp, Jennings, & Fischer, 1987), self-other differentiation, self-permanence, and the ability to consider the self as a separate entity are some of the features of this system. The ability to consider one's self – what has been called self-awareness or referential self – is one of the last features of self to emerge, occurring in the last half of the second year of life. The ability to consider one's self rather than the ability to differentiate or discriminate self from other is the cognitive capacity that allows for all self-conscious emotions such as embarrassment and empathy, although the development of standards is also needed for self-conscious evaluative emotions such as shame, guilt, and pride. Self-referential behavior has been defined operationally as the ability of the child to look at its image in the mirror and to show, by pointing and touching its nose, that the image in the mirror *there* is located in space *here* at the physical site of the child itself. In the results reported in both studies, embarrassment, in general, does not occur unless self-referential behavior exists.

While a third factor may be related to our findings, given the observed relation between embarrassment, but not wariness, and self-referential behavior, it would seem that self-recognition behavior represents an important milestone in the child's development of a self system and in its general cognitive and emotional development.

The relation between the primary emotions and the development of the self has been suggested (Lewis et al., 1985; Schneider-Rosen & Cicchetti, 1984; Stern, 1985), but little empirical work has been conducted relating these two systems. The mother-child relationship has been proposed to affect the development of self, but only two studies have shown any relation (Lewis et al., 1985; Schneider-Rosen & Cicchetti, 1984). While it appears likely that socioemotional behavior and its socialization affect the child's developing self system, there is only weak evidence to indicate any direct effect of early emotional life on the referential self. Nevertheless, the development of the self system impacts on the child's subsequent emotional life [...]

References

Amsterdam, B. K. (1972). Mirror self image reactions before age two. *Developmental Psychology, 5*, 297–305.

Bertenthal, F. I., & Fischer, K. W. (1978). The development of self-recognition in the infant. *Developmental Psychology, 11*, 44–50.

Borke, H. (1971). Interpersonal perception of young children: Egocentrism or empathy. *Developmental Psychology, 5*, 263–269.

Buss, A. H. (1980). *Self-consciousness and social anxiety.* San Francisco: W. H. Freeman.

Charlesworth, W. R. (1969). The role of surprise in cognitive development. In D. Elkind & J. H. Flavell (Eds.), *Studies in cognitive development: Essays in honor of Jean Piaget* (pp. 257–314). London: Oxford University Press.

Darwin, C. (1965). *The expression of emotion in animals and man.* Chicago: University of Chicago Press. (Original edition 1872)

Dixon, J. C. (1957). The development of self-recognition. *Journal of Genetic Psychology, 91*, 251–256.

Izard, C. E. (1977). *Human emotions.* New York: Plenum.

Izard, C. E. & Dougherty, L. M. (1982). Two complementary systems for measuring facial expressions in infants and children. In C. E. Izard (Ed.), *Measuring emotions in infants and children* (pp. 97–126). New York: Cambridge University Press.

Kagan, J. (1981). *The second year: The emergence of self-awareness.* Cambridge, MA: Harvard University Press.

Lewis, M., & Brooks-Gunn, J. (1979a). *Social cognition and the acquisition of self.* New York: Plenum.

Lewis, M., & Brooks-Gunn, J. (1979b). Toward a theory of social cognition: The development of self. In I. Uzgiris (Ed.), *New directions in child development: Social interaction and communication in infancy* (pp. 1–20). San Francisco: Jossey-Bass.

Lewis, M., Brooks-Gunn, J., & Jaskir, J. (1985). Individual differences in early visual self-recognition. *Developmental Psychology, 21*, 1181–1187.

Lewis, M., & Michalson, L. (1983). *Children's emotions and moods: Developmental theory and measurement.* New York: Plenum.

Lewis, M., & Rosenblum, L. (1974). (Eds.). *The origins of fear.* New York: Wiley.

Lewis, M., Sullivan, M. W., & Michalson, L. (1984). The cognitive-emotional fugue. In C. E. Izard, J. Kagan, & R. B. Zajonc (Eds.), *Emotions, cognition and behavior* (pp. 264–288). London: Cambridge University Press.

Piaget, J. (1954). *The origins of intelligence in children* (M. Cook, trans.). New York: Norton.

Pipp, S., Jennings, S., & Fischer, K. W. (1987). Acquisition of self and mother knowledge in infancy. *Developmental Psychology, 23*, 86–96.

Plutchik, R. (1970). Emotions, evolution and adaptive processes. In M. Arnold (Ed.), *Feelings and emotion* (pp. 384–402). New York: Academic Press.

Schneider-Rosen, K., & Cicchetti, D. (1984). The relationship between affect and cognitionin maltreated infants: Quality of attachment and the development of visual self-recognition. *Child Development, 55*, 648–658.

Schulman, A. H., & Kaplowitz, C. (1977). Mirror-image response during the first two years of life. *Developmental Psychology, 10*, 133–142.

Stenberg, C., Campos, J., & Emde, R. (1983). The facial expression of anger in seven-month-old infants. *Child Development, 54*, 178–184.

Stipek, D. J. (1983). A developmental analysis of pride and shame. *Human Development, 26*, 42–54.

Sullivan, M. W., & Lewis, M. (1989). Emotion and cognition in infancy: Facial expressions during contingency learning. *International Journal of Behavioral Development, 12*, 221–237.

Tomkins, S. S. (1963). *Affect, imagery and consciousness:* Vol. 2. *The negative affect.* New York: Springer.

CHAPTER *15*

Family Talk about Feeling States and Children's Later Understanding of Others' Emotions

J. Dunn, J. Brown, and L. Beardsall

Although emotions function as means of communication with others, only a few people study emotions in the context of relationships. Judy Dunn has been a pioneer of such study. She has shown that children show sophisticated cognitive capacities within their most intimate relationships. When children are arguing, teasing, trying to get their way in a conflict, justifying their actions to stay out of trouble, they reveal a complex understanding of the others' internal states (Dunn, 1988).

In recent years Dunn's interest has been in children's abilities to understand emotion and the kinds of interactions in families that promote such understanding (Brown & Dunn, 1996). In this selection she shows that talk about emotions and other internal states amongst family members promotes children's ability to understand emotion several years later. There are very marked differences in how much families engage in talk about emotions. For some mother–child dyads, emotion talk is a small proportion of their interaction, while for others it is a large proportion. Children whose mothers talk more to them about emotions when they are 3 years old show greater understanding of the emotions of an unfamiliar adult when they are 6. In another study Brown and Dunn have shown that talk between mother and child at age 3 predicts understanding of mixed emotions when the children are 6 (Brown & Dunn, 1996).

Through talk about emotion parents may promote children's abilities to think about, reflect on, and talk about emotions as entities. This has been called the metacognition of emotion, and may relate to how well emotional events are handled in people's lives (Gottman, Fainsilber-Katz, & Hooven, 1996).

J. Dunn, J. Brown, and L. Beardsall, Family talk about feeling states and children's later understanding of others' emotions. *Developmental Psychology, 27* (1991), 448–455. Copyright © 1991 by the American Psychological Association. Reprinted with permission.

References

Dunn, J. (1988). *The beginnings of social understanding*. Cambridge, MA: Harvard University Press.

Brown, J., & Dunn, J. (1996). Continuities in emotion understanding from three to six years. *Child Development, 67*, 789–802.

Gottman, J. M., Fainsilber-Katz, L., & Hooven, C. (1996). Parental meta-emotion philosophy and the emotional life of families: theoretical models and preliminary data. *Journal of Family Psychology, 10*, 243–268.

There is growing interest among psychologists in the nature of very young children's understanding of emotions – a core aspect of human development about whose early stages we still know little (see Harris, 1989; Miller & Aloise, 1989, for reviews). One important source of evidence for children's interest in emotions, and their grasp of cause and consequence of emotions, is their talk about feeling states. A number of studies have now provided converging evidence that from around 20 months children use emotion-descriptive terms in daily interaction with family members (Bretherton, Fritz, Zahn-Waxler, & Ridgeway, 1986; Bretherton, McNew, & Beeghly-Smith, 1981; Dunn, Bretherton, & Munn, 1987; Ridgeway, Waters, & Kuczaj, 1985). Using parental reports, Ridgeway and her colleagues documented a dramatic increase in children's vocabulary of emotion terms between 24 and 36 months. In addition, the studies show that children by 36 months talk about past and future emotions and discuss the antecedents and consequences of emotional states – findings further supported by recent studies of children's causal understanding of emotions (Huttenlocher & Smiley, 1990, Stein & Levine, 1989a).

The primary focus of these studies of children's talk about feeling states has been the description of normative development – the documentation of the frequency and range of emotion terms used by children of different ages. Although this research has clarified the achievements and limitations of the abilities of children of different ages, one major issue remains relatively unexplored. This is the question of the developmental significance of individual differences in very young children's participation in talk about feeling states. The extent of individual differences in children's talk about emotions and in their exposure to discussion of feeling states has been little considered, beyond one descriptive paper focused upon 24-month-olds (Dunn et al., 1987); we know nothing about the later correlates of such individual differences. Do children differ much in their participation in discussion of feeling states and their causes within the family, and are such differences in early family experiences associated with later differences in children's abilities to judge others' emotions? These questions are of considerable developmental importance; they center upon the relation of language experiences to conceptual development – a core aspect of human development.

Although differences in children's abilities to recognize and understand others' feelings are clearly important, we know relatively little about their origins. It is often assumed that early experience within the family must have a major impact; however, the nature of that influence is not yet well understood. It is important here to make a distinction between *recognizing/understanding* another's feeling state and *behavioral responses* to others' emotional expressions. With regard to the latter, there is evidence for connections between parental behavior and emotional expressiveness and children's later response to others' distress or anger. Zahn-Waxler and her colleagues found that parental reactions to a child's causing hurt or distress to another were related to later differences in the children's "reparative" behavior towards their victims (Zahn-Waxler, Radke-Yarrow, & King, 1979). There is also evidence for links between family emotional expressiveness and children's behavior with peers (Cassidy & Parke, 1989; Denham, McKinley, Couchoud, & Holt, 1990). A number of lines of evidence support the hypothesis that family discourse about feelings is important in relation to children's later social behavior. For instance, the studies by Zahn-Waxler and her colleagues showed verbal explanation concerning cause and consequence of emotions to be one feature of parental behavior that was associated with the later differences in child behavioral outcome. Secondly, associations between maternal talk about feelings to firstborn children and these children's later friendly behavior towards their infant siblings have been reported in two separate studies (Dunn & Kendrick, 1982; Howe & Ross, 1990).

On the issue of whether there are links between parental behavior and emotional understanding, however, little information is available. Studies of abused children indicate that in these extreme cases there may indeed be associations between parental behavior and the ability to recognize others' feelings (Camras, 1989). It remains unclear whether such connections apply within the normal range. Denham and Couchoud's (1988) finding that parents' self-reports of their socialization practices were associated with differences in preschool children's ability to identify emotions stands very much alone.

Whether differences in parental talk about affect and in explicit discussion of cause and consequences of feeling states are systematically related to differences in later emotional understanding is an intriguing but unexplored question, one which raises the central developmental issue of the relation between language experiences and conceptual development. It has been argued that the ability to talk about emotion serves the function of enabling children to "distance" themselves from, and to reflect upon, the experience of emotion (Bretherton et al., 1986; Stern, 1985). Stern argues that this allows children and their significant others to "negotiate shared meanings" about experience. If discourse serves this function, then discussion of feelings should play an important role in children's developing understanding of emotions; we might predict that in families in which mothers and children engage relatively frequently in such talk, the children's ability to understand the feelings of others would be fostered. That is, an association between the *language experience* and the later ability of the children to *understand* others' emotions might be expected. From this general prediction, more specific questions about which particular features of the language experience are related to later individual differences in conceptual development follow. Is the experience of discourse about emotions important because the child is encouraged to reflect on and articulate the causes and consequences of feeling states? Does its importance lie in the child's exposure to discussion of a diversity of emotional themes? Are discussions of negative and positive feeling states both related to later outcome, or does discourse about negative feelings have special significance? Do the families who discuss feeling states talk more frequently in general – and are later differences in conceptual ability attributable to these differences in family talk, rather than to differences in family talk about feelings per se?

A further issue to be explored is the significance of the context in which such discourse about feeling states takes place. For instance, do disputes, in which children are faced with the challenge of another's viewpoint, have special developmental significance? From Piaget's proposal that argument between peers is of special significance in the development of social understanding, social conflict has been highlighted as of particular importance (see Shantz, 1987). It has also been argued that angry emotions and situations of frustration and failure are more frequently associated with evaluative, thoughtful behavior than are situations in which people are happy or successful (Schwarz, 1988; Stein & Levine, 1990b). At present, little information is available on what social processes may be implicated in the development of the ability to understand others' feelings, even though this is such a central aspect of human development. In contrast to the proposal that disputes or contexts of thwarted self-interest (Dunn, 1988) are of special significance, it has also been proposed that discourse about the social world that takes place in the context of calm reflective discussion between family members, not directly concerned with immediate practical goals, is especially important in fostering social understanding (see, e.g., Tizard & Hughes, 1985). These different proposals each remain to be tested.

In this article these questions concerning the developmental significance of individual differences in family discourse about feelings are considered in light of data from a longitudinal study of children observed within the family. The children were observed at home in the toddler and preschool period and then were tested at $6\frac{1}{2}$ years on an affective perspective-taking task – Rothenberg's assessment of social sensitivity (Rothenberg, 1970). The study thus offers the opportunity to examine associations between individual differences in family talk about feelings in the preschool years and later differences in children's ability to grasp what others may be feeling.

Specifically, the article has two goals. The first is to present descriptive data on individual differences in a range of features of discourse about feeling states. We will consider differences in frequency, theme, and pragmatics of feeling state talk between 36-month-olds and their mothers at home, in the discussion of cause and consequence within such feeling-state conversations, and the significance of disputes as a context in which these causal discussions about feelings take place. The second goal is to examine associations between differences in each of these features of early talk about feelings and individual differences in performance on the Rothenberg assessment of social sensitivity 3 years later.

Method

Subjects

Forty-one sibling pairs and their mothers in Cambridge and surrounding villages in England were observed when the second child was 36 months old. The families were recruited either through Health Visitors or through a newspaper

171

advertisement. The social class of the families according to the Registrar General's (1973) classification was I/II (professional/managerial) for 26 families, III (white collar) for 4 families, III (skilled manual) for 8 families, and IV/V (semi-skilled or unskilled manual) for 3 families. There were 8 girl–girl pairs, 8 boy–boy pairs, 13 older boy-younger girl pairs, and 12 younger boy-older girls pairs. The mean difference between the siblings in age was 26 months (range 12–57 months). The families participated in a follow-up visit when the secondborn children were 6 years, 6 months old. In this article the secondborn child is referred to as the *child*, and the firstborn as the *sibling*.

Observations at Time 1

Observations were carried out when the child was 36 months old. Two observations of 1 hr each were carried out. All observations were made in the home at a time when the mother, child, and sibling were present. Audiotape and pencil-and-paper recording methods were used. To reduce the intrusive effect of the observer, one visit was paid to the home before conducting the first observation, and recording did not begin for at least 10 min after arrival. The same observer visited the family each time. The mothers continued to carry out their usual routine while the observer was present; it was emphasized to them that we wanted to study normal interaction between the siblings and to disrupt family patterns of interaction as little as possible. The frequency of conflict, arguments, and extended bouts of pretend play (Dunn & Dale, 1984; Dunn & Munn, 1985) suggests that attempts to minimize the intrusive effects of the observers' presence were reasonably successful. Family conversation during the observation was recorded on a small portable stereo taperecorder and transcribed by the observer following the observation.

Coding of transcripts

A categorization system was designed for the analysis of conversations in which family members referred to feeling states. References included conversational turns in which the speaker used a feeling state term (e.g. "sad" or "happy"), those in which the speaker used a phrase that connoted a feeling state (e.g. "make a fuss"), and those in which an expletive was used that connoted a particular feeling state (e.g. "Yuck!" [disgust]). Nonspecific expletives (e.g. "Aha!"), crying, laughter, and other nonverbal expressions of affect were not included. Because the analyses were limited to feeling state references, internal state terms indicating volition, motivation, or cognition were not included. Statements of a moral or evaluative nature were included only if their content specifically denoted or connoted a feeling state on the part of the speaker or referee (e.g. "That's disgusting!"). The label *nice* was included if it was used to express liking but excluded if it was used in the moral sense of "good" (i.e. well-behaved) or if it was used as a simple evaluative adjective. The term *like* was included only when it referred to a state of enjoyment or dislike, not when it indicated desire or volition, as in the example "Would you like to have this toy?" Terms that projected feeling states as attributes into the objects that elicited them (e.g. "poor" or "scary") were included. Both individual conversational turns in which feeling state references were made and conversations in which a feeling state was discussed were included in the analyses.

A conversational turn, referring to feeling states, was defined as all of one speaker's utterances bounded by the utterances of another speaker, in which an explicit reference to a feeling state was made. If an individual's utterances within one conversational turn referred to more than one emotional theme or to more than one individual's feelings, each reference was coded separately. Each conversational turn that referred to a feeling state was coded in terms of the following categories: (a) *conversational partners* – who the speaker was and to whom the turn was addressed; (b) *referent* – the person whose feeling state was referred to by the speaker; (c) *theme* – the emotion-descriptive theme of each turn; (d) *disputes* – whether the conversational turn involved a dispute over either the action, intentions, or beliefs or points of view of another (see Dunn & Munn, 1987); (e) *causal reference* – the occurrence of a turn within a feeling state conversation in which a causal relation was discussed. The turn was required to be related to the causal component of the conversation (e.g. as either the antecedent or consequent of the causal reference). The criteria used to determine whether a causal inference was made were based on those developed by Hood and Bloom (1979). Causal statements by young children and also by adults do not invariably contain causal connectives (see Hood & Bloom, 1979); thus turns coded as causal included, in addition to those in which an explicit causal term was used (e.g. "why" or "because"), turns in which a reference was made to two events or states that had a conditional relation (e.g. "Don't jump – you'll hurt yourself!"). (f) *pragmatic context* – the explicit or inferred intention of the speaker when making the reference to feeling states was coded. Twelve categories of pragmatic context were developed from studying the transcripts; these were then grouped into three broad categories each for children's and for mothers' turns. For children these were (a) *self-interest* – efforts to gain assistance or comfort and to meet own immediate needs; (b) *discussion/pretend* – commentary and discussion about past events, solo or shared pretend; (c) *influencing affect* – efforts to change the feelings of others, including friendly and provocative teasing, comforting others, and attempts to avoid blame and excuse own actions. Mothers' turns were grouped according to the following categories: (a) *control* – efforts to control or reinforce socially acceptable behavior; (b) *discussion/pretend* – commentary and discussion about past events, solo or shared pretend; (c) *influencing affect/other* – efforts to change the feelings of others (e.g. comforting and altruistic efforts; mother's efforts to get own needs met). Note that turns were coded independently with respect to disputes, causal, and pragmatic context categories. That is, disputes could and did occur in each pragmatic category, and conversely, nondisputed conversations occurred in each pragmatic category. Similarly, causal references were made in all of the pragmatic contexts.

Conversations about feeling states   In addition to coding individual speaker turns that included explicit reference to feeling states, we decided to include a measure of conversations about feeling states, on the grounds that the topic of the feeling state frequently continued over several turns in a conversation beyond the turn in which it was explicitly mentioned. That is, children were frequently participants in conversations about feelings that extended over several turns, turns that were not captured by the measure of explicit reference to feelings. Feeling state conversations were defined as those conversational turns that included a specific reference to a feeling state and those turns surrounding the explicit references that had the feeling state itself as their topic (following Dunn et al., 1987). Conversations were coded in terms of (a) who the speakers were, (b) the number of conversational turns each speaker made, (c) whether a dispute occurred in the conversation, and (d) whether a causal reference was made during the conversation.

Mean length of utterance (MLU)   The mean length and the upper-bound mean length of each child's utterances were coded (Shatz & Gelman, 1973) from the 100 consecutive child utterances that followed the child's first 10 conversational turns on the transcript. The number of words in the 10 longest of these utterances was used to determine the upper-bound mean length of each child's utterances.

Total talk   The total number of conversational turns, including feeling state turns, exchanged between mothers and children was counted for each observation.

Reliability of transcript coding

The transcripts were coded by Judy Dunn and Jane Brown. Intercoder agreement was assessed by both coders coding eight 1-hr transcripts. Cohen's kappa for the measures were as follows: Categorization of a turn as concerned with *feeling state* = .94; turns within a *conversation about feeling states* = .75; *participants* in a conversation about feeling states = .90; *referent* of feeling state reference = .75; *theme* of the feeling state reference = .73; *pragmatic context* of feeling state turn = .73; categorization of a turn as *causal* = .73; categorization of conversation as *dispute* = .73. After this assessment, each coder coded half the transcripts – that is, disagreements were not discussed.

Affective perspective taking: Rothenberg test of social sensitivity

At $6\frac{1}{2}$ years the children's ability to identify others' emotions was assessed with the Rothenberg (1970) test of social sensitivity. The children listened to four tape-recorded scenarios of a man and a woman interacting. The four emotions represented in the scenarios were happiness, anger, anxiety, and sadness. The child was asked to concentrate on one of the actors in each scenario – the woman in two of the scenarios and the man in the other two. Each scenario depicted a change of feelings for that actor from his or her initial comments to his or her later ones in which the target emotion was portrayed. Photos of a man and a woman depicting the appropriate feelings states were used in conjunction with the tapes. The child was then asked to identify how the actor felt at the start of the scenario and at the end. Transcripts of the scenarios are reported in Rothenberg (1970).

Scoring reflected the accuracy of the child's description of the actor's feelings. Most credit was given for accurately mentioning changes in the actor's feelings (+2). Accurate mention of one of the feelings portrayed by the actor received less credit (+1), no mention of feelings received no credit (0), and an inaccurate description of the actor's feelings lost credit (−1). Evidence for the validity of the measure was reported by Rothenberg: Positive correlations were found between high scores on the assessment and teacher ratings of the children on leadership, sensitivity to others and friendliness, and peer ratings on friendliness and leadership. Furthermore, in an observational and interview study of 6- and 9-year-olds, children scoring high on the Rothenberg test were observed to tease more frequently during conflict with siblings (behavior that entailed understanding what would upset the other child) and to use conciliation strategies more frequently (Beardsall, 1986).

Results

Descriptive data on individual differences in feeling-state talk

In table 15.1, the frequencies and ranges of the measures of talk about feeling states from the observations at 36 months are shown. It can be seen that the number of explicit feeling state turns by individual children varied a great deal; the frequency ranged from no turns to 27.2 turns per hour of observation. Individual differences between mothers in frequency of explicit references were marked too: They ranged from 0 to 21.5 turns per hour. Although on average there were 8.4 conversations per hour between mothers and children involving talk about feelings, the range was from 2.1 to 25.0. The frequency of talk about feelings between children and their siblings was much lower. In the analyses that follow we have focused, therefore, upon conversations about feelings between children and their mothers; the low frequency of sibling–child talk about feelings in many families meant that comparison by partner (mother vs. sibling) would not have been appropriate. The analyses do include those triadic conversations in which mothers, children, and siblings were involved. Table 15.1 shows that mothers referred equally frequently to the feelings of others and to the feelings of the child, and children referred most often to their own feelings. The frequency of conversational turns in each pragmatic category is also shown in table 15.1: Individual differences between families in each of these were marked. Table 15.1 shows that there were also notable differences between families in the frequency with which causality was discussed in these feeling-state conversations (range from 0.8 to 12.9 per hour). Causal discussions occurred on average in 52% (range: 13%–100%) of the conversations.

The issue of how frequently discussions of feeling states involved disputes between conversational partners was next considered. The wide range of individual differences was again evident here (range: 0 to 8.2 per hour). Twenty-two percent of all conversations in which feelings were discussed between mother and child or among mother, child, and sibling involved a dispute (range: 0%–75%). The relation between discussion of cause and the context of disputes was examined in light of the arguments that children begin to consider cause and consequences of others' feelings when in argument with others. The results showed

Table 15.1. Mean frequencies (per hour) of conversational turns and conversations referring to feeling states

Variable	M	SD	Range
Conversational turns referring to feeling states			
Child to mother	4.9	5.1	0–27.2
Mother to child	7.7	5.7	0–21.5
Child to sibling	1.9	2.4	0–8.7
Sibling to child	2.7	3.1	0–13
Conversations referring to feeling states			
Mother-child			
Mother-child-sibling	8.4	6	2.1–25.0
Total conversational turns			
Mother to child	133.4	69.8	17.8–372.1
Child to mother	128.3	66.8	22.8–375.7
References to child's feelings			
Child-to-mother turns	3.6	3.9	0–19.7
Mother-to-child turns	3.9	3.2	0–13.6
Reference to others' feelings			
Child-to-mother turns	1.2	1.7	0–7.6
Mother-to-child turns	3.8	3.7	0–15.5
Pragmatic category			
Child-to-mother turns			
Self-interest	1.6	2.0	0–8.3
Discussion/pretend	2.0	2.5	0–9.1
Influencing affect	1.1	2.0	0–9.1
Mother-to-child turns			
Behavior controlling	2.5	2.9	0–10.9
Discussion/pretend	3.6	2.9	0–13.1
Influencing affect/other	1.6	1.5	0–5.3
Feeling-state conversation measures			
Disputes	1.8	1.9	0–8.2
Causal references	4.1	2.9	.8–12.9

that in disputes, discussion of cause was particularly common: Overall 67% of the conversations in which a dispute took place included a causal turn. In contrast, only 45% of conversations in which no dispute occurred included a causal reference, a significant difference (*t* test for difference of two proportions, $t = 31.42, p < .001$).

Emotional themes

A number of different emotional themes were discussed by the 36-month-olds and their mothers and siblings, as summarized in table 15.2. There were marked individual differences in the number of different emotional themes discussed.

Table 15.2. Emotion descriptive themes: numbers of mothers and children who made reference to each theme and mean percentage of turns by theme

Theme	No. of mothers who referred to theme	Mean % of mother-to-child turns on theme	No. of children who referred to theme	Mean % of child-to-mother turns on theme
Pleasure[a]	28	24	19	22
Fatigue	13	6	7	6
Surprise	1	< 1	0	0
Anger[b]	13	7	4	2
Fear[b]	6	4	5	3
Distress[b]	14	6	8	6
Indifference	1	< 1	1	< 1
Concern	14	6	1	< 1
Affection[a]	4	1	4	2
Sympathy[a]	11	5	4	4
Dislike (people)[b]	3	< 1	2	< 1
Shyness	2	< 1	0	0
Disgust[b]	12	5	6	4
Pain[b]	29	28	23	38
Amusement[a]	4	1	5	3
Dislike (things)[b]	9	4	9	7
Remorse	3	< 1	1	< 1
Positive themes	30	32	23	28
Negative themes	29	38	23	31

Note. Superscript *a* refers to emotion themes included in category of positive themes; superscript *b* refers to emotion themes included in category of negative themes.

Although the mean number referred to by the children was 2.5 per hour, the range was from 0 to 9.5. For mothers, the mean was 4.1 (range: 0.7 to 10.3), and the mean for mother-child conversations was 4.9 (range: 1.2–13.1). These individual themes were grouped into two categories of *positive* and *negative* emotions for the subsequent analyses examining the relation of positive and negative feeling state discourse to later affective perspective taking.

Gender differences

Because an earlier study (Dunn et al., 1987) had reported differences between girls and boys in the frequency of their references to feeling states, and in their mothers' references to feeling states, each measure was examined for possible gender differences. None were found.

Relations between measures of feeling-state talk

The relations between the different measures of talk about feelings, the context of the feeling-state talk (dispute or nondispute), the children's verbal fluency as reflected in the MLU and upper-bound MLU, and the amount of verbal discussion in the family more generally was considered next. The correlations with MLU and upper-bound MLU were very similar; we report only those for the upper-bound measure. Table 15.3 shows the correlations between the different measures of feeling-state talk, children's upper-bound MLU, and the total amount of talk between mothers and children. Children's upper-bound MLU was related positively to the measures of feeling-state talk, but significantly only for talk to the mother. For simplicity of presentation, the pragmatic categories and referent of talk are not included in table 15.3. Each of these measures was significantly positively correlated with the total feeling-state talk measure, with causal talk, and with diversity of themes. The pragmatic categories were also each correlated positively with the frequency of disputes, with one exception: The pragmatic category of *discussion/pretend* was not significantly related to disputes in feeling-state talk for mother or for child. In summary, in families in which mothers and children talked frequently about feelings, they discussed a wide variety of emotional themes, referred to the feeling states of both child and others, discussed feelings in a variety of pragmatic contexts, discussed cause relatively frequently, and were often engaged in disputes in these conversations.

Relations between feeling-state talk and later performance on the Rothenberg assessment of social sensitivity

The second goal of the article was to examine the relations between the feeling-state talk measures and the children's later ability to identify the feelings of others in the Rothenberg test. The mean score for the children on the Rothenberg was 2.23 ($SD = 2.16$), with a range from -2.0 to 6.0. Correlations between these scores and the feeling-state talk measures are shown in table 15.3. Differences in scores on the Rothenberg assessment were correlated with a number of the earlier feeling-state talk measures: frequency of mothers' and children's talk about feelings, diversity of themes discussed, frequency of causal feeling-state conversations, and disputes in feeling-state conversations. Each of the pragmatic categories also

Table 15.3 Correlations between feeling state talk measures, child's upper-bound MLU, total talk (all at Time 1), and Rothenberg test of social sensitivity at Time 2

Variable	1	2	3	4	5	6	7	8	9
1 FST – Child to mother	—								
2 FST – Mother to child	.72*	—							
3 FST – Total mother & child	.92*	.94*	—						
4 FSC – Disputes	.60*	.63*	.66*	—					
5 FSC – Causal	.75*	.82*	.85*	.46*	—				
6 FSC – Diversity of themes	.57*	.85*	.77*	.39*	.65*	—			
7 Child's upper bound MLU	.38*	.24	.24	.06	.37*	.18	—		
8 Total mother-child talk	.41*	.51*	.50*	.26	.37*	.37*	.26	—	
9 Rothenberg test of social sensitivity	.42*	.40*	.45*	.34*	.36*	.47*	.13	.21	—

Note. FST = feeling-state turn; FSC = feeling-state conversation; MLU = mean length of utterance.
* $p < .05$.

showed positive correlations with later affective perspective taking. These were as follows: For children, *self-interest*, $r(40) = .30$; *discussion/pretend*, $r(40) = .33$; *influencing affect*, $r(40) = .33$. For mothers, *control*, $r(40) = .43$; *influencing affect/other*, $r(40) = .34$; all significant at $p < .05$. For mothers, *discussion/pretend*, $r(40) = .26$, $p < .11$. The referent of the conversations also showed positive correlations with the affective perspective-taking measure: Child refers to child, $r(40) = .42$; child refers to other, $r(40) = .30$; mother refers to child, $r(40) = .38$; mother refers to other, $r(40) = .32$; all significant at $p < .05$.

We next considered the broad categories of negative and positive feeling state themes. Correlations with later affective perspective taking did not reach significance for either of these general categories. For mother-to-child talk, the correlations were $rs(40) = .24$ and $.14$ for negative and positive, respectively; for child-to-mother talk, $rs(40) = .24$ and $.13$ for negative and positive, respectively.

Finally, the possibility was examined that the associations between the feeling-state talk measures and the children's later affective perspective taking were mediated by the children's verbal fluency, and general linguistic experience was examined. It should be noted from table 15.3 that the children's verbal ability and the total talk during the observation were not significantly correlated with the outcome measure. However, in light of the significant correlations between several of the feeling-state talk measures and child's upper-bound MLU and total mother-child talk, partial correlations were conducted to determine the extent to which feeling-state language was related to subsequent social sensitivity when these latter measures were controlled. With child's MLU controlled, the pattern of correlations between the Rothenberg scores and the feeling-state discourse measures remained very similar to that reported in table 15.3, $rs(40) = .41, .38, .42, .34, .35$, and $.45$ for the measures child-to-mother feeling-state turns, mother-to-child feeling-state turns, total feeling-state turns, disputes in feeling-state conversations, causal conversations, and diversity of themes, respectively (all significant at $p < .05$). With total mother-child talk controlled, the correlations between the Rothenberg scores and the feeling-state talk measures again were similar to those reported in Table 3, $rs(40) = .38, .35, .40, .31, .30$, and $.43$, respectively, for the measures listed above and in table 15.3.

Discussion

There was wide variation among the 36-month-old children in this study in the frequency with which they talked about feelings within the family, and there were related differences in their mothers' talk about feeling states. These individual differences were evident in each aspect of talk that we considered – the diversity of themes, the frequency of different pragmatic contexts of feeling-state talk, the causal content, and the extent to which conversational partners were in dispute. These different features of the feeling-state talk were correlated with one another. That is, children and mothers in families that engaged in discussion of a diverse range of feelings were also likely to discuss cause and consequence and to dispute the position held by other family members relatively frequently. The results showed that children were more likely to be engaged in discussion of cause of feelings when they were in dispute with others than when not in dispute – results that support arguments for the significance of social conflict as a setting in which the development of social understanding is likely to be fostered (Dunn, 1988; Shantz, 1987; Stein & Miller, 199-).

These differences in discourse about feelings were systematically linked to differences in outcome 3 years later. Children who grew up in families in which such feeling-state talk was frequent were as 6-year-olds better at making judgments about the emotions of unfamiliar adults in the affective perspective-talking task than were children who had not participated in feeling-state talk with such frequency as 3-year-olds. One possibility considered was that because the Rothenberg test depends on childrens' verbally describing the feelings of the adults in the scenarios, the association with the earlier measure simply reflected differences in children's verbal fluency. However, the upper-bound MLU at 36 months did not correlate significantly with the 6-year measure, and thus differences in verbal ability appear unlikely to be the whole explanation for the pattern of continuity. In one previous cross-sectional study employing the Rothenberg test, no significant correlation was found between verbal IQ and the Rothenberg assessment (Beardsall, 1986), though it should be noted that Rothenberg (1970) found a low positive correlation with verbal IQ. In considering the developmental implications of these findings, three issues in particular merit discussion.

The first concerns the inferences to be drawn about the significance of discourse for children's conceptual development. It would clearly be inappropriate to assume from such correlations that there was a simple causal link between these sets of measures, and a number of possible underlying or contributing processes remain to be considered in future research. It seems very likely that families who differ in the frequency of talk about feelings will differ in other respects – for instance, in parental emotional expressiveness or child-rearing patterns, in children's personality or expressiveness, or in their relationships with other family members. Any or all of such differences could contribute to later differences in the ability to judge others' feelings. These caveats are important; nevertheless, it should be noted that the findings do highlight a continuity between patterns of early family discourse and children's understanding of others' emotions – a continuity not explained by the children's verbal fluency as reflected in the upper-bound MLU or by the frequency of mother-child talk. The argument that engaging in verbal discussion about others' inner states may well encourage reflection and understanding of such states – that differences in conceptual development may be mediated through language – is supported by the results. To test for a *unique* contribution of discourse, further research will be needed. But at the very least, future studies of conceptual development aimed at documenting salient early experiences within the family should include measures of family discourse focused on the domains of interest, in addition to more traditional measures such as parental responsiveness and attentiveness.

The second issue concerns the questions raised in the introduction about the specific features of discourse that might be associated with later understanding. The associations over time that were found were comparable for each pragmatic category considered and for talk that was focused on the feelings of the child or of another. No special significance can be attributed to discourse about negative feelings from these results. That is, the results do not support the idea that particular contexts – such as calm reflective discourse or pretend – or particular emotional themes – such as negative emotions – have special developmental importance. Rather, the findings suggest that children may learn about this crucially important feature of other people in a wide variety of settings. By 36 months, those children who are discussing feeling states and their causes relatively frequently are doing so for a range of pragmatic purposes. However, some support for the significance of disputes in the development of this aspect of social understanding is found in the finding that children were more likely to be engaged in the discussion of cause of feelings when they were in dispute with others than when not in dispute – results in keeping with the arguments for the importance of social conflict in the development of social understanding. It should be noted that the dispute category employed here included not only conflict over behavior but also arguments over conflicting beliefs, ideas, and memories. Note, too, that Stein and Miller (1982) comment on their findings from an experimental study that "Argument is the one discourse type where significant conceptual change can occur."

The third issue concerns the distinction between understanding emotions and sympathetic or prosocial behavior. It is important to emphasize that the differences in understanding revealed in the Rothenberg assessment are not necessarily associated with particularly empathetic or prosocial behavior. As Shantz (1983) and Eisenberg (1986) have pointed out, skill at understanding others' feelings by no means guarantees friendly or prosocial behavior. Indeed, it is clear that a subtle understanding of what will provoke or upset another expands the possibilities for effectiveness in social conflict. A previous study indicated that success on the Rothenberg assessment was, in fact, correlated with frequent teasing and bossy assertive behavior toward the sibling during observations made at the time of the assessment of social understanding (Beardsall, 1986). In this study, an association was found between feeling-state talk during disputes and success on the Rothenberg assessment. However, because teasing behavior as well as disputes and the judgments of the Rothenberg can each entail relatively sophisticated appreciation of others' feelings, it is particularly important to exercise caution about inferring direction of causal influence. It remains unclear whether children learn about others' feelings through disputatious or teasing exchanges or whether a relatively sophisticated understanding of others contributes to the likelihood that children will become engaged in disputes.

Finally, it should be noted that in this study, discussions between children and their siblings that concerned feeling states were not frequent, and it was thus not possible to compare mother-child and sibling-child differences in discourse about feelings or to examine patterns over time that included dyadic sibling-child discourse about feelings. It could be that when children are only 3 years old, their mothers are more salient conversational partners with whom to talk about feelings – even when the talk arises out of conflict with siblings. Indeed, the children talked predominantly about their own feelings and discussed feelings most often in efforts to meet their own needs during these observations. They may have accurately deduced that their mothers were more likely to be of assistance and to be concerned with the children's own feelings than were their siblings. An important future step will be to explore whether sibling or peer influence on children's understanding of emotions is mediated through discourse about feelings at some later point in development. It may be, however that such influence is mediated – even with older children – through participation in particular kinds of social interaction – for instance, joint pretend play (see, e.g. Gottman & Parker, 1986) and through the emotional quality of the relationship between children, rather than through the discourse features studied here.

In conclusion, it is likely that individual differences in understanding others' feelings are influenced by many factors; what stands out from the results of this study is that discourse about feelings is, even with such young children, part of a pattern of interaction that shows continuity with this centrally important aspect of human development. The next step in understanding the nature of this continuity will be to examine in more detail the social processes implicated in these discourse differences.

References

Beardsall, L. (1986). *Conflict between siblings in middle childhood.* Unpublished doctoral dissertation, University of Cambridge.

Bretherton, I., Fritz, J., Zahn-Waxler, C., & Ridgeway, D. (1986). Learning to talk about emotions: a functionalist perspective. *Child Development, 57*, 529–548.

Bretherton, I., McNew, S., & Beeghly-Smith, M. (1981). Early person knowledge as expressed in gestural and verbal communication: When do infants acquire a "theory of mind"? In M. E. Lamb & L. R. Sherrod (Eds.), *Infant social cognition* (pp. 333–373). Hillsdale, NJ: Erlbaum.

Camras, L. (1989). *Maternal facial behavior and recognition of emotional expression by abused and nonabused children.* Paper presented at the biennial meeting [April] of the Society for Research in Child Development, Kansas City, MO.

Cassidy, J., & Parke, R. D. (1989). *Family expressiveness and children's social competence.* Paper presented at the biennial meeting [April] of the Society for Research in Child Development, Kansas City, MO.

Denham, S. A., & Couchoud, E. A. (1988). *Knowledge about emotions: Relations with socialization and social behavior.* Paper presented in symposium Emotion Knowledge and Emotional Development at biennial meeting [May] of the Conference on Human Development, Charleston, SC.

Denham, S. A., McKinley, M., Couchoud, E. A., & Holt, R. (1990). Emotional and behavioral predictors of peer status in young preschoolers. *Child Development, 61*, 1145–1152.

Dunn, J. (1988). *The beginnings of social understanding.* Cambridge, MA: Harvard University Press.

Dunn, J., Bretherton, I., & Munn, P. (1987). Conversations about feeling states between mothers and their young children. *Developmental Psychology, 23*, 132–139.

Dunn, J., & Dale, N. (1984). I a Daddy: 2-year-olds' collaboration in joint pretend with sibling and with mother. In I. Bretherton (Ed.), *Symbolic play: The development of social understanding* (pp. 131–158). San Diego, CA: Academic Press.

Dunn, J., & Kendrick, C. (1982). *Siblings: Love, envy and understanding.* Cambridge, MA: Harvard University Press.

Dunn, J., & Munn, P. (1985). Becoming a family member: Family conflict and the development of social understanding in the second year. *Child Development, 56*, 480–492.

—— (1987). The development of justification in disputes. *Developmental Psychology, 23*, 791–798.

Eisenberg, N. (1986). *Altruistic emotion, cognition and behavior*. Hillsdale, NJ: Erlbaum.

Gottman, J., & Parker, J. (1986). *Conversations of friends*. Cambridge: Cambridge University Press.

Harris, P. L. (1989). *Children and emotion*. Oxford: Basil Blackwell.

Hood, L., & Bloom, L. (1979). What, when and how about why: A longitudinal study of early expressions of causality. *Monographs of the Society for Research in Child Development, 44* (6, serial no. 181).

Howe, N., & Ross, H. (1990). Socialization, perspective-taking, and the sibling relationship. *Developmental Psychology, 26*, 160–165.

Huttenlocher, J., & Smiley, P. (1990). The development of the concept of person. In N. L. Stein, B. Leventhal, & T. Trabasso (Eds.), *Psychobiological approaches to emotion*. Hillsdale, NJ: Erlbaum.

Miller, P. H., & Aloise, P. A. (1989). Young children's understanding of the psychological causes of behavior: a review. *Child Development, 60*, 257–285.

Registrar General (1973). *Great Britain Summary Tables, Census 1971*. London: Her Majesty's Stationery Office.

Ridgeway, D., Waters, E., & Kuczaj, S. A. (1985). The acquisition of emotion descriptive language: Receptive and productive vocabulary norms for ages 18 months to 6 years. *Developmental Psychology, 21*, 901–908.

Rothenberg, B. (1970). Children's social sensitivity and the relationship to interpersonal competence, intrapersonal comfort and intellectual level. *Developmental Psychology, 2*, 335–350.

Schwarz, N. (1988). *Happy but mindless*. Paper presented at the 24th International Congress of Psychology, Sydney, Australia.

Shantz, C. U. (1983). Social cognition. In J. H. Flavell & E. M. Markman (Eds.), P. H. Mussen (Series Ed.), *Handbook of child psychology:* Vol. 3. *Cognitive development* (pp. 495–555). New York: Wiley.

Shantz, C. U. (1987). Conflicts between children. *Child Development, 58*, 283–305.

Shatz, M., & Gelman, R. (1973). The development of communication skills: Modifications in the speech of young children as a function of listener. *Monographs of the Society for Research in Child Development, 38* (5, serial no. 152).

Stein, N. L., & Levine, L. J. (1989a). The causal organization of emotional knowledge: a developmental study. *Cognition and Emotion, 3*, 343–378.

Stein, N. L., & Levine, L. J. (1990b). Making sense out of emotion: The representation and use of goal-structured knowledge. In N. L. Stein, B. L. Leventhal, & T. Trabasso (Eds.), *Psychological and biological approaches to emotion*. Hillsdale, NJ: Erlbaum.

Stein, N. L., & Miller, C. A. (1982). The process of thinking and reasoning in argumentative contexts: Evaluation of evidence and the resolution of conflict. In R. Glaser (Ed.), *Advances in instructional psychology*. Hillsdale, NJ: Erlbaum.

Stern, D. (1985). *The interpersonal world of the infant*. New York: Basic Books.

Tizard, B., & Hughes, M. (1985). *Young children learning*. London: Fontana.

Zahn-Waxler, C., Radke-Yarrow, M., & King, R. A. (1979). Child rearing and children's prosocial initiations towards victims of distress. *Child Development, 48*, 319–330.

CHAPTER *16*

Biological Bases of Childhood Shyness

J. Kagan, J. S. Reznick, and N. Snidman

Constitutional differences in behavior and mood have been called temperament. It is of course difficult to sort out how much of a baby's emotional state and behavior is attributable to constitutional make-up and how much to their environment, and this has made for active debate in temperament research. Findings from behavioral genetics make it clear that at least some of our emotionality is attributable to the genes (Goldsmith, 1993; Plomin, 1988).

Here we reprint some work that has been influential in how we think about the aspect of temperament called shyness or behavioral inhibition. Behavioral inhibition is when children become very frightened of new circumstances or people. Instead of being able to interact and join in with new activities, their fear is so strong that they are inhibited in activity and enjoyment. Such shyness shows considerable continuity over time. Kagan and his colleagues have found that children who were extremely shy at 2 years old were more likely to be socially avoidant at 7. The researchers identified a physiological response pattern of a high stable heart rate and greater sympathetic reactivity suggesting a lower threshold for limbic-hypothalamic arousal.

References

Goldsmith, H. H. (1993). Temperament: variability in developing emotion systems. In M. Lewis & J. M. Haviland (Eds.), *Handbook of emotions* (pp. 353–364). New York: Guilford.
Plomin, R. (1988). *Development, genetics and psychology*. Hillsdale, NJ: Erlbaum.

A child's initial reaction to unfamiliar events, especially other people, is one of the few behavioral qualities that is moderately stable over time and independent of social class and intelligence test scores. About 10 to 15 percent of healthy, 2- and 3-year-old children consistently become quiet, vigilant, and affectively subdued in such contexts for periods lasting from 5 to 30 minutes. An equal proportion is typically spontaneous, as if the distinction between familiar and unfamiliar were of minimal psychological consequence.[1] Empirical indexes of a pair of related, but not identical, constructs in adults, often called introversion and extroversion, are among the most stable and heritable in contemporary psychology.[2]

Comparative psychologists and behavioral biologists may be studying an analogous form of variation among members of a species or closely related strains. Mice, rats, cats, dogs, wolves, pigs, cows, monkeys, and even paradise fish differ intraspecifically in their initial tendency to approach or to avoid novelty.[3] Some investigators have explored the physiological correlates of these behavioral differences. For example, about 15 percent of kittens (*Felis catus*) show prolonged restraint before approaching novel objects and people and, as adults, do not attack rats. These avoidant cats, compared with a larger complementary group that does not retreat from novelty, show greater neural activity in the basomedial amygdala following exposure to a rat, as well as larger evoked potentials in the ventromedial hypothalamus following direct stimulation of the basomedial amygdala.[4] Laboratory born and reared rhesus monkeys also vary in their response to novelty. Those who are slow to explore show higher heart rates in unfamiliar settings and larger increases in plasma cortisol following separation from the mother or peers than do animals who are much less avoidant.[5] The total corpus of evidence suggests that both animals and children who consistently show an initial avoidance of or behavioral restraint to novelty display distinctive behavioral and physiological profiles early in development, implying the influence of genetic factors.

Inhibited and uninhibited children

Our laboratory has used a longitudinal design in the study of three cohorts of Caucasian children from working- and middle-class Boston homes. The first two cohorts were selected at either 21 or 31 months of age to include approximately equal numbers of children who were either consistently shy, quiet, and timid (inhibited) or consistently sociable, talkative, and affectively spontaneous (uninhibited) when exposed to unfamiliar people, procedures, and objects in unfamiliar laboratory settings. About 15 percent of a total sample of 400 children evaluated was classified as belonging to one of the two extreme groups with similar proportions of boys and girls in each group.[6]

Descriptions of procedures The children in cohort 1, selected at 21 months, were observed on two occasions with unfamiliar women and objects in several unfamiliar laboratory rooms. The major behavioral signs of inhibition coded from videotape were prolonged clinging to or remaining proximal to the mother, cessation of vocalization, and reluctance to approach or actual retreat from the unfamiliar events. The children who displayed these behaviors consistently across most incentives, as well as those who did not, were selected to form one group of 28 inhibited and another group of 30 uninhibited children.

The initial selection of children for cohort 2 at 31 months was based on behavior with an unfamiliar child of the same sex and age in the same laboratory playroom, with both mothers present, and a subsequent episode in which the child encountered an unfamiliar woman dressed in an unusual costume. The indexes of inhibition, similar to those used with cohort 1, were long latencies to play, speak, and interact with the unfamiliar child and woman, as well as long periods of time proximal to the mother. This selection process yielded 26 consistently inhibited and 23 consistently uninhibited children.

Each of these two cohorts was observed on three additional occasions. Cohort 1 was observed subsequently at 4, 5.5, and 7.5 years of age; cohort 2 at 3.5, 5.5, and 7.5 years, with about 20 percent attrition by the time of the last assessment at 7.5 years when there were 41 children in each cohort. The phenotypic display of the two temperamental tendencies changes with age because of learning and maturation. A 2-year-old will become uncertain in an unfamiliar room with unfamiliar objects, but older children require more potent incentives, especially unfamiliar children and adults. Thus, the specific laboratory procedures we used changed for the four evaluations.

The index of inhibition on the second assessment (3.5 or 4 years) was based on behavior in two, separate 40-minute laboratory play sessions with an unfamiliar child of the same sex and age with both mothers present. At 5.5 years the children in both cohorts were observed in four different unfamiliar situations. The indexes of inhibition, for each situation, were based on (i) long latencies to initiate play or interact with an unfamiliar child as well as time proximal to the mother in a laboratory playroom, (ii) spatial isolation and infrequent interaction with class-mates in the child's school setting, (iii) long latencies to talk and infrequent spontaneous comments with a female examiner who administered a 90-minute cognitive battery (including recall and recognition memory, match to sample, and discrimination of pictures), and (iv) reluctance to play with novel toys suggestive of risk in an unfamiliar laboratory room (a large black box with a hole or a beam set at an angle to the floor). The theoretically relevant variables from each situation were aggregated to form a composite index of behavioral inhibition.[7]

The index of behavioral inhibition at 7.5 years was based on two situations separated by several months. The first was a laboratory play situation involving seven to ten unfamiliar children of the same age and sex; a single unfamiliar child does not generate sufficient uncertainty in a child this old. Approximately 50 minutes was devoted to structured, competitive games and a total of 30 minutes to unstructured free-play intervals interposed between each of the games. The two variables indexing behavioral inhibition were infrequent spontaneous comments to the other children and long periods of playing or standing apart from any other child in the room. The second assessment context was an individual testing session with an unfamiliar female examiner. The two variables were latency to the sixth spontaneous comment to the examiner and the total number of spontaneous comments over the testing session. The results are similar if latency to any of the first six comments is used as the component of the index. The reliabilities between coders (correlation coefficients) for the variables quantified from video-tapes were generally above 0.90 at each age.

Preservation of behavioral differences The initial behavioral differences between inhibited and uninhibited children predicted theoretically reasonable derivatives at the older ages (the adjectives inhibited and uninhibited refer to the original classification at 21 or 31 months, unless stated otherwise). The slopes of the regression lines relating an index of inhibited behavior at one age to an index at a later age, which reflect the stability of behavior, ranged from 0.40 to 1.12 ($P < 0.01$). The standard error of the slopes ranged from 0.09 to 0.22 and the standard deviation of the values around the slope ranged from 0.45 to 0.83.[8] Each mother's rating of her child's shyness with unfamiliar people was only moderately related to the child's behavior in the laboratory (correlations between the two variables ranged from 0.3 to 0.6). Additionally, the mothers of inhibited children in both cohorts more often reported a history of excessive irritability, colic, and sleeplessness during the infant's first year.

Figure 16.1 illustrates values for children in each cohort on the two indexes of behavioral inhibition with the group of unfamiliar peers at age 7.5 – that is, the percentage of time distant from any other child during the free-play intervals and total number of spontaneous comments. More inhibited, than uninhibited, children were above the median on the first variable and below on the second ($X^2 = 7.9, P < 0.05$ for cohort 1; $X^2 = 5.2$, $P < 0.05$ for cohort 2; and $X^2 = 15.2$, $P < 0.001$ for the pooled cohorts). A frequent scene during the play sessions was a cluster of three or four children playing close to each other, often talking, and one or two children standing or playing alone one to several meters from the center of social activity. These isolated, quiet children were typically those who had been classified as inhibited 5 or 6 years earlier.[9]

After 4 years of age remaining quiet with an unfamiliar adult in an evaluative setting is an extremely sensitive sign of behavioral inhibition. The inhibited

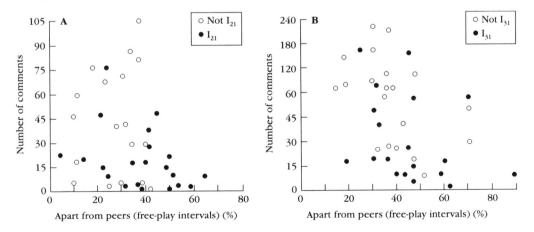

Figure 16.1. Relation between total number of spontaneous comments and the percentage of time each child was distant from a peer in a free-play situation at 7.5 years for (A) cohort 1 children selected at 21 months and (B) cohort 2 children selected at 31 months. The free-play intervals were longer for cohort 2; hence the larger number of spontaneous comments. I, inhibited; Not I, uninhibited.

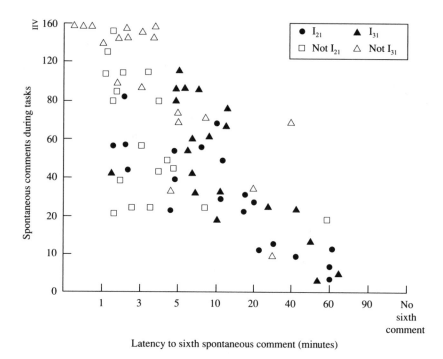

Figure 16.2. Relation between latency to the sixth spontaneous comment and total number of spontaneous comments at 7.5 years for cohort 1 children selected at 21 months and cohort 2 children selected at 31 months. I, inhibited; Not I, uninhibited.

children were much less talkative with the examiner than uninhibited children during the testing session at and 5.5 years. During the testing session with an unfamiliar female examiner at 7.5 years, 60 percent of the inhibited and 15 percent of the uninhibited children uttered their sixth spontaneous comment later in the session and, in addition, spoke less often than uninhibited children (based on median values for the two variables $X^2 = 20.9, P < 0.0001$) (figure 16.2).

The mean of the two standardized indexes of inhibited behavior from the peer play procedure (proportional amount of time distant from peers and total number of spontaneous comments) was combined with the mean of the two standardized indexes from the testing situation (latency to the sixth spontaneous comment and total number of spontaneous comments; $r = 0.40$ between the two indexes) to yield an aggregate index of inhibition for the 41 children in cohort 1 at 7.5 years. Figure 16.3 illustrates the relation between the aggregate score and the original behavioral index. The predictive relation between the indexes at 21 months and 7.5 years had a slope of 0.50 ($P < 0.001$), with a standard error of 0.09 and a standard deviation of the values around the regression line of 0.56. The comparable analysis of cohort 2 data revealed a slope of 0.5 ($P < 0.001$) between the indexes at 3.5 and 7.5 years with a standard error of 0.12 and a standard deviation of the points around the line of 0.45. Furthermore, the children in both cohorts who had the most extreme scores on the original index were most likely to have remained behaviorally consistent through 7.5 years.

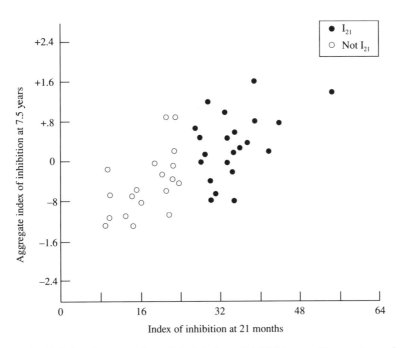

Figure 16.3. Relation between the original index of inhibition at 21 months and the aggregate index of inhibition (z score) at 7.5 years for cohort 1 children. I, inhibited; Not I, uninhibited.

An unselected cohort In a third longitudinal study, Caucasian middle-class children of both sexes were selected who were extreme on the two behavioral profiles. The children in cohort 3 were observed initially at 14 months $(n = 100)$, and again at 20 $(n = 91), 32(n = 76)$, and 48 months $(n = 77)$. The indexes of inhibition at 14 and 20 months were based on behavior with an unfamiliar examiner and with unfamiliar toys in laboratory rooms. The index of inhibition at 32 months was based on behavior in a 30-minute free-play situation with two other unfamiliar children of the same sex and age with all three mothers present. The index of inhibition at 48 months was based on behavior with an unfamiliar child of the same sex and age, with an unfamiliar examiner in a testing situation and in an unfamiliar room containing objects suggestive of risk. The original variation in inhibited behavior for the entire group at 14 months was correlated with the variation at 20 and 32 months $(r = 0.52$ and $0.44;$ $P < 0.01)$, but the indexes at 14 and 20 months did not predict differences in behavioral inhibition at 4 years of age. However, when we restricted the analysis to those children who fell at the top and bottom 20 percent of the distribution of behavioral inhibition at both 14 and 20 months (13 children in each group), the two groups showed statistically significant differences at 4 years of age $(t = 2.69, P < 0.01)$. Almost half the inhibited but 8 percent of the uninhibited group had a positive standard score on the index of inhibition at 4 years of age. This finding, together with the data from cohorts 1 and 2, implies that the constructs inhibited and uninhibited refer to qualitative categories of children. These terms do not refer to a behavioral continuum ranging from timidity to sociability in a volunteer sample of children, even though such a continuum can be observed phenotypically.

Physiology and inhibition

As noted, intraspecific variation in behavioral withdrawal to novelty in rats, cats, and monkeys is often related to physiological reactions that imply greater arousal in selected hypothalamic and limbic sites, especially the amygdala. If this relation were present in humans, inhibited children should show more activity in biological systems that originate in these sites. Three such systems are the sympathetic chain, reticular formation with its projections to skeletal muscles, and the hypothalamic-pituitary-adrenal axis.[10]

Sympathetic reactivity Five potential indexes of sympathetic reactivity include a high and minimally variable heart rate, as well as heart rate acceleration, pupillary dilation, and norepinephrine level to psychological stress and challenge. We measured each child's heart period and heart period variability under both minimally stressful baseline conditions as well as during moderately stressful cognitive tasks on every one of the four assessments. Heart period variability was the average standard deviation of the interbeat intervals during the trials of the test episodes. Mean heart period and heart period variability for a multitrial episode were based on the values for the separate trials of that episode. Although we use the terms heart rate and heart rate variability in the text, all statistical analyses were performed on the heart period values.

Mean heart rate and variability were always inversely correlated – a higher heart rate associated with lower variability – under both relaxed conditions as well as during cognitive activity (product moment correlations were between -0.6 and -0.7). Individual differences in heart rate and variability were preserved from 21 months to 7.5 years in cohort 1 ($r = 0.62, P < 0.001$ for heart rate; $r = 0.54, P < 0.001$ for variability); from 31 months to 5.5 years for cohort 2 ($r = 0.59, P < 0.001$ for heart rate and $r = 0.61, P < 0.001$ for variability). Correlations are reported because the children were not selected to be extreme on the cardiac variables and both heart rate and variability were normally distributed at all ages. Further, the index of inhibited behavior was typically associated with a higher and more stable heart rate on the early evaluations (average $r = 0.4$), but on the last assessment at 7.5 years this relation was less robust ($r = 0.3$). However, the inhibited children with the highest heart rates on the first two assessments were more likely to have remained inhibited through 7.5 years than the inhibited children who had lower heart rates earlier. We computed for each child in cohort 1 a standard score representing his or her index of inhibition and heart rate on each of the four assessments. At every age the consistently inhibited children (those with positive standard scores on the index of inhibition on each assessment) and the consistently uninhibited children had the highest and lowest heart rates, respectively (figure 16.4).

Unusual fears at 5.5 and 7.5 years (violence on television or in movies, kidnappers, or going to the bedroom alone in the evening) were most frequent

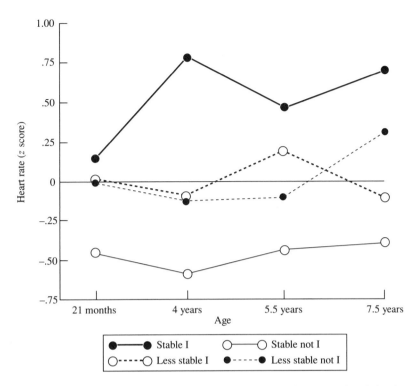

Figure 16.4. Mean heart rate (z score) for cohort 1 children at each of the four assessments (stable I refers to 12 children who were inhibited at every age; less stable I, to 10 children who were inhibited originally but were uninhibited on one or more of the later assessments; stable not I, to 12 children who were consistently uninhibited; and less stable not I, to 7 children who were classified as uninhibited originally but were inhibited on one or more of the later assessments). The standard errors of the mean for each of the four groups at the four ages averaged 0.29, 0.26 for the consistently inhibited children, and 0.34 for the consistently uninhibited children.

in inhibited children with the highest heart rates (60 percent of the group) and least frequent in uninhibited children with the lowest heart rates (no child in this group had any unusual or intense fears).

In addition, at every age inhibited children were more likely than uninhibited ones to show an increase in heart rate, about ten beats per minute, across the trials of a test or across the entire battery of cognitive tests.[11] This fact was also true for the cohort 3 children who had extreme scores on the index of inhibition at 4 years of age. The inhibited children were more likely to attain their maximal heart rate early in the testing session, usually during the first cognitive procedure following the initial baseline. We also evaluated, for the first time at 7.5 years in cohort 2 and 4 years in cohort 3, the change in heart rate when the child's posture changed from sitting to standing. Inhibited children showed a larger increase in mean heart rate (ten beats per minute) during a 60-second period than did uninhibited children, despite a slightly higher heart rate during the preceding sitting baseline. This result suggests that the inhibited children maintained a brisker sympathetic response to the drop in blood pressure that accompanies the rise to a standing position. In addition, the inhibited children in cohort 2 showed higher diastolic, but not a higher systolic, blood pressure during the testing session at 7.5 years, implying greater sympathetic tone in the vessels of the arterial tree.

Several months after the laboratory session with cohort 1 at 7.5 years we recorded the child's heart rate during one night of sleep. We eliminated the first and last hours of sleep on the assumption that sleep would be lighter during these times, and a continuous respiration record permitted elimination of epochs of active sleep. The mean quiet heart rate during sleep was 76 beats per minute, with a range of 59 to 92 beats, and there was no statistically significant relation between heart and respiration rate. The mean sleeping heart rate was correlated with heart rate obtained in the laboratory at each of the four ages ($r = 0.37, 0.40, 0.61,$ and $0.49, p < 0.05$). Although the sleep heart rate had only a low positive association with the aggregate index of inhibition at 7.5 years, two of the four components of the composite index of inhibition at 5.5 years (reluctance to play with novel toys suggestive of risk in an unfamiliar room and shy, restrained behavior with an unfamiliar peer) were associated with higher sleeping heart rates 2 years later ($r = 0.48, P < 0.01; r = 0.35, P < 0.05$).

Pupillary dilation, which is another potential index of sympathetic activity,[12] was assessed only at 5.5 years. Although both cohorts showed a reliable increase in pupil size of about 0.3 millimeter to cognitive test items (an increase of about 5 percent), the inhibited children in both cohorts had larger pupil diameters during test questions as well as during the intervals between test items [$F(1, 269) = 20.9, P < 0.1$ for test trials; $F(1, 154) = 17.3, P < 0.001$ for periods before trials; F values based on repeated measures analysis of variance].

Muscle tension   Projections from limbic structures to the skeletal muscles of the larynx and vocal cords also appear to be at higher levels of excitability in inhibited children. Increased tension in these muscles is usually accompanied by a decrease in the variability of the pitch periods of vocal utterances, which is called perturbation.[13] The increased muscle tension can be caused by discharge of the nucleus ambiguus as well as sympathetic activity that constricts arterioles serving the muscles of the larynx and vocal folds. Because the vocal cords do not maintain a steady rate as they open and close, the perturbations in the rate at which they open and close is a consequence of many factors, one of which is the degree of tension in the laryngeal muscles.[14] We measured the vocal perturbation of single-word utterances at 5.5 years in cohort 1 and 3.5 years in cohort 2. The inhibited, compared with the uninhibited, children showed a significantly greater decrease in vocal perturbation when the single words were spoken under moderate as opposed to low stress. The inhibited children also showed less variability in the fundamental frequency of all the single-word utterances spoken during the episode.[15]

Urinary norepinephrine   Norepinephrine is the primary neurotransmitter in the postganglionic synapses of the peripheral sympathetic nervous system. A urine sample collected from each child in cohort 1 at the end of the test battery at 5.5 years was tested for norepinephrine and its derivatives (normetanephrine, MHPG, and VMA) by mass fragmentography.[16] Concentrations of each compound were transformed to micrograms per gram of creatinine, and a composite index of total norepinephrine activity was computed. There was a modest correlation between this index and inhibited behavior at both 4 and 5.5 years ($r = 0.34, P < 0.05$ with the index at age 4; $r = 0.31, P < 0.05$ with the index at age 5.5 years).

Salivary cortisol In order to assess activity in the hypothalamic-pituitary-adrenal axis, samples of saliva were gathered on cohort 1 at 5.5 years when the child came to the laboratory, as well as at home on three mornings before breakfast and before the stress of the day had begun. Analysis of unbound cortisol in these saliva samples by a modification of the standard radioimmunoassy method revealed that the average cortisol level for the three morning home samples was correlated with the original index of inhibition ($r = 0.39, P < 0.05$).[17]

Aggregate of physiological variables With the exception of heart rate and heart rate variability, correlations among the remaining physiological variables were low, ranging from -0.22 to $+0.33$ with a median coefficient of $+0.10$. This phenomenon has been noted by others.[18] However, it is likely that an aggregate index of physiological activity might be more highly correlated with inhibited behavior because any single variable could be the result of a factor unrelated to the hypothetical processes mediating inhibited and uninhibited behavior. Pooling several indexes would dilute the contribution of any of these factors. For example, a child who did not belong to the inhibited category but who was highly motivated to solve the cognitive problems might show a high and minimally variable heart rate and a large pupil, but this child should show average cortisol levels and variability in the vocal perturbation index. Consider the following analogy. Body temperature, fatigue, thoracic discomfort, and pneumococci in the sputum are not highly correlated in a random sample of the population. But persons with high values on all four variables meet the criterion for a special disease category. We averaged the standard scores for eight peripheral psychophysiological variables gathered at 5.5 years on cohort 1 to create a composite index of physiological arousal (mean heart period, heart period variability, pupillary dilation during cognitive tests, total norepinephrine activity, mean cortisol level at home and in the laboratory, variability of the pitch periods of vocal utterances under cognitive stress, and the standard deviation of the fundamental frequency values of the vocal utterances). There was a substantial positive relation between this composite physiological index and the index of inhibition at every age ($r = 0.70$ with the index at 21 months and $r = 0.64$ with the index at 7.5 years of age).

Discussion

A majority of children who had been selected from a much larger sample at 1.5 or 2.5 years because they were extremely shy, quiet, and restrained in a variety of unfamiliar contexts became 7-year-olds who were quiet, cautious, and socially avoidant with peers and adults, whereas a majority of children who had been selected to be extremely sociable and affectively spontaneous were talkative and socially interactive at 7 years of age. However, the preservation of these two behavioral styles, albeit modest and different in form at the two ages, holds only for children selected originally to be extreme in their behavior. The data from cohort 3 indicate that there is no predictive relation in an unselected sample between indexes of inhibited behavior assessed during the second and fourth years. Only when we restricted the analysis to the behavioral extremes did we find preservation of the two behavioral categories as well as an association between inhibition and both heart rate acceleration to mild stress and high early morning levels of salivary cortisol.

The behavioral differences between the two groups were most consistently associated with peripheral physiological variables implying greater sympathetic reactivity among the inhibited children, especially larger cardiac accelerations to cognitive activity and to a postural change from sitting to standing. We suggest, albeit speculatively, that most of the children we call inhibited belong to a qualitatively distinct category of infants who were born with a lower threshold for limbic-hypothalamic arousal to unexpected changes in the environment or novel events that cannot be assimilated easily. This hypothesis is consonant with comparable data gathered on rhesus monkeys, the views of a number of physiologists,[19] and especially animal data implying that the amygdala is an important mediator of states which would be regarded as resembling anxiety or fear in humans.[20] Although the reasons for the lower thresholds in limbic-hypothalamic sites are unclear, and likely to be complex, tonically higher levels of central norepinephrine, greater density of receptors for norepinephrine in these areas, or both are possible contributing factors.[21] This suggestion is supported by evidence indicating a close covariation in free-moving cats between activity of the locus coeruleus, the main source of central norepinephrine, and acceleration of heart rate to the stresses of white noise and restraint.[22]

However, we suggest that the actualization of shy, quiet, timid behavior at 2 years of age requires some form of chronic environmental stress acting upon the original temperamental disposition present at birth. Some possible stressors include prolonged hospitalization, death of a parent, marital quarreling, or mental illness in a family member. These stressors were not frequent in our samples. However, in both longitudinal cohorts, two-thirds of the inhibited children were later born while two-thirds of the uninhibited children were first born. An older sibling who unexpectedly seizes a toy, teases, or yells at an infant who has a low threshold for limbic arousal might provide the chronic stress necessary to transform the temperamental quality into the profile we call behavioral inhibition. Thus, it is important to differentiate between those children and adolescents who are quiet and restrained in unfamiliar social situations because of the influence of temperamental factors and those who behave this way because of environmental experiences alone. Physiological measures might be helpful in distinguishing between these two groups. We suspect that the contemporary construct of introversion, usually applied to adults, contains both types.[23] Finally, we note that these data support Jung's claim, which Freud rejected, that temperamental factors contribute to the development of social anxiety and avoidance and to the symptoms of panic and agoraphobia that had been classified earlier in the century as components of hysteria.[24]

References and notes

1   J. Kagan, J. S. Reznick, C. Clarke, N. Snidman, C. Garcia-Coll, *Child Development, 55,* 2212 (1984); A. Thomas and S. Chess, *Temperament and development* (New York: Brunner Mazel, 1977).

2   J. J. Conley, *Journal of Personality and Social Psychology, 49,* 1266 (1985); R. Plomin, *Development, Genetics and Psychology* Hillsdale, NJ: Erlbaum, 1986); J. Kagan and H. A. Moss, *Birth to Maturity* (New York: Wiley, 1962); I. M. Marks, *Fears, Phobias and Rituals* (New York: Oxford University Press 1987).

3   D. A. Blizard, *Behavior Genetics, 11,* 469 (1981); R. T. Blanchard, K. J. Flannelly, D. C. Blanchard, *Journal of Comparative Psychology, 100,* 101 (1986); R. M. Murphey, F. A. M. Duarte, M. C. T. Penendo, *Behav. Genet. 10,* 170 (1980); K. McDonald, *J. Comp. Psychol. 97,* 99 (1983); V. Csanyi and J. Gervai, *Behav. Genet. 16,* 553 (1986); R. Dantzer and P. Mormede, *Animal stress,* G. P. Moberg, Ed. (Bethesda, MD. American Physiological Society, 1985), pp. 81–95; D. O. Cooper, Bethesda, MD:, D. E. Schmidt, R. J. Barrett, *Pharmacology, Biochemistry Behavior, 19,* 457 (1983); J. Stevenson-Hinde, R. Stillwell-Barns, M. Zunz, *Primates, 21,* 66 (1980); T. C. Schneirla, *Advances in the Study of Behavior,* D. S. Lehrman, R. A. Hinde, E. Shaw, Eds. (New York: Academic Press, 1965), pp. 1–74; J. P. Scott and J. L. Fuller, *Dog behavior: The genetic basis* (Chicago: University of Chicago Press, 1965); M. E. Goddard and R. G. Beilharz, *Behav. Genet. 15,* 69 (1985).

4   R. E. Adamec and C. Stark-Adamec, *The Limbic System,* B. K. Doane and K. E. Livingston, Eds. (New York: Raven, 1986), pp. 129–145.

5   S. J. Suomi, *Perinatal development: A psychobiological perspective,* N. A. Krasnegor, E. M. Blass, M. A. Hofer, W. P. Smotherman, Eds. (New York: Academic Press, 1987), pp. 397–420.

6   C. Garcia-Coll, J. Kagan, J. S. Reznick, *Child Development, 55,* 1005 (1984); N. Snidman, thesis, University of California, Los Angeles (1984). During the initial selection at 21 or 31 months, it was most difficult to find extremely inhibited boys.

7   J. S. Reznick et al., *Child Dev. 51,* 660 (1986).

8   Because the two groups of children in cohorts 1 and 2 were selected originally to represent behavioral extremes, the slope of the regression line, rather than the product moment correlation, is the more appropriate statistic to summarize the degree to which the children retained their relative position on the behavioral indexes of inhibition across the assessments at the different ages.

9   K. Miyake (personal communication) of the University of Hokkaido in Sapporo, Japan, who has been studying 13 children from the first week through 6 years of age, implemented this same procedure with one group of boys and one of girls. The two 6-year-olds who were the most distant from the other children in their play group had been extremely shy and fearful during the first 2 years of life while the two children who were most often proximal to a peer had been the least fearful.

10 A. S. Kling, R. L. Lloyd, K. M. Perryman, *Behavioral and Neural Biology 47,* 54 (1987); D. H. Cohen, *Limbic and autonomic nervous system research,* L. V. DiCara, Ed. (New York: Plenum, 1974), pp. 223–275; G. J. Mogenson, *Progress in psychobiology and physiological psychology,* A. N. Epstein and A. R. Morrison, Eds. (New York: Academic Press, 1987), pp. 117–170.

11 See B. Giordani, S. B. Manuck, and J. C. Farmer [*Child Dev. 52,* 533 (1981)] and J. W. Hinton and B. Craske [*Biological Psychology, 5,* 23 (1977)] for comparable findings with adult introverts and J. Kagan, J. S. Reznick, and N. Snidman [*Child Dev. 58,* 1459 (1987)] for details of the heart rate analyses.

12 J. Beatty, *Psychological Bulletin, 91*, 276 (1982); F. Richer and J. Beatty, *Psychophysiology*, *24*, 258 (1987); R. F. Stanners, M. Coulter, A. W. Sweet, P. Murphy, *Motivation and Emotion, 3*, 319 (1979).

13 K. N. Stevens and M. Hirano, *Vocal fold physiology* (Tokyo: University of Tokyo Press, 1981).

14 P. Lieberman, *Journal of the Acoustical Society of America, 33*, 597 (1961).

15 W. Coster, thesis, Harvard University, Cambridge (1986); N. Snidman, P. Lieberman, J. S. Reznick, J. Kagan, unpublished manuscript; see J. Kagan, D. R. Lapidus, and M. Moore [*Child Dev. 49*, 1005 (1978)] for evidence of a significant positive relation between frequency of crying to discrepant events in a laboratory setting at 4 and 8 months of age – a characteristic of inhibited infants – and resting electromyogram levels at 10 years of age.

16 F. Karoum, *Methods in biogenic amine research*, S. Parvez, T. Nagatsu, I. Nagatsu, H. Parvez, Eds. (Amsterdam: Elsevier, 1983), pp. 237–255.

17 R. F. Walker, *Steroid hormones in saliva*, D. B. Ferguson, Ed. (Basel: Karger, 1984), pp. 33–50; the inhibited children in cohort 2 also generated higher morning cortisol levels than uninhibited children at 5.5 and 7.5 years of age.

18 D. Kelley, C. C. Brown, J. W. Shaffer, *Psychophysiology, 6*, 429 (1970); J. Fahrenberg, F. Foerster, H. J. Schneider, W. Muller, M. Myrtek, *Psychophysiology, 23*, 323 (1986); R. M. Nesse et al., *Psychosom. Med. 47*, 320 (1985).

19 J. P. Aggleton and R. E. Passingham, *Journal of Comparative and Physiological Psychology*, *95*, 961 (1981); P. Gloor, *Limbic mechanisms*, K. E. Livingston and O. Hoznykiewicz, Eds. (New York: Plenum, 1978), pp. 189–209; M. Sarter and H. J. Markowitsch, *Behav. Neuroscience, 99*, 342, (1985); A. Tsuda and M. Tanaka, *Behavioral Neuroscience*, p. 802.

20 J. Hitchcock and M. Davis, *Behav. Neurosci. 100*, 11 (1986); D. H. Cohen, *Memory system of the brain*, N. M. Weinberger, J. L. McGaugh, G. Lynch, Eds. (New York: Guilford, 1985), pp. 27–48; L. T. Dunn and B. J. Everitt, *Behav. Neurosci. 102*, 3 (1988).

21 G. Aston-Jones and F. E. Bloom, *J. Neurosci. 1*, 887 (1981); A. Bandura et al., *Journal of Consulting and Clinical Psychology, 53*, 406 (1985); M. F. Reiser, *Mind, brain, body* (New York, Basic Books, 1984); D. S. Charney and D. E. Redmond, *Neuropharmacology, 22*, 1531 (1983); D. B. Cubicciotti, S. P. Mendoza, W. A. Mason, E. N. Sassenrath, *J. Comp. Psychol. 100*, 385 (1986).

22 E. D. Abercrombie and B. L. Jacobs, *Journal of Neuroscience, 7*, 2837 (1987).

23 H. J. Eysenck, *Personality, genetics and behavior* (New York: Praeger, 1982).

24 C. J. Jung, *Psychological types* (New York: Harcourt Brace, 1924).

CHAPTER *17*

Moving against the World

A. Caspi, G. H. Elder, and D. J. Bem

There has been a great deal of interest in psychology in the stability of people's personalities over time and across situations. Our great novels deal with the formation of character. How did this person come to be how we see them? At the center of character are emotional responses: What are the person's goals, where have those come from, how does the person react when those goals are thwarted?

In Joan Brady's Theory of War *the main character was brought up as a white slave. He was brutalized and humiliated as a child. As an adult he was cold and ruthless. His long-term goal was retaliation, not only towards those who caused his childhood trauma, but towards others with whom he came in contact. We see the trajectory of a life in which one event builds upon another. Along the way there are moments of affection and hope that might set him on a new trajectory. The emotional habits of a life, however, act as a magnet; often it is difficult to pull away to construct a different life around alternative life goals or emotional scripts.*

Caspi, Elder, and Bem have managed to capture these continuities quantitatively. The continuities have an emotional flavor. They talk about two kinds of continuity. One is continuity of an emotional state within the person: a tendency to anger. The second is the way in which people's temperaments constrain their environments. We make worlds for ourselves. These worlds then have an effect on our moods and feed back into those emotional states, so that they can actually become more stable with time as we construct environments that reinforce our more habitual emotions. Caspi and his colleagues have shown in this selection that such effects last into adulthood. The long-lasting effects of shyness have been examined in another paper (Caspi, Elder, & Bem, 1988). Quinton and others (1993) have also described how particular patterns of behavior can result in accumulation of risk to the individual over time.

References

Brady, J. (1994). *Theory of war*. London: Abacus.

Caspi, A., Elder, G. H., & Bem, D. J. (1988). Moving away from the world: life-course patterns of shy children. *Developmental Psychology, 24*, 824–831.

Quinton, D., Pickles, A., Maughan, B., & Rutter, M. (1993). Partners, Peers and pathways: Assortative pairing and continuities in conduct disorder. *Development and Psychopathology, 5*, 763–783.

The need to delay gratification, control impulses, and modulate emotional expression is the earliest and most ubiquitous demand that society places on the developing child, and success at many life tasks depends critically on the individual's mastery of such ego control. In this article, we looked back at the life histories of children who were failing to achieve such mastery, who, at age 10, were still reacting to childhood frustration and adult authority with explosive temper tantrums. We sought to discover whether such ill-tempered children become ill-tempered adults and, if they do, what the causes and consequences of such continuity are.

The continuity of maladaptive behavior has long been recognized as a challenge to psychological theory. If behavior is largely sustained by its consequences, then adaptive behaviors should show continuity almost by definition. (Research confirms that it is the adaptive or "ego resilient" individual whose personality displays the strongest continuity across the life course [Block, 1971].) But why should maladaptive behaviors persist? What are the processes that sustain them across time and circumstance?

These are ancient and enduring questions, but we believe that the recent emphasis in both personality and developmental psychology on the interaction between the person and the environment can provide a fresh perspective on them. In particular, we should like to focus on two of the many meanings of *interaction* that abound in the contemporary literature of interactional psychology (e.g. Magnusson & Endler, 1977). One of these meanings refers to interactions between dispositions of the person and characteristics of the environment. We are interested here in the special case in which the individual's dispositions systematically select him or her into particular environments, environments that, in turn, might reinforce and sustain those dispositions (e.g. Scarr & McCartney, 1983; Wachtel, 1977b). For example, when extraverts preferentially seek out social situations they thereby select themselves into environments that further nourish and sustain their sociability.

Maladaptive behaviors can similarly select individuals into environments, albeit more coercively. The ill-tempered boy who drops out of school may thereby limit his future career opportunities and select himself into frustrating life circumstances that further evoke a pattern of striking out explosively against the world. His maladaptive behaviors increasingly channel him into environments that perpetuate those behaviors; they are sustained by the progressive accumulation of their own consequences. We shall call continuity of this kind *cumulative continuity*.

A second meaning of interaction refers to the reciprocal, dynamic transaction between the person and the environment: The person acts, the environment reacts, and the person reacts back. This process provides another potential mechanism for sustaining maladaptive behaviors. For example, Patterson's work with aggressive boys has shown in elegant detail how family interactions can create and sustain destructive and aversive patterns of behavior (Patterson, 1982). By extension, we suggest that a child whose temper tantrums coerce others into providing short-term payoffs in the immediate situation may thereby learn a behavioral style that continues to "work" in similar ways in later years. The immediate reinforcement short-circuits the learning of more controlled interactional styles that might have greater adaptability in the long run.

In this analysis, we thus concur with Wachtel (1977a) and others before him (e.g. Cottrell, 1969; Sullivan, 1953) who have argued that it is not so much a personality trait or a psychoanalytic-like residue of early childhood that is maintained across time, but an interactional style that evokes reciprocal, maintaining responses from others. Accordingly, we shall call continuity of this kind *interactional continuity*.

In general, then, we propose that long-term continuities of personality through the life course are to be found in interactional styles that are sustained by the progressive accumulation of their own consequences over time (cumulative continuity) or by their contemporary consequences in reciprocal social interaction (interactional continuity) or by both.

This kind of interactional analysis also suggests the kinds of situations that will later evoke particular behavioral styles. For example, the explosive, undercontrolled interactional style that appears as temper tantrums in childhood may later manifest itself as ill-tempered, undercontrolled irritability when the individual again confronts frustration or controlling authority (e.g. in school, the armed services, or low-level jobs). In addition, such a style may manifest itself again in life situations that require frequent negotiation of interpersonal conflicts (e.g. in marriage or child rearing).

Accordingly, we have organized our subjects' life-course trajectories in terms of achievement patterns (in education, military, and work settings), marital careers, and parenting. These phenotypically diverse situations are all characterized by demands that may elicit previously established relational styles. Each requires the individual to delay gratification, control impulses, or modulate emotional expression in ways he or she could not manage in late childhood.

Method

Subjects

Data for this study were obtained from the archives of the Institute of Human Development (IHD) at the University of California, Berkeley. The subjects are members of the Berkeley Guidance Study (Eichorn, 1981), a study initiated in 1928 with every third birth in the city of Berkeley over a period of 18 months. The original sample included an intensively studied group of 113 subjects and a less intensively studied group of 101 subjects matched on social and economic characteristics. Both samples are combined in our study.

Most of the subjects came from white, Protestant, native-born families. Slightly more than 60 percent were born into middle-class homes.

The original sample contained 102 boys, of whom a maximum of 87 have been followed up into adulthood. There are no significant differences between those who were followed up and those who were not followed up in childhood temper tantrums ($t < 1$), adolescent measures of intelligence ($t < 1$), or family social class at the time of their births ($t = 1.23$, *ns*). Respondents were slightly better educated than nonrespondents, however ($t = 1.77, p = .08$).

Of the 112 girls in the sample, a maximum of 95 have been followed up into adulthood. There are no significant differences between those who were followed up and those who were not followed up in childhood temper tantrums ($t < 1$). Respondents did, however, score significantly higher than nonrespondents on adolescent measures of intelligence ($t = 3.84, p < .001$) and social class at the time of their births ($t = 2.99, p < .01$).

Temper tantrums

Childhood data on the Berkeley subjects were obtained from clinical interviews with their mothers and subsequently organized into ratings on 5-point behavior scales (see Macfarlane, 1938; Macfarlane, Allen, & Honzik, 1954). We have used two of these scales in our study: severity of temper tantrums and frequency of temper tantrums. Severe tantrums involved "biting, kicking, striking, and throwing things" as well as verbal explosions such as "swearing, screaming, and shouting accompanied by marked emotional reactions... anger completely dominated behavior." Tantrum frequency ranged from one per month to several times per day. For the analyses presented here, we have combined these two ratings into a single 5-point scale averaged across ages 8, 9, and 10 (1936–1938), designating any child with a score of 3 or above as having had a history of childhood temper tantrums. In all, 38% of the boys and 29% of the girls were so classified.

Adult assessment

The Berkeley subjects were interviewed when they were about 30 years of age (1960) and again when they were about 40 (1968–1971). These interviews provide a detailed record of each subject's education, work, marriage, and parenthood. In addition, at least two professional clinicians read each interview from the 1960 follow-up and provided a Q-sort description of the subject using the 100-item California Q-Set (Block, 1971). Additional information on marital and parenting roles was obtained from interviews conducted in 1970 with subjects' spouses and any of their children between the ages of 14 and 19.

Results and discussion

Male subjects

Do ill-tempered boys become ill-tempered men? The answer is yes. Correlations between the temper-tantrum scores in late childhood and the Q-sort ratings of judges 20 years later reveal that ill-tempered boys are later described as significantly more undercontrolled ($r = .45, p < .001$), irritable ($r = .27, p < .05$), and moody ($r = .29, p < .05$) than their even-tempered peers. Other Q-sort items reflect some of the occupational correlates described later: These men are also described as significantly less ambitious ($r = -.37, p < .05$), productive ($r = -.38, p < .01$), and dependable ($r = -.38, p < .01$) than their even-tempered peers.

Adult achievement   The Berkeley men reached the age of majority during the late 1940s, a period of significant social change in American life. A new middle class was emerging from a new white-collar workplace in which interpersonal skills often replaced technical or clerical skills as a requirement for success and advancement in institutional roles (Mills, 1951): "The child who is to be trained for the intricate human relations of the bureaucracy...must learn to be a 'nice guy' – affable, unthreatening, responsible, competent, adaptive" (Miller & Swanson, 1958: 202–203). An explosive, undercontrolled style would seem particularly ill-suited to this new world and might well have had the most severe implications for boys from middle-class origins, boys who were in the position to take first advantage of the new societal trends.

Some of these implications can be seen in tables 17.1, 17.2, and 17.3, which provide educational and occupational data for men with and without a history of childhood tantrums, stratified by their social class of origin.

The most striking finding across the three time periods reflected in these tables is the progressive deterioration of socioeconomic status for ill-tempered boys from the middle class. Thus, in addition to the expected effect of class origins on educational attainment, Table 17.1 shows that ill-tempered boys were somewhat more likely to lose out in formal education than their even-tempered peers, $F(1, 86) = 3.24, p = .07$. By the time they enter the labor force (table 17.2) their childhood tantrums become as strong a predictor of occupational status, $F(1, 81) = 11.07, p < .001$, as their social class, $F(1, 81) = 11.24, p < .001$. Although the interaction effect does not attain significance, the means show that men from the middle class with a history of childhood tantrums resemble men from the working class more than they do their even-tempered middle-class counterparts. By mid-life (table 17.3), ill-tempered boys from the middle class have become indistinguishable from their working-class counterparts; this is reflected in

Table 17.1.   Educational attainment of male subjects by childhood temper tantrums and social class origins

	Class origin		
Temper tantrum rating	Middle class	Working class	M
Low	7.03	5.43	6.35
High	6.38	5.07	5.83
Mean	6.77	5.29	

Note: 1 = Less than 7th grade; 5 = high school diploma; 8 = professional degree. For tantrums, $F(1, 86) = 3.24, p = .07$; for class, $F(1, 86) = 25.61, p < .001$; and for Tantrums × Class, $F(1, 86) < 1$.

Table 17.2. Occupational status of male subjects' first job following completion of education by childhood temper tantrums and social class origins

Temper tantrum rating	Class origin		M
	Middle class	Working class	
Low	5.48	3.95	4.84
High	3.95	3.00	3.54
Mean	4.86	3.56	

Note. 1 = unskilled employee; 7 = higher executive. For tantrums, $F(1, 81) = 11.07, p < .001$; for class, $F(1, 81) = 11.24, p < .001$; and for Tantrums × Class, $F(1, 81) < 1$.

Table 17.3. Mid-life (age 40) occupational status of male subjects by childhood temper tantrums and social class origins

Temper tantrum rating	Class origin		M
	Middle class	Working class	
Low	5.96	4.40	5.31
High	4.94	4.92	4.93
Mean	5.59	4.59	

Note. 1 = unskilled employee; 7 = higher executive. For tantrums, $F(1, 75) = 1.43, p = .24$; for class, $F(1, 75) = 10.64, p < .01$; and for Tantrums × Class, $F(1, 75) = 5.99, p < .05$.

the means and the significant interaction between childhood tantrums and class origins, $F(1, 75) = 5.99, p < .05$.

The downward mobility of these ill-tempered boys from the middle class is further confirmed by a comparison of their occupational status at age 40 with that of their fathers at a comparable age (1938–1939). A majority of them (53%) experienced downward mobility compared with only 28% of their even-tempered, middle-class peers, $\tau_b = .41, p < .001$. Other research has shown that the reverse process also takes place: Working-class boys who adopt the middle-class standard of ego control achieve upward occupational mobility (Haan, 1964; Snarey & Vaillant, 1985).

But what about the ill-tempered working-class boys in our study? Because of the strong effect of social class no additional debilitating effects of temper tantrums could be discerned for them in our analysis of occupational attainment. As it happens, however, history performed a control experiment for us by assigning nearly 70% of the Berkeley men to military service, mostly during the Korean War. And here we find that childhood tantrums predict equally well for both social classes. In particular, men with a childhood history of tantrums achieved significantly lower military rank at the time of their discharge than their even-tempered peers ($r = -.33, p < .05$), a relationship that obtains for men from both middle-class ($r = -.36, p < .05$) and working-class backgrounds ($r = -.32, p < .05$), and remains unaltered when controlled for adolescent IQ ($r = -.34, p < .05$).

Military service is also of conceptual interest here because it imposes the kind of frustration and controlling authority that probably provoked tantrums in the childhood years. As we proposed in the introduction, continuities in personality are most likely to appear in later life if and when circumstances re-create environments with similar interactional properties. Like military service, most low-status jobs are characterized by a low degree of autonomy and a high degree of supervision by authority (Kohn & Schooler, 1983), suggesting that the occupational consequences of an explosive interactional style should be especially marked for men in such jobs.

To test this hypothesis, we first examined each subject's work history from ages 18 to 40, calculating the number of months he was unemployed, the number of jobs held, the number of employers served, and the number of career switches made between functionally unrelated lines of work. These were converted to z scores and averaged into a single index of erratic work history. The sample was then divided into men holding high-status jobs (I and II on the Hollingshead index) and those holding low-status jobs (III–V). Table 17.4 displays the results.

As table 17.4 shows, there is a significant effect of childhood tantrums, $F(1, 70) = 16.97$, $p < .001$, and a near-significant effect of job status, $F(1, 70) = 3.67$, $p = .06$ on the erratic quality of men's work histories. But most important, there is a significant interaction effect between these variables, $F(1, 70) = 4.47$, $p < .05$. Men who had a history of childhood temper tantrums and who also held low-status jobs were more prone to erratic work lives than the remaining three groups, $t = 4.64$, $p < .001$. Moreover, regression analyses reveal that both the main effect of temper tantrums and the interaction effect between tantrums and job status remain significant when controlled for class origin, educational level, and adolescent IQ.

Parallel analyses of the components of this composite index yield similar results. Men with a history of childhood tantrums were likely to experience more unemployment, to hold more jobs, to change employers more often, and to suffer a greater number of breaks in their line of work than their even-tempered peers ($ps < .05$). Moreover, they are less satisfied with their careers, $r = -.37$, $p < .05$. Of particular pertinence to our conceptual analysis is the finding that these men are dissatisfied with the nature of supervision on the job, $r = -.28$, $p < .05$.

Table 17.4. Erratic work life of male subjects by childhood temper tantrums and adult job status

| Temper tantrum rating | Adult job status | | M |
	Low status	High status	
Low	−.18	−.23	−.21
High	.67	.05	.38
Mean	.15	−.17	

Note: The values are Z-scores from the erratic work-life index. For tantrums, $F(1, 70) = 16.97$, $p < .001$; for job status, $F(1, 70) = 3.67$, $p = .06$; for Tantrums × Job Status, $F(1, 70) = 4.47$, $p < .05$.

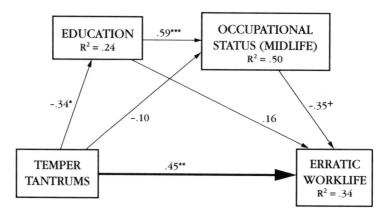

Figure 17.1 The effect of temper tantrums on occupational attainment and erratic work lives of men from middle-class origins. (IQ [Wechsler-Bellevue, age 18] is included as an exogenous variable in estimating this model. The correlation between IQ and temper tantrums is $-.09$. $\dagger p < .10$; $*p < .05$; $**p < .01$; $***p < .001$.)

These two indices of dissatisfaction are nonsignificantly higher for men in low-status jobs, $r = -.49$, $p < .05$, and $r = -.39$, $p < .10$, respectively.

Mechanisms of continuity   In the introduction we proposed that continuities in maladaptive behaviors across the life course may rest upon two mechanisms. First, the cumulative consequences of such behaviors can increasingly channel the individual into frustrating environments that provoke further maladaptive responding (cumulative continuity). Second, maladaptive behaviors may reflect an interactional style carried through life that evokes reciprocal, maintaining responses from others in social interaction (interactional continuity). Using the findings already reported on men with middle-class origins, the path analysis in figure 17.1 reveals evidence for both kinds of continuity.

Cumulative continuity is nicely illustrated by the effect of childhood tantrums on occupational status at mid-life: A history of childhood tantrums is as good a predictor of educational attainment as IQ ($\beta_{tantrums} = -.34$; $\beta_{IQ} = .32$; the correlation between childhood tantrums and IQ is $-.09$). In turn, educational attainment strongly predicts occupational status ($\beta = .59$). There is, however, no direct effect of temper tantrums on occupational status ($\beta = .10$). In other words, middle-class boys with a history of childhood tantrums arrive at lower occupational status at mid-life because they truncated their formal education earlier, not because they continue to carry an ill-tempered interactional style. Further cumulative continuity is seen in the subsequent link between occupational status and an erratic work life ($\beta = -.35$).

Interactional continuity is implied by the strong direct link between tantrums and an erratic work life ($\beta = -.45$). Men with a childhood history of tantrums appear to carry this interactional style with them through life, where it gets them into trouble in the world of work, particularly, as we saw earlier, in low-status jobs.

Marriage and parenthood   A history of childhood tantrums also affects the domestic sphere. Men with such a history were significantly less likely to have an intact first marriage at mid-life (age 40) by better than a 2:1 ratio: Almost half (46.4%) of these men had divorced, whereas only 22.2% of the men without such a history had done so ($\tau_b = -.25, p = .02$).

Information on parenting was obtained from the 1970 interviews with both spouses and children. Spouses rated the overall quality of the subject's parenting on a 5-point scale. From the children's interviews, an index of ill-tempered parenting was calculated by combining two items: One summarized the child's perception of how well-tempered the parent was, ranging from *exceptionally good-tempered* to *usually bad-tempered*. The other summarized the child's perception of the parent's self-control, ranging from *no evidence of parental loss of control* to *parent shows widespread loss of control – evidence of screaming or crying in front of child, physical abuse* (see Elder, Caspi, & Downey, 1986).

Neither the spouse ($r = .14$) nor the child index ($r = .08$) reveals a significant direct effect of childhood tantrums on parenting behavior for the male subjects. As we have seen, however, nearly half of the men with a history of childhood tantrums were no longer in their first marriages at the time of these interviews. It may be that their parenting is not harsh or ill-tempered, but remote or virtually nonexistent. However, to the extent that men with a history of childhood tantrums did become ill-tempered fathers, this relation is expressed through their work problems. A path analysis revealed this indirect link: A history of childhood tantrums was significantly related to an erratic work life ($\beta = .35$, $p < .05$), which was, in turn, significantly related to the spouses' report of inadequate parenting ($\beta = .36$, $p < .05$). (These path coefficients are corrected for social class and educational level.) Once again, we see evidence of cumulative continuity.

Female subjects

Do ill-tempered girls become ill-tempered women? If they do, it is not apparent from the interviews. None of the relevant Q-sort items in adulthood correlates with a history of childhood temper tantrums. The subjects' husbands and children, however, think otherwise.

Adult achievement   Analyses of women's achievement patterns (education, occupational attainment, worklives) do not show the significant connections between childhood temper tantrums and life disorganization that we found for men. Although a large majority of the women were employed at some point in their lives, there was little variation in their occupational status compared with the men. Over two-thirds of the women who were employed held clerical, sales, or technical jobs. A third stopped working following marriage or the birth of their first child, others returned to work after an extended period of homemaking, and others alternated between employment and homemaking. Thus, the key elements of adult achievement assessed for men were less applicable to the women in this historical period.

Table 17.5. Occupational status of female subjects' husbands at time of marriage by childhood temper tantrums and social class origins

| Temper tantrum rating | Class origin | | M |
	Middle class	Working class	
Low	5.50	4.00	5.00
High	4.88	2.43	4.17
Mean	5.32	3.59	

Note. 1 = unskilled employee; 7 = higher executive. For tantrums, $F(1, 80) = 5.76, p < .05$; for class, $F(1, 80) = 23.15, p < .001$; and for Class × Tantrums, $F(1, 79) = 1.35, p = .25$.

Although it is not possible to examine the direct effects of childhood temper tantrums on women's achievements, it is possible to trace the implications of this behavioral style on women's status achievements through their husbands' occupational status. This is shown in table 17.5 as a function of the women's own history of childhood tantrums and class of origin. As we see, there is both the expected effect of class origins, $F(1, 80) = 23.15, p < .0001$, and also a significant effect of childhood tantrums, $F(1, 80) = 5.76, p < .05$. Women with a history of childhood tantrums fared less well than their even-tempered peers in the marriage market. (Regression analysis reveals that the effect of tantrums remains significant when controlled for the woman's class origins, her educational attainment, and her adolescent IQ.) A similar analysis performed on the husbands' occupational status later in mid-life yields virtually identical results. The effect of class origins remains significant, $F(1, 71) = 11.96, p < .001$, as does the effect of childhood tantrums, $F(1, 71) = 4.11, p < .05$.

The downward mobility of ill-tempered girls is further confirmed by a comparison of their husbands' occupational status at mid-life with that of the girls' fathers at a comparable age (1938–1939). We find that 40% of women with childhood tantrums married down compared with only 24% of their even tempered peers, $\tau_b = .16, p = .09$.

Marriage and parenthood As we have seen, insufficient self-control in childhood consigned women to marriages "below their station." It also contributed to the deterioration of these relationships. Over a quarter (26.1%) of the women with a history of tantrums had divorced by mid-life compared with only 12.1% of women without such a history ($\tau_b = -.17, p = .06$). Moreover, in those cases where the marital relationship had not dissolved by mid-life, husbands of women with a history of childhood tantrums report more marital conflicts, $t(40) = 1.90, p = .06$, and were more dissatisfied with their marriages than husbands of women without such a history, $t(40) = 1.85, p = .07$.

As adults, women with a history of childhood tantrums became ill-tempered parents as well. The two parenting indexes derived from the 1970 interviews show that they are perceived by both their husbands and their children as less adequate, more ill-tempered mothers than women with no history of childhood tantrums (both $rs = .34, ps < .05$). Indeed, in our data a history of childhood tantrums is the best predictor of women's ill-tempered parenting. Thus, ill-tempered girls do become ill-tempered women.

General discussion

We have sought in this study to discover whether ill-tempered children become ill-tempered adults. They do. Children with a stable pattern of temper tantrums in late childhood experience difficulties across many life tasks. The early tendency toward explosive, undercontrolled behavior was evoked in new roles and settings, especially those involving subordination (in educational, military, and work settings) and in situations that required negotiating interpersonal conflicts (such as marriage and parenting). Ill-tempered boys experienced downward mobility and problems in the adult domain most central to men's lives, work. Ill-tempered girls experienced comparable downward mobility through marriage and did poorly in the role traditionally most salient to women's lives, parenting. Ill-tempered children of both sexes were likely to divorce and to have conflict-laden marriages.

The specific findings from this study must, of course, be viewed in cultural and historical perspective. For example, recent sex role changes in our society will probably cause the life-course consequences of childhood temper tantrums to become more similar for men and women in the future. Particular developmental patterns depend not only on the individual's pattern of approach and response (what Bronson, 1966, has aptly termed central orientations), but also on the structure of the environment in any given historical period. But, although social change may produce change in particular manifestations of a disposition in the life course, we can still hope to abstract the general principles of personality functioning that produce these manifestations.

Thus, we have suggested not only that early personality can shape the life course, but that long-term continuities of personality are to be found in interactional styles that are sustained both by the progressive accumulation of their own consequences (cumulative continuity) and by evoking maintaining responses from others during reciprocal social interaction (interactional continuity).

References

Block, J. (1971). *Lives through time*. Berkeley, CA: Bancroft.
Bronson, W. C. (1966). Central orientations: a study of behavior organization from childhood to adolescence. *Child Development, 37*, 125–155.
Cottrell, L. S. (1969). Interpersonal interaction and the development of the self. In D. A. Goslin (Ed.), *Handbook of socialization theory and research*. Chicago: Rand McNally.
Eichorn, D. H. (1981). Samples and procedures. In D. H. Eichorn, J. A. Clausen, N. Haan, M. P. Honzik, & P. H. Mussen (Eds.), *Present and past in middle life*. New York: Academic Press.
Elder, G. H., Jr., Caspi, A., & Downey, G., (1986). Problem behavior and family relationships: Life course and intergenerational themes. In A. Sorensen, F. Weinert, & L. Sherrod (Eds.), *Human development and the life course: Multidisciplinary perspectives*. Hillsdale, NJ: Erlbaum.

Haan, N. (1964). The relationship of ego functioning and intelligence to social status and social mobility. *Journal of Abnormal and Social Psychology, 69*, 594–605.

Kohn, M. L., & Schooler, C. (1983). *Work and personality: An inquiry into social stratification.* Norwood, NJ: Ablex.

Macfarlane, J. W. (1938). Studies in child guidance: 1. Methodology of data collection and organization. *Monographs of the Society for Research in Child Development, 3* (6, serial no. 19).

Macfarlane, J. W., Allen, L., & Honzik, M. P. (1954). *A developmental study of the behavioral problems of children between twenty-one months and fourteen years.* Berkeley: University of California Press.

Magnusson, D., & Endler, N. S. (1977). Interactional psychology: present status and future prospects. In D. Magnusson & N. S. Endler (Eds.), *Personality at the crossroads: Current issues in interactional psychology.* Hillsdale, NJ: Erlbaum.

Miller, D. R., & Swanson, G. E. (1958). *The changing American parent.* New York: Wiley.

Mills, C. W. (1951). *White collar.* New York: Oxford University Press.

Patterson, G. R. (1982). *Coercive family process.* Eugene, OR: Castallia.

Scarr, S., & McCartney, K. (1983). How people make their own environments: A theory of genotype-environment correlations. *Child Development, 40*, 424–435.

Snarey, J. R., & Vaillant, G. E. (1985). How lower and working class youth become middle-class adults: the association between ego defense mechanisms and upward social mobility. *Child Development, 56*, 899–910.

Sullivan, H. S. (1953). *The interpersonal theory of psychiatry.* New York: Norton.

Wachtel, P. L. (1977a). *Psychoanalysis and behavior therapy.* New York: Basic Books.

Wachtel, P. L. (1977b). Interaction cycles, unconscious processes, and the person-situation issue. In D. Magnusson & N. S. Endler (Eds.), *Personality at the crossroads: Current issues in interactional psychology.* Hillsdale, NJ: Erlbaum.

CHAPTER *18*

Script Theory: Differential Magnification of Affects

S. S. Tomkins

In the recent history of research on emotions, the work of Tomkins plays two important roles. First, it provides hypotheses about the relation of components of emotion to each other. Tomkins's hypothesis is that the components – facial expression, physiology, and feeling – come as packages. If you start up one component it will tend to entrain the others. Principal among the components are certain facial expressions which can start up a specific emotional feeling with its distinctive physiology (see, for instance, Ekman, Levenson, & Friesen, 1983). As well as the hypothesis of emotion-components each provoking each other by feedback, there is also the idea that as the package snowballs, it becomes amplified, and it is the amplification of emotions that gives life its power.

The second important role of Tomkins involves his idea of scripts. Scripts are emotional habits. Here Tomkins talks about how they are started, sustained, and become amplified. This selection includes some of Tomkins's discussion of how scripts start in childhood. They form important structures in development, based on making a characteristic and somewhat stereotyped kind of appraisal to a wide range of events, and generating amplified outline strategies for coping with such events.

Tomkins (e.g. 1995, in the chapter on script theory) describes some recognizable scripts. In commitment scripts a person limits what is possible by committing him- or herself to marriage, to a certain career, to a creed, to a nation ... Such scripts involve conforming to some social aspects and shunning others. They may arise by identification with admired people, or by avoiding something that seemed terrible in early life. Or consider affect management scripts that aim to control negative emotions: They might involve cigarettes, alcohol, travel, sex, TV ... aiming to reduce negative feelings, and also avoiding risk. So, like an emotion itself, an emotional script can amplify an emotional response, binding together the emotion and the circumstance in which it arises into a package over which there ceases to be much easy conscious control.

References

Ekman, P., Levenson, R. W., & Friesen, W. V. (1983). Autonomic nervous system activity distinguishes among emotions. *Science, 221,* 1208–1210.

Tomkins, S. S. (1962). *Affect, imagery, consciousness.* 4 vols New York: Springer.

——(1995). *Exploring affect: The selected writings of Sylvan S. Tomkins* (Ed. E. V. Demos). New York: Cambridge University Press.

The theory of affect I first presented at the Fourteenth International Congress of Psychology at Montreal, in 1954, and later expanded in *Affect, Imagery, Consciousness* in 1962, has since been modified in four essential ways. First, the theory of affect as amplification I now specify as analogic amplification. Second, I believe now that it is the skin of the face, rather than its musculature, which is the major mechanism of analogic amplification. Third, a substantial quantity of the affect we experience as adults is pseudo, backed-up affect. Fourth, affect amplifies not only its own activator, but also the response to both that activator and to itself.

I view affect as the primary innate biological motivating mechanism, more urgent than drive deprivation and pleasure and more urgent even than physical pain. That this is so is not obvious, but it is readily demonstrated. Consider that almost any interference with breathing will immediately arouse the most desperate gasping for breath. Consider the drivenness of the tumescent, erect male. Consider the urgency of desperate hunger. These are the intractable driven states that prompted the answer to the question "What do human beings really want?" to be "The human animal is driven to breathe, to sex, to drink, and to eat." And yet this apparent urgency proves to be an illusion. It is *not* an illusion that one must have air, water, food to maintain oneself and sex to reproduce oneself. What *is* illusory is the biological and psychological source of the apparent urgency of the desperate quality of the hunger, air, and sex drives. Consider these drive states more closely. When someone puts his hand over my mouth and nose, I become terrified. But this panic, this terror, is in no way a part of the drive mechanism. I can be terrified at the possibility of losing my job, or of developing cancer, or at the possibility of the loss of my beloved. Fear or terror is an innate affect which can be triggered by a wide variety of circumstances. Not having enough air to breathe is one of many such circumstances. But if the rate of anoxic deprivation becomes slower, as, for example, in the case of wartime pilots who refused to wear oxygen masks at 30,000 feet, then there develops not a panic, but a euphoric state; and some of these men met their deaths with smiles on their lips. The smile is the affect of enjoyment, in no way specific to slow anoxic deprivation.

Consider more closely the tumescent male with an erection. He is sexually excited, we say. He is indeed excited, but no one has ever observed an excited penis. It is a man who is excited and who breathes hard, not in the penis, but in the chest, the face, in the nose and nostrils. Such excitement is in no way peculiarly sexual. The same excitement can be experienced, without the benefit of an erection, to mathematics – beauty bare – to poetry, to a rise in the stock market. Instead of these representing sublimations of sexuality, it is rather that sexuality, in order to become possible, must borrow its potency from the affect of excitement. The drive must be assisted by affect as an *amplifier* if it is to work at all. Freud, better than anyone else, knew that the blind, pushy, imperious Id was the most fragile of impulses, readily disrupted by fear, by shame, by rage, by boredom. At the first sign of affect *other* than excitement, there is impotence and frigidity. The penis proves to be a paper tiger in the absence of appropriate affective amplification.

The affect system is therefore the primary motivational system because without its amplification, nothing else matters – and with its amplification, anything else *can* matter. It thus combines *urgency* and *generality*. It lends its power to memory, to perception, to thought, and to action no less than to the drives.

This theory of affect as amplification was flawed by a serious ambiguity. I had unwittingly assumed that in both electronic amplification and affective amplification there was an increase in gain of the signal. If that were the case, what was amplified would remain essentially the same except that it would become louder. But affects are separate mechanisms, involving bodily responses quite distinct from the other bodily responses they are presumed to amplify.

How can one response of our body amplify another response? It does this by being similar to that response – but also different. It is an analog amplifier. The affect mechanism is like the pain mechanism in this respect. If we cut our hand, saw it bleeding, but had no innate pain receptors, we would know we had done something which needed repair, but there would be no urgency to it. Like our automobile which needs a tune-up, we might well let it go until next week when we had more time. But the pain mechanism, like the affect mechanism, so amplifies our awareness of the injury which activates it that we are forced to be concerned, and concerned immediately. The biological utility of such analogic amplification is self-evident. The injury, as such, in the absence of pain, simply does not hurt. The pain receptors have evolved to make us hurt and care about injury and disease. Pain is an analog of injury in its inherent similarity. Contrast pain with an orgasm, as a possible analog. If instead of pain, we always had an orgasm to injury, we would be biologically destined to bleed to death. Affect receptors are no less compelling. Our hair stands on end, and we sweat in terror. Our face reddens as our blood pressure rises in anger. Our blood vessels dilate and our face becomes pleasantly warm as we smile in enjoyment. These are compelling analogs of what arouses terror, rage, and enjoyment. These experiences constitute one form of affect amplification. A second form of affect amplification occurs by virtue of the similarity of their profile, in time, to their activating trigger. Just as a pistol shot is a stimulus which is very sudden in onset, very brief in duration, and equally sudden in decay, so its amplifying affective analog, the startle response, mimics the pistol shot by being equally sudden in onset, brief in duration, and equally sudden in decay. Affect, therefore, by being analogous in the quality of the feelings from its specific receptors, as well as in its profile of activation, maintenance, and decay, amplifies and extends the duration and impact of whatever triggers the effect. Epileptics do not startle. They experience a pistol shot as sudden but *not* startling. A world experienced without any affect would be a pallid, meaningless world. We would know *that* things happened, but we could not care whether they did or not.

By being immediately activated and thereby co-assembled with its activator, affect either makes good things better or bad things worse, by conjointly simulating its activator in its profile of neural firing and by adding a special analogic quality which is intensely rewarding or punishing. In illustrating the simulation of an activating stimulus, e.g. a pistol shot by the startle response, I somewhat exaggerated the goodness of fit between activator and affect to better illustrate the general principle. Having done so, let me now be more precise in the characterization of the degree of similarity in profile of neural firing between activator and affect activated. I have presented a model of the innate activators of the primary affects in which every possible major general neural contingency will innately activate different specific affects. Thus, increased gradients of rising neural firing will activate interest, fear, or surprise, as the slope of increasing density of neural firing becomes steeper. I assume that enjoyment is activated by a decreasing gradient of neural firing and that distress is activated by a sustained level of neural firing which exceeds an optimal level by an as yet undetermined magnitude, and that anger is also activated by a nonoptimal level of neural firing but one which is substantially higher than that which activates distress. Increase, decrease, or level of neural firing are in this model the sufficient conditions for activating specific affects. Analogic amplification, therefore, is based upon *one* of these three distinctive features rather than all of them. It so happens that the startle simulates the steepness of gradient of onset, the brief plateau of maintenance, and the equally steep gradient of decline of profile of the pistol shot and its internal neural correlate – but that is not the general case. Analogic simulation is based on the similarity to the adequate activator, not on all of its characteristics. Thus it is the decay alone of a stimulus which is stimulated in enjoyment. If one places electrodes on the wrist of a subject, permits fear to build, then removes the electrodes suddenly, we can invariably activate a smile of relief at just that moment. This amplifies (or makes more so) the declining neural stimulation from the reduction of fear. Therefore, enjoyment amplifies by simulating decreasing gradients of neural stimulation. Interest, fear, and surprise amplify by simulating increasing gradients of neural stimulation. Distress and anger amplify by simulating maintained level of stimulation.

The second modification in my theory concerns the exact loci of the rewarding and punishing amplifying analogs. From the start, I emphasized the face and voice as the major loci of the critical feedback which was experienced as affect. The voice I still regard as a major locus and will discuss its role in the next section. The face now appears to me still the central site of affect responses and their feedback, but I have now come to regard the skin, in general, and the skin of the face, in particular, as of the greatest importance in producing the feel of affect. My original observations of the intensity of infantile affect, of how an infant was, for example, seized by his or her own crying, left no doubt in my mind that what the face was doing with its muscles, and blood vessels, as well as with its accompanying vocalization, was at the heart of the matter. This seemed to me not an "expression" of anything else but rather the major phenomenon. I then spent a few years in posing professional actors and others to simulate facial affect. McCarter and I were rewarded by a correlation of $+.86$ between the judgments of untrained judges as to what affects they saw on the faces of these subjects as presented in still photographs, and what I had intended these sets of muscular responses to represent (Tomkins & McCarter, 1964).

This success was gratifying, after so many years of indifferent and variable findings in this field, but it was also somewhat misleading in overemphasizing the role of innately patterned facial muscular responses in the production of affect. I was further confirmed in these somewhat misleading results by the successes of Paul Ekman and Carroll Izard. Paul Ekman, using some of my photographs, was able to demonstrate a wide cultural consensus, even in very primitive and remote societies (Ekman, Sorenson, & Friesen, 1969). Carroll Izard (1969), using different photographs but the same conceptual scheme, further extended these impressive results to many other societies. The combined weight of all these investigations was most impressive, but I continued to be troubled by one small fact. The contraction of no other set of muscles in the body had *any* apparent motivational properties. Thus, if I were angry, I might clench my fist and hit someone, but if I simply clenched my fist, this would in no way guarantee I would become angry. Muscles appeared to be specialized for action and not for affect. Why then was the smile so easily and so universally responded to as an affect? Why did someone who was crying seem so distressed and so unhappy?

Further, from an evolutionary point of view, we know that different functions are piled indiscriminately on top of structures which may originally have evolved to support quite different functions. The tongue was an organ of eating before it was an organ of speech. The muscles of the face were also probably involved in eating before they were used as vehicles of affect – though we do not know this for a fact. It is, of course, possible that the complex affect displays on the human face evolved primarily as communication mechanisms rather than as sources of motivating feedback. My intuition was, and still is, that the communication of affect is a secondary spin-off function rather than the primary function. This would appear to have been the case with a closely related mechanism, that of pain. The cry of pain does communicate – but the feeling of pain does not. It powerfully motivates the person who feels it, in much the same way that affect does. That someone else is informed of this is not, however, mediated by the pain receptors themselves, but by the cry of distress which usually accompanies it. I, therefore, began to look at affect analogs such as pain and sexual sensitivity and fatigue for clues about the nature of the motivating properties of the affect mechanisms.

I soon became aware of a paradox – that three of the most compelling states to which the human being is vulnerable arise on the surface of the skin. Torture via skin stimulation has been used for centuries to shape and compel human beings to act against their own deepest wishes and values. Sexual seduction, again via skin stimulation, particularly of the genitals, has also prompted human beings on occasion to violate their own wishes and values. Finally, fatigue to the point of extreme sleepiness appears to be localized in the skin surrounding the eyes. This area will sometimes be rubbed in an effort to change the ongoing stimulation and ward off sleepiness. But in the end, it appears to be nothing but an altered responsiveness of skin receptors, especially in the eyelids, which make it impossible for sleepy people to maintain the state of wakefulness. They cannot keep their eyes open, though they may be powerfully motivated to do so[...]

In my script theory, the scene, a happening with a perceived beginning and end, is the basic unit of analysis. The whole connected set of scenes lived in sequence is called the *plot* of a life. The script, in contrast, does not deal with all the scenes or the plot of a life, but rather with the individual's rules for predicting, interpreting, responding to, and controlling a magnified set of scenes.

Although I am urging what appears to be a dramaturgic model for the study of personality, it is sufficiently different in nature from what may seem to be similar theories to warrant some brief disclaimers. By scenes, scripts, and script theory, I do not mean that the individual is inherently engaged in impression management for the benefit of an audience, after Goffman. Such scenes are not excluded as possible scenes, but they are very special cases, limited either to specific person- ality structures who are on stage much of their lives or to specific occasions for any human beings when they feel they are being watched and evaluated. Nor do I mean that the individual is necessarily caught in unauthentic "games," after Berne, nor are these necessarily excluded. Some individuals' scripts may indeed be well described as a game, and any and all individuals may on occasion play such games, but they are a very special kind of scene and script. Nor is script theory identical with role theory. Roles seldom completely define the personality of an individual and when this does happen, we encounter a very specialized kind of script. The several possible relationships between roles and scripts, such as their mutual support, their conflicts, as well as their relative independence of each other, provide a new important bridge between personality theory and general social science. Indeed, what sociologists have called the definition of the situation and what I am defining as the script is to some extent the same phenomenon viewed from two different but related theoretical perspectives – the scene as defined by the society or as defined by the individual. These definitions are neither necess- arily, nor always, identical, but they must necessarily be related to each other rather than completely orthogonal to each other, if either the society or the individual is to remain viable. If the society is ever to change, there must be some tension sustained between the society's definition of the situation and the individual's script. If the society is to endure as a coherent entity, its definition of situations must in some measure be constructed as an integral part of the shared scripts of its individuals.

The closest affinity of my views is with the script theoretic formulation of Robert Abelson (1975) and Schank and Abelson (1977). Although their use of the concept of script is somewhat different from mine, the theoretical structure lends itself to ready mapping one on to the other, despite terminological differences which obscure important similarities of the entire two theoretical structures.

Let us examine how a set of scenes may become magnified sufficiently to prompt the generation of a script. The case we will use is that of Laura, a young girl studied by Robertson (note 1) in connection with a study of the effects of hospitalization on young children when they are separated from their parents. Laura was hospitalized for about a week. During this week, away from her parents, she was subjected to a variety of medical examinations and procedures and also photographed by a moving picture camera near her crib. Like many young children, she missed her parents, was somewhat disturbed by the medical procedures, and cried a good deal. The quality of her life changed radically this week from good to bad. But what of the more permanent effect of these bad scenes on the quality of her life? First, the answer to such a question will depend critically on the degree of magnification which *follows* this week. How many times will she rehearse these bad scenes? Will such rehearsals co-assemble them in such an order and with such spacing that they are experienced as magnifying or attenuating the negative affects connected with these scenes? Further, apart from her own imagination, what will be the quantity of good and bad scenes she experiences at home when she returns? Will her parents further frighten or reassure her, or in attempting to reassure her give her an implicit message that she has been through hell? Further, will this be the beginning of further medical problems, or will it be an isolated week in her life?

What is important from the point of view of script theory is that the effect of any set of scenes is *indeterminate* until the future happens and either further magnifies or attenuates such experience. The second point is that the consequence of any experience is not singular but plural. There is no *single* effect but rather there are *many* effects which change in time – what I have called the principle of *plurideterminacy*. Thus when Laura first returned home, she appeared to be disturbed. Therefore the effect, if we had measured it then, was deleterious. But in a few days she was her normal self again. Now if we assessed the effect, we would say that over the long term it was *not* so serious. However, some time later when Robertson visited her home to interview her parents, she became disturbed once again, so the magnification of the bad scene had now been increased. This illustrates a very important third principle of psychological magnification and script formation: Scenes are magnified not by repetition, but by repetition with a *difference*. It is, as in art, the unity in variety which engages the mind and heart of the person who is experiencing a rapid growth of punishment or reward. Sheer repetition of experience characteristically evokes adaptation which attenuates, rather than magnifies, the connected scenes. In the case of Laura, it is the very fact that Robertson now unexpectedly has invaded her home – the fortress of love and security – that has changed everything for the worse. Up to this point, the main danger appeared to be that her parents might take her from her home and leave her in an alien, dangerous environment. But now her parents appear to be either unwilling or unable to prevent the dangerous intrusion into what was, till then, safe space. Indeed, they may appear to be in collusion with the intruder. The whole matter appears to have become more problematic. Yet in a few days all is again well, and we would be tempted to think that the affair has been closed – that the long-term effects of the hospitalization are not serious.

All goes well for some time. Then Laura is taken to an art museum by her parents. They wish to see an exhibition of paintings. They leave Laura in a white crib which the museum provides. What will be the effect of this? Once before, they took her to a hospital and left her in a white crib. Will she become disturbed and cry? She does not – so we have been correct in supposing that the experience in the hospital is limited in its long-term effects. She has been left by her parents in a white crib; but the deadly parallel escapes her. A few minutes later, however, a man comes by with a camera and takes a picture of her. And now she *does* cry. The family of connected scenes has now again been critically enlarged. This man is *not* Robertson. He has a camera, not a moving picture camera. It is an art museum, not a hospital – but it smells like danger to Laura, and her own crying becomes self-validating. The scene, whether dangerous or not, has been made punishing by her own crying. Any scene which is sufficiently similar to evoke the same kind of affect is thereby *made* more similar, and increases the degree of connectedness of the whole family of scenes. Just as members of a family are not similar in all respects, yet appear to be recognized as members of the same family, so do connected scenes which are psychologically magnified become more similar as members of a family of scenes. The scene in the hospital, at home, and at the museum will now be sufficiently magnified to generate a script. What will this script be like?

First it should be noted that this series of scenes involves little action on the part of Laura. She responds affectively to the hospital and museum scenes, but is otherwise passive. There have not as yet developed action strategies for avoiding or escaping such threatening scenes. We do not know for sure that, or how much, she anticipates or rehearses these scenes. Therefore our examination of the dynamics of script formation in the case of Laura is limited to script formation which is primarily interpretive and reactive and is a simplified case of what normally includes more active reaction to and participation in the generation of scenes and scripts. It is, however, useful for us at this stage of our presentation of script theory to deal with the simplest type of script which emphasizes the attainment of understanding of what is happening in a scene, since more complex scripts necessarily always include such understanding before coping strategies can be developed.

A complete understanding of the formation of scripts must rest on a foundation of perceptual, cognitive, memory, affect, action, and feedback theory. Needless to say, none of these separate mechanisms has been entirely satisfactorily illuminated at a theoretical level and their complex modes of interaction in a feedback system is an achievement far from realization. Yet an understanding of the complexities involved in interpreting and perceptually and cognitively ordering constantly shifting information from one scene to the next requires just such a missing theory. I have elsewhere presented my theories of perception, cognition, memory and feedback mechanisms upon which I have based script theory (Tomkins, 1971, 1979). I will use some of these assumptions in an illustrative but incomplete way in the following attempts to understand script formation.

The perception of a scene, at its simplest, involves a partitioning of the scene into figure and ground. The figural part of the scene, as in any object perception, is the most salient and most differentiated part of it, separated from the ground by a sharp gradient which produces a contour or connected boundary which separates the figure from its less differentiated ground. Such a figure becomes figural characteristically as a conjoint function of sharply differentiated gradients of stimulation (of shape, texture, or color in the visual field, of loudness, pitch, or rhythm in the auditory field), internal gradients of experienced affect (so that, e.g. it is the object with contours which excites, and is experienced as "exciting," rather than the ground), correlated gradients of experienced internal images and/or thoughts and/or words so that the object is experienced as fused with recruited images or imageless compressed thoughts or is fused with a word (e.g. that is "mother"), and with actions taken or with action potentials (e.g. That object is touchable, can be put in the mouth, or dropped to make a sound). These separate sources of information, converging conjointly in what I have called the central assembly, interact intimately and produce an organization of a simple scene into a salient figure differentiated from a more diffuse background.

Differentiation of a scene involves shifting centration away from one figure to another aspect of the same scene which now becomes figural. The first figure characteristically becomes a compressed part of the ground but capable of later expansion so that it may produce a more complex awareness of the now more differentiated scene. Ultimately, the whole scene is compressed and perceived as a habitual skill so that very small alternative samplings tell individuals all they think they then want to know about a repeated scene. After achieving some knowledge of the general characteristics of a scene with respect to its beginning (what started the scene), its cast (who is in the scene), its place (where is it), its time (when did it take place), its actions (who did what), its functions (did I see it, dream it, think about it, move around in it), its events (what happened – e.g. it snowed, there was an accident), its props (what things are in the scene – e.g. trees, automobiles), its outcomes (what happened at the end of the scene) and its end (what terminated the scene), the individual through memory and thought is then in a position to compare total scenes with each other – to co-assemble them and to begin to understand their several possible relationships to each other. Such comparisons between two or more scenes may go on in a third scene quite distinct from the scenes being compared, or the preceding scenes may be recruited simultaneously with another apparent repetition of one or more of the earlier scenes, in an effort to understand the similarities and differences between the present scene and its forerunners.

The human being handles the information in a family of connected scenes in ways which are not very different from the ways in which scientists handle information. They attempt to maximize the order inherent in the information in as efficient and powerful a way as is consistent with their prior knowledge and with their present channel capacity limitations. Since the efficiency and power of any theory is a function of the ratio of the number of explanation assumptions in the numerator relative to the number of phenomena explained in the denominator, human beings, like any scientist, attempt to explain as much of the variance as they can with the fewest possible assumptions. This is in part because of an enforced limitation on their ability to process information, and in part because some power to command, understand, predict, and control their scenes is urgently demanded if they are to optimize the ratio of rewarding positive and punishing negative affect in their lives.

In their attempt to order the information and produce a script from a set of scenes, they will first of all partition the variance into what they regard as the major variance and the residual variance – the big, most important features of the set of scenes – the constants of their script equation as differentiated from the related more differentiated variables of their script equation. In this respect, the procedure resembles factor analytic procedures whereby a general factor of intelligence is first extracted, followed by more specific factors which account for less and less of the variance. It resembles analysis of variance procedures in its strategy of first asking if there is a main effect, and then asking about more specific interactions.

What is the general script factor, or the main effect script question likely to be? It is characteristically determined by three conjoint criteria: (1) What is experienced with the most dense, i.e. the most intense and enduring affect? (2) What are experienced as the sharpest gradients of change of such affect? (3) What are the most frequently repeated sequences of such affect and affect changes? Whenever these three criteria are conjointly met in any series of scenes, they will constitute the first major partitioning of the variance within and between scenes. The most repeated changes in dense affect may occur either within any scene or between scenes or both. It should be noted that any one of these principles might operate in the organization of a *single* scene. An individual would, of course, pay attention to anything which deeply distressed him or her or to anything which suddenly changed, or to anything which was repeated within a scene. When, however, the task shifts to ordering a complex set of changes, both within and between scenes, his or her ability to deal with the totality of such information is sharply reduced. It is for this reason, I think, that the criteria for judging what is most important become more selective by requiring that conjoint conditions be met in a hierarchical order. The big picture must first be grasped before it can be fleshed in. An important, repeated change is the general script factor. This includes internal repetition, in past rehearsal and future anticipation[...]

Note

1   Robertson, J. *Case history of a child undergoing short separation from mother in a hospital.* Unpublished report, Tavistock Institute, London. Undated.

References

Abelson, R. (1975). Concepts for representing mundane reality in plans. In D. G. Bobrow & A. Collins (Eds.), *Representation and understanding.* New York: Academic Press.

Ekman, P., Sorenson, E. R., & Friesen, W. V. (1969). Pan-cultural elements in facial displays of emotions. *Science, 164,* 86–88.

Izard, C. (1969). The emotions and emotion constructs in personality and culture research. In R. B. Catell (Ed.), *Handbook of modern personality theory.* Chicago: Aldine.

Schank, R., & Abelson, R. (1977). *Scripts, plans, goals and understanding.* Hillsdale, NJ: Erlbaum.

Tomkins, S. S., & McCarter, R. (1964). What and where are the primary affects? Some evidence for a theory. *Perceptual and Motor Skills, 18,* 119–158.

CHAPTER *19*

Marital Disharmony and Children's Behavior Problems

J. M. Jenkins and M. A. Smith

Here we discuss how interactions in a family can also encourage the development of emotional styles or scripts that are carried into new situations and new relationships. Marital disharmony has been known to be associated with the development of emotional and behavioral problems in children (Cummings & Davies, 1994). In the work presented here by one of the editors of this book, with Marjorie Smith, the idea was to identify the particular aspect of an unhappy marriage that was problematic for children. A measure of anger-based marital conflict was a much stronger predictor of disturbance in children than other aspects of the parental marital relationship.

How does this notion of disturbance in children relate to their emotions? Externalizing disorder is a term used to talk about a configuration of behaviors that occur together such as lying, stealing, verbal and physical aggression, defiance, cruelty to animals, etc. Although these are behaviors rather than emotions they seem to come out of an anger organization. The person seems angry with the world, and these behaviors are an expression of that anger. Internalizing disorder on the other hand is made up of shyness, withdrawal, fearfulness, crying, sulking, and seems to come out of experiences of fear and sadness. For the work described in this selection as well as more recent work on marital conflict and children's emotion (Jenkins, 1995) it is clear that anger-based interactions between parents are associated with anger-based psychopathology in children.

What the authors have also shown is that when anger-based conflict between parents was higher, so too were anger interactions in the parent–child relationship. One possibility to explain such associations is that children learn emotion-based scripts (see selection 18) from their families. For children constantly exposed to anger-based marital conflict and their parents' anger

J. M. Jenkins and M. A. Smith, Marital disharmony and children's behavior problems: aspects of a poor marriage that affect children adversely. *Journal of Child Psychology and Psychiatry*, *32* (1991), 793–796, 796–803, 804–807. Copyright © 1991 Association for Child Psychology and Psychiatry. Reprinted by permission of Cambridge University Press.

expressions towards them may conclude that a large element of relationships is about trying to get the better of another person, getting them to submit at all costs, retaliating against perceived slights, etc.

References

Cummings, E. M., & Davies, P. T. (1994). *Children and marital conflict: The impact of family dispute and resolution.* New York: Guilford Press.

Jenkins, J. M. (1995). Parental conflict, children's peer relations and affective expression. Paper presented at Society for Research in Child Development, April 1995, Indianapolis.

Introduction

Aspects of poor parental marriage which affect children adversely

The association between poor parental marriage and children's psychiatric disturbance is well established. Children living in disharmonious homes show more emotional and behavioral problems than children living in harmonious homes (Block, Block, & Morrison, 1981; Emery, 1982; Rutter et al., 1975). Most of the research documenting the relationship between poor parental marriage and children's psychiatric problems has used a global assessment of marital disharmony (Emery & O'Leary, 1984; Richman, Stevenson, & Graham, 1982). Little research has been done on what it is within the global concept of disharmonious marriage which has an adverse impact on children. A number of studies indicate that various specific factors within the broader framework of marital disharmony might be implicated.

Quinton, Rutter, and Rowlands (1976) found that child psychiatric disorder was more strongly associated with poor marriages characterized by discord than poor marriages characterized by apathy and distance. Porter and O'Leary (1980), investigating a sample of children attending a psychiatric clinic, found that boys' externalized or antisocial problems were more strongly associated with a measure assessing the extent of marital hostility observed by the child (defined by quarrelling, sarcasm, and physical abuse), than a more general measure of marital satisfaction. Hess and Camara (1979) found that parental conflict was a stronger predictor of children's adjustment than whether the family was intact or divorced. There is, therefore, some evidence that overt conflict is one of the elements of an unhappy parental relationship which is particularly deleterious to children.

Another possible factor within parental disharmony explaining children's emotional and behavioral problems is parental discrepancy on child-rearing issues such as discipline. If parents are in disagreement over child rearing they will not be consistent in handling children and this may be linked to the development of behavioral disorders. Block and others (1981) found that parental discrepancy on child-rearing issues was associated with problems of undercontrol in boys and problems of overcontrol in girls. Chess, Thomas, Korn, Mittleman, and Cohen (1983) found that a scale of parental conflict (composed mainly of items related to disagreement over child management) when the child was 3 years old was significantly related to adaptation as an adult, assessed when the child had reached early adult life (18 and 22 years old). Camara and Resnick (1987), investigating family process predictors of children's post-divorce adjustment, found that inter-parental cooperation in the parental role was a strong predictor of children's behavioral problems, self-esteem, and prosocial behavior. Family therapists also stress the importance of parents agreeing on issues related to children so that children do not get caught up in the parental conflict (Haley, 1976; Minuchin, Rosman, & Baker, 1978).

The relationship between marital disharmony, the parent–child relationship, and children's behavioral and emotional problems

Parental disharmony may have a direct effect on children's behavior or it may operate indirectly through a third variable, which covaries with parental disharmony. In order to illustrate how a direct effect might operate, consider the following example in relation to parental conflict. The sight of people arguing, with raised voices and angry facial expressions, may in itself be frightening or distressing to children. There is some support for this hypothesis in that children who watch two adults, who are not their parents, in a simulated argument, show distress during the episode and increased aggression with peers directly after it (Cummings, Ianotti, & Zahn-Waxler, 1985; Cummings, 1987; Cummings, Pellegrini, Notarius, & Cummings, 1989a).

It may be, however, that disharmony distorts family relationships and it is these family relationships rather than the disharmony itself which are active in contributing to children's emotional problems. Destructive family alliances may develop as a consequence of two parents not getting on (Emery, 1988).

Parental disharmony may affect how one parent feels and acts toward the child, which in turn affects the child's behavior. Jouriles, Barling, and O'Leary (1987) found that violence between parents was associated with increased parent–child violence. Parent–child violence was a stronger predictor of children's behavioral problems than marital violence and after controlling for parent-child violence the association between marital violence and children's behavioral problems was not significant. Easterbrooks and Emde (1988), in a longitudinal study of marital quality, parenting, and children's behavior, found a significant relationship between marital quality and fathers' child-rearing attitudes, but no relationship between marital quality and mothers' child-rearing attitudes, nor marital quality and observational measures of mothers' and fathers' parenting behaviors in a laboratory setting. Thus as yet there is mixed evidence on the link between marital quality and parenting behaviours.

In this study we were interested to examine the impact of parental disharmony on parent–child relationships and to examine whether these parent–child relationship variables played an important role in mediating the relationship between parental disharmony and children's problems. Several aspects of the parent–child relationship were hypothesized to covary with marital disharmony and be associated with an increased level of behavioral problems in children. Richman and colleagues (1982) found that maternal criticism of the child at age 3 predicted behavioral disorders at age 8. They did not examine the relationship between parent–child criticism and parental disharmony but it would be plausible to hypothesize that these covaried. Lack of parental structure and supervision of the child has been found to be associated with increased antisocial behaviors (Patterson, 1982; Robins & Ratcliff, 1978) and is more common in homes in which the parents have recently separated than in intact homes (Hetherington, Cox, & Cox, 1978). In any study attempting to determine which aspects of a poor marital relationship affect children adversely it is important to control for aspects of the parent–child relationship which covary with negative aspects of the marital relationship.

One further methodological issue to consider is that many of the studies finding a link between marital disharmony and children's problems rely on data collected from the same respondent (usually the mother) to assess marital disharmony and children's behavioral problems. It may be that the positive correlation is due to one person reporting on both variables rather than because a real relationship exists between the two variables. For instance, a mother in a disharmonious marriage who is feeling miserable about a variety of issues in her life may experience her child's behavior as problematic, when his or her behavior is normal. It is therefore important to have a measure of child behavioral disturbance which is independent of parental support.

Aims of this study

The aims of this study were: (a) to examine the relative strengths of association between children's emotional and behavioral problems and the following three aspects of parental marriage in a general population sample: overt parental conflict, covert and unexpressed tension between parents, parental discrepancy on child-rearing practices; (b) to examine the impact of marital disharmony on aspects of the parent–child relationship, and (c) to control for aspects of the parent–child relationship when assessing the link between marital disharmony and children's behavior [. . .]

Method

One hundred and thirty-nine families took part in the study. This included 139 primary caretakers (this was the mother in all but three families and this dataset will be referred to as the mothers' data), 102 fathers, and 136 children. The 139 families included 16 families in which the parents had separated or divorced since the initial interview and 4 families in which one of the spouses had died. Only those families which remained intact between the first and second interview were included in the following analyses ($n = 119$).

Mothers and fathers were interviewed in their homes simultaneously but separately using a semi-structured interview. The children were interviewed approximately 1 week later. All interviewers were blind to any previous knowledge of the family and the children's interviewer was blind to all details of the present family circumstances. All three respondents reported on the children's emotional and behavioral problems, but only mothers and fathers reported on the parental marriage. The information collected from mothers was more comprehensive than that collected from either fathers or children and details of this are outlined in the measures section. Interviews with the parents took approximately 3 hours and those with the children $1\frac{1}{2}$ hours. Inter-rater reliability was assessed by two interviewers rating the same interview and was carried out on 15 mothers and 10 children. Cronbach's alpha (Cronbach, Gleser, Nanda, & Rajaratnam, 1972) was used to calculate reliability and was between $a = 0.73$ and $a = 1.0$ for measures described in this paper. Test-retest reliability trials were not carried out on the mothers' or fathers' interviews as most of the measures were taken from interviews with previously well established reliability and validity (Brown & Rutter, 1966; Rutter, Tizard, & Whitmore, 1970; Rutter & Brown, 1966; Quinton et al., 1976; Richman et al., 1982).

In order to give some overall indications of the validity of this interview assessment of the parental marital relationship used in the larger study, longitudinal data are presented. There was a strong correlation between the present marital rating (1985–1986) and the past one assessed between 1979 and 1982 ($r = 0.61, p < 0.001$). Eighty percent of families remained in the same marital grouping, i.e. they were harmonious and remained harmonious (rated 1, 2, or 3) or were disharmonious and remained disharmonious (rated 4, 5, or 6). Ten percent that were disharmonious became harmonious and 10% that were harmonious became disharmonious. This suggests a high level of continuity in parental marriage. Of the 16 families in which a separation/divorce had taken place, 12 (75%) had previously been rated as disharmonious. A significant relationship was found between the past marital rating and children's present behavioural and emotional problems ($r = 0.29, p < 0.001$). More information on the continuity of children's behavior and parental marriage can be found in Smith and others (199-).

Children's emotional and behavioral problems

Information was obtained from mothers, fathers, and children about their children's behavior and emotional state. Some items were taken from the interview developed by Graham and Rutter (Graham & Rutter, 1968; Rutter & Graham, 1968) and supplemented with items covered in ICD9 (World Health Organization, 1978) and DSM-III (American Psychiatric Association, 1980). Thirty-one aspects of behavior were covered in the parents' interviews and included: sadness, irritable moods, anxiety, school refusal, fears and phobias, sleep problems, stealing at home and at school, disobedience, temper tantrums, aggressive behavior towards peers or sibs, attention seeking, lying, enuresis, encopresis, eating disorder, hyperactivity, poor concentration, headaches, stomach aches, nausea and any other problems. Thirty items were covered in the children's interview. Only half overlapped with the parents' items. Items were omitted to save children embarrassement (e.g. encopresis) and children were asked in more detail about aspects of behavior that they were thought to have more information on (e.g. disobedience at school). Each item was rated from 0 to 3, according to the frequency and severity of the behavior over the last year, with a higher score indicating a more severe problem.

The coding scheme reflected the degree of handicap that the behavior caused the child and family. Codings on the 31 items were summed to yield a total symptom score. High symptom scores indicated many minor problems, a smaller number of serious problems or both. Inter-rater reliability for the mothers' report of symptoms was $a = 0.84$ and for the children's symptoms was $a = 0.89$. The children's interview was repeated with 20 children 1 month apart. Test-retest reliability on the children's symptom score was $a = 0.87$.

Internalized and externalized problems

On the basis of prior hypothesis, consultation with a child psychiatrist and the statistical correlation of each individual item with the rest of the scale, symptoms were grouped into internalized and externalized problems. A separate score was computed for each. The scale for internalized behaviors included specific fears, anxieties, miserable and irritable moods, temper tantrums, school refusal, and aches and pains. Internal consistency of this scale as measured by Cronbach's alpha was $a = 0.65$ (mothers' data), $a = 0.59$ (fathers' data) and $a = 0.75$ (children's data). The scale for externalized behaviors included lying, stealing, aggression to siblings and peers, disobedience, overactive behavior, poor concentration, and soiling. Internal consistency was $a = 0.70$ (mothers' data), $a = 0.36$ (fathers' data), and $a = 0.68$ (children's data).

Marital dimensions

For the present paper we supplemented the interview based assessment of marriage (Quinton et al., 1976) with questions on discrepancy in child-rearing views and covert tension and more detailed codings about the severity of quarrels, as these were not covered in the original measure.

Overt parental conflict　Mothers and fathers were asked about the frequency of conflict over the last year. For a difference of opinion to be rated as a conflict it had to last for a minimum of 5 minutes, with raised voices. They were then asked detailed questions about the characteristics of quarrels including the amount of shouting, swearing, throwing objects, and threatening to walk out. A global rating was made combining the frequency and severity information (range 1–4). This global rating of conflict was more strongly related to children's symptom scores than the simple frequency rating and is the rating used in this paper. In some of the analyses that follow this variable is dichotomized into high and low conflict. "Low" conflict includes no or mild conflict defined as less than monthly conflict or conflicts of short duration and low severity. Medium and high ratings of conflict were combined into the "high" category and included conflict that was monthly or more often, or severe in degree, i.e. prolonged with shouting, swearing, etc.

Covert tension　This was based on mothers' and fathers' reports on how often they were tense and angry with one another, when they did not quarrel about the source of the tension. It was rated in terms of frequency and duration of episodes over the past year (range 1–4).

Discrepancy in child-rearing practices   Parents were asked about the extent to which they disagreed on three aspects of child-rearing: discipline, children's education, and everyday childcare (e.g. what the child should wear, how often they should be bathed). Each area was rated individually in terms of frequency of disagreement and then summed (range 1–7).

Parent-child relationship variables

Lack of care   Parents were questioned on the amount of supervision that they exercised when the child was playing outside and how far the child was allowed to go on their own, the number of rules and the extent to which these were enforced, and the extent of family activities such as organized mealtimes (range 1–9).

Parental physical aggression toward the child was based on the mother's report of her and her husband's loss of physical control with the child over the previous 6 months (range 1–9).

Maternal verbal aggression toward the child was based on global ratings of the mothers' level of criticism and hostility toward the child during the entire interview and was assessed on the basis of voice tone and content (range 1–7).

Results

Agreement between parents

Agreement between parents on aspects of the marital relationship as assessed by Pearson correlation was as follows: overt parental conflict ($r = 0.45$), covert tension ($r = 0.30$), and discrepancy in child-rearing practices ($r = 0.25$). Fathers reported fewer problems than mothers both in relation to the marriage and in relation to the children's behavior (Jenkins & Smith). Agreement on children's symptoms was as follows: mothers and fathers ($r = 0.36$), mothers and children ($r = 0.33$), and fathers and children ($r = 0.16$). As agreement between parents was low, combining both parents' reports of the marital dimensions would just give an unreliable measure. Each parent's report of the marital dimensions was used separately, and compared with their own report of children's symptoms. Children's assessments of their own symptoms are included in the analyses in order to supply an account of children's symptoms which is independent of the parents' report of their marriage.

Which aspect of parental marriage is most strongly associated with children's symptoms?

The intercorrelation between the three marital dimensions was examined. Mothers' report of overt parental conflict was significantly related to mothers' report of covert tension ($r = 0.41$) and to mothers' report of discrepancy in child-rearing practices ($r = 0.48$); mothers' report of discrepancy in child-rearing practices was significantly related to mothers' report of covert tension ($r = 0.31$).

Multicollinearity was tested for by examining the combination of two variables in predicting the third using multiple regression. No combination of two variables was found to predict more than 25% of the variance of the third.

Fathers' report of overt parental conflict was weakly but significantly related to fathers' report of covert tension ($r = 0.20$) and to fathers' report on discrepancy in child-rearing practices ($r = 0.42$); fathers' report on discrepancy in child-rearing practices was weakly related to fathers' report of covert tension ($r = 0.22$).

We had initially intended to include frequency of short parental separation over the last 2 years in intact marriages as one of the marital dimensions to be examined. There were, however, too few instances of the parents separating for short periods of time and then getting back together ($n = 8$) to make inclusion meaningful.

In order to determine which marital dimension was the most significant in predicting children's disturbance, the relationship between the children's symptoms and the three marital dimensions was examined using Pearson product moment correlation. Results for mothers', fathers', and children's data using the total symptom score, children's internalized and children's externalized problems can be seen in table 19.1.

The marital dimension most strongly related to children's total symptom score, their externalized problems, and internalized problems in mothers', fathers', and

Table 19.1   Pearson product moment correlations of mothers' and fathers' reports of each marital dimension with mothers', fathers', and children's reports of children's total symptom score, children's internalized problem score, and children's externalized problem score

	Mothers' report: total score	Mothers' report: internal problems	Mothers' report: external problems	Child's report: total score	Child's report: internal problems	Child's report: external problems
Mothers' report of overt parental conflict	0.43***	0.36***	0.42***	0.27**	0.12	0.32***
Mothers' discrepancy in child-rearing practices	0.32***	0.34***	0.32***	0.09	0.05	0.10
Mothers' covert tension	0.31***	0.26**	0.35***	0.12	0.02	0.29***
	Fathers' report: total score	Fathers' report: internal problems	Fathers' report: external problems	Child's report: total score	Child's report: internal problems	Child's report: external problems
Fathers' report of overt parental conflict	0.39***	0.30**	0.33***	0.19*	0.09	0.24**
Fathers' report of discrepancy in child-rearing practices	0.27**	0.27**	0.22*	0.09	0.04	0.11
Fathers' report of covert tension	0.08	0.08	0.11	0.10	0.00	0.11

$*p < 0.05; **p < 0.01; ***p < 0.001.$

children's accounts is overt parental conflict. The more frequent and severe the conflict, the more difficulties mothers, fathers, and children report with children's behavior. Overt parental conflict is more consistently related to children's externalized behavioral problems than their internalized behavioral problems in mothers', fathers', and children's accounts of children's symptoms.

Discrepancy in child-rearing practices is related to mothers' and fathers' accounts of children's symptoms but not to children's accounts. Covert tension is related to mothers' accounts of children's symptoms and the children's accounts of their externalized problems but not to the children's account of their total symptom score or any of the fathers' reports of the children's symptoms.

As the measures were not strictly continuous, Spearman rank correlations were performed using the different accounts of symptoms as the outcome variable, and conflict was confirmed as the variable most strongly and consistently related to children's symptoms, particularly externalized problems.

There was some intercorrelation between the different dimensions of parental marriage. Simple correlation coefficients do not allow us to assess the unique impact of overt parental conflict, as separate from the impact of covert tension or discrepancy in child-rearing practices. In order to examine the unique impact of overt parental conflict it was important to control for the impact of the other marital dimensions.

A partial correlation was therefore carried out on each factor controlling for the effect of the other two factors. For example, a partial correlation was carried out between overt parental conflict and children's symptoms controlling for covert tension and discrepancy in child-rearing practices. The results of these partial correlations can be seen in table 19.2.

In mothers', fathers', and children's data, overt parental conflict is the only marital dimension associated with children's symptoms after controlling for the other two variables (in this case discrepancy in child-rearing practices and covert tension). Thus, covert tension and discrepancy over child-rearing practices do not in themselves have an association with children's emotional and behavioral problems after controlling for the effects of overt parental conflict.

In order to give some indication of the levels of symptoms and their range that children were showing in response to overt parental conflict, this variable was dichotomized into high and low overt conflict. The means, standard deviations, and ranges of children's symptom scores as reported by mothers, fathers, and children as a function of high and low conflict are given in table 19.3.

It can be seen from this that by no means all children who experienced parental conflict were showing emotional and behavioral problems. As a group, children in high conflict homes experienced significantly more problems (see below) than children in low conflict homes, but it is still the case that some children living in conflictual homes show no problems.

Relationship between parental conflict, problems in the parent–child relationship, and children's symptoms

It may be that frequent and severe conflict has a direct effect on children's behavior or that frequent and severe parental conflict is associated with a third

Table 19.2. Partial correlations between each marital dimension (as reported by mothers and fathers) and children's total symptom score as reported by mothers, fathers and children controlling for the remaining two marital dimensions

	Mothers' report: children's symptoms	Children's report: children's symptoms
Mothers' report of overt parental conflict controlling for discrepancy in child-rearing practices and covert tension	0.28**	0.24**
Mothers' report of discrepancy in child-rearing practices controlling for overt parental conflict and covert tension	0.14	−0.03
Mothers' report of covert tension controlling for overt parental conflict and discrepancy in child-rearing practices	0.09	−0.02
	Fathers' report: children's symptoms	Children's report: children's symptoms
Fathers' report of overt parental conflict controlling for discrepancy in child-rearing practices and covert tension	0.32***	0.16
Fathers' discrepancy in child-rearing practices controlling for overt parental conflict and covert tension	0.13	0.00
Fathers' covert tension controlling for overt parental conflict and discrepancy in child-rearing practices	−0.01	−0.06

** $p < 0.01$; *** $p < 0.001$.

Table 19.3. Mean, standard deviation, and range of children's symptoms as reported by mothers, fathers, and children as a function of high and low overt parental conflict

	Low overt conflict	*High overt conflict*
Mothers' report		
Mean	8.3	14.4
SD	4.8	9.0
Range	0–27	1–34
Fathers' report		
Mean	7.6	9.7
SD	5.7	8.8
Range	0–26	0–40
Children's report		
Mean	9.5	13.7
SD	5.3	7.0
Range	2–26	3–32

Table 19.4. Pearson product moment correlations of parental conflict and children's symptoms (as reported by mothers above and children below), with lack of care, parental physical aggression, and parental verbal aggression

Mothers' data	Overt parental conflict as reported by mothers	Children's symptoms as reported by mothers
Lack of care	0.24**	0.44***
Parental physical aggression	0.31***	0.33***
Parental verbal aggression	0.08	0.30**

Children's data	Children's symptoms as reported by children
Lack of care	0.06
Parental physical aggression	0.14
Parental verbal aggression	0.12

** $p < 0.01$; *** $p < 0.001$.

variable, e.g. problems in the parent–child relationship, and that it is this third variable which is the active element in promoting higher levels of disturbance in children. Variables which were hypothesized as mediating variables were: the parents being physically aggressive to the child, the parents being critical toward the child, and lack of parental care of the child.

In order to assess whether aspects of the parent–child relationship covaried with parental conflict and children's symptoms, Pearson product moment correlations were carried out and the results can be seen in table 19.4.

As parental conflict increased, there was an increase in lack of care of the child, and parental aggression toward the child. There was no significant relationship between parental conflict and parental criticism of the child.

Lack of parental care of the child, parental criticism, and parental aggression toward children were found to be significantly associated with increased child behavior problems as reported by mothers, but not when children's reports of their symptoms were used.

In order to examine the hypothesis that the relationship between parental conflict and children's symptoms was mediated by aspects of the parent–child relationship, an analysis of covariance was carried out. Parental conflict was dichotomized into low and high conflict groups. Lack of parental care of the child, parental criticism, and parental aggression toward children were entered as covariates in an ANCOVA with children's total symptom score as reported by mothers as the outcome variable and parental conflict and children's sex as main effects. Covariates were assessed before main effects or interactions. Parental physical aggression was dropped as a covariate and the analysis was repeated, as parental physical aggression was not found to be significantly related to children's symptoms when the other two covariates were in the analysis.

Lack of care [$F(1, 112) = 31.7$, $p < 0.001$] and parental criticism [$F(1, 112) = 11$, $p < 0.001$] were both found to be significantly related to children's symptoms. Parental conflict was found to be significantly related to children's emotional and behavioral problems, after controlling for covariates [$F(1, 112) = 15.3$, $p < 0.0001$]. Children's sex was not significantly related to children's symptoms [$F(1, 112) = 1.9$, NS] but the interaction between sex and parental conflict was significant [$F(1, 112) = 7.0, p < 0.009$] with boys more affected by parental conflict than girls. Thus parenting variables, although significantly related to children's symptoms, were not found to account for the relationship between parental conflict and children's symptoms.

In relation to the children's data, an analysis of covariance was unnecessary as none of the hypothesized covariates were found to be significantly associated with the children's report of their symptoms. A two-way ANOVA with parental conflict and children's sex as main effects showed that parental conflict was related to children's symptoms [$F(1, 112)12.8, p < 0.001$] but neither the children's sex [$F(1, 112) = 1.9$, NS] nor the interaction between sex and parental conflict were significantly related to children's symptoms [$F(1, 112) = 1.07$, NS] demonstrating that on the basis of children's own reports children are adversely affected by parental quarrelling but boys are not more affected than girls [...]

Discussion

This is the first study in a general population sample to examine systematically what it is about parental marital disharmony that is damaging to children. Other studies have compared the differential impact of single dimensions of the parental marital relationship such as conflict versus apathy (Quinton et al., 1976), or disagreement on child-rearing practices (Block et al., 1981). This study used multiple respondents for the reporting of children's emotional and behavioral problems, which allowed for a measure of the children's disturbance which was independent of the reporting of parental marriage. This is only rarely achieved in studies of the effects of marriage on children (Emery, 1982).

Parental conflict emerged as the strongest predictor of children's problems in mothers', fathers', and children's accounts of emotional and behavioral problems. Parental conflict was also found to be more strongly and more consistently related to children's antisocial or externalized behaviors than their emotional or internalized behaviors. Parental conflict remained the only variable associated with children's problems after controlling for the influence of other aspects of the marriage. Covert tension between the parents and discrepancy on child-rearing practices were significantly related to children's problems but not after controlling for the influence of parental conflict. It should be noted, however, that the relationship between parental conflict and children's symptoms found in this study is not strong. Many children in high-conflict homes were showing low symptom scores. Many factors other than parental disharmony are known to contribute to the development of emotional and behavioral problems in children (Rutter, 1979). It has been demonstrated that some factors act to protect children in disharmonious homes from showing emotional and behavioral problems (Jenkins & Smith, 1990). Including such ameliorating or protective factors in the analysis increases levels of prediction of the outcome variable. Further, Rutter (1979) has shown that stresses potentiate one another with the combination of two stresses providing a much higher risk of psychiatric disorder than one would expect by summing the effect of the individual stresses.

It is important to exercise some caution in interpreting the finding that parental conflict is the aspect of a poor parental marriage most deleterious to children. The difference between correlations of marital dimensions and children's symptoms is not large. Further, there was some covariation between the different marital dimensions. Disharmonious marriages tended not to be problematic on one dimension but on a range of dimensions. This makes it harder to estimate the unique impact of any one variable. Although an attempt was made to identify statistically the unique impact of different marital dimensions, this was only partially successful, given that these dimensions are intercorrelated in the real world.

However, the fact that conflict was confirmed as the strongest predictor of children's problems in each of three combinations of independent and dependent variables across respondents, and that conflict was the only dimension which remained significantly associated with children's problems after controlling for the other marital dimensions lends support to the finding that conflict is the element in a disharmonious marriage which is most deleterious to children. The results of this study are in agreement with the findings of Quinton and others (1976) who found that children demonstrated behavioral problems only when parents had a conflictual poor marriage, not when they had a poor marriage that was characterized by distance and apathy toward one another. We confirmed Block and colleagues' (1981) finding that discrepancy in child-rearing practices was associated with emotional and behavioral problems in children, but we took the inquiry one stage further by controlling for other aspects of the marriage and finding that discrepancy in child-rearing practices was only deleterious when it was associated with high overt parental conflict. Other researchers have also found a strong relationship between emotional and behavioral problems in children and parental conflict (Long, Slater, Forehand, & Fauber, 1988; Hess & Camara, 1979; Porter & O'Leary, 1980; Wolfe, Jaffe, Wilson, & Zak, 1985) [...]

Mechanisms underlying association between parental conflict and children's behavioral and emotional problems

On the basis of the findings from this study, it is likely that parental conflict is deleterious to children, both directly in terms of children reacting negatively to being exposed to displays of anger and indirectly in terms of its association with parenting problems and problematic family relationships.

Direct effects   The experience of seeing and hearing a display of anger between parents is itself aversive to children. Cummings and colleagues (Cummings et al., 1985; Cummings, 1987) have found that children show an increase in aggressive behavior toward their peers after they have watched two people that they do not know getting angry with one another. The children report feelings of anger and boys show a more aggressive response than girls. These effects are not mediated by adult–child relationship variables as the experimenters are unknown to the children and have no direct interaction with them. A variety of explanations have been put forward (Cummings et al., 1985) to explain the distress and anger that children show in response to background anger, including modelling effects, the lifting of a prohibition on the expression of negative emotion, some kind of contagion of emotion, etc.

Indirect effects   One hypothesis, put forward by Jouriles and colleagues (1987), was that parental conflict was deleterious to children only insofar as it was associated with raised levels of parent–child aggression. In the present study it was found that there was still a significant relationship between parental conflict and children's symptoms after controlling for parental aggression toward the child. The subjects in Jouriles and others' study were attending a treatment center for mothers and children experiencing marital violence, and were probably showing much higher levels of violence than the level we found in a general population sample. This might account for the difference in our findings. In any case, it would seem that the association between parental conflict and children's problems does not operate primarily through aggression in the parent–child relationship in families in the general population.

As overt parental conflict increased in this study, children also experienced less parental care and monitoring, and higher levels of physical aggression directed toward them. Factors such as lack of care and monitoring and parental physical aggression are known to be associated with increased risk of behavioral problems, particularly externalized or antisocial problems (Henggeler, 1989; Patterson, 1982; Robins & Ratcliff, 1978). Parental conflict may make it more likely that these negative parenting behaviors occur.

For instance, Hetherington and colleagues (1978) found that in the first year following divorce, divorced parents provided less structure in preschool children's lives such as mealtimes, bedtimes, etc. than the parents in a non-divorced group. It may be that when the parental relationship is problematic, evidenced by a high level of conflict or divorce, the parents become too preoccupied to provide children with the level of structure and supervision that they need. In this circumstance children will be experiencing several stressors, which are consequent on one another. From the present cross-sectional data, it is not possible to determine whether parental conflict is increasing the risk of physical aggression and lack of monitoring or vice versa, or indeed whether personality factors in the parents are responsible for generating high parental conflict and a high level of problems in the parent–child relationship. But the hypothesis that parental conflict is implicated in raising the occurrence of other negative factors needs further investigation [...]

References

American Psychiatric Association (1980). *Diagnostic and statistical manual of mental disorders* (DSM-III). 3rd edn. Washington, DC: American Psychiatric Association.

Angold, A., Weissman, M. M., John, K., Merikanagas, K. R., Prusoff, B. A., Wickramaratne, P., Davis Gammon, G. & Warner, V. (1987). Parent and child reports of depressive symptoms in children at low and high risk of depression. *Journal of Child Psychology and Psychiatry, 28*, 901–915.

Block, J. H., Block, J. & Morrison, A. (1981). Parental agreement-disagreement on child-rearing orientations and gender-related personality correlates in children. *Child Development, 52*, 965–974.

Brown, W. & Rutter, M. (1966). The measurement of family activities and relationships: a methodological study. *Human Relations, 19*, 241–263.

Camara, K. A. & Resnick, G. (1987). Marital and parental subsystems in mother custody, father custody and two parent households: effects on children's social development. In J. Vincent (Ed.), *Advances in family intervention, assessment and theory.* Vol. 4. Greenwich, CT: JAI.

Chess, S., Thomas, A., Korn, S., Mittleman, M. & Cohen, H. (1983). Early parental attitudes, divorce and separation and young adult outcome: findings of a longitudinal study. *Journal of the American Academy of Child and Adolescent Psychiatry, 22*, 47–51.

Cronbach, L. J., Gleser, G. C., Nanda, H. & Rajaratnam, N. (1972). *The dependability of behavioural measurements: theory of generalisability for scores and profiles.* New York: Wiley.

Cummings, E. M. (1987). Coping with background anger in early childhood. *Child Development, 58*, 976–984.

Cummings, E. M. and Cummings, J. S. (1988). A process-oriented approach to children's coping with adults' angry behavior. *Developmental Review, 8*, 296–321.

Cummings, E. M., Ianotti, R. J. & Zahn-Waxler, C. (1985). The influence of conflict between adults on the emotions and aggression of young children. *Developmental Psychology, 21*, 495–507.

Cummings, J. S., Pellegrini, D. S., Notarius, C. I. & Cummings, E. M. (1989a). Children's responses to angry adult behaviour as a function of marital distress and history of interparent hostility. *Child Development, 60*, 1035–1043.

Cummings, E. M., Vogel, D., Cummings, J. S. & El Sheikh, M. (1989b). Children's responses to different forms expression of anger between adults. *Child Development, 60*, 1392–1404.

Earls, F. (1980). The prevalence of behaviour problems in 3 year old children. *Journal of the American Academy of Child Psychiatry, 19*, 439–452.

Easterbrooks, M. A. & Emde, R. N. (1988). Marital and parent-child relationships: the role of affect in the family system. In R. A. Hinde & J. S. Stevenson-Hinde (Eds), *Relationships within families: Mutual influences.* Oxford: Clarendon Press.

Edelbrock, C., Costello, A. J., Dulcan, M. K., Kalas, R. & Conover, N. C. (1985). Age differences in the reliability of the psychiatric interview of the child. *Child Development, 56*, 265–275.

Edelbrock, C., Costello, A. J., Dulcan, M. K., Conover, N. C. & Kalas, R. (1986). Parent-child agreement on child psychiatric symptoms assessed via structured interview. *Journal of Child Psychology and Psychiatry, 27*, 181–190.

Emery, R. (1982). Interpersonal conflict and the children of discord and divorce. *Psychological Bulletin, 92*, 310–330.

—— (1988). *Marriage, divorce and children's adjustment.* Newbury Park, CA: Sage.

Emery, R. E. & O'Leary, D. K. (1982). Children's perceptions of marital discord and behavior problems of boys and girls. *Journal of Abnormal Child Psychology, 10*, 11–24.

—— (1984). Marital discord and child behavior in a non-clinic sample. *Journal of Abnormal Child Psychology, 12*, 411–420.

Graham, P. J. & Rutter, M. (1968). The reliability and validity of the psychiatric assessment of the child. II. Interview with the parents. *British Journal of Psychiatry, 114*, 581–592.

Haley, J. (1976). *Problem-solving therapy: new strategies for effective family therapy.* San Francisco: Jossey-Bass.

Hengeller, S. W. (1989). *Delinquency in adolescence.* Newbury Park, CA: Sage.

Hess, R. D. & Camara, K. A. (1979). Post divorce family relationships as mediating factors in consequences of divorce for children. *Journal of Social Issues, 35,* 79–96.

Hetherington, E. M., Cox, M. & Cox, R. (1978). The aftermath of divorce. In J. H. Stevens & M. Matthews (Eds), *Mother-child relations.* Washington, DC: N.A.E.Y.C.

Jenkins, J. M. & Smith, M. A. (1990). Factors protecting children in disharmonious homes. *American Academy of Child and Adolescent Psychiatry, 29,* 60–69.

Jenkins, J. M. & Smith, M. A. Mothers', fathers' and children's reporting differences on family relationships and children's behaviour.

Jenkins, J. M. Smith, M. A. & Graham, P. J. (1989). Coping with parental quarrels. *Journal of the American Academy of Child and Adolescent Psychiatry, 28,* 182–189.

Jouriles, E. N., Barling, J. & O'Leary, K. D. (1987). Predicting child behavior problems in maritally violent families. *Journal of Abnormal Child Psychology, 15,* 165–173.

Jouriles, E. N., Pfiffner, L. J. & O'Leary, S. G. (1988). Marital conflict, parenting and toddler conduct problems. *Journal of Abnormal Child Psychology, 16,* 197–206.

Long, N., Slater, E., Forehand, R. & Fauber, R. (1988). Continued high or reduced interparental conflict following divorce: relation to young adolescent adjustment. *Journal of Consulting and Clinical Psychology, 56,* 467–469.

Minuchin, S., Rosman, B. L. & Baker, L. (1978). *Psychosomatic families: Anorexia nervosa in context.* Cambridge, MA: Harvard University Press.

Patterson, G. R. (1982). *Coercive family process.* Eugene, OR: Castalia.

Porter, B. & O'Leary, K. D. (1980). Marital discord and childhood behavior problems. *Journal of Abnormal Child Psychology, 80,* 287–295.

Quinton, D., Rutter, M. & Rowlands, O. (1976). An evaluation of an interview assessment of marriage. *Psychological Medicine, 61,* 577–586.

Richman, N., Stevenson, J. & Graham, P. J. (1982). *Pre-school to school: A behavioural study.* London: Academic Press.

Robins, L. N. & Ratcliff, K. S. (1978). Risk factors in the continuation of childhood antisocial behaviour in adulthood. *International Journal of Mental Health, 7,* 96–116.

Rutter, M. (1970). Sex differences in children's responses to family stress. In E. J. Anthony & C. Koupernik (Eds), *The child and his family.* Vol. 1. New York: John Wiley.

—— (1979). Protective factors in children's responses to stress and disadvantage. In M. W. Kent & J. E. Rolf (Eds), *Primary prevention of psychopathology,* Vol. 3. *Social competence in children* (pp. 49–74). Hanover, NH: University Press of New England.

Rutter, M. & Brown, G. (1966). The reliability and validity of measures of family life and relationships in families containing a psychiatric patient. *Social Psychiatry, 1,* 38–53.

Rutter, M. & Graham, P. J. (1968). The reliability and validity of the psychiatric assessment of the child. I. Interview with the child. *British Journal of Psychiatry, 114,* 563–579.

Rutter, M., Tizard, J. & Whitmore, K. (1970). *Education, health and behaviour.* London: Longman.

Rutter, M., Yule, B., Quinton, D., Rowlands, O., Yule, W. & Berger, M. (1975). Attainment and adjustment in two geographical areas. III. Some factors accounting for area differences. *British Journal of Psychiatry, 126,* 520–533.

Smith, M. A., Delves, T., Lansdown, R., Clayton, B. & Graham, P. (1983). The effects of lead exposure on urban children: the Institute of Child Health/Southampton Study. *Developmental Medicine and Child Neurology, 25,* Suppl. 47, 5.

Smith, M. A., Jenkins, J. M. & Graham, P. J. Continuities in children's behaviour, parental marriage and maternal depression.

Whitehead, L. (1979). Sex differences in children's responses to family stress: a re-evaluation. *Journal of Child Psychology and Psychiatry, 20,* 247–254.

Wolfe, D. A., Jaffe, P., Wilson, S. K. & Zak, L. (1985). Children of battered women: the relation of child behaviour to family violence and maternal stress. *Journal of Consulting and Clinical Psychology*, *53*, 657–665.

World Health Organization (1978). *Mental disorders. Glossary and guide to their classification in accordance with the 9th revision of the international classification of disorders*. Geneva: WHO.

PART IV

*Functions of Emotions in Society
and in the Individual*

Functions of Emotions in Society and in the Individual

For a long time in the history of research on emotions, function was barely considered. Now it is clear that we cannot understand emotions without understanding their functions. But these functions are important not just in evolutionary terms, but in current everyday life. The first set of everyday functions in this section concerns interactions among people, the second occurs within individuals.

Effects of emotions among people

Catherine Lutz in *Unnatural Emotions*, the book she wrote about her nine-month visit to the Pacific atoll of Ifaluk, said that in this very interdependent society people's "emotional lives *are* their social lives" (p. 101, emphasis in original). Shaver, Wu, and Schwartz (1992) argued that essentially the same is true of the emotional lives of Americans, as well as of the Chinese.

In interdependent societies (such as Ifaluk or China) it is clear that people's most important concerns are social. And though people in individualistic societies, such as the USA, seem more independent, here too people's most important concerns are social – think of the importance of falling in love, of anger toward others at wrongdoing, of social anxieties. So although emotional life has been studied specifically in only a limited number of societies, it seems a likely hypothesis that within all cultures the majority of emotions will be social. In the selections of this section, therefore, we start with some of these socially structuring emotions. Think of it like this: Positive emotions tend to provide outline structures for cooperation; negative emotions structure groups of people in other ways.

The paper by Sherif depicts affection, happiness, and honor within groups of 11- and 12-year-old boys at summer camps. The groups have many of the characteristics of the hierarchies seen among other species of primates. Emotions within the group provide outline structures for the group's cooperative activity. But Sherif's paper also depicts the emotions of anger and contempt as they occur between groups. Both positive and negative emotions easily occur among us human beings. If happiness is the emotion that promotes cooperation, then anger and contempt are the emotions of conflict, and even of war.

Contempt is the corrosive emotion of social exclusion. Between social groups it is often accompanied by anger. But within social groups, at least in the West, anger has a different function: As Averill (1982) has proposed, this emotion provides a temporary social role – the role of the angry person whose rights have been violated in some way and who is demanding redress.

Averill's idea of emotions as temporary social roles is an inviting one. For the most part, when we meet, we enact roles that are familiar to us and to those with whom we interact. With a child we are nurturant, with a friend we are friendly, with the greengrocer we are cooperative in making a purchase. But if anything unexpected should occur, emotions emerge, and the social structuring set up by these emotions offers each person a new role, and a new piece of the social drama is played out.

In some societies, including Ifaluk as described by Lutz and the Inuit group described by Briggs (selection 5), people are suspicious of anger. For an adult to display anger in such societies would be equivalent in a Western society to being introduced to a stranger and dissolving in embarrassment, staring at the floor, and remaining silent. On Ifaluk and among the Inuit anger is not unknown, but it is socially incompetent. Similarly in America and Europe social embarrassment is not unknown, but for an adult to exhibit it at the mere event of meeting someone new would be enough to label the person as unable to take part in ordinary interactions.

By contrast, in the West anger is seen as sometimes necessary to protect one's rights, and to maintain a respect for self. So – surprisingly perhaps – anger in Western societies is not primarily the emotion of rejection. It is the emotion of conflict, but also of renegotiation, as Averill (1982) found. Anger provides temporary roles for both people involved in the incident, within which the terms of the relationship can be renegotiated.

In relation to the question of how far emotions are biologically based or socially constructed, Averill's work shows how emotions are constructed within specific societies. Members of the societies studied by Lutz and Briggs that are strongly interdependent do not get angry at incidents that would make Westerners angry. By contrast, we who live in a society oriented to the assertion of individual rights become angry when these rights are infringed. Western individualist societies, in other words, seem to have taken the emotion of anger and forged from it something useful – the temporary, but conflictual, role of renegotiating a relationship between individuals with rights.

But, as we discussed in part I, social constructivism does not imply construction solely from language and social convention. Biological givens are also elements in the constructive process. Darwin's idea of emotional expressions was of pieces of behavior that could be triggered whether or not they are of any use, and Berkowitz

(1990) has shown that in the case of anger this behavior may be directed at someone whether or not they had anything to do with causing the event that made the person angry. Such features make some societies and some individuals altogether suspicious of anger, and they avoid it. Even within Western society – with its ubiquitous television and movie stories of action and revenge for wrong doing both in the realm of fiction and under the aegis of foreign policy – it seems that there is something about angry violence that fascinates us, perhaps because we like to identify with the powerful. Perhaps too, fascination depends on there being something about anger that we do not fully understand or accept.

Moving from the potentially constructive functions of anger, the next selection in this part, from Gottman, shows again the distinction between the emotions of conflict, which can be constructed into socially useful functions, and the emotions of contempt, which are more difficult to reconcile with a rosy view of human nature. If in the studies of Sherif we saw contempt between boys of 11, Gottman shows this same emotion occurring in the heart of marriage. Let us once again take a post-Darwinian view: Contempt is the emotion of rejection of others. In its extreme forms, which seem distressingly easy for even civilized human beings to reach, it can lead to treating others as non-human. This is indeed how people were treated in Nazi concentration camps (e.g. Levi, 1958). In conflicts with others outside the circle of friends and loved ones, the function can easily become not renegotiation but complete separation of the self from the other, in extreme cases by extermination.

We can imagine that during the several million years of human evolution in which our ancestors lived in smallish groups, they travelled nomadically over large areas. We can imagine conflicts between groups of individuals in the line that led to modern humans, and conflict too with groups of other human-like creatures of that era, such as the Neanderthals. Only one line of these species survived, the line that has led to ourselves. We can imagine too that if a contempt-based conflict should emerge within bands of humans, then the group would split. So vast were the spaces and so sparse and mobile the human population in those ancient times that there need not be occasion for the two sub- groups to meet again.

So it is likely that selective evolutionary advantages were conferred on individuals possessing the genes for contempt. These would tend to bind together individuals of a particular species, and bind together also individuals who were alike in groups that were not too large, and therefore perhaps make such groups more successful. We know that when groups become too large cooperation within the group becomes less likely (Dunbar, 1996) so that the human adaptive advantage of working in social groups is lost.

It seems easier to accept contemptuous antagonisms between species than among members of our own species, but the evidence points to the cues for contempt being almost as easily roused for members of our own species as they are for members of other species. We get a sense of how this contempt works from Jane Goodall, who studied chimpanzees over many years in a reserve in Gombe, Tanzania. In her book of 1986 she recounts a sinister sequence of incidents. The large, socially intercommunicating group of chimpanzees at Gombe split into two sub-groups, which ceased to communicate. When by chance they met there was edginess between the sub-groups, even between individuals who had previously been friends. The two sub-groups started occupying two distinct territories. Parties of the larger sub-group started patrolling the boundaries of their territory, and making forays into the territory of the other sub-group. When a member of the smaller sub-group happened to be discovered alone, or if several individuals in a numerically weaker party were found, then the individual or the small party from the smaller sub-group was hunted down and killed.

Just as love is part of the biologically given repertoire of human emotions, so too is this kind of internecine contempt. Part of the social construction that we humans have managed is that only occasionally does it reach the murderous proportions that occurred among the chimpanzees of Gombe. But it does not take very much, as Sherif shows (selection 20) for a set of individuals to cease to be treated as "one of us" and start to be treated as "one of them." It can be as little as dividing a group into two on the shallowest of bases – getting twenty people into a room and tossing a penny for each and creating a group who are "heads" and a group who are "tails" will do it (Tajfel, 1978). And when superficial but discernible characteristics like skin color, or dialect, come under the influence of the emotions of contempt, the contempt even seems to many to have the compelling quality of reason.

What Gottman shows in his paper is how, between some husbands and wives, the mood of cooperation prevails. Some couples even do well though they argue a lot, when they also have ways of making up. In other couples, however, an emotion from the open fastnesses of our ancestral environment of evolutionary adaptedness has been imported into modern households. Destructive emotions of contempt, which Gottman calls hostility, can prompt couples towards that increasingly common kind of event in our society – costly in almost every way for couples and their children – marital separation. At the end of his paper Gottman offers a description derived from predator–prey relations – the emotional relationships between people can form a dynamic self-organizing system: The dynamic systems approach is likely to be increasingly important in understanding emotions (see e.g. Lewis, 1996).

Effects of emotions within the individual

As well as structuring our relationships, emotions constrain us as individuals, and they do so in what might be thought of as lawful ways. The next set of articles in this section all illustrate and explore this function. The first in this set, by Frijda (selection 22) is the best general article we know on the constraints that emotions impose on us and our actions.

Different emotions and moods structure the mind in different ways. In evolutionary terms, if we think of happiness as the emotion of confidence and optimism, of being in a safe and relatively non-threatening environment. It is the emotion not just of social cooperation, as we have discussed above, but of making progress individually in some plan, of being engaged in some activity. One of the earliest researchers to show this effect was Alice Isen. Selection 23 is one of her most striking findings – that happy people are more creative in solving certain kinds of problem.

What happiness does is to induce a particular arrangement of the cognitive architecture that will facilitate making progress, when nothing too negative is at hand. It is an architecture that allows the person to focus attention on the task at hand, not to be put off by small setbacks, to think optimistically, expansively, and trustingly, to bring to mind examples of previous successes.

But there is some evidence that being happy may not always be beneficial to thinking. There is now a large number of experiments in which positive and negative moods have been induced, and subjects have performed tasks of various kinds, such as making social judgments about people, or judging the goodness of an argument. Negative mood-states are good for certain kinds of cognitive tasks in which persistence and careful analytical processing are involved (Mackie & Worth, 1991).

Some of the clearest intra-personal effects have been found in the area that relates normal and abnormal psychology. The next selection by Andrew Mathews shows this. A mood of anxiety brings the attentional focus predominantly upon safety and danger, so during fear and anxiety we tend to stop other tasks, we may freeze into inactivity. We often check what we have done, looking carefully for signs of danger or safety. We prepare to avoid or escape, or sometimes to combat the danger if it should occur. Fear and anxiety, then, are the emotion and mood which structure the brain to meet with threats and danger (see also selection 10). By contrast, as Mathews goes on to explain, the emotions of depression have their effects not primarily on attention but on memory, bringing to mind previous occasions when losses or failures have occurred. One can imagine here that the brain is adapted to bringing forward, from memory, information about how setbacks have been handled in the past.

We end part IV with an excerpt from an article that has become very influential (selection 25, by Salovey and Mayer), on the idea that to be sensitive to our own and others' emotions is a form of intelligence.

References

Berkowitz, L. (1990). On the formation and regulation of anger and aggression: a cognitive-neoassociationsistic analysis. *American Psychologist, 45*, 494–503.

Dunbar, R. I. M. (1996). *Grooming, gossip and the evolution of language.* London: Faber & Faber.

Goodall, J. (1986). *The chimpanzees of Gombe: Patterns of behavior.* Cambridge, MA: Harvard University Press.

Levi, P. (1958). *If this is a man* (S. Woolf, Trans.). London: Sphere (1987).

Lewis, M. D. (1996). Self-organizing cognitive appraisals. *Cognition and Emotion, 10*, 1–25.

Lutz, C. A. (1988). *Unnatural emotions: Everyday sentiments on a Micronesian atoll and their challenge to Western theory.* Chicago: University of Chicago Press.

Mackie, D. M., & Worth, L. T. (1991). Feeling good, but not thinking straight: the impact of positive mood on persuasion. In J. P. Forgas (Ed.), *Emotion and social judgements* (pp. 201–219). Oxford: Pergamon Press.

Scherer, K. R. Wallbott, H. G., & Summerfield, A. B. (1986). *Experiencing emotion: A cross-cultural study.* Cambridge: Cambridge University Press.

Shaver, P. R., Wu, S., & Schwartz, J. C. (1992). Cross-cultural similarities and differences in emotion and its representation. In M. S. Clark (Ed.), *Review of Personality and Social Psychology*, Vol. 13: *Emotion* (pp. 175–212). Newbury Park, CA: Sage.

Tajfel, H. (1978). Differentiation between social groups: studies in the social psychology of intergroup relations. In H. Tajfel (Ed.), *European Monographs in Social Psychology, No. 14.* London: Academic Press.

CHAPTER *20*

Experiments in Group Conflict

M. Sherif

Muzafer Sherif conceived a famous series of studies of intergroup relations among boys at summer camps. The article we reprint here is an accessible short description of the experiments. For more details see his book with Carolyn Sherif, Groups in Harmony and in Tension. *In these studies we see the formation of groups with bonds of affectionate friendship within the group but then, when competing for a scarce resource, the formation of antagonisms to members of the other group, antagonisms that have all the marks of destructive contempt.*

  Sherif had first-hand experience of war and revolution in his native Turkey. He had also seen the deterioration of intergroup relationships in Germany, and seen too the social decay in prewar France. These experiences touched him deeply, leading him, as he said, to strive for a social psychology "which would embody the main features of actual life events, pointing if possible to realistic solutions to such problems." Sherif describes psychological studies that do indeed fulfill this aim. His proposed solution to the violence of intergroup tensions – that it is no good people in rival groups merely meeting each other and talking but that they need to collaborate on joint tasks in which they come to rely on each other and trust each other – is profoundly important.

Reference

Sherif, M., & Sherif, C. W. (1953). *Groups in harmony and in tension.* New York: Harper & Row.

Conflict between groups – whether between boys' gangs, social classes, "races", or nations – has no simple cause, nor is mankind yet in sight of a cure. It is often rooted deep in personal, social, economic, religious, and historical forces. Nevertheless it is possible to identify certain general factors which have a crucial influence on the attitude of any group toward others. Social scientists have long

M. Sherif, Experiments in group conflict. *Scientific American, 195* (November 1956), 54–58. Reprinted by permission of *Scientific American*, NY.

sought to bring these factors to light by studying what might be called the "natural history" of groups and group relations. Intergroup conflict and harmony is not a subject that lends itself easily to laboratory experiments. But in recent years there has been a beginning of attempts to investigate the problem under controlled yet lifelike conditions, and I shall report here the results of a program of experimental studies of groups which I started in 1948. Among the persons working with me were Marvin B. Sussman, Robert Huntington, O. J. Harvey, B. Jack White, William R. Hood, and Carolyn W. Sherif. The experiments were conducted in 1949, 1953, and 1954; this article gives a composite of the findings.

We wanted to conduct our study with groups of the informal type, where group organization and attitudes would evolve naturally and spontaneously, without formal direction or external pressures. For this purpose we conceived that an isolated summer camp would make a good experimental setting, and that decision led us to choose as subjects boys about 11 or 12 years old, who would find camping natural and fascinating. Since our aim was to study the development of group relations among these boys under carefully controlled conditions, with as little interference as possible from personal neuroses, background influences, or prior experiences, we selected normal boys of homogeneous background who did not know one another before they came to the camp.

They were picked by a long and thorough procedure. We interviewed each boy's family, teachers, and school officials, studied his school and medical records, obtained his scores on personality tests, and observed him in his classes and at play with his schoolmates. With all this information we were able to assure ourselves that the boys chosen were of like kind and background: all were healthy, socially well-adjusted, somewhat above average in intelligence, and from stable, white, Protestant, middle-class homes.

None of the boys was aware that he was part of an experiment on group relations. The investigators appeared as a regular camp staff – camp directors, counselors, and so on. The boys met one another for the first time in buses that took them to the camp, and so far as they knew it was a normal summer of camping. To keep the situation as lifelike as possible, we conducted all our experiments within the framework of regular camp activities and games. We set up projects which were so interesting and attractive that the boys plunged into them enthusiastically without suspecting that they might be test situations. Unobtrusively we made records of their behavior, even using "candid" cameras and microphones when feasible.

We began by observing how the boys became a coherent group. The first of our camps was conducted in the hills of northern Connecticut in the summer of 1949. When the boys arrived, they were all housed at first in one large bunkhouse. As was to be expected, they quickly formed particular friendships and chose buddies. We had deliberately put all the boys together in this expectation, because we wanted to see what would happen later after the boys were separated into different groups. Our object was to reduce the factor of personal attraction in the formation of groups. In a few days we divided the boys into two groups and put them in different cabins. Before doing so, we asked each boy informally who his best friends were, and then took pains to place the "best friends" in different groups so far as possible. (The pain of separation was assuaged by allowing each group to go at once on a hike and camp-out.)

As everyone knows, a group of strangers brought together in some common activity soon acquires an informal and spontaneous kind of organization. It comes to look upon some members as leaders, divides up duties, adopts unwritten norms of behavior, develops an *esprit de corps*. Our boys followed this pattern as they shared a series of experiences. In each group the boys pooled their efforts, organized duties, and divided up tasks in work and play. Different individuals assumed different responsibilities. One boy excelled in cooking. Another led in athletics. Others, though not outstanding in any one skill, could be counted on to pitch in and do their level best in anything the group attempted. One or two seemed to disrupt activities, to start teasing at the wrong moment, or offer useless suggestions. A few boys consistently had good suggestions and showed ability to coordinate the efforts of others in carrying them through. Within a few days one person had proved himself more resourceful and skillful than the rest. Thus, rather quickly, a leader and lieutenants emerged. Some boys sifted toward the bottom of the heap, while others jockeyed for higher positions.

We watched these developments closely and rated the boys' relative positions in the group, not only on the basis of our own observations but also by informal sounding of the boys' opinions as to who got things started, who got things done, who could be counted on to support group activities.

As the group became an organization, the boys coined nicknames. The big, blond, hardy leader of one group was dubbed "Baby Face" by his admiring followers. A boy with a rather long head became "Lemon Head." Each group developed its own jargon, special jokes, secrets, and special ways of performing tasks. One group, after killing a snake near a place where it had gone to swim, named the place "Moccasin Creek" and thereafter preferred this swimming hole to any other, though there were better ones nearby.

Wayward members who failed to do things "right" or who did not contribute their bit to the common effort found themselves receiving the "silent treatment," ridicule or even threats. Each group selected symbols and a name, and they had these put on their caps and T-shirts. The 1954 camp was conducted in Oklahoma, near a famous hideaway of Jesse James called Robber's Cave. The two groups of boys at this camp named themselves the Rattlers and the Eagles.

Our conclusions on every phase of the study were based on a variety of observations, rather than on any single method. For example, we devised a game to test the boys' evaluations of one another. Before an important baseball game, we set up a target board for the boys to throw at, on the pretense of making practice for the game more interesting. There were no marks on the front of the board for the boys to judge objectively how close the ball came to a bull's-eye, but, unknown to them, the board was wired to flashing lights behind so that an observer could see exactly where the ball hit. We found that the boys consistently overestimated the performances by the most highly regarded members of their group and underestimated the scores of those of low social standing.

The attitudes of group members were even more dramatically illustrated during a cook-out in the woods. The staff supplied the boys with unprepared food and let them cook it themselves. One boy promptly started to build a fire, asking for help

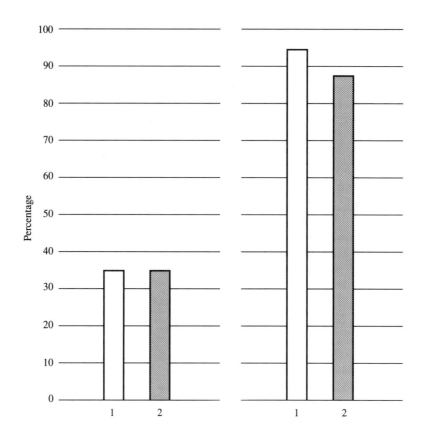

Figure 20.1 Friendship choices of campers for others in their own cabin are shown for Red Devils (white) and Bulldogs (grey). As first a low percentage of friendships were in the cabin group (left). After five days, most friendship choices were within the group (right).

in getting wood. Another attacked the raw hamburger to make patties. Others prepared a place to put buns, relishes and the like. Two mixed soft drinks from flavoring and sugar. One boy who stood around without helping was told by the others to "get to it." Shortly the fire was blazing and the cook had hamburgers sizzling. Two boys distributed them as rapidly as they became edible. Soon it was time for the watermelon. A low-ranking member of the group took a knife and started toward the melon. Some of the boys protested. The most highly regarded boy in the group took over the knife, saying, "You guys who yell the loudest get yours last."

When the two groups in the camp had developed group organization and spirit, we proceeded to the experimental studies of intergroup relations. The groups had had no previous encounters; indeed, in the 1954 camp at Robber's Cave the two groups came in separate buses and were kept apart while each acquired a group feeling.

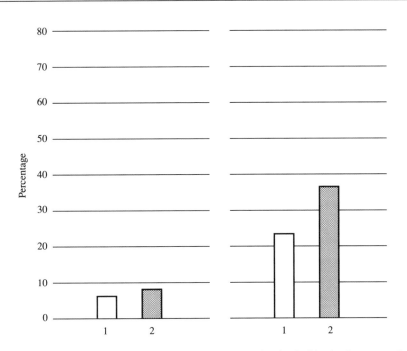

Figure 20.2 During conflict between the two groups in the Robber's Cave experiment there were few friendships between cabins (left). After cooperation toward common goals had restored good feelings, the number of friendships between groups rose significantly (right).

Our working hypothesis was that when two groups have conflicting aims – i.e. when one can achieve its ends only at the expense of the other – their members will become hostile to each other even though the groups are composed of normal well-adjusted individuals. There is a corollary to this assumption which we shall consider later. To produce friction between the groups of boys we arranged a tournament of games: baseball, touch football, a tug-of-war, a treasure hunt, and so on. The tournament started in a spirit of good sportsmanship. But as it progressed good feeling soon evaporated. The members of each group began to call their rivals "stinkers," "sneaks", and "cheaters." They refused to have anything more to do with individuals in the opposing group. The boys in the 1949 camp turned against buddies whom they had chosen as "best friends" when they first arrived at the camp. A large proportion of the boys in each group gave negative ratings to all the boys in the other. The rival groups made threatening posters and planned raids, collecting secret hoards of green apples for ammunition. In the Robber's Cave camp the Eagles, after a defeat in a tournament game, burned a banner left behind by the Rattlers; the next morning the Rattlers seized the Eagles' flag when they arrived on the athletic field. From that time on name-calling, scuffles, and raids were the rule of the day.

Within each group, of course, solidarity increased. There were changes: One group deposed its leader because he could not "take it" in the contests with the adversary; another group overnight made something of a hero of a big boy who had previously been regarded as a bully. But morale and cooperativeness

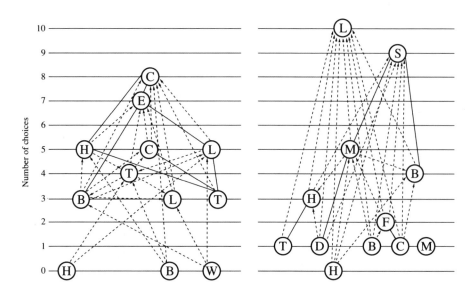

Figure 20.3 Sociograms represent patterns of choices within the fully developed groups. One-way friendships are indicated by broken arrows; reciprocated friendships by solid lines. Leaders were among those highest in the popularity scale. Bulldogs (left) had a close-knit organization with good group spirit. Low-ranking members participated less in the life of the group but were not rejected. Red Devils (right) lost the tournament of games between the groups. They had less group unity and were sharply stratified.

within the group became stronger. It is noteworthy that this heightening of cooperativeness and generally democratic behavior did not carry over to the group's relations with other groups.

We now turned to the other side of the problem: How can two groups in conflict be brought into harmony? We first undertook to test the theory that pleasant social contacts between members of conflicting groups will reduce friction between them. In the 1954 camp we brought the hostile Rattlers and Eagles together for social events: going to the movies, eating in the same dining room and so on. But far from reducing conflict, these situations only served as opportunities for the rival groups to berate and attack each other. In the dining-hall line they shoved each other aside, and the group that lost the contest for the head of the line shouted "Ladies first!" at the winner. They threw paper, food, and vile names at each other at the tables. An Eagle bumped by a Rattler was admonished by his fellow Eagles to brush "the dirt" off his clothes.

We then returned to the corollary of our assumption about the creation of conflict. Just as competition generates friction, working in a common endeavor should promote harmony. It seemed to us, considering group relations in the everyday world, that where harmony between groups is established, the most decisive factor is the existence of "super-ordinate" goals which have a compelling appeal for both but which neither could achieve without the other. To test this

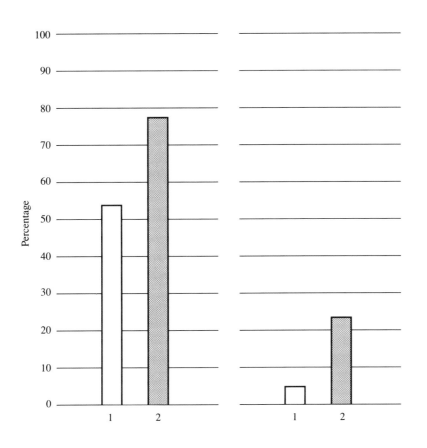

Figure 20.4 Negative ratings of each group by the other were common during the period of conflict (left) but decreased when harmony was restored (right). The graphs show percent who thought that *all* (rather than *some* or *none*) of the other group were cheaters, sneaks, etc.

hypothesis experimentally, we created a series of urgent, and natural, situations which challenged our boys.

One was a breakdown in the water supply. Water came to our camp in pipes from a tank about a mile away. We arranged to interrupt it and then called the boys together to inform them of the crisis. Both groups promptly volunteered to search the water line for the trouble. They worked together harmoniously, and before the end of the afternoon they had located and corrected the difficulty.

A similar opportunity offered itself when the boys requested a movie. We told them that the camp could not afford to rent one. The two groups then got together, figured out how much each group would have to contribute, chose the film by a vote, and enjoyed the showing together.

One day the two groups went on an outing at a lake some distance away. A large truck was to go to town for food. But when everyone was hungry and ready to eat, it developed that the truck would not start (we had taken care of that). The boys got a rope – the same rope they had used in their acrimonious tug-of-war – and all pulled together to start the truck.

These joint efforts did not immediately dispel hostility. At first the groups returned to the old bickering and name-calling as soon as the job in hand was finished. But gradually the series of cooperative acts reduced friction and conflict. The members of the two groups began to feel more friendly to each other. For example, a Rattler whom the Eagles disliked for his sharp tongue and skill in defeating them became a "good egg." The boys stopped shoving in the meal line. They no longer called each other names, and sat together at the table. New friendships developed between individuals in the two groups.

In the end the groups were actively seeking opportunities to mingle, to entertain and "treat" each other. They decided to hold a joint campfire. They took turns presenting skits and songs. Members of both groups requested that they go home together on the same bus, rather than on the separate buses in which they had come. On the way the bus stopped for refreshments. One group still had five dollars which they had won as a prize in a contest. They decided to spend this sum on refreshments. On their own initiative they invited their former rivals to be their guests for malted milks.

Our interviews with the boys confirmed this change. From choosing their "best friends" almost exclusively in their own group, many of them shifted to listing boys in the other group as best friends (see figure 20.3). They were glad to have a second chance to rate boys in the other group, some of them remarking that they had changed their minds since the first rating made after the tournament. Indeed they had. The new ratings were largely favorable (see figure 20.4).

Efforts to reduce friction and prejudice between groups in our society have usually followed rather different methods. Much attention has been given to bringing members of hostile groups together socially, to communicating accurate and favorable information about one group to the other, and to bringing the leaders of groups together to enlist their influence. But as everyone knows, such measures sometimes reduce intergroup tensions and sometimes do not. Social contacts, as our experiments demonstrated, may only serve as occasions for intensifying conflict. Favorable information about a disliked group may be ignored or reinterpreted to fit stereotyped notions about the group. Leaders cannot act without regard for the prevailing temper in their own groups.

What our limited experiments have shown is that the possibilities for achieving harmony are greatly enhanced when groups are brought together to work toward common ends. Then favorable information about a disliked group is seen in a new light, and leaders are in a position to take bolder steps toward cooperation. In short, hostility gives way when groups pull together to achieve overriding goals which are real and compelling to all concerned.

CHAPTER *21*

The Roles of Conflict Engagement, Escalation, and Avoidance in Marital Interaction

J. M. Gottman

For some time it has been possible to imagine the perfect study of interpersonal emotions. What you would do is to bring to the laboratory people who know each other well, say, people who are married. You would wire them up to polygraphs to record heart rate, the slight sweating that occurs when people are aroused (skin conductance), skin temperature, and other variables controlled by the autonomic nervous system, of the kind that James postulated to be the bases for our feelings of emotions. You would link your polygraphs to your computer, and you would make video recordings of the faces and audio recordings of the words of both husband and wife. You would have the couple discuss various things – something neutral, and something conflictual between them. Next day you would have the subjects come back to the laboratory individually to view the video recordings, to indicate what emotions they had felt from moment to moment during their interactions.

There you have the perfect set-up – social interaction, conversation, and emotions measured by facial expression, physiological response, and self-report. This, indeed, is the research arrangement that John Gottman has been working with since 1979. In it some 2000 couples have been studied. The paper we reprint here is one of a recent set of results derived from this method. Physiological recording in these studies was under the direction of Robert Levenson. Reports of this work are to be found in Levenson & Gottman (1983), and more recently in Gottman and Levenson (1992).

Using measures of the kind described in these papers it has been possible to predict with 90 percent accuracy which marriages will succeed, and which will fail. Recently Gottman

(1993) has published a popular book in which he recommends couples to avoid doing the things which he has found are associated with marital breakdown. The results of Gottman's studies are correlational. Whether marital therapy based on having couples avoid the behavior associated with failure would improve marital satisfaction is a research question for the future.

References

Gottman, J. (1993). *Why marriages succeed or fail.* New York: Simon & Schuster.

Gottman, J. M., & Levenson, R. W. (1992). Marital processes predictive of later dissolution: behavior, physiology and health. *Journal of Personality and Social Psychology, 63*, 221–133.

Levenson, R. W., & Gottman, J. M. (1983). Marital interaction: physiological linkage and affective exchange. *Journal of Personality and Social Psychology, 49*, 587–597.

There have been many previous attempts at marital typologies (e.g. Bell, 1975; Cuber & Harroff, 1965; Fitzpatrick, 1988; Margolin, 1988; Olson, 1981). Most of these classifications of marriages were not based on direct observation of how couples behaved, but rather they were based on self-report data concerning beliefs, lifestyles, or interaction patterns (Gottman, 1979). It would also be useful to have an external criterion validity test of a proposed classification system. This article proposes longitudinal stability of the marriage or divorce as the external validity criterion. To date, there have been only four prospective studies of divorce (Bentler & Newcomb, 1978; Block, Block, & Morrison, 1981; Constantine & Bahr, 1980; Kelly & Conley, 1987); these studies have produced weak and inconsistent results, and none have used interview or observational data.

In a previous report, Gottman and Levenson (1992) proposed a preliminary typology that divided married couples into two groups a "regulated" group, whose interactive speaker behaviors during a 15-min conflict discussion were generally more negative than positive, and a "nonregulated" group, whose interactions were more positive than negative. The goal of this article is to extend this typology by considering additional behavioral data that have recently become available for the same sample. The behavior of the listener as well as the behavior of the speaker will be considered, as will the coding of affect. This article also attempts to combine quantitative methods of data analysis with admittedly more speculative clinical observations to suggest a typology of five groups of couples that differ in marital interaction patterns, in marital satisfaction at two time points, and in marital stability.

It would also be useful if a proposed typology were organized around theoretical questions. The typology proposed here is organized around a behavioral balance theory of marriage, in which it is assumed that marriages function with a kind of set point that balances positivity with negativity. Balance theories of marriage have been implicit in marital research from two traditions, the behavioral tradition (Gottman, 1979; Wills, Weiss, & Patterson, 1974) and the behavior exchange tradition (Gottman et al., 1976; Thibaut & Kelley, 1959). The assumption in the proposed balance theory is that the set point makes a difference in predicting the future course of the marriage.

Method

Subjects

Seventy-nine couples were originally recruited in Bloomington. Indiana, using newspaper advertisements. A demographic summary is provided in Gottman and Levenson (1992).

Procedure

Interaction session   Couples had three 15-min conversations: (a) events of the day, (b) conflict resolution (discussion of a problem area of continuing disagreement), and (c) pleasant topic.

Follow-up   Four years after the initial assessment, the original 79 couples were recontacted, and at least one spouse (70 husbands and 72 wives) from 73 of the couples (92.4%) agreed to participate in the follow-up. Spouses completed a set of questionnaires assessing marital satisfaction and items relevant to possible marital dissolution. The two dichotomous variables, serious considerations of divorce in the 4 years since Time 1 and Time 2 and actual divorce, will serve as the external criterion variables in this article.

Coding and analysis of the data

The videotapes of the problem area interaction were coded using three observational coding systems: the Marital Interaction Coding System (MICS), which in this study was used to focus on persuasion attempts; the Rapid Couples Interaction Scoring System (RCISS), which focused on problem solving (both speaker and listener behaviors); and the Specific Affect Coding System (SPAFF), which focused on specific emotions. The RCISS provided the means for classifying couples into the initial groups.

Marital interaction coding system   The MICS (Weiss & Summers, 1983) was used in this study to obtain an estimate of attempts at persuasion used by the couples for each third of the 15-min conflict marital interaction; the sum of two MICS subcodes, disagreement plus criticism (labeled *engagement* by Gottman & Krokoff, 1989), was used to provide a crude index of persuasion attempts. MICS codes were assigned continuously by coders for 30-s blocks. Double codes, which are used with more recent versions of the MICS, were treated as additional single codes for this research. Means reported for the MICS are the total number of persuasion attempts in each 5-min block. A sample of every videotape was independently coded by another observer, and a confusion matrix was computed. The average weighted Cohen's kappa for this coding (all subcodes of the MICS summed over all couples) was 0.60.

Specific affect coding system   For greater description of the affective portion of the interactions beyond the positive and negative dimensions, the SPAFF (Gottman &

Krokoff, 1989) was used. Coders classified each turn at speech as affectively neutral, as one of five negative affects (*anger, disgust/ contempt, sadness, fear*, or *whining*), or as one of four positive affects (*affection/ caring, humor, interest/ curiosity*, or *joy/ enthusiasm*). The kappa coefficient of reliability, controlling for chance agreements, was equal to 0.75 for the entire SPAFF coding.

SPAFF sequential analyses   SPAFF codes were also lumped into positive, negative, and neutral affect, and z scores were computed (see Allison & Liker, 1982; Gottman & Roy, 1991) for six sequences: (a) two (one for husband to wife and one for wife to husband) *startup* sequences (Patterson, 1982), or the transition from one partner's neutral affect to the other partner's negative affect; (b) two *continuance* sequences (Patterson, 1982), or the transition from one partner's negative affect to the other partner's negative affect; and (c) two *positive reciprocity* sequences (Gottman, 1979), or the transition from one partner's positive affect to the other partner's negative affect.

Rapid couples interaction scoring system   The RCISS uses a verbatim transcript of the videotape and the actual videotape. A checklist of 13 behaviors are scored for the speaker and 9 behaviors are scored for the listener on each turn at speech (for more detail, see Krokoff, Gottman, & Hass, 1989). RCISS behavioral codes can be scored in terms of underlying positive-negative dimension. The data are coded each turn at speech and later summarized into the following scales: (a) *complain/ criticize;* (b) *defensiveness;* (c) *contempt;* (d) *stonewalling*, a set of behaviors that describe the listener's withdrawal and disengagement from the interaction (e.g., not looking at the speaker, no facial movement, no vocal responses showing the speaker that the listener is tracking the speaker); (e) *positive presentation of issues;* (f) *assent*, including simple agreements and positive vocal listener backchannels; (g) *humor;* and (h) *positive listener*, a set of behaviors that are the opposite of stonewalling and that suggest an engaged and positive listener. We also computed, for each spouse, the overall speaker slopes for the variable (i) *positive–negative*. Using Cohen's kappa, reliability for all RCISS codes was 0.72. Because of the checklist nature of this system, codes are independent of one another in the coding process.

Using RCISS point graphs to classify couples   RCISS speaker and listener codes were used to classify couples into a 2×2 factorial design. This classification scheme was based on a method proposed originally by Gottman (1979) for use with the Couples Interaction Scoring System, a predecessor of the RCISS. On each conversational turn, the total number of positive RCISS items minus the total number of negative items coded was computed for each spouse. Then the cumulative total of these points was plotted for each spouse. The slopes of these plots were determined using linear regression analysis. Gottman (1979) found that speaker slopes were related to marital distress or satisfaction; distressed or dissatisfied couples had more negative speaker slopes; the listener's behavior was not studied. In the present study, four groups were defined as shown in figure 21.1. The initial experimental design of this article and the *N*s thus derived are shown in figure 21.1. Figure 21.1 represents the first step in forming the typology. The following analyses of SPAFF variables will make a case for the summary names given to couples in figure 21.1.

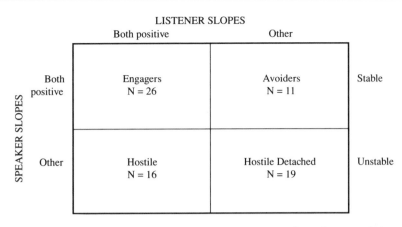

Figure 21.1 Design of the study as a function of listener and speaker cumulative point graph slopes.

Results

Typology and marital stability

The following results will justify the summary terms *stable* and *unstable* to the right of the two rows in figure 21.1.

Serious consideration of divorce For the dichotomous variables of serious considerations of divorce in the 4 years between Time 1 and Time 2 and the divorce variable, a series of chi-square tests were performed for both main and interaction effects of listener and speaker slopes. For the husbands' serious considerations of divorce, there was a significant main effect for speaker slope, $\chi^2(1, N = 73) = 7.75, < .01$; no significant effect for listener slope, $\chi^2(1, N = 73) = 0.01, ns$; and a significant interaction effect, $\chi^2(3, N = 73) = 8.50, p < .05$. Among positive speaker slope couples, husbands were significantly less likely to seriously consider divorce than negative speaker sloped husbands (18% vs. 52%); for wives the percentages were 33% and 48%, respectively. Individual cells of a contingency table can be examined statistically to test which cells contribute to the effect (Bishop, Fienberg, & Holland, 1975). The cells contributing significantly to the interaction effect showed that when the listeners are engaged there is a bigger difference between whether the speaker is positive or not in terms of the husband's serious considerations of divorce, when the listeners were engaged (60% of nonpositive speaker slope husbands seriously considered divorce, compared with 17% of positive speaker slope couples). For the wives' serious considerations of divorce, none of the effects were significant: speaker slope, $\chi^2(1, N = 73) = 1.50$; listener slope, $\chi^2(1, N = 73) = 0.28$; and interaction, $\chi^2(3, N = 73) = 1.20$.

Actual divorce For the divorce variable, there was a significant main effect for speaker slope, $\chi^2(1, N = 73) = 4.37, p < .05$; no significant effect for listener slope, $\chi^2(1, N = 73) = 0.72 ns$; and no significant interaction effect, $\chi^2(3, N = 73) = 4.10, ns$. Couples who had positively sloped speaker point graphs at Time 1 were significantly less likely to divorce in the intervening 4 years than other couples (3% vs. 19%).

Table 21.1. SPAFF codes as a function of speaker slope (G), listener slope (L), and their interaction $(G \times L)$

Effect	G	L	$G \times L$
		Husband positive	
Multivariate[a]	1.10	3.05*	0.81
Univariate			
Neutral	0.02	0.06	1.51
Humor	1.24	1.86	0.24
Affection	4.64*	2.35	0.49
Interest	2.15	5.70*	0.30
Joy	1.58	1.40	0.03
		Husband negative	
Multivariate[b]	2.66*	1.01	1.58
Univariate			
Anger	4.33*	0.31	3.69
Disgust	0.01	0.02	7.56**
Whining	4.99*	0.71	0.00
Sadness	0.02	0.72	0.03
Fear	2.17	2.78	0.54
		Wife positive	
Multivariate[a]	2.76*	1.81	1.01
Univariate			
Neutral	1.73	0.08	2.01
Humor	2.34	2.96	0.02
Affection	3.73	0.78	1.86
Interest	5.18*	4.95*	0.32
Joy	7.60**	0.89	0.88
		Wife negative	
Multivariate[b]	2.98*	0.62	2.25
Univariate			
Anger	6.72*	0.40	2.89
Disgust	2.73	0.05	7.62**
Whining	1.82	0.29	1.93
Sadness	0.92	0.09	0.31
Fear	1.76	1.78	0.61

Note. SPAFF = Specific Affect Coding System.
[a]Multivariate *dfs* = $(3, 66)$; univariate *dfs* = $(1, 68)$. [b]Multivariate *dfs* = $(5, 61)$; univariate *dfs* = $(1, 65)$.
* $p < .05$. ** $p < .01$.

Description of marital processes

The following results will justify the terms *engager, avoider, hostile,* and *hostile/detached* in the boxes of figure 21.1. Table 21.1 summarizes the multivariate analyses of variance (MANOVAs) and analyses of variance (ANOVAs) for the SPAFF variables for the 2×2 design. RCISS subscales are not analyzed here to avoid confound with the couples' classification scheme itself. Comparisons between groups were performed using two-tailed *t* tests between groups.

Stable and unstable couples and hostility　There is support for the contention that unstable couples at Time 1 could be described as more hostile than stable couples. Husbands in stable couples displayed more affection ($M = 3.00$ vs. 1.55), were less angry ($M = 12.72$ vs. 24.48), and whined less ($M = 1.28$ vs. 1.55). Wives in stable couples showed more interest ($M = 13.39$ vs. 6.61), more joy ($M = 1.31$ vs. .24), and less anger ($M = 15.19$ vs. 29.48). The listener main effects could be interpreted as a manipulation check on the RCISS listener dichotomy: There were significant listener slope main effects for husband interest ($M = 12.00$ vs. 6.18) and wife interest ($M = 12.90$ vs. 6.11). There were also significant interaction effects between speaker and listener slope for husband and wife disgust; surprisingly, husbands who were positive speakers and listeners showed the highest levels of disgust. There were no significant main effects or interaction effects for the sequences.

Engagers versus avoiders　Although stable couples were more positive and less negative than unstable couples, there are some systematic differences between the groups labeled *engagers* and *avoiders* in figure 21.1. Because avoiders and engagers differed only on RCISS listener behavior, RCISS speaker codes and affects were examined by comparing engagers and avoiders. For the RCISS, engagers significantly exceeded avoiders on both husband's and wife's complain/criticize score: husband, $t(27) = 3.08$, $p < .01$, engager $M = 0.12$, avoider $M = 0.01$; wife $t(28) = 3.28$, $p < .01$, engager $M = 0.12$, avoider $M = 0.02$; as well as on positive agenda building; husband, $t(35) = 2.57$, $p < .05$, engager $M = 0.70$, avoider $M = 0.49$; wife, $t(35) = 2.11$, $p < .05$, engager $M = 0.68$, avoider $M = 0.52$. Hence, both in positive and in negative presentation of issues, engagers exceeded avoiders. Combined with the fact that avoiders show greater listener withdrawal, there is justification for the contention that the upper left-hand cell should be called *conflict engagers* and the upper right-hand cell should be called *conflict avoiders*. For the SPAFF variables, engager husbands showed more disgust and contempt than avoiders, $t(33) = 2.19$, $p < .05$, engager $M = 8.00$, avoider $M = 2.45$, whereas engager wives showed more disgust and contempt, $t(30) = 2.34$, $p < .05$, engager $M = 5.68$, avoider $M = 1.45$, and engager husbands whined more, $t(32) = 2.20$, $p < .05$, engager $M = 5.08$, avoider $M = 1.45$, than avoider wives. For the sequences, engagers were higher than avoiders on negative continuance, husband to wife, $t(33) = 2.08$, $p < .05$, engager $M = 6.11$, avoider $M = 3.77$; wife to husband, $t(33) = 2.26$, $p < .05$, engager $M = 6.42$, avoider $M = 3.69$, and on positive reciprocity, wife to husband, $t(29) = 2.24$, $p < .05$, engager $M = 4.90$, avoider $M = 2.56$. Engagers were more likely to reciprocate both positive and negative affect than avoiders.

Hostile versus hostile/detached couples　The *detached* in the label *hostile/detached* is warranted by the fact that hostile detached couples are far less engaged as listeners. However, are there differences between groups in speaker behavior? Again, because one axis of the design is based on listener behavior, only RCISS speaker codes and affects were examined in comparing hostile and hostile/

detached couples. There was evidence that hostile/detached couples were more negative and less positive than hostile couples. On the RCISS, hostile/detached husbands showed more verbal contempt, $t(22) = 3.06$, $p < .01$, hostile $M = 0.04$, hostile/detached $M = 0.15$, and less positive agenda building, $t(33) = 2.95$, $p < .01$, hostile $M = 0.58$, hostile/detached $M = 0.33$, whereas hostile/detached wives showed more verbal contempt, $t(23) = -2.46$, $p < .05$, hostile $M = 0.06$, hostile/detached $M = 0.21$. On the SPAFF, hostile/detached husbands showed less interest, $t(33) = 3.01$, $p < .01$, and more disgust, $t(33) = 2.73$, $p < .01$, than hostile husbands; hostile/detached wives also showed les interest, $t(33) = 2.80$, $p < .01$, and more disgust, $t(33) = 2.46$, $p < .01$, than hostile husbands. There were no significant differences between hostile and hostile/detached couples for any of the sequences.

Two types of conflict engagers The high means for husband and wife disgust for the positive-engaged cell of the design were quite unexpected and puzzling and led to a review of the videotapes for the couples in this cell. On the basis of clinical intuitions in viewing the videotapes, without benefit of an additional coding system, there appeared to be two distinct types of couples in this cell, who differed in terms of how emotional they were. This observation led to a division of the couples in the engager cell at the cell's median for husband plus wife SPAFF neutral affect, which produced the final experimental design shown in figure 21.2.

Comparing volatile and validating couples Because these two groups were classified in the same cell of the design using the RCISS speaker and listener slopes, I would not expect them to differ on RCISS subscales. Hence, a comparison of groups using RCISS subscales is unconfounded. On the RCISS, volatile husbands were significantly greater than validating husbands in positive agenda building, $t(18) = 4.19$, $p < .001$, volatile $M = 0.84$, validating $M = 0.57$; they smiled and laughed more, $t(24) = 2.25$, $p < .05$, volatile $M = 0.19$, volidating $M = 0.10$;

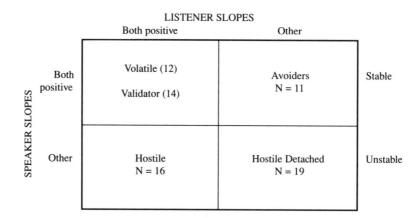

Figure 21.2 Final design of the typology, showing five groups of couples, three stable couples (volatile, validating, and avoiding), and two unstable couples (hostile and hostile/detached).

but assented less, $t(20) = -3.40$, $p < .01$, volatile $M = 0.06$, validating $M = 0.20$; and were less engaged listeners, $t(15) = -2.89$, $p < .05$, volatile $M = 1.69$, validating $M = 2.39$. Volatile wives were more defensive, $t(24) = 2.77$, $p < .05$, volatile $M = 0.25$, validating $M = 0.14$; assented less, $t(16) = -3.60$, $p < .01$, volatile $M = 0.04$, validating $M = 0.21$; were greater on positive agenda building, $t(19) = 3.51$, $p < .01$, volatile $M = 0.81$, validating $M = 0.57$; smiled and laughed more, $t(24) = 2.25$, $p < .05$, volatile $M = 0.18$, validating $M = 0.10$; and were less engaged listeners, $t(15) = -2.13$, $p < .001$, volatile $M = 1.95$, validating $M = 2.58$. On the SPAFF, volatile husbands displayed more tension, $t(15) = 3.10$, $p < .01$, volatile $M = 40.33$, validating $M = 9.46$, whereas wives displayed more anger, $t(16) = 2.42$, $p < .05$, volatile $M = 26.58$, validating $M = 8.23$; more tension, $t(13) = 4.18$, $p < .001$, volatile $M = 39.00$, validating $M = 8.00$; and more joy, $t(13) = 2.55$, $p < .05$, volatile $M = 0.84$, validating $M = 0.57$. Volatile couples were higher than validators on negative continuance, husband to wife, $t(14) = 3.03$, $p < .01$, volatile $M = 8.99$, validating $M = 3.69$; wife to husband, $t(15) = 2.88$, $p < .05$, volatile $M = 9.15$, validating $M = 4.11$; and on positive reciprocity, husband to wife, $t(22) = 3.14$, $p < .01$, volatile $M = 7.34$, validating $M = 2.89$; wife to husband, $t(22) = 2.21$, $p < .05$, volatile $M = 6.59$, validating $M = 3.47$. Volatile couples were both more positive and more negative than validating couples.

Discussion Gottman (1979) divided each conflictual marital interaction into thirds. In general, there were three distinct phases to a conflict discussion. The first phase was agenda building, in which among happily married couples both people tended to present their views and feelings on a problem; the second phase was the arguing phase, in which both people usually tried to persuade one another; the third phase was the negotiation phase, in which compromise was the apparent goal. It is useful to consider the findings in terms of these phases.

For the conflict avoider couples (who were also low in emotion), the interviewer had a great deal of difficulty setting up the conflict discussion. Although conflict avoiders did not describe themselves as avoidant of conflict, these couples did not have specific strategies for resolving conflict. For example, they often referred to the passage of time alone as solving problems, and to working things out alone. One wife said, "Well, Jim says he just likes to let things go and 'go with the flow' and just let problems work themselves out and that problems usually work themselves out without a lot of deep discussion about it." When avoiding couples refer to "talking things out" there is an emphasis on common ground rather than on differences, an acceptance of differences and disagreements as just not very important, so that they can be ignored. The interactions are not psychologically minded or introspective. Once each person has stated his or her case, they tend to see the discussion as close to an end. They consider accepting these differences as a complete discussion. Once they understand their differences, they feel that the common ground and values they share overwhelm these differences and make them unimportant and easy to accept. Hence, there is very little give and take and little attempt to persuade one another. The discussion has very little emotion, either positive or negative. Often the proposed solutions to issues are quite nonspecific.

On the other hand, for engagers, it was quite easy for the interviewer to set up the conflict discussion. These couples confronted conflict openly, disagreed, and tried to persuade one another. For volatile couples, there was a high level of both positive and negative affect in these marriages. The husbands were extremely expressive and involved. There was a great deal of negativity in these interactions, and also a lot of humor and affection. There seems to be a premium placed on arguing in these couples, apparently in the service of preserving their individuality and separateness. What appears to be characteristic of these couples is that the usual persuasion part of the discussion comes very early, and it pervades the entire discussion, even in the early agenda building phase when feelings are usually being expressed (Gottman, 1979). As a result there are many communications that say, in effect, "Your feelings are wrong." For example, a wife may express her concern about the family budget, saying that she thinks that they do not save enough. The volatile husband may respond by saying something like, "You are wrong. We do not have a problem with finances." Then the persuasion begins, but it surrounds her expression of feelings.

Validating couples, who were intermediate in expressing emotion, had conversations that involved conflict, but there was a lot of ease and calm in the discussion. The conversation was initially characterized by one spouse validating the other's description of a problem. Validation can be as minimal as vocal listener backchannels such as "mmhmm" and "yeah." When listening to this interaction, it does not necessarily seem that the validating husband is in agreement with his wife but is simply saying, "OK, go on, I'm interested and I'm listening to your feelings. I may have my own point of view on this issue, but I want to hear you out." That is sufficient to count as validation. At a more extreme level, the validating spouse provides support, perhaps empathy for the partner's feelings, communicating that he or she understands expressed feelings, that it makes sense for the partner to feel that way, given his or her position and vantage point. The validator still may not feel the way the partner does, but he or she communicates, verbally or nonverbally, that he or she understands and accepts the expressed feelings as valid. This communication can be nonverbal, as in mirroring facial expressions of worry and distress, or it can be direct and verbal. In the conversation of validating couples, there is often the sense that, although there is disagreement between them, they are both working together on a problem. However, in the disagreement part of the interaction there is a great deal of belligerent argument by each person for his or her position.

The conversations of unstable couples were quite negative. For example, the conversations of hostile couples were characterized not only by a great deal of direct engagement in conflict and an attentive listener but also by defensiveness, usually on the part of both people. One sequence that indexes defensiveness is the mindreading to disagreement sequence. In this sequence, one person attributes a motive, feeling, or behavior to the other person. At times this statement is accompanied by a "you always" or "you never" phrase, and it usually has a negative voice tone or facial expression that gives the mindreading a blaming or judgmental quality. For example, one person may say, "You never clean up the house. You just don't care how we live!" This will be followed by disagreement and elaboration, such as, "I do so clean up a lot. Just the other day I straightened the house before your mother came over!" Hostile/detached couples were detached and emotionally uninvolved with one another, but they got into brief episodes of reciprocated attack and defensiveness, often ostensibly about trivial matters.

Hypothesis to be tested   On the basis of these observations, one would predict that three stable groups would differ by the amount and timing of persuasion attempts. This hypothesis will now be spelled out.

Discriminating among types of stable marriages

For each 5 min of the interaction, the amount of conflict engagement, which is the sum of disagree and criticize codes on the MICS, was computed. Because persuasion episodes were relatively rare within couples, data were combined across couples and subjected to log-linear analysis. If the clinical observations are correct about the three groups of couples, the following pattern should be observed. The volatile couples should be highest in persuasion attempts, and these attempts should begin at the start, in the agenda-building phase. What this means is that the spouses are trying to persuade each other even at the stage of expressing feelings. Volatile couples then are expected to continue their persuasion attempts unabated throughout all parts of the interaction. The shape of their curve should be a straight line, at a higher elevation than the other two groups. Validating couples are expected to listen to one another in the agenda-building stage and to validate feelings with agreement or assent, so that their persuasion attempts should be high only in the middle third, or arguing phase, of the discussion. Validating couples are also expected to compromise and negotiate in the final third of the interaction. Hence, the amount of persuasion should fall for this group, and it ought to have an inverted-V shape. Avoiders are expected to avoid persuasion attempts throughout the interaction, so their curve should be at a low level, and it should be flat throughout the interaction. Figure 21.3 is a summary of the results. This figure, by visual inspection, does follow the predictions made. Essentially the same pattern of results held for husbands and for wives. If I examine the proportion of persuasion attempts in each phase of the discussion, validators and volatile couples showed essentially no gender differences across the three phases of the discussion. However, avoiders did show a gender difference. Most of the persuasion attempts by avoiding wives were in the first third, whereas most of the persuasion attempts of avoiding husbands were in the last third.

A log-linear analysis of the data in figure 21.3 was performed. The statistical tests are likelihood ratio chi-square tests for main effects and interactions and specific contrasts (see Gottman & Roy, 1991). There was a statistically significant effect for groups, $\chi^2(2, N = 73) = 65.44$, $p < .001$; a statistically significant effect for gender, $\chi^2(1, N = 73) = 4.26$, $p < .05$; but no significant effect by thirds, $\chi^2(2, N = 73) = 2.41\,ns$. The Group × Thirds interaction was statistically significant, $\chi^2(2, N = 73) = 19.20$, $p < .001$. Next, consider the data separately by spouse for each third of the interaction. I used contrasts (see Gottman & Roy, 1991). In the first third, persuasion attempts for volatile husbands were significantly greater than those for validating husbands ($z = 3.19$), and volatile husbands were greater than avoiders ($z = 3.41$), but avoiders and validators were not significantly

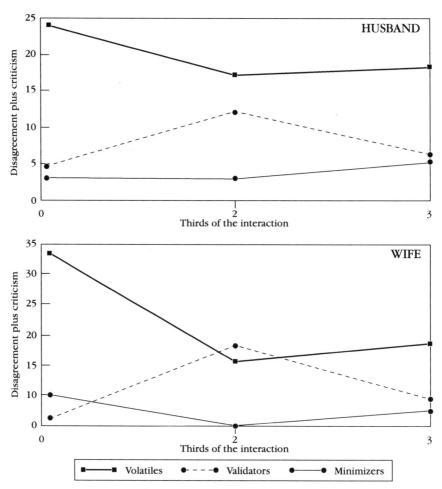

Figure 21.3 Graphs of Persuasion × Time differences across the three stable types of couples. (Top panel = husband's data; bottom panel = wife's data.)

different ($z = 0.73$). In the second third, persuasion attempts for volatile husbands were not significantly greater than those for validating husbands ($z = .92$), volatile husbands were greater than avoiders ($z = 2.78$), and validators significantly exceeded avoiders ($z = 2.15$). In the final third, volatile husbands were significantly greater than validating husbands ($z = 2.29$), and volatile husbands were greater than avoiders ($z = 2.51$), but avoiders and validators were not significantly different ($z = 0.29$). For wives, in the first third, volatile wives were significantly greater than validating wives ($z = 3.82$), and volatile wives were greater than avoiders ($z = 3.33$), but avoiders and validators were not significantly different ($z = 1.14$). In the second third, volatile wives were not significantly different than validating wives ($z = .50$), volatile wives were greater than avoiders ($z = 2.14$), and validators also exceeded avoiders ($z = 2.51$). In the final third, volatile wives were significantly greater than validating wives ($z = 2.10$), volatile wives were not significantly different from avoiders ($z = 1.70$), and neither were avoiders and validators significantly different ($z = 0.48$).

A balance theory of marriage

The classifications in this article are based on the relative balance of positive and negative speaker and listener behaviors. It is possible that the three types of stable couples described represent the entire range of adaptations that exist to balancing or regulating positive and negative behaviors in a marriage. If this were the case, then other adaptations would prove to be unstable longitudinally. Let us examine the nature of the three stable adaptations to balancing negativity and positivity. In the volatile case, the adaptation includes a lot of negativity. This tends to be balanced by a lot of laughter, positive presentation of issues, and a passionate, romantic marriage. This is the adaptation with a lot of nonneutral affect. There are two other adaptations that involve much less negative and positive affect and much more neutral interaction. One adaptation, represented by the validators, involves carefully picking and choosing when to disagree and confront conflict and then conveying some measure of support when one's partner expresses negative feelings about an issue. The other adaptation with high levels of neutral affect is the avoider adaptation. It appears to involve a minimization of the importance of disagreement. It results in a good deal of calm interaction, but pays the price with emotional distance in the marriage. We may think of these three adaptations as balancing some quantity of positivity against negativity.

Test of the balance theory Using only RCISS codes, all husband and wife positive speaker codes and all husband and wife negative speaker codes were separately summed, and the ratio was computed. The statistical comparison between stable and unstable couples resulted in $F(1, 68) = 29.20$, $p < .001$: Whether comparing stable and unstable husbands, $F(1, 68) = 19.51$, $p < .001$, or comparing wives, $F(1, 68) = 24.69$, $p < .001$, the results were significant. For husbands across all three stable groups, the ratio was 5.10; for wives the ratio was 5.06. For husbands in unstable marriages, the mean ratio was 1.06; for wives, the ratio was 0.67. There was no significant difference in the ratio between stable couples, for husbands, $F(2, 32) = 0.39$, and for wives, $F(2, 32) = 0.40$.

Extensions into affect These balance theory results have been specific to one observational coding system, the RCISS. The RCISS is a combination of both problem solving and affect. There are two interesting questions one may ask. First, would the results hold if only affect were examined with the SPAFF? Second, an advantage of the SPAFF is that all three marital interactions can be examined. Would the results obtained hold for interactions other than conflict resolution? Is there evidence for some other constant in these contexts? Or would roughly the same constant be obtained? To answer the first question, the ratio of positive to negative SPAFF affects for the conflict interaction was computed. There were again no significant differences between types of couples within the stable group; for husbands, $F(2, 32) = 0.39$, and for wives, $F(2, 32) = 0.40$. However, again according to prediction, the ratio discriminated stable from unstable couples on the conflict interaction; for husbands, $F(1, 64) = 7.93$, $p < .01$; for wives, $F(1, 64) = 6.16$, $p < .05$. Furthermore, the mean for stable husbands was 4.16, and that for unstable husbands was 0.91; the mean for stable wives was 5.26, and that for unstable wives was 0.46. Hence, on the conflict interaction this constant held as characteristic of stable couples when only pure affect was considered, as measured by the SPAFF.

To answer the second question, the same ratio was computed for the events of the day interaction and for the positive interaction. On the events conversation, again the husband ratio did not discriminate among stable types, and the same was true for the wife ratio: For husbands, $F(2, 21) = 0.37$, *ns*; for wives, $F(2, 27) = 0.22$, *ns*. However, again as predicted, the ratios did discriminate stable from unstable couples. For husbands, the mean for stable couples was 4.16 and the mean for unstable couples was $0.91, F(1, 64) = 7.93$, $p < .01$. For wives, the mean for stable couples was 5.26 and the mean for unstable couples was 0.46, $F(1, 67) = 6.16$, $p < .05$. Again, the constant of nearly 5.0 was obtained as the ratio of positive to negative affects for stable couples on the events of the day conversation, and a ratio of less that 1.0 was obtained for unstable couples. In the positive conversation, once again the ratio did not discriminate among stable subtypes. For husbands, the ratio was not significantly different across the groups, $F(2, 22) = 0.68$, *ns*, as was the case for wives, $F(2, 24) = 0.58$, *ns*. Once again, the ratio did discriminate between stable and unstable subtypes, for both husbands and wives: For husbands, $F(1, 64) = 7.93$, $p < .01$, and for wives, $F(1, 67) = 6.16$, $p < .05$. The mean for stable husbands was 4.16, and for unstable husbands the mean was 0.91. The mean for stable wives was 5.26, whereas the mean for unstable wives was 0.46. During conflict, the wives in the hostile group had a higher ratio of positive to negative affects than wives in the hostile/detached group (0.73 compared with 0.20; the F ratios for the conflict conversation were, for wives, $F(1, 31) = 10.03$, $p < .003$, and for husbands, $F(1, 29) = 0.95$, *ns*.

Summary: toward an ecology of behavior   The results can be summarized with contour graphs that display all five groups on one graph and show the degree of separation achievable with some of the measures. Figure 21.4 (left panel) is an illustration of a

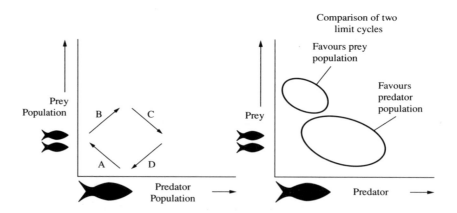

Figure 21.4   Predator-prey diagrams. (Left panel shows a stable limit cycle that is actually composed of regions of changing predator and prey populations. Right panel shows limit cycles, one favoring the predator and one favoring the prey.)

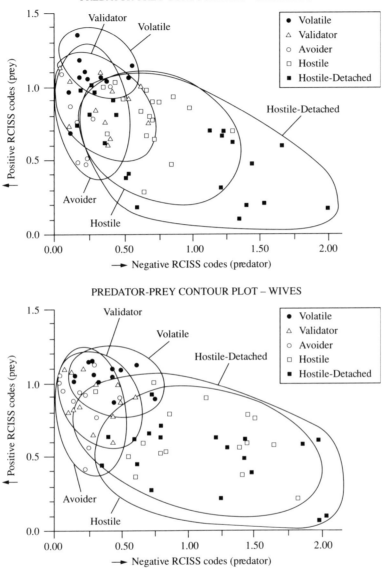

Figure 21.5 Predator-prey contour plots of positive and negative RICSS points. (RCISS = Rapid Couples Interaction Scoring System. Left panel = husbands' scores; right panel = wives' scores. Figure illustrates the five groups of couples.)

standard predator-prey diagram showing that what is called a *stable limit cycle* is actually composed of regions of changing predator and prey populations. Region A is one in which both populations are low and the population of the predator decreases because of lack of food, while the population of the prey increases because of the lack of predation. In Region B, there are lots of small fish but relatively few predators, and hence both populations can increase; this is shown by the direction of the vector B. In Region C, both populations are large, and the big fish are multiplying, which results in a reduction of the number of small fish. In Region D, there are few small fish and many larger fish, and both populations must decline.

The figure explains how one obtains a closed loop, or *limit cycle*, in this manner. Figure 21.4 (right panel) shows a predator–prey model illustrating two stable limit cycles, one favoring the predator and one favoring the prey. To apply these plots to the data of this study, in our data the species population will be replaced by a behavior frequency. In our case, negativity is the predator and positivity is the prey. Figure 21.5 illustrates the predator–prey contour plots of positive and negative RCISS points for husbands and wives. Each point represents the husbands' or wives' data for one particular couple. The figure illustrates the five groups of couples: contours have been drawn to encircle each group. It is clear from this figure that for stable couples the limit cycle favors the prey (positivity), whereas for unstable couples the limit cycle favors the predator (negativity).

Discussion

There seems to be a rough constant that is invariant across each of the three types of stable couples. This constant, the ratio of positive to negative RCISS speaker codes during conflict resolution, is about 5, and it is not significantly different across the three types of stable marriages. The volatile couples reach the ratio of 5 by mixing a lot of positive affect with a lot of negative affect. The validators mix a moderate amount of positive affect with a moderate amount of negative affect. The avoiders mix a small amount of positive affect with a small amount of negative affect. Each group does so in a way that achieves roughly the same balance between positive and negative. I can speculate that each type of marriage has its risks, benefits, and costs. The volatile marriage tends to be quite romantic and passionate, but it has the risk of dissolving into endless bickering. The validating marriage (which is consistent with current models of marital therapy) is calmer and intimate; these couples appear to value a companionate marriage and shared experiences, not individuality. The risk may be that romance will disappear over time, and partners will become merely close friends. The third type avoids the pain of confrontation and conflict, but the risk may be emotional distance and loneliness.

References

Allison, P. D., & Liker, J. K. (1982). Analyzing sequential categorical data on dyadic interaction: a comment on Gottman. *Psychological Bulletin, 91*, 393–403.

Bell, R. R. (1975). *Marriage and family interaction.* Homewood, IL: Dorsey Press.

Bentler, P. M., & Newcomb, M. D. (1978). Longitudinal study of marital success and failure. *Journal of Consulting and Clinical Psychology, 46*, 1053–1070.

Bishop, Y. M. M., Fienberg, S., & Holland, P. W. (1975). *Discrete multivariate analysis.* Cambridge, MA: MIT Press.

Block, J. H., Block, J., & Morrison, A. (1981). Parental agreement–disagreement on child-rearing and gender-related personality correlates in children. *Child Development, 52*, 965–974.

Constantine, J. A., & Bahr, S. J. (1980). Locus of control and marital stability: a longitudinal study. *Journal of Divorce, 4*, 11–22.

Cuber, J. F., & Harroff, P. B. (1965). *The significant Americans.* New York: Appleton-Century-Crofts.

Fitzpatrick, M. A. (1988). *Between husbands and wives: Communication in marriage.* Newbury Park, CA: Sage.

Gottman, J. M. (1979). *Marital interaction: Experimental investigations.* San Diego, CA: Academic Press.

Gottman, J. M., & Krokoff, L. J. (1989). The relationship between marital interaction and marital satisfaction: a longitudinal view. *Journal of Consulting and Clinical Psychology, 57*, 47–52.

Gottman, J. M., & Levenson, R. W. (1992). Toward a typology of marriage based on affective behavior: preliminary differences in behavior, physiology, health, and risk for dissolution. *Journal of Personality and Social Psychology, 63*, 221–233.

Gottman, J. M., Notarius, C., Markman, H., Bank, S., Yoppi, B., & Rubin, M. E. (1976). Behavior exchange theory and marital decision making. *Journal of Personality and Social Psychology, 34*, 14–23.

Gottman, J. M., & Roy, A. K. (1991). *Sequential analysis.* Cambridge: Cambridge University Press.

Kelly, L. E., & Conley, J. J. (1987). Personality and compatibility: a prospective analysis of marital stability and marital satisfaction. *Journal of Personality and Social Psychology, 52*, 27–40.

Krokoff, L. J., Gottman, J. M., & Hass, S. D. (1989). Validation of a global rapid couples interaction scoring system. *Behavioral Assessment, 11*, 65–79.

Margolin, G. (1988). Marital conflict is not marital conflict is not marital conflict. In R. DeV. Peters & R. J. McMahon (Eds.), *Social learning and systems approaches to marriage and the family* (pp. 193–216). New York: Brunner/Mazel.

Matthews, K. A., Weiss, S. M., Detre, T., Dembroski, T. M., Falkner, B., Manuck, S. B., & Williams, R., Jr. (1986). *Handbook of stress, reactivity, and cardiovascular disease.* New York: Wiley.

Olson, D. H. (1981). Family typologies: Bridging family research and family therapy. In E. E. Filsinger & R. A. Lewis (Eds.), *Assessing marriage: New behavioral approaches* (pp. 74–89). Newbury Park, CA: Sage.

Patterson, G. R. (1982). *Coercive family process.* Eugene, OR: Castalia Press.

Thibaut, J. W., & Kelley, H. H. (1959). *The social psychology of groups.* New York: Wiley.

Weiss, R. L., & Summers, K. J. (1983). Marital Interaction Coding System-III. In E. Filsinger (Ed.), *Marriage and family assessment* (pp. 85–116). Newbury Park, CA: Sage.

Wills, T. A., Weiss, R. L., & Patterson, G. R. (1974). A behavioral analysis of the determinants of marital satisfaction. *Journal of Clinical and Consulting Psychology, 42*, 802–811.

CHAPTER *22*

The Laws of Emotion

N. H. Frijda

The title of this paper by Nico Frijda hints at the idea that research on emotions has attained scientific standing. At the same time it echoes the proposals of the Dutch rationalist philosopher Baruch Spinoza, whose 1675 book on ethics was about emotions. Spinoza's main idea was that the universe is an expression of the mind of God, actuated according to what we call laws. The universe is everything that is. As an expression of God it cannot be imperfect. We human beings are part of this universe. The task for our rational minds, then, is to understand this. When we feel bitter at something that did not go as we wished, or angry at someone, Spinoza calls these passive emotions. They are based on confused ideas, of seeing our desires rather than the universe as causes of what happens.

It was Spinoza who coined the memorable phase "Of human bondage." And it was he who seems to have been the first in relatively modern times to have proposed the engaging idea that to accept and understand our emotions and their laws, rather than trying to escape them or pretend they do not exist, is to be freed from their bondage. Frijda's paper, then, is a modern version, setting out the laws of emotion that seem to constrain us. Or is it that in understanding these laws, we might take a step to becoming free?

One of Frijda's innovations has been to point out, and then show empirically (Frijda, Kuipers, & ter Schure, 1989), how the core of an emotion is what he calls "action readiness" – a preparedness to act in a certain kind of way in response to a certain kind of situation. If, as is claimed by Frijda and other cognitive researchers such as Oatley & Johnson-Laird, and Stein & Trabasso (selections 9 and 28) as well as developmental researchers like Campos and colleagues (1994) the emotions function to manage goal priorities, then these types of action readiness will be at least as important as the appraisals that have occupied much recent cognitive research on emotions.

N. H. Frijda, The laws of emotion. *American Psychologist, 43* (1988), 349–358. Copyright © 1988 by the American Psychological Association. Reprinted with permission.

References

Campos, J. J., Mumme, D. L., Kermoian, R., & Campos, R. G. (1994). A functionalist perspective on the nature of emotion. In N. A. Fox (Ed.), *The development of emotion regulation. Monographs of the Society for Research in Child Development* (Vol. *59*, 2–3, serial no. 240, pp. 284–303).

Frijda, N. H., Kuipers, P., & ter Schure, E. (1989). Relations among emotion, appraisal, and emotional action readiness. *Journal of Personality and Social Psychology, 57,* 212–228.

Spinoza, B. (1675). *The ethics* (R. H. M. Elwes, Trans.). New York: Dover (reprinted 1955).

When formulating "laws" in this article, I am discussing what are primarily empirical regularities. These regularities – or putative regularities – are, however, assumed to rest on underlying causal mechanisms that generate them. I am suggesting that the laws of emotion are grounded in mechanisms that are not of a voluntary nature and that are only partially under voluntary control. Not only emotions obey the laws; we obey them. We are subject to our emotions, and we cannot engender emotions at will.

The laws of emotion that I will discuss are not all equally well established. Not all of them originate in solid evidence, nor are all equally supported by it. To a large extent, in fact, to list the laws of emotion is to list a program of research. However, the laws provide a coherent picture of emotional responding, which suggests that such a research program might be worthwhile.

The law of situational meaning

What I mean by laws of emotion is best illustrated by the "Constitution" of emotion, the *law of situational meaning: Emotions arise in response to the meaning structures of given situations; different emotions arise in response to different meaning structures.* Emotions are dictated by the meaning structure of events in a precisely determined fashion.

On a global plane, this law refers to fairly obvious and almost trivial regularities. Emotions tend to be elicited by particular types of event. Grief is elicited by personal loss, anger by insults or frustrations, and so forth. This obviousness should not obscure the fact that regularity and mechanism are involved. Emotions, quite generally, arise in response to events that are important to the individual, and which importance he or she appraises in some way. Events that satisfy the individual's goals, or promise to do so, yield positive emotions; events that harm or threaten the individual's concerns lead to negative emotions; and emotions are elicited by novel or unexpected events.

Input some event with its particular kind of meaning; out comes an emotion of a particular kind. That is the law of situational meaning. In goes loss, and out comes grief. In goes a frustration or an offense, and out comes anger. Of course, the law does not apply in this crude manner. It is meanings and the subject's appraisals that count – that is, the relationship between events and the subject's concerns, and not events as such. Thus, in goes a personal loss that is felt as irremediable, and out comes grief, with a high degree of probability. In goes a frustration or an offense for which someone else is to blame and could have avoided, and out comes anger – almost certainly. The outputs are highly probable, but are not absolutely certain because the inputs can still be perceived in different fashions. One can view serious, irremediable personal loss as unavoidable, as in the nature of things; there will be resignation then instead of grief. Frustration or offense can be seen as caused by someone powerful who may have further offenses in store, and fear then is likely to supplant anger as the emotional response. These subtleties, rather than undermining the law of situational meaning, underscore it. Emotions change when meanings change. Emotions are changed when events are viewed differently. Input is changed, and output changes accordingly.

The substance of this law was advanced by Arnold (1960) and Lazarus (1966). Evidence is accumulating that it is valid and that a number of subsidiary laws – for the elicitation of fear, of anxiety, of joy, and so forth – can be subsumed under it. The evidence is indirect because it consists mainly of correlations between subjects' reports of their emotional states and their conscious appraisals of events, which are not faithful reflections of the cognitive antecedents. Still, the correlations are strong (see, e.g. Frijda, 1987; Smith & Ellsworth, 1987) and suggest mechanisms. In fact, a computer program has been written that takes descriptions of event appraisals as its input and that outputs plausible guesses of the emotion's names. It shows the beginnings of success. When given the descriptions by 30 subjects of affective states corresponding to 32 emotion labels, the computer achieved a hit rate of 31% for the first choice and of 71% for the first five choices (with chance percentages of 3% and 17% respectively; Frijda & Swagerman, 1987).

The law of situational meaning provides the overarching framework to organize findings on the cognitive variables that account for the various emotions and their intensity (see also Ortony, Clore, & Collins, 1988). These cognitive variables pertain not merely to how the individual thinks the events might affect him or her but also to how he or she might handle these events. They include secondary as well as primary appraisals, in Lazarus's (1966) terms. Fear involves uncertainty about one's ability to withstand or handle a given threat; grief involves certainty about the impossibility of reversing what happened. Analyses of self-reports and of the semantics of emotion terms offer converging conclusions on the major variables involved (see Scherer, 1988, for a review). Experimental studies corroborate the importance of many of them. Outcome uncertainty affects fear intensity (e.g. Epstein, 1973). Causal attributions have been shown to influence emotions of anger, pride, shame, and gratitude (Weiner, 1985). Unpredictability and uncontrollability contribute to the shaping of emotional response (Mineka & Hendersen, 1985). They may lead to depressive mood (Abramson, Seligman, & Teasdale, 1978) or reactance (Wortman & Brehm, 1975), depending on one's cognitive set. Erratic behavior in one's friends enrages when one is used to control and saddens when one is used to being controlled.

The workings of the law of situational meaning are not always transparent because they can be overridden by conscious control or by less conscious counterforces that I will discuss later. The law is most evident when resources for control and counterforces fail, such as in illness or exhaustion. Posttraumatic syndromes show that, under these conditions, almost every obstruction is a stimulus for angry irritation, every loss or failure one for sorrow, every uncertainty one for insecurity or anxiety, and almost every kindness one for tears.

Under more normal circumstances, too, the automatic workings of the law of situational meaning are evident. I mention two examples. One is "sentimentality," the almost compulsive emergence of tearful emotions when attachment themes are touched on in films or stories about miracle workers (Efran & Spangler, 1979), brides marrying in white, or little children who, after years of hardship, find a home or are lovingly accepted by their grandfathers. Tears are drawn, it seems, by a precise kind of sequence: Latent attachment concerns are awakened; expectations regarding their nonfulfillment are carefully evoked but held in abeyance; and then one is brusquely confronted with their fulfillment. The sequence is more potent than the observer's intellectual or emotional sophistication, a fact to which probably every reader can testify.

The other example concerns falling in love. Data from questionnaire studies (Rombouts, 1987) suggest that it is also triggered by a specific sequence of events, in which the qualities of the love-object are of minor importance. A person is ready to fall in love because of one of a number of reasons – loneliness, sexual need, dissatisfaction, or need of variety. An object then incites interest, again for one of a number of reasons, such as novelty, attractiveness, or mere proximity. Then give the person a moment of promise, a brief response from the object that suggests interest. It may be a confidence; it may be a single glance, such as a young girl may think she received from a pop star. Then give the person a brief lapse of time – anywhere between half an hour or half a day, the self-reports suggest – during which fantasies can develop. After that sequence, no more than a single confirmation, real or imagined, is needed to precipitate falling in love.

In the emergence of emotions people need not be explicitly aware of these meaning structures. They do their work, whether one knows it or not. One does not have to know that something is familiar in order to like it for that reason (Zajonc, 1980). Distinct awareness comes after the fact, if it comes at all.

Emotions

In the preceding section, I have not specified what I mean by "emotions" nor what it is that the laws of emotion involve. There is no consensus about the definition of emotion; one may quarrel endlessly about the word. The issue can be approached somewhat empirically, however, in bootstrapping fashion, by first assuming that what we loosely call "emotions" are responses to events that are important to the individual, and then by asking of what the responses to such events consist. Those responses are what the laws are about.

First of all, those responses – "emotions" – are subjective experiences. Their core is the experience of pleasure or pain. That core is embedded in the outcome of appraisal, the awareness of situational meaning structure. Emotional experience contains more, however, that emotion psychology seems to have almost forgotten.

Introspections produce a wealth of statements that refer to what I call "awareness of state of action readiness." Subjects report impulses to approach or avoid, desires to shout and sing or move, and the urge to retaliate; or, on occasion, they report an absence of desire to do anything, or a lack of interest, or feelings of loss of control (Davitz, 1969; Frijda, 1986, 1987).

What is interesting about these felt states of action readiness is that the kinds of states reported correspond to the kinds of state of action readiness that are manifest in overt behavior, for instance, facial expression and organized action. Awareness of state of action readiness is a rough reflection of state of action readiness itself [...]

The law of situational meaning can now be phrased more precisely. Meaning structures are lawfully connected to forms of action readiness. Events appraised in terms of their meanings are the emotional piano player's finger strokes; available modes of action readiness are the keys that are tapped; changes in action readiness are the tones brought forth.

The keys, the available modes of action readiness, correspond to the behavior systems and general response modes with which humans are endowed. These include the programs for innate behavioral patterns, of which elementary defensive and aggressive behaviors, laughter and crying, and the universal facial expressions (Ekman, 1982) are elements. They further include the general activation or deactivation patterns of exuberance, undirected excitement, and apathetic response, and the pattern of freezing or inhibition. They also include the various autonomic and hormonal response patterns – those of orienting, of active or passive coping, and the like, described by the Laceys (Lacey & Lacey, 1970), Obrist (1981), and Mason (1975), among others. These physiological patterns form, so to speak, the logistic support of the action readiness changes involved. And last, the response modes include the action control changes that are manifest in behavioral interference and that we experience as preoccupation and urgency; sometimes, these are the only aspect of our change in action readiness that we feel or show.

The law of concern

The law of situational meaning has a necessary complement in the *law of concern: Emotions arise in response to events that are important to the individual's goals, motives, or concerns.* Every emotion hides a concern, that is, a more or less enduring disposition to prefer particular states of the world. A concern is what gives a particular event its emotional meaning. We suffer when ill befalls someone because, and as long as, we love that someone. We glow with pride upon success and are dejected upon failure when and because we strive for achievement, in general or in that particular trade. Emotions point to the presence of some concern. The concern may be different from one occurrence of an emotion to another. We fear the things we fear for many different reasons. Note that the law of concern joins different and even opposite emotions. One suffers when a cherished person is gravely ill; one feels joy at his or her fortune or recovery; one is angry at those who harm him or her. Emotions arise from the interaction of situational meanings and concerns.

One may question whether a concern can be found behind every single instance of emotion. It would not be meaningful to posit a "concern for the unexpected" behind startle (but, also, it may not be meaningful to regard startle as an emotion; cf. Ekman, Friesen, & Simons, 1985). But by and large, the law of concern holds and is of considerable value in understanding emotions. Why does someone get upset at the news of another person's illness? Because he or she seems to love that person. Why does someone feel such terrible jealousy? Because, perhaps, he or she yearns for continuous possession and symbiotic proximity. Emotions form the prime material in the exploration of an individual's concerns.

The law of apparent reality

According to the law of situational meaning, emotions are dictated by the way a person perceives the situation. One aspect of this perception is particularly important for the elicitation of emotion. I will call it the situation's "apparent reality." Emotions are subject to the *law of apparent reality: Emotions are elicited by events appraised as real, and their intensity corresponds to the degree to which this is the case.*

What is taken to be real elicits emotions. What does not impress one as true and unavoidable elicits no emotion or a weaker one. The law applies to events taken to be real when in fact they are not. It also applies to events that are real but that are not taken seriously. Whatever is present counts; whatever lies merely in the future can be taken lightly or disregarded, however grim the prospects. Mere warnings usually are not heeded. Examples are found in the responses to nuclear energy dangers that tend to evoke emotions only when consequences are felt. Unrest arose when restrictions on milk consumption were imposed after Chernobyl. Symbolic information generally has weak impact, as compared to the impact of pictures and of events actually seen – the "vividness effect" discussed in social psychology (Fiske & Taylor, 1984). A photograph of one distressed child in Vietnam had more effect than reports about thousands killed. Although people have full knowledge of the threat of nuclear war, they tend to remain cool under that threat, except for the emotions rising during a few weeks after the showing of a film such as *The Day After* (Fiske, 1987).

Examples abound from less dramatic contexts. Telling a phobic that spiders are harmless is useless when the phobic sees the crawling animal. Knowing means less than seeing. When someone tells us in a friendly fashion that she or he does not appreciate our attentions, we tend not to heed her or him. Words mean less than tone of voice. When someone steps on our toes, we get angry even when we know that he or she is not to blame. Feeling means more than knowing.

I call this the law of apparent reality and use the word *reality* to characterize the stimulus properties at hand; Ortony, Clore, and Collins (1988) extensively discuss the issue under the same heading. The preceding anecdotal examples are paralleled by experimental results. Bridger and Mandel (1964) showed that a conditioned fear response, established by the warning that shock would follow a signal light, extinguished at once when shock electrodes were removed. It did not, however, when a single strong shock reinforcement had actually been delivered. Conditioned electrodermal response persisted indefinitely after shock, in the same way that a smell of burning evokes a sense of panic in anyone who has ever been in a conflagration. The powerlessness of verbal reassurance to diminish phobic anxiety contrasts with the abatement of phobia sometimes obtained by "live modeling plus participation," that is, by making the subject actually touch the snake or spider after seeing a model do it (Bandura, 1977). Smaller effects, but still effects, are obtained by having the subject imagine touching the snake or spider, provided that true, vivid imagery is achieved (Lang, 1977).

The law of apparent reality applies to numerous instances of strong emotion in everyday life and explains important phenomena, such as the absence of strong emotions where one might have expected them. Grief dawns only gradually and slowly after personal loss. Emotions often do not arise when being told of loss, and the loss is merely known. They break through when the lost person is truly missed, when the arm reaches out in vain or the desire to communicate finds its target to be absent (Parkes, 1972). The law also accounts for the weakness of reason as opposed to the strength of passion. "Reason" refers to the consideration of satisfactions and pains that are far away and only symbolically mediated. "Passion" refers to the effects of the present, of what is actually here to entice or repel.

What is the source of the law of apparent reality? What do actual stimuli such as shock, fires, live encounters, truly missing someone, and actions such as touching a snake have in common? It is, I think, their "reality." Stimuli appraised as "real" include (a) unconditioned affective stimuli such as pain, startle stimuli, and perceived expressive behaviors (Lanzetta & Orr, 1986; Ohman & Dimberg, 1978); (b) sensory stimuli strongly associated to such stimuli; and (c) events involving the actual ineffectuality of actions, such as not receiving an answer to one's calls. Several guesses can be made as to why these are the emotionally effective stimuli; a plausible one is that the modes of action readiness are biological dispositions that need sensory stimuli as their unconditioned releasers. It is sensory stimulations that have the proper input format for the emotion process. Notice that vivid imagination, too, has the properties of "reality." It is capable of eliciting or abating strong emotions. Imagination, conceivably, serves to transform symbolic knowledge into emotionally effective stimulation. The effects of imaginal stimuli – fantasies, films, songs, pictures, stories – underline the major problem behind the law of apparent reality: to explain why one kind of cognition is not equivalent to another.

The laws of change, habituation, and comparative feeling

The nature of events that elicit emotions must be still further specified because emotions obey the *law of change: Emotions are elicited not so much by the presence of favorable or unfavorable conditions, but by actual or expected changes in favorable or unfavorable conditions.* It is change that does it – change with respect to current adaptation level. Everyday examples of the importance of change abound. Subjective satisfactions, these days, are not superior to those in, say, 1937, when economic conditions were incomparably inferior. They probably are not superior to subjective satisfactions in any developing country that suffers no outright famine or oppression. Or, take the common observation that spouses who were taken for granted and were even felt to be sources of irritation are gravely missed after they die or leave. "One never stops to wonder, until a person's gone," as Dory Previn (1970) put it, "one never stops to wonder, 'til he's left and carried on."

The greater the change, the stronger the subsequent emotion. Having overcome uncertainty results in a pleasure of considerably larger magnitude than that produced by the same event without prior challenge or suspense. Basketball fans enjoy the victory of their team most when both teams' chances of winning are even (Ortony & Clore, 1988). Laughter generally follows what has been called the "suspense-mastery" or "arousal- safety" sequence (Rothbart, 1973): During infants' rough-and-tumble play, for instance, laughter is evoked only at the stage of development in which the event is just on the verge between being under control and being beyond control (Sroufe & Waters, 1976). A similar sequence accounts for the enjoyment of suspense in crime and adventure tales and perhaps even for that of mountain climbing and stunt riding where, on occasion, it results in peak experience (Piët, 1987).

The law of change can take treacherous forms, because adaptation level is not its only frame of reference. Hopes and perspectives on the future contribute. Goal-gradient phenomena seem to find their root herein. War pilots went on their missions with bravura, which tended to shift to anxiety and depression when possible survival once again became a real option toward the end of their tour of duty (Janis, 1951).

The law of change, to a large extent, is based on the *law of habituation: Continued pleasures wear off; continued hardships lose their poignancy.* Habituation is known experimentally mainly from the orienting response. There is more evidence, however, from repeated exposures to phobic objects or electric shocks (e.g. Epstein, 1973). Daily life offers ample illustrations again, partly consoling ones, partly saddening ones. The pains of loss of love abate with time, but love itself gradually loses its magic. Continued exposure to inhumanities blunts both suffering and moral discernment.

The law of change has many variants. One is the law of affective contrast. Loss of satisfaction does not yield a neutral condition, but positive misery. Loss of misery does not yield a sense of normality, but positive happiness. The law of affective contrast was formulated by Beebe-Center (1932) as resulting from adaptation level shifts and by Solomon (1980) as due to "opponent processes." Whatever its source, it is a law of considerable practical consequence. It is the basis of the play of take-and-give that proves so effective in, for instance, brainwashing. One takes privileges away and subsequently gives them back in part, and the emotions of gratitude and attachment result.

The law of change itself expresses a more encompassing generality that we can name the *law of comparative feeling: The intensity of emotion depends on the relationship between an event and some frame of reference against which the event is evaluated.* The frame of reference is often the prevailing state of affairs, but it can also be an expectation, as it is in the conditions for relief, disappointment, or the enhancement of joy by previous suspense. Or it can be provided by the fate and condition of other people. Ratings of subjective well-being have been shown to vary with prior exposure to descriptions of the past as times of poverty or as times of personal closeness. One tends to feel less well off when others fare better. Envy and *Schadenfreude* are names for emotions rooted in comparisons of this kind.

Generally speaking, the frame of reference that determines what counts as an emotional event consists of that which is deemed possible. This holds with considerable generality. Those who wring their hands in despair still entertain hopes; they have not really abandoned desiring. Those who grieve and mourn have not really taken their leave from the departed person; they still expect him or her at the other end of their arms, bed, or table. Those who feel that they should be able to cope suffer when they cannot cope. The point needs to be stressed and elaborated because internal locus of control, achievement motivation, and being in control are generally held to be factors that contribute to coping with stress. They are and do as long as there exist ways to cope. They bring extra burdens when there are no such ways. Anecdotal evidence from concentration camps and trauma research, as well as experimental studies with animals and humans (Rothbaum, Weisz, & Snyder, 1982; Weiss, 1971; Wortman & Brehm, 1975), support this conclusion.

The law of hedonic asymmetry

The laws of habituation and comparative feeling operate only within certain limits. There exists, it would seem, misery that one does not get used to; there is deprivation to which one does not adapt. This fact has, it appears, no counterpart for positive emotions. Joy, bliss, and fascination invariably tend to fade toward neutrality or some pale contentment. One must, I think, posit a *law of hedonic asymmetry*, the law of asymmetrical adaptation to pleasure or pain: *Pleasure is always contingent upon change and disappears with continuous satisfaction. Pain may persist under persisting adverse conditions.* One gets used to the events that, earlier, delighted and caused joy; one does not get used to continuous harassment or humiliation. Fear can go on forever; hopes have limited duration. The law predicts a negative balance for the quality of life, unless self-deceit and self-defense intervene, which of course they do. It may not be as bad as that when life is not filled with adverse conditions, but for many people life is filled in that manner. Remember that the joys of freedom, for those who suffered oppression, do not last as long as the sorrows of oppression did. True enough, the situations underlying these examples are not altogether transparent. It is difficult to disentangle the effects of repetition, accumulation, and sheer persistence of a given state of affairs. Oppression makes itself known each day; liberty, as an event, occurs only at the day of liberation. Be that as it may, at a gross level the law appears to hold and to manifest itself in many ways, dramatic as well as commonplace. The grief upon one's partner's being gone is much, much more poignant and enduring than the joy caused by his or her presence a month before or the joy after his or her return one month later.

The law of hedonic asymmetry is a stern and bitter law. It seems almost a necessary one, considering its roots, which, theoretically, are so obvious. Emotions exist for the sake of signaling states of the world that have to be responded to or that no longer need response and action. Once the "no more action needed" signal has sounded, the signaling system can be switched off; there is no further need for it. That the net quality of life, by consequence, tends to be negative is an unfortunate result. It shows the human mind to have been made not for happiness, but for instantiating the blind biological laws of survival.

On the other hand, the law's outcomes are not unavoidable. Adaptation to satisfaction can be counteracted by constantly being aware of how fortunate one's condition is and of how it could have been otherwise, or actually was otherwise before – by rekindling impact through recollection and imagination. Enduring happiness seems possible, and it can be understood theoretically. However, note that it does not come naturally, by itself. It takes effort.

The law of conservation of emotional momentum

The law of change, or at least the law of habituation, shows a further restriction. One of its consequences seems to be that emotions diminish with time. This supposition, or one of its forms, is expressed in the common adage that time heals all wounds. That adage, however, is untrue. Time heals no wounds. On the contrary, what accounts for habituation is repeated exposure to the emotional event within the bounds of asymmetry of adaptation. It is repetition that does it, when it does, not time. Time does not really soften emotions. We may phrase the *law of conservation of emotional momentum thus: Emotional events retain their power to elicit emotions indefinitely, unless counteracted by repetitive exposures that permit extinction or habituation, to the extent that these are possible.*

The law will be difficult to prove because it asserts resistance against change when nothing happens. Yet, it is of value to propose it, and there is evidence to support it. As regards its value, behavior therapy and trauma theory both appear to hold the silent supposition that enduring trauma effects need explanation in terms of avoidance, denial, secondary gain, or whatever. Yet, traditional extinction theory as well as the interference theory of forgetting make it more reasonable to assume that the emotional impact of traumatic events never really wanes; it can only be overwritten. As regards the evidence, it is ample, although only clinical or anecdotal. Loss of a child never appears to become a neutral event (Lehman, Wortman, & Williams, 1987). The persistence or recurrence of other trauma effects is of course well-known. Emotions surge up when stimuli resembling the original stimuli are encountered or when aroused by "unbidden" images (the term is Horowitz's, 1976) in nightmares or even while awake. The sudden fear – shivering, palpitations, a sense of panic – upon the smell of burning in former fire victims is a more common occurrence. Equally common is the unexpected outburst of tears when, many years later, a letter, a toy, or a piece of clothing belonging to a child who died is stumbled upon, or the blood that rushes to one's face when recalling an embarrassing act committed years ago. The emotional experiences tend to be fresh, as poignant and as articulable as they were at the original occasion, or perhaps even more so. Certain old pains just do not grow old; they only refer to old events.

The law of closure

In the preceding sections, I have discussed the lawful determination of emotional reactions, mentioning the determinants of situational meaning, concerns, apparent reality, change, and momentum. Emotional response itself, too, has its lawful properties, which can be subsumed under the *law of closure: Emotions tend to be closed to judgments of relativity of impact and to the requirements of goals other than their own.* They tend to be absolute with regard to such judgments and to have control over the action system.

It may be, according to the law of change, that the causes of emotion are relative ones, relative, that is, to one's frame of reference – emotional response does not know this relativity and does not recognize it. For someone who is truly angry, the thing that happened is felt to be absolutely bad. It is disgraceful. It is not merely a disgraceful act but one that flows from the actor's very nature and disposition. Somebody who has acted so disgracefully *is* disgraceful and thus will always be. The offense and the misery it causes have a character of perpetuity. In strong grief the person feels that life is devoid of meaning, that life cannot go on without the one lost. Each time one falls in love, one feels one never felt like that before. One dies a thousand deaths without the other. Every feature or action of the love object has an untarnishable gloss for as long as the infatuation lasts. In the presence of strong desires – think of trying to lose weight, stop smoking, or get off drugs – one feels as if one will die when they are not satisfied and that the pain is insupportable, even while one knows that the pang of desire will be over in a minute or two. Verbal expressions of emotions tend to reflect this absoluteness in quality and time: "I could kill him" or "I cannot live without her."

The closure of emotion is manifest not only in the absoluteness of feeling but also in the fact that emotions know no probabilities. They do not weigh likelihoods. What they know, they know for sure. Could it be that your friend is meeting someone else? Your jealousy is certain. Could it be that your partner is an inattentive person? Your anger is certain. Does she love me? Love now is certain that she does, and then is certain that she does not. When jealous, thoughts of scenes of unfaithfulness crop up, and one suffers from images self-created. It is the same for the delights and the anxieties of love. Love is consummated ten times before it actually is, and, when one is uncertain whether the loved one will be at the rendezvous, one prepares the reproachful speech over the telephone in advance.

The absoluteness of feelings and thinking is mirrored by what people do. They tend to act upon this absoluteness. The primary phenomenon of emotion, one may argue, is what can be called the "control precedence" of action readiness (Frijda, 1986). The action readiness of emotion tends to occupy center stage. It tends to override other concerns, other goals, and other actions. It tends to override considerations of appropriateness or long-term consequence. Control precedence applies to action as well as to nonaction, to fear's impulse to flee as well as to grief or despair's lethargy. It applies to single actions, such as shouting or crying, as well as to the execution of long-term plans, such as when passionate love makes a person neglect his or her obligations. It applies to attentional control (Mandler, 1984). It also applies to the information processing involved in action preparation and execution, where it shows in the effects of emotion on performance – activating under some conditions and interfering under others.

Closure, or control precedence, may well be considered the essential feature of emotion, its distinguishing mark, much more so than autonomic arousal or the occurrence of innate responses such as crying or facial expressions. The notion of control precedence captures in some sense the involuntary nature of emotional impulse or apathy, its characteristic of being an "urge," both in experience and in behavior.

The law of closure expresses what I think is the major, basic, theoretical fact about emotion: its modularity (Fodor, 1981). Emotion can be considered the outflow of a module serving the regulation of activity for safeguarding the satisfaction of the individual's major goals or concerns. Modularity is the conception that best accounts for the central properties of emotional response hinted at in this section (see Frijda & Swagerman, 1987).

The law of care for consequence

Emotion is not always as absolute as just sketched. Emotions do manifest deliberation, calculation, or consideration. Infatuation can be stingy, and anger can be prudent. However, I argue, closure and absoluteness reflect the basic modular shape of emotion. The manifestations of that basic shape may run into opposite tendencies, though, that stem from the *law of care for consequence: Every emotional impulse elicits a secondary impulse that tends to modify it in view of its possible consequences*. The major effect is response moderation. Its major mechanism is response inhibition.

Presence of a tendency toward moderation or inhibition of response – that is, presence of emotion control – must be considered a ubiquitous fact of emotion. Its ubiquity, and thus the validity of the law, paradoxically is evident in those rare instances when control power fails, as happens in blind panic or anger, with neurological interferences such as temporal epilepsy (Mark & Ervin, 1970) or experimental decortication (Bard, 1934), and under toxic influences like those of alcohol. Normal fury or passion, however violent, is nonetheless controlled. In anger, one rarely smashes one's truly precious objects. When madly in love, one still waits to get home before consummating. Something snaps when going from there to frenzy, to blind impulse.

The law of care for consequence, too, is a law of emotion. Control, in large measure, is an emotional response. Anxiety – rigid anxiety, freezing – in fact is its most complete expression; the drying up of emotional freedom before critical onlookers is a more moderate version. Like other emotional responses, control is elicited or maintained by stimuli. The stimuli for control are the signals for possible adverse consequences of uninhibited response such as retaliation, reprobation, or miscarriage of plans. The notion that inhibition is triggered by anticipation of adverse response consequences, of course, comes from Gray (1982).

The fact that involuntary emotion control itself is an emotional response implies that the other laws of emotions apply to it, notably the law of apparent reality. One cannot at will shed restraint, as little as one can at will shed anxiety or timidity. Emotional spontaneity is a function of how the environment is perceived to respond. Environmentally induced inhibition is illustrated by audience effects like the one just mentioned, familiar from examinations or auditions and from social facilitation research. Opposite, disinhibitory effects are found in the surprising emotional responsiveness, the increase in susceptibility to weeping and sexual excitement, in groups that are sympathetic toward such impulses. Therapy groups, sensitivity training groups, and meetings in sects like those led by Baghwan Rajneesh illustrate what is meant. The point is of much more relevant consequence because it provides a basis for explaining certain aspects of mass behavior. According to deindividuation theory (e.g. Zimbardo, 1970), mass enthusiasm, mass ecstasy, and mass violence are consequences of decreases in self-monitoring and of focusing attention on a leader and a common objective. These mass phenomena, in other words, result from a decrease in control due to the absence of stimuli that signal adverse response consequences and to the presence of stimuli that signal approbation of unhampered impulse expression.

The laws of the lightest load and the greatest gain

Emotion control is not dictated entirely by external cues, or, more precisely, to the extent that it is dominated by external cues, those cues themselves are, within limits, at the subject's discretion. One can focus now upon this, then upon that, aspect of reality. One can complement reality with imagination or detract from it by not thinking of particular implications. The construction of situational meaning structures, in other words, offers leeway for emotional control that has its origins within the object himself or herself. Situational meaning structures can be chosen in ways that decrease emotional intensity, prevent occurrence of emotion, or make events appear more tolerable or more pleasing. The situational meaning structure that dictates emotion, in accordance with our first law, is in part shaped and transformed by its own expected outcomes and consequences. Transformation follows various principles. One of these can be phrased as the *law of the lightest load: Whenever a situation can be viewed in alternative ways, a tendency exists to view it in a way that minimizes negative emotional load.* "Negative emotional load" refers to the degree to which a situation is painful and hard to endure.

Defensive denial is commonplace and has been widely described (see Lazarus & Folkman, 1984). The many ways to minimize emotional load, however, merit emphasis; mechanisms exist to ensure it at different levels of the process by which meaning structures are constructed. Denial, avoidant thinking, and entertaining of illusionary hopes operate at almost the conscious, voluntary level (see Weisman's, 1972, concept of "middle knowledge"). People often claim that they had always known that their illness would be fatal, that the loss they suffered would be permanent, or that the malfunctioning in the nuclear plant was dangerous, their earlier denials notwithstanding. Note that such knowledge does not prevent the denials from being resistant to correction, presumably because the load reduction they effect is so considerable.

Other mechanisms of load lightening operate at a much more elementary level. This applies particularly to the mechanisms that transform one's sense of reality and block the occurrence of hedonic appreciations. What I am referring to are the mechanisms of depersonalization, the occurrence of the sense of unreality, the veil over emotional feeling. Depersonalization occurs under all conditions of shock, severe trauma, severe threat, and severe pain. It has been described contingent upon accidents, serious loss or failure, torture, and sexual abuse (e.g. Cappon & Banks, 1961).

Denial and depersonalization are by no means the only ways in which load minimizing operates. The interplay of emotion and cognition can take many shapes that often are, for the subject, as difficult to recognize as they are difficult to bear. Examples are provided by the occurrence of painful emotions that, there are reasons to suppose, replace still more devastating ones. Sometimes, for instance, people entertain a "worst case hypothesis," preferring the apparent certainty of a disastrous prospect over the uncertainty of a future unknown. They convince themselves, for instance, that they are suffering from fatal illness in order to shield themselves from the possible shock of being told unpreparedly. An even more complex interplay is found in the cognitive strategy that leads people to view themselves as responsible when in fact they have been victims of arbitrary mal-treatment. The guilt feelings that, paradoxically, are so common in victims of sexual or other child abuse appear to serve to retain the view that adults are dependable and right in what they do. These guilt feelings are the lesser price to pay compared to the utter despair and disorientation that would otherwise follow. They permit the victim to see sense in a fate that contains none (Kroon, 1986).

The law of the lightest load blends into the *law of the greatest gain: Whenever a situation can be viewed in alternative ways, a tendency exists to view it in a way that maximizes emotional gain.* Emotions produce gains that differ from one emotion to another. Anger intimidates and instills docility. Fear saves the efforts of trying to overcome risks. Guilt feelings for misdeeds done confer high moral standing. Grief provides excuses, confers the right to be treated with consideration, and gives off calls for help. Often, when crying in distress or anger, one casts half an eye for signs of sympathy or mollification. Anticipation of such consequences, it can be argued, belongs to the factors that generate one particular situational meaning structure rather than another, and thus brings one particular emotion rather than another into existence. The mechanism involved is transparent. One focuses, for instance, on the idea that another is to blame in order to permit emergence of an anger that makes the other refrain from what he or she is doing. The mechanism operates in jealousy, and the coercive effects perpetuate much marital quarreling. Even if the pains of jealousy may not originate in the wish to prevent the partner from being unfaithful, that wish strongly sustains jealousy; it does so particularly when the partner yields and gives up part of his or her freedom of action. Who would wish to make one suffer so? Here, too, certain painful emotions appear to result from something resembling choice – choice of a painful emotion over a still more painful one. That process in fact is rather general. Grief upon loss, for instance, tends to be willfully prolonged, not only because it provides excuses but also because it keeps the lost person nearby, so to speak. When grief is over, true loneliness sets in.

Concluding remarks

[. . .] Even if not subjected blindly to the laws of emotion, still we are subjected to them. When falling in love, when suffering grief for a lost dear one, when tortured by jealousy, when blaming others or fate for our misfortunes, when saying "never" when we mean "now," when unable to refrain from making that one remark that will spoil an evening together, one is propelled by the big hand of emotion mechanism. I would like, in conclusion, to return to the issue touched on in the beginning of this article: the opposition one may feel between the lawfulness of emotions and the sense of personal freedom.

Note, first, that there is comfort in the notion of the lawfulness of emotion and in one's participation in the laws of nature that that notion implies. It is the comfort that resides in the recognition of necessity generally. I mentioned previously the law of comparative feeling – emotions are proportional to the difference between what is and what is deemed possible. Recognizing necessity where there is necessity, where nature limits one's control, can considerably decrease emotional load. More important, there is, I think, no true opposition between lawfulness and freedom. Personal freedom, wrote Spinoza (1677/1955) consists in acting according to one's own laws rather than to those imposed by someone else.

Second, as I hinted at earlier in this article, neither is there a fundamental opposition between Emotion and Reason. It may be argued that reason consists of basing choices on the perspectives of emotions at some later time. Reason dictates not giving in to one's impulses because doing so may cause greater suffering later. Reason dictates nuclear disarmament because we expect more sorrow than pleasure from nuclear war, if not for ourselves then for our children, whose fate fills us with emotion. The only true opposition is that between the dictates of the law of apparent reality, which tend to attach to the here and now, and the anticipations of later emotions, which tend not to be so dictated and thereby lack emotional force.

It is here that the laws of emotion and reason may meet and where both emotion and reason can be extended so as to make them coincide more fully with one's own laws. Following reason does not necessarily imply exertion of the voluntary capacities to suppress emotion. It does not necessarily involve depriving certain aspects of reality of their emotive powers. On the contrary, our voluntary capacities allow us to draw more of reality into the sphere of emotion and its laws. They allow us to turn the law of apparent reality into a law of reality, that is, to let reality – full reality, including long-term consequences – be what determines emotion. They allow one's emotions to be elicited not merely by the proximal, or the perceptual, or that which directly interferes with one's actions, but by that which in fact touches on one's concerns, whether proximal or distal, whether occurring now or in the future, whether interfering with one's own life or that of others. This is accomplished with the help of imagination and deeper processing. These procedures, as I have suggested, can confer emotive power on stimuli that do not by their nature have it. They can extend the driving forces of emotion to the spheres of moral responsibility, for instance. The laws of emotion can extend to the calls of reason as much as to those of immediate interests.

References

Abramson, L., Seligman, M., & Teasdale, J. (1978). Learned helplessness in humans: critique and reformulation. *Journal of Abnormal Psychology, 87*, 49–74.

Arnold, M. B. (1960). *Emotion and personality*. 2 vols. New York: Columbia University Press.

Bain, A. (1859). *The emotions and the will*. London: Longmans.

Bandura, A. (1977). *Social learning theory*. Englewood Cliffs, NJ: Prentice Hall.

Bard, P. (1934). On emotional expression after decortication with some remarks on certain theoretical views. *Psychological Review, 38*, 309–329; 424–449.

Beebe-Center, J. G. (1932). *The psychology of pleasantness and unpleasantness*. New York: Van Nostrand.

Bridger, W. H., & Mandel, J. J. (1964). A comparison of GSR fear responses produced by threat and electrical shock. *Journal of Psychiatric Research, 2*, 31–40.

Cappon, D., & Banks, R. (1961). Orientation perception: a review and preliminary study of distortion in orientation perception. *Archives of General Psychiatry, 5*, 380–392.

Davitz, J. R. (1969). *The language of emotion*. New York: Academic Press.

Dijker, A. J. M. (1987). Emotional reactions to ethnic minorities. *European Journal of Social Psychology, 17*, 305–325.

Efran, J. S., & Spangler, T. J. (1979). Why grown-ups cry: a two-factor theory and evidence from *The Miracle Worker*. *Motivation and Emotion, 3*, 63–72.

Ekman, P. (Ed.). (1982). *Emotion in the human face*, 2nd edn. New York: Cambridge University Press.

Ekman, P. E., Friesen, W. V., & Simons, R. C. (1985). Is the startle reaction an emotion? *Journal of Personality and Social Behavior, 49*, 1416–1426.

Epstein, S. (1973). Expectancy and magnitude of reaction to a noxious UCS. *Psychophysiology, 10*, 100–107.

Fiske, S. T. (1987). People's reactions to nuclear war: implications for psychologists. *American Psychologist, 42*, 207–217.

Fiske, S. T., & Taylor, S. E. (1984). *Social cognition*. New York: Random House.

Fodor, J. (1981). *The modularity of mind*. Cambridge, MA: MIT Press.

Frijda, N. H. (1986). *The emotions*. London: Cambridge University Press.

—— (1987). Emotions, cognitive structure and action tendency. *Cognition and Emotion, 1*, 115–144.

Frijda, N. H., & Swagerman, J. (1987). Can computers feel? *Cognition and Emotion, 1*, 235–258.

Gray, J. (1982). *The neuropsychology of anxiety: Inquiry into the septo-hippocampal system*. Oxford: Clarendon Press.

Horowitz, M. J. (1976). *Stress response syndromes*. New York: Jason Aronson.

Izard, C. E. (1977). *Human emotions*. New York: Plenum Press.

Janis, I. L. (1951). *Air war and emotional stress*. New York: McGraw-Hill.

Kroon, R. M. C. (1986). *De wereld op zijn kop: Een literatuurstudie naar parentificatie en incest* [The world upside down: A literature survey on parentification and incest]. Unpublished master's thesis, Amsterdam University.

Kuipers, P. (1987). *Appraisal and action readiness in emotions*. Unpublished doctoral dissertation, Amsterdam University.

Lacey, J. I., & Lacey, B. C. (1970). Some autonomic-nervous system relationships. In P. Black (Ed.), *Physiological correlates of emotion* (pp. 205–227). New York: Academic Press.

Lang, P. (1977). Imagery and therapy: an information processing analysis of fear. *Behavior Therapy, 8*, 862–886.

Lanzetta, J. T., & Orr, S. P. (1986). Excitatory strength of expressive faces: Effects of happy and fear expressions and context on the extinction of a conditioned fear response. *Journal of Personality and Social Behavior, 50*, 190–194.

Lazarus, R. S. (1966). *Psychological stress and the coping process*. New York: McGraw-Hill.

Lazarus, R. S., & Folkman, S. (1984). *Stress, appraisal and coping*. New York: Springer.

285

Lehman, D. R., Wortman, C. B., & Williams, A. F. (1987). Long-term effects of losing a spouse or child in a motor vehicle crash. *Journal of Personality and Social Behavior, 52,* 218–231.

Mandler, G. (1984). *Mind and body: The psychology of emotion and stress.* New York: Norton.

Mark, V. H., & Ervin, F. R. (1970). *Violence and the brain.* New York: Harper & Row.

Mason, J. W. (1975). Emotion as reflected in patterns of endocrine integration. In L. Levi (Ed.), *Emotions: Their parameters and measurement* (pp. 143–181). New York: Raven Press.

Mineka, S., & Hendersen, R. W. (1985). Controllability and predictability in acquired motivation. *Annual Review of Psychology, 36,* 495–529.

Obrist, P. A. (1981). *Cardiovascular psychophysiology: A perspective.* New York: Plenum Press.

Öhman, A., & Dimberg, U. (1978). Facial expressions as conditioned stimuli for electro-dermal responses: A case of "preparedness"? *Journal of Personality and Social Psychology, 36,* 1251–1258.

Ortony, A., & Clore, G. L. (1988). *Report on emotions in basketball fans.* Manuscript in preparation.

Ortony, A., Clore, G. L., & Collins, A. (1988). *The cognitive structure of emotions.* New York: Cambridge University Press.

Parkes, C. M. (1972). *Bereavement: A study of grief in adult life.* New York: International Universities Press.

Piët, S. (1987). What motivates stuntmen? *Motivation and Emotion, 11,* 195–213.

Plutchik, R. (1980). *Emotion: A psychoevolutionary synthesis.* New York: Harper & Row.

Previn, D. (1970). Scared to be alone (Song). In D. Previn, *On my way to where* (Album, UAG 29176). United Artists.

Rombouts, H. (1987). *The emotion of being in love.* Manuscript submitted for publication.

Rothbart, M. K. (1973). Laughter in young children. *Psychological Bulletin, 80,* 247–256.

Rothbaum, F., Weisz, J. R., & Snyder, S. S. (1982). Changing the world and changing the self: A two-process model of perceived control. *Journal of Personality and Social Psychology, 42,* 5–37.

Scherer, K. R. (1988). Criteria for emotion antecedent appraisal: a review. In V. Hamilton, G. H. Bower, & N. H. Frijda (Eds.), *Cognition, motivation and affect* (pp. 89–126). Dordrecht: Nijhoff.

Simon, H. A. (1973). *The sciences of the artificial.* Cambridge, MA: MIT Press.

Smith, C. A., & Ellsworth, P. C. (1987). Patterns of appraisal and emotion related to taking an exam. *Journal of Personality and Social Psychology, 52,* 475–488.

Solomon, R. L. (1980). The opponent-process theory of acquired motivation. *American Psychologist, 5,* 691–712.

Spinoza, B. (1955). *Ethics* (R. H. M. Elwes, Trans.). New York: Dover Books. (Original work published 1677.)

Sroufe, L. A., & Waters, E. (1976). The ontogenesis of smiling and laughter: a perspective on the organization of development in infancy. *Psychological Review, 83,* 173–189.

Weiner, B. (1985). An attributional theory of achievement motivation and emotion. *Psychological Review, 92,* 548–573.

Weisman, A. D. (1972). *On dying and denying.* New York: Behavior Publications.

Weiss, J. M. (1971). Effects of punishing a coping response (conflict) on stress pathology in rats. *Journal of Comparative and Physiological Psychology, 77,* 14–21.

Wortman, C. B., & Brehm, J. W. (1975). Responses to uncontrollable outcomes: an integration of reactance theory and the learned helplessness model. In L. Berkowitz (Ed.), *Advances in experimental social psychology* (Vol. 8, pp. 277–336). New York: Academic Press.

Zajonc, R. B. (1980). Thinking and feeling: preferences need no inferences. *American Psychologist, 35,* 151–175.

Zimbardo, P. G. (1970). The human choice: individuation, reason and order versus deindividuation, impulse and chaos. In W. J. Arnold & D. Levine (Eds.), *1969 Nebraska Symposium on Motivation* (Vol. 16). Lincoln: University of Nebraska Press.

CHAPTER *23*

Positive Affect Facilitates Creative Problem Solving

A. M. Isen, K. A. Daubman, and G. P. Nowicki

Alice Isen has been influential in developing the experimental study of effects of emotions. She made people mildly happy by telling them they had been good at a task, or by offering a small gift, or by arranging some small monetary reward. She found that subjects became more socially cooperative – making larger donations to charity and being more likely to help a stranger – and also recalling more positive memories (Isen et al., 1978).

The principal conclusion of Isen and colleagues' paper excerpted here is that positive mood helps insightful problem solving. The explanation, as suggested for instance by Schwarz and Bless (1991), is that happiness implies a safe environment, so that less constrained and more expansive mental processing can occur. Generally this kind of explanation is widely accepted.

A useful recent review of studies of the effects of mood on solving problems that require insight is by Kaufman and Vosburg (1997). They conclude that most published studies support Isen and colleagues' conclusions, but they also report two studies of students trying to solve pencil-and-paper insight problems as well as analytical problems.

Although the pencil-and-paper insight problems were formally similar to the problem used by Isen and her colleagues (in this selection), Kaufman and Vosburg found in their studies that positive mood was associated with less frequent solution of problems. What could account for this discrepancy? One possibility is that whereas Isen's subjects were set to solve their problem individually with real objects, experiencing effects of their progressive attempts at solution, Kaufman and Vosburg's subjects sat in groups in a classroom, and worked with a written problem and a diagram. Perhaps this made their task more like an analytical task. Kaufman and Vosburg suggest that, in their setting, subjects who were happy gave up more quickly, in order to preserve their happy mood.

A. M. Isen, K. A. Daubman, and G. P. Nowicki. Positive affect facilitates creative problem solving. *Journal of Personality and Social Psychology, 52,* (1987), 1122–1123, 1124–1126, 1128–1129. Copyright © 1987 by the American Psychological Association, Reprinted with permission.

There is substantial evidence that moods do affect problem solving as well as social cooperation, but some of the conditions for replicating the effects are as yet unclear.

References

Isen, A. M., Shalker, T., Clark, M., & Karp, L. (1978). Affect, accessibility of material in memory and behavior: a cognitive loop? *Journal of Personality and Social Psychology, 36*, 1–12.

Kaufman, G., & Vosburg, S. K. (1997). "Paradoxical" mood effects on creative problem-solving. *Cognition and Emotion, 11*, 151–170.

Schwarz, N., & Bless, H. (1991). Happy and mindless, but sad and smart? The impact of affective states on analytic reasoning. In J. Forgas (Ed.), *Emotion and social judgment* (pp. 55–71). Oxford: Pergamon Press.

Recent research has suggested that positive affect can influence the way cognitive material is organized and thus may influence creativity. Studies using three types of tasks (typicality rating, sorting, and word association) indicated that persons in whom positive affect had been induced differed from those in control conditions in the associations that they gave to common, neutral words (Isen, Johnson, Mertz, & Robinson, 1985) and in the pattern and degree of relatedness that they depicted among stimulus elements (Isen & Daubman, 1984). It has been suggested that these differences are due to differences between the groups in the tendency to relate and integrate divergent material. This process of bringing together apparently disparate material in a useful or reasonable but unaccustomed way is central to most current conceptualizations of the creative process (e.g. Koestler, 1964; S. A. Mednick, 1962). Thus, it seems likely that positive affect may promote creativity.

In one of these series of studies, it was found that persons in whom positive affect had been induced (in any of three ways) tended to categorize stimuli more inclusively than did persons in the control conditions (Isen & Daubman, 1984). This tendency was reflected by performance on both a rating task and a sorting task. On the sorting task, positive-affect subjects tended to group more stimuli together than control subjects did, thus indicating that, for them, more of the items could be seen as related. On the rating task, persons in whom positive affect had been induced tended to rate nontypical exemplars of a category more as members of the category than control subjects did. For example, in a task similar to that used by Rosch (1975) in assessing the prototypicality of category exemplars, persons in whom positive affect had been induced – by refreshments at the experimental session, receipt of a small gift, or viewing 5 min of a comedy film – gave higher ratings to the atypical exemplars *elevator, camel*, and *feet* as members of the category *vehicle* than did subjects in control conditions. That is, they gave evidence of being better able than control subjects to see the relatedness between these exemplars and the category or to see aspects of these exemplars that would make them like members of the category.

In a second series of studies, persons in whom positive affect had been induced – by having refreshments (juice and cookies) at the experimental session, giving word associations to positive words, receiving a small gift, or viewing 5 min of a comedy film – gave more unusual first associates to neutral words, according to the Palermo and Jenkins (1964) norms, than did persons in the control conditions (Isen et al., 1985).

Both of these effects have been interpreted as indicating an influence of positive affect on cognitive organization because they reflect the relatedness that people see among ideas or cognitive elements. One shows how persons organize stimuli set before them when they set out to do so; the other indicates the concepts that are cued for people by given stimulus words. In each type, there is evidence of greater integration or perception of interrelatedness of stimuli among people who are feeling happy.

Either of the effects of positive feelings on cognitive organization that has been observed thus far (atypical categorization and word association) might also be seen as reflective of an influence of affect on creativity. The categorization task involves either seeing nontypical yet plausible ways of relating items, or seeing aspects of the items that are real and useful but not usually focal in people's attention; these processes are central to creativity. Likewise, responding with related but nontypical word associations can be seen as creative, and in fact word association tasks have often been explicitly linked with creativity (e.g. Freedman, 1965; Maltzman, Simon, Raskin, & Licht, 1960; M. T. Mednick, S. A. Mednick, & E. V. Mednick, 1964; S. A. Mednick, 1962).

Moreover, S. A. Mednick's (1962) theory of creativity specifically relates word associations to cognitive representation and defines creativity in terms of the formation of new associations or combinations of cognitive elements that are in some way useful. Thus, this theory of creativity is also compatible with the process suggested to result from positive affect, a process involving making new associations and combining cognitive elements in new ways.

Our studies are designed to test more directly the proposition that positive affect promotes creativity, and to extend the evidence beyond that available in the word association and categorization studies. In these experiments, we investigate whether the creativity promoted by positive affect includes problem-solving innovation.

The task that we used in the first two studies was the candle task used by Karl Duncker (1945) in his demonstrations of creative problem solving (actually, his demonstration of what he termed functional fixedness). In this task, the subject is presented with a box of tacks, a candle, and a book of matches and is asked to attach the candle to the wall (a corkboard) in such a way that it will burn without dripping wax on the table or floor [...]

Experiment 2

Experiment 2 was conducted to replicate and extend the finding that one's affective state can influence creative problem solving. First, we wanted to explore the conditions of affect that might produce the same result, in order to learn more about the specific aspects of feeling states that might be responsible for the effect. We examined whether positive affect other than feelings of amusement might have the same effect, we included a negative-affect condition, to begin investigation of the impact of negative affect on creativity, and we included an arousal-control group, to get some idea about whether arousal, independent of affect, might influence performance on this task. The prediction that arousal alone might improve performance on tasks such as these has an intuitive appeal to many people, and it may also follow from a theory such as spreading activation, as described by, for example, Anderson (1983).

We predicted that the second means of positive-affect induction (a small gift) would facilitate solution of the candle problem, as would the humorous film. Because we conceptualized this effect as attributable to cognitive processes resulting from positive affect, rather than to a process of general activation, we expected the arousal condition to have no effect. We did not predict the deficit in performance due to arousal that some might have expected on this complex task requiring innovative responding, in part because success rates were already so low in the control conditions.

We did not expect negative affect to improve creative problem solving, because it has often been associated with constricted thinking and reduced cue utilization (e.g. Bruner, Matter, & Papanek, 1955; Easterbrook, 1959). At the same time, we did not expect impaired performance, because of the relatively low success rates in the control conditions. Moreover, recent research on the impact of negative affect on social behavior, memory, other cognitive processes, and performance has indicated complex effects, with negative affect sometimes facilitating, sometimes impairing, and sometimes leaving unaffected behaviors of interest (see, e.g., Isen, 1984, for discussion). Thus, the prediction regarding the impact of negative affect relative to the control group was difficult to make; we did, however, expect a difference between the negative-affect condition and the comparable positive-affect group.

Method

Subjects   Subjects were 33 male and 83 female students who participated in this experiment for extra credit for their introductory psychology classes. Male-female composition was roughly equivalent in each of the conditions (between 26% and 32% men).

Manipulations   In one positive-affect condition, subjects each received a junior candy bar as an expression of thanks for their participation. In the other positive-affect condition, participants viewed the same segment of *Gag Reel* that was shown in Experiment 1. The negative-affect manipulation consisted of viewing 5 min of *Night and Fog*, a documentary film depicting Nazi concentration camps. To control for the effects of watching a film on performance, one control group watched the same segment of the math film (*Area Under a Curve*) that was shown in Experiment 1. Again, subjects were told that the films were being pretested for use in another study the following term and that our interest was in people's general reactions to them.

To control for the effect of simple arousal on performance, another control group exercised for 2 min by stepping up on and down from a cement block. This exercise is similar to that known as the Step Test and results in elevated heart rate. The third control group received no manipulation.

Procedure Subjects assigned randomly to one of the conditions described (two positive-affect, one negative-affect, and three affect-control conditions) were admitted to the laboratory in groups of 1 to 3. The same instructions and procedures used in Experiment 1, including precautions against interaction among subjects, were used in this study.

After undergoing the assigned manipulation, some randomly selected subjects from each condition indicated their feelings on five 7-point Likert scales representing five affective dimensions. In the film conditions, subjects were asked to indicate how the film had made them feel; in the other affect-induction conditions, subjects were asked just to indicate their feelings. Thus, the manipulation check was slightly but meaningfully different in the two types of conditions (films vs. no film).

Four of the scales in the questionnaire were intended only as filler items (refreshed vs. tired, calm vs. anxious, alert vs. unaware, and amused vs. sober). The other scale (positive vs. negative) was included for the purpose of checking whether the appropriate affective states had been induced. We expected that subjects in the comedy-film condition would feel more positive, and subjects in the negative-film condition more negative, than subjects in the neutral-film condition and that subjects in the candy condition would feel more positive than subjects in the no-manipulation control condition; the exercise condition was not expected to differ from the control condition in rated affect.

Subjects, seated at individual tables approximately 20 ft (6 m) apart, with dividers positioned between them so that they could not see each other. The materials for the candle task were on the table, in the appropriate display, but under a cover until the task was explained by the experimenter. The following instructions were read to subjects in Conditions 1, 2, and 3:

> On the table are a book of matches, a box of tacks, and a candle. Above the table on the wall is a corkboard. Your task is to affix the candle to the corkboard in such a way that it will burn without dripping wax onto the table or the floor beneath. You will be given 10 minutes to work on the problem. [Instructions inserted from Experiment 1. Eds.]

Subjects in Condition 4 heard the same instructions except that the box and the tacks were listed separately as items on the table. The problem as usually presented can be solved if the box is emptied, tacked to the wall, and used as a platform (candle holder) for the upright candle.

At the end of the session the purpose of the study was explained to the subjects, they were shown the solution to the problem, and the experimenter thanked the subjects for participating.

Results and Discussion

Manipulation check Tables 23.1 and 23.2 present the mean affect ratings (manipulation check) in each condition (film and no film separately). Two separate analyses of variance (ANOVAS), one including the film conditions and the

Table 23.1. Study 2: Manipulation check and mean affect ratings (positive-negative scale) in each film condition

Condition	M	MS_e	n
Comedy	3.11	1.29	11
Neutral	3.90	1.04	10
Negative	5.52	2.12	12

Note. Ratings were made on 7-point scales (1 = *positive*, 7 = *negative*).

Table 23.2. Manipulation check and mean affect ratings (positive-negative scales) in each nonfilm condition

Condition	M	MS_e	n
Candy bar	2.69	1.27	18
No manipulation	3.18	2.07	18
Exercise	3.10	2.88	12

Note. Ratings were made on 7-point scales (1 = *positive*, 7 = *negative*).

other including the candy, exercise, and no-manipulation conditions, were performed on the data. Separate analyses were performed because the manipulation check question (as described in the Procedure) was different for the two types of conditions. The analysis contrasting the three film conditions indicated a significant effect, $F(2, 30) = 11.44$, $p < .01$. Subsequent t tests revealed that subjects in the comedy-film condition reported that they felt more positive, $t(19) = 1.68$, $p = .056$, one-tailed, and those in the negative-film condition more negative $t(20) = 3.05$, $p < .01$, one-tailed, than did subjects in the neutral-film condition. However, the analysis contrasting the candy, exercise, and no-manipulation conditions indicated no significant differences among these three groups, $F(2, 45) = .60$. Thus, contrary to expectation, subjects in the candy condition did not report that they felt more positive than subjects in their comparison group, the no-manipulation condition, $t(34) = 1.17$, $p > .10$. Subjects in these no-film conditions were not compared with subjects in any of the film conditions on the affect manipulation check because, as noted, the affect-rating tasks were differently focused in these two distinct contexts and therefore should be distinguished from one another.

The manipulation check data confirm the expected positive-affect and negative-affect induction in the film conditions but not in the gift (candy bar) condition. This suggests that our gift, a small (junior) candy bar in nothing but its commercial wrapper, was not successful in inducing pleasant feelings in subjects. Perhaps it was too small a gift or inappropriately packaged.

Moreover, in retrospect, it is clear to us that this type of manipulation check (self-reported mood) is especially inappropriate for persons who have received treatments such as a gift of candy. The measure is simply too reactive and may even cause subjects to be suspicious of the experimenter's intent in giving them the candy and resentful rather than elated in the remainder of the session. It is probably inappropriate also for treatments such as the exercise condition, in which, again, there is no apparent reason for the question and it is therefore too reactive. (In the film conditions, in contrast, the affect question is an integral part of the task of pretesting the film.)

Problem solving Table 23.3 presents the percentage of subjects in each condition who solved the problem. We predicted that a higher proportion of subjects in the positive-affect conditions than in their respective control conditions (neutral film and no manipulation) would solve the problem correctly. As expected, a χ^2 test indicated that a higher percentage of subjects who had viewed the comedy film solved the problem than of subjects who had viewed the control film, $\chi^2(1, N = 38) = 9.46$, $p < .01$;[1] however, subjects who had received a candy bar did not perform better than subjects in the no-manipulation condition, $\chi^2(1, N = 39) < 1$. We did not expect any of the other conditions to facilitate solution of the problem, and in fact chi-squares comparing the exercise condition with its appropriate control (no manipulation) and the negative-affect condition with its control group (neutral film) revealed no significant difference, $\chi^2(1, N = 38) < 1$ and $\chi^2(1, N = 39) = 2.27$, $p > .1$, respectively. Moreover, subjects in the positive-affect film condition performed significantly better than subjects in all of these comparison conditions, combined, $\chi^2(1, N = 96) = 10.41$, $p < .01$, or singly, $\chi^2(1, N = 38) = 3.89$, $p < .05$; $\chi^2(1, N = 39) = 3.09$, $p < .05$;[2] and $\chi^2(1, N = 38) = 7.24$, $p < .01$, for exercise, negative affect, and no-manipulation, respectively.

Although no specific prediction was made regarding time to reach a solution, we thought that positive affect might reduce solution time (among those solving the problem) as well as facilitate problem solution, as had been observed. Individual *t* tests revealed, however, that there were no significant differences among the conditions in the amount of time taken to solve the problem correctly (see table 23.4 for means and variances). These results should be interpreted with caution, however, because of the extremely small sample sizes, especially in some of the conditions where only two or three persons solved the problem.

The results of this experiment support and extend those of the preceding one. Subjects in whom positive affect had been induced through viewing a comedy film were more likely to find a creative solution than were subjects who viewed a negative film or subjects in any one of three neutral-affect conditions (neutral film,

Table 23.3. Study 2: Number and percentage of subjects obtaining correct solution in each condition

Condition	*n*	%
Positive film	11/19	58
Neutral film	2/19	11
Negative film	6/20	30
Candy bar	5/20	25
No manipulation	3/19	16
Exercise	5/19	26

Table 23.4. Study 2: Mean amount of time in minutes to solve problem in each condition

Condition	M	MS_e	n
Comedy film	4.30	11.29	8[a]
Neutral film	4.20	8.14	2
Negative film	4.29	7.27	6
Candy bar	5.81	14.44	5
No manipulation	3.06	9.01	3
Exercise	6.71	11.68	5

a Three data points were lost because of a malfunction of timing devices

no manipulation, and no-film arousal). Furthermore, this experiment suggests that the superior performance of subjects in the positive-affect condition is not due to a relatively high arousal level, as subjects in the exercise condition performed no better than subjects in the other control conditions and significantly worse than subjects in the comedy-film condition. We chose to represent arousal by means of exercise, even though this may seem questionable on some counts, because there is a growing body of literature that conceptualizes arousal in this way (e.g. Zillmann, 1979). If the meaning of arousal is taken to be better represented by the negative-affect condition than the exercise condition, then again there is no evidence that the effect of positive affect in our study is attributable only to arousal.

Contrary to expectation, subjects in the gift condition did not show improved performance as those in the comedy-film condition did. Thus, it may be specifically humor, and not positive affect more generally, that gives rise to improved creative problem solving. On the other hand, the manipulation check data suggest that positive affect may not have been induced in that condition. Moreover, as we have speculated, the rather heavy-handed technique of inexplicably inquiring about subjects moods after giving them a gift may have ruined the lighthearted affect induction that was intended. Previous research has indicated that some affect inductions cannot withstand a manipulation check questionnaire (e.g. Frost & Greene, 1982; Isen & Gorgoglione, 1983), and this may be another instance of a similar phenomenon, if for a slightly different reason [...]

General Discussion

Results of these four studies taken together show that positive affect, induced by a comedy film or a small gift of candy, can facilitate creative responding on tasks usually thought to reflect creativity. At the same time, a manipulation designed to induce negative affect (negative film) and one promotive of arousal devoid of any particular affective tone (exercise) had no effect on these measures. Thus, it appears that elation, if it involves arousal, is unlike some other aroused states in that it seems to lead to the kinds of thinking that enable people to solve problems that require ingenuity or innovation.

It has been proposed that a creative-problem-solving task is one involving the ability to see relatedness in diverse stimuli that normally seem unrelated. This is the essence of the definition of creativity provided by a number of theorists: S. A. Mednick (1962), for example, has proposed that creativity involves the combination of elements that are remotely associated; Koestler (1964) spoke of bisociation, the association and combination of two different frames of reference; and the mathematician Poincaré (cited in Martindale, 1981) suggested that creativity involves useful new combinations of associative elements. At the same time, a similar process – one of seeing relatedness in stimuli that are not usually seen as related to one another – has been proposed and demonstrated to result from the induction of a happy affective state (e.g. Isen, 1984; Isen & Daubman, 1984; Isen et al., 1985). Thus, it makes sense that a person who is feeling good might be more creative than others (or than she or he might be at another time).

These results indicate that creativity, an important skill that is often thought of as a stable characteristic of persons, can be facilitated by a transient pleasant affective state. Moreover, the affective state sufficient to do this can be induced subtly, by small everyday events. This suggests that creativity can be fostered by appropriate modification of the physical or interpersonal environment.

Our findings have potential application to several domains. Their implications for the educational enterprise are clear: Teachers (and the students themselves) should regard everyone as potentially creative, and an effort should be made to provide the conditions that are conducive to creativity. One of those conditions is a happy feeling state. Although we induced this state by means of a small gift of candy and a comedy film in these experiments, it is likely that other inductions of good feeling might also be effective in facilitating creativity. We would suggest, for the educational context, that an atmosphere of interpersonal respect conducive to good self-esteem might be the kind of condition that would promote creativity.

These results are also potentially relevant to other settings, including other organizational settings such as businesses, in which leaders seek to promote creativity or innovative problem solving. Once again, the most important way of inducing good feelings may be by allowing workers to achieve a sense of competence, self-worth, and respect. Pleasant surprises may also be effective, but if used too frequently, they will become expected and may lose their ability to induce happy feelings.

Finally, our findings may bear on interpersonal problem solving more generally. A recent study has reported that persons in whom positive affect was induced negotiated more effectively and obtained higher joint benefits on an integrative bargaining task that required finding an innovative solution (Carnevale & Isen, 1986). The creation and maintenance of good interpersonal relationships often involves finding ways of resolving disputes or negotiating arrangements of various kinds. When these would benefit from a creative approach, positive feelings might facilitate the interpersonal process. Thus, it may be possible to extend our findings regarding the facilitative effect of good feelings on creative problem solving to many organizational and interpersonal domains [. . .]

References

Anderson, J. R. (1983). *The architecture of cognition*. Cambridge, MA: Harvard University Press.

Bruner, J. S., Matter, J., & Papanek, M. L. (1955). Breadth of learning as a function of drive level and mechanization. *Psychological Review, 62*, 1–10.

Duncker, K. (1945). On problem solving. *Psychological Monographs, 58* (5, whole no. 270).

Easterbrook, J. A. (1959). The effect of emotion on cue utilization and the organization of behavior. *Psychological Review, 66*, 183–201.

Freedman, J. L. (1965). Increasing creativity by free-association training. *Journal of Experimental Psychology, 69*, 89–91.

Frost, R. O., & Greene, M. L. (1982). Duration and post-experimental removal of Velten Mood Induction Procedure effects. *Personality and Social Psychology Bulletin, 8*, 341–347.

Isen, A. M. (1984). Toward understanding the role of affect in cognition. In R. Wyer & T. Srull (Eds.), *Handbook of social cognition* (pp. 174–236). Hillsdale, NJ: Erlbaum.

—— (1987). Positive affect, cognitive processes, and social behavior. In L. Berkowitz (Ed.), *Advances in experimental social psychology*. New York: Academic Press.

Isen, A. M., & Daubman, K. A. (1984). The influence of affect on categorization. *Journal of Personality and Social Psychology, 47*, 1206–1217.

Isen, A. M., & Gorgoglione, J. M. (1983). Some specific effects of four affect-induction procedures. *Personality and Social Psychology Bulletin, 9*, 136–143.

Isen, A. M., Johnson, M. M. S., Mertz, E., & Robinson, G. F. (1985). The influence of positive affect on the unusualness of word associations. *Journal of Personality and Social Psychology, 48*, 1–14.

Koestler, A. (1964). *The act of creation*. New York: Macmillan.

Maltzman, I., Simon, S., Raskin, D., & Licht, L. (1960). Experimental studies in the training of originality. *Psychological Monographs, 74*, 1–23.

Martindale, C. (1981). *Cognition and consciousness*. Homewood, IL: Dorsey Press.

Mednick, M. T., Mednick, S. A., & Mednick, E. V. (1964). Incubation of creative performance and specific associative priming. *Journal of Abnormal and Social Psychology, 69*, 84–88.

Mednick, S. A. (1962). The associative basis of the creative process. *Psychological Review, 69*, 220–232.

Palermo, D. S., & Jenkins, J. J. (1964). *Word association norms*. Minneapolis: University of Minnesota Press.

Rosch, E. (1975). Cognitive representations of semantic categories. *Journal of Experimental Psychology: General, 104*, 192–233.

Zillmann, D. (1979). *Hostility and aggression*. Hillsdale, NJ: Erlbaum.

CHAPTER *24*

Biases in Emotional Processing

A. Mathews

Andrew Mathews pioneered one of the first successful cognitive-behavioral treatments for agoraphobia (Mathews, Gelder, & Johnson 1981). It involved recruiting the patient's spouse to act as a co-therapist, and having the patient gradually exposed to the places and activities in the outside world that she or he feared. The reason this therapy was so interesting and effective was twofold. First, agoraphobia, a social anxiety of leaving home and of going alone into public places, is often sustained with the cooperation of a spouse or parent who fulfills those functions in the outer world that the patient is too anxious to perform. The condition is, in other words, a syndrome not of one but of two people: One is too anxious to go out while the other is so helpful that the other does not need to go out. So recruiting the patient's partner as a co-therapist, as Mathews and his colleagues did, was a brilliant stroke. Secondly, although the earlier versions of behavior therapy, which involved imagining feared scenes, claimed success, it has subsequently been found that having the patient actually do progressively more feared versions of the things he or she avoids is more effective.

Mathews moved from developing therapy to studying the fundamental cognitive processes of anxiety, which he has been successful in disentangling. He and his collaborators have been in the forefront of exploring laboratory methods with anxious and non-anxious people to see how in anxiety the brain becomes biased to process signs of safety and danger, and becomes attentionally preoccupied with these kinds of information.

Reference

Mathews, A. M., Gelder, M. G., & Johnson, D. W. (1981). *Agoraphobia: Nature and treatment.* London: Tavistock.

At the beginning of the last decade, there was a public debate in the pages of the *American Psychologist* on the subject of cognition and emotion. On one side Zajonc (1980) argued that emotion is independent of cognition. Some emotional reactions, such as the fear elicited by accidentally stepping on a snake, seem to occur rapidly and before detailed cognitive analysis could possibly be completed. Furthermore, preference for novel stimuli can be increased by repeated exposure to them, even when subjects fail to recognize that they have seen them at all. For example, abstract shapes repeatedly displayed at speeds too fast for them to be recognized were subsequently preferred to control shapes that were never displayed (Seamon et al., 1984). On the other side, Lazarus (1982) argued that cognition not only precedes emotional reactions, but is the principal agent in bringing them about. If emotional reactions are rapid it is because they are the outcome of an automatic appraisal that is equally rapid. People cannot report on this primary appraisal because the cognitive processes involved are involuntary and non-conscious in nature.

Most psychologists believe this argument is now over, and that the cognitive side has won. A similar theoretical shift has taken place in our views about emotional disorders, such as anxiety and depression. Cognitive theories about the etiology and treatment of clinical conditions are now part of mainstream clinical psychology. For example, David Clark and his colleagues have presented persuasive evidence that panic attacks can be triggered by the catastrophic misinterpretation of bodily symptoms (Clark et al., 1988). This theory has already lead to the application of a novel form of cognitive therapy designed specifically for panic disorder.

But how much do we know for certain about the causal role of cognitive processes in emotion and emotional disorders? Are the worrying thoughts reported by anxious patients a *cause* of their condition, or are they just an irrelevant by-product of a non-cognitive etiology? Despite the impressive growth of knowledge in this area, causal hypotheses remain speculation rather than fact. In this presentation I will review research illustrating what we now know (or think we know) about the relationship between cognitive processes and emotional disorder, and consider what more we will need to know before such causal hypotheses should be accepted.

When feeling depressed about something, we become more likely to remember negative events. In experimental studies, the induction of sad mood leads to a greater proportion of sad personal events being recalled from autobiographical memory (Teasdale, 1988). Similarly, fear makes us more likely to notice cues warning that the feared event is about to happen. In a number of experiments, we have found that anxious subjects preferentially attend to cues related to threat, and interpret ambiguous information as being threatening. A paradigm that we have used in several of these experiments involves simultaneously displaying one threatening word (e.g. "failure" or "disease") and one neutral word on a computer screen. On occasional trials a small dot appears in the prior location of one of these words and subjects are instructed to press a button as soon as they see it. Generally anxious patients were speeded when the dot probe appears in the location of a threatening word, indicating that they were more likely to be attending to it than to a neutral word (MacLeod et al., 1986; Mogg et al., 1992). The basic finding is not confined to

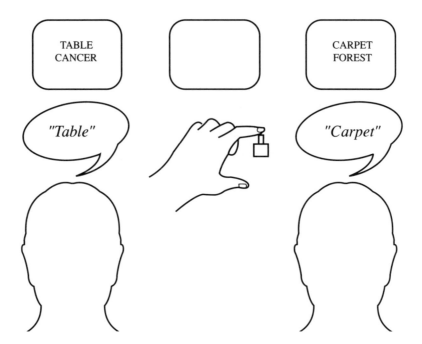

Figure 24.1   A schematic sequence of computer screen displays.

clinical groups: normal subjects with extremely high trait anxiety scores show a similar effect (Broadbent & Broadbent, 1988).

Circular relationship

The nature of these processing biases strongly suggests the potential for a circular relationship between cognition and mood. Anxious or depressed mood acts so as to give processing priority to the type of information that is most likely to enhance or maintain that mood state. Any further deterioration in mood that results will presumably lead to the intake of more mood-congruent information, and so on. In the case of fear aroused by an immediate physical threat, such as that of being attacked by a mugger, increased sensitivity to warning cues is obviously adaptive. It is not too difficult, however, to imagine that this circular process could get out of hand and become over-sensitive, leading to pathological conditions such as generalized anxiety or panic disorder.

Emotional processing biases seem intuitively understandable, and are also predicted by the mood and memory network theory proposed by Bower (1981). All events experienced in a particular emotional state are said to be connected in the memory network. Thus, if an emotional representation in memory is activated, it will lead to activation automatically spreading to all other information that was acquired in the same emotional state. As is now well-known, however, this attractive theory has run into a number of problems. For example, it has proved difficult reliably to reproduce mood-state-dependent learning, in which material learned in one mood is better recalled in the same rather than in a different mood

(Bower, 1987). Secondly, although many experiments have found evidence of mood-congruent recall (better memory for *sad* information in sad subjects) there have been occasional reports of significant mood *in*congruent recall (better memory for *happy* information in sad subjects; Parrott & Sabini, 1990). At the very least, this suggests that normal subjects can sometimes override the supposedly automatic effects of spreading activation, perhaps by virtue of their voluntary efforts to control their own mood.

Another problem for spreading activation theory has been the failure to find emotional effects in some tasks, such as making lexical decisions. It was expected that subjects in a sad or anxious mood would be faster at identifying stimuli as words, if the words match their current mood. This is because spreading activation should have already primed the representation of congruent emotional words in memory, thus speeding these subjects' ability to identify them, relative to neutral words. With occasional exceptions, however, the general finding has been of no such emotional effect on the lexical decision task (Clark et al., 1983). In our own research with anxious patients we also failed to find the predicted effect of a faster lexical decision for threatening words, despite having found evidence of selective attention for the same stimuli in the attention measure described earlier. One potentially important feature of the attentional deployment task is that it involves competition for cognitive resources, in that one of the two stimuli displayed has to be selected in preference to the other. If emotional bias arises from giving priority to congruent information, then the failure to find a lexical decision effect might be due to the lack of competition for resources in this task.

Allocation of resources

Accordingly, we (MacLeod & Mathews, 1991) designed a lexical decision task in which either a single stimulus, a word or word-like letter string, could be presented; or two stimuli could be presented simultaneously, one above the other. Subjects were instructed to respond "yes" if any word was present in either type of display, or "no" if only non-words were present. On trials when only one stimulus was present, both anxious and control subjects were faster to identify threatening words; but as expected, there was no difference in this respect between the groups. However, when two stimuli were present, one word and one non-word, the groups were influenced differently by the type of word that was present. Specifically, anxious subjects were relatively speeded when a threatening rather than a neutral word was present, whereas controls were not. This basic finding was replicated in a second experiment (Mogg et al., 1991) although the effect was most marked when the word appeared in the lower of the two positions. Putting the results of the two studies together, we can conclude that:

1 there are no mood effects on single lexical decision speed for congruent words;
2 there is relative speeding effect for threatening words in anxious subjects when two stimuli are present; and
3 this latter result may depend on attentional competition effects.

Threatening information appears to be given processing priority by anxious subjects. This is reassuringly consistent with the earlier conclusion from the dot-probe task, but it also implies that an automatic spreading activation account of emotional bias is likely to prove insufficient. Rather, it suggests that emotional states control how processing resources are allocated within the cognitive system.

Selective processing

If we assume that emotional information is given priority for processing, a further question arises. Does all mood-congruent information attract resources in emotional states, or are only certain kinds of information selected? In fact, there is already a great deal of evidence indicating that only personally relevant information is selectively processed. Early on, it became clear that depressed subjects do not selectively recall all negative information; rather, they tend to recall negative information that has been encoded in relation to themselves. For example, depressed subjects tend to recall relatively more negative trait adjectives if they have been asked whether the words describe themselves. However, if asked to decide if the same words describe an acquaintance, they then recall more positive adjectives, just as non-depressed subjects do (Bradley & Mathews, 1983). Similarly, if anxious subjects are asked about the risk of future negative events, they typically estimate the probability as being higher than do non-anxious controls (Butler & Mathews, 1983, 1987). However, the risk of the same unpleasant events happening to other people is not overestimated to the same extent.

We can go further than saying that it is only personally-related information which attracts selective processing. The material concerned must also be relevant to the individual's current concerns. To justify this claim, consider the now numerous findings of interference from emotional words in the modified Stroop

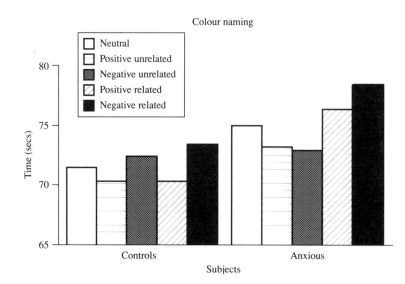

Figure 24.2   Histogram showing results from Mathews and Klug (1993).

test. When anxious or depressed subjects are required to name the color of the ink in which different types of emotional words are written, they are slowed most when the words to be ignored match their current concerns. Subjects who report worrying about physical threats are slowed more by words like "disease" or "fatal", while those who worry about social threats are most slowed by words like "foolish" or "lonely". Patients with panic disorders are slowed most by words describing physical symptoms or catastrophic disease (Ehlers et al., 1988; McNally et al., 1992), while social phobics show more interference from socially threatening words (Hope et al., 1990). Patients with eating disorders are slowed by food-related words (Cooper & Fairbairn, 1992) and those with post-traumatic stress disorder are slowed by words related to their traumatic experience (McNally et al., 1990; Foa et al., 1991). However, it is not just the traumatic event that causes the interference: Vietnam veterans and rape victims who coped relatively well with the experience did not show any slowing effect. The conclusion seems clear: Selective processing is specific to material that matches the content of the individual's current concerns.

However, one recent finding seems to challenge this conclusion. Martin and others (1991) found that anxious patients were slowed as much by positive as by negative threatening words, and suggested that the critical variable was emotionality, rather than threat. In a subsequent examination of this issue, we (Mathews & Klug, 1993) replicated this result, but only for words that were closely related to the likely concerns of anxious patients (see figure 24.2). For example, positive words such as "confident" or "healthy" may be related to the concerns of anxious patients, because they feel *lacking* in confidence or good health. Unrelated positive words (such as "mercy" or "romantic") caused no interference. On the surface all these words appear positive in emotional valence, but only some of them are semantically linked to a personally threatening concern.

It would surely be wrong to conclude that the effect of emotion on attention is confined to stimuli linked to personal threat. Suppose the emotion in question was intense love for another person: Presumably, attention will be captured by positive stimuli associated with that person. Rather, the claim is that emotional processing biases operate on information that is associated with the *function* of the emotion concerned, but only when that information is related to the current concerns of the individual. Thus, in the case of anxiety states, the claim is that attention is directed to the general class of threatening stimuli, and within this class, towards stimuli that match current concerns.

Nodes or modes?

In spreading activation theory, different emotions are represented as nodes in a memory network. These emotion nodes differ mainly by virtue of the content of the information attached to that node. In contrast, some biological theories of emotion propose that there are a limited number of basic emotions, each having a specific evolutionary function. A cognitive version of this view has been put forward by Oatley and Johnson-Laird (1988), who argue that emotions impose a specific mode of operation on the cognitive system, serving to determine priorities

303

when conflicts arise between ongoing plans or goals. In the case of fear, for example, when ongoing behavior conflicts with the background goal of ensuring safety and survival, the imposed cognitive mode gives priority to processes that facilitate vigilance for danger and avoidance. Sadness is the response to the failure of a major plan or loss of a goal, and gives priority to the processing necessary to abandon it. Basic emotions such as fear, sadness, and anger may thus differ not just in terms of the associated cognitive content, but also in the type of cognitive process that operates on that content. Our contention is that anxiety and depression share cognitive configurations with fear and sadness, based on their original evolutionary function. Anxiety, like fear, should thus facilitate perceptual processes involved in vigilance for future danger, while depression, as a pathological extension of sadness, might facilitate processes involved with thinking about the causes of past failure.

What evidence is there for this claim? Research on anxious patients shows that selective attention to emotional material is a fairly robust effect, and yet it has proved difficult to find as strong effects in depression (see, for example, MacLeod et al., 1986; Gotlib et al., 1988). In contrast, it is easy to show that depressed patients recall relatively more negative words related to themselves (e.g. Watkins et al., 1992), but surprisingly difficult to show the same thing in anxious subjects. Some studies do show a tendency for better recall or word related to anxious mood or symptoms (e.g. Mogg & Mathews, 1990; McNally et al., 1989), but others show no differences or even poorer recall of threatening words in anxious patients (e.g. Mogg et al., 1987).

While the results are not completely clear, there does seem a consistent trend for stronger attentional effects to be found in anxiety, and more robust negative recall effects in depression. More evidence is needed before we can be certain but at present it seems likely that emotions differ in the type of cognitive *process* that is involved, as well as in the *content* that is selectively processed and stored in memory. Differences between emotions in terms of cognitive process make little sense in terms of a simple memory network model, in which all emotions are basically the same apart from the content of information linked with that emotion. They would make very good sense, however, if emotions evolved to serve specific functions, requiring the imposition of specific modes of operation on the cognitive system.

Automatic and strategic processes

It was noted earlier that cognitive theories of emotion based on automatic spreading activation are embarrassed by findings of mood-*in*congruent recall, implying that the retrieval of emotional information can be controlled strategically. Evidence of strategic influences on the recall of emotional information does not, of course, show that all selective encoding is strategic. Indirect tests, of implicit memory, in which no deliberate attempts to remember are involved, demonstrate that performance can be influenced by previous experience, even in the absence of conscious recollection (Roediger, 1990). Evidence of emotional effects on indirect tests would thus argue for the involvement of automatic processes.

One widely used test of implicit memory requires subjects to complete word stems or word fragments with whatever word first comes to mind. Subjects are more likely to produce a word that they have encountered recently, even when they do not recall having seen it before. For example, if I asked you to complete the letters sel... with the first word to come to mind you might say "selective", because you read it recently, rather than, for example, "seldom." Word completion might thus reveal selective encoding of threatening information in anxious subjects, consistent with their attentional bias favoring the same material, despite lack of a similar bias in recall. Consistent with this expectation, we found that completions by anxious patients were more likely to match previously encountered threatening words, while recovered patients and normal controls showed the reverse trend. In contrast, when the same subjects were asked to use the word stem as a cue to recall a previously seen word, the groups did not differ significantly (Mathews et al., 1989). Subsequent experiments with other groups of anxious subjects have produced mixed results; some supporting this pattern, but others failing to show significant word completion differences. However, a consistently different pattern of results has been obtained when the same method was applied to depressed patients. As expected, depressed patients recalled more negative words that they had seen previously, but did not differ significantly from normals in their pattern of word completion (Watkins et al., 1992).

One way of accounting for these differences follows on from the earlier argument about differences in the type of selective processing involved in anxiety and depression. We could suppose that the function of fear or anxiety, that is, to identify and then avoid danger, is best served by rapid perceptual encoding of threatening information, rather than more time-consuming controlled elaboration on the semantic properties of that stimulus. By this argument, anxious subjects should form a better perceptual representation of a threatening stimulus, leading to greater automatic priming effects, but do not necessarily have an advantage when trying to use semantic associations to aid recall. In contrast, elaborative processing of negative personal information is central to the proposed function of sadness or depression, leading to an advantage in recall for that material for depressed subjects.

The evidence based on word completion is not completely convincing however, partly because of some replication failures with anxious groups, and partly because there is no way to be certain that subjects do not use conscious recall during completion, even when instructed otherwise. An alternative approach is to investigate if any interference effects can be detected at a pre-attentive stage of processing, before subjects can report on the presence or nature or the stimuli responsible. There is now quite good evidence of priming effects attributable to stimuli that are presented very briefly, and then masked by covering them with random letter shapes. For example, decisions about the emotional valence of target words are significantly speeded if they follow masked primes sharing the same valence, despite the inability of subjects to report on the prime (Greenwald et al., 1989). Similarly, several recent studies of color-naming have used both masked and unmasked words to test if interference due to emotional stimuli will persist when subjects cannot report on the interfering words.

In one of these studies, words rated as being relevant to the concerns of anxious and depressed subjects, some masked and some unmasked, were displayed on a

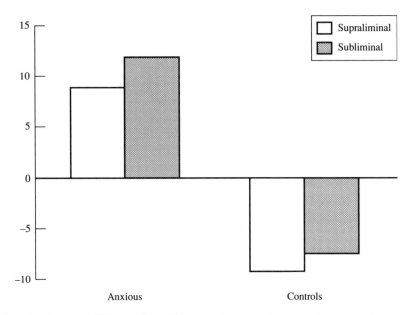

Figure 24.3 Mean difference in milliseconds between time to color name threat versus neutral words presented supra- or subliminally.

background patch of color. Results showed that color-naming interference effects were present in masked trials when either type of negative word was displayed, compared with neutral words, but only for the anxious group. Neither control nor depressed subjects were found to show significant interference relative to neutral words, for either masked or unmasked presentations (Mogg et al., 1993). Awareness of masked words was tested by requiring subjects to guess whether a word or non-word was present in a similar series of trials. Very few subjects performed better than chance, and eliminating these subjects from the analysis did not change the results. The selective interference effect found is therefore difficult to account for in terms of strategic processes that depend on subjects knowing which stimuli are emotional and which are not. Rather, it seems that interference due to early selective processing of emotional information in anxious subjects must be automatic, and pre-attentive in origin. Depressed subjects may not show an equivalent automatic bias, or at least not at such an early stage of processing.

Another interesting implication of these results is that the specificity of attentional effects to relevant personal concerns, which was documented earlier, may not apply so strongly to pre-attentive processing. This is because no differences were detected in the interference due to masked words that had been judged relevant to either anxious or depressed patients. Similar results were found in another study of interference from masked words, this time involving high and low trait-anxious students anticipating a stressful examination (MacLeod & Rutherford, 1992). In highly trait-anxious students there was as much interference in masked trials involving generally threatening words, as from words chosen to be relevant to the source of stress. In contrast, stimuli that were not masked produced interference only when the words were related to examinations. It appears that clinically anxious patients and high-trait normals under stress are alike in showing interference effects from threatening stimuli presented out of awareness, and these effects are less specific than those found in studies of post-attentional interference. One possible explanation is that the early pre-attentive process may be relatively crude, involving only the classification of stimuli into threat or non-threat categories. Those classed as potential threats presumably then receive more detailed processing in subsequent stages to determine their relevance to current concerns.

To summarize, there is evidence that some types of selective emotional processing depend on automatic processes, while others involve more controlled strategic operations. Although I have emphasized automatic processes in anxiety states, and strategic processes in depression, it is quite likely that both are involved in most emotions. For example, even if the initial tendency for sad subjects to make negative judgments about themselves is a controlled elaborative process, it may become automated through practice as depression becomes chronic (Bargh & Tota, 1988). Equally, after initial automatic perceptual identification of threat cues, anxious subjects may then intentionally avoid further elaborative processing in order to minimize their discomfort (Mogg et al., 1987).

Emotional vulnerability

So far, the evidence presented supports the presence of both automatic and strategic processing biases in emotional states, and shows that they operate so as to give priority to personally relevant information that is related to the function of that emotion. None of this, however, demonstrates that selective processing *causes* emotional disorders, nor does it make explicit exactly how such processing might relate to either trait emotionality and current mood state. The hypothesis advanced here is that individuals vary in their tendency to encode negative or threatening information, and that this trait factor interacts with stressful life events to determine emotional reactions.

Measures of selective processing typically correlate with both state and trait measures, making it difficult to disentangle their respective relationships. One approach to this problem is to see what happens to selective processing after recovery from an emotional disorder: If it is an enduring trait-like factor, then one might expect it to remain unchanged. In general, this has not been found. After recovery, patients typically resemble normal controls on measures of attentional, interpretative and memory bias. There are two exceptions to this rule however: In one case anxiety patients were more slowed than controls by threatening distractors, while they were searching for target stimuli, even after recovery (Mathews et al., 1990). In the other, previously depressed subjects were more negative in self-description and recall than were never-depressed controls (Teasdale & Dent, 1987). Although these results could be used to support the idea that selective processing is an enduring characteristic, they are isolated findings. Even if they were replicated, it would be difficult to rule out rival hypotheses; for example, that the experience of emotional disorder changes patients permanently in some way.

An alternative approach is to examine normal groups varying in trait anxiety level, when under conditions of high or low stress. Here the results support the interactional view that high trait-anxious subjects react differently to stress than do low trait subjects. Using the dot-probe method of assessing attention, we found that a high trait-anxious group of students became more attentive to threatening words just before an important examination, whereas low trait-anxious students did not (MacLeod & Mathews, 1988). Thus, although both groups appeared to be the same on baseline testing, as the examination approached, they differed sharply in their reaction to cues related to the source of threat. Only the high-trait subjects reacted to stress by selectively attending to information likely to worsen their emotional state. A recent replication of these findings indicates that they are probably reliable. It is thus plausible that the tendency selectively to encode threatening cues when under stress represents the cognitive substrate for vulnerability to anxiety states.

It may be important to note that these results were found in subjects anticipating a real stressful event over a relatively long time period. By contrast, the results of studies in which subjects have been subjected to short-term contrived stress in the laboratory have been much more variable. Students made to think they had failed in a simple test of ability sometimes become more attentive to relevant threat cues, irrespective of trait anxiety level (Mogg et al., 1990), but sometimes the effects of induced stress are more complex (MacLeod & Rutherford, 1992). Indeed, in some recent experiments with normal subjects we have found that acute stress can paradoxically decrease the interference effects attributable to threatening distractors (Mathews & Sebastian, 1993).

In one of these studies we selected students reporting extremely high or low fear of non-poisonous snakes, and required them to color-name words that were related or unrelated to snakes. To ensure that they were fearful at the time of testing, they were shown a small boa-constrictor in a glass tank, and informed that after the color-naming task they would be asked to approach the snake as closely as possible. To our surprise, there was no significant interference effect, and the trend for slower color-naming of snake words was if anything larger in low-fear subjects. In contrast, Watts et al., (1986) had previously found interference effects from spider words in phobic subjects, even without the additional stress of a spider being present. When we repeated the experiment without a snake being present, the expected interference effect in high-fearful subjects was clearly present. Finally, when we aroused fear in another group of similar subjects by having a tarantula spider present in the room, the interference effect was once more eliminated.

How are such unexpected results to be explained? Clearly, interference effects are not automatic consequences of emotional state, although they occurred only in the high-fearful subjects. Perhaps emotional arousal has some global effect attributable to narrowing of attention, but if so, it does not seem to eliminate the pervasive distraction effects seen in highly anxious patients. Alternatively, perhaps arousal of fear in non-clinical subjects can sometimes lead to effortful avoidance of threatening cues, in the same way that induced sadness can sometimes produce mood-incongruent recall. If so, then we might speculate further that, at least in normal subjects with high levels of negative emotionality, pre-attentive detection of threatening stimuli can be opposed at a post-awareness stage by selective ignoring or inattention. This effortful inattention could be seen as one strategy for coping with stress, aimed at keeping negative affect under control.

Further support for this possibility is provided by the otherwise confusing pattern of color-naming interference found in a study of female patients undergoing a threatening diagnostic procedure (colposcopy). Prior to knowing their diagnosis, they were tested using both masked and unmasked words, and the two corresponding interference indices were correlated with questionnaire measures of emotional reaction. Only the index derived from masked words was significantly correlated with trait anxiety, and the same measure was the best predictor of distress in those subjects who later received a positive diagnosis (MacLeod & Hagan, 1991). The implication of these results would seem to be that pre-attentive interference is a more direct measure of emotional vulnerability, because post-attentional measures can be influenced by strategic effects, such as effortful avoidance.

Causal models

As was admitted at the outset, none of this data proves that emotional reactions, whether normal or abnormal, are actually caused by the selective processing of emotional information. However, the type of causal model that is required has become clearer, and perhaps this will help in deciding what sort of tests would be more definitive. A model based only on automatic activation of all mood-congruent representations in memory is insufficient, as it not only ignores strategic processes that may be relevant, but more importantly, does not account for individual differences in vulnerability or differences between emotions. Instead, it is proposed that emotions correspond to functional configurations of the cognitive system that are adopted more readily by some individuals than by others.

Differences in trait anxiety, for example, could be modelled as the readiness to adopt a vigilant mode, in which processes involved in the detection of threat are favoured. In the alternative (defensive) mode, mildly threatening cues are not selected and thus do not interrupt performance, unless they are so pressing as to require an adaptive shift into vigilant mode. The vigilant processing mode is assumed to influence automatic operations such as pre-attentive detection, although the later post-attentional consequences may be modified by controlled strategies such as avoidance. Because such strategies are effortful, however, and draw on limited resources, attempts to oppose the selective encoding of threatening information will become increasingly difficult as the perceived threat increases. Eventually this will exceed the resources available and become impossible. Such a catastrophic failure of attentional control might provide a useful model for the onset of an anxiety disorder.

This type of model can account for variations in processing bias across emotional states, and for individual differences in vulnerability to emotional reactions. In allowing for an interaction between automatic and controlled processes, an explanation can also be given for pre-attentive detection without post-attentional interference effects under some conditions. Similarly, the presence of both pre- and post-attentional interference in clinical patients can be attributed to a breakdown in effortful control. Testing such a model will not be easy, but one approach might be to measure interference from masked words in patients before and after treatment, and to determine if automatic detection of threat cues under stress is predictive of subsequent relapse.

In conclusion, even without being certain about the causal role of cognitive processes in emotion, we know a great deal more about how they operate than we did a decade ago. Such knowledge puts important constraints on the type of theory that is viable, and will thus surely contribute towards the formulation of a more satisfactory model than is possible today. The successful application of cognitive-behavioral treatments for emotional disorders is some indication of the usefulness of existing models. If the research that I have discussed does contribute to the evolution of more powerful theories, it should also help in the development of the next generation of psychological treatments.

References

Bargh, J. A., & Tota, M. E. (1988). Context-dependent automatic processing in depression: Accessibility of negative constructs with regard to self but not to others. *Journal of Personality & Social Psychology, 54*, 925–939.

Bower, G. H. (1981). Mood and memory. *American Psychologist, 36*, 129–148.

—— (1987). Commentary on mood and memory. *Behaviour Research and Therapy, 25*, 443–456.

Bradley, B.P., & Mathews, A. (1983). Negative self-schemata in clinical depression. *British Journal of Clinical Psychology, 22*, 173–181.

Broadbent, D. & Broadbent, M. (1988). Anxiety and attentional bias: State and trait. *Cognition and Emotion, 2*, 165–183.

Butler, G., & Mathews, A. (1983). Cognitive processes in anxiety. *Advances in Behaviour Therapy, 5*, 51–62.

—— (1987). Anticipatory anxiety and risk perception. *Cognitive Therapy and Research, 91*, 551–565.

Clark, D.M., Teasdale, J.D., Broadbent, D.E., & Martin, M. (1983). Effect of mood on lexical decisions. *Bulletin of the Psychonomic Society, 21*, 175–178.

Clark, D.M., Salkovskis, P.M., Gelder, M., Koehler, C., Martin, M., Anastasiades, P., Hackmann, A., Middleton, H., & Jeavons, A. (1988). Tests of a cognitive theory of panic. In I. Hand & H.-U. Wittchen (Eds.) *Panics and Phobias* (pp. 149–158). Berlin and Heidelberg: Springer-Verlag.

Cooper, M.J., & Fairburn, C.G. (1992). Selective processing of eating and shape related words in patients with eating disorder and dieters. *British Journal of Clinical Psychology, 31*, 363–366.

Ehlers, A., Margraf, J., Davies, S., & Roth, W.T. (1988). Selective processing of threat cues in subjects with panic attacks. *Cognition and Emotion, 2*, 201–219.

Foa, E.B., Feske, U., Murdock, T.B., Kozak, M.J., & McCarthy, P.R. (1991). Processing of threat-related information in rape victims. *Journal of Abnormal Psychology, 100*, 156–162.

Gotlib, I.H., McLachlan, A.L., & Katz, A.N. (1988). Biases in visual attention in depressed and non-depressed individuals. *Cognition and Emotion, 2*, 185–200.

Greenwald, A.G., Klinger, M.R., & Liu, T.J. (1989). Unconscious processing of dichoptically masked words. *Memory & Cognition, 17*, 35–47.

Hope, D.A., Roper, R.M., Heimberg, R.G., & Dombeck, M.J. (1990). Representations of the self in social phobia: vulnerability to social threat. *Cognitive Therapy & Research, 14*, 177–189.

Lazarus, R. S. (1982). Thoughts on the relations between emotion and cognition. *American Psychologist, 37*, 1019–1024.

MacLeod, C., & Hagan, R. (1992). Individual differences in the selective processing of threatening information, and emotional responses to a stressful life event. *Behaviour Research and Therapy, 30*, 151–161.

MacLeod, C., & Mathews, A. (1988). Anxiety and the allocation of attention to threat. *Quarterly Journal of Experimental Psychology, 40A*, 653–670.

—— (1991). Biased cognitive operations in anxiety: Accessibility of information or assignment of processing priorities. *Behaviour Research Therapy, 6*, 599–610.

MacLeod, C., & Rutherford, E. M. (1992). Anxiety and the selective processing of emotional information: mediating roles of awareness, trait and state variables, and personal relevance of stimulus materials. *Behaviour Research and Therapy, 30*, 479–491.

MacLeod, C., Mathews, A., & Tata, P. (1986). Attentional bias in emotional disorders. *Journal of Abnormal Psychology, 95*, 15–20.

McNally, R. J., Foa, E. G., & Donnell, C. D. (1989). Memory bias for anxiety information in panic disorder. *Cognition & Emotion, 3*, 27–44.

McNally, R. J., Kaspi, S. P., Riemann, B. C., & Zeitlin, S. B. (1990). Selective processing of threat cues in post-traumatic stress disorder. *Journal of Abnormal Psychology, 99*, 398–402.

McNally, R., Rieman, B., Louro, C., Lukach, B., & Kim, E. (1992). Cognitive processing of emotional information in panic disorder. *Behaviour Research and Therapy, 30*, 143–150.

Martin, M., Williams, R., & Clark, D. M. (1991). Does anxiety lead to selective processing of threat-related information? *Behaviour Research and Therapy, 29*, 147–160.

Mathews, A., & Klug, F. (1993). Emotionality and interference with color-naming in anxiety. *Behaviour Research and Therapy, 31*, 57–62.

Mathews, A., & Sebastian, S. (1993). Suppression of emotional Stroop effects by fear-arousal. *Congition and Emotion, 7*, 517–530.

Mathews, A., May, J., Mogg, K. & Eysenck, M. (1990). Attentional bias in anxiety: selective search or defective filtering. *Journal of Abnormal Psychology, 99*, 166–173.

Mathews, A., Mogg, K., May, J. & Eysenck, M. (1989). Implicit and explicit memory bias in anxiety. *Journal of Abnormal Psychology, 98*, 236–240.

Mogg, K., & Mathews, A. (1990). Is there a self-referent mood-congruent bias in anxiety? *Behaviour Research and Therapy, 28*, 91–92.

Mogg, K., Mathews, A., & Eysenck, M. (1992). Attentional bias to threat in clinical anxiety states. *Cognition and Emotion, 6*, 149–159.

Mogg, K., Mathews, A. & Weinman, J. (1987). Memory bias in clinical anxiety. *Journal of Abnormal Psychology, 96*, 94–98.

Mogg, K., Mathews, A., Eysenck, M. W., & May, J. (1993). Biased cognitive operations in anxiety: Artefact, processing priorities or attentional search? *Behaviour Research and Therapy, 5*, 459–467.

Mogg, K., Mathews, A., Bird, C. & MacGregor-Morris, R. (1990). Effects of stress and anxiety on the processing of threat stimuli. *Journal of Personality and Social Psychology, 59*, 1230–1237.

Mogg, K., Mathews, A., May. J., Grove, M., Eysenck, M., & Weinman, J. (1991). Assessment of cognitive bias in anxiety and depression using a Colour Perception Task. *Cognition and Emotion, 5*, 221–238.

Oatley, K., & Johnson-Laird, P. (1987). Towards a cognitive theory of emotions. *Cognition and Emotion, 1*, 29–50.

Parrott, W. G., & Sabini, J. (1990). Mood and memory under natural conditions: Evidence for mood incongruent recall. *Journal of Personality and Social Psychology, 59*, 321–336.

Roediger, H. L. (1990). Implicit memory: retention without remembering. *American Psychologist, 45*, 1043–1056.

Seamon, J. G., Marsh, R. L., & Brody, N. (1984). Critical importance of exposure duration for affective discrimination of stimuli that are not recognized. *Journal of Experimental Psychology: Learning, Memory and Cognition, 10*, 465–469.

Teasdale, J. D. (1988). Cognitive vulnerability to persistent depression. *Cognition and Emotion, 2*, 247–274.

Teasdale, J. D. & Dent, J. (1987). Cognitive vulnerability to depression: An investigation of two hypotheses. *British Journal of Clinical Psychology, 22*, 163–171.

Watkins, P., Mathews, A., Williamson, D. A., & Fuller, R. (1992). Mood congruent memory in depression: Emotional priming or elaboration? *Journal of Abnormal Psychology, 101*, 581–586.

Watts, F. N., McKenna, F. P., Sharrock, R., & Trezise, L. (1986). Colour naming of phobia related words. *British Journal of Psychology, 77*, 97–108.

Zajonc, R. B. (1980). Feeling and thinking: Preferences need no inferences. *American Psychologist, 35*, 151–175.

CHAPTER *25*

Emotional Intelligence

P. Salovey and J. M. Meyer

If you write a book it is good to choose a suggestive title. Emotional Intelligence *has proved to be a wonderful title for Daniel Goleman's 1995 book, which made the* New York Times *bestseller list. It is a wide-ranging account of the importance of emotions in people's personal and social lives. But the title itself, as Goleman acknowledges, was taken from an article published by Peter Salovey and John Mayer in 1990. This original article is not easy to obtain, and we are pleased to reprint an excerpt here.*

Howard Gardner has for some time been proposing that there is not just one kind of intelligence, but multiple intelligences (e.g. Gardner, 1983). Emotional intelligence is one aspect, but until Salovey and Mayer's article, this idea was (in comparison with the other kinds of intelligence described by Gardner) relatively unelaborated. Salovey and Mayer's proposal indicates how to approach the issue – they show that this is a kind of intelligence with five principal features (i) being aware of one's own emotions, (ii) being able to manage one's own emotions, (iii) being sensitive to the emotions of others, (iv) being able to respond to and negotiate with other people emotionally, (v) being able to use one's own emotions to motivate oneself.

References

Gardner, H. (1983). *Frames of mind.* New York: Basic Books.
Goleman, D. (1995). *Emotional intelligence.* New York: Bantam.

Emotional intelligence: conceptualization and scope

There is an exciting body of research that, for lack of a theoretical concept, is dismembered and scattered over a diversity of journals, books, and subfields of

P. Salovey and J. M. Meyer, Emotional intelligence. *Imagination, Cognition, and Personality, 9* (1990), 189–191, 193, 195, 198–200. Reprinted by kind permission of Baywood Publishing Co. Inc., New York.

psychology. This collection of studies has in common the examination of how people appraise and communicate emotion, and how they use that emotion in solving problems. It is different from research on the interaction of cognition and affect, traditionally conceived (see notes 1–5) because it concentrates not on memory or judgment per se, but on more general contributions of emotionality to personality. As long as this research remains scattered without a guiding framework, its contribution to psychology will be minimal. But by integrating this research conceptually, its contribution to psychology will be readily grasped.

Much of the research to be studied is descriptive in nature. And the descriptive qualities of the work have been developed through the agency of scale development and measurement. For this reason, some sections of the current review will integrate a number of instances of scale development, such as those concerning alexithymia, emotional expression, and empathy. Although we are not interested in the scales per se, we are interested in the constructs that underlie them and the means by which they operationalize portions of what we will call emotional intelligence.

We hope to reveal the implications of this scattered set of findings that have not yet been appreciated: that there is a set of conceptually related mental processes involving emotional information. The mental processes include: (a) appraising and expressing emotions in the self and others. (b) regulating emotion in the self and others, and (c) using emotions in adaptive ways. An outline of these components is provided in figure 25.1. Although these processes are common to everyone, the present model also addresses individual differences in processing styles and abilities. Such individual differences are important for two reasons. First, there has been a century-long tradition among clinicians recognizing that people differ in the capacity to understand and express emotions. Second,

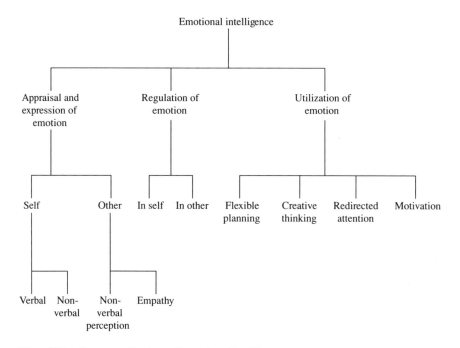

Figure 25.1 Conceptualization of emotional intelligence.

such differences may be rooted in underlying skills that can be learned and thereby contribute to people's mental health.

In the next portion of the article, each of these processes is discussed in turn, operationalizations are described, and pertinent experimental results are presented [...]

Appraisal and expression of emotion

Emotion in the Self

Summary We have suggested that appraising and expressing emotions accurately is a part of emotional intelligence. This is the case because those who are more accurate can more quickly perceive and respond to their own emotions and better express those emotions to others. Such emotionally intelligent individuals can also respond more appropriately to their own feelings because of the accuracy with which they perceive them. These skills are *emotionally* intelligent because they require the processing of emotional information from within the organism, and because it is clear that some level of minimal competence at these skills is necessary for adequate social functioning [...]

Emotion in others

Summary We have included the skillful recognizance of others' emotional reactions and empathic responses to them as a component of emotional intelligence. These skills enable individuals to gauge accurately the affective responses in others and to choose socially adaptive behaviors in response. Such individuals should be perceived as genuine and warm by others, while individuals lacking these skills should appear oblivious and boorish [...]

Regulation of emotion

Summary We have included the regulation of emotion in the construct of emotional intelligence because it may lead to more adaptive and reinforcing mood states. Most people regulate emotion in themselves and others (note 6) Emotionally intelligent individuals, however, should be especially adept at this process and do so to meet particular goals. On the positive side, they may enhance their own and others' moods and even manage emotions so as to motivate others charismatically toward a worthwhile end. On the negative side, those whose skills are channelled antisocially may create manipulative scenes or lead others sociopathically to nefarious ends.

Utilizing emotional intelligence

Individuals also differ in their ability to harness their own emotions in order to solve problems. Moods and emotions subtly but systematically influence some of the components and strategies involved in problem solving (see notes 7 and 8 for reviews). First, emotion swings may facilitate the generation of multiple future plans. Second, positive emotion may alter memory organization so that cognitive material is better integrated and diverse ideas are seen as more related (note 8). Third, emotion provides interrupts for complex systems, "popping" them out of a given level of processing and focusing them on more pressing needs. Moods such as anxiety and depression, for example, may focus attention on the self (notes 9–11). Finally, emotions and moods may be used to motivate and assist performance at complex intellectual tasks (notes 12–14).

Flexible planning

One central aspect of personality is the mood swing wherein individuals differ in the frequency and amplitude of their shifts in predominant affect (notes 15–16). Those with the strongest mood swings will experience concomitant changes in their estimates of the likelihood of future events depending upon the valence of those events. People in good moods perceive positive events as more likely and negative events as less likely to occur and that the reverse holds true for people in unpleasant moods (notes 17–22). Mood swings may assist such people in breaking set when thinking about the future and consider a wider variety of possible outcomes. As a consequence, they may be more likely to generate a larger number of future plans for themselves and thereby be better prepared to take advantage of future opportunities (note 7).

Creative thinking

Mood may also assist problem solving by virtue of its impact on the organization and use of information in memory. For example, individuals may find it easier to categorize features of problems as being related or unrelated while they experience positive mood (note 23). This clarity in categorizing information may have positive impact on creative problem solving (note 24).

Standard creativity tasks such as the remote associates task and cognitive categorization tests have commonly been used as the dependent variables in this research. For example, Isen and others (note 24) demonstrated that positive mood can facilitate more creative responses to Duncker's candle task. It seems that subjects experiencing positive mood are more likely to give especially unusual or creative first associates to neutral cues (note 25). Moreover, happy individuals may be more likely to discover category organizing principles and use them to integrate and remember information (note 26)

Mood redirected attention

The third principle states that attention is directed to new problems when powerful emotions occur. Thus, when people attend to their feelings, they may be directed away from an ongoing problem into a new one of greater immediate importance. The salesperson who is undergoing a divorce may be directed away from trivial work-related problems and toward understanding of her own interpersonal relations through the pain that emerges from her marital situation (notes 27–29). In this fashion, individuals learn to capitalize on the capacity of emotional processes to refocus attention on the most important stimuli in their environment. Rather than merely disrupting ongoing cognitive activities, affect can help individuals to reprioritize the internal and external demands on their attention, and allocate attentional resources accordingly.

Motivating emotions

Finally, moods may be used to motivate persistence at challenging tasks. For example, some individuals can channel the anxiety created by evaluative situations (such as tests and impending performances) to motivate them to prepare more thoroughly and attain more exacting standards (note 13). Others may imagine negative outcomes as a method of motivating performance (notes 12,14). People may use good moods to increase their confidence in their capabilities and thus persist in the face of obstacles and aversive experiences (notes 22, 30–32). Finally, individuals with positive attitudes toward life construct interpersonal experiences that lead to better outcomes and greater rewards for themselves and others (note 33).

Summary

When people approach life tasks with emotional intelligence, they should be at an advantage for solving problems adaptively. And it is for this reason that such skills are included within the construct of emotional intelligence. The sorts of problems people identify and the way they frame them will probably be more related to internal emotional experience than will be the problems addressed by others. For example, such individuals are more likely to ask not how much they will earn in a career, but rather whether they will be happy in such a career. Having framed a problem, individuals with such skills may be more creative and flexible in arriving at possible alternatives to problems. They are also more apt to integrate emotional considerations when choosing among alternatives. Such an approach will lead to behavior that is considerate and respectful of the internal experience of themselves and others [. . .]

Notes and references

1   P. Blaney, Affect and memory: a Review, *Psychological Bulletin*, 99, 229–246, 1986.
2   M. S. Clark and S. T. Fiske, *Affect and cognition*, Hillsdale, NJ: Erlbaum, 1982.
3   C. E. Izard, J. Kagan, and R. B. Zajonc, *Emotions, cognition, and behavior*, Cambridge: Cambridge University Press, 1984.
4   J. D. Mayer and P. Salovey, Personality moderates the effects of affect on cognition. In *Affect, cognition, and social behavior*. J. Forgas and K. Fiedler (Eds.). Toronto: Hogrefe, pp. 87–99, 1988.
5   J. A. Singer and P. Salovey, Mood and memory: evaluating the network theory of affect, *Clinical Psychology Review, 8*, 211–251, 1988.

6   J. D. Mayer and Y. N. Gaschke, The experience and meta-experience of mood, *Journal of Personality and Social Psychology*, 55, 102–111, 1988.

7   J. D. Mayer, How mood influences cognition, In *Advances in cognitive science*. Vol. 1, N. E. Sharkey (Ed.). Chichester: Ellis Horwood, pp. 290–314, 1986.

8   A. M. Isen, Positive affect, cognitive processes, and social behavior. In *Advances in experimental social psychology*, vol. 20, L. Berkowitz (Ed.), New York: Academic Press, pp. 203–253, 1987.

9   T. Pyszczynski and J. Greenberg, Self-regulatory perseveration and the depressive self-focusing style: a self-awareness theory of reactive depression, *Psychological Bulletin, 102*, 122–138, 1987.

10 P. Salovey and J. Rodin, Cognitions about the self: connecting feeling states to social behavior. In *Self, situations, and social behavior: Review of personality and social psychology*. Vol. 6, P. Shaver (Ed.). Beverly Hills CA: Sage, pp. 143–166, 1985.

11 J. V. Wood, J. A. Saltzberg, and L. A. Goldsamt, Does affect induce self-focused attention?, *Journal of Personality and Social Psychology, 58*, 899–908, 1990.

12 N. Cantor, J. K. Norem, P. M. Niedenthal, C. A. Langston, and A. M. Brower, Life tasks, self-concept ideals, and cognitive strategies in a life transition, *Journal of Personality and Social Psychology, 53*, 1178–1191, 1987.

13 R. Alpert and R. Haber, Anxiety in academic achievement situations. *Journal of Abnormal Psychology, 61*, 207–215, 1960.

14 C. Showers, The effects of how and why thinking on perceptions of future negative events, *Cognitive Therapy and Research, 12*, 225–240, 1988.

15 H. J. Eysenck, *Personality, Genetics, and Behavior*, New York: Praeger, 1982.

16 R. J. Larsen, E. Diener, and R. A. Emmons, Affect intensity and reactions to daily life events, *Journal of Personality and Social Psychology, 51*, 803–814, 1986.

17 G. H. Bower, Mood and memory, *American Psychologist, 36*, 129–148, 1981.

18 E. J. Johnson and A. Tversky, Affect, generalization, and the perception of risk. *Journal of Personality and Social Psychology, 15*, 294–301, 1983.

19 J. D. Mayer and D. Bremer, Assessing mood with affect-sensitive tasks, *Journal of Personality Assessment, 49*, 95–99, 1985.

20 J. D. Mayer and A. J. Volanth, Cognitive involvement in the emotional response system, *Motivation and Emotion, 9*, 261–275, 1985.

21 J. D. Mayer, M. Mamberg, and A. J. Volanth, Cognitive domains of the mood system, *Journal of Personality, 56*, 453–486, 1988.

22 P. Salovey and D. Birnbaum, Influence of mood on health-relevant cognitions, *Journal of Personality and Social Psychology, 57*, 1989.

23 A. M. Isen and K. A. Daubman, The influence of affect on categorization, *Journal of Personality and Social Psychology, 47*, 1206–1217, 1984.

24 A. M. Isen, K. A. Daubman, and G. P. Nowicki, Positive affect facilitates creative problem solving, *Journal of Personality and Social Psychology, 52*, 1122–1131, 1987.

25 A. M. Isen, M. M. S. Johnson, E. Mertz, and G. Robinson, The influence of positive affect on the unusuainess of word associations, *Journal of Personality and Social Psychology, 48*, 1413–1426, 1985.

26 A. M. Isen, K. A. Daubman, and J. M. Gorgoglione, The influence of positive affect on cognitive organization: implications for education. In *Aptitude, Learning, and Instruction: Affective and Cognitive Factors*. R. Snow and M. Farr (Eds.). Hillsdale, NJ: Erlbaum, 193.

27 J. A. Easterbrook, The effects of emotion on cue utilization and the organization of behavior, *Psychological Review, 66*, 183–200, 1959.

28 G. Mandler, *Mind and emotion*, New York: Wiley, 1975.

29 H. A. Simon, Comments, In *Affect and cognition*, M. S. Clark and S. T. Fiske (Eds.), Hillsdale, NJ: Erlbaum, pp. 333–342, 1982.

30 A. Bandura, *Social foundations of thought and action*, Englewood Cliffs, NJ: Prentice-Hall, 1986.

31 D. J. Kavanagh and G. H. Bower, Mood and self-efficacy: impact of joy and sadness on perceived capabilities, *Cognitive Therapy and Research, 9*, 507–525, 1985.

32 P. Salovey, The effects of mood and focus of attention on self-relevant thoughts and helping intention. Unpublished doctoral dissertation, Yale University, 1986.

33 S. Epstein and G. J. Feist, Relation between self- and other-acceptance and its moderation by identification. *Journal of Personality and Social Psychology, 54*, 309–315, 1988.

PART V

Emotional Disorders in Childhood and Adulthood

Emotional Disorders in Childhood and Adulthood

Imagine Michael, a 10-year-old boy who is having serious problems at home and at school. He gets into a temper whenever he is crossed. He can be heard swearing and yelling at his peers, parents, and teachers. He often steals things and has been in trouble with the police. He is cruel and hostile to other children. This boy suffers from what is known as an externalizing disorder.

Now imagine another person, Ann, 28 years old, who has two preschool children. She lives on the nineteenth floor of a high-rise apartment block in a poor neighborhood. For a year she has been clinically depressed. This is not the first time that she has felt so low. When she was a child, living with her father and then later her stepmother, she often felt that no one cared much for her. Her husband left just over a year ago. His departure precipitated her episode of depression, because although their relationship was not a good one, after he left she had no means of financial support and felt unable to cope with her two small children alone. She could see no way out of her desperate situation.

These disorders have characteristic emotional flavors. Michael seems angry much of the time. Ann is anxious and sad. Unlike many of the emotional states that we have been considering, these emotional states last a long time. A child who has a serious externalizing disorder in childhood has a strong chance of growing into an adult who is aggressive and hostile with serious antisocial tendencies (Robins, 1978), and will often end in prison. Although depression and anxiety are usually more intermittent, even disappearing for periods of time, once someone has had one bout of depression he or she is more likely to suffer another (Harrington et al., 1990; Kovacs et al., 1984). Although psychiatric disorders have a characteristic emotion at their base, understanding is just beginning about how short-term emotions relate to long-term patterns of psychopathology.

Many recent theories of emotion stress the functional role of emotions. Emotions help us to organize our priorities. They also serve as a signalling system helping us to communicate with others about the status of our goals. They serve useful functions. Emotions in psychopathology seem quite the opposite. The repeated bouts of anger and aggression that Michael displays, and the disabling sadness and fear that Ann experiences, seem to operate against their interests. So, are emotions in psychopathology functional or are the concepts that we use for thinking about normal emotions inadequate for understanding emotional disorders?

We take the view that understanding normal emotions is, with some elaboration, applicable to the understanding of emotional disorder (see Cole et al., 1994 for a useful discussion). There are two kinds of argument and evidence, one about habits of emotion, the other about stressful circumstances.

Habits of emotion

Long-lasting patterns of emotional habit are built up from temperamental biases and environmental influences to deal with life in a particular place of upbringing. A person – any person – develops habits of emotional responsiveness.

What is a habit? It is a repeated pattern of responsiveness that becomes difficult to change consciously. Consider this metaphor: Suppose you buy some new shoes. As you wear them, they become more comfortable, but they change shape and become creased – the creases are like habit.

Like comfortable shoes, habits are useful, changes in response to the environment. Rather than having to think through each situation anew, habits enable us to respond automatically, and without spending too much time thinking. Learning to read fluently, for instance, instills habits that enable us to decode words without thinking and to concentrate on the meanings.

But habits bring problems. The main one, like the creases of comfortable shoes, is that they are difficult to undo. The whole of Darwin's argument about emotional expressions (selection 1) was of this kind: Emotional expressions are habitual actions from earlier phases of evolutionary or individual development that can not be deleted.

Emotional habits, then, enable us to respond automatically to recurring situations. Tomkins (selection 18) proposed how emotional scripts may be formed and then sustained. What a script does is to set up and make more likely a particular pattern of appraisal of events, and also amplify the kind of response to these appraisals. For instance, events in Ann's childhood left her with a low threshold for feeling unloved and worthless. These feelings were reawakened and further amplified when her husband displayed his lack of love for her. Such patterns can be thought of as exaggerations of individual differences as described by Kagan and Caspi and their colleagues (selections 16 and 17). In this part, Patterson and others (selection 26) show how such patterns of emotional organization, which are the bases of disorder, emerge from adaptations to aversive environments.

Thus children who are in adverse circumstances may develop strategies or ways of dealing with their circumstances in which certain emotions are augmented, other emotions are avoided. Such strategies help to maintain functioning in an environment, even though this environment is less than optimal.

Attachment patterns have been described in comparable ways (Cassidy, 1994). The avoidant attachment pattern (involving a lack of exhibited emotional distress on separation with a parent) has been called a strategy for dealing with the disappointment of a psychologically unavailable parent. In the work of Patterson and others (selection 26) we see how an angry and aggressive emotional pattern is functional in the environment of a certain kind of family, but dysfunctional in the wider social world. Patterson has shown how children's aggression can get parents to give up what they were trying to get the child to do. It serves to help the child meet his or her goal. But at school it is less functional, and because of the habitual nature of certain kinds of response, the child lacks the flexibility to develop other strategies to meet goals in new circumstances.

Emotions can be dysfunctional in some aspect of our lives but functional in other aspects. Through carrying out sequential analyses in families in which mothers were suffering from depression, Hops and others (1987) found that depression attenuated the fathers' and the children's aggression toward mothers. So the mothers' depressed moods, although difficult for them as individuals, functioned to protect them in their families. Biglan and others (1989) have shown that aggressive versus depressive emotions have different effects on subsequent responses from other people. In response to anger people back away, give in to the other person, but can also become more aggressive. In response to depression partners attenuate aggression and offer more comfort. So one of the things that children learn in their early environments is how emotions operate for them in their interactions.

One answer to the question of the relationship of shorter-term emotions to longer-lasting traits is that as some kinds of emotions are experienced and expressed in any environment, some become more likely, and then habitual, so that long-lasting and rigid patterns of emotional responsiveness are set up.

Some emotional habits, such as those that Michael displays, are formed in punitive or unsupportive environments, and as Caspi and colleagues (selection 17) showed, they then tend to last into adulthood. Others occur, perhaps, largely for temperamental reasons, and also tend to continue. For most of us, the effects of such patterns on ourselves and others are relatively mild. In some cases the emotional habit makes it impossible for the person to cope with living an ordinary life, and that is when we think of it as an emotional disorder.

Stresses of the immediate social environment

There is another way in which normal emotions are connected with emotional disorders. If we suffer a loss, perhaps we do poorly in an examination or fail to land a job we applied for, we might feel sad. But if an event is very serious – a marriage or long-standing relationship splits up, or we lose our job with no prospects of other employment – we may become not just sad but depressed. In Ann's story, as well as from the literature on psychiatric epidemiology, we see that both children and adults show psychiatric disorder when very negative events occur in their lives.

But the idea as stated in the above paragraph needs refinement. A stressor does not act in and of itself. It acts selectively to amplify pre-existing habitual kinds of emotional scripts (selection 18). For one person, with a generally internalizing script, loss of a relationship or of essential employment may make them depressed and anxious. For people with an externalizing script, such events may make them angry. They will form plans of retribution and havoc.

Life in any society involves adverse events. The form of emotional response will differ according to the culture, and according to the scripts and emotional habits of individuals within it.

So what are the risks? In both adults and children living in an aversive environment increases the risk of developing disorders. For adults, economic poverty (Kessler et al., 1994) and life events (selection 27) are associated with increased psychiatric illness. For children, aversive environments include having parents who are frequently angry with them (Pettit, Dodge, & Brown, 1988) or with one another (Jenkins & Smith, 1990). The more aversive factors a child has to cope with, the more likely the child is to show disorder (Rutter, 1979). Temperamental vulnerability (see selection 16) and cognitive impairments raise the risk for children too.

Emotions in psychopathology are elicited in the same kind of way that short-term emotions are elicited. Things happen in people's lives that do not fit with the goals that they have for themselves. When conditions remain the same, with the person feeling that they have no way to improve their situation, these emotions can persist.

Aversive environments also contribute to relapse in non-affective psychiatric disorder, as well as affective psychiatric disorder (Hooley, Orley, & Teasdale, 1986). We present a review by Kavanagh (selection 30) showing that when families are hostile and overinvolved with a family member who is recovering from a psychotic episode, the person will relapse more quickly than if his or her relatives are not hostile and overinvolved.

To understand such effects, let us return to Tomkins's idea of emotion scripts. One affect is more readily experienced than another. In a script, emotions become magnified through events that elicit similar elements of experience. Ann had an early experience of feeling unloved and worthless. In her adult life she contributes by choosing a man who is not very supportive, and by having children young. When things become difficult she finds that her husband makes her feel as rejected as she felt in her childhood. The combination of feeling vulnerable in childhood and major life events in adulthood is potent in the development of affectively based psychiatric disorder in adulthood (Brown & Harris, 1993).

What might these emotional scripts be that we construct in childhood and refashion through the course of our lives? Stein and others (selection 28) give us some insight into this through the use of narrative analysis of interviews carried out with men who had just lost their partners to AIDS. They used ideas of appraisal, with which some of part I was concerned, to predict whether the bereaved person would be depressed a year later. This paper shows how the loop – from appraisals, to scripts, to reactivations of scripts in serious events – is closed.

Therapy for the emotional disorders

Scripts are not fate. Though we know that some unfortunate temperaments or some aversive environments are likely to direct a person toward paths that can last throughout life (selections 16, 17, and 26), we cannot predict how most lives will turn out. There are choices, and the psychological therapies are all those methods that people use to help make them.

Therapies based on regulation

Throughout the ages there have been recognizable strands of therapy. One has been based on the idea that emotions are unruly and must be regulated. In the late Greek era, and in the Roman period of Western civilizations, these methods were highly developed by Epicureans and Stoics, philosophers influenced by Aristotle. They sought therapies for the soul (Nussbaum, 1994).

In modern times, descendants of these ways of thinking have become embodied in forms of therapy, most notably cognitive behavioral therapy, in which the therapist identifies mistaken ways of thinking that lead to strong and uncontrollable emotions, so that the client can recognize them and see them as mistaken. So, for instance, if Ann were a client, she might say: "You see, my husband left me, that proves I am worthless, and if I am so unlovable I may as well be dead." This is a typical kind of thought of a depressed person. Together the therapist and Ann would work together to identify such thoughts, seeing how they lead to feelings of despair, and then see where the conclusions are mistaken: because she was rejected by one person does not mean Ann is worthless. As shown by Mathews (selection 24) such thoughts can bring to mind memories and more thoughts of defeat and despair, which amplify the depressed feelings and make them yet more convincing.

Escaping such patterns does not, in itself, help the external situation. If Ann can overcome some of the compulsiveness of her self-denigrating thoughts and emotions, she is still a single mother with very little money. But the idea is that appraisal patterns amplify the negative feelings, and make it less easy to solve problems or experience positive aspects of a situation.

Greenberg and Safran (1989) have illustrated how emotions become a target for regulative psychotherapy. Modern drugs, such as Prozac and other antidepressants, can also help regulate moods, diminishing sadness and increasing more assertive moods, so cutting into the amplifying cycles of depressive breakdown. Trials of such drugs, and of cognitive behavioral therapies, indicate they are about equally effective in relieving episodes of depression (Robinson, Berman, & Neimeyer, 1990). Comparable and similarly effective therapies exist for anxiety disorders, and here too there is a special set of drugs, tranquillizers, designed to diminish fearful, anxious moods.

Therapies based on insight

Alongside regulative therapies have been therapies of insight, based on understanding our emotions. In some ways these are similar to regulative therapies, in that regulation often involves understanding causes of emotions, with the idea that when these are understood the power of the emotions diminishes. Nonetheless, it is worth distinguishing this second type of therapy.

Insight therapies are represented here by Freud (selection 3), and Pennebaker and others (selection 29). Pennebaker and colleagues argue that the essential ingredients of their therapy are open to all, thinking deeply about our emotions and confiding them to someone. Rimé and others (1992) have shown that most incidents of emotion are confided to someone else. Writing about emotions in such a way that we can reflect upon them is also helpful. Notice too how the results of such reflection not only bring a person into closer harmony with himself or herself, but increase psychological well-being as well as resistance to physical disease.

Therapies based on reintegration with the social group

In many societies religious and shamanistic healing practices have involved people whose emotions have cut them off from other members of their society, undertaking ceremonies or rituals to re-integrate them with their community. Such practices, long seen as quaint, are now more often recognized as important, even as ideals with which our Western individualistic society has lost touch.

Consider schizophrenia, widely seen as among the most severe and intractable of mental illnesses. It came as a shock to researchers that although schizophrenia probably has a strong genetic basis, and although it occurs with about the same prevalence of 1 percent of the population in all societies that have been studied, it is on average far less severe and much briefer in rural societies of the developing world than in industrialized societies (Leff et al., 1992). Could it be that the processes of re-integration in traditional societies are better than the hostility which members of Western societies tend to hold for the disease, which is accompanied by removing the sufferer to a hospital, and applying the label "schizophrenia" – a condition considered to last a lifetime (see Kuipers & Bebbington, 1988)?

In our last selection, Kavanagh reviews the concept of "expressed emotion" in which family members are both overinvolved with a patient returning from mental hospital, as well as expressing angry and contemptuous emotions to or about that person. In therapy based on this concept, and in combination with drugs (e.g. Hogarty et al., 1986), relapses of schizophrenia have been markedly diminished.

Though psychotherapy is no magic cure for emotional disorders, by seeing emotions as the main focus of psychotherapy, and by distinguishing among the different effects of emotions in disorder as Greenberg and Safran (1989) recommend, the ancient idea of being able to modulate our emotions by understanding them comes closer to realization.

References

Biglan, A., Rothlind, J., Hops, H., & Sherman, L. (1989). Impact of distressed and aggressive behavior. *Journal of Abnormal Psychology, 98*, 218–228.

Brown, G. W., & Harris, T. O. (1993). Aetiology of anxiety and depressive disorders in an inner-city population. 1. Early adversity. *Psychological Medicine, 23*, 143–154.

Cassidy, J. (1994). Emotion regulation: influences of attachment relationships. In N.A. Fox (Ed.) *The development of emotion regulation. Monographs of the Society for Research in Child Development* (serial no. 214, Vol. *59*, pp. 228–249).

Cole, P., Michel, M. K., & O'Donnell-Teti, L. (1994). The development of emotion regulation and dysregulation: a clinical perspective. *Monographs of the Society for Research in Child Development, 59* (serial no. 240), 73–103.

Greenberg, L. S., & Safran, J. D. (1989). Emotion in psychotherapy. *American Psychologist, 44*, 19–29.

Harrington, R., Fudge, H., Rutter, M., Pickles, A., & Hill, J. (1990). Adult outcomes of childhood and adolescent depression. *Archives of General Psychiatry, 47*, 465–473.

Hogarty, G. E., Anderson, C. M., Reiss, M. A., Kornblith, S. J., Greenwald, D. P., Javna, C. D., & Madonia, M. J. (1986). Family psychoeducation, social skills training, and maintenance chemotherapy in the aftercare treatment of schizophrenia. One-year effects of a controlled study of relapse and expressed emotion. *Archives of General Psychiatry, 43*, 633–642.

Hooley, J. M., Orley, J., & Teasdale, J. (1986). Levels of expressed emotion and relapse in depressed patients. *British Journal of Psychiatry, 148*, 642–647.

Hops, H., Biglan A., Sherman L., Arthur J., Friedman L., & V., O. (1987). Home observations of family interactions of depressed women. *Journal of Consulting and Clinical Psychology, 55*, 341–346.

Jenkins, J. M., & Smith, M. A. (1990). Factors protecting children living in disharmonious homes: maternal reports. *Journal of the American Academy of Child and Adolescent Psychiatry, 29*, 60–69.

Kessler, R. C., McGonagle, K. A., Zhao, S., Nelson, C. P., Hughes, M., Eshleman, S., Wittchen, H.-U., & Kendler, K. S. (1994). Lifetime and 12-month prevalence of DSM-III-R psychiatric disorders in the United States: Results from the National Comorbidity Survey. *Archives of General Psychiatry, 51*, 8–19.

Kovacs, M., Feinberg, T. L., Crouse-Novak, M. A., Paulauskas, S. L., & Finkelstein, R. (1984). Depressive disorder in childhood: a longitudinal prospective study of characteristics and recovery. *Archives of General Psychiatry, 41*, 229–237, 643–649.

Kuipers, L., & Bebbington, P. (1988). Expressed emotion research in schizophrenia: theoretical and clinical implications. *Psychological Medicine, 18*, 893–909.

Leff, J., Sartorius, N., Jablensky, A., Korten, A., & Ernberg, G. (1992). The international pilot study of schizophrenia: five-year follow-up findings. *Psychological Medicine, 22*, 131–145.

Nussbaum, M. C. (1994). *The therapy of desire*. Princeton, NJ: Princeton University Press.

Pettit, G. S., Dodge, K. A., & Brown, M. M. (1988). Early family experience, social problem solving patterns and children's social competence. *Child Development, 59*, 107–120.

Rimé, B., Mesquita, B., Philippot, P., & Boca, S. (1991). Beyond the emotional event: six studies on the social sharing of emotions. *Cognition and Emotion, 5*, 435–465.

Robins, L. N. (1978). Sturdy childhood predictors of adult antisocial behavior: replications from longitudinal studies. *Psychological Medicine, 8*, 611–622.

Robinson, L. A., Berman, J. S., & Neimeyer, R. A. (1990). Psychotherapy for the treatment of depression: a comprehensive review of controlled outcome studies. *Psychological Bulletin, 108*, 30–49.

Rutter, M. (1979). Protective factors in children's responses to stress and disadvantage. In M. W. Kent & J. E. Rolf (Eds.), *Primary prevention in psychopathology*, Vol. 3: *Social competence in children* (pp. 49–74). Hanover, NH: University Press of New England.

CHAPTER 26

Antisocial Boys

G. R. Patterson, J. B. Reid, and T. J. Dishion

Gerald Patterson has spent over thirty years researching family interaction and aggression in children. In this selection the outcome with which he is concerned is delinquency.

You may think delinquency is rather a long way away from emotion, yet it is not. Externalizing disorders – conduct disorder in children, antisocial personality disorder in adults – are based on an affective organization in which anger is frequent in comparison to other emotions such as sadness and happiness. People with these disorders are easily angered, and they use verbal and physical aggression to retaliate against perceived injustices (Dodge, Bates, & Pettit, 1990). Although in early childhood the behavior may be mainly oppositional, in some children it escalates to delinquent and more antisocial activity.

Two types of delinquent children have been differentiated: those who show problems with aggression in their families and those who show normal early development, but take to delinquent activity in adolescence (Moffitt et al., 1996). The article presented here is concerned with the former group of children.

One of the important findings for emotion researchers is the way in which anger organizations are established and maintained. Patterson and his colleagues have found that aggressive children come from highly coercive homes. One person's aggression elicits another's aggression, which elicits a further aggressive response from the first person, and the cycle continues. People relate to one another in patterns of trying to force others to fall in with their goals. Also important is the way in which such coercive behaviors are reinforced. In cycles of escalating coercion between parent and child, the parent often pulls out, deciding it is not worth the struggle and the child can do whatever he or she originally wanted to do. Escalating anger and aggression has resulted in the child achieving his or her goal. Patterson and his colleagues argue that this expectation of anger resulting in goal reinstatement is taken into other relationships.

G. R. Patterson, J. B. Reid, and T. J. Dishion, *Antisocial Boys*. Eugene, OR: Castalia, 1992, pp. 10–14.
Reprinted with the permission of Castalia Publishing Co.

References

Dodge, K. A., Bates, J. E., & Pettit, G. S. (1990). Mechanisms in the cycle of violence. *Science, 250*, 1678–1683.

Moffitt, T. E., Caspi, A., Dickson, N., Silva, P., & Stanton, W. (1996). Childhood onset versus adolescent-onset antisocial conduct problems in males: natural history from ages 3 to 18 years. *Development and Psychopathology, 8*, 399–424.

The four stages

Retrospective accounts of problem children's development have suggested a patterned sequence of effects that seem to be repeated in many cases. The parents usually described the child's preschool years as difficult, and they mentioned that he was noticeably different from his siblings. The label we have given to this developmental milestone is *basic training*. The parents often commented that they didn't think the child was "disturbed" or "in need of help" until he started school. Within a few months, the parents began to receive telephone calls from distraught school personnel who reported that he was disruptive in class. Later still, the parents were told that the child was not acquiring academic skills. This is the second stage in the development of coercive behaviors. The hypothesis is that the child's abrasive behavior leads to peer rejection and academic skill deficits. In effect, *the social environment reacts*. The child's failures at stage 2 limit the social experiences available to him, and he begins to seek out a supportive environment. This places the child at risk for involvement with *deviant peers and polishing antisocial skills*, which is the third stage. Each small step increases the risk that the child will fail as an adult in the areas of work and human relationships. We believe that the eventual outcome is *the career antisocial adult*.

The four stages have been arranged in what is basically an action–reaction sequence. The child's coercive actions initiate state 1, the social environment reacts in stage 2, and so on. The following section briefly reviews the empirical findings and hypotheses that relate to each of the four stages.

Stage 1: Basic training

The key hypothesis is that the basic training for patterns of antisocial behavior prior to adolescence takes place in the home, and family members are the primary trainers. It begins with a breakdown of parental effectiveness in disciplinary confrontations. This breakdown permits an increase in coercive exchanges between the target child and all other family members. The target child finds that aversive behaviors such as whining, crying, yelling, hitting, or having temper tantrums are effective. Typically, the training involves a "dance" of at least three steps that changes the behaviors of both participants over time. We use the term *process* to describe these gradual changes. The details of the training process are presented in Patterson (1982) and briefly reviewed in Chapter 4. Essentially, the child learns that his own aversive behaviors turn off the aversive behaviors of other family members and may also directly produce positive reinforcers.

After several hundred trials, we hypothesize that the coercive exchanges increase in duration. Studies have shown that these extended exchanges are accompanied by commensurate increases in amplitude (e.g. the likelihood of hitting increases). We call this *escalation*. The escalation is dyadic in the sense that, as might be expected, it occurs not only for the target child but also for siblings and parents.

It is difficult to monitor the whereabouts of a child who is extremely coercive. The child literally coerces the rest of the family into allowing additional unsupervised street time, which leads him to a deviant peer group. The child's patterns of antisocial behavior then include both overt (e.g. fighting, temper tantrums) and clandestine acts (Loeber & Schmaling, 1985a, b). This coercive process characterizes approximately two-thirds of the families referred to OSLC for treatment. The children in these families are most at risk for arrest during early adolescence.

The training trials occur dozens of times every day, but they go unnoticed because they are embedded in the daily stream of interactions among family members. Why is it that the training process begins and continues in some families and not others? We believe that ineffective parenting practices are the primary (but not the only) determinants. For the younger child, ineffective parental discipline seems to be the primary determinant, and the child's temperament is a secondary determinant (Bates & Bayles, 1988). For the adolescent, a combination of ineffective discipline and a lack of parental monitoring seems to characterize the coercive process in the home. Ineffective discipline consists of scolding and nagging about relatively trivial matters and threatening to use punishment without following through. A lack of monitoring means that the parent often doesn't know where the child is, who the child is with, what the child is doing, or when the child will be home. If these parenting skills are suspended for weeks, months, or years, the natural contingencies found in coercive exchanges will prevail, and there will be a steady increase in antisocial behavior. On the other hand, increasing the effectiveness of parental monitoring and discipline reduces the rate of antisocial behavior.

It is hypothesized that three other parental family management skills relate to the child's social competence: (1) the contingent use of positive reinforcement, (2) group problem-solving skills, and (3) parental involvement. The models presented in Chapter 8 describe the relation between parenting practices and child adjustment. Figure 26.1 summarizes the relations between parenting skill variables and child adjustment variables. Each concept is measured with multiagent, multimethod indicators. The arrows in figure 26.1 represent path coefficients that describe the connection between two concepts. For example, the correlations between measures of parental family management skills and child behavior (i.e. outcome) are expected to be significant.

The basic training concept includes the idea that family process occurs within a context, which has a significant impact on what happens within the family. Figure 26.1 summarizes some of the contextual variables we have examined in the past few years. These variables and their relation to family process are discussed in greater detail in Chapter 7. Each variable has been identified as having some relation to poor child adjustment. For example, families with lower socioeconomic

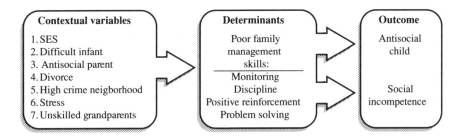

Figure 26.1   The effect of context on child adjustment.

status and those coping with divorce or high levels of stress are at risk for producing antisocial boys.

The figure summarizes the expected relations among three sets of variables. It shows that the relation between context and child adjustment is thought to be indirect. The a priori model indicates that the effect of context on child problem behavior is mediated by its disruptive effect on child-rearing practices. Most children who live in ghettos or in divorced families do not become chronic delinquents, but the child who lives in a ghetto with parents who are marginal in their family management practices is at much greater risk for becoming delinquent.

Parents with a difficult infant may be at least marginally skilled in raising their other children, but they may find that they are unable to discipline the difficult child as he grows older. Similarly, parents may do quite well in raising several children and then have their parenting skills seriously disrupted by marital conflict or other major stressors.

The relations specified in figure 26.1 would require significant correlations between measures of risk variables and measures of parental family management skills. Substance abuse, marital conflict, or changes in parental stress level would be followed by corresponding changes in the family management skills.

Stage 2: The social environment reacts

Stage 2 describes the outcome of the child's efforts to cope with a major developmental hurdle. When he enters school, will he be able to relate to normal peers and develop at least minimal academic skills? Failure at these two developmental tasks presumably has profound implications for the child's adjustment as an adolescent and as an adult. The hypothesis is that coercive or antisocial behaviors learned in the home place the child at grave risk for dual social failure.

The abrasive style of these children in their interpersonal exchanges at home places them at serious risk for rejection by their parents (Patterson, 1986a). It is difficult to teach these children social or academic skills. Their explosive tempers and refusal to accept negative feedback eventually make them spectators, rather than participants, in peer group activities. Their status as relatively unskilled youngsters becomes more pronounced as the gap between them and their normal peers widens over time.

These children avoid difficult tasks and demanding settings by coercing those who try to teach them to be "responsible." They soon learn to evade doing homework and chores. They eventually learn to avoid school and all its demands, and they are often tardy or truant. Even when they are in the classroom, they spend little time on task. It is not surprising, then, to find that they tend to be identified early on as problem children at school. The literature and empirical findings that relate to this stage are reviewed in Chapters 6 and 8.

We hypothesize that rejection by peers and parents contributes to recurring bouts of sadness in the child and that by age 10 or 11 the dysphoria is acute enough to be noticed by adults who interact with the child at both home and school.

Stage 3: Deviant peers and polishing antisocial skills

Stage 3 describes the probable outcome of stages 1 and 2. Recurring academic failure and rebuffs by parents, teachers, and normal peers induce unskilled children to seek out peers who are mirror images of themselves. By the time the children are 12 or 13 years old, parents and teachers can readily identify which peer groups are deviant. They are characterized by negative attitudes about school and adult authority. Recent studies have strongly implicated the contribution of a deviant peer group to increases in later delinquency and substance abuse (Elliott et al., 1985). We hypothesize that the problems associated with antisocial children and the failure of their parents to discipline and monitor them provide a basis for identifying which boys are at risk for membership in deviant peer groups. This involvement increases the risk for substance abuse, truancy, and delinquency later in adolescence (Patterson & Yoerger, 1991). One hypothesis to be tested with the longitudinal data set now being collected is that boys who are antisocial at age 10 are at greater risk for involvement in a deviant peer group two to four years later.

Although the stages of the coercion process seem to define a progression, we are not suggesting that *all* antisocial children move through each stage in succession. We view the connection between adjacent stages as transitive in a probabilistic sense. This implies that if a child is at a particular stage, there is a strong likelihood that he has already moved through the previous stage(s). The coercion process is a flexible, probabilistic sequence that applies to many extremely antisocial children. The progression concept will be presented at several different points in this volume. In the present context, it suggests that many boys who are failing in school and have been rejected by peers also will be identified as antisocial at home. On the other hand, not all boys who are antisocial fail in school, nor are they all rejected by peers. Each stage is more extreme in terms of risk, but the number of children at each successive stage is commensurately smaller. Those children who are at the more advanced stages are at increased risk for status as career antisocial adults.

Stage 4: The career antisocial adult

This stage reflects the findings from several longitudinal studies of antisocial individuals that include their overall adjustment as adults (Caspi, Elder, & Bem,

1987; Huesmann, Eron, Lefkowitz, & Walder, 1984; Magnusson, 1984; Robins & Ratcliff, 1978–1979; West & Farrington, 1977). The studies consistently indicate a marginal existence in adulthood. Antisocial children often have trouble staying employed as adults, and they tend to be downwardly mobile. Caspi and his colleagues also showed that unhappy marriages and higher risk of divorce are in store for antisocial children. Robins and Ratcliff found the same combination of erratic employment and marital difficulties in adulthood, as well as a higher risk for alcohol and drug problems and multiple arrests, for antisocial children. Their lack of social skills leads them to an increasingly marginal existence characterized by a constant stream of crises, many of which are of their own making. Antisocial children are at more serious risk than any other subgroup (with the possible exception of autistic and schizophrenic children) for a wide spectrum of adult adjustment problems such as substance abuse, institutionalization for crimes or mental disorders, disrupted marriages, and marginal employment records (Caspi, Bem, & Elder, 1989; Robins, West, & Herjanic, 1975). Antisocial people tend to be lonely and loved by few.

One could attempt to romanticize such children as being the stuff of which cultural rebels are formed. Nevertheless, theirs is not the selective resistance to authority that characterizes the effective rebel. Instead, they defy all authority figures and rules that restrict them. They are not even very good at fighting or stealing. These boys are losers. It is the combination of extremely high rates of antisocial behavior and incompetence that places them at risk for being arrested as preadolescents (Hood & Sparks, 1970).

A primary objective for our programmatic intervention and modeling studies has been to provide a solid empirical base for preventing antisocial problems in children. One basic requirement is to develop a long-range method of identifying the children who are at risk for becoming chronic delinquent adolescents. This critical prerequisite for effective prevention was considered carefully by Loeber and Dishion (1983) and Loeber, Dishion, and Patterson (1984). This again emphasizes the importance of developing models, because the ability to predict is determined by the adequacy of the underlying model.

The processes relating to coercion seem to be as ubiquitous as the common cold. From one month to the next, minor fluctuations probably occur in this process all the time. This volume is not designed to address the important topic of maintenance; that requires a systematic study of longitudinal data. The focus is on evaluating the coherence of the structure within stages and, in so doing, to establish a solid empirical foundation for the process studies that are now in progress.

References

Bates, J. E., & Bayles, K. (1988). Attachment and the development of behavior problems. In J. Belsky & T. Nezworski (Eds.), *Clinical implications of attachment* (pp. 253–294). Hillsdale, NJ: Erlbaum.

Caspi, A., Bem, D. J., & Elder, G. H., Jr. (1989). Continuities and consequences of interactional styles across the life course. *Journal of Personality, 57*, 375–406.

Caspi, A., Elder, G. H., & Bem, D. J. (1987). Moving against the world: life course patterns of explosive children. *Developmental Psychology, 23*, 308–313.

Elliott, D. S., Huizinga, D., & Ageton, S. S. (1985). *Explaining delinquency and drug use.* Beverly Hills, CA: Sage.

Hood, R., & Sparks, R. (1970). *Key issues in criminology.* London: Weidenfeld & Nicolson.

Huesmann, L. R., Eron, L. D., Lefkowitz, M. M., & Walder, L. O. (1984). Stability of aggression over time and generations. *Developmental Psychology, 20,* 1120–1134.

Loeber, R., & Dishion, T. J. (1983). Early predictors of male delinquency: a review. *Psychological Bulletin, 94,* 68–99.

Loeber, R., Dishion, T. J., & Patterson, G. R. (1984) Multiple gating: a multistage assessment procedure for identifying youths at risk for delinquency. *Journal of Research in Crime and Delinquency, 21,* 7–32.

Loeber, R., & Schmaling, K. B. (1985a). Empirical evidence for overt and covert patterns of antisocial conduct problems: A meta-analysis. *Journal of Abnormal Child Psychology, 13,* 337–352.

—— (1985b). The utility of differentiating between mixed and pure forms of antisocial child behavior. *Journal of Abnormal Child Psychology, 13,* 315–336.

Magnusson, D. (1984). *Early conduct and biological factors in the developmental background of adult delinquency.* Lecture presented at Oxford University, September 1984.

Patterson, G. R. (1982). *A social learning approach.* Vol. 3: *Coercive family process.* Eugene, OR: Castalia.

—— (1986). Maternal rejection: Determinant or product for deviant child behavior? In W. W. Hartup & Z. Rubin (Eds.), *Relationships and development* (pp. 73–94). Hillsdale, NJ: Erlbaum.

Patterson, G. R., & Yoerger, K. (1991). *The development of antisocial behavior.* Paper presented at the NATO Advanced Study Institute, "Crime and Mental Disorder," Ciocco, Italy, August 1991.

Robins, L. N., & Ratcliff, K. S. (1978–1979). Risk factors in the continuation of childhood antisocial behaviors into adulthood. *International Journal of Mental Health, 7* (3–4), 96–116.

Robins, L. N., West, P. A., & Herjanic, B. L. (1975). Arrests and delinquency in two generations: A study of black urban families and their children. *Journal of Child Psychology and Psychiatry, 16,* 125–140.

West, D. J., & Farrington, D. P. (1977). *The delinquent way of life.* New York: Crane, Russak.

CHAPTER 27

Loss, Humiliation, and Entrapment among Women Developing Depression

G. W. Brown, T. O. Harris, and C. Hepworth

George Brown, Tirril Harris, and their colleagues, have been widely influential in helping understanding of how negative environments increase risk of disorder. Through extensive interviewing of women in the community, they have demonstrated that it is life events such as marital separation, being evicted from home, losing the family's only income, that provoke depression. Brown and Harris's (1978) first striking finding was that 89 percent of the women who had become depressed had experienced, just before the onset of depression, a very severe event or difficulty in the presence of a vulnerability factor such as having no intimate relationships, or having too many small children to look after, or having lost her own mother before she was aged 11.

The methods that Brown and Harris developed to examine the relationship between life events and emotional disorders were innovative. Instead of counting up stressful life events, they rated events on the basis of the context in which they occurred, and the meaning that they had in people's lives. Taking into account such meanings led to a much better prediction of who would, and who would not, become depressed following a life event.

The other major contribution of the work from Brown and Harris is the way that they have been able to refine the definition and meaning of events that lead to depression. Initially, following an attachment perspective, they thought that losing someone close was the main precipitant of depression. In the paper presented here the definition of loss has been refined. There are losses of people, but there are also losses of cherished ideas or roles. A person can feel deeply humiliated or

G. W. Brown, T. O. Harris, and C. Hepworth. Loss, humiliation, and entrapment among women developing depression: a patient and non-patient comparison. *Psychological Medicine*, 25 (1995), 7–18. Copyright © 1995 Cambridge University Press. Reprinted with permission.

diminished in their interaction with others. They lose their sense of themselves. Or they can feel that they lose possibilities for themselves so that they have no way forward. In this selection, Brown, Harris, and Hepworth suggest that humiliation and entrapment may be more significant than the simple loss of a person in leading people to depressive breakdown.

Reference

Brown, G. W., & Harris, T. O. (1978). *Social origins of depression: A study of psychiatric disorder in women.* London: Tavistock.

Introduction

The role of psychosocial stress in provoking clinical depression was confirmed on a sound basis with the refinement of the concepts of "exit event" in New Haven (Paykel et al., 1969) and "severe event" in London (Brown et al., 1973) as central depressogenic stressors. Most depressive episodes appear to be provoked in this way. (For recent reviews see Brown & Harris, 1986; Monroe & Depue, 1991; Paykel & Cooper, 1992.) It can be added that a loss is usually involved if this concept is extended beyond that of a person to that of a role (e.g. being made redundant) or a cherished idea (e.g. finding out about a child's delinquency) (Brown et al., 1987). Furthermore, severe events that "match" a role to which a woman is highly committed or match an ongoing marked difficulty are particularly likely to provoke a depressive disorder.

The importance of loss in depression is widely accepted. There has also been emphasis on the role of helplessness, powerlessness, and defeat brought about by the event. Bibring's (1953) key psychoanalytical paper was the first to give an unequivocal role to the lowering of self-regarding feelings following such an event. Particularly interesting are views that concern ranking derived from ethological observations of evolutionary-based response tendencies – that is, responses of the same order as those involving anxiety and attachment. Those deriving from the experience of defeat have been argued to be particularly important and to have originated from either the activity of defending territory or submission that follows being "out-ranked" in a group-living species (Price & Sloman, 1987). While observations have derived from non-human species, their possible relevance for human populations has also been emphasized (Price et al., 1994). Gilbert (1989), with this in mind, has emphasized in addition the importance of a sense of belonging and has outlined a number of depressogenic situations that follow fairly closely those reached by life-event research: (i) direct attacks on a person's self-esteem that force them into a subordinate position; (ii) events undermining a person's sense of rank, attractiveness and value, particularly via the consequences of the event for core roles, and (iii) blocked escape. He notes that one consequence of "fresh-start events" that have been shown to relate to recovery (Brown et al., 1988, 1992) is a reduced feeling of being trapped in a punishing situation.

Such ideas go beyond the concept of loss of person or object, and serve to pinpoint particular features of the notion of loss of cherished idea. In discussing human despair Unger (1984) also underlines the key importance of the experience of imprisonment. This can occur in the "blocked escape" described by Gilbert when we are unable to free ourselves from an unrewarding setting, but also in grief when despair arises from a disbelief in our ability to reaffirm an identity in the absence of the lost relationship.

While the experience of loss is certainly common prior to a depressive onset, it is by no means necessarily associated with the experience of defeat and entrapment which may well arise from experiences other than loss. Is loss, therefore, of fundamental importance for depression or merely a likely correlate of a more basic set of experiences? In approaching this question we follow the tradition of rating life events in contextual terms (i.e. by ignoring self-reports of feelings), using a descriptive scheme that characterizes events in terms of their probability of arousing certain kinds of feeling in an individual with similar biographical circumstances surrounding the event. We have concentrated on the three broad themes of devaluation of self, entrapment, and loss, bearing in mind that in practice they are likely to overlap a good deal. While we see the experience of defeat as possibly central, we do not attempt to measure it directly. We assume, however, that it is likely to be closely linked with devaluation of self and entrapment but not with loss as such. While contextual ratings of these can be no more than approximate, they have the advantage of allowing minimal estimates of causal effects while ruling out obvious sources of bias (Brown, 1989) [...]

Method

Samples

Patients   The patient series is based on a prospective study of women aged 18–60 attending psychiatric departments of two North London hospitals. They were either in-patient, day-patient, or out-patient during a defined period in the mid-1980s with a target episode of primary depression. They were seen in most instances after their condition had shown some improvement, and were followed up with a second interview 2 years later. The broad aim was to see how far the findings with regard to depression in an earlier general population enquiry, of women living in Islington in North London carried out in the early 1980s, would hold for a patient series.

Patients with a previous episode of schizophrenia, or with organic disorder of a possible depressogenic type (either directly or through the medication prescribed for it) were not included; neither were patients with alcoholism or drug abuse that predated the onset of their depressive episode [...]

General community sample, Islington   The sample of Islington mothers has been described elsewhere (Brown et al., 1985, 1987). On the basis of general practitioners lists, 404 Islington mothers with a child (under the age of 18) living at home were interviewed and 353 of these agreed to be interviewed again 1 year later. Married/cohabiting women were selected if their partners were in manual occupations, and all single mothers were interviewed regardless of class consideration. A quarter of the total sample were single mothers. Details were collected concerning psychiatric state and various psychosocial measures during the prior year. At follow-up, 1 year later, psychiatric disorder was again measured along with details of life events and difficulties. For the present analyses a 2-year study period covering the year before first interview as well as the follow-up year will be considered.

I Clinical measures

Caseness of depression   A shortened version of the Present State Examination (PSE) was used in both enquiries (Wing et al., 1974, 1977) extended to date onset and offset of episodes of depression and anxiety, as well as assessing severity of symptoms for the 12 months before each interview (Brown & Harris, 1978; Finlay-Jones et al., 1980). The Bedford College threshold for "caseness" has been found similar to, if not a little more severe than, probable major depression according to RDC criteria (Dean et al., 1983) [...]

II Psychosocial measures

Measurement of provoking factors: life events and difficulties   The Life Events and Diffi-culties Schedule (LEDS) employs a semi-structured interview and is based on a system of contextual measures reflecting the likely meaning of events and diffi-culties. This takes into account relevant biographical information, but ignores any reported emotional response (Brown & Harris, 1978, 1986, 1989). The date of each event is recorded in terms of week of occurrence.

A   Severe events   Only one type of event has proved to be of etiological import-ance – those which, based on a contextual judgment of likely long-term threat, are considered severe. (Threat is used here in the sense of overall unpleasantness, not in its more restricted sense of danger.) Severe events are defined by two rating scales. They must be rated "1-marked" or "2-moderate" on a 4-point scale of long-term threat judged in contextual terms at a point some 10 to 14 days after date of occurrence. In addition, they must be focused on the subject – either alone or jointly with someone else.

B   Marked difficulties   Likewise, only a restricted class of difficulty, termed marked, appears to be of etiological significance. These must be rated on the top 3 points of a 6-point scale of unpleasantness (see Brown & Harris, 1978, ch. 8 and 9). The term "major" is used to reflect those lasting at least 2 years.

C   Loss, disappointment and danger   Only severe events are considered for rating loss and danger. Loss is defined broadly to include not only a person, but also loss of a role, of resources, or of a cherished idea (e.g. learning of a daughter's delinquency), and disappointment as a return of trouble that there had been reason to expect was a thing of the past. Disappointment was rarely rated and for the present analysis was treated as equivalent to a loss. Danger is defined as an event suggesting a future loss (Finlay-Jones & Brown, 1981). The top two points of 4-point scales were used to reflect a definite loss, disappointment or danger (1-marked, 2-moderate, 3-some, 4-none/little). As noted, disappointment is combined with loss, and takes the higher of the two ratings on the two scales.

D New hierarchial classification of events   A new set of ratings reflects the likely response to a severe event, using the details collected about each event, but excluding what the woman said about her response. Raters were blind to whether the event was associated with an onset.

The scheme is dealt with hierarchically – only if the first point is unrated is the second considered and so on. Therefore, while an event might meet the definition of several scale points it is rated on only one. It should be borne in mind that all of the following examples have been rated severe, and that it has not always been possible in a brief description to convey the justification for this severity rating as such.

The hierarchical rating scheme was developed because we wished to test the hypothesis that once the humiliation and entrapment aspects of severe events were taken into account events that concerned only loss or danger would play a far less important aetiological role. Given that previous analyses had shown that the great majority of severe events before onset of depression involved a loss of some kind, there was no question of ruling out the involvement of loss. We wished to test how far it played a role without accompanying humiliation or entrapment.

(a) Humiliation/trapped   The term humiliation is used to convey the likelihood of an event rendering a person devalued in relation to others or self. Entrapment is only considered if criteria for humiliation are not met. The four sub-categories require at a minimum a rating of at least "2-moderate" on loss or danger.

(i) _Humiliation: separation_   This deals with rifts with a close tie (in most instances a household member or a sexual relationship). Some element of failure and rejection must also be involved – e.g. a 14-year-old daughter who insists on going to live with her father, but not an offspring who leaves home to get married. Rifts that follow the initiative of the other person are included – e.g. a boyfriend who decides that he did not "want an exclusive relationship." Subject-initiated breaks are not considered humiliating (see (vi) below). However, 'forced' separations in response to an infidelity or marked violence are included.

(ii) _Humiliation: other's delinquency_   In most instances this involves behavior of a child – e.g. an adolescent daughter found stealing from her mother's purse and playing truant. The assumption is that the subject may well feel devalued by the event.

(iii) _Humiliation: put down_   This should involve what is likely to be a central aspect of self identity. All discoveries of infidelity (or being told of a wish to be unfaithful), for example, have been included. Otherwise most events involve some direct verbal or physical attack. Typical examples are a woman being told by her husband that she is abnormal (because of her epilepsy) and not fit to be a mother, in a row that later led to a marital separation; a single mother criticized by a magistrate for failing to keep up payments for a fine incurred by her teenage son and told she could in future be sent to prison; a 9-year-old daughter who said she wanted to leave her mother and go back to live in the West Indies. (Eventually she got her way.)

(iv) *Trapped*   Entrapment events must arise from an ongoing marked difficulty of at least 6 months duration and serve at the same time to underline that the situation will persist or even get worse – e.g. being told that a paralyzed and bedridden husband will not improve would be included, but leaving a feckless husband who had created large debts would not be included since the event may well lead to some improvement. Since the event must "match" an ongoing marked difficulty, possible feelings of entrapment following a new crisis (such as birth of a handicapped child) would not be included.

Inter-rater reliability for the 9-point scale was 0.90 weighted kappa (Kw).

(b) Loss alone   There are four subcategories of loss, using the existing Life Events and Difficulties Schedule (LEDS) ratings, without humiliation or entrapment. An event with any loss rating (i.e. 1, 2, or 3) has been included irrespective of its rating on danger. Categories (v), (vi), and (vii) must have a rating of at least "2-moderate" on loss.

(v) *Death*

(vi) *Separation-subject initiated*   These are separations where the subject plays a major part in bringing it about. (But excluding those following discovery of infidelity or extreme violence placed in category (i).)

(vii) *Other key loss*   This covers all other instances of a "2-moderate" or higher loss. Typical examples are: an abortion where the pregnancy had resulted from a relationship that had ended, and giving up a valued job in order to return to Ireland because of her husband's health.

(viii) *Lesser loss*   This is rated only "3-some" on loss. Typical examples are death of a mother not seen for years and attending her funeral in the West Indies, or a husband told he will no longer receive overtime pay, which resulted in a significant fall in income for a poor family.

(c) *Non-humiliation/ non-loss*
(ix) *Danger alone*   This covers events not meeting criteria for categories (i) to (viii) – e.g. "worst-ever asthma attack" with a one-day hospital stay, or a violent ex-husband sends a telegram to say he has found out where she lives.

E   "Atypical" provoking events   The above scheme was supplemented by a rating of how far a severe event appeared to involve a serious threat to a core role or relationship. Events not doing so were considered "atypical" in terms of provocation. The rating is only seen as tentative and exploratory.

Analysis

Two strategies have been used in the analysis of events. The first assumes that antecedent events in the individual case have etiological significance in order to estimate the minimum number of cases in whom no such event can be recognized. The analysis concentrates on whether at least one severe event occurred in a defined period before onset (section I). The second strategy considers all severe events and seeks to establish the strength of the causal relationship based on different categorization of events (section II).

In the community series all onsets in the 2-year study period are considered, but in the patient series only the target episode [...]

Results [...]

II The role of loss

The second analysis dealing with the causal relationship of different types of severe event and onset starts with the Islington population series, as this provides essential data about women who do not develop a depressive disorder. The analyses for both are based on a consideration of how often an onset follows a particular type of event within 6 months. (For this question we have taken the more conservative 6-month definition of provoking event.) Severe events occurring during an episode of depression have been ignored. Only the nearest event before onset in this 6-month period has been considered. In the community series all onsets in the 2-year study period are examined, but in the patient series again only the target episode.

About a fifth of severe events in both community and patient series were part of a linked sequence – for example, the diagnosis of a husband's cancer and a subsequent major operation. Such events have only been counted once and called an event sequence with the highest rating in the hierarchy taken to define type. One exception has been made. In order to see whether loss of a person carries more risk than other types of loss, separations have been rated separately – e.g. learning of a husband's infidelity and a separation a few weeks later has not been counted as part of a sequence. An earlier report showed that some three-quarters of provoking severe events involved a significant loss (i.e. "2-moderate" or higher), and this also held when sequences were considered.

The new descriptive scheme, while incorporating the loss rating, gives priority to experiences of humiliation (i.e. devaluation of self) and entrapment. Findings for the Islington women for the 2-year study period provide a direct estimate of risk for the various categories of event based on a defined population and period of time.

(a) Onset in the general population A total of 202 of the 404 Islingon women experienced at least one severe event in the 2-year period while they were not depressed. The number of severe events was 457, but this was reduced to 377 when those events which formed part of a sequence were counted as one event (see earlier). There were 68 episodes of depression occurring to 61 women with

85% (58/68) of the episodes preceded by a severe event (or sequence) in the prior 6 months. Overall risk of an onset of depression following the 377 event sequences was approximately 1 in 7 (58/377).

Table 27.1 shows risk by event type. The broad threefold classification of humiliation/trapped, loss alone and danger alone is highly related to onset. Women humiliated or trapped were three times as likely to develop depression (31%, 41/131) compared with those with a loss alone (9%, 14/157). The large danger alone category contained few onsets (3%, 3/89), $\chi^2 = 40.39$, 2df, $P < 0.001$. (An analysis excluding the seven extra episodes among women with multiple onsets arrived at a similarly highly significant difference.)

The somewhat lower risk among the second humiliation category that deals with delinquency was expected as a number of the events were relatively less severe – e.g. discovery that a 17-year-old son had been "smoking pot" compared with a husband's infidelity. Otherwise there is nothing to suggest a difference in risk between these categories designed, albeit crudely, to reflect experiences of devaluation of self, entrapment, or powerlessness. A special exercise in which the three humiliation categories were also rated for entrapment gave no hint of an additive effect. Only about a third (44/131) of the events involving humiliation or entrapment did not involve a loss at a "2-moderate" level. (The same held for the humiliation and entrapment events actually leading to onset – only 37% (15/41) were without "moderate" or "marked" loss.)

In practically all instances the provoking severe event involved a core role or relationship. The only possible exceptions were neighbors who threatened to set

Table 27.1. Rate of onset by humiliation–entrapment–loss–danger following 377 event sequences during a 2-year period among Islington community women

1. Humiliation/Trapped % provoking onset (41/131) 31%	2. Loss alone % provoking onset (14/157) 9%
i. Humiliation: separation (12/34) 35%	v. Death (7/24) 29%
ii. Humiliation: other's delinquency (7/36) 19%	vi. Separation – subject initiated (2/18) 11%
iii. Humiliation: put down (12/32) 38%	vii. Other key loss (4/58) 7%
iv. Trapped (10/29) 34%	viii. Lesser loss (1/57) 2%
3. Danger/Distress alone % provoking onset ix. (3/89) 3%	
4. Total % provoking onset (58/377) 15%	

fire to the patient's house in the context of a long history of trouble ("trapped"), a birth with painful complications ("danger"), and a husband made redundant ("other key loss"). Among "humiliation" events, those that involved husbands, lovers, and children were highly represented – 27 out of 31, with 18 involving a partner or lover and nine a child. Four involved a sister or mother. Four of the 10 provoking events that involved entrapment concerned a husband or lover (e.g. a husband very unlikely to recover), two housing problems (e.g. alternative accommodation falling through), three the woman's health or employment (e.g. in a difficult marriage when told that her crippling arthritis would not improve) and one a child (told he should see a psychiatrist about his over-activity). The seven onsets associated with a death involved a husband (3), a friend (2), a parent (1), and a child (1), and the seven remaining losses, a husband (2), boyfriend (2), or the subject losing a job (1), or a miscarriage or birth in a difficult ongoing situation (2).

There are also some important differences in risk by subtype. A separation that involved either humiliation or death was four times more likely to be followed by an onset than a separation made either on the subject's initiative or any other key loss. There is also, as suggested by this last result, some indication of the importance of an element of control on the woman's part. When the "separation: humiliation" category is further divided into those where it was entirely the other person's doing compared with those that involved the subject taking some initiative, albeit in response to extreme provocation, the onset rate is 53% (8/15) versus 21% (4/19). In addition, it is only 11% (2/18) among those where initiative was taken by the subject without such provocation ($\chi^2 = 7.93, 2\mathrm{df}, P < 0.02$). Also notable is the overall gradient in risk for events that do not involve humiliation or entrapment. Risk following a death is around a quarter with other critical losses 8% (vi or vii), lesser loss 2%, and danger alone 3%.

To sum up, a chi-squared test revealed that there were significant differences between the proportions of depression onsets in the three severe event categories, humiliation/trapped, loss alone, and danger alone ($\chi^2 = 40, 2\mathrm{df}, P < 0.001$). Orthogonal (Helmert, see Norusis, 1990) contrasts indicated that the proportion of onsets was higher in the humiliation/trapped category than the other two ($z = 5.5, P < 0.001$), while the proportion of onsets in loss alone did not differ significantly from that in danger alone ($z = 1.50, NS$). Within the loss alone category, however, death was associated with a significantly higher proportion of depression onsets than the other categories of loss ($z = 2.13, P0.05$ for the corresponding contrast). Therefore, losses leading to depression are mainly associated with humiliation, entrapment or a death.

(b) Onset in the patient series The 84 provoking events that occurred within 6 months of onset in the patient series are shown in table 27.2. As with the general population sample, provoking events that involved a significant loss (i.e. a rating of "2-moderate" or higher) were common – two-thirds (56/84) of the provoking events. In terms of the descriptive humiliation–entrapment–loss–danger the results are very close to those of the community onsets (table 27.2). It is, however, of interest that 5 of the 9 severe events that occurred before onset in the melancholic/psychotic previous subgroup were in the "danger alone" category,

Table 27.2. Onsets by type of provoking severe event within 6 months of onset – comparison of community and patient series

	Community		Patients	
1. Humiliation				
Separation	(12)		(20)	
Other's delinquency	(7)		(5)	
Put down	(12)	71%	(16)	62%
		(41 / 58)		(52 / 84)
2. Trapped	(10)		(11)	
3. Loss alone				
Death	(7)		(9)	
Separation – subject initiated	(2)		(3)	
		24%		25%
Other key loss	(4)	(14 / 58)	(7)	(21 / 84)
Lesser loss	(1)		(2)	
4. Danger	(3)	5%	(11)	13%
		(3/58)		(11/84)
	(58)		(84)	
	$\chi^2 = 2.60, 2\text{df}, \textit{NS}$			

compared with only 8% (6/75) in the other diagnostic group ($\chi^2 = 12.06, 1\text{df}$, $P < 0.01$).

(*c*) Multiple severe events   So far the assumption has been made that only the severe event or event sequence nearest onset played an etiological role. Taking other events into account made very little differences to the analysis in terms of hierarchy. It was necessary not to extend the period too far back since the other severe events would then fall more than 26 weeks before onset. Taking a 12-week period before the key event, only three of the 58 events in the community series were preceded by one higher in the hierarchy: two deaths were preceded by a humiliation and an entrapment respectively, and an entrapment was preceded by a humiliation. In the patient series a danger was preceded by a humiliation in one instance.

2   *Sexual/cohabiting status of patients and events*

One further difference in event-type emerged when sexual/cohabiting status was considered. Sexual/cohabiting status of the patients has been classified in terms of living with partner ($N = 63$), child alone ($N = 8$), lover and child ($N = 7$), alone with parent ($N = 21$) or having a lover who is non-resident ($N = 28$). Non-married women had to have been cohabiting for 1 year to be rated with their partner. All but five of the 21 women in the alone/parental category were, in fact, living alone: four were with a parent, and one with a daughter of 35 who was staying with her temporarily during a marital crisis. Those with a child alone (all under 25) had been in a cohabiting relationship within 6 years of onset.

As many as 70% (44/63) of those with a partner and 91% (31/35) of those with a sexual relationship with someone who was not a partner had a clearly unsatisfactory relationship at the time of the target onset. The provoking experience had either involved a major marital or sexual crisis (usually a separation or discovery of infidelity) or the quality of the marriage was already "poor" – i.e. a score of at least 4 on the Camberwell Family Study Marital Scale (Quinton et al., 1976). This dismal picture tended to persist – almost half (30/63) of those living with a partner (in practice, all male) prior to onset were no longer together at the end of the follow-up period and three-quarters (27/35) of the non-partner sexual relationships no longer existed. As would be expected therefore for those with a partner or boyfriend two-thirds of the provoking events concerned this relationship.

Sexual/cohabiting status also related to the experience of an event in the 6 months before onset appearing to fall short of the type found in the community series, where they almost without exception involved a core role or relationship. The 20 "events" that were atypical in this sense in the patient series are listed in Appendix 2 (including one that consisted of the start of a marked difficulty) – for example, a woman prevented temporarily from going to work after scaffolding fell on her in the street. Only 5% (3/58) of the provoking events in the general population, compared with 24% (20/84) among patients were atypical $-\chi^2 = 7.76$, 1 df, P < 0.01.

This difference is explained by the frequency of such events in the alone/parental group among patients. Just over half (11/21) were atypical compared with 8% (9/106) among the remainder $-P < 0.001$. (The comparison cannot be made for the community series: since they were all selected on the basis of having a child who lived at home, none of the mothers lived alone and in practice none lived with a parent.) As might be expected, 14 of the 20 atypical "events" concerned the final three, least severe, descriptive categories – i.e. "other key loss," "lesser loss" or "danger alone."

III Major difficulties

Only one of the 68 community episodes and ten of the 106 onsets among the patients were associated with a major difficulty without a provoking event. Among the patients seven involved the experience of being persistently humiliated or "put down" by a husband (5) or father (2) – for example. "He (husband) puts me down continually, shouting and swearing, walking out of the room if I try and discuss anything"; and "My father is always very cruel. He invents new mental tortures and throws and smashes things." (He had sexually molested her in the past.)

Only two of the five women in the small melancholic/psychotic previous episode group had a difficulty involving humiliation and put down compared with all five in the main diagnostic group. However, this difference is not statistically significant.

Discussion

The role of loss

The importance of severe events for the majority of episodes of clinical depression seen by psychiatrists has been confirmed, bearing in mind that they were comparatively rare for a small subset of melancholic/psychotic conditions with a prior episode of depression (Brown et al., 1994). Three-quarters of the main diagnostic group (i.e. non-melancholic/non-psychotic previous) had a severe event or equivalent in the 6 months before onset, which is not much different from that obtained in the general population – 85%. The actual impact of the provoking experiences for the non-melancholic/non-psychotic series is probably somewhat greater. The importance of a loss experience has also been confirmed when this is extended to cover loss of a role or cherished idea as well as loss of a person. Earlier research in extending the idea of exit to this broader idea of loss enabled events that provoked depression to be distinguished from those that provoked anxiety disorders. The latter events often appear to involve danger without loss (Finlay-Jones & Brown, 1981; Brown, 1993). However, the development of a new descriptive measure covering the experience of being humiliated (i.e. devalued) or trapped with the addition of the concept of atypical event, has enabled fresh light to be thrown on the role of loss.

In the Islington community series almost all of the severe events which actually provoked onset turned out to concern a major role or relationship. Using a hierarchical descriptive scheme, almost three-quarters (41/58) involved being humiliated or trapped, with most of the remaining (22%) involving a loss alone, and only 5% danger alone. Events rated as a LEDS severe loss played a comparatively minor role after losses that involved humiliation, entrapment or death had been taken into account (table 27.1). Much the same held for the patient series (table 27.2). Almost two-thirds (52/84) of the severe events in the 6 months before onset involved being humiliated and trapped. These estimates of the role of this particular experience may turn out to be conservative, given that self-reports of feelings actually experienced were not taken into account.

About three-quarters of onsets in both series were preceded by a severe event that involved a loss. However, several results suggest that this experience might not be primary. A quarter of humiliating and entrapment events did not involve loss – for example, a birth in the context of an alcoholic boyfriend who for several years had consistently given little by way of economic or emotional support. Furthermore, except for the small number with a death, other losses did not often lead to depression. It is also clear that once events involving humiliation and entrapment are excluded the large category of danger events in the community (a fifth of severe events) contains few onsets. Given that the LEDS definition of loss is broad, the results as a whole suggest that the experience of defeat and the lack of a way forward (frequently linked to a loss), may be primary. Here it should be borne in mind that the LEDS definition of loss may, in any case, at times be too broad. For example, a woman who manages to leave a partner who for many years had been violent and abusive would be rated as having a loss. But it may be asked what has been lost? Any depressogenic effect is likely to come from recognizing the hopelessness of finding the kind of relationship she desires, rather than from the loss of something that in a real sense had been largely lost long before.

Such an emphasis is consistent with the much lowered risk of depression associated with separation initiated by the subject. This would be expected if such control lessened any sense of humiliation or defeat. In the community the significance of this is underlined by the results concerning separations from a core tie (usually a partner or boyfriend). Approximately half with least control (the other person almost entirely initiating it), a quarter with some control (the subject initiating it in response to marked provocation), and a tenth with most control developed depression. The significance of control is also seen in the high rate of depression (56%, 5/9) where discovery of infidelity was not followed by separation.

The importance of lack of control as a risk factor is the one unequivocal finding to emerge from the extensive research on the reformulated learned helplessness model of depression (Hammen, 1988). Both community and patient results therefore support Bibring's formulation in 1953 that it is feelings of helplessness and powerlessness that are critical – both of which he saw as coinciding with loss of self-esteem. They are also consistent with the recent formulations of Price and Sloman (1987) and Gilbert (1989, 1992) in terms of evolutionary-based "social mentalities" that involve ranking and power being activated in depression. While the experience of loss when defined broadly is very common, it usually appears to be necessary for this to lead to a further experience summed up in terms such as helplessness and powerlessness (Bibring, 1953; Lazarus, 1966; Beck, 1967; Melges & Bowlby, 1969; Brown et al., 1975; Seligman, 1975), seeing no way forward (Becker, 1964; Fredin, 1982), and defeat (Price & Sloman, 1987; Price, 1988). Our contextual ratings of humiliation and entrapment, of course, only reflect the likelihood of the experience of powerlessness, defeat, and the like. In practice, a number of elements are likely to converge in the production of depression. The event is also likely, for example, to be ego-involving. The risk of depression in the Islington sample was much higher in the follow-up period for those roles where marked commitment had been rated at first interview (Brown, et al., 1987). In terms of the themes just reviewed that of defeat has the advantage of conveying that something central to the person has been involved. Oatley and Bolton (1985) have emphasized the importance of seeing provoking events in terms of threats to a core role or relationship, and the present analysis has confirmed this. In addition to loss and ego-involvement it is possible to add a sense of being devalued and lack of control. Previously we have emphasized the mediating role of generalized hopelessness (Brown & Harris, 1978), and it is easy to see how the experience of defeat even more than that of loss could promote this. The various elements are also likely at times to interact in complex ways. It is possible to visualize a humiliation forced on a person not proving to be depressogenic because, by the time it was effected, it came to be seen by the victim as beneficial – for example, a husband forcing a divorce settlement on his wife, much against her will, but which in practice gave her tangible benefits such as ownership of the family home.

The possible exception to these conclusions concerns deaths which were associated with a high rate of depression (table 27.1). However, in practice these may often involve the experience of defeat. In grief, despair can arise from a disbelief in our ability to reaffirm a valued identity in the absence of the lost relationship (Parkes, 1971; Unger, 1984) [...]

References

Alnaes, R. & Torgersen, S. (1991). Personality and personality disorder among patients with various affective disorders. *Journal of Personality Disorders, 5*, 107–121.

Bebbington, P. E., Brugha, T., MacCarthy, B., Potter, J., Sturt, E., Wykes, T., Katz, R., & McGuffin, P. (1988). The Camberwell Collaborative Study I. Depressed probands: adversity and the form of depression. *British Journal of Psychiatry, 152*, 754–765.

Beck, A. T. (1967). *Depression: Clinical, experimental and theoretical aspects.* London: Staples Press.

Becker, E. (1964). *The revolution in psychiatry.* New York: Free Press.

Bibring, E. (1953). Mechanisms of depression. In A. Greenacre (Ed.), *Affective Disorders: Psychoanalytic Contributions to their Study* (pp. 13–48). New York: International Universities Press.

Brown, G. W. (1989). Life events and measurement. In G. W. Brown and T. Harris (Eds.), *Life Events and Illness* (pp. 3–46). New York: Guilford.

——(1993). Life events and affective disorder: replications and limitations. *Psychosomatic Medicine, 55*, 248–259.

Brown, G. W. & Harris, T. O. (1978). *Social origins of depression: A study of psychiatric disorder in women.* London: Tavistock.

——(1986). Establishing causal links: the Bedford College Studies of Depression. In H. Katschnig (Ed.), *Life Events and Psychiatric Disorders* (pp. 107–187). Cambridge: Cambridge University Press.

——(1989). *Life events & Illness.* New York: Guilford.

Brown, G. W., Sklair, F., Harris, T. O. & Birley, J. L. T. (1973). Life events and psychiatric disorders: 1. Some methodological issues. *Psychological Medicine, 3*, 74–78.

Brown, G. W., Ni Brolchain, M. & Harris, T. O. (1975). Social class and psychiatric disturbance among women in an urban population. *Sociology, 9*, 225–254.

Brown, G. W., Craig, T. K. J. & Harris, T. O. (1985). Depression: disease or distress? Some epidemiological considerations. *British Journal of Psychiatry, 147*, 612–622.

Brown, G. W., Bifulco, A. & Harris, T. O. (1987). Life events, vulnerability and onset of depression: some refinements. *British Journal of Psychiatry, 150*, 30–42.

Brown, G. W., Adler, Z. & Bifulco, A. (1988). Life events, difficulties and recovery from chronic depression. *British Journal of Psychiatry, 152*, 487–498.

Brown, G. W., Lemyre, L. & Bifulco, A. (1992). Social factors and recovery from anxiety and depressive disorders: a test of the specificity hypothesis. *British Journal of Psychiatry, 161*, 44–54.

Brown, G. W., Harris, T. O. & Hepworth, C. (1994) Life events and "endogenous" depression: a puzzle re-examined. *Archives of General Psychiatry, 51*, 525–534.

Dean, C., Surtees, P. G. & Sashidharan, S. D. (1983). Comparison of research diagnostic systems in an Edinburgh community sample. *British Journal of Psychiatry, 142*, 247–256.

Finlay-Jones, R., Brown, G. W., Duncan-Jones, P., Harris, T. O., Murphy, E. & Prudo, R. (1980). Depression and anxiety in the community. *Psychological Medicine, 10*, 445–454.

Finlay-Jones, R. & Brown, G. W. (1981). Types of stressful life event and the onset of anxiety and depressive disorders. *Psychological Medicine, 11*, 803–815.

Fredin, L. (1982). *Psychosocial Aspects of Depression: No Way Out?* Chichester: Wiley.

Gilbert, P. (1989). *Human nature and suffering.* Hove: Erlbaum.

—— (1992). *Depression: The evolution of powerlessness.* Hove: Erlbaum.

Hammen, C. (1988). Depression and cognition about personal stressful life events. In L. B. Alloy (Ed.), *Cognitive Processes in Depression* (pp. 77–108). New York: Guilford.

Harris, T. O. & Brown, G. W. (1994) Interpersonal style and onset of depression: an NHS patient series. (Manuscript.)

Harris, T. O., Brown, G. W., Craig, T. J. K., Hepworth, C. & Robinson, R. (1994). Past loss and symptom morphology in depression: The mediating role of childhood adversity and current personality. (Manuscript.)

Lazarus, R. S. (1966). *Psychological stress and the coping process.* New York: McGraw-Hill.

Melges, F. T. & Bowlby, J. (1969). Types of hopelessness in psychopathological process. *Archives of General Psychiatry, 20,* 690–699.

Monroe, S. M. & Depue, R. A. (1991). Life stress and depression. In J. Becker and A. Kleinman (Eds.), *Psychosocial Aspects of Depression* (pp. 101–130). Hillsdale, NJ: Erlbaum.

Norusis, M. (1990). *SPSS/PC+ Advanced Statistics 4.0.* Chicago: SPSS.

Oatley, K. & Bolton, W. (1985). A social theory of depression in reaction to life events. *Psychological Review, 92,* 372–388.

Parkes, C. M. (1971). Psycho-social transitions: a field for study. *Social Science and Medicine, 5,* 101–15.

Paykel, E. S. & Cooper, Z. (1992). Life events and social stress. In E. S. Paykel (Ed.), *Handbook of Affective Disorders.* 2nd edn. (pp. 149–170). Edinburgh: Churchill Livingstone.

Paykel, E. S., Myers, J. K., Dienelt, M. N., Klerman, G. L., Lindenthal, J. J. & Pepper, M. P. (1969). Life events and depression: a controlled study. *Archives of General Psychiatry, 21,* 753–760.

Post, R. M. (1990). Sensitization and kindling perspectives on the course of affective illness: toward a new treatment with the anticonvulsant carbamazepine. *Pharmacopsychiatry, 12,* 3–17.

Price, J. S. (1988). Alternative channels for negotiating asymmetry in social relationships. In M. R. A. Chance (Ed.), *Social Fabrics of the Mind* (pp. 157–195). London: Erlbaum.

Price, J. S. & Sloman, L. (1987). Depression as a yielding behaviour: an animal model based on Schjelderup-Ebbe's pecking order. *Ethology and Sociobiology, 8,* 85–98.

Price, J., Sloman, L., Gardner, Jr, R., Gilbert, P. & Rohde, P. (1994). The social competition hypothesis of depression. *British Journal of Psychiatry, 164,* 309–315.

Quinton, D., Rutter, M. & Rowlands, O. (1976). An evaluation of an interview assessment of marriage. *Psychological Medicine, 6,* 577–586.

Seligman, M. E. P. (1975). *Helplessness: On depression, development and death.* San Francisco: W. H. Freeman.

Spitzer, R. L., Endicott, J. & Robins, E. (1978). Research Diagnostic Criteria: rationale and reliability. *Archives of General Psychiatry, 35,* 773–782.

Unger, R. M. (1984). *Passion: An essay on personality.* New York: Free Press.

Wing, J. K., Cooper, J. E. & Sartorious, N. (1974). *The Measurement and Classification of Psychiatric Symptoms: an Instruction Manual for the Present State Examination and CATEGO Program.* Cambridge: Cambridge University Press.

Wing, J. K., Nixon, J. M., Mann, S. A. & Leff, J. P. (1977). Reliability of the PSE (ninth edition) used in a population study. *Psychological Medicine, 7,* 505–516.

Wing, J. K., Babor, T., Brugha, T., Burke, J., Cooper, J. E., Giel, R., Jablensky, A., Regier, D. & Sartorius, N. (1990). SCAN. Schedules for Clinical Assessment in Neuropsychiatry. *Archives of General Psychiatry, 47,* 589–593.

CHAPTER *28*

Appraisal and Goal Processes as Predictors of Psychological Well-being in Bereaved Caregivers

N. Stein, S. Folkman, T. Trabasso, and
T. A. Richards

Nancy Stein and Tom Trabasso have proposed an appraisal model of emotion process (Stein, Trabasso, & Liwag, 1993). When desired goals are blocked, threatened, or attained, emotions are experienced, and these prompt new plans. Stein and her colleagues argue that we are constantly engaged in an evaluation of our environment about whether the things that are important to us are happening or being interfered with. If a goal is thwarted, to what extent do we think that we can recover, based on our beliefs about ourselves, our situation, other people?

This model has been used to examine reactions to bereavement. As we have seen in Brown and Harris's work (selection 27) negative life events have profound effects on well-being. Stein and her colleagues attempt to understand how people's thinking about these events mediates between event and well-being. Are some ways of making sense of events in the context of a life less harmful to well-being than others? They studied a group of men whose partners had just died of AIDS, and below there are excerpts from this work.

An important contribution of this work is the methodology developed for the analysis of the narrative accounts given by the subjects. We see how people appraise aspects of their lives that are relevant to their goals, and how the salience of particular goals affects outcome. This research suggests that people who focus more on the positive aspects of stressful situations will be less at risk of debilitating emotional states in the future.

Reference

Stein, N. L., Trabasso, T., & Liwag, M. (1993). The representation and organization of emotional experience: unfolding the emotion episode. In M. Lewis & J. M. Haviland (Eds.), *Handbook of emotions* (pp. 279–300). New York: Guilford.

In this article, we examine appraisal and goal processes associated with psychological well-being in response to the loss of a partner to AIDS. We used a narrative analysis (Stein & Liwag, 1997; Stein & Trabasso, 1982; Stein, Trabasso, & Liwag, 1992, 1994; Trabasso & Stein, 1994) of bereavement interviews to identify appraisal and goal processes that would explain psychological well-being at the time of bereavement and predict it 12 months later. Our analysis focused on three aspects of appraisal – beliefs, emotions, and goal outcomes – and future goals and plans that caregivers reported in coping with the death and loss of their partner. The maintenance or recovery of psychological well-being by a caregiver who provided care to a partner and then suffered his loss was hypothesized to depend on the activation of beliefs and goals that hold positive personal meaning, the revision of untenable beliefs and goals, the construction of concrete plans for the future, the experiences of positive emotions, and successful goal outcomes in the recounting of past events associated with care-giving and the partner [...]

A basic tenet of both positions is that the understanding of an event, whether stressful, traumatic, or an everyday occurrence, is based on the event's personal significance to an individual's well-being. Personal significance is determined by the individual's inferences about the ways in which an event directly affects valued beliefs, goals, and psychological and physical states (Folkman & Lazarus, 1990; Lazarus & Folkman, 1984; Stein & Levine, 1987, 1990). Changes in the status of well-being occur when desired goals are blocked, attained, or threatened. Individuals experience positive emotions and pleasurable states of well-being when they overcome obstacles that blocked their desired goals or when they avoid or escape from undesired states. *Goals* are defined as imaginable states of existence that are desired, and refer to any valued object, activity, or state that a person wants to attain. To activate a goal implies movement and directionality from one state to another or the initiation of an effort to maintain a current state. When people fail to attain or maintain desired goals or when they cannot prevent undesired states from occurring or continuing, they experience negative emotions and aversive states.

The terms *appraisal* and *goal processes* refer to the sequence of causal thinking, evaluation, emotional experience, goal setting, planning, and enactment that occurs as a stressful event unfolds over time. Our narrative analysis of appraisal and goal processes describes how a person represents and appraises a stressful event in relation to past experience (Folkman & Stein, 1997; Stein, Trabasso, & Liwag, 1992; Trabasso & Stein, 1994) and how a person uses past experience to generate goals and plans for the future [...]

Aims of the present research

An overall objective of the present research was to determine the extent to which an analysis of the appraisal and goal processes in narratives would provide an account of the caregiver's psychological well-being both at the time of his partner's death and 12 months later. Caring for a partner who is dying and losing that partner are highly stressful events. These events have great personal significance and are beyond an individual's personal control (Lazarus & Folkman, 1984).

This research had three specific aims. The first was to identify through narrative analysis the extent to which caregivers reported both positive and negative appraisals about their beliefs, goal outcomes, and emotional states during the highly stressful days leading up to and following a partner's death as a result of AIDS. Although the overall circumstances are universally regarded as highly stressful, the question is, will the caregiver's day-to-day experiences all be negative or will his experiences be more varied in terms of the inclusion of both positive and negative evaluation? The second aim was to examine the extent to which beliefs, goal outcomes of success or failure, and emotion states as appraisals predict the caregivers' formulation and use of future-oriented goals and plans. The ability to generate such goals and plans is widely acknowledged as an indicator of good psychological functioning. Does the narrative analysis identify which caregivers generate future-oriented plans and goals? The third aim was to determine the extent to which appraisal and goal process variables, including beliefs, goal outcomes, emotion states, as well as future goals and plans, predict psychological well-being at the time of the partner's death and 12 months later.

Method

Participants

This study examined data from the University of California, San Francisco (UCSF) Coping Project, a longitudinal study of the effects of caregiving and bereavement on the mental and physical health of 86 HIV-positive and 167 HIV-negative partners of men with AIDS. Participants were recruited between April 1990 and June 1992 from the San Francisco bay area. To be included in the cohort of bereaved caregivers selected for the present study, participants had to be HIV-negative caregivers whose partners died during the study and who had been interviewed at least once prior to their partner's death. Further, each participant had to have been interviewed three times following the partner's death: at approximately 2 weeks, 4 weeks, and 12 months after the death. These data had to have been collected by February 1993, the month in which the Rashomon project began.

The data of 30 caregivers who met the above criteria were selected. The average length of time the selected caregivers were involved in a relationship with their partners was 6.27 years. Their average age was 39.33 years, their median educational level was college graduate, and 97% ($N = 29$) were white.

Procedures

The first and second bereavement interviews began with the assessment of psychological well-being. At the first interview, the interviewer asked the caregiver to describe what had happened at the time of his partner's death, what he was feeling, what he was thinking, what helped him, and what made things difficult for him. In the second interview, the caregivers were free to review the same events as they reported in the first interview, and some did so, usually with an update on what was happening to them. Some caregivers talked only about those events that had occurred since their first interview. The narrative portions of these interviews were tape-recorded and later transcribed verbatim. Transcriptions were checked for accuracy against the recordings. As was done at the beginning of the first and second interviews, psychological well-being was assessed at the beginning of the third interview, which occurred 12 months following the partner's death. Each caregiver had the same interviewer throughout the study.

Measures of psychological well-being

There were four measures of psychological well-being:

1 *Depressive mood* was assessed with the 20-item Centers for Epidemiological Studies Depression measure (CES-D; Radloff, 1977) of cognitive, affective, and vegetative symptoms of depression. Participants indicated on a 4-point scale that ranged from *rarely or none of the time* (0) to *most or all of the time* (3) how frequently each of 20 symptoms had occurred during the previous week (possible scores ranged from 0 to 60; Cronbach's $\alpha = .89$).

2 *Positive morale* was assessed with a modified version of the Positive Morale subscale from Bradburn's (1969) Affect Balance Scale. The subscale consists of 8 items assessing positive mood states that are rated on a 4-point Likert scale that ranges from *none* (0) to *often* (3) for how often the person felt a particular mood during the previous week (possible scores ranged from 0 to 24; Cronbach's $\alpha = .90$). Examples of items include feeling "on top of the world," "optimistic," "pleased about having accomplished something," and "cheerful."

3 *Positive states of mind* were assessed with the Positive States of Mind Scale (Horowitz, Adler, & Kegeles, 1988), a 6-item scale that focuses on positively valued states such as pleasure, productivity, focused activity, and connection to others. Participants rated on a 4-point Likert scale that ranged from *unable to have it* (0) to *have it easily* (3) how much trouble, if any, they had in having the given state of mind during the previous week (possible scores ranged from 0 to 18; Cronbach's $\alpha = .81$).

4 *Impact of death* was measured with the Impact of Event Scale (Horowitz, Wilner, & Alvarez, 1979), a 15-item measure that includes subscales of intrusive and avoidant thoughts. The measure was administered with respect to the partner's death. A summary score was used in the present analysis (possible scores ranged from 0 to 32; Cronbach's $\alpha = .87$).

Two scores on each of the four measures of psychological well-being served as dependent measures. The first score was the average of a caregiver's total score on each of the four measures of psychological well-being obtained during the first and second interviews, 2 and 4 weeks following the partner's death. The second score for each measure was the total score 12 months following the partner's death. On all measures, higher scores represent greater amounts of the psychological state being assessed.

Narrative analysis

All transcribed narratives from the two bereavement interviews were coded as to their appraisals, goals, and plans. The narratives ranged in length from a few paragraphs to over 20 single-spaced, typewritten pages. Transcribed narratives were parsed into clausal units by five researchers. Four coders were then trained on the narrative coding scheme by Nancy L. Stein. For the purpose of training, all four coded the same 10 narratives. Each coder achieved from 85% to 90% agreement with Nancy L. Stein.

Parsing into clauses The first analysis involved parsing each of the 60 narratives into clausal units. Clauses contained one main verb predicate along with its arguments. Verbs included infinitives, discrete verbs, and auxiliaries plus infinitives. A clause often corresponded to a simple active sentence. The following episode has been parsed into clauses with the verb phrase italicized:

> It *was* a very stressful day
> because we *wanted to try*
> *to get* things moving
> and *needed to deal* with him [a nurse]
> in order *to do* that.
> And (he) *didn't call*
> so it's like we *waited* all day
> and finally at 4:30 he *got* around to us.
> I *asked* him
> *to come* over
> And he *did.*

Relative clauses joined with a main clause were treated as single clausal units. Relative clauses often refer to internal states or memories of conversations. The following statements exemplify these complex verb cases:

> He decided not to take the prednisone
> He thought about not taking the medication.
> The woman made him feel scared.
> And I said, 'If you don't want to be involved in this...'

Note that the clauses containing what was decided, thought about, felt, and said were the contents of interest in our analysis.

Parsing into episodes   After clausal parsing, the clauses of each narrative were further analyzed and organized into a series of goal-based episodes. An episode always included the following functional categories: an initiating event, goal, action, and outcome (Stein & Glenn, 1979; Trabasso et al., 1989). Episodes also may have included internal states other than goals, such as emotions, cognitions, and perceptions. Episodic boundaries were determined by the presence of an initiating or precipitating event at the beginning and by a goal outcome of success or failure at the end. After episodic parsing was carried out, the episodes and their clauses were arranged according to the inferred temporal order in which the events were likely to have occurred. Each episode was classified into one of three mutually exclusive time periods (a) prior to the death of the partner, (b) during and surrounding the death of the partner, or (c) subsequent to the death of the partner.

Parsing into functional categories   Linguistic and semantic criteria then were used to determine the specific functional category membership of each clause in an episode. Identifying the functional significance of each clause was essential for carrying out the narrative analysis. For the present set of narratives, we used the following eight category classifications (Folkman & Stein, 1997; Stein, Trabasso, & Liwag, 1992, 1994): *precipitating events, beliefs, values, preferences, emotions, goals, plans of action*, and *goal outcomes*.

Precipitating events   Episodes always begin with precipitating events. These events are called precipitators because they challenge the narrator's current set of beliefs about the world. Physical events, human actions, memories of past events, or images of future events can all serve as precipitating events. In most instances, precipitating events contain some type of novel information about changes and force an appraisal of current beliefs and goals.

The main criterion that was used to identify a precipitating event was the explicit report of a state change in some aspect of the narrator's personal experience. As we indicated above, when caregivers spoke about their partner's death, they often began by talking about events that signaled the final decline of their partner. We now present two illustrations of such narratives. Note that in each case, three clauses comprise the precipitating event. Each of the three clauses describes an aspect of the state changes that were perceived by the caregiver:

Example 1.
He went into the hospital one last time.
Basically, they started chemotherapy,
and couldn't keep his bone marrow working.

Example 2.
A couple of weeks before he died,
they did a couple of procedures on him,
and I think that did him in.

Precipitating events were retold throughout the narrative and always signaled the beginning of a new episode. These, other than the first precipitating event, served a double function: they began an episode but they also functioned as the outcome of goal success or failure at the end of the previous episode. For example, one caregiver reported that he was looking for an urn in which he could store his partner's ashes. He told of going to an art fair, finding a woman who made urns, talking to her, and having her offer to make an urn for him. The woman's offer to make an urn was the outcome of the caregiver's request to have an urn made. The offer, however, then enabled future action by the caregiver. Thus, the outcome in the first episode served as the initiating event in the second episode.

Beliefs Beliefs were defined as organized forms of knowledge that carry an expectation about some aspect of the world. Beliefs reflect what people think was, is, or could be true about their world (Stein & Levine, 1987, 1990; Stein, Trabasso, & Liwag, 1992). When a precipitating event occurs, people activate relevant beliefs (knowledge) in an attempt to understand the personal significance of the event under consideration. In this way, they can determine how an event has affected or will affect them in the future. In describing an event's impact, caregivers reported the following types of beliefs:

1 Beliefs that described their knowledge about past and current states of the world:

> He did not want to die in the hospital, absolutely.
> He loved that kind of massage.
> I have had the same attitude for the past two months:
> This is his life and death,
> I'm merely a conduit
> to see that it happens gracefully.
> I feel particularly honored
> that I've been able to participate in each [the life and death process]
> of them.

2 Past and current beliefs that were challenged or violated:

> I couldn't believe what was happening to him.
> He was not the person I knew.
> I couldn't tolerate it.
> I hadn't expected him to get sick this fast.
> This was it – it was different.
> I took the wrong approach (and I changed it).

3 Beliefs about future states of affairs, including the need to revise current beliefs:

> I don't think they [doctors] should do that.
> If I don't change, I'll be hopeless.
> Some gaps need to be filled [in] and some don't.

That's one of the things my work does – I can develop it
[caregiver's behavior] into a positive compulsion.
I'll get going in a while (I am not in any rush).

Belief appraisals   Belief appraisals almost always follow the reporting of an initiating event or an outcome, and they function to assess its impact. Belief appraisals
are evaluations about people, places, precipitating events, internal states, actions,
and outcomes that affect the status of goals and well-being (Lazarus & Folkman,
1984; Stein & Levine, 1987; Stein, Trabasso, & Liwag, 1992, 1994). The appraisal
of a belief involves a judgment about the value of the belief to the individual. This
value can be expressed in terms of valence (good, bad) or a preference (liking and
disliking), such as:

(a) I really liked it when we could just spend some quiet time, without any more
painful things occurring; or
(b) I really hate the way doctors talk to you about these visits.

Belief appraisals often preceded statements of wishing or desiring something (a
goal). Belief appraisals, however, are different from goals. Belief appraisals, unlike
goals, do not encode directionality or active movement toward an end state.
However, belief appraisals often lie in close proximity to statements of goals
because they provide the motivation for activating goals.

Thematic classification of belief appraisals   Because all caregivers experienced the loss of
their partner, similar thematic classes of belief appraisals were found in all caregiver
narratives. Other classes of appraisals were reported in the narratives of only a few
caregivers. To capture the commonalty and diversity of thematic patterns of belief
appraisals, all belief appraisals in all narratives were listed and systematically
classified into 1 of 18 categories. Ten categories were identified as positive in
valence, and 8 were negative in valence. The valence of each belief appraisal was
determined by semantic criteria (e.g. good, bad, wonderful, it was the right thing to
do, it was not considerate). Care was taken to separate positive and negative belief
appraisal statements from the reporting of specific emotion responses, goals, and
goal outcomes. Table 28.1 lists the 10 positive and 8 negative categories of belief
appraisals. Specific examples of each category are presented in the Appendix.

Goals   Goals were defined in terms of desired or undesired states. Goals imply
movement and directionality. A goal is a desire to go from one state to another or
to maintain a current state. Goals referred to any valued object, activity, or state
that the participant or his partner with AIDS wanted to attain or maintain. Goals
can be identified by the use of auxiliaries such as *wish, want, decide, going to do, try to
do, must do* (e.g. "I really wish he weren't in so much pain and suffering," "I wish I
could transform him back to his old self," "I really don't want him to go through
all of this suffering," "I wish he would have a more positive attitude so he could
beat this thing.")
Goals were also identified by the use of a prepositional phrase attached to
an action statement. Goals motivate action and are often joined to them by

Table 28.1. Corresponding positive and negative thematic categories for belief appraisals

Positive belief appraisals	Negative belief appraisals
Beneficial quality of the relationship	Regrets about quality of relationship
Helping partner to die	Regrets about caregiving
Positive attitude toward death	Fear of death or dying
Belief in the persistence of relationship	Negative consequences of caregiving and relationship with partner
Spirituality	—
Letting go of the relationship	Failure to accept partner's death
Positive aspects of social support	—
Positive memories of partner	Dealing with the negative consequences of loss of the relationship
Self-growth from past events	Fear of future
Feelings of personal strength	Awareness and persistence of psychological vulnerability

Note. Dashes indicate there was no corresponding negative category.

prepositions such as *to, for,* or *in order to* plus a verb and arguments in clauses (e.g. "I read some of his favorite short stories to him *in order to relax him,*" "I tried *to give him a soothing massage,*" and "I was taking him *to the doctor,* when…").

In the bereavement narratives, goals were talked about with respect to past events leading to the death of the partner, to events surrounding the death, or to the caregiver's future. A distinction was made between those goals the caregiver had already carried out (past goals) and those goals that remained to be accomplished (future goals). The verb tense of the auxiliary was used to discriminate between past goals (*I was going to, I wanted to, I tried to*) and future goals (*I'm going to consider doing it, I'll try to get involved again, I won't rush things*).

Future goals varied widely in their specificity and term. Some goals incorporated the caregiver's needs for the moment; others were formulated to span a longer period. Therefore, two goal categories were created: Short term and long term. Short-term goals pertained to the immediate future – that is, the present day or the next few weeks – and were highly specific and discrete, such as writing an obituary, notifying friends of the partner's death, or planning a memorial service. Long-term goals were described more globally and pertained to more situations and the more distant future. Examples included getting back into physical shape, remaining in touch with the deceased partner's family, reconnecting with friends, attempting to derive pleasure from physical or sexual activity, taking a vacation, renovating a house, or changing jobs.

We also made a distinction between goals that were focused primarily on the self and those that were focused on the partner. Examples of self-goals were "I had to think about how this was going to affect me," "I decided that I had to let go of the relationship." Examples of goals pertaining to the partner were "I promised him that I would take care of the cats" and "He was really devoted to those people, and so I went to their place."

Goal outcomes   Goal outcomes were defined as success or failure at attaining, maintaining, escaping from, or avoiding states, activities, or objects. Two different outcomes were identified, success and failure. The language of completion was used to identify outcomes: "I did it," "I got it," "I really accomplished a lot" or "I really blew it," and "It just didn't happen." Thus, goal outcomes include reference to the result or ending of an action. "I gave him a massage, and he felt better" or "Although I gave him the medicine, he got worse."

Emotion states   A taxonomy of emotions and related internal state words developed by Stein and Carstensen (1993) was used to identify emotion states. The taxonomy distinguishes among specific emotion states, general affective states, metaphors for emotional experiences, mood states, dispositional states (personality traits), mental states, and preferences. Only words that expressed specific emotion responses to a shift in a status of a current goal were included. Other types of affective responses (e.g. preferences, positive and negative assessments of personal dispositions) were included in the belief appraisal category. We created a separate category for specific emotional state appraisals because they are indicators of the value of shifts in goals and their status. We excluded other types of affective responses (e.g. statements of mood, statements of personality dispositions, statements of mental states) from our emotion category to avoid confounding our narrative measures with the outcome measures of psychological well-being, which include assessments of more long-term, enduring positive and negative mood and mental states.

Plans   Plans focused on future actions that the participant considered necessary to the attainment of his goals. Plans were identified by the use of verbs that were conditional or future oriented, such as "I want to get going, and here's what I'd really like to do"; "I am joining a support group so I can help others and meet new people"; "I need companionship, so I hope to meet someone on this trip and get into a new relationship." The classification of plans paralleled the classification of goals in terms of a short-and long-term focus. Some plans were immediate and focused on actions to be taken in only one situation. Others covered a wider number of related situations and actions and focused on the more distant future. Like goals, plans were focused either on the self or on the partner, both in the short term and long term.

Results

We considered three types of appraisal: appraisals of beliefs, appraisals of goal outcomes, and appraisals of goal-related emotion states. We first present results regarding the relative frequency of positive and negative appraisals of beliefs, goal outcomes, and emotion states, and the intercorrelations among these variables. Second, we present the results of our examination of the relationships between appraisals of beliefs, goal outcomes, and emotion states with the ability to formulate and carry out future goals and plans. We then present the relationship between the appraisal variables (beliefs, goal outcomes, and emotion states), future-oriented goals and plans, and the psychological well-being of the caregiver at the time of the partner's death and 12 months later.

Positive and negative appraisals

The total numbers of positive or negative belief appraisals, successful or failed outcomes, and positive or negative emotional states were found for each caregiver

Table 28.2. Measures of appraisal: summary of descriptive statistics

Appraisal measure	Valence	
	Positive	Negative
Beliefs		
M	5.50	2.90
SD	1.98	1.06
Range	2–10	1–6
t(29)	8.31**	
Proportion	.65	.35
SD	.09	.09
Range	0.40–0.80	0.20–0.60
t(29)	9.17**	
Goal outcomes		
M	30.83	10.87
SD	16.93	6.31
Range	6–73	0–32
t(29)	7.85**	
Proportion	.75	.25
SD	.13	.13
Range	0.49–1.00	0.00–0.51
t(29)	10.93**	
Emotions		
M	7.80	13.70
SD	6.40	11.59
Range	0–27	1–46
t(29)	−2.60**	
Proportion	.39	.61
SD	.24	.24
Range	0.00–0.90	0.10–1.00
t(29)	−5.90**	
Positive appraisals		
Proportion	.60	
SD	.12	
Range	0.37–0.84	
t(29)	5.60**	

**p < .01.

in his two bereavement narratives. The means, standard deviations, and ranges for each type of appraisal are shown in table 28.2, as is the proportion of the positive or negative reports for each type of appraisal. Proportion scores were used to control for differences in verbosity and length of narrative. Table 28.2 also reports the average proportion of the three types of positive appraisals, matched t tests comparing the means of negative and positive scores on each appraisal measure, and a t test of the mean proportion of positive appraisals equal to chance (.50).

The results indicate that caregivers, on average, reported more positive than negative appraisals of beliefs and goal outcomes. However, caregivers reported more negative than positive emotions. Thus, caregivers reported proportionately more positive beliefs about the impact of caregiving events and goal outcomes despite consistently reporting more negative emotions.

Correlations were computed among the three types of appraisal – beliefs, goal outcomes, and emotional states. All measures were positively related, with correlations ranging from .16 to .39. However, only the correlation between beliefs and emotion states reached statistical significance ($r = .39, p = .05$).

Partial correlations of each of the three types of appraisal with the mean proportion of positive appraisals indicated that the proportion of positive emotions accounted for 68% of the variance in this measure; goal outcomes accounted for an additional 21%, beliefs accounted for an additional 1%. Thus, our measure of positive appraisals was influenced primarily by emotions and goal outcomes.

Relations between positive appraisals and future goals and plans

The average proportion of positive appraisals correlated significantly with long-term plans for the self ($r = .46, p = .01$), marginally with long-term plans for the partner ($r = .35, p = .06$), and significantly with long-term goals for the self ($r = .36, p = .05$). Thus, positive appraisals were highly related to the caregiver's reports of long-range plans for the partner and long-range goals and plans for the self.

To show the relationships between goals and plans with appraisals, the caregivers were classified as to whether their proportion of positive appraisals was in the lower, middle, or upper third of the distribution. Then, for each third, the mean numbers of goals and plans per caregiver were found. The means for short-term and long-term goals and plans for each third of the caregivers are displayed in figure 28.1.

Caregivers whose proportion of positive appraisals ranked in the upper third of the distribution reported more plans for themselves than they did for their partners. They also reported more goals and plans overall than did the other two groups. Positive appraisals about caregiving and events surrounding bereavement apparently may have enabled these caregivers to focus on plans to get on with their own lives following the loss of their partner and their role as caregiver. Caregivers who reported proportionately more positive appraisals also reported more concurrent and future-oriented goals and plans of long duration that focused on work, relationships, housing, and recreation. In contrast, those caregivers who ranked in the lower third focused more on short-term goals such as the immediate demands and consequences of bereavement (e.g. taking care of details for the funeral or for the household). Those caregivers who were in the middle third of

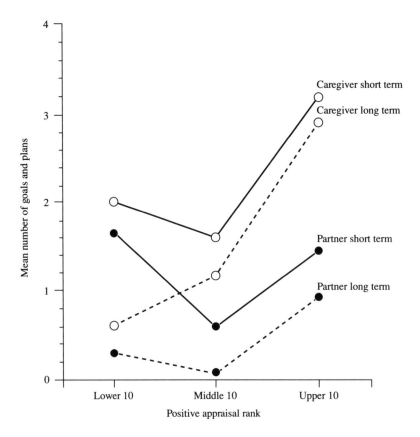

Figure 28.1   Mean number of short- and long-term goals and plans reported by caregivers in terms of three levels of positive appraisals.

the distribution of the proportions of positive appraisals appeared to be in transition; they focused less on their partner and more on their own goals and plans. They did so, however, less often in comparison to caregivers who generated proportions of positive appraisals in the upper third.

Positive appraisals and psychological well-being

The measures of psychological well-being at bereavement and 12 months later were correlated with the mean proportion of positive appraisals. The results are presented in table 28.3.

The mean proportion of positive appraisals was significantly correlated with all psychological well-being measures at bereavement and at 12 months later, except for the impact of death measure. To understand these findings, we constructed four different graphs to illustrate the slope magnitude and direction of the relationships between the proportion of positive appraisals and scores on each of the four psychological well-being measures. The average score was found for each of the four measures of psychological well-being at the time of the bereavement and 12 months later for caregivers falling in the lower, middle, and upper

Table 28.3. Correlations between caregiver's overall proportion of positive appraisals and his psychological well-being at bereavement and at 12 months following his partner's death

	Measure of psychological well-being			
Overall appraisal score	Positive morale	Positive states of mind	Depressive mood	Impact of death
At bereavement	.42*	.35†	−.43*	−.26
At 12 months following partner's death	.63**	.67**	−.51**	−.12

† $p < .10$ (marginally significant). *$p < .05$. **$p < .01$.

thirds of the distribution of the proportion of positive appraisals. These results are displayed in figure 28.2.

Note in the upper left panel of figure 28.2 that positive morale increased with positive appraisals. Caregivers who were in the lower third of the positive appraisal distribution and whose proportion of positive appraisals averaged less than 50% at bereavement showed little or no gain in positive morale 12 months later. Those in the middle and upper groups of the distribution, who averaged 58% or 72% of positive appraisals, respectively, showed substantially more gain.

The top right panel of figure 28.2 illustrates that positive states of mind and the proportion of positive appraisals were positively related at bereavement and 12 months later. Again, scores on positive states of mind at bereavement were lower than those obtained 12 months later. The group that generated the lowest proportion of positive appraisals showed little or no gain at bereavement, whereas the middle and upper-level groups showed substantial improvements in positive states of mind at 12 months following bereavement.

The bottom panels of figure 28.2 focus on negative psychological well-being. The correlations between impact of death and depressive mood with the proportion of positive appraisals were negative. Increases in the proportion of positive appraisals were associated with decreases in impact of death or depressive mood scores. Caregivers also received higher scores on impact of death and depressive mood measures at bereavement than they did 12 months later. The curves for each negative well-being measure were parallel to one another such that these assessments of negative psychological well-being were inversely related to the proportion of positive appraisals.

Future goals, plans, and psychological well-being

Regression analyses of the four measures of psychological well-being with future goals and plans as predictor variables showed that long-term goals for the partner accounted for significant variance in positive states of mind at bereavement ($R^2 = .15$, $p = .04$), whereas long-term goals for the self marginally accounted for a significant amount of variance ($R^2 = .03$, $p = .10$). Long-term goals for the partner ($R^2 = .17$, $p = .02$) and short-term plans for the partner ($R^2 = .14$, $p = .04$) accounted for significant amounts of variance in depressive mood. These

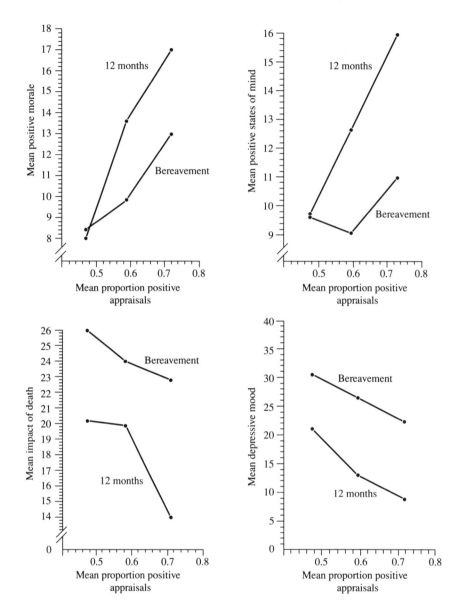

Figure 28.2 The relationship between two positive and two negative measures of psychological well-being at bereavement and 12 months later with the proportion of positive appraisals in bereavement narratives.

correlations indicated that the relation between long-term goals for the partner and depressive mood was negative, and the relation between short-term plans for the partner and depressive mood was positive. At 12 months, short-term plans for the partner accounted for marginal variance in positive morale ($R^2 = -.10$, $p = .08$) and for marginal variance in depressive mood ($R^2 = .12$, $p = .07$). These findings indicate that developing long-range goals for both the partner and self was related to psychological well-being at bereavement, whereas focusing on short-term goals related to the partner's death was a negative predictor of psychological well-being 12 months later.

Using appraisals and future goals and plans to predict psychological well-being at 12 months

A multivariate analysis was carried out to determine whether the proportion of positive appraisals and short-term goals for the partner predicted psychological well-being of caregivers at 12 months, controlling for the same measure of well-being at bereavement. The independent variables entered were the measure of psychological well-being at the time of bereavement, the mean proportion of positive appraisals, and the number of short-term goals for the partner with AIDS. A backward stepwise regression analysis was then performed to determine how much of a reduction in the variance was accounted for by removing each factor while retaining the other two factors. Table 28.4 summarizes the results of these multivariate analyses.

The total and adjusted R-squares for the full model with three independent variables are displayed in table 28.4 for each measure of psychological well-being. As table 28.4 illustrates, the statistical model that was based on the narrative analysis of appraisals and goal plans accounted for substantial amounts of variance for positive morale, positive states of mind, and depressive mood. The standardized beta coefficients for positive appraisal were all statistically significant

Table 28.4. Predictions of a caregiver's psychological well-being at 12 months following the partner's death, controlling for caregiver's well-being at time of death

Variable	β	Prob.	Change in R^2 if removed	Total R^2	Adjusted R^2
Positive morale				.49	.43
Positive morale at bereavement	.06	.69	< .01		
Short-term plans and goals for partner with AIDS	−.30	.04	.09		
Positive appraisals	.61	< .01	.31		
Positive states of mind				.59	.54
Positive states at bereavement	.25	.07	.05		
Short-term plans and goals for partner with AIDS	−.26	.05	.07		
Positive appraisals	.59	< .01	.30		
Depressive mood				.44	.37
Depressive mood at bereavement	.29	.09	.07		
Short-term plans and goals for partner with AIDS	.29	.06	.08		
Positive appraisals	−.39	.02	.13		
Impact of event				.32	.30
Impact of event at death of partner	.57	< .01	.32		

Note. Prob. = probability.

(*ps* < .02). Those for short-term goals and plans for the partner with AIDS reached borderline levels of significance (*p* < .06). The appraisal and goal variables did not predict the impact of death at 12 months. The only significant predictor of the impact of death at 12 months was the score on this measure at bereavement.

The reduction in explained variance produced by forced removal of each predictor variable is presented in the center column of table 28.4. Here, corresponding to the results on the beta coefficients, the most substantial reduction occurred for positive morale, positive states of mind, and depressive mood when positive appraisal was removed. The next largest reduction was that due to short-term goals for the partner. The smallest reduction occurred when the same psychological well-being measure at bereavement was removed, with the exception of the measure of impact of death.

Discussion

The analysis of the narratives with the appraisal and goal process model focused on (a) valenced beliefs and expectations; (b) specific situation goals and their outcomes; (c) emotions associated with goals having been challenged, goal success, and goal failure; and (d) future goals and plans. A measure of appraisal composed of the proportion of positive beliefs, goal outcomes, and emotions accounted for substantial variance in psychological well-being at bereavement and predicted well-being 12 months later. The substantial variance accounted for in well-being at 12 months by positive appraisals was independent of the measures of psychological well-being at bereavement. In addition, this single measure of positive appraisals accounted for variation in caregivers' long-term goals and plans for themselves at the time of the partner's death.

In their narratives, caregivers appraised just about everything that happened to them. They evaluated their relationship with the partner; their partner as a person; their beliefs about death, dying, and spirituality; their viewpoint of themselves as caregivers; whether they were helpful to their partners; the difficulties associated with caregiving; the consequences of their loss; the things they learned from past experience; and their progress in recovering from bereavement. To an observer, caring for a partner with AIDS and then losing him might be perceived as a uniformly grim, negative experience. The results showed, however, that in the midst of this experience, caregivers made positive appraisals with respect to their beliefs about how things were, are, and will be; their goals; the outcomes of their goals; and the emotions related to their goals. In the midst of the stress that characterized the ill partner's last days and the days immediately following his death, caregivers reported proportionately more positive than negative beliefs and more successful than unsuccessful goal outcomes while reporting more negative than positive emotion states. Through their positive appraisals, individuals confronted with the stress of providing care to a dying partner and then losing that partner were able to sustain their psychological well-being at bereavement and 1 year later.

Empirically, the three aspects of appraisal that we assessed – beliefs, goal outcomes, and emotions – were relatively independent of each other. The relative independence of these appraisal dimensions was consistent with our theory of appraisal and goal processes. This theory states that each dimension characterizes part of the appraisal and goal process and serves a function in evaluating constituents of an episode. Precipitating events elicit beliefs that reflect what people hold to be true about the world, what they like, and, more important, what they expect in terms of how they think their world should function. Goals formulated in response to evaluations of precipitating events indicate a person's desires. The plans that are generated indicate courses of action that could actualize them. The outcomes reflect evaluations of goal successes or failures. Emotions in response to precipitating events indicate that the status of a person's existing goals has changed, whereas emotions in response to the outcome of goal-directed actions indicate whether goals were successfully attained or maintained. It is possible that within an episode, a caregiver could express negative belief violations and negative emotions to a precipitating event, formulate and carry out goals successfully, and express positive emotions over successfully meeting a goal. Thus, positive and negative appraisals co-occurred and were distributed over the course of the clauses that described the unfolding of an episode.

Positive emotions and successful goal outcomes accounted for the majority of the variance in our central measure of appraisal (average proportion of positive appraisals). Belief appraisals accounted for a negligible amount of the variance in this appraisal measure. The contribution of the belief appraisals may have been limited by a restriction of range in this measure compared to the other two (see table 28.2). In addition, some beliefs have been more significantly related to psychological well-being than others. For example, a review of the belief appraisal content suggested that caregivers with high well-being scores were less likely to express relationship regrets, voice nonacceptance of their partner's death, report psychological vulnerability, focus on wishful thinking about reinstating aspects of their relationship with their partner, and express beliefs about spirituality and the persistence of the relationship with their partner. They also appeared more likely to report that they had been a good caregiver or that they had eased the death of their partner, and they expressed the belief that they had to "let go" of their memories of their relationship with their partner and get on with their lives.

At bereavement, the goals and plans that focused on the self and on the long term were correlated with positive appraisals. Thus, caregivers who evaluated events relatively more positively also were future oriented in a constructive fashion. They were able to formulate realistic goals and plans with respect to getting on with their lives, for example, resuming relationships, work, and leisure activities. Long-term and self-oriented goals and plans were also associated with the recovery of psychological well-being at bereavement. In contrast, those caregivers who focused relatively more on short-term goals and plans for the partner did less well psychologically 12 months later. Goals and plans, therefore, served as both indicators of current well-being and as predictors of future well-being.

The unique variance accounted for by emotions, goal outcomes, and beliefs was therefore not just a proxy for mood or morale. Positive appraisals and plans predicted psychological well-being (mood and morale) 12 months after the partner's death independent of measures of these variables at the time of bereavement. The positive appraisals included emotions, but these emotions were situated and meaningfully related to ongoing events, goals, actions, and outcomes in the everyday lives of the caregivers. We also distinguished positive (and negative) appraisals from underlying traits such as positive and negative emotionality (Tellegen, 1985) or negative affect (e.g. Watson & Clark, 1984). Although these dimensions may influence appraisals, as we noted, appraisals were characterized by specific cognitive and affective content related to a specific context [...]

References

Bradburn, N. (1969). *The structure of psychological well-being.* Chicago: Aldine.

Carver, C. S., & Scheier, M. F. (1990). Origins and functions of positive and negative affect: A control-process view. *Psychological Review, 97,* 19–35.

Emmons, R. A. (1992). Abstract versus concrete goals: Personal striving level, physical illness, and psychological well-being. *Journal of Personality and Social Psychology, 62,* 292–300.

Emmons, R. A., & McAdams, D. P. (1991). Personal strivings and motive dispositions: exploring the links. *Personality and Social Psychology Bulletin, 17,* 648–654.

Folkman, S., & Lazarus, R. S. (1990). Coping and emotion. In N. L. Stein, B. Leventhal, & T. Trabasso (Eds.), *Psychological and biological approaches to emotion* (pp. 313–332). Hillsdale, NJ: Erlbaum.

Folkman, S., & Stein, N. L. (1997). Adaptive goal processes in stressful events. In N. Stein, P. A. Ornstein, B. Tversky, & C. Brainerd (Eds.), *Memory for everyday and emotional events.* (pp. 113–137). Hillsdale, NJ: Erlbaum.

Harber, K. D., & Pennebaker, J. W. (1992). Overcoming traumatic memories. In S. A. Christianson (Ed.), *The handbook of emotion and memory: Research and theory* (pp. 359–387). Hillsdale, NJ: Erlbaum.

Horowitz, M., Adler, N., & Kegeles, S. (1988). A scale for measuring the occurrence of positive states of mind: a preliminary report. *Psychosomatic Medicine, 50,* 477–483.

Horowitz, M., Wilner, N., & Alvarez, W. (1979). Impact of Event Scale: a measure of subjective stress. *Psychosomatic Medicine, 41,* 209–218.

Janis, I. J., & Mann, L. (1977). *Decision making.* New York: Free Press.

Klinger, E. (1977). *Meaning and void: Inner experience and the incentives in people's lives.* Minneapolis: University of Minnesota Press.

—— (1987). Current concerns and disengagement from incentives. In F. Halisch & J. Kuhl (Eds.), *Motivation, intention, and volition* (pp. 337–347). Berlin: Springer

—— (1996). Emotional influences on cognitive processing with implications for theories of both. In P. M. Gollwitzer & J. A. Bargh (Eds.), *The psychology of action* (pp. 168–189). New York: Guilford.

Lazarus, R. S., & Folkman, S. (1984). *Stress, appraisal, and coping.* New York: Springer.

Nolen-Hoeksema, S. (1991). Responses to depression and their effects on the duration of depressive episodes. *Journal of Abnormal Psychology, 100,* 569–582.

Nolen-Hoeksema, S., & Morrow, J. (1991). A prospective study of depression and post-traumatic stress symptoms after a natural disaster: The 1989 Loma Prieta earthquake. *Journal of Personality and Social Psychology, 61,* 115–121.

—— (1993). Effects of rumination and distraction on naturally occurring depressed mood. *Cognition and Emotion, 7,* 561–570.

Pennebaker, J. W. (1985). Traumatic experience and psychosomatic disease: exploring the roles of behavioral inhibition, obsession, and confiding. *Canadian Psychology, 26,* 82–95.

—— (1989). Confession, inhibition, and disease. In L. Berkowitz (Ed.), *Advances in experimental social psychology* (Vol. 22, pp. 211–244). New York: Academic Press.

Radloff, L. S. (1977). CES-D Scale: A self-report depression scale for research in the general population: *Applied Psychological Measurement, 1,* 385–401.

Scheier, M. F., & Carver, C. S. (1985). Optimism, coping, and health: assessment and implications of general outcome expectancies. *Health Psychology, 4,* 219–247.

Silver, R. L., Boon, C., & Stones, M. H. (1983). Searching for meaning in misfortune: making sense of incest. *Journal of Social Issues, 39,* 81–102.

Stein, N. L., & Carstensen, L. (1993). *Natural language descriptions of the face: A working internal state and event taxonomy.* Unpublished manuscript, University of Chicago.

Stein, N. L., & Glenn, C. G. (1979). An analysis of story comprehension in elementary school children. In R. O. Freedle (Ed.), *New directions in discourse processing: Vol. 2. Advances in discourse processes* (pp. 53–120). Norwood, NJ: Ablex.

Stein, N. L., & Levine, L. (1987). Thinking about feelings: the development and use of emotional knowledge. In R. E. Snow & M. Farr (Eds.), *Aptitude, learning, and instruction: Vol. 3, Cognition, conotation, and affect* (pp. 168–198). Hillsdale, NJ: Erlbaum.

—— (1990). Making sense out of emotional experience: The representation and use of goal-directed knowledge. In N. L. Stein, B. Leventhal, & T. Trabasso (Eds.), *Psychological and biological approaches to emotion* (pp. 45–74). Hillsdale, NJ: Erlbaum.

Stein, N. L., & Liwag, M. D. (1997). A goal-appraisal process approach to understanding and remembering emotional events. In P. van den Broek, P. Bauer, & T. Bourg (Eds.), *Development spans in event comprehension and representation* (pp. 199–235). Hillsdale, NJ: Erlbaum.

Stein, N. L., & Trabasso, T. (1982). What's in a story? An approach to comprehension. In R. Glaser (Ed.), *Advances in the psychology of instruction* (vol. 2, pp. 212–267). Hillsdale, NJ: Erlbaum.

—— (1992). The organization of emotional experience. *Cognition and Emotion, 6,* 225–244.

Stein, N. L., Trabasso, T., & Liwag, M. (1992). The representation and organization of emotional experience. In M. L. Lewis & J. Haviland (Eds.), *Handbook of emotion* (pp. 279–299). New York: Guilford.

—— (1994). The Rashomon phenomenon: Personal frames and future oriented appraisals in memory for emotional events. In M. M. Haith, J. B. Benson, R. J. Roberts, & B. F. Pennington (Eds.), *Future oriented processes* (pp. 409–435). Chicago: University of Chicago Press.

Stroebe, M. S., Stroebe, W., & Hansson, R. O. (1993). *Handbook of bereavement.* New York: Cambridge University Press.

Taylor, S. E., & Brown, J. D. (1988). Illusion and well-being: a social psychological perspective on mental health. *Psychological Bulletin, 103,* 193–210.

—— (1994). Positive illusions and well-being revisited: Separating fact from fiction. *Psychological Bulletin, 116,* 21–27.

Tellegen, A. (1985). Structures of mood and personality and their relevance to assessing anxiety, with an emphasis on self- report. In A. H. Tuma & J. Mason (Eds.), *Anxiety and the anxiety disorders* (pp. 681–706). Hillsdale, NJ: Erlbaum.

Trabasso, T., Secco, T., & Van den Broek, P. (1984). Causal cohesion and story coherence. In H. Mandl, N. L. Stein, & T. Trabasso (Eds.), *Learning and comprehension of text* (pp. 83–111). Hillsdale, NJ: Erlbaum.

Trabasso, T., & Stein, N. L. (1994). Using goal-plan knowledge to merge the past with the present and the future in narrating on- line events. In M. M. Haith, J. B. Benson, R. J. Roberts, & B. F. Pennington (Eds.), *Future oriented processes.* Chicago: University of Chicago Press.

Trabasso, T., & Suh, S. (1993). Understanding text: achieving explanatory coherence through on-line inferences and mental operations in working memory. *Discourse Processes, 16*, 3–34.

Trabasso, T., Van den Broek, P., & Suh, S. (1989). Logical necessity and transitivity of causal relations in stories. *Discourse Processes, 12*, 1–25.

Walsh, F., & McGoldrick, M. (1991). *Living beyond loss: Death in the family.* New York: Norton.

Watson, D., & Clark, L. A. (1984). Negative affectivity: the disposition to experience aversive emotional states. *Psychological Bulletin, 96*, 465–490.

Wortman, C. B., & Silver, R. C. (1987). Coping with irrevocable loss. In G. R. VandenBos & B. K. Bryant (Eds.), *Cataclysms, crises, and catastrophes: Psychology in action.* The Master Lectures (Vol. 6, pp. 185–235). Washington, DC: American Psychological Association.

—— (1990). Successful mastery of bereavement and widowhood: a life course perspective. In P. B. Baltes & M. M. Baltes (Eds.), *Successful aging* (pp. 225–264). New York: Cambridge University Press.

Wortman, C. B., Silver, R. C., & Kessler, R. C. (1993). The meaning of loss and adjustment to bereavement. In M. S. Stroebe, W. Stroebe, & R. O. Hansson (Eds.), *Handbook of bereavement* (pp. 349–366). New York: Cambridge University Press.

CHAPTER *29*

Disclosure of Traumas and Immune Function

J. W. Pennebaker, J. K. Kiecolt-Glaser, and R. Glaser

How do people handle emotional experience? Some think about their emotions a lot and are very articulate about their internal experiences. Others talk little about their feelings spontaneously and, when asked, seem to find it difficult to identify or analyze them. The skill of thinking and talking about emotions has been called the metacognition of emotion, an aspect of emotional intelligence (selection 25). There is a growing interest in how it relates to psychological (Gottman, Fainsilber-Katz, & Hooven, 1996) and physical well-being.

Stressful and traumatic events in people's lives have been shown to be associated with increased onsets of illness (O'Leary, 1990). Pennebaker and his colleagues have been examining an intervention that involves having people write about negative experiences for 20 minutes a day for four days – this leads to better functioning of the immune system and fewer visits to doctors. People who disclosed experiences they had not previously discussed with others showed the most marked improvements in immune system functioning. Why was writing about traumatic experience so beneficial? Probably because it affords the opportunity to restructure experience, gain a different understanding of events. It may even be, as Pennebaker and his colleagues argue, that one cause of stress is expenditure of resources to inhibit thoughts or feelings of specific events. When people confront their distressed emotions around the event, that form of stress diminishes. These data imply that we need to look more closely at the metacognition of emotion in predicting emotional and physical well-being.

J. W. Pennebaker, J. K. Kiecolt-Glaser, and R. Glaser, Disclosure of traumas and immune function: health implications for psychotherapy. *Journal of Consulting and Clinical Psychology, 56* (1988), 239–245. Copyright © 1988 by the American Psychological Association. Reprinted with permission.

References

Gottman, J. M., Fainsilber-Katz, L., & Hooven, C. (1996). Parental meta-emotion philosophy and the emotional life of families: Theoretical models and preliminary data. *Journal
of Family Psychology, 10*, 243–268.

O'Leary, A. (1990). Stress, emotion, and human immune function. *Psychological Bulletin, 108*,
363–382.

There is little doubt that psychotherapy reduces subjective distress and yields
positive behavioral outcomes. In recent years, a small group of researchers
has sought to learn whether psychotherapy can also reduce health problems.
Two promising reviews have indicated that the use of mental health services is
associated with fewer medical visits, fewer days of hospitalization, and lower
overall medical costs. In a summary of 15 studies published between 1965 and
1980, Mumford, Schlesinger, and Glass (1981) found that individuals who under-
went psychotherapy evidenced a 13 percent decrease in medical utilization relative
to nonpsychotherapy control subjects. Similarly, in a review of 13 studies of
mental health services that were introduced into organizations, Jones and Vischi
(1980) found that psychotherapy was associated with a 20% drop in medical
utilization.

Although promising, these findings leave open the question of why medical
use drops following psychotherapy. Kiesler (1983), for example, urged caution
in blindly accepting a causal interpretation because we do not know if these
effects generalize across practitioners and sites. Furthermore, individuals
who seek psychotherapy in an organized health system, such as a Health Maintenance Organization (HMO), tend to be some of the highest users of the medical
system (see also Tessler, Mechanic, & Diamond, 1976). Finally, these studies
have not distinguished between actual health problems and unnecessary medical
visits.

Ironically, in the fields of psychosomatics and health psychology, researchers
have long known that psychological disturbance can lead to health problems.
Alexander (1950), Selye (1976), and other pioneers have provided overwhelming
evidence that psychological conflict, anxiety, and stress can cause or exacerbate
disease processes. It follows that the reduction of conflict or stress should reduce
illness.

An important predictor of illness is the way in which individuals cope with
traumatic experiences. It has been well-documented that individuals who have
suffered a major upheaval, such as the death of a spouse or a divorce, are more
vulnerable to a variety of major and minor illnesses. However, the adverse effects
of stress can be buffered by such things as a social support network (e.g. Cohen &
Syme, 1985; Swann & Pridmore, 1985) and by a predisposition toward hardiness
(Kobasa, 1982).

A common theme in the psychotherapy literature is that individuals tend to deal
with trauma most effectively if they can understand and assimilate it. Indeed,
Breuer and Freud (1895/1966), in their development of the cathartic method,
emphasized the value of talking about the thoughts and feelings associated with

upsetting events in the reduction of hysterical symptoms. To examine the links between confronting traumatic events and long-term health, Pennebaker and Beall (1986) asked healthy college students to write about either personally traumatic experiences or trivial topics for 4 consecutive days. Subjects who wrote about traumatic events were required to discuss either the relevant facts (trauma–fact condition), their feelings about the events (trauma–emotion), or both their thoughts and feelings (trauma–combination). In the months following the study, subjects in the trauma–combination condition visited the student health center for illness significantly less often than people in any of the other conditions.

Confronting a trauma may be beneficial from at least two perspectives. First, individuals no longer need to actively inhibit or hold back their thoughts and feelings from others. Indeed, several studies have indicated that actively inhibiting ongoing behavior is associated with both short-term autonomic activity (cf. Fowles, 1980; Gray, 1975) and long-term stress-related disease (Pennebaker & Susman, 1988). Confronting a trauma, then, may reduce the long-term work of inhibition. Second, by confronting the trauma, individuals may assimilate, reframe, or find meaning in the event (Horowitz, 1976; Meichenbaum, 1977; Silver, Boon, & Stones, 1983).

A major problem in evaluating the health effects of confronting a trauma is that most measures are relatively subjective or are susceptible to demand characteristics, such as self-reported symptoms or physician visits. Furthermore, studies such as these fail to identify the underlying mechanisms that influence health. Recent research in psychoneuroimmunology has indicated that the central nervous system can directly influence the functioning of the immune system. For example, the psychological stress associated with exams, loneliness, and divorce can lead to adverse immunological changes (e.g. Bartrop, Luckhurst, Lazarus, Kiloh, & Penny, 1977; F. Cohen, 1980; Kiecolt-Glaser, Garner, Speicher, Penn, & Glaser, 1984; Kiecolt-Glaser et al., 1987). Similarly, relaxation interventions can enhance some aspects of immunocompetence (Kiecolt-Glaser et al., 1985).

Although there is no single, general measure of immune function, many psychoimmunological studies have examined the lymphocyte (white blood cell) response to stimulation by substances foreign to the body, called *mitogens*. *Blastogenesis*, the measurement of the proliferation of lymphocytes in response to stimulation, is thought to provide an in vitro model of the body's response to challenge by infectious agents, such as bacteria or viruses. Because different mitogens stimulate different subpopulations of lymphocytes, two types of mitogens – phytohemagglutinin (PHA) and concanavalin A (ConA) – were used. Both PHA and ConA stimulate the proliferation of T-lymphocytes. Whereas PHA stimulates the proliferation of helper cells, ConA stimulates both helper and suppressor T-cells (e.g. Ader, 1981; Glaser et al., 1985; Reinherz & Schlossman, 1980).

The present project examined the effects of writing about a traumatic experience on immunological function and on other measures of distress. We predicted that individuals assigned to write about traumatic experience would demonstrate a heightened proliferative response to PHA and ConA assays relative to control subjects who merely wrote about superficial topics.

Method

Overview

Fifty healthy undergraduates were randomly assigned to write about either personal traumatic events or trivial topics for 20 min on each of 4 consecutive days. Lymphocytes, which were prepared from blood samples obtained the day before, the last day, and 6 weeks after writing, were assayed for their blastogenic response to PHA and ConA. Health center illness records, self-reports, autonomic measures, and individual difference measures were collected before and during the experiment.

Subjects

Thirty-six women and 14 men who were enrolled in undergraduate psychology courses participated as part of an extra-credit class option. Prior to agreeing to participate, all subjects were told that the experiment might require that they write about extremely personal material and that they have their blood drawn. All subjects participated in the pretest and in the 4 writing days. Two subjects missed the 6-week follow-up blood draw. Two subjects' immunological data were excluded from the analyses: 1 for taking cortisone, the other for pregnancy. In addition, three blood samples for the second draw and one for the third draw were lost during the assaying process.

Procedure

The day prior to the actual writing, subjects met as a group and completed a battery of questionnaires. During the session and after sitting quietly for at least 10 min, subjects' blood pressure levels, heart rates, and skin conductance levels were measured. At assigned times, subjects were escorted to the adjacent Student Health Center building where blood was drawn by the nursing staff. After the blood was drawn and all questionnaires were completed, subjects met individually with the first experimenter, who randomly assigned them to conditions with the provision that an equal ratio of men to women be in each of the two conditions. All subjects were told that they would be required to write about specific topics on each of the following 4 days. Subjects in the trauma condition were informed as follows:

> During each of the four writing days, I want you to write about the most traumatic and upsetting experiences of your entire life. You can write on different topics each day or on the same topic for all four days. The important thing is that you write about your deepest thoughts and feelings. Ideally, whatever you write about should deal with an event or experience that you have not talked with others about in detail.

Those in the no-trauma condition were informed that they would be asked to write on an assigned topic during each of the 4 writing days. The experimenter emphasized that subjects were to describe specific objects or events in detail without discussing their own thoughts or feelings.

On each of the 4 writing days, subjects first met individually with the first experimenter, who reiterated the instructions. For subjects in the no-trauma cell, the specific writing topic was assigned. Depending on the day of the study, subjects were variously asked to describe their activities during the day, the most recent social event that they attended, the shoes they were wearing, or their plans for the remainder of the day. Each day, subjects were escorted to individual private rooms by an experimenter blind to condition, where they were given 20 min to write on their assigned topics. Immediately before and after writing, subjects completed a brief questionnaire that assessed their moods and physical symptoms. After writing only, subjects evaluated their day's essay. The questionnaires and writing samples were stapled and deposited in a large box by the subjects as they left.

After writing on the 4th day, blood pressure, heart rate, and skin conductance were measured before subjects went to the health center for the second blood draw. After the draw, subjects completed a brief questionnaire. Six weeks later, subjects returned to the health center, where autonomic levels and blood samples were collected for a third time. Subjects completed a postexperimental questionnaire and were extensively debriefed about the experiment.

At the conclusion of the study, the health center provided data regarding the number of visits each student had made for illness for the 5 months prior to the study and for the 6 weeks of the study. Approximately 3 months after the writing phase of the study, all subjects were mailed a final questionnaire in order to assess the possible long-term effects of the experiment. The long-term follow-up questionnaire included items assessing subjective distress and daily habits (e.g., smoking and exercise patterns) that had been completed earlier in the study. Of the 50 subjects, 2 did not receive the questionnaire (due to incorrectly listed mailing addresses) and 4 failed to return the questionnaire. All subjects were mailed a follow-up letter that provided the study's outcome, their own immune data, and an interpretation of these data. All essays, physiological data, and self-reports included only subject numbers. Immune assays were collected, performed, and analyzed blind to condition.

Immune assays

In the study, each subject's blood was drawn at the same time each day to control for possible diurnal variations. For each blood draw, whole blood treated with ethylenediominetetra-acetic acid (EDTA) to prevent clotting was collected from each subject. The blood samples were sent to the laboratory the following morning and assayed for their ability to respond to PHA and ConA (Kiecolt-Glaser et al., 1984). Lymphocytes were separated from whole blood samples on Hypaque-Ficall gradients.

The PHA and ConA were used at three different concentrations: 5, 10, and 20 $\mu g/ml$ for PHA and 2, 5, and 10 $\mu g/ml$ for ConA. Each assay was performed in triplicate. Complete medium was used for baseline controls. One tenth milliliter of mitogen was added to 1×10^6 lymphocyte (in 0.1 ml medium) in 96 well plates and was incubated at 37 °C for 48 hr. Fifty microliters of tritiated thymidine (10 $\mu Ci/ml$, specific activity 82 Ci/mM) were added to each well and the plates were incubated at 37 °C for 4 hr. Cells were harvested onto GF11A filters. Radioactivity was measured using a Beckman LS7000 scintillation counter. The mean stimulation value (expressed in counts per minute) was subtracted from the control value and transformed to log (base 10).

Results

Three general classes of data were collected: evaluations of and responses to the essays, long-term effects of the experiment, and individual differences mediating responses to the essays. Each will be discussed separately.

Parameters of essay writing

Subjects disclosed highly personal and upsetting experiences in the trauma condition. Overall, the primary topics of the essays were coming to college (19%), with 10% focusing on the loss and loneliness associated with leaving home; conflicts associated with members of the opposite sex (15%); parental problems (14%), including divorce (6%), family quarrels (6%), and family violence (2%); death (13%) of either a relative (6%), friend (4%), or pet (3%); injury or illness (12%), including eating disorders (4%), car accidents (4%), alcohol/drug abuse (2%), or other causes; sexual abuse (9%) by family member (4%) or stranger (5%); serious thoughts of suicide (6%); public humiliation (5%), such as learning that others suspected the subject of homosexuality; and miscellaneous concerns about religion (4%) and the meaning of life (3%).

Two independent judges rated each essay for the degree to which the content was personal, using a 7-point unipolar scale on which 7 = *personal*. Interjudge correlations across essays averaged .89. In addition, objective parameters of each essay were tabulated, including the total number of words, number of self-references (I, me, my, mine), and number of emotion words. An overall multivariate analysis of variance (MANOVA) was initially computed on the objective and self-ratings of the essays. As expected, a highly significant condition effect was obtained, $F(9, 40) = 72.31, p < .01$. As can be seen in table 29.1, simple one-way analyses of variance (ANOVAS) indicated that trauma subjects' essays were rated as more personal than those of control subjects, $F(1, 48) = 215.94, p < .01$. Finally, relative to control subjects, trauma subjects wrote more words and included more self-references and more emotion words (all $ps \leq .01$) on each essay.

After completing each writing session, subjects rated how personal they considered their essay to be, the degree to which they revealed emotions in their essay, and the degree to which they had previously held back telling others about the subject covered in their essay. Subjects rated each question along a 7-point unipolar scale on which 7 = *a great deal*. Averaging across the 4 days of writing, subjects in the trauma group considered their essays to be far more personal, $F(1, 48) = 279.89, p < .01$, and revealing of their emotions, $F(1, 48) = 266.73, p < .01$, than those in the control group. As depicted in table 29.1, subjects in the trauma group wrote about topics that they had previously held back from telling others relative to those in the control group, $F(1, 48) = 73.80, p < .01$.

Table 29.1. Parameters and responses to essays

Variable	Condition	
	Trauma (n = 25)	Control (n = 25)
Essay parameter		
No. words/essay	465.8	388.8
No. self-references/essay	46.8	30.2
No. emotion words/essay	11.7	0.6
Personal rating	4.69	1.08
Self-report essay rating		
Personal	5.87	2.14
Revealing of emotions	5.18	1.34
Previously held back	4.58	1.52
Response to essay		
Physical symptoms		
Before writing	12.3	12.2
After writing	15.4	11.4
Negative moods		
Before writing	13.4	13.1
After writing	17.8	11.4

Note. Means for the two groups were all significantly different ($p \leq .01$) except for ratings of symptoms and moods before writing.

Each day, immediately before and after writing, subjects completed a brief questionnaire assessing the degree to which they felt each of eight common physical symptoms (e.g. headache, pounding heart, tense muscles) and six negative moods (e.g. frustrated, guilty, depressed). The self-report items were summed to yield separate physical symptom and mood scales. The two scales were subjected to separate $2 \times 2 \times 4$ (Condition $\times$ Time [before vs. after writing] $\times$ Day) repeated-measures ANOVAS. Contrary to a simplistic catharsis or venting view, subjects in the trauma group reported higher levels of physical symptoms and negative moods following the writing compared with the control subjects. Significant Condition $\times$ Time interactions emerged for both symptoms, $F(1, 48) = 37.21, p < .001$, and negative moods, $F(1, 48) = 61.27, p < .001$. Although significant main effects for condition and time for the negative moods were obtained (both $ps < .01$), these effects were attributable to the interaction. No other effects attained significance.

Long-term effects of essay writing

Four types of data assessed the long-term effects of disclosing traumatic experiences: mitogen responses, health center visits, self-reports of subjective distress, and autonomic changes. The immune, subjective distress, and autonomic data were collected the day before the experiment began (and before assignment to condition was made), approximately 1 hr after the final writing sample was collected, and 6 weeks after the conclusion of the writing portion of the study.

Immunological data The blastogenic data for PHA and ConA stimulation were analyzed separately. A 2 × 3 × 3 (Condition × Day × Concentration [of mitogen; 5, 10, and 20 μ g/ml]) repeated-measures ANOVA was computed on the PHA data. Significant effects emerged for day, $F(2, 80) = 79.10, p < .001$, concentration, $F(2, 80) = 29.94$, $p < .001$, and Concentration × Day interaction, $F(4, 160) = 5.25$, $p = .001$. Most important, however, was the emergence of the Condition × Day interaction, $F(2, 80) = 3.36, p = .04$, indicating that trauma subjects demonstrated an overall higher mitogen response following baseline in comparison with control subjects.

The writing phase of the experiment took place during the first week of February immediately prior to midterm exams. According to annual health center records, this period is marked by one of the highest illness rates of the entire school year. The follow-up blood draw, 6 weeks later, took place 4 days before the school's spring break vacation, a time when the incidence of illness visits is much lower. In short, the highly significant increase in immune response for the follow-up period may reflect, in part, both normal seasonal variation and normal fluctuations in the mitogen stimulation assays.

The ConA data, which were only available from the first two blood draws (due to a problem with the ConA preparation), were subjected to a 2 × 2 × 3 (Condition × Day × Concentration [mitogen stimulation level]) ANOVA. As with the PHA findings, significant day, concentration, and Day × Concentration effects emerged (all $ps \leq .01$). Although it occurred in the same direction as the PHA means, the Condition × Day interaction did not attain significance, $F(1, 43) = 2.03, p = .16$. No other effects approached significance.

Health center data The number of health center visits for illness were tabulated by the student health center over two time periods: from the beginning of the school year until the beginning of the study (covering a 4-month interval) and from the

Table 29.2. Mean lymphocyte response to PHA stimulation over sample points in counts per minute, $\log_{10}$

Group	5 μg/ culture	10 μg/ culture	20 μg/ culture
Trauma ($n = 20$)			
Before writing	4.93	4.99	4.90
After writing	4.96	5.00	4.94
6-week follow-up	5.43	5.42	5.34
Control ($n = 22$)			
Before writing	5.01	5.07	4.97
After writing	4.82	4.88	4.81
6-week follow-up	5.37	5.39	5.30

Note. PHA = phytohemagglutinin. Higher numbers reflect greater lymphocyte response. The writing period took place during the first week of February. Average standard deviation within mitogen concentration levels was .260 for the trauma group and .262 for the control group.

beginning of the study until the debriefing period (a 6-week interval). The number of health center visits was adjusted to reflect visits per month and was subjected to a 2 × 2 (Condition × Time) ANOVA.

Consistent with the Pennebaker and Beall (1986) findings, a significant Condition × Time interaction emerged for health center visits for illness, $F(1, 48) = 4.20, p < .05$. As depicted in figure 29.1, trauma subjects evidenced a drop in visits relative to control subjects. No other effects attained significance. As with the immune data, it is important to note that the apparent increase in illness visits for the control group probably reflects normal seasonal illness rates during the month of February.

Subjective distress   Questionnaires pertaining to the effects of the experiment were completed 1 hr after the last writing session, 6 weeks later prior to the final blood draw, and again at the end of the semester approximately 3 months after the writing phase of the study. Two general types of information were included on the questionnaires. The first included subjects' general attitudes about the experiment. The second focused on the health-related behaviors that had changed since the experiment.

Although the experiment was associated initially with some negative feelings among the trauma subjects, they were significantly happier than control subjects at the 3-month follow-up, $t(42) = 2.09, p < .05$. In response to the question, "Looking back on this experiment, to what degree has this experiment been valuable or meaningful for you?" trauma subjects were far more positive than control subjects, $t(42) = 4.50, p < .001$ (on a 7-point scale on which $7 = $ *a great deal,* trauma

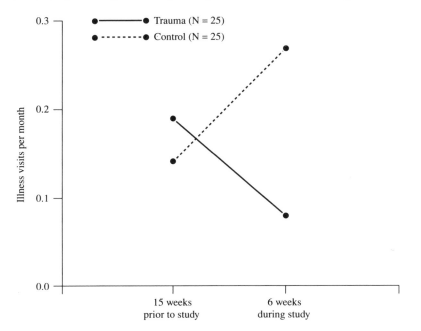

Figure 29.1   Mean health center illness visits for the periods before and during the experiment. (Note that the standard deviation for visits per month ranged from .12 to .40, averaging .26 over the four observations.)

mean = 4.35, control mean = 2.33). Whereas subjects in the trauma group reported feeling more depressed than control subjects on the last day of writing, $t(48) = 2.81, p < .01$ (trauma mean = 3.80, control mean = 2.68), this difference disappeared by the follow-up questionnaire, $t = .09$ (trauma mean = 2.70, control mean = 2.67). No other simple effects attained significance.

A series of repeated-measures ANOVAS were computed on questions assessing the following health-related behaviors: cigarettes smoked per day, caffeinated and alcoholic beverages consumed per day, aspirin and sleeping pill use, and hours of strenuous exercise per week. No significant main effects or interactions approached significance. In short, the experiment did not appear to influence long-term behavior.

Other relevant data   Resting levels of systolic and diastolic blood pressure, heart rate, and skin conductance level were measured approximately 1 hr prior to each of the three blood draws. Repeated-measures ANOVAS on each autonomic index yielded no significant effects.

Finally, simple correlations were computed between changes in immune response and changes in health center visits and autonomic levels from the first to the final day of the study. Although PHA and ConA changes over the first 5 days of the study were correlated with each other, $r(43) = .88, p < .01$, changes in PHA and ConA were unrelated to all other variables. Similarly, changes in illness visits were unrelated to autonomic levels.

Who benefits most: exploring individual differences

Do all individuals who write about a traumatic experience benefit equally? We have argued here and elsewhere (cf. Pennebaker, Hughes, & O'Heeron, 1987) that the failure to confront traumatic experience is stressful. A significant form of stress is associated with the work of inhibiting or actively holding back the disclosure of important traumas. All participants in the present study rated the degree to which they had written about an event that they had "actively held back in discussing with others" after each writing session. According to our conception, those individuals in the trauma condition who had addressed issues that they had previously held back should have benefited most.

To test this idea, subjects in the trauma condition were split at the median into two groups based on their mean response to the actively-holding-back question. Those who reported that they had written about topics that they had previously held back were labeled high disclosers ($n = 11$) and the remainder were labeled low disclosers ($n = 14$). A series of ANOVAS was computed on the primary variables of interest using the three groups (trauma, high discloser; trauma, low discloser; control) as the between-subjects factor. Contrasts using the mean square error term compared high versus low disclosers.

Overall, high disclosers wrote significantly more words, $t(48) = 3.53, p < .01$ (high mean = 505.3, low mean = 435.5) on each essay than low disclosers. Although high disclosers reported that their essays were more personal than low disclosers, $t(48) = 2.94, p < .05$ (Ms = 6.13 vs. 5.68, respectively), independent judges rated the two groups equivalently, $t < 1.0$. No other significant essay characteristics emerged that separated high and low disclosers.

More interesting were the physiological correlates of disclosure. Analyses of the immune data indicated that, overall, high disclosers had a marginally higher response to PHA stimulation than low disclosers, $t(39) = 1.96, p = .06$ (high mean $= 5.18$, low mean $= 5.00$). An ANOVA on the ConA data, on the other hand, yielded a significant Condition $\times$ Day $\times$ Concentration interaction, $F(4, 84) = 2.99$, $p = .02$. As can be seen in figure 29.2, high disclosers demonstrated an improved mitogen response across all mitogen concentrations relative to low disclosers and control subjects from before the study to the last day of writing (recall that follow-up ConA data were lost). No other interactions with the discloser variable attained significance for either PHA or ConA.

Although there were no initial differences in autonomic levels as a function of type of discloser or condition prior to the study, repeated-measures ANOVAS yielded Condition $\times$ Day effects for systolic blood pressure, $F(4, 84) = 2.68, p < .05$, and a marginal effect for heart rate, $F(4, 84) = 1.97, p = .10$. Indeed, from the beginning of the study to follow-up, high disclosers showed a greater decline than low disclosers in both systolic blood pressure, $t(44) = 3.42$, $p < .01$ (change from before study to follow-up: high disclosers $= -5.5$ mm/hg, low disclosers $= 8.7$ mm/hg), and diastolic blood pressure, $t(44) = 2.50$, $p < .05$ (high disclosers $= -5.8$ mm/hg, low disclosers $= 1.0$ mm/hg). Similar nonsignificant trends were found for heart rate (high disclosers $= -1.2$ beats per minute, low disclosers $= 1.1$) and skin conductance (high disclosers $= -2.6 \mu$mhos, low disclosers $= 0.3$).

Discussion

The results indicate that writing about traumatic experience has positive effects on the blastogenic response of T-lymphocytes to two mitogens, on autonomic levels,

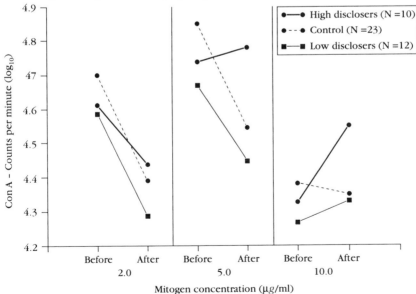

Figure 29.2 Lymphocyte response to three levels of concanavalin A (Con A) stimulation before and after the writing sessions.

on health center use, and on subjective distress. The results are important in (a) supporting an inhibitory model of psychosomatics, (b) pointing to the effectiveness of using writing as a general preventive therapy, and (c) promoting an awareness that psychotherapy can bring about direct and cost-effective improvements in health.

Within psychology, it has been generally accepted that stress can increase the incidence of illness. We have proposed that one form of stress is associated with the failure to confront traumatic experience. Specifically, the inhibition or active holding back of thoughts, emotions, or behaviors is associated with physical work that, over time, can become manifested in disease. The present study supports this idea. Individuals who are forced to confront upsetting experiences in their lives show improvements in physical health relative to control subjects. More important, in our study the individuals who showed the greatest health improvements were those who wrote about topics that they had actively held back from telling others.

One important remaining question concerns the specific dimensions of writing that actively promote health. Based on previous work (e.g. Pennebaker & O'Heeron, 1984; Wegner, 1989), we believe that the failure to confront a trauma forces the person to live with it in an unresolved manner. Indeed, not disclosing a recent trauma such as the death of a spouse is associated with increased obsessions about the spouse. It follows, then, that actively confronting a trauma allows for the understanding and assimilation of that trauma.

In the present study, for example, several subjects who wrote about the same traumas day after day gradually changed their perspectives. One woman, who had been molested at the age of 9 years by a boy 3 years older, initially emphasized her feelings of embarrassment and guilt. By the third day of writing, she expressed anger at the boy who had victimized her. By the last day, she had begun to put it in perspective. On the follow-up survey 6 weeks after the experiment, she reported, "Before, when I thought about it, I'd lie to myself...Now, I don't feel like I even have to think about it because I got it off my chest. I finally admitted that it happened...I really know the truth and won't have to lie to myself anymore."

Clinical psychologists within the cognitive and psychodynamic traditions are currently addressing some of the processes underlying this confrontational strategy (Horowitz, 1976; Meichenbaum, 1977). Through writing or talking about an upsetting experience, the person can come to understand the causes and effects of the trauma better, which may ultimately eliminate the need for inhibition.

Although some therapists have asserted the value of writing about one's problems, such as in bibliotherapy (cf. Lazarus, 1984), very little systematic work has been done on it. Within the context of the present study, psychologically healthy individuals were initially upset about disclosing personal and upsetting experiences. That is, immediately after writing, trauma subjects reported more physical symptoms and negative moods. Writing about traumas, then, appears to be painful in the short run. Indeed, in a recent study by Lamnin and Murray (1987) comparing a writing therapy with a client-centered approach, clients were found to be more depressed immediately after each writing session than after a live therapy session.

There are clear disadvantages as well as advantages to writing versus talking with another person about traumas. Writing about intensely personal experiences does not allow for an objective outside opinion, support from others, or objective coping information. Alternatively, writing is tremendously cost-effective, allows people to confront traumas at their own rates, and encourages them to devise their own meaning and solutions to their problems. Above all, writing may provide an alternative form of preventive therapy that can be valuable for individuals who otherwise would not enter therapy.

Previous archival studies have indicated that medical use decreases once psychotherapy begins (e.g. Mumford et al., 1981). Although encouraging, meta-analyses such as these have not been able to pinpoint the direct causal mechanisms. The present study offers experimental evidence linking the confronting of traumas with health improvement. Obviously, we have only examined the responses of a psychologically healthy population. Nevertheless, the present findings, along with those from conceptually similar experiments (e.g., Pennebaker & Beall, 1986), suggest that the disclosure of traumas is simultaneously associated with improvement in certain aspects of immune function and physical health.

References

Ader, R. (1981). *Psychoneuroimmunology*. New York: Academic Press.

Alexander, F. (1950). *Psychosomatic medicine*. New York: Norton.

Bartrop, R. W., Luckhurst, E., Lazarus, L., Kiloh, L. G., & Penny, R. (1977). Depressed lymphocyte function after bereavement. *Lancet, 1*, 834–836.

Breuer, J., & Freud, S. (1966). *Studies on hysteria*. New York: Avon. (Original work published 1895).

Cohen, F. (1980). Personality, stress, and the development of physical illness. In G. C. Stone, F. Cohen, & N. E. Adler (Eds.), *Health psychology* (pp. 77–111). San Francisco: Jossey-Bass.

Cohen, S., & Syme, S. (Eds.). (1985). *Social support and health*. Orlando, FL: Academic Press.

Fowles, D. C. (1980). The three arousal model: implications of Gray's two-factor theory for heart rate, electrodermal activity, and psychopathy. *Psychophysiology, 17*, 87–104.

Glaser, R., Kiecolt-Glaser, J. K., Stout, J. C., Tarr, K. L., Speicher, C. E., & Holliday, J. E. (1985). Stress-related impairments in cellular immunity. *Psychiatric Research, 16*, 233–239.

Gray, J. (1975). *Elements of a two-process theory of learning*. New York: Academic Press.

Horowitz, M. J. (1976). *Stress response syndromes*. New York: Jacob Aronson.

Jones, K., & Vischi, T. (1980). Impact of alcohol, drug abuse and mental health treatment on medical care utilization: a review of the literature. *Medical Care, 17* (Suppl. 2), 1–82.

Kiecolt-Glaser, J. K., Fisher, L., Ogrocki, P., Stout, J. C., Speicher, C. E., & Glaser, R. (1987). Marital quality, marital disruption, and immune function. *Psychosomatic Medicine, 49*, 13–34.

Kiecolt-Glaser, J. K., Garner, W., Speicher, C., Penn, G., & Glaser, R. (1984). Psychosocial modifiers of immunocompetence in medical students. *Psychosomatic Medicine, 46*, 7–14.

Kiecolt-Glaser, J. K., Glaser, R., Williger, D., Stout, J., Messick, G., Sheppard, S., Ricker, D., Romisher, S. C., Briner, W., Bonnell, G., & Donnerberg, R. (1985). Psychosocial enhancement of immunocompetence in a geriatric population. *Health Psychology, 4*, 25–41.

Kiesler, C. A. (1983). Psychology and mental health policy. In M. Hersen, A. E. Kazdin, & A. S. Bellack (Eds.), *The clinical psychology handbook* (pp. 63–82). New York: Pergamon Press.

Kobasa, S. (1982). The hardy personality: toward a social psychology of stress and health. In G. S. Sanders & J. Suls (Eds.), *Social psychology of health and illness* (pp. 3–32). Hillsdale, NJ: Erlbaum.

Lamnin, A. D., & Murray, E. (1987). *Catharsis versus psychotherapy.* Unpublished manuscript, University of Miami.

Lazarus, A. A. (1984). Multimodal therapy. In R. J. Corsini (Ed.), *Current psychotherapies.* 3rd edn. (pp. 491–530). Itasca, IL: Peacock.

Meichenbaum, D. H. (1977). *Cognitive-behavior modification: An integrative approach.* New York: Plenum Press.

Mumford, E., Schlesinger, H. J., & Glass, G. V. (1981). Reducing medical costs through mental health treatment: research problems and recommendations. In A. Broskowski, E. Marks, & S. H. Budman (Eds.), *Linking health and mental health* (pp. 257–273). Beverly Hills, CA: Sage.

Pennebaker, J. W., & Beall, S. (1986). Confronting a traumatic event: toward an understanding of inhibition and disease. *Journal of Abnormal Psychology, 95,* 274–281.

Pennebaker, J. W., Hughes, C., & O'Heeron, R. C. (1987). The psychophysiology of confession: Linking inhibitory and psychosomatic processes. *Journal of Personality and Social Psychology, 52,* 781–793.

Pennebaker, J. W., & O'Heeron, R. C. (1984). Confiding in others and illness rate among spouses of suicide and accidental death victims. *Journal of Abnormal Psychology, 93,* 473–476.

Pennebaker, J. W., & Susman, J. R. (1988). Disclosure of traumas and psychosomatic processes. *Social Science and Medicine, 26,* 327–332.

Reinherz, E. L., & Schlossman, S. F. (1980). Current concepts in immunology: regulation of the immune response – Inducer and suppressor T-lymphocyte subsets in human beings. *New England Journal of Medicine, 303,* 370–373.

Selye, H. (1976). *The stress of life.* New York: McGraw-Hill.

Silver, R. L., Boon, C., & Stones, M. H. (1983). Searching for meaning in misfortune: making sense of incest. *Journal of Social Issues, 39,* 81–102.

Swann, W. B., & Pridmore, S. C. (1985). Intimates as agents of social support: sources of consolation or despair? *Journal of Personality and Social Psychology, 49,* 1609–1617.

Tessler, R., Mechanic, D., & Diamond, M. (1976). The effect of psychological distress on physician utilization. *Journal of Health and Social Behavior, 17,* 353–364.

Wegner, D. M. (1988). Stress and mental control. In S. Fisher & J. Reason (Eds.), *Handbook of life stress, cognition, and health* (pp. 683–697). Chichester: Wiley.

CHAPTER *30*

Recent Developments in Expressed Emotion and Schizophrenia

D. J. Kavanagh

Emotion-based interactions with people to whom we are close affect the course of several kinds of psychiatric illnesses. Work began thirty years ago on what is now called "expressed emotion." The term refers to how a relative of a person with psychiatric illness talks about that person to an interviewer. If the relative speaks with high hostility, criticism, and overinvolvement, the psychiatrically ill person is found to be more likely to suffer an earlier relapse of illness than if the relative expresses less criticism, hostility, and overinvolvement. This effect has been widely replicated in different countries for people with schizophrenic illness (Jenkins & Karno, 1992). The same effects occur when people are treated with antipsychotic drugs and when they are not (Vaughn & Leff, 1976). A similar pattern occurs when people have been hospitalized for depressive episodes (Hooley et al., 1986).

Learning a different way of interacting in a family around emotional issues can have far-reaching consequences for people with serious psychiatric disorder as has been shown in a number of therapy outcome studies. See, for example, the section entitled "Implications for management" at the end of this selection.

References

Hooley, J. M., Orley, J., & Teasdale, J. (1986). Levels of expressed emotion and relapse in depressed patients. *British Journal of Psychiatry, 148,* 642–647.

Jenkins, J. H., & Karno, M. (1992). The meaning of expressed emotion: theoretical issues raised by cross-cultural research. *American Journal of Psychiatry, 149,* 9–21.

Vaughn, C. E., & Leff, J. P. (1976). The influence of family and social factors on the course of psychiatric illness: a comparison of schizophrenic and depressed patients. *British Journal of Psychiatry, 129*, 125–137.

The last thirty years of research into schizophrenia has seen considerable interest in the role of social and situational factors in relapse (Brown & Birley, 1968; Birley & Brown, 1970; Katschnig, 1986). An influential part of this research has focused on the concept of expressed emotion (EE; Brown et al., 1962, 1972). Although the early studies examined the role of both positive and negative emotions, subsequent research has effectively narrowed the concept to negative or intrusive attitudes that relatives express about the patient.

Since those early studies, EE assessments have usually been derived from a single instrument, the Camberwell Family Interview (CFI), which is a standard interview that is administered separately to each relative and is typically administered during an exacerbation of symptoms (Vaughn & Leff, 1976b). The interviews now take 1–1$\frac{1}{2}$ hours and ratings are made from audiotapes. The key scores for EE are a frequency count of critical comments about the patient, and global ratings of hostility and "emotional overinvolvement" (EOI). Critical comments are unambiguous statements of disapproval or resentment, rejecting remarks, or statements that are delivered with a critical tone of voice. Hostility is present when there is rejection of the patient or expression of a global criticism. EOI refers to self-sacrifice, overprotection, or overidentification with the patient. An interview is rated high in EE if there is one or more of the key features: a high level of criticism (usually 6 comments or more), a score above 3 or 4 on the 6-point EOI scale, or any degree of hostility. Only one high-EE interview is required for the family assessment to score as high EE.

Most of the research on EE has focused on the prediction of schizophrenic relapse, but it soon became evident that EE could be a more generalized risk factor for relapse in psychiatry and health psychology. There is now some evidence that EE predicts outcomes in depression (Vaughn & Leff, 1976a; Hooley et al., 1986; Hooley & Teasdale, 1989), bipolar disorder (Miklowitz et al., 1986, 1988; Priebe et al., 1989), and weight reduction (Fischman-Havstad & Marston, 1984; Flanagan & Wagner, 1991). A number of other studies are currently in progress.

Even within schizophrenia, not all of the studies have supported the EE hypothesis, and the notion that EE might be a determinant of relapse has attracted scientific controversy (Hogarty et al., 1986; MacMillan et al., 1986, 1987; J. Mintz et al., 1987). Families and health researchers have also expressed concern that EE may be used to blame families for the disorder (Hatfield et al., 1987; Kanter et al., 1987). The present paper reviews these issues and discusses implications for practitioners.

Outcome studies on schizophrenia

Studies on the prediction of the course of schizophrenia from EE are shown in table 30.1. Twenty-six are displayed, with a total sample size of 1323. The median

Table 30.1. Relapse data from prospective outcome studies on expressed emotion

| | Percentage relapses and sample size | | | |
| | 0 to 9–12 months | | 0 to 24 months | |
	low EE % (n)	high EE % (n)	low EE % (n)	high EE % (n)
Brown et al. (1962)[1]	28 (47)	76 (50)***	–	–
Brown et al. (1972)	16 (56)	58 (45)***	–	–
Vaughn & Leff (1976*a*), Leff & Vaughn (1981)	6 (16)	48 (21)**	20 (15)	62 (21)*
Vaughn et al. (1984)	17 (18)	56 (36)*	–	–
Moline et al. (1985)[1]	29 (7)	71 (17)[2]	–	–
Dulz & Hand (1986)	65 (17)	48 (29)	–	–
MacMillan et al. (1986)[1]	41 (34)	68 (38)*[3]	–	–
Nuechterlein et al. (1986)[1]	0 (7)	40 (20)*	–	–
Karno et al. (1987)	26 (27)	59 (17)*	–	–
Leff et al. (1987, 1990*a*)	9 (54)	31 (16)*[4]	33 (46)	50 (14)
McCreadie & Phillips (1988)[1]	20 (35)	17 (24)	–	–
Parker et al. (1988)	60 (15)	48 (42)	–	–
Cazullo et al. (1988)	27 (11)	63 (8)*[5]	–	–
Gutiérrez et al. (1988)[1]	10 (21)	54 (11)*	–	–
Tarrier et al. (1988*b*, 1989)[6]	21 (19)	48 (29)*	33 (18)	59 (29)
Rostworowska et al. (1987), Budzyna-Dawidowski et al. (1989)[1]	9 (11)	60 (25)**	18 (11)	72 (25)**
Mózný et al. (1989)[1]	29 (38)	60 (30)**	–	–
Montero et al. (1990)[7]	19 (36)	33 (24)	–	–
Arévalo & Vizcarro (1989)	38 (13)	44 (18)	–	–
Ivanović & Vuletić (1989)	7 (31)	66 (29)**	–	–
Buchkremer et al. (1991)	28 (40)	37 (59)[8]	–	–
Barrelet et al. (1990)	0 (12)	33 (24)*	–	–
Vaughan et al. (1992)	25 (40)	53 (47)**	–	–
Median relapses[9]	21	48	27	61
High-EE control groups in treatment studies				
Leff et al. (1982, 1985)	–	50 (12)	–	75 (12)
Falloon et al. (1982, 1985)	–	44 (18)	–	83 (18)
Hogarty et al. (1986, 1987)	–	28 (29)	–	66 (27)
Median relapses across studies[9]	21	48	27	66
Totalling subjects across studies	23 (605)	50 (718)	29 (90)	66 (146)

* $p \leqslant 0.05$, ** $p \leqslant 0.01$, *** $p < 0.001$.
1 These studies measured relapses over 12 months. All other studies had follow-ups lasting 9 months. A 12-month follow-up in Leff et al. (1987) was measured from admission and approximated 9 months from discharge.
2 High EE was based on critical comments $\geqslant 6$ and EOI $\geqslant 4$. The result using a cut-off point of $\geqslant 10$ critical comments was low EE 31% (13), high EE 91% (11)**.

3 Follow-up varied from 6 months to 2 years. The calculation excluded five subjects who were lost during follow-up; if they did not relapse, the rates would be low EE 39% (36), high EE 63% (41).
4 Rates are based on clinical diagnosis from all known information. The rates based on PSE and CATEGO diagnoses were: low EE 14% (37), high EE 33% (12).
5 These rates were for exacerbations of symptoms, using critical comments $\geqslant 6$ and EOI $\geqslant 4$. There was no significant predictive effect for EE when the EOI cut-off point was 3. If psychiatric admissions were used as the criterion for relapse, low EE had 9% and high EE 63%*.
6 The Tarrier et al. (1988, 1989) results are from control groups in a treatment study.
7 With a criterion of critical comments $\geqslant 4$ and EOI $\geqslant 3$, the results became low EE 10% (30), high EE 40% (30)*.
8 These data are 9-month re-admission rates read from a graph.
9 A study by Straube et al. (1989) could not be included in this table because relapse proportions were not reported. EE had a correlation of *0.22, P < 0.10*, with relapses over 2 years.

relapse rate over 9–12 months is 21% for low EE, or less than half of the 48% rate in the high-EE group. This suggests that a phenomenon as valuable clinically as medication (30% relapse on neuroleptics, 65% on placebo; Davis, 1975). Among the studies that presented data on both high and low EE, 87% had higher absolute values for relapse when EE was high, and the difference in relapse rates was statistically significant in 70%. These results do not seem to be strongly affected by a publication bias in favour of significant results, since Table 1 is thought to provide an almost exhaustive list of the research at the time of preparation.

Given that the small sample sizes in these studies provided limited opportunity to detect binary outcomes, this is substantial support for the predictive utility of EE. If the true difference in outcomes for low v. high EE were 0.20–0.50, a sample size of 43 in each group is required before 70% of the studies are reliably expected to show a significant difference at $P < 0.05$ (Fleiss, 1973). Only four studies approach this number in each group, and the median number is only 21 (low EE) to 25 (high EE) [...]

The nature of EE

The predictive status of EE appears to be on relatively firm ground, even if its application is more limited than was first thought. But what is the nature of EE, and what could be the mechanism for the predictive results?

Components of EE

As we might expect, critical comments and ratings of hostility are significantly correlated, and criticism is usually more common (Vaughn et al., 1984). However, cultural factors can result in hostility being evidenced even when levels of criticism are low (e.g. Leff et al., 1987).

While criticism and hostility are usually related, the data offer dubious support for a global EE concept that encompasses both criticism and EOI (Vaughn et al., 1984; Szmukler et al., 1987). In the study by Vaughn et al. (1984) the correlation between the two components was 0.30 for fathers, but only −0.03 for mothers. Psychophysiological measures have been unable to distinguish between subjects from households of high EOI and those from households of high criticism (Tarrier et al., 1988a), but this does not mean that the variables are equivalent in other respects.

The limited correlation between EOI and criticism has probably had little impact on the predictive studies. Criticism usually exerts more power over EE classification than does EOI, because of its greater frequency in most samples (e.g. Brown et al., 1972; MacMillan et al., 1986; cf. Vaughn et al., 1984). There is also a substantial overlap between households that are above the cut-off points for EOI and criticism (Brown et al., 1972). A low correlation between the components as continuous variables is of little detriment to a dichotomous EE assessment.

Among the EE variables, criticism seems to make the greatest contribution to relapse in most of the studies that have examined the issue (e.g. Moline et al., 1985; MacMillan et al., 1986; Hogarty et al., 1986; Barrelet et al., 1990). However, some studies have found hostility (Parker et al., 1988; Leff et al., 1990a) or EOI (Gutiérrez et al., 1988) to be more sensitive predictors. The relative effects of components may differ across samples according to their relative frequency and the sensitivity of the assessment to cultural differences in their expression [...]

Cultural variations in EE

High EE is much more frequent in the West than in India. Among rural Indian families the incidence of high EE was only 8% (Wig et al., 1987). Kuipers & Bebbington (1988) present an analysis that uses the low incidence of EE to explain the reduced risk of relapse that is seen in developing countries (World Health Organization, 1979; Waxler, 1979). Part of the reason for reductions in EE and relapse rates may be the greater involvement of extended families in these cultures (Wig et al., 1987). El-Islam (1982) found that extended families in an Arab culture were more tolerant of eccentric behaviour and temporary withdrawal than were nuclear families. They also encouraged more social activity without overly taxing the patient's social resources. Such behaviour is similar to low-EE responses to the patient's problem. Reactions like these by the extended family not only would produce a less stressful environment for the patient, but would model low-EE behaviour of members of a nuclear family. If these results transfer to other cultures, they would emphasise the importance of maintaining traditional links with extended families.

EE and affective responses

Brown and others (1972) suggested that EE produces relapse by raising the patients' arousal beyond an optimal level. Data on emotional arousal and EE are particularly interesting, because they attempt to test this proposition. Reviews are presented by Turpin and others (1988) and Tarrier (1989). When patients are first tested, subjects from high-EE settings either have a higher frequency of skin conductance responses (Sturgeon et al., 1984), or they show less adaptation after the relative enters the room (Tarrier et al., 1979, 1988a). As already mentioned, the differences are present even when the CFI assessment had been undertaken a considerable time before. However, the differences do not recur when subjects are retested three to nine months later (Tarrier et al., 1979, 1988b) unless the subjects are in high contact with their relatives. The authors argue that the stress of an initial testing allows more sensitive measurement of affective reactions to high EE.

Support for the view that these negative emotions are implicated in relapse is provided by the observation that features such as depression and hostility frequently precede a relapse (Herz & Melville, 1980; Subotnik & Nuechterlein, 1988; Birchwood et al., 1989). However, there is little information on the process by which relapse might be triggered by these emotions. One possibility is that the emotional states could have direct effects on the biochemical course of the disorder. An alternative view looks at psychological effects of the emotions. Increases in anxiety, depression or anger that are sustained or severe evoke behavioural sequelae such as insomnia, lack of interest in activities, social withdrawal, and aggression (Herz & Melville, 1980). When such behaviour triggers aversive social interactions, it may provide apparent substantiation for paranoid ideas. When the behaviour cuts the person off from social contact, it reduces the patient's sources of assistance and corrective information. Negative emotions also colour interpretations of events and are likely to undermine the client's ability to concentrate, test the validity of ideas, and control emerging symptoms (Falloon & Talbot, 1981; Breier & Strauss, 1983; Glynn et al., 1990). If these effects of the emotions occurred when the person was physiologically vulnerable to positive symptoms, they would increase the probability of relapse.

One apparent problem with this hypothesis is that people with schizophrenia are, in laboratory tests, notoriously prone to error in verbally identifying emotional reactions of other people (e.g. Cramer et al., 1989), but there are several reasons for caution in interpreting these data. One is that much of the research has been undertaken with in-patients or with ratings being made of people who are unknown to the client. Naturalistic interactions also differ from the laboratory tasks in the presence of a substantial degree of redundancy and of emotion labelling by others in the social environment. Further potential problems involve the verbal facility of subjects and their willingness to confide their true reactions to a tester. All of these factors could lead to exaggerations of deficits if the studies are used to predict everyday perceptions of emotion and emotional reactions by people with schizophrenia.

The psychophysiological evidence demonstrates that people with schizophrenia do experience powerful emotional reactions in response to negative interactions. The restriction of predictive effects in the EE literature to interactions that have a critical, hostile or intrusive character provides further support for the proposition that patients are perceiving the interactions accurately on sufficient occasions for this to have a substantial effect [...]

Implications for management

From the social interaction model we would expect that relapses associated with high EE would be reduced if patients and relatives could develop more effective coping strategies to deal with the problems that are posed by schizophrenia. Consistent with this view, skills-orientated family interventions have significantly improved the immediate course of schizophrenia when they are compared with routine or individual treatments. Detailed reviews of the literature are provided by Barrowclough & Tarrier (1984), Strachan (1986), Smith & Birchwood (1990), and Kavanagh (1992), and results of the key studies are summarized in table 30.2. Control subjects from high-EE settings had a median relapse rate of 48% over nine months, but only 9% of the family-intervention subjects relapsed over the same period. If these results are compared with table 30.1; they show that a family intervention drops the high-EE risk to a level expected for low EE. Over 24 months the relapse figures substantially increase (71% for controls and 33% for family intervention), but they continue to parallel the outcomes of high and low EE in the naturalistic studies. Family interventions can reduce EE or lower contact time for most families (Leff et al., 1982; Tarrier et al., 1988*b*). Consistent with the EE hypothesis, reductions in relapse are particularly marked when EE becomes low (Hogarty et al., 1986; Leff et al., 1989). The main impact of the intervention seems to be on prevention of major episodes: minor exacerbations of symptoms may still occur (Falloon et al., 1984).

Although there were distinctive features to each of the treatments used in the intervention trials, they had a number of elements in common. Almost all of them included education of the family about schizophrenia and assistance in controlling stress. Most of them trained the families in systematic techniques to set goals and solve problems more effectively, and some also included communication training and behaviour management strategies when required. Detailed treatment manuals are provided by Anderson et al. (1986), Falloon et al. (1984) and Piatkowska et al.

Table 30.2. Percentage of relapses in treatment studies that preselected for high EE

	0–9 months		0–24 months	
	Family intervention	*Routine or individual treatment*	*Family intervention*	*Routine or individual treatment*
Leff et al. (1982, 1985)	8%	50%	50%[1]	75%[1]
Falloon et al. (1982, 1985)	6%	44%	17%	83%
Köttgen et al. (1984)	33%	50%	–	–
Hogarty et al. (1986, 1987)[2]	19%	28%	32%	66%
Tarrier et al. (1988*b*, 1989)	12%	48%[3]	33%	59%[3]
Leff et al. (1989, 1990*b*)	8%	–	33%	–
Median	10%	48%	33%	71%

1 The percentages include subjects who stopped medication and counts suicides as relapses. If those subjects are omitted, the outcomes are: 20% (family treatment), 78% (routine care).
2 Social skills training to individual clients produced a 9- month relapse rate of 20% and a 2-year rate of 42%. A combined intervention of family and social skills training gave 0% relapse in 9 months and 25% in 2 years.
3 Combined results for the brief education and routine treatment conditions

(1992). As we would expect from an interactional model of relapse, similar improvements can be achieved either by an educational family intervention or by sessions with individual patients that increases their skills in reducing conflict with the family (Hogarty et al., 1986). An intervention that combines the individual and family strategies may be better than either of them alone (Hogarty et al. 1986), although further research is needed to check that the result is not due to increased contact with therapists in the joint intervention.

There is little evidence that effects from a brief family intervention are maintained once sessions are stopped altogether (Goldstein & Kopeikin, 1981). All of the interventions with sustained effects have continued low-level contact with families and clients (Falloon et al., 1985: Tarrier et al., 1989). Continued sessions are probably required to remind patients and relatives about the strategies they learned, to prompt the application of the strategies to new situations, and to encourage families to keep trying in the face of setbacks.

At present we do not know which aspects of the family interventions are responsible for its effect. Current studies fail to exclude effects of participation in a special treatment, increased therapist contact with the family, or the provision of non-specific support. Nor do we know which ingredients in the interventions are most effective, although brief didactic programmes do not seem to have a marked effect by themselves (Tarrier et al., 1988b). We do know that the effects are unlikely to occur through increased medication. Although medication compliance may be better after family intervention (Falloon et al., 1982), ingested amounts are lower because of reductions in the prescribed dosage (Falloon et al., 1985).

The evidence on family interventions is currently built on a relatively small group of studies and leaves many questions unanswered. However, the current work suggests that these interventions may prove to be the most significant treatment breakthrough in schizophrenia since the discovery of neuroleptic medication. If the concept of EE contributed nothing else, it may be credited with inspiring this potentially important advance.

References

Anderson, C. M., Reiss, D. J. & Hogarty, G. E. (1986). *Schizophrenia in the family: A practitioner's guide to psychoeducation and management.* New York: Guilford.

Arevalo, J. & Vizcarro, C. (1989) "Emocion expresada" y curso de la esquizofrenia en una muestra espanola. *Analisis y Modificacion de Conducta, 15*, 3–23.

Barrelet, L., Ferrero, F., Szigethy, L., et al. (1990). Expressed emotion and first-admission schizophrenia: nine-month follow-up in a French cultural environment. *British Journal of Psychiatry, 156*, 357–362.

Barrowclough, C., & Tarrier, N. (1984). "Psychosocial" interventions with families and their effects on the course of schizophrenia: a review. *Psychological Medicine, 14*, 629–642.

Birchwood, M, Smith, J., & MacMillan, F. (1989). The development and implementation of an early warning system to predict relapse in schizophrenia. *Psychological Medicine, 19*, 649–656.

Birley, J. L. T., & Brown, G. W. (1970). Crises and life changes preceding acute schizophrenia. *British Journal of Psychiatry, 116*, 327–333.

Breier, A., & Strauss, J. S. (1983) Self-control in psychotic disorders. *Archives of General Psychiatry, 40*, 1141–1145.

Brewin, C. R., MacCarthy, B., Duda, K., et al. (1991) Attributions and expressed emotion in the relatives of patients with schizophrenia. *Journal of Abnormal Psychology, 100*, 546–554.

Brown, G. W., Monck, E. M., Carstairs, G. M., et al. (1962). Influence of family life on the course of schizophrenic illness. *British Journal of Preventative Social Medicine, 16*, 55–68.

Brown, G. W., & Birley, J. L. T. (1968). Crises and life changes and the onset of schizophrenia. *Journal of Health and Social Behaviour, 9*, 203–214.

——, —— & Wing, J. K. (1972). Influence of family life on the course of schizophrenic disorders: a replication. *British Journal of Psychiatry, 121*, 241–258.

Buchkremer, G., Stricker, K., Holle, R., et al. (1991). The predictability of relapses in schizophrenic patients. *European Archives of Psychiatry and Clinical Neurosciences, 240*, 292–300.

Budzyna-Dawidowski, P., Rostworowska, M. & de Barbaro, B. (1989). Stability of expressed emotion: a 3 year follow-up study of schizophrenic patients. Paper presented to the XIX Congress of the European Association of Behaviour Therapy, Vienna, September 1989.

Cazullo, C. L., Bertrando, P., Bressi, C., et al. (1988). Emotività expressa e schizofrenia: studio prospettico di replicazione. *Notizie ARS* (suppl. 3/88), 16–21.

Cramer, P., Weegmann, M., & O'Neil, M. (1989). Schizophrenia and the perception of emotions – How accurately do schizophrenics judge the emotional states of others? *British Journal of Psychiatry, 155*, 225–228.

Davis, J. (1975) Overview: maintenance therapy in psychiatry: I. Schizophrenia. *American Journal of Psychiatry, 132*, 1237–1245.

Dulz, B. & Hand, I. (1986). Short-term relapse in young schizophrenics: can it be predicted and affected by family (CFI), patient and treatment variables? An experimental study. In *Treatment of schizophrenia: Family assessment and intervention* (eds M. J. Goldstein, I. Hand & K. Hahlweg), (pp. 59–75). Berlin: Springer.

El-Islam, M. F. (1982) Rehabilitation of schizophrenics by the extended family. *Acta Psychiatrica Scandinavica, 65*, 112–119.

Falloon, I. R. H. & Talbot, R. E. (1981) Persistent auditory hallucinations: coping mechanisms and implications for management. *Psychological Medicine, 11*, 329–339.

——, Boyd, J. L., McGill, C. W., et al. (1982) Family management in the prevention of exacerbations of schizophrenia: a controlled study. *New England Journal of Medicine, 306*, 1437–1440.

——, —— (1984) *Family Care of Schizophrenia.* New York: Guilford Press.

——, ——, ——, et al. (1985) Family management in the prevention of morbidity of schizophrenia: clinical outcome of a two-year longitudinal study. *Archives of General Psychiatry, 42*, 887–896.

Fischman-Havstad, L. & Marston, A. R. (1984). Weight loss maintenance as an aspect of family emotion and process. *British Journal of Clinical Psychology, 23*, 265–271.

Flanagan, D. A. J. & Wagner, H. L. (1991). Expressed emotion and panic-fear in the prediction of diet treatment compliance. *British Journal of Clinical Psychology, 30*, 231–240.

Glynn, S. M., Randolph, E. T., Eth, S., et al. (1990) Patient psychopathology and expressed emotion in schizophrenia. *British Journal of Psychiatry, 157*, 877–880.

Gutierrez, E., Escudero, V., Valero, J. A., et al. (1988). Expresion de emociones y curso de la esquizofrenia: II. Expresion de emociones y curso de la esquizofrenia en pacientes en remisión. *Análisisy modificación de Conducta, 14*, 275–316.

Hatfield, A. B., Spaniol, L. & Zipple, A. M. (1987) Expressed emotion: a family perspective. *Schizophrenia Bulletin, 13*, 221–235.

Herz, M. I. & Melville, C. (1980) Relapse in schizophrenia. *American Journal of Psychiatry, 137*, 801–805.

Hogarty, G. E. Anderson, C. M. & Reiss, D. J. (1987) Family psycho-education, social skills training, and medication in schizophrenia: the long and the short of it. *Psychopharmacology Bulletin, 23*, 12–13.

——et al. (1986) Family psychoeducation, social skills training, and maintenance chemotherapy in the aftercare treatment of schizophrenia. 1. One-year effects of a controlled study on relapse and expressed emotion. *Archives of General Psychiatry, 43*, 633–642.

Hooley, J. M., & Teasdale, J. D. (1989). Predictors of relapse in unipolar depressives: expressed emotion, marital distress, and perceived criticism. *Journal of Abnormal Psychology, 98*, 229–235.

Ivanović, M., & Vuletić, Z. (1989). Expressed emotion in families of patients with frequent types of schizophrenia and influence on the course of illness: nine months follow-up. Paper presented to the XIX Congress of the European Association of Behaviour Therapy, Vienna, September 1989.

Kanter, J., Lamb, H. R., & Loeper, C. (1987). Expressed emotion in families: a critical review. *Hospital and Community Psychiatry, 38*, 374–380.

Karno, M., Jenkins, J. H., de la Selva, A., et al. (1987). Expressed emotion and schizophrenic outcome among Mexican- American families. *Journal of Nervous and Mental Disease, 175*, 143–151.

Katschnig, H. (ed.) (1986). *Life events and psychiatric disorders: Controversial issues.* Cambridge: Cambridge University Press.

Kavanagh, D. J. (1992). Interventions for families and social networks. In *Schizophrenia: An overview and practical handbook* (ed. D. J. Kavanagh). London: Chapman & Hall.

Kupiers, L., & Bebbington, P. (1988) Expressed emotion research in schizophrenia: theoretical and clinical implications. *Psychological Medicine, 18*, 893–909.

Leff, J. & Vaughn, C. (1980) The interaction of life events and relatives' expressed emotion in schizophrenia and depressive neurosis. *British Journal of Psychiatry, 136*, 146–153.

——(1981) The role of maintenance therapy and relatives' expressed emotion in relapse of schizophrenia: a 2-year follow-up. *British Journal of Psychiatry, 139*, 102–104.

——(1985) *Expressed emotion in families: Its significance for mental illness.* New York: Guilford.

——Kuipers, L., Berkowitz, R., et al. (1982) A controlled trial of intervention in the families of schizophrenic patients. *British Journal of Psychiatry, 141*, 121–134.

——, ——, ——, et al. (1985) A controlled trial of social intervention in the families of schizophrenic patients: two year follow-up. *British Journal of Psychiatry, 146*, 594–600.

——, Wig, N. N., Ghosh, A., et al. (1987) Influence of relatives' expressed emotion on the course of schizophrenia in Chandigarh. *British Journal of Psychiatry, 151*, 166–173.

——, Berkowitz, R., Shavit, N., et al. (1989) A trial of family therapy v. a relatives group for schizophrenia. *British Journal of Psychiatry, 154*, 58–66.

——, Wig, N. N., Bedi, H., et al. (1990*a*) Relatives' expressed emotion and the course of schizophrenia in Chandigarh: a two-year follow-up of a first-contact sample. *British Journal of Psychiatry, 156*, 351–356.

——, Berkowitz, R., Shavit, N., et al. (1990*b*) A trial of family therapy versus a relatives group for schizophrenia. Two-year follow-up. *British Journal of Psychiatry, 157*, 571–577.

MacMillan, J. F., Gold, A., Crow, T. J., et al. (1986) The Northwick Park study of first episodes of schizophrenia. IV. Expressed emotion and relapse. *British Journal of Psychiatry, 148*, 133–143.

——, Crow, T. J., Johnson, A. L., et al. (1987) Expressed emotion and relapse in first episodes of schizophrenia. *British Journal of Psychiatry, 151*, 320–323.

McCreadie, R. G., & Phillips, K. (1988) The Nithsdale schizophrenia survey. VII. Does relatives' high expressed emotion predict relapse? *British Journal of Psychiatry, 152,* 477–481.

Miklowitz, D. J., Goldstein, M. J., Nuechterlein, K. H., et al. (1986) Expressed emotion, affective style, lithium compliance, and relapse in recent-onset mania. *Psychopharmacology Bulletin, 22,* 628–632.

Mintz, J., Mintz, L. & Goldstein, M. (1987). Expressed emotion and relapse in first episodes of schizophrenia: a rejoinder to MacMillan et al. (1986). *British Journal of Psychiatry, 151,* 314–320.

Moline, R. E., Singh, S., Morris, A., et al. (1985). Family expressed emotion and relapse in schizophrenia in 24 urban American patients. *American Journal of Psychiatry, 142,* 1078–1081.

Montero, I., Gomez Beneyto, M., Ruiz, I., et al. (1990). Emotional expressiveness and development of schizophrenia: a reply to the work of Vaughn. *Actas Luso-Espanolas de Neurologia, Psiquiatria y Ciencias Afines, 18,* 387–395.

Mozny, P., Petrikovitsová, A., Lavická, Z., et al. (1989). Expressed emotions, relapse rate and utilization of psychiatric hospital care in schizophrenia. Paper presented to the XIX Congress of the European Association of Behaviour Therapy, Vienna, September 1989.

Nuechterlein, K. H. & Dawson, M. E. (1984) A heuristic vulnerability-stress model of schizophrenic episodes. *Schizophrenia Bulletin, 10,* 300–312.

Parker, G., Johnston, P. & Hayward, L. (1988). Parental 'expressed emotion' as a predictor of schizophrenic relapse. *Archives of General Psychiatry, 45,* 806–813.

Piatkowska, O., Kavanagh, D., Manicavasagar, V., et al. (1992) *Cognitive-Behavioral Family Intervention for Schizophrenia.* Pergamon.

Priebe, S., Wildgrube, C. & Muller-Oerlinghausen, B. (1989) Lithium prophylaxis and expressed emotion. *British Journal of Psychiatry, 154,* 396–399.

Rostworowska, M., Barbaro, B. & Cechnicki, A. (1987) The influence of expressed emotion on the course of schizophrenia: a Polish replication. Poster presented at the 17th Congress of the European Association for Behaviour Therapy, Amsterdam, 26–29 August.

Smith, J. V. & Birchwood, M. J. (1987) Education for families with schizophrenic relatives. *British Journal of Psychiatry, 150,* 645–652.

—— (1990) Relatives and patients as partners in the management of schizophrenia: the development of a service model. *British Journal of Psychiatry, 156,* 654–660.

Strachan, A. M. (1986) Family intervention for the rehabilitation of schizophrenia. *Schizophrenia Bulletin, 12,* 678–698.

Sturgeon, D., Turpin, G., Berkowitz, R., et al. (1984) Psychophysiological responses of schizophrenic patients to high and low expressed emotion relatives: a follow-up study. *British Journal of Psychiatry, 145,* 62–69.

Subotnik, K. L. & Nuechterlein, K. H. (1988) Prodromal signs and symptoms of schizophrenic relapse. *Journal of Abnormal Psychology, 97,* 405–412.

Szmukler, G. I., Berkowitz, R., Eisler, I., et al. (1987) Expressed emotion in individual and family settings: a comparative study. *British Journal of Psychiatry, 151,* 174–178.

Tarrier, N. (1989) Electrodermal activity, expressed emotion and outcome in schizophrenia. *British Journal of Psychiatry, 155* (suppl. 5), 51–56.

——, Vaughn C., Lader, M. H., et al. (1979) Bodily reactions to people and events in schizophrenia. *Archives of General Psychiatry, 36,* 311–315.

——, Barrowclough, C., Porceddu, K., et al. (1988*a*) The assessment of physiological reactivity to the expressed emotion of the relative of schizophrenic patients. *British Journal of Psychiatry, 152,* 618–624.

——, ——, Vaughn, C., et al. (1988*b*) The community management of schizophrenia: a controlled trial of a behavioural intervention with families to reduce relapse. *British Journal of Psychiatry, 153*, 532–542.

——, ——, ——, et al. (1989) Community management of schizophrenia: a two-year follow-up of a behavioural intervention with families. *British Journal of Psychiatry, 154*, 625–628.

Turpin, G., Tarrier, N. & Sturgeon, D. (1988) Social psychophysiology and the study of biopsychosocial models of schizophrenia. In *Social Psychophysiology: Theory and Clinical Applications* (ed. H. Wagner). Chichester: Wiley.

Vaughn, C. E. & Leff, J. (1976*a*) The influence of family and social factors on the course of psychiatric illness. *British Journal of Psychiatry, 129*, 125–137.

——(1976*b*) The measurement of expressed emotion in the families of psychiatric patients. *British Journal of Social and Clinical Psychology, 15*, 157–165.

——, Snyder, K. S., Jones, S., et al. (1984) Family factors in schizophrenic relapse: replication in California of British research on expressed emotion. *Archives of General Psychiatry, 41*, 1169–1177.

Waxler, N. (1979) Is outcome for schizophrenia better in nonindustrial societies? The case of Sri Lanka. *Journal of Nervous and Mental Diseases, 167*, 144–158.

Wig, N. N., Menon, D. K., Bedi, H., et al. (1987) Expressed emotion and schizophrenia in North India: I. Cross-cultural transfer of ratings of relatives' expressed emotion. *British Journal of Psychiatry, 151*, 156–173.

World Health Organization (1979) *Schizophrenia: An international follow-up study*. New York: Wiley.

Index